THE
PSYCHOTIC
PROCESS

THE
PSYCHOTIC
PROCESS

John Frosch, M.D.

Professor of Psychiatry, N.Y.U. School of Medicine
Editor Emeritus, Journal of the American Psychoanalytic Association
Emeritus Director of Psychiatry, Brookdale Hospital Medical Center

INTERNATIONAL UNIVERSITIES PRESS, INC.
New York

Library of Congress Cataloging in Publication Data

Frosch, John.
    The psychotic process.

    Bibliography: p.
    Includes index.
    1. Psychoses.   2. Psychoanalysis.   I. Title.
RC512.F76 1982   616.89   82-21392
ISBN 0-8236-5690-X

Manufactured in the United States of America

To My Dear Wife Ann

Whose devotion and dedication
really made this work possible

CONTENTS

Acknowledgments

It is customary to express one's appreciation to those who have been of help in the preparation of any work. Yet how is it possible with mere words, or the mention of a name, to do full justice to the feeling of gratitude I have for the many who, in one way or another, were of assistance? More than the usual executive assistant was Julia de Clemente. Her dedication, sincere involvement, and interest in assuming the drudgery of the necessary secretarial load lightened my own load considerably. She was assisted from time to time in the typing chores by Deloris Johnson. Unfortunately due to external circumstances she had to relinquish this role. In stepped Ellie Gipson, who graciously took over the onerous typing chore. She was assisted from time to time by a member of her staff, Claudette Andrade.

Occasionally I called on colleagues for their opinions on one or the other section of the book. Dr. William Frosch, my nephew, reviewed the original manuscript and made many cogent suggestions. My son, Dr. James P. Frosch, made valuable constructive criticisms from time to time. However, no work can evolve without the substantial backing of a good librarian. Such was Sophie Winston of the Brookdale Hospital Medical Center, who hawkshaw-like traced many references.

Now the manuscript is ready for the publisher. Every author has a narcissistic investment in his work, which creates a defensive attitude against any suggestions by an editor. These are viewed as an attack on his offspring. Such was the case with Sue Heinemann, who was assigned as editor by the publisher. However, what started out in the customary adversarial relationship, eventually evolved into a good working alliance. The publishers, Martin Azarian and Margaret Emery Azarian, created such a climate of full cooperation and patience, as to justify fully my original decision to have International Universities Press publish this book.

And yet a fundamental role was that of my wife, Ann, who had participated actively in the publication of the *Annual Survey of Psychoanalysis* and the *Journal of the American Psychoanalytic Association*. She participated fully as actively in the preparation of this manuscript at all levels. Above all, however, was how she bore with my many mood swings and irritable reactions to the frequent periods of frustration. It was, however, completely in keeping with her whole relationship to me.

Every author, at some point, begins to have many doubts about his work. Should it be allowed to see the light of day? At this point I share these feelings. Nonetheless, at this stage I have to accept full responsibility for what is both good and bad, and I hope the former will outweigh the latter.

Preface

For 40 some years I worked with psychotic patients and those designated borderline, both in institutions and in private practice. Although an appreciable portion of this work was in clinical psychiatry, it was extensively augmented by my psychoanalytic work with such patients. It was quite natural for me, as an analyst, to view my psychiatric data with a psychoanalytic eye. This view permeates my approach.

As my interest in the psychoses grew, I was asked to give courses in this area to psychoanalytic candidates at the New York Psychoanalytic Institute, as well as at the Psychoanalytic Institute of the Downstate Medical Center. At the New York Psychoanalytic Institute Edith Jacobson taught the first part (on depression), while I taught the second part (on the other psychoses and the borderline). In addition to teaching, I participated in scientific meetings devoted to the psychoses, published articles in scientific journals, and presented material on the psychoanalytic concepts of psychoses before several psychoanalytic societies.

In 1962 and 1964, I organized and chaired the first panel discussion held by the American Psychoanalytic Association on the nature of the psychotic process. The list of participants attested to the intense interest of many prominent figures in psychoanalysis in the psychoses. It may be of more than historical interest to name the participants, since there is by no means unanimity among analysts about the psychoanalytic view of psychosis. The participants included Charlotte Babcock, Robert C. Bak, Donald L. Burnham, Gustav Bychowski, Kurt R. Eissler, O. Spurgeon English, Jan Frank, Edward D. Hoedemaker, Edward Hornick, Edith Jacobson, Maurits Katan, Sylvan Keiser, Charles Kligerman, Sidney Kligerman, Sidney Levin, Ruth Lidz, Theodore Lidz, Sydney G. Margolin, William G. Niederland, Lewis L. Robbins, Robert Rubenstein, David L. Rubinfine, Philip F. Seitz, Elvin V. Semrad, Herman

M. Serota, Julian L. Stamm, Manuel Stapen, Arthur F. Valenstein, H. G. van der Walls, Robert S. Wallerstein, and Otto A. Will, Jr.

Extensive reports of these discussions were prepared by Abraham Freedman, but unfortunately they were never published. I will make ample reference to these discussions, and am grateful for Freedman's record of these exciting interchanges.

Over the years I have been repeatedly urged to integrate my contributions into a book, but I have procrastinated for many reasons. Much of my thinking was constantly being enriched and expanded by my own and others' experiences. Somehow, putting ideas and concepts into book form places a stamp of finality which was not congruent with the evolving state of this highly complex field.

As I sat in the chair as Editor of the *Journal of the American Psychoanalytic Association* and surveyed the many contributions submitted for publication, as well as contributions in other journals and books, I saw how many of my colleagues were grappling with the problems I had been trying to understand for years. I finally felt it was appropriate for me to share my thoughts and join the other contributors.

During my many years of exposure to the various clinical manifestations of psychosis, I encountered a bewildering array of phenomena requiring constant revisions in my thinking. I found myself searching for common denominators to unite these psychotic manifestations. Increasingly I moved in the direction of trying to understand the underlying features that brought about these manifestations. Others were also moving in this direction.

Rather than concentrating on the various clinical symptoms, I chose to focus on processes, the continuous interplay of factors and operations moving toward an end product. Obviously, growing out of these processes are various phenomena, clinically observable, either in isolated manifestations or more organized clinical syndromes, be they characterological distortions or more defined clinical syndromes. But it is only through a study of these processes that our understanding of the clinical manifestations can be deepened. I have therefore chosen to direct the main thrust of this book to the *psychotic process*. If we look for a common frame of reference for psychoses, we need not get hung up over the differences between one and the other psychosis, but rather, having established what they share as psychosis, we may then go on and discuss how they differ. It is this approach that is the leitmotif of this contribution. The impact of the psychotic process on character structure brings about what I call the psychotic character. Although I will refer to this condition, a detailed discussion of this syndrome must remain the subject of another book.

My experience in teaching medical students, psychiatric residents, psychiatrists, and other mental health professionals has led me to gear my psychoanalytic understanding of the psychoses to many levels.[1] This approach is partially reflected in this book. Although primarily addressed to psychoanalysts, it will be of interest to psychiatrists and mental health professionals who need to understand the dynamic aspects of the psychoses. I shall inevitably here and there refer to the descriptive and phenomenological aspects of the psychoses, but my essential concern will be the dynamic and genetic aspects, as well as the psychoanalytic treatment of the psychoses. This book, I believe, will therefore be especially useful for the experienced psychoanalyst searching for greater understanding of the psychoses.

[1] Such teaching took place over many years, at various institutions, among them the Departments of Psychiatry at the New York University School of Medicine, the Downstate Medical Center, and the Brookdale Hospital Medical Center.

Prologue

It is the specific nature of the patient's problems and modes of dealing with these problems, influenced by the available tools, that add up to clinical phenomena. Reworded, it is the interplay of the specific danger and conflict, the techniques used to deal with this danger and conflict, and the available ego functions, as well as the impact on the ego of all these factors, that produces the clinical picture. As we shall see, differences between the psychotic and neurotic processes can be found in all three areas, and these unique aspects determine the "choice" of illness.

It might be worthwhile, at this point, to see how the concept of the psychotic process evolved psychoanalytically and what the present thinking is in this area. Contributions to the psychoanalytic understanding of the psychoses have, from the beginning, looked at the various components that enter into the psychotic process. These components are not, however, alluded to as such, nor are they seen as a whole. Quite early, for instance, Freud dealt with the nature of the defenses as well as the fate of reality. Subsequently, he examined the nature of the conflict, and only later did he turn to disturbances in the ego, ego boundaries, and ego functions vis-à-vis reality. Other authors also focused on one or the other component. It is the integration of these components into the concept of a psychotic process that is the essential contribution of this volume.

To do this, I shall turn to three questions: (1) What is the nature of the danger and conflict that characterizes the psychotic process (in contrast to the neurotic process)? (2) What are the means used to cope with this danger and conflict? And (3) are there ego and ego function impairments unique to the psychotic process? I intend to demonstrate that the basic anxiety deriving from fear of dissolution and disintegration of the self is crucial to understanding the danger in the psychotic process. Various mechanisms are used to cope with this danger, such as

1

fragmentation, splitting, denial, introjection, projection, and projective identification. We find ego fragility and blurring of ego boundaries, as well as defects in ego functions involved in the relationship with reality and the sensing of reality. But, above all, what is paradigmatic for the psychotic process is the loss of reality testing.

My survey of the psychoanalytic contributions to the understanding of the psychotic process will not be inclusive. In focusing on the structure of the psychotic process and its impact on psychic functioning, I shall attempt to show not only what characterizes the psychotic process, but also how it differs from the neurotic process. Attention will be given to psychoanalytic contributions on the symptom psychoses, which derive from the psychotic process. Here, however, it should be kept in mind that while, given certain circumstances, pathological processes may bring about symptom neurosis or psychosis, this is only one possibility. They may also result in various distorted character structures, character traits, or idiosyncratic manifestations. One patient, for example, remarked that while she was at a concert she felt the floor tremble: "I asked the lady on my right whether she felt the floor tremble and she said, 'No.' So I asked the lady on my left and she said the same. I therefore concluded that it was a projection of my vaginal orgasm." In this case, there is no question that closeness of the id to the ego — one of the characteristic features of the psychotic process — permitted an invasion into consciousness of a pathological idea. But the patient, in evaluating external reality, was able to recognize that this was an internally derived experience. When questioned about her statement that this was a projection of a vaginal orgasm, she agreed it was a peculiar way of viewing what had happened and wavered in this belief. It was clear that her perception had been distorted, but she revealed the persistence of an important ego function — reality testing — which kept her on this side of psychosis. In my opinion, she was therefore not clinically psychotic, although what took place derived from a psychotic process.

The attitude of psychoanalysis toward the psychoses has for some been influenced by Freud's pessimism about the psychoanalytic treatment of psychotics. In his view, their inability to develop a transference in the true sense and their extreme narcissism made them unsuitable for psychoanalytic treatment. In the *Outline* (1940), he pointed out:

> If the patient's ego is to be a useful ally in our common work, it must, however hard it may be pressed by the hostile powers, have retained a certain amount of coherence and some fragment of understanding for

the demands of reality. But this is not to be expected of the ego of a psychotic, it cannot observe a pact of this kind, indeed it can scarcely enter into one. It will very soon have tossed us away and the help we offer it and sent us to join the portions of the external world which no longer mean anything to it. Thus we discover that we must renounce the idea of trying our plan of cure upon psychotics — renounce it perhaps only for the time being, till we have found some other plan better adapted for them [p. 173].

As we shall see, this position has not been supported by many who have worked with psychotic patients. Searles (1963), in discussing transference psychosis, asserts: "To be sure we have long ago outgrown the position in this regard of Freud and Abraham, who held that the schizophrenic patient has regressed to an autoerotic level of development and is incapable therefore of forming a transference" (p. 250). In a somewhat similar vein, the psychoanalytic glossary (Moore and Fine, 1968) explains: "Originally it was felt that 'no transference' relationship could develop in such cases because of the degree of narcissism; however, a more accurate description is that quite intense and distorted transferences (sometimes described as transference psychosis) develop which have to be handled and resolved with great care since they often represent the patient's initial and very tenuous efforts to re-establish a genuine object relationship with another human being" (p. 82).

But it was not only his doubts about treatment that turned Freud away from psychosis. He openly expressed his dislike for the psychotic. In a letter to Hollós in 1928, he remarked: "I finally confessed to myself that... I do not like those patients, that they irritate me, that I find them foreign to me and to all that is human" (Schur, 1966, p. 21). He expressed a similar aversion in his correspondence with Simmel (see Deri and Brunswick, 1964, p. 106).

This is a strange attitude for one who in his earlier writings contributed so much to the psychoanalytic understanding of the psychoses. Perhaps a clue to Freud's aversion may be found in the last line of the letter to Hollós. He himself asked: "is it the consequence of an ever increasing preference for the primacy of the intellect, the expression of animosity toward the id?"

Freud's animosity toward the id was reflected in his attitude toward abstract art and artists. In a letter to Pfister in 1920, he stated: "For I think you ought to know that in actual life I am terribly intolerant of cranks, that I see only the harmful sick of them and that so far as these 'artists' are concerned I am almost one of those whom at the outset you castigate as philistines and lowbrows. And in the end you explain quite clearly and exhaustively why these people lack the right to claim the name of artist" (1873–1939, p. 331; also in Gombrich, 1966, p. 34). In 1938, after meeting Salvador Dali through Stefan Zweig, he confessed: "up to then I was inclined to consider the Surrealists, who appear to have chosen me as their patron saint; pure lunatics or, let us say 95 percent, as with 'pure' alcohol" (1873–1939, p. 448; Gombrich, 1966, p. 34). And in a letter to Karl Abraham, who had sent him a drawing by an expressionist artist, he commented: "People such as he should be the last to be allowed access to analytic circles for they are the all-too-unwelcome illustration of Adler's theory that it is precisely people with severe inborn defects of vision who become painters and draughtsmen" (Gombrich, 1966, p. 34).

To Freud, there was no artistic value in the primary process as such. "Far from looking in the world of art only for its unconscious content of biological drives and childhood memories, he insisted on that degree of adjustment to reality that alone turns a dream into a work of art" (Gombrich, 1966, p. 36). Freud's attitude toward unmodified id derivatives was expressed in his attitude toward surrealism, as seen in an exchange of letters with André Breton. In one letter he explained: "A mere collection of dreams, without the dreamer's associations, without the knowledge of the circumstances in which they occur, tells me nothing, and I can hardly imagine what it could tell anyone" (Gombrich, 1966, p. 31).

In a letter written in 1929 to Theodor Reik, Freud expressed what would appear to be, given his early interest in the unconscious, an inconsistent attitude toward crude instinctual manifestations unmodified by the ego. Referring to Dostoyevsky, he wrote:

> I might also have charged against him that his insight was so entirely restricted to the workings of the abnormal psyche. Consider his astounding helplessness before the phenomena of love; he really only understands either crude, instinctive desire or masochistic submission and love from pity. You are also quite right in your assumption that I do not really like Dostoyevsky, despite all my admiration for his power and nobility. That comes from the fact that my patience with pathological natures is completely exhausted in my daily work. In art and life, I am intolerant toward them. That is a personal trait, not binding on others [Reik, 1949, p. 175].

Anna Freud (personal communication, 1972) seems to confirm her father's "animosity to the id" in indicating that Freud's paramount interest in the ego played a large role in his denigration of the id. Nonetheless, as we shall see, it was through his studies of the ego and disturbances in its functioning that he found one of the keys to the understanding of the psychoses.

In an attempt to understand Freud's attitude, Kohut (1977) discusses certain personality traits which may have influenced Freud's reaction to primitive, archaic expressions. He proposes that Freud had a basic narcissistic vulnerability which made him fearful of overstimulation by things he did not understand or control. There was a special fear of overstimulation in the area of exhibitionism. As Kohut puts it: "It was his personality that determined his preference for the content of thought, for the clearly defined and definable; it was his personality that made him shun the areas of contentless forms and intensities and unaccountable emotions" (p. 294). Kohut points out that Freud's was a personality defined by the need for the steadfast predominance of rationality. "Freud was not able or willing to devote himself in close empathic immersion to the vicissitudes of the self as he had been able to do with regard to the vicissitudes of object-instinctual experiences" (p. 297).

I am not sure that all this adds up, as Kohut and others seem to imply, to the claim that Freud was afraid of id-derived material. If so, how could one explain his fearless facing of his own unconscious and instinct-derived influences on his own personality? Furthermore, what is there about Kohut's self psychology that would be frightening to Freud in terms of archaic states and the power of the id? It would seem to me that the very language of self psychology should be reassuring to one afraid of the id.

A contrasting view regarding the importance of psychoanalytic involvement in the study and treatment of psychoses came out at a conference held in 1954 on the "Widening Scope of Indications for Psychoanalysis." Both Leo Stone and Edith Jacobson contended that there was enough of an ego left to work with in both the borderline and the psychotic. In Stone's opinion:

> ... psychoanalysis may legitimately be invoked and indeed should be invoked, for many very ill people of good personality resources, who are probably inaccessible to cure by other methods, who are willing to accept the long travail of analysis, without guarantees of success. There is always a possibility of helping, where all other measures fail. With the progressive understanding of the actions of psychotherapeutic admixtures or of large scale "parameters" in the psychoanalytic method, now

so largely intuitive in their application, we can hope that such successes will be more frequent [1954, p. 593].

Anna Freud (1954), however, regretted what she believed was an enormous expenditure of time and energy in the treatment of borderline and psychotic cases.

> For years now, our most experienced and finest analysts have concentrated their efforts on opening up new fields for the application of analysis by making the psychotic disorders, the severe depressions, the borderline cases, addictions, perversions, delinquency, etc. amenable to treatment. I have no wish to underestimate the resulting benefits to patients, nor the resulting considerable gains to analysis as a therapy and science. But I regret sometimes that so much interest and effort has been withdrawn from the hysteric, phobic and compulsive disorders, leaving their treatment to the beginners or the less knowledgeable and adventurous analytic practitioners. If all the skill, knowledge and pioneering effort which was spent on widening the scope of application of psychoanalysis had been employed instead on intensifying and improving our technique in the original field, I cannot help but feel that, by now, we would find the treatment of the common neuroses child's play, instead of struggling with their technical problems as we have continued to do. How do analysts decide if they are given the choice between returning to health half a dozen young people with good prospects in life but disturbed in their enjoyment and efficiency by comparatively mild neuroses, or devoting the same time, trouble and effort to one single borderline case, who may or may not be saved from spending the rest of his life in an institution. Personally, I can feel the pull in both directions, perhaps with a bias toward the former task; as a body, the Psychoanalytic Association has inclined in recent years toward the latter. Let us hope that the future analysts, who occupy our Training Institutes now as candidates, will be numerous enough to spread their energies over both fields [p. 610].

Foreshadowing Anna Freud's views to some extent, Glover (1945) had stated:

> A similar situation threatens to develop regarding the importance of the study of psychoses to psychoanalysis. The fact that the regressions, restitutive symptom-formations and disintegration products observed in the psychoses are of a primitive type tends to give the observer the impression that he is in especially close touch with the unconscious mental processes, and encourages him in the belief that he may speak with special authority on psychoanalytic matters. Whereas the plain fact is that up to the present the study of psychoses remains for the largest part

an observational field in which the essential techniques of psychoanalytic research are almost as limited as they are in the study of early infancy
[p. 76].

And yet, although Freud did not publish anything fundamentally new
about the psychoses after his 1924 papers, I have been assured in personal
communications (A. Freud, 1972; M. Katan, 1971) that until the later
years of his life, he still had many patients who were quite ill, some borderline and some psychotic. Moreover, he discussed Katan's concept of
restitution with him with a great deal of interest and some disagreement.

We might expect that Freud's dislike for psychotics and his animosity
toward the id would limit psychoanalytic interest in the psychotic process and in therapeutic approaches to the resulting conditions.[1] This,
however, appears *not* to have been the case. Despite Freud's attitude,
psychoanalytic interest in the psychoses has not only continued un-
abated through the years, but appears to be increasing. Contributions
to this area both theoretically and therapeutically have been made not
only by nonclassical analysts such as Sullivan, Fromm-Reichmann,
Will, and Searles, but by many classical analysts, including Jacobson,
Freeman, Kernberg, Arlow, Brenner, and Mahler, as well as by Kleinian adherents. Some have focused on borderline problems, discussions
of which invariably involve the psychotic process. Panels, discussion
groups, books, papers, all attest to the ongoing interest in understanding and treating the psychoses.

Nonetheless, in the field of psychoanalysis, it has not been as easy to
study psychosis as neurosis since flagrant borderline and psychotic disorders are generally not treated analytically on the outside. In recent
years, most psychoanalysts have not concerned themselves as much
with institutionalized patients, aside from those who have a special
interest in the severely disturbed, hospitalized psychotic or borderline
patient. The psychotic patients psychoanalysts today see tend to be
those who are still able to get along in the community or so-called
borderline cases, although there are some analysts who work within

[1] Whatever its significance, for many years the various psychoanalytic training institutes, with a few exceptions, did not conduct courses on the psychoses. As a matter of
fact, when I gave courses on the psychoses and allied states at the New York Psychoanalytic Institute and the Division for Psychoanalytic Education of the Downstate
Medical Center, I received many visitors from other institutes seeking guidance in
establishing such courses, as well as invitations to share my experiences through visits
to various institutes.

structured situations with much more disturbed psychotic patients. Yet
the problem of psychosis seems to fascinate psychoanalysts. One finds
much in psychotic symptomatology that seems to contribute toward an
understanding of both normal and pathological behavior and psychic
development, despite Glover's opinion. At the same time, the impact of
the psychotic process on character disturbances, character traits, and
idiosyncratic behavior requires an understanding of this process.

The extent to which the psychoanalytic study of the psychoses has
enriched our understanding of psychoanalytic concepts is well summarized in the psychoanalytic glossary:

> The investigation of the psychoses led Freud and other observers into a
> re-evaluation of the earlier libido and topographic theories. A better
> understanding of narcissism, the aggressive drive and the concept of the
> self contributed to the development of the structural theory and the
> dual instinct theory, resulting finally in the more significant place of ego
> psychology in psychoanalysis. It has also encouraged and facilitated the
> study of early ego states and development because of their significance in
> psychotic regression [Moore and Fine, 1968, p. 82].

PART I

BACKGROUND
CONSIDERATIONS

1.
Terminology, Methodology, and Nosology

Terminological Considerations

There is by no means consistency in the use of psychoanalytic terms. Any attempt to evaluate the psychoanalytic contributions on the various psychotic syndromes is met by terminological and methodological confusion. This is especially the case when one attempts to delineate what characterizes the psychoses as distinct from the neuroses. The psychoanalytic glossary, for instance, defines psychosis as a form of mental disorder associated with some personality disorganization and characterized by marked ego and libidinal regression. In describing neurosis, on the other hand, the glossary points to manifest disturbances "in thoughts, feelings, attitudes and behavior, which have their primary origin within the mind and are only secondarily related to events and stimuli of the current real world" (Moore and Fine, 1968, p. 82). This is hardly a clear distinction. Nor would these definitions find universal concurrence.

In a delightful brief historical survey of the use of the terms "neurosis" and "psychosis," Macalpine and Hunter (1955) indicate that "the term neurosis derived from the Greek, meaning nerve or tendon, and a neurotic was a substance having an action on the nervous system, usually a bracing action" (p. 16). The term "psychosis" is generally attributed to Feuchtersleben, who used it to describe diseases of the mind or soul (the brain was considered the organ of the mind, but not the mind itself). Romberg, in 1846, classified both diseases of the nervous system and mental diseases as neurosis. By the turn of this century, however, mental disease with no neuropathology had been split off from this group, and the term "neurosis" was applied to such functional disorders. The division on the basis of organic pathology led to the

11

lumping together of many diseases which are kept apart today: for instance, hysteria and epilepsy. Actually, even this distinction was mud-
dled, as the terms came to be combined, with "neuropsychosis" used
when the major development was in the nervous system, and "psychoneurosis," when the mental factor was more important. As we read the
early psychoanalytic literature, we see that neurosis and psychosis were
considered by some as separate entities, by others as interchangeable.
Indeed, Freud himself refers to psychotic conditions as neurosis (for instance, in his use of the term "narcissistic neurosis"), and he examines
the Schreber case with neurosis as a frame of reference.

In the discussion groups on the nature of the psychotic process at the
meetings of the American Psychoanalytic Association (Freedman,
1962, 1964), several questions were posed relating to this subject:
Should we differentiate psychoanalytically between neurosis and psychosis? Are there any distinctive features that characterize psychosis
genetically, dynamically, structurally, etc., and are these different
from those in neurosis? If so, are these differences qualitative or quantitative? If they are qualitative, what are the essential features of those
processes which eventuate in psychosis rather than neurosis? If one
views these conditions as conflict-derived, is the conflict the same or
different in neurosis and psychosis? If one sees the conflict as essentially
the same and the difference as lying in the modes of coping with the
conflict, how are the modes different in the two conditions? If either or
both of the above factors play a role in producing psychotic conditions,
what are the genetic aspects that make it possible for these factors to
develop in the way they do? What are the therapeutic implications of
these concepts?

These questions have been addressed through the years, but today
there is still confusion among psychoanalysts as to whether there is any
basic *qualitative* difference between neurosis and psychosis. Indeed,
some believe that it is pointless to try to differentiate between the two.
Arlow and Brenner (1964, 1969, 1970), for instance, argue that essentially the basic processes and therapy in the two are the same, the difference being primarily quantitative.

This issue is not only a topic of debate in psychoanalysis, but represents an ongoing controversy in clinical psychiatry as well. A good illustration is the heated discussion regarding the inclusion of psychodynamic concepts in *DSM-III* (American Psychiatric Association, 1981).
Some contended that the term "neurosis" should be excluded since this
concept could not be clearly defined clinically. Although the term

"psychosis" was retained, this was via a listing of symptoms commonly associated with what is considered a psychotic condition. No attempt was made to define the psychotic process or psychosis as such. This classification aimed to present the diagnosis of various clinical syndromes on a descriptive level, something which, it was claimed, could not be done for neurosis.

The situation is further confused by inconsistent and overlapping terminology in discussions of psychosis. Many of the psychoanalytic contributions, ostensibly made on the topic of psychosis, have dealt primarily with schizophrenia. There has been a subtle, and at other times a not so subtle, attempt to apply concepts evolved in the study of schizophrenia to the psychoses in general.[1] This slipping over from explanatory concepts about schizophrenia to psychosis (and vice versa) is a perennial problem in psychiatry as well. Methodologically, to interchange concepts of schizophrenia with psychosis leads to difficulties. Indeed, Beck (1959, 1965) and others have indicated that schizophrenia may occur without psychosis. Grotstein (1977) indicates that although schizophrenia and psychosis have much in common, such as the precocious closure of chaos and confusion, as well as a probable psychosomatic nature, "the schizophrenic's personality develops, allegedly, from a defective neurophysiological personality in respect of the stimulus barrier and to defective sensory integration; whereas psychosis seems to involve biochemical alterations in the disengaged neural systems" (p. 433). To illustrate the dilemma in the use of the concept "psychosis" by psychoanalysts, one might cite Jacobson's (1953) objections to Katan's use of the term "prepsychotic" for much of the symptomatology of the cyclothymic disorders. In her opinion, much of what he calls prepsychotic is gross psychosis.

Looking at the early psychoanalytic literature, it is often difficult to differentiate among contributions on paranoia, paranoid mechanisms, paraphrenia, and schizophrenia. The way these concepts were used interchangeably is exemplified by a statement Freud (1911b) made: "And we can understand how a clinical picture such as Schreber's can come about and take the name of a paranoid dementia from the fact that in its production of a wish phantasy and of hallucinations, it shows paraphrenic traits, while in its exciting cause, in its use of the mecha-

---

[1] Knight (1953, 1954), in his seminal contributions on the problem of the borderline, tries to delineate psychotic features in two patients by using schizophrenic symptomatology as his essential frame of reference, slipping back and forth in his use of these terms.

nism of projection and in its final issue it exhibits a paranoid character"
(p. 78).

Freud refers to a case in his "Further Remarks on the Neuropsychoses of Defence" (1896) as a case of chronic paranoia, only to question
this diagnosis in a subsequent footnote, changing it to dementia paranoides (p. 174n). In his earlier paper on the defense neuropsychoses
(1894), he interchanges such terms as defense psychoses, defense psychoneuroses, defense neuropsychoses, and neuroses. At times Freud
equates neurosis with what Feuchtersleben meant by psychosis, namely,
a disease of the mind; at other times, however, he underlines the
organic toxic factor in neurosis. As I already noted, Freud repeatedly
refers to psychotic conditions with the term "neurosis." He looks at
Schreber's pathology with neurosis as the basic frame of reference.[2]
Equally confusing is his attempt to combine illnesses such as dementia
praecox and schizophrenia by use of the term "paraphrenia."

Further confusion has, in my opinion, been generated in the psychoanalytic literature by the fact that the terminology is not consistent
in all areas (phenomenological, dynamic, genetic, etc.). An example is
the use of the term "narcissistic neurosis" in relation to psychosis. Freud
at first conceptualizes narcissistic neurosis as the counterpart of transference neurosis. In the *Introductory Lectures* (1916–1917), he at times
equates narcissistic neurosis with psychosis and generally indicates a
close relationship. Later, in his paper on "Neurosis and Psychosis"
(1924b), Freud locates the conflict structurally, saying that conflict between the ego and the id reflects psychoneurosis; between the superego
and ego, narcissistic neurosis; between the ego and reality, psychosis.
But as far as I know, the term "narcissistic neurosis" is not applied exclusively to the melancholias.

The term has become somewhat denigrated by the rather broad
frame of reference within which the concept of narcissism is used. To
quote Glover: "A 'narcissistic' organization could be postulated in all
psychoses without any indication of the state of ego-structure to which
any one psychosis regressed" (1932b, p. 161). In this regard, we might
also ask whether it is not essential for us to distinguish clearly between
those regressions to narcissism in which considerable ego cathexis, and
therefore capacity for object interest, remains, and those deeper regres-

[2] As we shall see, Arlow and Brenner (1964, 1969, 1970) and London (1973), in
using concepts of neurosis as a frame of reference for psychosis, have further contributed to the controversy between those who adhere to a unitary theory of psychosis and
those who believe that a specific defect (or defects) accounts for psychosis.

sions, such as one sees in neglected patients in state hospitals, in which almost no object interest remains and the patient is virtually inaccessible by way of the ego (see Freedman, 1962, 1964).

Waelder (1960) expresses the problem well:

> The application of this fruitful concept [narcissism] by analysts has so far suffered from a careless use of language that uses the term narcissistic equally without qualification for the phenomena of satisfied, as for those of frustrated, self-love; the self-contented person who does not seem to need anybody else is equally called narcissistic as is the person in constant need of moral support [pp. 68–69].

Hartmann (1953) also refers to the limitations of narcissism as a frame of reference.

> A description from the angle of narcissism does not account for the distinction between "sexual overestimation" of the self as we find it, e.g., in megalomania and other forms of self-cathexis. Nor for the differences of "ego" and "self," or between the cathexis of the self-image (a complex of representations) and ego functions, a distinction that is relevant in developmental psychology and in the pathology especially of the psychoses [p. 185].

This ambiguity has led to the use of the concepts of self and self-representation to account for many of the phenomena previously considered under the concept "ego." The situation is further compounded by Kohut's (1971, 1977) view of narcissism as a separate line in psychic development, with especial importance for self development.

Kanzer (1964) discusses the confusion between the terms "auto-erotism" and "narcissism" which permeated the early psychoanalytic literature. In his opinion, some of the confusion derived from a failure to clarify the frames of reference used, i.e., whether the term referred to the source of instinctual energy, the mode of instinctual activity, or the object of instinctual energy. Kanzer points out that at first auto-erotism was considered a pre-ego instinctual activity. With the development of ego theory, autoerotism became the mode of satisfaction characteristic of, but not preceding, the narcissistic organization. Yet "autoerotism" was also used to describe a mode of satisfaction resorted to during later life. Moreover, sometimes the term was used to characterize preoedipal as opposed to phallic modes of libidinal development.

Freud, for instance, believed that the autism Bleuler described was really autoerotism and that Bleuler had misused this term when he called it "autism." This opinion reflected the thinking of the time. Both

Freud and Abraham had in mind the undifferentiated stage in psychic development, which was equated with primary narcissism and primary identification. It might be well to reserve the term "autoerotic" for instinct-gratifying activity that seeks the self or parts of the self as the object, and to use the concept of narcissism to describe a stage in object relations where the self is the frame of reference. Certainly using these concepts to denote a psychotic process is confusing. We ought to consider whether the term "narcissistic neurosis" has any real value for us today as a nosological entity.

The difficulty in establishing a uniform definition of psychosis reminds me of Janet's (1906) remarks regarding the multiplicity of definitions of hysteria:

> Do not forget that we are speaking of medicine, and that this is rather a special domain, less calm and serene than high mathematics. You should not ask too much of the virtue of a physician, or hope that he will confine himself to repeating the definition of a predecessor, even if he does not cite his name. What would be left for him? He must needs change something in these definitions, were it but a single word, in order to appear to innovate, which, in medicine, is indispensable. I do not exaggerate in telling you that, nowadays, three-fourths of the definitions of hysteria are nearly identical [p. 321].

I would not like to think that in our attempts to define and describe the psychotic process we are merely changing a few words. I hope that our attempts will result in a picture that adds to our understanding of and way of conceptualizing psychosis.

Methodological Considerations

In examining psychotic phenomena, I should like to emphasize some basic methodological considerations. The violation of certain important principles is not infrequent, leading to unending controversy and confusion. We may examine a phenomenon at three levels: descriptive, dynamic, and genetic. The first step is to describe *what* we see and to achieve some degree of agreement on this — the so-called descriptive level. We may then direct ourselves to an examination of *how* the interplay of various forces produces what we see, how what we see comes about — i.e., the dynamic factors. Finally, we may turn to *why* it happens and why in this way. We are now talking of causality, of genetic factors.

Psychoanalysis has contributed to all three areas, but it is the latter two, the dynamic and the genetic, that have been the focus of most psychoanalytic contributions. It is important to remember, however, that the dynamic and genetic features lend understanding to phenomenology and have implications for prognosis and therapy. Although Janet (1906) proposed to examine clinical phenomena from a dynamic point of view, he contended:

> The psychological interpretation should not suppress what is good, what is excellent, in our ancestors' works. Now the last century produced a monumental work; namely, clinical work. With infinite patience and penetration, all those great clinicians introduced order into a real chaos; they ranged the diseases in groups, they enabled us to recognize these groups. Improvements should consist in consolidating this edifice and not in throwing it down [p. 323].

Ernst Kris once pointed out in a personal communication that one of the important contributions of psychoanalysis lies in asking the right question. Such a question, insofar as psychosis is concerned, might be: What do we in psychoanalysis have to contribute to the understanding of the psychotic process? Perhaps we should concern ourselves with setting up frames of reference to examine the nature of the basic psychotic process. We should then concern ourselves with the role this process plays in the various clinical conditions, whether gross psychotic syndromes, characterological disorders, or idiosyncratic manifestations.

Having done this, will it be possible to spell out any common denominators which tie together the clinical pictures deriving from this process, such as a psychotic syndrome? Can we postulate that, regardless of the form of psychosis, an individual who possesses the common denominator(s) is psychotic? Can we then tease apart which factors, be they biological or psychological or both, constitute such a common denominator, and how these constituents have an impact on the common denominator? Once we have determined what is similar in the clinical pictures, we need to look at the differences, at those features which account for the one or the other clinical manifestation. In other words, we must ask: In what way does the psychosis in one condition differ from another and what accounts for the difference?

The difficulty in finding a unified concept of a given process underlying all psychoses is revealed by examining the psychoanalytic contributions on the organic brain disorders, psychoses associated with somatic disorders, and psychotic affective disorders. Psychoanalytic contributions on the organic brain disorders are few. Perhaps one of the earliest and most thought-provoking was Ferenczi and Hollós's (1922) contribution on the psychological symptomatology of general paresis.

They viewed the brain as the seat of the ego. Ferenczi's (1917, 1919) "pathopsychoses" and Meng's (1934; Meng and Stern, 1955; Stokvis, 1952) "organ psychoses" referred to psychotic somatic syndromes. More recently, Freeman (1973) has applied Anna Freud's profile to psychotic organic brain syndromes. But it is unclear what it is that ties these syndromes together as psychoses. Moreover, Jacobson (1953) has indicated that the psychoanalytic literature on psychoses lacks studies of schizophrenia and cyclothymia from a common and comparative point of view. We shall see, however, that since then several authors (including Jacobson) have attempted to do this. There do appear to be attempts to weave our understanding of these disorders into the framework of psychoanalytic theory and coordinate it with prevailing frames of reference. Still, at some point, we need to ask: What is the common denominator that the condition known as schizophrenia shares with the depressive psychoses, or the organic psychoses?

If, for instance, we accepted Hartmann's (1953) observation that in schizophrenia there is a defect in the capacity for neutralization, then we would have to move in two directions. We would need to explore what it is that interferes with the capacity for neutralization and how this defect contributes to those pathological features which constitute the common denominator for schizophrenia (let alone for other psychoses). To step back for a moment and examine the first of these, namely, what it is that engenders this defect, one might conceptualize certain biological factors (e.g., biochemical abnormalities). But then one would have to demonstrate how these biological factors produce a defect in the capacity for neutralization, or with which components of this capacity these biological factors are involved, even in normal conditions. For instance, does a defect in catecholamine receptivity have some impact on the capacity for neutralization? Do these biological factors contribute to building up those components which eventuate in a capacity for neutralization, and because of some inherent biological defect these components cannot perform their usual role in contributing to the capacity for neutralization? One could raise the question whether the overabundance or lack of a given biochemical directly affects a particular area of the brain, which reacts by producing a clinical symptom (e.g., depression, delusions, hallucinations). Or does this biochemical aberration affect certain building blocks of psychic operations, whose malfunctioning then plays a role in creating that setting in which specific problems, such as depression, hallucinations, or delusions, come to expression in a clinical picture? In my discussion of impairments of perception and the role of the stimulus barrier in such impairments, I shall examine these questions further.

I should like to open still another area for exploration. Let us take the capacity to see connections, which if hypertrophied, may eventuate in an unusual ability to develop metaphors and analogies. In one individual this hypertrophied capacity may eventuate in creativity. Yet, in another, it may eventuate in ideas of reference, delusions of persecution, etc. Id-derived fantasies may in one individual contribute to creative bursts and in another to impulsive behavior. In a certain sense, the capacity to see connections requires some degree of loosening of differentiation. Overdeveloped lines of differentiation may interfere with the flowing over that makes connections possible. Here one can even raise the question of the difference between abstract art and the paintings of a psychotic, as was done by Freud.

Let us pursue this from a somewhat different direction and start out with the statement that the ego is ultimately a body ego. Can one broaden this inquiry to encompass the question of whether the evolution of psychic functions is not intimately tied up with the development of the body image? Certainly the development of the ego and the self must be coeval with the development of the body image, which they ultimately encompass. The capacity for differentiation, which plays a role in the ultimate development of the body image, is particularly important for the development of psychic functions. As noted above, the flowing over which one encounters in both creativity and psychosis reflects a certain amount of dedifferentiation. One finds body-image disturbances and alterations in the latter. Are they equally present in the former? Are the processes that enter into creative dedifferentiation under the control of other ego operations, not available to the psychotic?

Clearly, as one tries to establish agreed-upon common denominators, one must consider that to a large extent contributions are influenced by the nature of the patient material studied. It is certainly relevant whether the patients are ambulatory and in analytic treatment or whether they are hospitalized (the kind of hospitalization must also be considered). Jacobson (1967) emphasized this in alluding to her differences with Searles, who worked with hospitalized, severely disturbed schizophrenic patients. The treatment problems with these patients, she indicated, are quite different in nature from those with the group of ambulatory patients with whom she customarily worked. Whereas these factors may not affect the *basic* findings in different contributions, they may have some impact not only on the therapeutic implications but also on *some* of the theoretical formulations.

Nosological Considerations

Rather early in the history of psychoanalysis attempts were made to differentiate various clinical conditions from each other, including the various psychoses. Inherent in the earlier studies of the psychoses were attempts to differentiate the various psychoses from each other, within the framework of existing concepts. In other words, to develop a nosology, although this intent was not specifically expressed. Any attempt to establish a psychoanalytic nosology, let alone to define concepts within such a nosology, encounters many problems. Not the least of these is the lack of agreement on the heuristic value of even establishing a nosology, as well as on which frames of reference should be used. Stärcke (1920), for instance, did not see any value in differentiating among the various psychotic syndromes. He argued:

> In all this I take no account of any fundamental distinction between melancholic, schizophrenic, and paranoic delusions of persecution. Conditions are frequently met with, which can as easily be classified in one group as in another. Since Freud has enabled us to study the elementary syndrome analytically, we no longer have any excuse for the game of pouring cases out of one diagnostical pot into another. There is only this to be said of the systematic division of the psychoses: all actual cases are highly variegated mixtures of every sort of syndrome in every sort of relation. The recognized clinical types of "diseases" only represent a series of typical combinations [p. 234].

Nonetheless, I feel a psychoanalytic nosology fulfills many needs (see Rangell, 1965). It enables us to discern clinical similarities and differences between psychotic manifestations. A psychoanalytic nosology, however, should go beyond the descriptive level. It should enable us to clarify psychodynamic variations between and among psychotic manifestations. As such it encompasses etiological variations and specific differences in intra- and interstructural psychological processes. It considers drives and conflicts, as well as the self and object relations. Such a nosology should enable us to focus our psychotherapeutic endeavors more clearly. What is necessary, therefore, is not to dispense with nosology but rather to clarify our thinking in establishing a nosology.

As I have already intimated, a critical determinant in our approach will be the frame of reference we choose. Both the questions we ask and our ordering of data will be affected by this framework. Psychoanalytic developmental studies, for instance, have been criticized for not using a normative frame of reference, but rather a pathological one, although this has shifted somewhat under the purview of psychoanalytic ego psychology. The definition of normality is of course a highly controversial one; yet one does have frames of reference to which one can turn. Although "ego weakness" was at first easier to define, one can now equally define "ego strength."

Glover (1932b) believes that any classification of the psychoses must relate them to normal development. "But," he comments, "to do this we must realize how psychotic normal development is" (p. 165). The remark is telling. It is this use of psychosis language which leads Glover, Melanie Klein, and others to distort normal developmental stages. Addressing himself to the kind of approach which, like the descriptive Schneiderian classification, selects specific symptoms and symptom clusters as a frame of reference for psychopathology, Glover explains: "it appears reasonable to suppose that the rigid interlocking which hampers one system of classification may prove to be the firm groundwork of an unknown grouping. For example, if we find a delusional element common to schizophrenia and paranoia, or an affective system common to schizophrenia, it is always possible that the common element should have been the main factor in classification." He adds, however, that "an end product classification in psychiatry is. . . inadequate and must give way to a more 'functional approach'" (pp. 163–164).

Glover uses the fate and development of ego-nuclei as his frame of reference, saying that: "any psychic system which a) represents a positive libidinal relation to objects or part objects, b) can discharge reactive tension (i.e., aggression and hate against objects), and c) in one or other of these ways reduces anxiety, is entitled to be called an ego system or ego-nucleus" (p. 169). He goes on to explain: "At the beginning is a cluster formation of ego-nuclei converging on a consecutive series, the elements of which show an increasing degree of organization. The cluster and the first few nuclei that follow represent the fixation-points of the psychoses; the last organized nuclei represent the fixation-points of the neuroses" (pp. 170–171).

Glover coordinates the various levels of ego-nuclei development with the mechanisms of introjection and projection as well as with the sense of reality. Out of the interrelationship of these factors he evolves his classification of mental disorders. Yet he quite readily admits that other frames of reference might be equally useful:

> I have tried to suggest the possibility of a terminology based on important mechanisms, but others might well suggest that all psycho-pathological states could be accurately named after specific disturbances in the function of the super-ego. Thus melancholia, whilst essentially an introjective psychosis, might well be called a 'hypertrophy of the oral super-ego' possibly the 'second oral.'. . . The claims of 'isolating' or 'circumscribing' psychic mechanisms are certainly very great, as may be seen in the case of drug addictions and fetishisms. And the same is true of the spreading mechanisms (displacement). But on the other hand, there might be some advantage in arranging sub-groups by reference not only to the instincts involved in the condition, but the degree of completeness of the object. Conceivably also the example of psycho-analysis may be followed in naming certain instincts after the zonal component chiefly concerned. In their characterological studies, for example, psycho-analysts have not hesitated to describe an 'oral' or 'genital character,' and there are many character states that might be called 'sadistic hyperaemias' [pp. 185–186].

Clearly, the frames of reference used will determine the nature of a nosology. Since these vary so much, an agreed-upon nosology is difficult to achieve. For instance, with libido theory and economic factors as a frame of reference, stress is laid on fixation points, the aims of the sexual instinct, and object cathexis. From this perspective, the concept of withdrawal and restitution is used to explain the patient's relationship to persons and objects. In the case of withdrawal, there is a decathexis of the object. With the so-called restitution, attempts are made to recathect and to reestablish contact with the object — attempts which frequently miscarry. Historically, it was within this framework that the concept of narcissism was elaborated. Yet one might equally explore the role of object relations from this point of view. If, on the other hand, one were to take the dual instinct theory as the frame of reference, one might concentrate on the impact of aggression on the self and object relations. Taking yet another tack, if the psychoses are viewed within the framework of the structural model of the mind, the role of the superego, the ego and its functions, the type of object relations and self-object differentiation, become the areas of focus.

Thus, in arriving at an understanding of the psychotic process, I believe it is important to specify which frame of reference is being used. One may review contributions to the psychotic process chronologically, look at specific clinical entities within the framework of prevailing concepts and their subsequent development, or pursue the evolution of specific concepts over the years. Whichever way one surveys these contributions, there is bound to be a certain degree of overlap. One of the most comprehensive surveys of psychoanalytic contributions to the psychoses is that by Rickman (1926–1927), who summarizes the contributions from 1894 to 1926. He tries to do so chronologically, as well as by syndromes and concepts, but eventually has to abandon any attempt to reconcile these two approaches, and opts to focus on a given trend of thought, for instance, the concept of narcissism as applied to psychosis, and then trace its development. In many ways, his approach has guided my own.

If, then, in my survey of contributions there seems to be no consistent development, it is due to the methodological difficulty in doing so. Generally, I will try to survey the contributions within a chronological frame of reference, following the history of ideas, so as to give some sense of evolution and continuity. Approaching the contributions from the point of view of specific clinical syndromes may do violence to the chronological sequence of the contributions. Nonetheless, some cognizance must be taken of specific clinical syndromes, which may therefore lead to some confusion, although I will try to minimize this.

It struck me as I made a gross survey of psychoanalytic contributions to psychopathology that they fell under several main headings with subheadings, which I shall list, not necessarily chronologically. Each of these headings conveys the prevailing frame of reference, which, however, was repeatedly revised over the years.

    I. Freud's early concepts revolving around trauma and defense.
    II. The topographic model of the mind.
    III. The libido theory, emphasizing cathectic shifts and fixation points as a frame of reference and the concepts of withdrawal and restitution.
    IV. The dual instinct theory and the role of aggression.
    V. The structural model of the mind.
       A. The position of reality and the object in relation to the various psychic structures (the problem of self-nonself differentiation, as well as problems in identity).
       B. The state of the psychic structures
          1. Intersystemic (e.g., differentiation or dedifferentiation of psychic structures from each other)
          2. Intrasystemic
             a. State of the ego, id, and superego
             b. Disturbance in ego functions
                i. Defensive
                ii. Primary and secondary autonomous ego functions.
    VI. Object relations theory.
    VII. The defect-defense controversy.

It seems to me that most psychoanalytic contributions would fall into one area or the other, with the emphasis being determined by the theoretical orientation of the contributor. It should be clear, however, that there is by no means a clear separation of these contributions. As was pointed out above, there is a great deal of overlap. For instance, while many of the later contributions on the psychoses dealing with the fate of the object use self-nonself differentiation as a frame of reference, they can be tied to earlier contributions using the framework of levels of regression and the concepts of withdrawal and restitution. It will not be possible to do full justice to all the contributions; nonetheless, I shall try to relate the contributions to the delineated areas, as well as to the many questions raised above.

2.
Early Historical Background

Let me begin by sketching in some of the historical background of the psychoanalytic concepts ultimately incorporated into an understanding of the psychotic process. One can sense, without its being spelled out specifically, that these early contributions are dealing with the three frames of reference I have proposed for the psychotic process: the nature of the danger and conflict, the modes of dealing with this, and the specific disturbances in the ego and ego functions.

When Freud stepped onto the psychiatric stage in the 1880s and 1890s, the thinking on psychoses was dominated by the contributions of Kraepelin and Kahlbaum. It is of interest that Bleuler, who also formulated his ideas in this climate, generally accepted that psychotic productions stemmed from unconscious cerebration.[1] Freud's own early contributions on the psychoses were somewhat fragmentary, appearing here and there in his correspondence with Fliess, and subsequently with Ferenczi and Abraham. Much of this correspondence is devoted to the concepts of conflict and compromise formation, the nature of different defenses, and the roles these play in the choice of illness. Indeed, in the Fliess letters (1887–1902), we find many of the ideas which later found their way into Freud's published papers.

During this period, Freud's hypothesis of sexual trauma predominated. His early contributions on the neuropsychoses of defense (1894, 1896) reflected his thinking at the time about the neuroses, especially hysteria and the obsessions. His concept of trauma and defense against unbearable ideas and fantasies was the main frame of reference, the

---

[1] Bleuler's monograph on dementia praecox (published in 1911) was written some time between 1904 and 1908. His work on *Affectivity, Suggestibility and Paranoia* (published in English in 1912) was written in 1906.

term "defense" being used synonymously with "repression." In fact, I would suggest that this frame of reference was never really abandoned by Freud. Rather, his thinking on trauma and defense became more refined and sophisticated as his psychoanalytic theory developed.

In his early contributions Freud attempted to differentiate hysteria, obsession, paranoia, and hallucinatory confusion in terms of the age at which traumatic experiences occurred (see 1895a, p. 206). As far as I can tell, the traumatic experiences per se were not specific for one or the other illness (although he did at first speak of active and passive sexual experiences).[2] In any case, the ages were pushed back further and further, and the concept of trauma began to be diluted with that of wishful fantasy. More and more, the essential concept became that of defense against unbearable (incompatible) thoughts and affects (see 1894, 1895a). The clinical picture was then determined by the fate of the repressed which had returned — in other words, by the nature of the defense, and how it was carried out. In paranoia, this was by projection; in hallucinatory confusion, it was through denial of reality combined with hallucinatory wish fulfillment.

Freud's trauma-defense view of paranoia is clarified in his paper of 1896. After pointing out that the repressed memory determines the form of the symptoms in paranoia, he indicated that this is effected in part by the mechanism of projection, which serves as a defense against intolerable sexual ideas. He wrote:

> One is therefore justified in saying that the ego has fended off the incompatible idea through a flight into psychosis. The process by which this has been achieved once more eludes the subject's self-perception as it eludes psychologico-clinical analysis. It must be regarded as the expression of a pathological disposition of a fairly high degree and it may be described more or less as follows. The ego breaks away from the incompatible idea, but the latter is inseparably connected with a piece of reality, so that, insofar as the ego achieves this result, it, too, has detached itself wholly or in part from reality [p. 59].

[2] Abraham (1907, 1908), on the other hand, in discussing the impact of trauma in hysteria and dementia praecox, claimed: "Experiences of a sexual nature, whether they have the true value of a trauma, or produce a less severe impression upon infantile sexuality, are not the causes of illness, but merely determine its symptoms. They are not the cause of delusions and hallucinations; they merely give them their particular content. They are not responsible for the appearance of stereotyped words and postures; they merely determine the form which such manifestations take in an individual" (1907, p. 19).

It should be noted that Freud here was already talking about a break with reality and about how anything that contradicts the break with reality is removed, i.e., denied or replaced. For this to take place the capacity to test reality must be impaired (something Freud did not, however, elaborate upon at this point). It should also be noted that Freud did not really deal with the concept of psychosis as such. He seemed to accept the then-existing definition of clinical entities and chose to discuss the dynamics that resulted in these clinical pictures.

In relation to this discussion of the defense mechanism projection, it is informative to look at some even earlier remarks by Freud (1895a). He described paranoia as an "intellectual psychosis," with a pathological mode of defense. In his opinion, people became paranoid about things they could not tolerate, provided they had a certain psychic disposition toward the use of projection. Freud's ideas here were based on a case referred to him by Bleuler. A paranoid patient had run away from the treatment situation when Freud confronted her with a "scene" she did not want to face. Apparently she could not tolerate the self-reproach of being a bad woman. What happened was that what had been an internal reproach was now seen as an accusation coming from the outside. The source of judgment about her character had been transposed. Freud pointed out that something was gained by this reversal, for she could more easily reject an accusation from the outside. In this way the judgment, the reproach, was kept away from her ego. Again, we see that there is some reference to the denial of reality. I shall discuss this idea of a break with reality, as well as the concept of projection, more extensively later on.

The next major development in Freud's thinking was the topographic model of the mind. Insofar as the psychoses were concerned, Freud (1900) looked at their relationship to dreams, a topic I shall take up in the next chapter. The role of the unconscious in psychoses in a sense deals with one aspect of the psychotic process, namely, the closeness of the ego to the id (although this was not yet spelled out in those terms).

By 1911, Freud had formulated his libido theory, in which changes are explained by the shifting of libido rather than by defenses as such. Although Freud did not emphasize the defense concept again until 1925, let us be clear that the shifting of libido is actually defensive in nature. If libido is withdrawn from the outer world because that world is too painful, in the broad sense this is a defensive operation.

The application of the libido theory to the understanding of the psy-

choses was already alluded to by Freud in an 1897 draft he sent to Fliess
and in a 1908 letter to Ferenczi. It was ultimately crystallized in his
report on Schreber (1911b) and in his paper "On Narcissism" (1914a).
The Schreber case can be studied as a major example of changing developments in Freud's thinking on the structuring of psychosis and psychotic symptomatology in general. It also makes special reference to the
paranoid constellation. Actually, after the Schreber study, Freud himself made only a few additional contributions to the understanding of
the psychoses as such. In the main, it appears that he used the Schreber
material as a jumping-off point in evolving his ego psychological and
metapsychological concepts.[3] It is of course obvious that the Schreber
study itself also reflects many of Freud's earlier theoretical interests.
(Note that it was published in the same year as the "Two Principles"
paper [1911a].)

Let me underline at this point that it was within the framework of
libido theory that the concepts of withdrawal and restitution, as well as
narcissism, were developed. Abraham, in his contribution on hysteria
and dementia praecox (1908), highlighted the libidinal shifts from the
external world back to the self, as well as the diffusion in the sublima-
tion of the component sexual instincts. Indeed, Freud and Abraham
corresponded a great deal on this subject. They agreed that in hysteria
there is a withdrawal of libido from the outside world, but there is no
loss of the object. The withdrawal in dementia praecox, on the other
hand, is to "autoeroticism" and thus entails object loss.[4]

A good deal of the material dealt with by Abraham was already
alluded to in many of Freud's letters to Fliess, in which he discussed the
choice of neurosis. For instance, in Letter 125 from 1899, in discussing
what makes a person hysterical or paranoid, Freud said that at first he
thought it was the age at which the sexual trauma occurred. Later,
however, he gave up this idea and turned his thoughts in a different
direction. As he explained:

[3] To a large extent, the same is true of many of the psychoanalytic contributions to
the understanding of the psychoses. They are so intimately interwoven with metapsychological concepts that we might say the psychotic mechanisms are really used as
reference points to shed light on general theory by many authors.

[4] Note again the confusion in the use of the terms "autoeroticism" and "narcissism"
which I indicated in my discussion of terminology (Chapter 1). This confusion is also
apparent in Abraham's discussion of delusions of persecution and megalomania,
which he saw as evolving out of a withdrawal of libido. In the former, he said, the
withdrawal of libido to the self alienates the individual from the outside world so that
it appears hostile (Abraham used "self" and "ego" interchangeably here). Although the
problem of ambivalence is touched upon, it is not developed too clearly.

The lowest of the sexual strata is autoeroticism which renounces any psychosexual aim and seeks only local gratification. This is superseded by alloeroticism (homo and hetero) but undoubtedly survives as an independent tendency. [*This idea is interesting in view of the later views on autoplasticity and alloplasticity.*] Hysteria is alloerotic, the main highway it follows is identification with a loved person. Paranoia dissolves the identification again, re-establishes all the loved persons of childhood, and dissolves the ego itself into extraneous persons. So I have come to regard paranoia as a surge forward of the autoerotic tendency of a regression to a former state [1887–1902, p. 304].

In the Schreber case Freud attempted to be a little more specific about the nature of the conflict in paranoia. He proposed regression to autoeroticism for schizophrenia and to homosexuality for paranoia. As I shall detail in Chapter 4, it was within the framework of the libido theory, using the concepts of withdrawal and restitution, that Freud came to pinpoint the role of unconscious homosexuality in the paranoid constellation and to clarify the use of projection in dealing with the conflict.

It should be noted that at this time Freud was already struggling with the role of the ego in the psychotic picture. At first, the ego was depicted as a passive recipient of libido in the back and forth movement related to the object, and the need for the object. Symptomatology was thus related to various attempts to either withdraw from or reestablish contact with the object (the process of restitution). Indeed, a good deal of the overt symptomatology was construed as related to attempts to re-establish contact with the object. Somewhere along the line, however, Freud mentioned that along with the libidinal disturbances we must search for the characteristic ego disturbances that make for psychosis. In fact, near the end of the Schreber paper he made an important observation about the mutual influence of the ego and the id, implying that the ego defects should be studied in psychosis. He alluded to the same idea in a letter to Ferenczi a few years later (1913), when he stated: "I have always thought that sexual physiology lies behind psychoneuroses just as ego psychology lies behind paraphrenia." Also on Freud's mind at the time was the role reality plays in psychic functioning, as evidenced by his "Two Principles" paper (1911a).

Between the Schreber report and the next contributions dealing explicitly with psychosis (1924a, 1924b), Freud followed up on many of the metapsychological implications of the Schreber case. The dual instinct theory, developed during this time, contributed to an understanding of many aspects of depression. Particularly relevant in this regard is Freud's classic work on *Mourning and Melancholia* (1917b).

Freud's two 1924 papers use the structural hypothesis as the frame of reference. They point to psychosis as the outcome of a disturbance in the relation between the ego and the outer world. As I have indicated, however, Freud had alluded to this much earlier, for instance, in his papers on the defense neuropsychoses. This concept of a disturbance in the relation to reality underwent several modifications, so that in the *Outline* (1940), Freud said that the conflict with reality and the ensuing break with reality was associated either with painful pressure from reality or with pressure from the id, or both. Essentially, then, the difference here between psychosis and neurosis is that in the former the ego gives into the id, bows to the id, and lets itself be pushed around by it. (Of course, this is an oversimplification.)

Freud's 1924 papers left several questions unanswered. For instance, is there anything specific to the conflict with reality in psychosis which makes it so painful and so difficult to deal with? If not, then why do some individuals appear to be able to deal with it and others not? This question, of course, opens the way to the study of the ego and its functions to see if there are any specific disturbances in these which are unique for psychosis. Side by side with this question is the one about whether there is anything specific about reality, that is, the nature of object relations, which is genetically unique for the psychoses. In this area we find a host of recent contributions on the nature of early object relations and the disturbances in these relationships which may be typical of psychosis, whether it develops in childhood or later in life. Some of these studies focus on the infant-mother relationship. Others are generally concerned with the genetic factors that result in disturbances in the ego and its functions that may be unique for psychosis. Many authors seem to see specific disturbances in crucial ego functions and defenses as making it difficult for the ego of the psychotic to cope with increased conflictual pressure.

All of the above points to the importance of the three aspects I have underlined in relation to the psychotic process — the nature of the conflict, the mode of dealing with it, and the role of defects in the ego and its functions. As I turn now to a more detailed discussion of the various frames of reference cited above, I hope to show how the diverse contributions reflect on these three issues and add to our understanding of the psychotic process.

PART II

THE IMPACT OF DEVELOPING PSYCHOANALYTIC THEORIES

3.
The Topographic Model
of the Mind

Freud discusses his ideas on the relationship between dreams and psychosis and on schizophrenic language within the framework of the topographic model of the mind (1900, 1915d, 1917a). His application of the topographic model, however, is at time difficult to follow since he uses it in many different senses. To give but one example: In topographic regression we are dealing with the turning of thoughts into percepts and the prevalence of primary process. In temporal regression we are concerned with the return of older structures. In formal regression we encounter primitive modes of expression and representations. Although, according to Freud, these are all essentially at bottom the same, he somewhat inconsistently differentiates these various forms of regression when he applies them to dreams and schizophrenia (1917a).[1] Still, despite such points of confusion, the topographic model has contributed to certain aspects of our understanding of the psychotic process.

[1] Modell (1968), in discussing the role of topographic regression in psychoses, defines it as a shift in cathexis from the outer to the inner world: "If we then consider that there are two functional systems within the ego corresponding to the source from which gratification is achieved, we can then conceptualize a shift of interest from the outer to the inner world as a shift in cathexis from the outer to the inner portions of the ego" (p. 127).

A.
Dreams and Psychoses

Drawing on my previous paper on dreams and psychoses (Frosch, 1976), I intend in this chapter to discuss not only those aspects of the relationship between dreams and psychosis derived from the topographic model, but also those which go beyond it. This will avoid a certain degree of fragmentation of this important subject, although violating our attempt to relate developing concepts to their coeval theoretical frames of reference.

Similarities between Dreams and Psychosis

In *The Interpretation of Dreams* (1900), Freud raises several questions concerning the relationship between dreams and psychosis: (1) What are the etiological and clinical connections between dreams and psychosis? Can, for instance, a dream presage or usher in a psychosis? (2) What are the dreams of the psychotic like? Are there identifiable psychotic dreams? (3) What analogies are there between the structure of dreams and that of psychosis? What Freud essentially emphasizes is the similarity between the dream world and the waking life of the psychotic. He discusses this analogy in relation to consciousness and the role of the "censor" as the guardian of health. During dreaming, he points out, external action is eliminated. In contrast, psychosis occurs during the waking state, when the "gateway" to action is open. As Freud puts it:

> The position is less harmless when what brings about the displacement of forces is not the nightly relaxation in the critical censorship's output of force, but a pathological reduction in that force or a pathological intensification of the unconscious excitations while the preconscious is still cathected and the gateway to the power of movement stands open. When this is so, the watchman is overpowered, the unconscious excitations overwhelm the *Pcs.*, and then obtain control over our speech and actions; or they forcibly bring about hallucinatory regression and direct

34

the course of the apparatus (which was not designed for their use) by virtue of the attraction exercised by perceptions on the distribution of our
psychical energy. To this state of things we give the name of psychosis
[p. 568].

It is apparent that at this point Freud makes little distinction between
the processes involved in psychoses and those involved in dream states.
He leaves open the question of the nature of the factors that enter into
the relaxation of censorship during the waking state. Nor does he
elaborate on how an increase in the drives may overpower the censor,
eventuating in psychosis.

Freud retains his analogy between dreams and psychosis to the very
end. In the *Outline* (1940), he explains: "A dream, then, is a psychosis,
with all the absurdities, delusions and illusions of a psychosis. A
psychosis of short duration, no doubt, harmless, even entrusted with a
useful function, introduced with the subject's consent and terminated
by an act of his will. Nonetheless, it is a psychosis" (p. 172).

It is at times difficult to keep one's bearings in Freud's discussion of
this subject. This may be due to more than the inadequacies of the
topographic model. The fact is that the analogy between dreams and
psychosis is more apparent in some uses of the concept of the unconscious than in others. The analogy is clearer when the term "unconscious" is used in a descriptive rather than in a dynamic or systemic
sense. Moreover, there are many other inconsistencies Freud had to account for when he used the topographic hypothesis as a frame of reference. Subsequent theories thus required the reexamination of many
other phenomena seen in psychosis.

Varying views exist about the relationship between dreams and
psychosis, although most authors agree that there is a close similarity in
their structures. Federn (1952), like Freud, draws an analogy between
the two, postulating that in both the dream state and schizophrenia
there is a lowering of ego cathexis. Lewin (1950) interprets some of the
classic symptoms of mania, such as elation, flight of ideas, and hyperac-
tivity, as if they were dream elements. He compares benign stupors to
blank dreams. At one point he says: "Mania thus could be a kind of
sleep even if it is not a deep stupor. So considered, a typical elation or
mania is seen to resemble the dream of a small child with its playful
fantasy wish fulfillments" (p. 85).

Although Katan (1960) sees many superficial similarities between
dreams and psychosis, he argues that basically they are different, both

in structure and in the dynamic factors which enter into their production. In regard to the latter point, Freud (1933) states:

> The state of sleep involves a turning-away from the real external world, and there we have the necessary condition for the development of a psychosis. The most careful study of the severe psychosis will not reveal to us a single feature that is more characteristic of those pathological conditions. In psychosis, however, the turning away from reality is brought about in two kinds of ways; whether by the unconscious repressed becoming so excessively strong so that it overwhelms the conscious which is attached to reality, or because reality has become so intolerably distressing that the threatened ego throws itself into the arms of the unconscious instinctual forces in a desperate revolt. The harmless dream psychosis [*sic*] is a result of a withdrawal from the external world which is consciously willed and only temporary, and it disappears when relations to the external world are resumed [p. 16].[2]

Katan (1960), however, contends that the underlying cause of a dream is different from that of psychosis. In the dream the ego is governed by the principle of economy in order to sleep. This is not the case in psychosis, where danger arises from conflicts which force the ego to regress. Furthermore, he believes that the wish-fulfilling tendency which is so characteristic of the dream is completely lacking in psychosis.[3]

What underlies the psychotic's delusional system, according to Katan, is that the psychotic, in attempting restitution, must cope with a danger that calls for breaking off the ties with reality. This conflict is then mastered by unrealistic means. Dangerous urges from the id are projected. In other words, what we see in psychosis is not wish fulfillment but the attempt to master a danger by unrealistic means. On the other hand, according to Katan, dreams facilitate the ego's attempts to avoid reality in order to keep cathexis as low as possible. The dream ego does not want to return; the psychotic ego cannot return to normal reality. (Although Katan does not say so explicitly, this is because the reality is dangerous and is responsible for the break and withdrawal to begin with.) Nevertheless, Katan does believe that the ego in what he calls the

[2] We can see here how the ego's relationship with reality, a component of the psychotic process, is already being dealt with, albeit within a different framework.

[3] It is my view that wish-fulfilling tendencies are *not* lacking in psychosis. I would say that the wishful thinking in the psychotic is utilized in the service of constructing a subjective "reality," one which is different from the reality from which the psychotic has taken flight. Freud (1894) describes a patient who imagined her lover had returned. One might say that this hallucination was preceded by a withdrawal from a painful reality. Then the forces pushing for reality contact exerted themselves and the woman created a wish-fulfilling hallucination (by means of a hysterical mechanism).

"prepsychotic" phase and the ego in the dream state are in certain respects similar.

The consensus of psychoanalytic contributions is that, despite the apparent similarities, dreams and psychoses differ in certain basic respects, particularly in regard to the factors that play a role in their production. Which differences are highlighted depends of course on the frame of reference used (e.g., the topographic model, ego cathexis, ego functioning vis-à-vis reality). Psychophysiological studies (E. Hartmann, 1967; Kety, 1959), on the other hand, tend to emphasize the difference between the two states.

Psychotic Dreams

It might be appropriate to turn to the questions of whether there are identifiable psychotic dreams. Freud (1900, 1922) takes the position that whether or not psychosis can penetrate into dreams is not really the true question. The dream work can be applied to preconscious ideas which may contain obsessional, hysterical, or paranoid material. In other words, when we undo the dream work, we may find delusional elements or other fantasies. A pathological idea which exists in the preconscious can be transformed into a dream, just as anything else which exists in the preconscious. In both cases, the dream takes up material that has been forced into the background in waking life. Both Van Ophuijsen (1920) and Arlow (1949) report on patients in whom paranoid trends of a persecutory nature could be established through an understanding of the latent dream content. According to this viewpoint, it would seem that the latent content of the dream and the latent wish may be more closely identified with the nature of the psychosis than the manifest form of the dream.

Richardson and Moore (1963) submitted manifest dreams of schizophrenic and nonschizophrenic patients to a panel of analysts, who were asked to differentiate the schizophrenic from the nonschizophrenic dreams. The degree of correlation was not high, and the criteria used by the panel seemed as valid for one type of dream as the other. Nevertheless, with some degree of correction, the authors indicated that there was a significant difference in accuracy in judging the nonschizophrenic. They found that the presence of unusual, strange, uncanny, and bizarre qualities was more common for the schizophrenic than for the nonschizophrenic dream.

Katan (1960) has suggested that during sleep psychotics are more normal than when they are awake, that they are in the same state of mind as other people. On the other hand, Langs (1966) has compared the manifest content of three clinical groups — severe hysterical character disorders, paranoid schizophrenic reactions, and psychotic depressive reactions. He indicates that the differences in the dreams of these patients are consonant with the clinical pictures. Yet E. Hartmann (1967) asserts that the consensus of most reports is that manifest dream content does not provide a useful diagnostic test for schizophrenia, depression, or any other mental illness.

The relationship between nightmares and psychosis has been of recurrent interest. Do nightmares reflect psychosis? Indeed, might they be indicators of impending psychosis? Mack (1965, 1969a, 1969b, 1969c, 1970) sees similarities between the manifest features of childhood nightmares and certain acute psychoses in adults. A terror of overwhelming intensity, the perception of external danger, violence, the use of projection and distorting mechanisms, the helplessness and vulnerability of the ego — all these characteristics seem to be shared by the two conditions. Mack then depicts the nightmare as an encapsulated or delineated state, intermediate between normal dreaming and acute psychosis. He indicates that a history of repeated nightmares in childhood ("micro-psychoses") may be found in individuals who subsequently develop acute paranoid psychoses. In both instances, he suggests, what we may be dealing with is the ego's struggle to integrate an overwhelming experience. The ego becomes overwhelmed and reality testing may be lost for the child experiencing a severe nightmare, in a way that is quite similar to what occurs in an acute paranoid psychosis. For the child, whether the nightmares will furnish the anlage of later acute psychoses depends on the fate of childhood conflicts, how the parents deal with early anxiety situations, how the ego defenses develop during adolescence, and how development progresses during young adult life.

The relationship of nightmares to later psychosis has also been discussed by M. Sperling (1958), who describes a type of nightmare associated with hypermotility, psychoticlike behavior (with delusions and hallucinations), and retrograde amnesia. She views the recurrence of these nighttime psychotic episodes as having prognostic significance for later psychosis. More recently, E. Hartmann (1979) has presented studies of patients with a lifelong history of nightmares. These patients were clinically quite disturbed; some had a borderline diagnosis, and many, in Hartmann's opinion, were vulnerable to schizophrenia. Most had what Hartmann calls "permeable ego boundaries."

The subject of fluid ego boundaries will be discussed in detail later, in Chapter 9. One manifestation of this condition is the patient's difficulty in separating dreams from reality. I am inclined to believe that the inability to distinguish a dream from reality is a more important sign than the dream content as such. Freud (1907), in his study of Jensen's *Gradiva*, indicates that the inability to differentiate dreams from reality created a delusional system in the waking state. Yet Freud does not direct himself to the question of whether Harold the Dreamer was therefore a true psychotic. What he does say is:

> If a belief in the reality of the dream-images persists unusually long, so that one cannot tear oneself out of the dream, this is not a mistaken judgement provoked by the vividness of the dream images, but is a psychical act on its own; it is an assurance, relating to the content of the dream, that something in it is really as one has dreamt it; and it is right to have faith in this assurance [p. 57].

It is interesting to note that it is this kind of assurance which, Freud (1937) subsequently states, accounts for the fixity of delusions.

Leveton (1961) uses the term "night residue" to designate those aspects of the dream which "persist in some form into waking" state. One manifestation of this is the failure to separate the dream from waking thought so that, in extreme cases, sleep and waking are indistinguishable. The dream acquires a marked feeling of reality and at times may not even be seen as a dream. Rochlin (Mack, 1969b) believes that in the case of the person who is on the verge of psychosis the nightly regression that occurs in the dream cannot be shrugged off during the daytime with the assurance "it is only a dream." Rather, the regression runs from the dream at night into the day.

Mack (1969a, 1969b, 1969c) and others have called attention to the state of confusion and the inability to distinguish internal from external perceptions seen in the dreamer who awakens from a nightmare. Mack describes a woman who, several days before hospitalization, had a dream in which an enormous man without a face and wearing a pointed hat and brown cape was trying to destroy her. She woke up screaming in terror, but the image persisted in the corner of the room. Her husband had to comfort her and to take her to the spot where she hallucinated the man before the image receded. In Mack's opinion, the capacity to distinguish dreams from reality facilitates the maintenance of sanity. He suggests that the confusion may operate in two directions.

The patient may be unsure whether a dream has actually occurred or may have difficulty establishing that an actual traumatic situation was not a dream.

In my own experience, borderline and psychotic patients not infrequently have dreams of a strikingly real and vivid quality, so much so that it is difficult for them to say what is real and what is a dream. In a previous communication (1967b), I referred to a patient who showed a marked tendency to regression. Often, after a night's dreaming, there was a carryover of both the ego state of sleep and the contents of the dream. Throughout the day, events and situations from the dream continued to have a vivid quality, barely differentiated from reality. On one such occasion, this woman said, "My body feels awake, but my mind is still fuzzy-wooly, like it's still with my dream" (p. 611).

One of my borderline patients agitatedly reported a dream in which her mother was lying on top of her, having intercourse with her. What troubled her was that the sensation was so vivid that she was not sure that it was just a dream and kept wavering about the reality of the experience. Another acutely psychotic patient came to the hospital in a panic, thinking that he had murdered his brother-in-law. It turned out that he had had a dream of choking his brother-in-law to death. The feeling in his hand was so real that he began to wonder whether he had really committed the deed and rushed to the hospital in panic. During a psychotic state, one patient dreamt she was a prostitute. She was quite disturbed by the implication that she was dissolute. In contrast, as she was recovering from her psychotic state, she dreamt she was having an affair with someone who clearly represented me. She did not feel too upset by this, saying, "After all, it's only a dream." In all these patients the vividness of the dream contributed to ego states while they were awake which contained many of the ingredients of the nightmare. Although in some sense these patients recognized their "experiences" as dreams, the anxiety, the apprehension, the feeling tone, and the terror persisted.

A transitional state has been reported by Leveton (1961). He describes a patient who complained of increasing tension and fears of going to sleep because of a terrifying recurring dream. The patient became more and more agitated in the morning, finally becoming acutely psychotic, with the delusional content the same as his reported dream. He exclaimed: "Then all of a sudden one night I just lose all trace of time and I can't tell night from day, because the dream just goes on all the time. I can't wake up at all. Sleeping or waking, it's all the same to me."

It appears from the foregoing that there is no consensus on whether the manifest dream itself is a meaningful guide to the presence of psychosis. Viewpoints range from those who see the latent content as most tale-telling, to those who believe that certain features of the manifest dream may be significant in indicating the presence of psychosis. Still others suggest that the patient's attitude toward the dream, difficulties in differentiating dream from reality, and the persistence of dreamlike states in waking life may offer clues to the psychotic nature of a dream.

In my own work on the relationship of dreams to psychosis, I have directed myself to the question of the nature of the conflict or danger with which the patient is struggling and to what extent this is reflected in the content and form of the latent and manifest dream. In addition, I have been concerned with the context within which the dream occurs, i.e., whether the patient is in treatment, which stage in treatment, what the state of the awakened ego is following the dream (e.g., can the dream be distinguished from reality?). My assumption is that, as the symptomatology of the psychotic reflects attempts to deal with certain urges and conflicts, the dream of the psychotic may equally in one form or another reflect such attempts.

Dreams Presaging Psychosis

This brings us to another question raised by Freud (1900): whether dreams may presage or usher in psychosis. After reviewing the literature, he decided that this was the case and that certain dreams represent the first outbreak of a delusion. It is probable, Freud indicates, that in the dream the patient is already struggling with the material which comes into the psychosis. As he explains: "In these instances the dreams are represented as the etiology of the disorder, but we should be doing equal justice to the facts if we said that the mental disorder made its first appearance in dream life, that it first broke through in a dream" (p. 89).

Some time before the onset of his second illness, Schreber dreamt that his previous illness had returned; he then wondered, when he was still in a half-waking state, what it would be like to be copulated with as a woman. Freud (1911b) discusses this dream as a reactivation of Schreber's homosexual wishes about Flechsig and the wish to see Flechsig again. However, one might well ask whether this was not a variant of an examination dream, namely, that it may have reflected an awareness of the oncoming illness and its underlying conflict, and a reassurance that Schreber would recover from this illness and master the conflict just as he did previously. To some extent Katan (1960) hints at this idea when he says that "every initial dream which is emphasized by the patient as the starting point of his psychosis still contains the wish to be able to prevent the outbreak of a psychosis. . . . Upon awakening, the patient may discover that his ego is no longer able to manage the situation by reality means. This wish in the dream was the last barricade which the ego could erect against the oncoming psychosis" (p. 349).

Of particular interest in relation to impending psychosis are dreams that reflect the ego's inability to cope with a threatening danger, a loss of control, a sense of helplessness. Atkins (Mack, 1969b), for instance, suggests that a psychosis may be anticipated by certain dreams which in their manifest content reflect the ego's response to danger. Many writers have considered dreams that reflect ego disintegration and fragmentation prodromal of psychosis. On the other hand, such dreams *may* represent the ego's reaction to instinctual drives directed against the outside and the self. In this case, we are dealing with a much higher level of psychic development and the basic psychotic fear of loss of self is not the area of conflict (Frosch, 1967b). My own experience has been that when such dreams are encountered during analysis, they do not necessarily presage a psychotic break. Several reports have in fact stressed the relationship of such dreams to frightening aspects of the transference. More significance may be attached to these dreams when they occur outside the therapeutic setting.[4]

At the beginning of her illness, for instance, a psychotic patient expressed some end-of-the-world ideas as well as delusions of persecution. In the course of her illness, these ideas recurred in florid form, but, as she improved, they eventually disappeared. Sometime afterward, following a series of disturbing events which brought a beginning resurgence of anxiety, withdrawal, and agitated behavior, she reported this dream:

> There is a beautiful tree with lovely golden leaves. [Both the patient and her mother had blonde hair.] The bark begins to peel off this tree and the tree begins to rot inside and gradually the earth begins to seep up into the tree, the branches, and the leaves. The leaves turn brown and the

[4] Another caution about the interpretation of ego disintegration or world destruction dreams as indicative of psychosis is in order. I am inclined to believe that such dreams must be evaluated within the total context of the person's health. For instance, they may occur in connection with physical illness, fever, or other similar conditions.

tree begins to pulsate and throb, and it turns into the beating of waves and water, and the waves have sharp spikes.

It was immediately after this that the patient had another psychotic episode, in which world destruction delusions were prominent.

Merging of Dreams into the Psychosis

Many instances have been reported in which a dream not only ushers in a psychosis but is incorporated into the psychosis and the delusional system. Fisher and Dement (1961), for instance, report on a patient who had a nightmarish dream which recurred over a period of many weeks and was later incorporated into the content of the delusions that appeared in his psychotic period. This patient's dream reflected an already pressing conflict, namely, unconscious passive homosexual feelings toward the experimenter.

I have already alluded to a patient who dreamt she was a prostitute — a dream that disturbed her very much. Subsequently, after a brief period of remission, there was a flare-up of psychotic behavior and she actually became a prostitute for two weeks. However, this behavior, as I point out elsewhere (p. 97), was related to her underlying conflict about homosexuality.

It is interesting to note that in both Fisher and Dement's patient and in mine it was the manifest content that was incorporated into the psychotic behavior. To me, this would suggest that just as the manifest content of a dream is a distortion of latent conflict, so are delusions and psychosis compromise operations which attempt to preserve the psyche by means of distortion. In other words, the dreams and subsequent psychotic manifestations may represent a struggle with the same unconscious conflict. Does this, then, indicate a point of similarity between the dream work and what we might designate the "psychosis work"? Freud (1907) alludes to this when he comments:

> a delusion very often arises in connection with a dream, and, after what we have learned about the nature of dreams, there is no need to see a fresh riddle in this fact. Dreams and delusions arise from the same source — from what is repressed. Dreams are, as one might say, the physiological delusions of normal people. Before what is repressed has become strong enough to break through into waking life as a delusion, it may easily have achieved a first success, under the more favorable conditions of the state of sleep, in the form of a dream with persisting effects [p. 62].

Freud (1900) had already suggested that in the dream the patient is already struggling with the essential material of the psychosis. We need to ask, however: What makes it possible for such a dream to break into the awakened state in the form of psychosis?

Several authors have tried to account for the breakthrough of the dream in the psychosis by hypothesizing an increase in instinctual pressure, which makes for a weakening of ego functioning, especially if, to begin with, there is an ego defect in neutralization. Fisher and Dement (1961, 1963) propose that the dream may represent a safety valve for partial discharge of instinctual drives. On the basis of this assumption, they maintain that an increase in instinctual drive pressure will bring both qualitative and quantitative alterations in dreaming. Qualitatively, one would expect more direct expressions of instinctual gratification as opposed to disguised ones.

One might, however, take a different view of this seeming increase in instinctual drive pressure. I have already mentioned Leveton's (1961) idea that "as waking repression fail[s] to separate dream from waking thought . . . sleep and waking are indistinguishable." It is as though the important process of secondary elaboration, which generally distorts the latent dream wish, failed to operate both during sleep and in the awakened state, facilitating psychotic behavior.

Of course, these observations raise many questions. Is it purely a matter of a quantitative increase in drive pressure, or are there certain qualitative defects in the ego that permit the breakthrough into waking life? My inclination is to underline the role of ego defects. Under certain circumstances, for instance, the differentiation between sleeping and waking may be lost by virtue of such ego defects. I would refer here to the general dedifferentiation in the psychotic process, which brings in its wake severe disturbances in certain ego functions concerned with reality, affecting the ego's relationship to reality, the sense of reality, and the capacity to test reality (Frosch, 1964). The confusion between dream and reality is a logical counterpart of this lack of differentiation, with the consequence that the dream flows into the waking state. In psychosis, because of the disturbances in the ego, especially with regard to reality, the dream may be accepted as reality. The dedifferentiation between sleep and wakefulness in some schizophrenics, alluded to by E. Hartmann (1967), may find its analogy in the *schlaftrunkenheit*, which we see in some cases where the state of sleep and the state of wakefulness merge.

Another view is that the psychosis following a dream represents a continuing attempt, by a severely impaired ego, to deal with reactivated unresolved childhood conflicts. Katan (1960) contends that the dream ushering in a psychosis has a special function, and that, in a sense, the subsequent delusions amount to associations to the dream. They represent a working over of childhood memories, which ordinarily would have come to the fore in simple associations to the dream. It is from this understanding that Katan attempts to reconstruct the childhood situations from Schreber's delusions.

It might be relevant at this point to refer to the Wolf Man's psychosis following a dream during his analysis with Ruth Mack Brunswick (1928). For a time, before he came to Brunswick, he had had numerous somatic preoccupations with a paranoid flavoring. At one point in the analysis, Brunswick began to undermine his grandiosity, whereupon, following a dream, a full-blown paranoid psychosis broke out. He talked wildly, seemed cut off from reality, and threatened to shoot both Freud and Brunswick. The essential feature of the dream, which underlined the persecutory trend, was the gleaming eyes of the wolves. As Brunswick describes it:

> Their eyes gleam, and it is evident that they want to rush at the patient, his wife and the other woman. The patient is terrified fearing that they will succeed in breaking through the wall. The shining eyes of the wolves now remind the patient that for some time following the dream of four years he could not bear to be looked at fixedly. He would fly into a temper and cry "why do you stare at me like that?" An observant glance would recall the dream to him with all its nightmare quality [pp. 460–461].

Brunswick repeatedly refers to this as a persecutory dream: "Of course the dream derives its chief significance from its persecutory content... With the destruction of the patient's ideas of grandeur his full persecution mania made its appearance" (p. 461). Yet, it is not too clear why a psychosis developed following this dream, or whether the dream per se could be viewed as presaging psychosis.

In a critique of Brunswick's understanding of what transpired during this analysis, Harnik (1930) expresses the opinion that the wolves' gleaming eyes were related to a childhood situation. He believes that the outbreak of psychosis following the dream could be related to a regressive reactivation of earlier oral factors which represented the fixation point necessary for projection to take place. He points out that the Wolf Man's aversion to being looked at and his current anxiety about his nose had essentially the same meaning. In his opinion, the psychosis

following the dream constituted a negative reaction to a correct interpretation; as a matter of fact, he observes, a negative response seemed
to appear for a short time after every correct interpretation. But why in
this case there was a psychotic reaction is not explained by Harnik,
although he does postulate that the Wolf Man's oral ambivalence,
which played an important role in the paranoid mechanism, had been
reactivated in the analysis.

In rebuttal, Brunswick (1930) asserts that the aversion to being
stared at represented a projection of the Wolf Man's own observation of
the primal scene. This projection led to his ideas of reference. Brunswick denies that the psychotic reaction was a transient, negative reaction to a positive interpretation. She argues that it was the feeling of
passivity engendered by the primal-scene experience that reached such
proportions as to seek a way out in paranoid pathways. In response,
Harnik (1931) again insists on the reactivated oral factors as the specific
determinants of the paranoia. To him, orality was the crucial feature of
the Wolf Man's character structure.

In all of this discussion, the question I have raised is not really
answered. That question is: What in the dream itself, either in the
manifest or latent content, presaged the outbreak of a full-blown psychosis? It seems clear that the megalomania protected the Wolf Man
against many fears and was a cloak for his passive homosexuality. For
him to accept this was apparently unbearable, but it is not clear why
this should result in a psychotic break. If, however, one assumes that
the Wolf Man was a borderine personality (Blum, 1974; Wolberg,
1973), or, as I believe, a psychotic character (Frosch, 1964), then manifestations of severe ego defects were already present and played a role in
the continuing inability to deal with an ongoing childhood problem.
(See also my discussion of transference psychosis in Chapter 18.)

As one reviews the various contributions on whether there are
dreams that presage psychosis, there is some suggestive evidence that
this is the case. It seems that in such instances the psyche is struggling
with a conflict under the impact of ever-increasing instinctual pressure.
The psyche tries to deal with this in an ongoing way, in a manner appropriately related to the ego state (i.e., during sleep or waking).
Where the instinctual pressures related to the conflict are too great, the
struggle will continue into the awakened state. Further, where there
are ego defects which prevent repression, or existing difficulties in the
ego's position vis-à-vis reality, breakthrough into the awakened state

may eventuate in psychosis and even merge into the psychosis. The dreams may assume a terrifying, nightmarish, and ego-disintegrative aspect with undisguised instinctual qualities.

On the other hand, at a panel (Mack, 1969b), the consensus was that it is difficult in the course of analysis to predict whether a particular dream presages the outbreak of a psychosis without taking many other factors into consideration. As I indicated above, it is necessary to understand what is occurring during the analysis at the time. Knowledge of the state of the transference or the course of events in the patient's life may be of help in evaluating whether the dream presages psychosis. Previous evidence of ego defects suggesting difficulties in relating to reality may also be of help.

To summarize, it is difficult in the course of analysis to identify dreams as either presaging or representing psychosis without taking other factors into consideration. For instance, repetitive nightmares in childhood and during analysis indicate ego weakening, which may have psychotic implications. Some authors indicate that if dreams reflecting ego disintegration or loss of ego control occur at certain periods in the analysis, they may be of some significance. (It should be emphasized that whether the dream occurs during analysis or depth-exploratory psychotherapy, or whether the dream occurs spontaneously in a nontreatment setting, is not without import. The latter should be viewed as more malignant and carrying psychotic implications.) It is generally agreed that if a patient has difficulties in differentiating dreams from reality, or if dreamlike states persist in waking life, this is highly significant and usually reflcts already-existing severe ego defects vis-à-vis reality. There is also general agreement that the psychosis following a dream represents the ongoing work of a defective ego which is trying to deal with a dangerous threat, frequently deriving from childhood. Nonetheless, most recent contributors would contend that a dream during analysis, taken out of the context of the overall clinical situation, cannot in itself be seen as either presaging or representing a psychosis, despite the fact that certain dreams may suggest this state.

B.
Schizophrenic Language

In discussing the import of Freud's topographic model for an under-standing of psychosis, I have so far emphasized the analogy he draws between the dream state and psychosis. Yet there is another aspect of Freud's topographic hypothesis that has relevance for our study of the psychotic process — his discussion of the relationship between the thing presentation and the word presentation (1915d). Here Freud begins to make some rather interesting distinctions between dreams and schizo-phrenia using schizophrenic language as the frame of reference.

Perhaps at this point I might inject one or two thoughts on the ques-tion of whether there is anything more specific for schizophrenia than for any of the other psychoses. If I were to designate what this is, I would say it is the disturbance in language, in the use of words, which reflects disturbances in the thought processes. I do not mean that we do not find such disturbances in other psychoses, but I believe they are central to schizophrenia.

Although thought disturbances may express themselves in many ways, it is obvious that it is through the language of patients, how they speak and what they say, that we get some clue as to what is going on in their minds. Indeed, one of the most intriguing aspects of schizophrenia is the way the patient uses language and words, how he deals with the whole problem of communication. Certainly the schizophrenic uses language in a way that is often very difficult to follow.

The general consensus has been that we do not follow these patients because a good deal of their speech is autistically derived. Many of their ideas are influenced by emotionally charged complexes which have no meaning for us because we do not know what they are. The impact of these, it is thought, lends an air of unintelligibility to what the patient is saying. Yet the intrusion of emotional factors and personally charged items into an individual's thinking and speech does not always even-tuate in the peculiar, bizarre, idiosyncratic form of speech so often seen in the schizophrenic. Moreover, as we listen to the schizophrenic patient, we become aware that some of the unintelligibility derives from the omission of connections between phrases and sentences. The schizophrenic does not tell these to us, so we don't know what's involved.

A gross example of this phenomenon occurred with a patient who repeatedly exclaimed: "Oh, the boat from Russia — got my European goat — reaping comes and goes." This statement seems thoroughly incomprehensible. Some light is shed, however, when we learn that the patient came to the U.S. from Russia in the early part of this century. She gave birth to a child who died on the voyage. Allegedly, someone had told her that if the baby had been given goat's milk it would have lived. The first phrase, then, may refer to the trip. Does the second phrase allude to the goat's milk and her baby's death? Yet the omission of connections does not entirely account for the peculiarities of schizophrenic language. Returning to our example, we might note that the word "reaping" expresses "life" which comes and goes, but also contains a reference to the Grim Reaper, i.e., death. One word conveys both. This use of one word to express antithetical concepts is quite characteristic of the schizophrenic.

Another example clearly indicates the multiple meanings condensed in a single word. When I indicated to a patient that I couldn't quite follow him, he responded:

You seem to me to think that I could converse with you in some other way, in some other way we could talk.

How could I converse with you in other ways than in English?

You seem to think I could converse with you in some other way, some more fruity way. Fruity in the sense of productive.

Fruity in the sense of productive?

Yeh, fortuitous, meaning good luck.

What has that got to do with fruity?

Fruity is very good. It is like harvest.

I'm not quite clear about this word "fruity." I've never heard it used in this sense — a fruity conversation. What does it mean?

It means a conversation that gives a great amount of stimulation to the people who are involved and engaged in it. And it produces — which produces certain states of pleasure — pleasurable states.

Where did you come on this term — "fruity conversation"? How did it present itself to you? Where did you get the idea to use the word that way?

It arose in the situation we are in right now.

It just occurred to you now? You never used it before?

I've used it before on another occasion.

What occasion was that?
In the men's room at the place I used to work.
How did it come up — could you tell me?
We were talking about a third person. We were just washing up after a
lot of work and we were talking about this third person who had just
come to work. And I said I thought the person was sort of fruity. Was
sort of a fruit.
Meaning?
Meaning a person who was given to overabundance and to ample-type
conversations — to a person who was very talkative and given to high
great state experiences.
Great state experiences?
High state experiences in conversation.
You mean he was kind of exuberant in his conversation?
Yes.

Obviously this patient used the word "fruity" in several different
ways. His tendency to lend different meanings to this word could not
immediately be accounted for by the content of his conflict. It could
be said, however, that the patient was quite angry with me. He felt
pressed by my questioning him about his way of speaking. It is likely
that this touched on some passive-feminine problems. Yet, even
though we may follow the line of reasoning he resorts to in using the
word "fruity" in so many different ways, we still don't know what
makes it necessary, if you will, to structure his language in this idiosyncratic way.

Not only do schizophrenics lend special meanings to words, but
they sometimes confront us with a new language, with new words
and phrases (the so-called neologisms). These are frequently constructed out of parts of words, which have been given an independent
meaning, or combinations of parts of words. This kind of fragmentation, in which parts of words acquire a degree of autonomy, was seen
in a schizophrenic patient who referred to himself as a homo sexual.
By this he meant that he was a very virile man. By fragmenting the
word "homosexual" into separate parts, namely, "homo" meaning
man and "sexual" meaning virile, he used it to define a virile man.

The peculiar ability to combine words in a special way by taking
one fragment and linking it to another, or by making connections via
part components, is beautifully illustrated in an example given by
Ferenczi (1912b). Ferenczi asked a patient: "Can you speak German?"
(*tud németül* in Hungarian). The patient interpreted Ferenczi's ques-

tion as a command that he should take his penis in his hand and as a punishment for this he would be forced to sit (be imprisoned in a hole). According to his enemies' accusations, he wanted to insert his penis in another hole (i.e., strange women). The patient arrived at this interpretation by fragmenting and rearranging the word *németül* in Ferenczi's question:

> ném — nimm, which is German for "take"
> et — und, German for "and"
> ül — sitz, German for "seat" (ül is Hungarian for "to sit")
> [pp. 181–182].

Taking this peculiar meaning, he then wove it into his delusional system.

In an attempt to account for some of the structural oddities of schizophrenic language, several observers in recent years have suggested that one of the defects in schizophrenia lies in the representational function. Some, for instance, have indicated that the capacity for conceptualization and abstraction is somehow impaired and thus the schizophrenic uses language in a concrete manner. But what is meant by these terms? "Concrete" implies we are bound to the immediate experience of a given thing or situation and to its particular qualities. Abstraction allows us to go beyond the specific aspects or sense impressions and evolve a concept, a category or class, under which the particular is subsumed. We grasp the essential of a given whole.

Proverbs have sometimes been used to test the capacity for abstraction, although this has been questioned by some. Let us see how my "fruity" patient dealt with proverbs.

> *Would you mind telling me what this means? "Birds of a feather flock together." You've heard that. What does it mean?*
> Sure. It means that creatures of a similar species are likely to be found in sets characterized by their own characteristics.
> *Could you give me an example?*
> Yeh. A box of pencils.
> *Let's take another one. "A rolling stone gathers no moss."*
> It is more difficult for me.
> *Well, do the best you can with it.*
> It is difficult for life to take root under conditions of instability characterized by a rolling stone. [*He seems to start out all right but cannot tear himself away from the "rolling stone."*]
> *Could you give me an example, for instance?*
> [*He now personalizes it:*] It is difficult for me to get into a normal set and

into a working environment as long as I'm a patient on the 07 ward
at Bellevue.
*Let me ask one more then. "People who live in glass houses should not
    throw stones."*
Shall I give a definition of this one?
What do you understand by it?
I understand it to mean: When things are going well for you, it's very
    good to be extremely careful and make even greater efforts to do the
    correct thing and be the most helpful person you possibly can.
Could you give me an example of how this operates?
I'll give you a story. A man has a nice house with glass windows; it's a
    nice glass house. There is plenty of work for him to do in it and good
    companions for him to work with. It's a respectable job. He should
    not go and insult the boss. Particularly if it's a glass house that he
    works in. If it's a floral, a florist.

It is clear that this very bright patient could not tear himself away
from the specific components of the proverbs and, when he did, it was
to personalize them in a very concrete way.

It has also been postulated that we cannot follow the schizophrenic's speech because a good deal of it is autistically derived. This
brings us to the concept of autism. As I indicated in Chapter 1, Freud
believed that the autism Bleuler described was really autoerotism.
Following Freud's terminology, then, we can say that a withdrawal
from reality and regression to the stage of autoerotism brings with it a
dedifferentiation equated with primary narcissism. This stage facilitates the primary-process thinking so characteristic of schizophrenia.[5]
Thoughts and affects deriving form this world, which have highly personal implications, are incomprehensible to us. They lend an idiosyncratic cast to language and behavior.

In a letter of 1914 to Abraham (in Jones, 1955), Freud specifically
addresses the subject of the schizophrenic's treatment of words. His
explanation, couched in the framework of the topographic model, is
colored by libido theory and presages the significance of disturbed object relations in emotional disorders:

I think one can discern a simple solution of the relation of dementia
praecox to reality. The system unconcious is composed of the cathexes of

[5] Arieti (1974) has referred to paleologic thinking in the schizophrenic, which is
essentially primary-process thinking. Out of this evolves predicate thinking. He gives
as an example: "The Virgin Mary was a virgin. I am a virgin. Therefore I am the
Virgin Mary." This requires a loss of self-nonself differentiation, as well as early infantile fragmentation, in which parts of the self can substitute for other parts of the self.
See also Storch (1924).

material objects [*the thing*]. The system conscious corresponds to the association of these unconscious ideas with verbal ideas and this makes them able to become conscious. Repression in the transference neurosis consists of the withdrawal of libido from the system conscious, that is, in detachment of the concepts of objects from those of words; repression in the narcissistic neuroses [*psychoses*] signifies the withdrawal of libido from the unconscious ideas of objects, naturally a far more profound disturbance. So dementia praecox produces changes in language and in general treats the concepts of words just as hysteria treats those of objects, i.e., they are subjected to the primary process with condensation, displacement, discharge, etc. [p. 456].

Freud continues this discussion in his paper on "The Unconscious" (1915d). Looking at the schizophrenic's speech, he points to its stilted, almost precious quality and its peculiar disorganization of sentences. He also cites the prominence given to bodily organs or innervations, referring to the organ or hypochrondriacal speech found in schizophrenics. Yet he goes on to say:

More important than this is that in schizophrenia, words are subjected to the same process as that which makes the dream images out of latent thought processes, to what we have called the primary psychical process. Words undergo condensation and displacement and transfer their cathexes to one another in their entirety. The process may go so far that a special word, especially suitable on account of its numerous connections, takes over the representation of the whole chain of thought [p. 199].

At a later point in this paper Freud suggests that the cathexis of the word presentation is not part of the act of repression, but represents a first attempt at recovery of the lost object. It may well be that schizophrenics set off on a path that leads to the object via the verbal part of it, but then find themselves having to accept words as objects.

This relationship between the word presentation and the thing presentation is further elaborated in Freud's "Metapsychological Supplement to the Theory of Dreams" (1917a). Here Freud highlights an essential difference between the dream work and schizophrenia. In schizophrenia what becomes the subject of modification by the primary process is the word itself in which the preconscious thought was expressed. In dreams the subject of modification is not the word but the thing presentation, to which the word has been taken back. (In other words, it has been taken back to the original perception.) In dreams there is free communication between preconscious word cathexes and unconscious thing cathexes, while in schizophrenia this communication has been cut off.

In a brilliant tour de force, Freud, incorporating the libido theory as a frame of reference, summarizes the differences between dreams and psychosis: "In dreams, the withdrawal of cathexis [*libido or interest*] affects all systems equally. In the transference neuroses, the *Pcs.* cathexis is withdrawn; in schizophrenia, the cathexis of the *Ucs.*; in amentia, that of the *Cs.*" (p. 235). While Freud's first statement here— that "the withdrawal of cathexis affects all systems equally"—is of course not true (as he himself later admits), the other points are of interest. With the transference neurosis, he suggests there is a withdrawal from thoughts or ideas about the object to the unconscious object representation. With schizophrenia, Freud is referring to the nonhallucinatory aspects of the disease, where there is withdrawal from the thing or object representation. This results, among other things, in the kind of indifferent relation to the environment so common in schizophrenia, in which human relations are impaired, yet the environment remains in some way as part of a perceptual experience. A person's name or the name of an object remains without too much meaning, dissociated from the person or object; so it (i.e., the word) may be linked to anything and everything. With amentia, what Freud implies is a break with and denial of reality. There is a loss of reality testing, a function of the *Cs.* Wish fulfillment plays the main role in replacing reality. What Freud also means here, I think, is that the system *Pcs.*, insofar as it relates to external sensory stimuli, is decathected.

Of course, this is only a model, and Freud himself has to qualify it to account for various clinical phenomena, such as hallucinations in schizophrenia (whose *proferred* explanation would appear inconsistent with a strict application of the model). In the dream state, discharge through motility is not available and regressive perceptual modes are necessary. Yet Freud cannot simply say that hallucinations in schizophrenia, as in dreams, arise from a regression to more primitive modes of perception. What he does is to hypothesize that in schizophrenia the hallucinations constitute an attempt to reestablish contact with the object: "The hallucinatory phase of schizophrenia. . . might well correspond to a fresh attempt at restitution, designed to restore a libidinal cathexis to the idea of the object" (pp. 229–230). This is similar to his explanation of the schizophrenic's use of language.

In keeping with Freud's ideas, Hartmann (1953) proposes: "In the course of the schizophrenic process, while the ideas of the objects lose their cathexis, the preconscious verbal presentations connected with the object become hypercathected" (p. 182). From the perspective of ego psychology, we can see that if words are treated as if they were things, there must be a loss in the representational function of the ego, which normally allows for the differentiation of the signs from what they signify.

But how does all this look clinically? Do these ideas enable us to understand the language disturbance in the schizophrenic, which, as I have suggested, must reflect a thought disturbance? Let me cite a conversation with a patient who had certain delusional ideas of her husband's infidelity. When I asked her, "Are you jealous of your husband?" she said to me blandly, "No, I love perfume." The word "perfume" is puzzling until one realizes that she took the name of the perfume called "Jealousy" and made the relationship via words. In expressing her love for perfume, she in effect denied my question. For her, the thing (perfume) and the word ("jealousy") were identical and thus could be related to other words.

That the word begins to be treated almost independently can also be seen when the patient attaches extreme affects to certain words. A patient of mine at one point became exceedingly tense, anxious, even belligerent and assaultive, in relation to the mention of certain colors. The connection was with her husband. Yet the relationship to her husband was not apparent; it was the words for these colors that were laden with anxiety, rage, etc. (equal to her feelings toward her husband). The representational function of language was lost. The words became the husband, not a representation or symbol of the husband. She also connected parts of the words for these colors with other words, and these words, too, became laden with affect. Her attitude toward her husband was rather bland, alternating with periods of concern and anxiety. Was this simply a shifting of affect from one object to another as a form of displacement? Not entirely. What we see is a withdrawal of libido from the original object, with certain words (which were in some way related to it) now treated as the object. Connections between things are no longer made via their object representations as such, but via word representations. For my patient, even color connections were no longer made with regard to the color per se, but in terms of the word belonging to the color. These words were treated concretely as objects with accompanying affects.

The treatment of words as objects in an attempt to reconstitute the object and reality in a sense reflects a primitive way of relating to objects. The need and the struggle to hold onto objects were illustrated by my patient, who used her "color" words in identifying goodness and badness. Specific objects (her parents) then became the indicators of goodness and badness. Her parents were good. If she concentrated very hard on her parents, this would help defend against hostile and aggressive destructive thoughts (and, I might add, prevent her parents' destruction). There was an urge to stay at home with them, to be constantly in their presence.

A similar point is made by Nunberg (1920) in his discussion of a psychotic patient. He sees the patient's whole delusional system, with its various transformations, as an attempt to cathect anew the objects of the outside world with an overflow of narcissistic libido. Since this libido could not go back to the objects themselves, parts of the body represented themselves to the ego as objects and the patient libidinized these, resulting in various somatic phenomena. The patient used his body to communicate and his verbal expressions involved "organ speech." A good example was the patient's use of his bowel movements to "pay off debts." He attempted to regain the object of the external world via verbality: his verbal representations were objectivized and relations to the external world were expressed in organ speech. Words were concrete and endowed with affect. They sometimes took on the value of a sexual or aggressive act (omnipotence of thought). For instance, the patient felt that words could literally do damage.[6] As a result, at times he would not even speak.

A transitional stage in the use of words as objects was illustrated by a patient who was a psychotic character. In several of her obsessional-like preoccupations, she spoke of words and thoughts as objects. On one occasion she remarked: "Words are necessary to life. They are the means of holding onto an individual — my bridge of life to the real world." Yet it soon became clear that at times the words themselves became the individuals.

So far I have been discussing schizophrenic language primarily within the framework of the topographic model, supplemented by libido theory. I would now like to take a more structural-developmental approach and see how the concepts of faulty integration and dedifferentiation may add to our understanding. From this perspective, we would take as our point of departure the idea that at its earliest stage of development the psyche exists in an undifferentiated state, and only

[6] Although the obsessional, too, may feel that a word itself can do damage, in the obsessional there *is* a relationship with the object.

gradually integrates its component parts into a cohesive self- and body-image. At first, then, there is no distinction between what belongs to the self and what to the nonself. The source of stimuli cannot be pinpointed. Gradually, with some degree of differentiation, attempts are made to do this, although not too accurately at first. Stimuli stemming from different parts of the self may for some time be viewed as stemming from an external object. Organs may be endowed with an autonomy and considered as objects. The same may apply to thought processes (including language), so that in the beginning fragmented parts, representing the raw material of language, may operate quite autonomously and independently. To rephrase this somewhat, I would say that at the earliest stages of psychic development we are dealing with molecular parts, including not only the body fragments, but also the early components of thought and language. Just as the representations of organs and parts of organs may be treated as autonomous bodies, so may thought and language (Tausk, 1919; Schilder, 1935).

Freud (1891) discusses how visual, acoustic, kinesthetic, and other sensory components contribute to shaping words, which then become linked with object images (which themselves originate from a variety of representations). Before language development takes place, the individual source elements (acoustic, visual, etc.) remain unrelated and in themselves constitute independent objects, if you will. The sounds a child makes may at first lead an independent existence, without the purpose of communication. We have all seen children intrigued by the sound of a word and playing with this sound, without connecting the sound to communication. That is, before the "word" is linked to an object, it leads a kind of separate existence and in a sense is itself an object. Side by side with this fragmentation of language components, there is also a certain nondifferentiation or spilling over, facilitated by primary-process features (e.g., displacement, condensation). Thus, one "word" may cover a host of phenomena ("da-da," for instance, can mean bigness, a deep voice, pick me up, etc.).

From this perspective, then, the schizophrenic's treatment of words (or body parts) as objects could be compared to the earliest stage in psychic development, characterized by nondifferentiation and microfragmentation, if you will. We might hypothesize that if, for one reason or another, there is an interference with the appropriate integration of these fragments into coherent wholes, this raw material (the prototypes of language) may be used by the schizophrenic for various purposes. Yet schizophrenic speech is much more than a reinstitution of early defective ego states and processes. These are borrowed by the schizophrenic, in combination with factors from later psychic development, in the service of many needs — for instance, defense.

From all I have said, it should be obvious that many of the manifestations of psychosis cannot be explained solely by the topographic model of the mind. As we have already seen, several authors resorted to libido theory to supplement this model in explaining psychotic phenomena. I should thus like to turn to an examination of this theory and the understanding it lends to several aspects of the psychotic process.

4.
The Libido Theory

Introduction

Certainly many of the early psychoanalytic contributions were made with an eye to libidinal vicissitudes. But it is as the libido theory began to crystallize that the concepts of cathectic shifts, defense mechanisms, and fixation points became a central focus. As we shall see, the libido theory has contributed to an understanding of the psychotic process in several areas. In this chapter I shall select some of these areas for detailed discussion. In particular, I shall look at the role of unconscious homosexuality, the concepts of withdrawal and restitution, and the mechanism of projection, as well as at some of the clinical manifestations evolving out of these processes — namely, the paranoid constellation, delusions, and hypochondriasis. Although I shall to some degree try to pursue a chronological course with the libido theory as a frame of reference, I shall veer from this to develop particular concepts.

In addition to Freud's writings (see below), Abraham's contributions (1907, 1908, 1911, 1924) were important in relating libido theory to a psychoanalytic understanding of the psychoses. In 1907 he indicated that in hysteria and dementia praecox the symptoms are elaborations of sexual fantasies. By 1908 he was applying the libido theory to the psychoses. He highlighted the libidinal shifts from the external world back onto the self and advanced the idea that dementia praecox destroys the capacity for sexual transference, for object love, since this has been transferred to the self. The sexual overestimation thus becomes autoerotic (in the sense of narcissism) and is the source of the delusion of grandeur. According to Abraham, the distortion goes much deeper in dementia praecox than in hysteria, with the patient tending to slip back more and more into the "autoerotic" stage of development.

As I have indicated, the Schreber report (1911b) was the crystallization point for Freud's libido theory. Schreber had reached a relatively high position in the German judicial system when, at age 51, he had a breakdown which kept him hospitalized for some time. Near the end of his hospitalization he wrote his *Memoirs* (1900). (In a sense, Schreber was the Clifford Beers of psychoanalysis.) Freud used these *Memoirs* to develop his thinking on libidinal vicissitudes and the paranoid constellation. He directed himself to the dynamic and genetic aspects of delusions, for instance, rather than to their descriptive phenomenology. In doing so, he pointed out that the grandiosity viewed by many as the ultimate stage in the development of a delusional system is really a regressive reactivation of the common denominator in all such individuals — an extreme narcissism, with feelings of omnipotence, deriving from the earliest stages in psychic development. What we see as delusional persecutory systems in such individuals are, in a way, already later stages in paranoid development — an attempt at dealing with and resolving basic fears and anxieties. Delusions are reparative efforts at cure, at holding onto reality, which do not quite succeed.

Freud believed that unconsciously these individuals have not resolved the struggle over their sexual identity, specifically over their passive homosexuality, but have reached some kind of precarious balance which enables them to get along. Then, for some reason, this struggle is reactivated. This reactivation makes them particularly sensitive to their surroundings, to what they feel are humiliations. They may even always have been hypersensitive by virtue of the underlying nonresolution of their sexual identities. This suspicion and hypersensitivity reflect a narcissistic vulnerability. Hidden behind this is a sense of grandiosity, which can be seen as laying the groundwork for the narcissistic vulnerability. The result is a withdrawal of libido from the outside world, and it is at this stage that one begins to see the evidence of the heightened self-preoccupation which brings in its wake the hypochondriasis and eventually the somatic delusions. (During attempts at restitution, hypochondriasis may also manifest itself.) Freud believed the individual tries to combat this withdrawal and return to reality via the mechanism of projection, thus bringing into the forefront all sorts of delusions. At the same time, material is derived from the early narcissistic period, out of which the grandiosity evolves.

In the Schreber report, then, Freud arrived at a dynamic formulation of the paranoid constellation, using the libido theory as his frame of reference. It is in this sense that his contribution should be viewed, rather than as a description of a specific clinical entity, and it is in this sense that it contributes most to our understanding of the psychotic process. I should add, however, that I do not find anything inconsistent between Freud's dynamic formulation and the clinical descriptions of others, such as Magnan. What are viewed by clinicians as early stages in the clinical picture are apparently already later stages in the dynamic development of the illness.

Before I turn directly to an examination of the paranoid constellation, let me briefly outline some of Freud's other essential contributions in the Schreber paper (all of which will be detailed in the sections that follow). Of particular importance is the central role Freud assigned to unconscious homosexual conflict in paranoid formation. Further light is shed on our understanding of the nature of the conflict by Freud's detailed discussion of the choice of illness. And the question of how the conflict is dealt with is illumined by his remarks on projection, repression, fixation points, withdrawal and restitution, narcissism, and hypochondriasis. (Unlike Magnan, for instance, Freud did not see redemption ideas as simply an explanatory delusion or rationalization.) Finally, his focus on the position of the object and his concept of restitution open up a consideration of the role of reality and, by implication, the position of the ego. Yet, although he suggested that ego disturbances play a role in psychotic manifestations, he was not specific about the nature of these disturbances or about the particular ego functions involved.

Freud's contribution left many other questions open, and these became the subject of subsequent writers' contributions. For instance, Freud did not examine the specificity of the unconscious homosexual conflict for paranoia, nor did he discuss the role of the mother. The latter omission may have been due to the fact that at the time Freud's frames of reference were involved with a higher stage of development, and the preoedipal factors were not too clear. As we shall see, several later contributions look at these early factors (e.g., Macalpine and Hunter, 1953; Fairbairn, 1956; White, 1961). Other subsequent contributions focus more sharply on the role of aggression — another area Freud had not developed at this time. Questions also arise regarding the mechanism of projection — i.e., what makes for paranoid and psychotic projection versus other forms of projection? We also need to look at how hypochondriasis fits into the picture or into psychotic symptomatology in general.

A.
The Role of Unconscious Homosexuality
in the Paranoid Constellation

Paranoid delusions are one of the most common clinical manifestations. They may be quite frank and direct or very subtle; highly organized or more diffuse. Some are transient phenomena; others persistent and chronic. Through the years, there have been numerous attempts to arrive at a clinical systematization of disorders showing paranoid delusions. The various diagnostic categories include paranoid personality, paranoia, paranoid condition, paranoid state, paranoid reaction, paraphrenia, and paranoid schizophrenia. Efforts to differentiate among and sharpen these classifications are associated with well-known names in the history of psychiatry: Heinroth, Kahlbaum, Kraepelin, Bleuler, Magnan, Adolph Meyer, and Kretschmer. More recent contributors include Cameron, Ovesey, and others. I shall not, however, attempt to discuss in detail the various arguments for the one or the other classification. Rather, my focus will be on the structure and dynamics of the paranoid delusion, with attention to its development and evolution, as well as its raison d'être.

Nonetheless, I would like to begin with Magnan's (1936) description of *délire chronique.* I have selected his formulation because, by and large, it fits in clinically with most of the other formulations, even though it differs in some details. Moreover, it was against this clinical concept that Freud directed his remarks in the Schreber case (1911b). Magnan depicted specific stages in the development of delusional systems. In his opinion, the delusional development could become fixed at any particular stage, thus accounting for the varying clinical pictures. Specifically, Magnan outlined (1) a hypochondriacal stage, or stage of subjective analysis; (2) a stage of persecution; (3) a transformation of the personality characterized by the expression of ideas of grandeur; and (4) occasionally a stage of deterioration. All of this may be set into motion by some precipitating factor, whether a social setback or slight humiliation. A sensitivity to external contacts develops and brings in its wake a kind of withdrawal with subjective preoccupations, which may present themselves in many forms (e.g., hypochondriacal complaints).

To illustrate this idea, let me present a composite case. A man becomes increasingly concerned about some bodily function. He goes from doctor to doctor and has all sorts of tests. Temporarily he is reassured by the negative findings. Eventually, however, he returns to the same symptoms and complaints, or variations thereof. Little by little, his bodily functioning becomes his main preoccupation, in a sense his whole life and whole concern. If the patient remains at this stage, his clinical condition is characterized as hypochondriasis.

But further developments may ensue. The patient may become extremely worried about his drowsiness, his headaches, the way his stomach feels, etc. Suddenly one day, in a flash, it becomes clear to him when all this began. It was the day his neighbor offered him a cup of coffee. Now that he thinks back, he remembers that it really did taste kind of funny and as soon as he drank it he did notice a slight dizziness and confusion. The coffee was poisoned; it affected his brain, his stomach, and other parts of his body. They have begun to disintegrate and deteriorate. Here we see the emergence of somatic delusions. With this retrospective falsification of the origins of his physical complaints, a familiar mechanism comes into play—projection. The patient's somatic sensations, the peculiar way he feels, are attributed to external forces; they are something that someone caused to happen to him.

It is with this sudden realization—"Now I understand it"—that we see the beginning development of the systematized delusion. Yet this burst of clarification brings in its wake a shift of anxiety, and the confusional state may subside. It is not beside the point that sometimes the initiation of a delusional system brings a kind of reintegration of the personality in other areas. Systematized delusions are sometimes considered to have an integrative effect on the ego.

The process may stop here. But let us see what happens if the condition progresses. The plot thickens. Groups of people are involved. The patient is the focus of a conspiracy, involving at first a few, then more people (both close to him and not). It may grow into a worldwide conspiracy. These people are out to get him, to hurt him, to stop some important function he has to perform. But why pick on him? Why has he been made the focus of a worldwide conspiracy? Obviously he must be an important person. Now we begin to see the beginning evolution of the delusion into the grandiose stage. The patient's own importance expands. Why are so many people involved? Little by little, the idea takes shape that this is all an attempt to interfere with an important mission entrusted to him. He is to save the world. He begins to see himself as the messenger of God, or even God Himself. If he carries this delusion all the way, it becomes: "I am the universe." (In this the original state of nondifferentiation in psychic development makes itself evident again.)

Obviously this presentation is highly schematic and oversimplified. For instance, we never see a total regression. Instead, we generally see evidence of subsequent development side by side with derivatives of early stages in development. Nor can one always follow all of these steps in a given patient. Sometimes the earliest steps are quite subtle, and the patient does not talk about them. Nevertheless, this picture may serve as a frame of reference for some of what we see in our patients clinically.

Let us now ask ourselves a question. Why do these paranoid systems evolve in the way they do, almost with a degree of monotonous regularity? It is here that Freud made his contribution in trying to understand the meaning and structure of delusions, what function they perform for the human psyche, their raison d'être, if you will. As I noted above, using Schreber's *Memoirs* as a jumping-off point, he attempted to describe the paranoid constellation, rather than paranoia per se (i.e., a specific clinical entity).[1] This examination of the paranoid constellation touched on three questions: (1) What is the nature of the conflict that underlies the disturbance? (2) What are the mechanisms by which repression (defense) is enacted? (3) What are the mechanisms of symptom formation? I believe these three questions lead into a consideration of three specific areas: (1) the role of unconscious homosexuality in the paranoid constellation, (2) the import of withdrawal and restitution, and (3) the use of projection.

The Role of Unconscious Homosexuality

Many of the more recent contributions view the unconscious homosexual features in the paranoid constellation as secondary to other fac-

[1] Nonetheless, Freud did attempt to differentiate between dementia praecox and paranoia. At one point he merged the two and called them paraphrenia. At another point he referred to them separately, using the term "paraphrenia" for dementia praecox. He indicated that paranoia should be maintained as an independent clinical entity. Yet he was unsure of this and changed his mind many times. I believe that what he described in the Schreber report was the paranoid constellation rather than paranoia as such.

tors, as pseudo-phenomena. I intend, however, to reaffirm the role of unconscious homosexuality as the organizing principle in the paranoid constellation. I propose that not only the forms of object choice, but also the vicissitudes of the modes of gratification represent a danger against which the ego has to defend itself. These are determining factors, eventuating in the paranoid constellation. In the male, unconscious homosexuality is denied, rejected, and projected because the passive anal-sadomasochistic aspects are felt to be degrading and humiliating. In the female, unconscious homosexuality is also experienced as degrading and humiliating. Furthermore, real humiliating experiences, during critical phases in psychic development, become part of the anal-sadomasochistic complex of unconscious homosexuality and play a significant role in the ultimate development of the paranoid constellation in the male. Degrading and humiliating experiences also contribute to the development of the paranoid constellation in the female.

Terminology

Before I address the role of unconscious homosexuality, however, I should like to direct myself to the confusion around the terms "unconscious" and "latent" homosexuality. The *Random House Dictionary of the English Language* (1966) defines "latent" as "existing in concealed or dormant form but potentially able to achieve expression" (p. 809). Following this definition of "latent," it would mean the potential for becoming an overt (practicing) homosexual and would thus be inappropriate in explaining the underlying conflict in the paranoid constellation. A case in point involves a 23-year-old social work student. During a course on psychoanalytic concepts, he became very tense and anxious when the concept of unconscious homosexuality was discussed. When I saw him, he was panicked by recollections of incidents in his life that pointed in the direction of overt homosexuality. For instance, as an adolescent he had found himself fascinated by the genitals of the other boys while taking showers at the gym. On occasion he had had erotic feelings, had begun to have an erection, and had rushed out of the shower in embarrassment. Other experiences also suggested a homosexual orientation which, while not overt, nonetheless had the potential of becoming overt. The patient had not recognized the homosexual nature of his feelings until he took the course and the concept of unconscious homosexuality was discussed. Retrospectively, however, he began to wonder whether all these experiences implied he was a homo-

sexual. Over a short period of time he began to accept this as his preference and eventually became a practicing homosexual; his latent homosexuality became overt.

In other words, in both latent and overt homosexuality we are dealing with what I believe to be different psychic constellations, in which
the genetic, dynamic, and therapeutic implications are different from
those in unconscious homosexuality. The latter may be encountered in
disguised or manifest form in the analysis of characterological disturbances, neuroses, dreams, and psychoses. Yet it is clear that these patients will not become overt homosexuals. Often I have told the patient
this, at the same time emphasizing the importance of exploring why
homosexual features arise.

A further element to be clarified is that in studying such patients it is
of no purpose whatever to search for evidence of overt homosexual behavior, either to prove or disprove the role of unconscious homosexuality in the paranoid constellation. Freud himself called attention to this
when he pointed out:

> Paranoia is precisely a disorder in which a sexual aetiology is by no
> means obvious; far from this, the strikingly prominent features in the
> causation of paranoia, especially among males, are social humiliations
> and slights. But if we go into the matter only a little more deeply, we
> shall be able to see that the really operative factor in these social injuries
> lies in the part played in them by the homosexual components of emo-
> tional life. So long as the individual is functioning normally and it is con-
> sequently impossible to see into the depths of his mental life, we may
> doubt whether his emotional relations to his neighbors in society have
> anything to do with sexuality, either actually or in their genesis. But
> delusions never fail to uncover these relations and to trace back the social
> feelings to their roots in a directly sensual erotic wish. So long as he was
> healthy, Dr. Schreber, too, whose delusions culminated in a wishful
> phantasy of an unmistakably homosexual nature, had, by all accounts,
> shown no signs of homosexuality in the ordinary sense of the word
> [1911b, p. 60].

In other words, we should not expect to find signs of overt homosexuality. Indeed, this is one of the methodological fallacies of questionnaire
studies of the paranoid constellation which use these signs as a frame of
reference. The term "unconscious homosexuality" applies to the *conflict* in paranoid symptomatology, and it has very specific connotations
of dangerous and unacceptable passivity, which must be rejected and
disavowed. Perhaps the term "homosexual" should not be used, but
rather the passive-feminine position, insofar as it applies to the male. (I

shall direct myself to the question of unconscious homosexuality in the female subsequently.)

HISTORICAL BACKGROUND

As I have already indicated, Freud's formulation of the unconscious homosexuality in paranoia was made within the context of libido theory. Strachey (1958) points out that Freud presented a case of female paranoia before the Vienna Psychoanalytic Society in 1906 (see also Jones, 1955, p. 281). At that date, he had apparently not yet arrived at the connection between paranoia and repressed passive homosexuality. Yet, only a little over a year later, he was putting forward that hypothesis in letters to Jung (January 27, 1908) and Ferenczi (February 11, 1908). Indeed, in his letter to Ferenczi of 1908, Freud explicitly discussed the relationship of unconscious homosexuality to paranoia.

The Schreber case (1911b) presented Freud with an opportunity to expand this idea. Freud attempted to account for two important aspects of Schreber's delusions, namely, the role of the redeemer and the transformation into a woman. He indicated that resistance to the feminine wishful fantasy, whose object was Flechsig, was defended against through projection in delusions of persecution. The persecutor, Flechsig, was replaced by God and ultimately Schreber's emasculation and femininity were no longer a disgrace, but were instrumental in the re-creation of humanity. Freud believed that this delusional outcome was a kind of compromise, an outlet that provided satisfaction for both contending forces. The ego found compensation in Schreber's megalomania while his feminine wishful fantasy made its way through and became acceptable.[2] Schreber's sense of reality, in the meantime, had become stronger, and Freud ultimately looked on the outcome as asymtotic.

In developing this thinking in relation to paranoia, Freud suggested that unconsciously such individuals have not resolved the struggle with their passive homosexuality, but have reached some kind of fragile sublimated balance which enables them to get along. As I mentioned above, Freud believed that if this tenuous balance is disrupted, hyper-

---

[2] Other authors have also viewed resistance to the feminine wishful fantasy as central to Schreber's psychopathology. Niederland (1968) points out that both of Schreber's illnesses started out with hypochondriacal complaints and both probably represented a withdrawal from the masculine position, with a succumbing to passive-feminine fantasies about Flechsig and von Weber. Moreover, both came on after Schreber had had to assume an active-masculine role. The first illness arose after Schreber failed to be elected to the Reichstag and the second after his appointment to the presidency of the Senate. (The climacteric apparently played a role only in the second illness.)

sensitive reactions will appear. In a letter to Fliess, he said that since many social feelings have their roots in early erotic wishes, it is in this area that the paranoid is particularly sensitive. The withdrawal of libido in response to this hypersensitivity and the attempts to return to reality via projection bring into the foreground the characteristic paranoid delusions. Freud's famous "I love him" proposition (1911b), with its various denials of unconscious homosexuality, serves as the frame of reference for four types of delusions: persecutory, erotomanic, jealous, and grandiose. (This is equally applicable to men and women.)

VARIOUS MANIFESTATIONS OF UNCONSCIOUS HOMOSEXUALITY

Before continuing with my historical perspective on the role assigned to unconscious homosexuality in the paranoid constellation, I would like to enter into what may at first seem a digression. My aim in what follows is to expand our understanding of how unconscious homosexuality may operate as an organizing principle in diverse clinical pictures and thus to set the stage for a more detailed look at its specific import in the paranoid constellation.

To begin with, I would like to take up Freud's "I love him" formula, which I just mentioned. I wonder whether there might not be a variant, combining a denial with projection: I do not love him (her) — he (she) loves him (her). In this variant, the homosexuality is projected and the other is accused of being homosexual. In the context of this projected homosexuality, I have in certain instances found a special kind of delusional idea and acting out. This special idea may not evolve into a full-blown delusional system. The patient may not make any overt accusations or indulge in any behavior that suggests to others that he entertains these ideas. Yet there may be a kind of acting out that suggests the underlying unconscious homosexuality.

An example of this was seen in a patient in analysis who temporarily thought that his wife might be having homosexual relations with a masseuse who came to give her treatment at the house. He wondered, when he left the house, whether more was going on than he was aware of. The patient assiduously inquired about the specific hour of the massage, but he never voiced his suspicions. What became clear was that this idea represented the outer leg of his own unconscious homosexual feelings.

This man had what appeared to be a rescue fantasy, which was reflected in his very choice of a wife. His wife, who was of a different faith, had been exposed to cruel treatment by her father. Before their marriage, when the patient would take her home, he would frequently, on leaving, hear her being chastised and abused by her father for being a "bum" and a "tramp." Moreover, it was rumored that the father had sexually abused his children and, in particular, the patient's future wife. The patient decided to marry her and save her from this fate. At the same time he had a persistent curiosity about what had actually transpired, asking his wife for details about what exactly the father did. From time to time after his marriage, he alluded to this situation and asked for details. On occasion, when he was angry with his wife, he called her a "tramp" — the very appellation her father had used. What emerged during his analysis was that here, too, there was a projection of an underlying unconscious homosexuality (see Appendix).

Another neurotic patient flew into angry outbursts against his wife when she was "unusually" friendly with other females in a social context. At first the patient attributed his rage to jealousy; his wife was not paying enough attention to him. Yet the vehemence of the patient's reaction suggested the need for further exploration. What we uncovered was his own unconscious homosexual wish, which he had projected onto his wife.

A variant of this direct projection of homosexuality has been reported by Miller (1962), who discusses the case of an overt homosexual who accused the analyst of being a homosexual or having been one. A kind of projective identification appeared to be at work. This patient frequently accused the analyst of what he (the patient) was feeling — attacking the analyst for being a fraud, a person who always played a role. Miller suggests that these reactions derived from a defense against anxiety provoked by separation. In order not to be separated from the analyst both had to feel the same. Miller recast the "I love him" formula to read: "He (the analyst) hates me exactly as much in the same manner as I hate him and since we are reflecting one another, we are not separated by that hate. Indeed he loves me exactly as much as I love him."

There seems to be a peculiar fascination that men have in the activities of lesbians. I treated a manic-depressive woman who during her manic phase had both hetero- and homosexual experiences. During her depressed phase, she felt very guilty about these experiences and confessed them to her husband. During subsequent sexual relations, he made her recount, in great detail, what actually went on during these experiences, especially the homosexual ones. This recounting was very exciting for him, culminating in orgasm. His wife indicated that his potency difficulties were resolved by these narrations.[3]

I have also seen a related manifestation in several manic-depressive women who were very hostile and aggressive toward their husbands during their manic episodes, but were quite submissive during their depressive periods. In their manic phases, the patients revealed that they suspected their husbands were homosexuals, that the husbands showed tremendous attachment and undue friendliness to one or the other male individual. Usually these were husbands of very close and intimate female friends of the patients, a relationship resented by the husbands. (It should be noted that this awareness of the husband's unconscious homosexuality was, in some instances, not without some degree of fine perception on the part of the patient.) In one case, the husband had been impotent for 10 years so that the patient had not had any relations with him. During her well periods and during her depressions, she never alluded to this as a factor, nor did she bring anything up about her suspicions of his homosexuality (to which she alluded during her manic episodes). Certainly, there was no conscious awareness of how her fear of her own attachments to women reinforced this projection.

The explanation of some of these instances of projection of unconscious homosexuality has led me to an understanding of still another variant of unconscious homosexuality. This was especially evident in the first patient described above, who had projected his unconscious homosexuality onto his wife, whom he suspected of having an affair with her masseuse. Behind this lay an intense interest in her alleged childhood sexual relations with her father. His sedulous inquiries about the details of these experiences evolved into what I have chosen to call a pimp fantasy. Here the man, either in fantasy or actual activity, uses the female to effect contact with another male. This projection is not accompanied by delusions of jealousy; on the contrary, it is consciously gratifying. It is my formulation that the woman is used both as a sacrificial object to ward off attack from the male and to make sexual contact with him. Although this fantasy does not necessarily produce specific delusions, it may be accompanied by hypersensitivity and paranoid trends. Most important, however, it is my belief that the wish to share a woman, and through her make contact with a man, reflects un-

---

[3] One of the demands of some customers in houses of prostitution is to have two women engage in sexual intercourse. The customer will watch this very avidly and urge them on, with mounting excitement, culminating in ejaculation. The man's identification with the woman seems obvious.

conscious homosexuality as an organizing principle. (For a detailed account of this manifestation of unconscious homosexuality, I refer the reader to the Appendix on "The Pimp Fantasy.")

FURTHER CONTRIBUTIONS TO FREUD'S FORMULATIONS

After this bypass I should like to return to the discussion of the role of unconscious homosexuality in the paranoid constellation. Freud adheres to the importance of unconscious homosexuality in the paranoid mechanism — although with several modifications and amplifications. There have, however, been many criticisms of Freud's concept of homosexuality as the focal conflict in the paranoid constellation. While some have clearly supported Freud's point of view, others have introduced additional components, augmenting or modifying the role of unconscious homosexuality. Still others have minimized or rejected this idea. Bleuler (1913), for instance, in reviewing Freud's contributions, accepts the important role that unconscious homosexuality plays in symptomatology, but he does not quite go along with its role in the etiology of paranoid schizophrenia. Two points need to be clarified here. Freud (1911b) himself is quite specific that the unconscious homosexual conflict is more unique for paranoia than for other psychiatric illnesses, such as schizophrenia. Again, I would underline that the usefulness of Freud's Schreber study lies in its contribution to understanding what I call the paranoid constellation, rather than a specific clinical entity. It should also be mentioned that Freud indicates that unconscious homosexuality is not the only determining factor in the development of paranoia, although it underlies it. It is also the way the person deals with the conflict (i.e., through projection and other mechanisms) that determines the paranoid manifestations — a point I shall return to later.

Among the early contributions confirming Freud's views is Ferenczi's paper "On the Part Played by Homosexuality in the Pathogenesis of Paranoia" (1912b). The first part of this paper gives ample indication that Ferenczi and Freud had been discussing this topic for quite some time before Freud published the Schreber case. Indeed, Ferenczi essentially recapitulates many of the points we have discussed. He also points out something interesting, namely, that in the case Freud described in his 1896 paper on the defense neuropsychoses, Freud did not adequately appreciate the role unconscious homosexuality played.

Ferenczi presents a number of cases in an attempt to demonstrate "that in the pathogenesis of paranoia, homosexuality plays not a chance part but the most important one, and that paranoia is perhaps nothing

else at all than disguised homosexuality, and that the paranoid defense
mechanism is directed only against 'homosexual cathexes'" (p. 157).
Near the end of this article, however, Ferenczi raises a question that
began to trouble many contributors. Ferenczi, who set out to demonstrate the role of homosexuality in paranoia, states: "The establishment
of this process would naturally bring us face to face with a larger problem, that of the choice of neurosis, with the question, namely, what
conditions have to be fulfilled for the normal preponderance of heterosexuality, a homosexual neurosis, or paranoia, to proceed from the
infantile bisexuality of ambisexuality" (p. 185). This, of course, touches
on a crucial question: If there is a basic bisexuality, why do differing
clinical pictures result, and what determines the choice?

In general, the attempts to resolve this dilemma revolved around
the question of whether there was any difference in the nature of the
unconscious homosexuality. Is there, for instance, a difference in the
vicissitudes of the instinctual drive in its relation to the object which
lends uniqueness to the various pictures? In other words, is there a
special mode of gratification in relation to a specific object? Or is it
ultimately a question of basic trends and object choices being reacted to
and dealt with differently by the psyche? And if so, to what is this
difference related?

Unconscious Homosexuality in a Neurotic

To highlight the question of choice of illness, I should like to present
material from the analysis of a neurotic patient. He was not a homosexual and did not reveal paranoid trends. Nonetheless, his analysis was
replete with homosexual fantasies, which from time to time would
come into the forefront with some intensity. The patient was essentially
a neurotic character with phobias in connection with his work, marked
anxiety, hysterical features (vomiting), as well as depression. As a child
he had been a finicky eater, looked pale, and was called a "green frog."
Much of the basic conflictual material revolved around castration anxiety, orality, fears of loss of money—all of which were expressed in his
fear of loss of sustenance as a result of being found to be inadequate in
his work. I shall, however, allude only to that material which is relevant to the subject under discussion, i.e., the role of the homosexual
fantasies. The question is: Why did these not eventuate in paranoid
features?

To begin with, I should point out that the homosexual material that
came up was primarily orally oriented and rarely anal. Once, the patient did mention that in years past he had occasionally inserted his

finger rectally to stimulate a bowel movement. Essentially, however, he was not an anally oriented person. The homosexual material was usually accompanied by passing fellatio fantasies or involved remarks such as "suck my cock." For instance, the patient described seeing the genitals of men in a shower room and having thoughts of fellatio. Occasionally he came into the office with a pseudo-angry thought against me and the thought "suck your cock" would follow. There were other oral fantasies of swallowing semen, and from time to time he had coprophagic fantasies, as well as cannibilistic ones.

I am going to bypass a great deal and concentrate on a given period in the analysis in which unconscious homosexual material was quite prominent. For a period of a few weeks, there was an upsurge of homosexual feelings, reflecting themselves in conscious thoughts as well as in dreams. The dreams showed confusion in sex identity (in one dream, for instance, he wasn't sure whether it was he or a female hermaphrodite). Castration anxiety was evident, with an increase in defensive feelings and concern about his penis. He would find himself stroking his testicles and holding onto them when he awoke. At one point, after reading about a famous explorer who had studied the sex life of primitive tribes (discussing the size of their genitals) and who also was suspected of homosexuality, the patient had a dream of a phallic mother. Among his associations was a recollection of frequently looking underneath his mother's skirt.

In the next session the patient reported the following events. He had had an accident after he left my office. Someone stopped short and he hit the other person's car. It might have been mine, he thought. He began to have his usual fears of being sued, loss of sustenance, etc., and he would think of this in an obsessive ruminative manner, especially during the early hours of the morning. Sunday night he had reread something by James Joyce describing fellatio experiences and that night he had had a dream from which he awoke anxious and concerned about loss of sustenance in connection with the accident. Earlier, on Friday night, he had had an impulse during sexual relations to have his wife perform fellatio on him. He had this wish constantly, but he could never bring himself to ask, although he would make suggestive movements. He then mentioned a childhood game called "milking the cow," which he had played with his brother when he was nine years old and his brother five. The brother would perform fellatio on him, and occasionally he would do the same on his brother, but only to fulfill the terms of the bargain. (In a current business partnership with his brother, there had been disagreements over payments, etc.) At this point the patient remarked on the upsurge of homosexual thoughts and their oral component. It was his impression that homosexual activity was only oral sucking, not anal activity.

In the light of this and previous material, I brought up his guilt about masturbation fantasies which (among other features) related to hostility toward the brother who had displaced him at the mother's breast. His fellatio wishes were overdetermined by the early experiences and longing for the maternal breast. In the transference his frequent allusion to performing fellatio on me and his wish to be closely related to me after the analysis served as the jumping-off point for this interpretation.

The following week the patient brought in dreams and material relating to castration anxiety, fear of touching the vagina, oral regressive trends, and sadistic elements. During one session he became very sleepy while I was talking about the partnership with his brother in connection with a dream. I had again pointed out the connection to his hostility toward his brother for taking mother's breast away, his anger at his mother, and his sexual play with his brother.

I would like to stop at this point and underline the following: (1) This man is not a homosexual and will not become one. (2) He has no more than the normal allotment of paranoid reactions. (3) Although anal material comes up, it is generally associated with oral-sadomasochistic material, with the masochistic elements dominating. But why is he not a homosexual? Why is he not paranoid? Why is he not psychotic? With these questions in mind, let us turn to the role of anality in homosexual conflict.

THE ROLE OF ANALITY

Many authors have attempted to assess the specific and significant features within the unconscious homosexual conflict that contribute to a paranoid outcome. Almost from the beginning, the role of anality and the fecal mass, at first in its erotic and subsequently in its sadistic aspects, was focused on. Yet the perception of the fecal mass as a bad internalized object is rather ubiquitous; it does not always eventuate in delusions of persecution. What determines when the bowel and its activities become a persecutor?

The question of when anality eventuates in persecutory delusions is underlined by patients who present a great deal of anal material but do not show paranoia. As an example, I would like to discuss a patient who attached hostile fantasies to his feces. He was an obsessive-compulsive character with periods of morning depression, which had been linked to oral deprivation and feeding times. (His sleep cycle had begun to pattern itself to these; he awoke every morning at 4 A.M. during this period in analysis.) The analysis, as is often the case with obsessional patients, highlighted the issue of maintaining control. This issue was reflected in the way he brought up material, in the transference, in his work, and in his relations with others. Like most obsessionals, he couldn't really delegate work, as people were seen as extensions of himself, whom he had to control. Elements of grandiosity were present in his fantasies with counterphobic features (he had flirted with danger even as a child). There was a constant search for perfection, with an inability to compromise.

This man's fear of his aggressive and hostile impulses was reflected in his sexual fantasies during masturbation. For instance, he imagined tearing the woman apart (although this fantasy also had passive elements). Later, in trying to pinpoint when these fantasies had arisen during the analysis, he associated them to my suggestion that he discontinue his weekly enemas. This remark had followed his mentioning that he had been constipated for years and that Saturday morning was enema time. At the time he had brought this up together with material relating to retention of the fecal mass within him. There were many mixed feelings associated with the fecal mass. The main theme, however, was the need to control it, not wanting to let anything which belonged to him leave him. On the one hand, he felt that the fecal mass was bad (the toxic theory of constipation) and that if it remained within him, it would harm him. If he left it inside, it meant he had something bad inside which could control him; in other words, he would have to give up control. In addition, since the feces stood for badness, it was attached to guilt, which he thought he could get rid of by "getting rid of the bad thing in me." At the same time he had some concern about the damage his feces could do to others. He thus wanted to be the one who determined when and under what circumstances this bad thing left him, to be the one in control. Yet somehow, even when the fecal mass was out of his body, it was still related to him, a part of him. The same was true for other parts of his body, like his hair. When he had a haircut, he considered the cut-off hair on the floor as still belonging to him. (Like many anal erotics, he was unable to get rid of things.) He also felt this about his thoughts, and even about his co-workers. They were all really parts of himself — his feces — which he had to control.

This patient also had passive-feminine fantasies related to his body image. Although a big powerful man, much taller than I am, he for some time in analysis viewed himself as small in relation to me. Because he was heavy, he considered his body as rounded like a woman's rather than angular like a man's. He saw his sexual parts as small in comparison with those of his older brother and a partner. He had a "schmekel," not a "schmuck." (This reflected his mother's teasing of him.)

My point in all this is that this patient's anal sadism was that of the obsessional neurotic. It is true that, in contrast to the oral homosexual fantasies of the patient I described above (p. 72), this patient's views on homosexual relations were anal. Yet his underlying fear of passivity and his need to control lest he be controlled did not produce any real paranoid trends. Why not?

Let me refer to still another patient who, although not psychotic, did show paranoid trends. This man was more openly anal-sadistic than the last patient. He had considerable difficulty with hemorrhoids as well as constipation. Interestingly enough, although he took cathartics for his constipation, he was disappointed when they were effective, for he felt a particular pleasure in pressing out a more formed and even hardened fecal mass. He liked to work against some resistance in the anal area. In this case, the anal difficulties were clearly associated with anger, as well as unconscious homosexuality. A connection could be made to his distrust of others, which bordered on the paranoid. It got so that when he reported incidents reflecting this distrust, I would ask him about his hemorrhoids and would learn that they had been acting up. Moreover, this patient invited anal assault by trying to convince his physician that he should be operated on, although at the same time he wondered about the "motives" of surgeons who always want to operate. On one occasion he reported that while having intercourse, at the point of orgasm, he had been aware of a fullness at his anal opening. It turned out that his hemorrhoids had blown up.

In this regard, one might recall Katan's (1950) report that in one of his borderline paranoid patients the fear of orgasm was related to a fear of helplessness, that an abandonment to the orgasm would leave him at the mercy of anyone who wanted to attack him anally. Yet aside from the feelings of distrust that cropped up from time to time, my patient was not paranoid to the point of delusions of persecution. Even here, then, certain questions have to be raised. At what point do anal and homosexual features eventuate in the full-fledged paranoid constellation? What determines when the bowel and its activities become the persecutor?

The Anal Persecutor

The role of anality in the development of delusions of persecution is brought up by Freud (1911b) in discussing Schreber's preoccupation with delusions about his bowel activities. Schreber felt that he was being prevented from moving his bowels, that whenever he had the urge to do so, someone else would occupy the bathroom. He thought his fecal mass was being manipulated by external forces; it was forced either forward or backward into his intestines.[4]

Ferenczi (1911) also brings attention to the importance of anality in paranoia. He presents the case of a 45-year-old peasant who had delusions of persecution in which people ridiculed him, enemies wanted to poison him, etc. Apparently this paranoid reaction surfaced after two operations for an anal fistula. Following the second operation, several hypochondriacal ideas appeared, with the patient reporting "noises in the chest" and suffering from anxiety attacks. He felt as if the fistula had suddenly climbed up into his stomach and was convinced he would die. The delusional ideas set in after the paresthesias and the anxiety brought on by the operation had passed. Ferenczi hypothesized that the surgeons' manipulation of his rectum stimulated this patient's hitherto hidden or poorly sublimated homosexual tendencies. With this in mind, he questioned the patient and learned that he had had a boyhood homosexual experience, in which he had played the passive role. Ferenczi then concluded that the stimulation of the anal erotic zone in the operation had awakened the wish to repeat this infantile homosexual play. The patient first attempted to defend himself against these impulses by converting them into the paresthesias and anxiety attacks. Subsequently, they were projected from the ego onto the outer world as delusional ideas. In Ferenczi's words: "The same unconscious passive pederastic fantasies underlay both the delusional idea and the paresthesias which had preceded the outbreak of these ideas" (p. 298). Were the paresthesias reproductions of the sensations of the operative procedure, which were then reacted to by delusions? (see Ferenczi's remarks on "one-day neurasthenia" in "On Onanism" [1912a]).

Ferenczi obviously believes that this patient attempted to deal with his homosexual conflict by means of a "paraphrenic" mechanism. The question of course remains: Why this mechanism rather than another?

[4] The role of anality and the fecal mass, and their position in the evolution of delusions of persecution, has been developed further by several authors (Ferenczi, 1911; Stärcke, 1920; Van Ophuijsen, 1920; Abraham, 1924; M. Klein, 1932; Bender, 1934; Alexander and Menninger, 1936; Arlow, 1949).

In his other paper (1912b), Ferenczi does look at the specific way of dealing with unconscious homosexuality in the paranoid. He points to a complete turning away from men, a regression to autoerotism, and a return of the repressed, with recathexis of the long-sublimated, but completely rejected male love object.

Whereas Ferenczi focuses on anal erotism and the precipitation of psychosis by external anal manipulation, Van Ophuijsen (1920) refers to the "skybalum" as the internal anal persecutor. Essentially the patients he discusses were not psychotic but revealed paranoid trends. They had fears, for instance, of being attacked from behind and couldn't bear to have anyone walk behind them. Based on his work with these patients, Van Ophuijsen arrives at the formulation, "The most important thing is that persecutor and skybalum are simply treated as equivalent things" (p. 237). He views the feeling of being assaulted or persecuted as a displacement outward of the feeling of being disturbed by the sensation called up by the skybalum.[5]

From a somewhat different perspective, Melanie Klein (1932) argues that the bad object, representing the bad sadistic impulse, becomes identified with feces and it is this internal sadistic object that becomes the persecutor. Yet Van Ophuijsen's concept of the skybalum as the persecutor has much about it that is suggestive of Klein's projective identification. This is expecially so if one views the skybalum within the context of something that is a part of you, in your body, and still remains part of you, even if expelled from your body. The hardened, painful fecal mass, this part of the self to which the patient reacts by projecting it onto an external persecutor, still remains a part of the self. Thus, the persecutor is a part of the self—a bad self. Even if the mass is expelled, it is not lost but returns in the form of the anal persecutor. This process would seem to be a special instance of what Klein calls projective identification.

In a brief communication, Arlow (1949) also links feelings of persecution to the fecal mass. He reports on a nonpsychotic patient who showed some paranoid tendencies, with ideas of reference and suspiciousness. The dreams of this patient, as well as the transference material, seemed to confirm that the persecutor might be unconsciously equated with the subject's feces. Arlow explains: "Tormenting anal sensations are projected to the homosexual object in the external world and transformed into feelings of persecution" (p. 81). The correlation of con-

---

[5] Abraham (1924) equates the loved objects in the paranoid with feces that cannot be gotten rid of, viewing this part of the loved object as an introject.

stipation with feelings of persecution, as well as the analysis of the transference, leads Arlow to conclude that there was an unconscious form of anal masturbation, in which the fecal mass aroused sensations in the subject's rectum in response to masochistic feminine fantasies. The fecal mass also represented the homosexual object's penis and, in a fantasy of pregnancy, the fetus.

The transformation of hostility toward the bowels and their activity into feelings of anal persecution was illustrated by one of my patients, a psychotic character, who could not tolerate any infirmity or sickness in himself. He showed many grandiose tendencies side by side with persecutory trends and homosexual preoccupations. Once when he was ill with diarrhea, he became exceedingly perturbed. He could not tolerate any indication that he was weak and at the mercy of a part of his body. He took it as a personal attack. That "son of a bitch," he said of his bowels, "why doesn't he leave me alone?" At other times this patient voiced concern about people coming too close to him on subways and buses; he sometimes felt he was being observed and watched. These concerns were accompanied by anger, but were also marked by almost paralyzing anxiety at times. Yet he was not psychotic during these periods.

Stärcke (1920) takes up the question of why it is that the loved one returns as the persecutor. He believes that the reversal of the sign—the positive one to the negative one—is to be found in ambivalence. As his jumping-off point, he observes that many delusions of persecution revolve around anal persecutions. According to Stärcke, patients at first are very vague about this; they only hint at it. But the core of the delusion is, as a rule, concerned with anal acts of lust and violence. Sometimes, after speaking of this, the patients seem relieved. Very frequently, however, they transfer the delusion to the physician, developing a strong attachment, or even viewing the physician as the persecutor. Stärcke's examination of various cases leads him to believe that there is an unconscious identification of the loved object with the skybalum, and that this identification provides the basis for the special ambivalence found in the paranoid's makeup. The skybalum, then, is the primary persecutor.

Stärcke suggests that the fecal mass is identified with the child's own body, as well as with the people who care for the child during the anal period. Toward the fecal mass, as well as toward the child's caretakers, there are generally ambivalent feelings. Ambivalence toward the fecal mass arises from the close association of pain and pleasure; ambivalence is felt toward the caretakers because approval and disapproval of anal activities are related to love and hatred. The anal aspect of narcissism is also emphasized by Stärcke — namely, feelings of heightened esteem as well as inferiority, with memories of being a dirty child. He claims Freud's formula might then be amplified in the following way. Part at least of the sublimated homosexuality regresses to anal erotism. Insofar as the latter is positive, it is reconstructed in the shape of delusions of grandeur, and insofar as it is negative, it is diverted by being projected as a delusion of persecution.

All of the above highlights my question about the specificity of the unconscious conflict that results in the paranoid reaction. The homosexual implications of anal sadism do appear to have some relationship to paranoid development, but how and why is as yet unclear. The anality appears to take on a special significance of a sadistic nature. Sometimes this is precipitated by experiential factors, as for instance in the case Ferenczi (1911) reports involving an anal operation.

Still, what is it that determines this way of reacting to the unconscious homosexual conflict? Ferenczi does not really discuss this. There was in this case an actual anal assault. Nonetheless, anal surgery is not generally followed by a psychotic reaction. I believe we are now venturing into my second and third questions about the psychotic process, but especially the latter, i.e., which specific ego disturbances set the stage for a psychotic reaction to the unconscious homosexual conflict? This point will become clearer in my own case material below.

At this point I should like to present illustrative material from a patient in psychoanalytically oriented psychotherapy, who developed a psychotic reaction following an ileostomy. The patient, in his late thirties, had worked for many years at a health club. He had suffered from ileitis since the age of 19 and had had a resection about nine years previously. A few months before the ileostomy he had been kicked in the abdomen while interceding in an altercation. This incident was followed by extreme pain and local manifestations. He was soon hospitalized and the ileostomy was performed.

The patient had not been informed that this was going to be the nature of the surgery, although this possibility had been mentioned. It was his wife who told him the next day that he had had an ileostomy. The implications of this did not quite sink in, but he felt very tense and restless. A few days later he had nightmares all night. He dreamt he was being destroyed, run through a grinder. People with his condition were being sprinkled with bread crumbs and made into cookies. Moreover, there was continuous sexual activity of an anal nature between males and males, as well as males and females, and he was one of the subjects. In the background somewhere was the sound of a large bird screaming. As the sexual orgy went on, the sound of the bird got louder and louder. He would awaken frightened, realize he had been dreaming, fall asleep again, only to continue the dream.

The following day a paranoid psychotic reaction occurred. He was frightened that there was a plot going on to liquidate him — that he was doomed. Everybody was in on the plot — people were watching him, making remarks about his ileostomy. He cried a lot and repetitively recounted his fears and the whole story to his wife and his physician. Although he continued to be frightened, gradually the delusions subsided. When I saw him the next day, while he was still somewhat shaken and fearful of going to sleep, he was no longer psychotic. Nonetheless, he focused on his ileostomy and his apprehension that people looking at him would know he had had an ileostomy. He was concerned about how he could keep this hidden.

In the course of analytically oriented psychotherapy over a year, this trend continued. He refused to accept the fact that the ileostomy was permanent and, in spite of medical opinion to the contrary, persisted in the belief that he could have a resection and this hole, this defect, would be closed up. His attempts at denial included a refusal to go to the ileostomy club to learn better management of what he felt was a temporary condition. But behind this was a fear of having to stand up and talk about himself and reveal himself to be inadequate — not only by virtue of his defect, but also sexually inadequate. Although at first he ascribed this to his ileostomy and his embarrassment at having sexual relations while wearing an ileostomy bag, it turned out that he had been impotent for years. He claimed he had had an adequate sex life early in marriage, but it was not long before he began to have difficulties, which ultimately culminated in total impotence. His impotence was a source of ongoing contention with his wife, who belittled him, sometimes in the presence of others, by making thinly veiled jokes. (I shall not pursue his own underlying hostility toward his wife, who had been a nurse and upon whom, on the surface, he was exceedingly dependent for his care throughout their 10 years of marriage. She resented this, saying "I'm married to a child not a man.")

I would like to concentrate on the many ramifications of the ileostomy for this patient. There was the realistic fear of having an "accident," and when this happened from time to time, he felt tremendously humiliated and ashamed. But there were also other, rather powerful feelings of hatred toward this opening in the body. He spoke quite openly of feeling persecuted by this enemy and wanting to devise ways of conquering it. He was never free of this persecutor, who made him feel helpless and inadequate, who threatened him constantly and weakened his manliness. It was clear that he had transferred to the ileostomy much that he had felt anally. In connection with his ileitis, he had had to have repeated anal procedures (barium enemas, colonoscopy, sigmoidoscopy, etc). Beyond the usual distress at these procedures, he developed an inordinate anxiety, a fear of being penetrated. He found these procedures humiliating. He felt helpless. I was able to relate these feelings to his feelings about the ileostomy and concerns about his virility.

This patient had always been a body person, concentrating on the development of his body. He was described by both his wife and physician as macho, constantly trying to demonstrate his manliness. His career ambitions also reflected this trend. He had tried to become a security guard but had been rejected because of ileitis. This was a grave disappointment which heightened his feelings of inadequacy. A great deal of other material confirmed his macho self-image and ego ideal. It is worth mentioning in passing that his father, although not physically punitive, was thoroughly unrelated to the patient. There was a total lack of warmth and a constant tendency to belittle the patient. This had continued into the present, with the father minimizing the patient's business ventures and other activities. The patient expressly disliked his father, who he felt had humiliated all the members of his family, but especially the patient's mother.

In the course of therapy the patient had ongoing sleep difficulties, which were eventually associated to a fear of dreaming. He had repeated nightmares of violent struggles, of being chased or being engaged in battle in which someone was being killed, although he was unsure who. (In the dream before his psychotic break, remember, there had been no doubt that he was the one who was to be killed and eliminated as useless and no longer essential.)

As the anniversary of his accident and surgery approached, he became anxious and depressed. His nightmares became more vivid. He dreamt of being shot at and killed. Indeed, death became a constant preoccupation. At this time he was engaged in litigation in connection with his injury, and it is of interest that this began to acquire a querulous quality. He felt that all the forces were ganging up on him, medical and legal, and that he was being treated unfairly and with disdain. I might mention that this was not an infrequent theme song in his life. He showed a marked sensitivity to criticism, or what he felt was criticism — although, truth to tell, both his wife and father were not above belittling him. He tended, however, to overreact. As I noted above, throughout his life, leading back to early childhood, there had been a constant fear of humiliation at the hands of his father. Subsequently his wife was added to the humiliators.

It is also of interest that he had a dream about gay people, and being surrounded by both males and females who were making eyes at him. During this period, he attended a basketball game with his son and insisted on sitting in the back row with the wall at his back. In this way, he could guard against attack.[6] In connection with this, he brought up his deathly fear of the medical anal procedures he had had to go through. Eventually, as the anniversary passed, and a good deal of the material was worked through, the anxiety subsided.

The case just described illustrates the role of the anal component in the unconscious homosexuality that eventuates in the paranoid constellation. Obviously anal preoccupations per se do not make for the paranoid constellation. When anal concerns do play a role in the formation of the paranoid constellation, there have usually been experiential factors leading to specific meanings becoming attached to the anal area, as well as to the fecal mass — generally of a sadistic nature. What role does the aggression and hostility so prevalent in the paranoid play in this picture? Is the element of humiliation, which seemed to be present in this patient, a significant one?

ANAL SADISM AND AGGRESSION

Even though Freud's original concept that homosexual wishful fantasies have an ultimate relationship to paranoia was greatly enlarged by explorations of the role of anality, there was still room for further expansion in light of the dual instinct theory and the role of aggression. Baumeyer (1956), in his discussion of the Schreber case, criticizes Freud's (1911b) formulation for not attaching sufficient significance to aggressive impulses. He argues that the repeated frustrations Schreber experienced before his psychotic breaks mobilized not only his uncon-

---

[6] Parenthetically, I would like to comment on the back and the behind aspects of the body as the feared area of attack. The body image rarely includes any clear image of the back. We ordinarily do not see our backs (except in a mirror). The back is also difficult to defend. One can more readily visualize what is going on in front. Does this, then, lend itself to such concerns as: "What's going on behind me?"

scious homosexuality but also his aggressive impulses. Baumeyer then quotes Schultz-Heincke (1931), who "advanced the opinion that the homosexual is characterized largely by the fact that, as a result of early suppression of the active fighting impulses, softness and surrender develop" (p. 73). Of course we have to bear in mind that he is probably referring to overt homosexuality; Freud (1922) and Nunberg (1938) also make this point about overt homosexuals.

The role of aggression and ambivalence in paranoia is in fact alluded to by Freud in some of his early writings. For instance, he notes: "In paranoia the worst delusions of persecution (pathological distrust of rulers and monarchs) correspond to these impulses [hostile and death wishes against the parents]" (1897, p. 207). Subsequently, he deals with this component within the framework of unconscious homosexuality, for instance, in the "I love him" variations described in the Schreber case. Nevertheless, aggression and ambivalence do not receive major emphasis until the formulation of the dual instinct theory. It is in the interplay of defensive aspects in relation to homosexuality that Freud (1922) deals with aggression. On the one hand, he depicts the use of overt aggression as a defense against unconscious homosexuality and indicates that ambivalence is always present in the persecuted paranoid as a defense against the homosexual conflict. On the other hand, he speaks of overt homosexuality as a defense against unconscious aggression. He points to a form of overt homosexuality that arises out of the repression of hostile aggressive feelings and death wishes, directed toward other family members of the same sex, generally brothers. With repression, these impulses undergo a transformation, so that the earlier rivals become the first homosexual love objects. Here we see the opposite dynamics from the paranoid, in which the original love object later becomes the hated object. Discussing the paranoid's ideas of reference, Freud suggests that because of their tremendous need for love and their extreme narcissism, they cannot tolerate indifference. To them, this is hate. In 1923, Freud reaffirms this two-sided picture of aggression as a defense against unconscious homosexuality and overt homosexuality as a defense against unconscious aggression. It should, however, be emphasized again that in discussing overt homosexuality we are dealing with something different from unconscious homosexuality (see my remarks on terminology).

Nunberg (1938) discusses the role of aggression in overt homosexuals who express sadistic fantasies in direct action both sexually and non-sexually. He believes this aggression derives from the patient's relationship with both parents. From this he draws an analogy to the homosexual component in paranoia and concludes that "aggression plays an important part not only in the object choice of the paranoid but also in homosexuality in general, and is at least to be regarded as characteristic of a certain type of homosexual" (p. 163). Nunberg indicates that in many aggressive overt homosexuals there are paranoid trends even though they are not psychotic. He sees this type of homosexual as standing in close relationship to the paranoid (in whom, however, the sadism is transformed into masochism). Yet he leaves unanswered the crucial question of why "out of the same fundamental situation paranoia develops in one instance and in another does not" (p. 164). It must also again be emphasized that Nunberg is primarily talking about overt homosexuals, and a particular kind of overt homosexual at that. I think that to analogize simply on the basis of finding aggressive components in both these conditions is methodologically questionable.

Taking Nunberg's formulations as a jumping-off point, Bak (1946) presents case material to demonstrate that paranoia is delusional masochism. In his patient there was a regression from sublimated homosexuality to masochism, with the wish to be castrated and humiliated. This was followed by a withdrawal of love, as the ego tried to protect itself from the masochistic threat. The result was an increase in hostility, with a shift from love to hatred. When this became too great to deal with, it was projected. But not only was the hatred projected, the patient also had to be the subject of this hatred — it still had to be related to him. It was thus still an extension of himself, reflecting an early ego state and early modes of ego functioning. Bak points out that it is in the projection of sadism that masochism is bound to return, and that the delusion represents a return of the repressed, leading to the conclusion that paranoia is delusional masochism. It should be noted, however, that Bak's patient had experienced overt sadistic behavior at the hands of his father, his mother, and other members of the family. The expression of this actual situation of humiliating experiences in the delusions suggests an almost real element in the patient's delusional system, as I believe is true for the psychotic paranoid constellation.

The increased appreciation of the impact of ambivalence and aggression also expanded understanding of the role of anality in the paranoid constellation. A cogent contribution along these lines has been made by Knight (1940b), whose thoughts can be summarized as follows: In the paranoid there is a tremendous ambivalence toward the father as a result of his preference for the mother. This ambivalence derives from the anal-sadistic expulsive stage (which heightens the tendency to projection).[7] The homosexuality is necessary to defend against hatred and hostility. Yet, coming closer to others via a homosexual attachment also represents an extreme danger, namely, the potential destruction of the love object because of the tremendous hostility. While the intense homosexual wish is needed to neutralize the aggression, the homosexual wishes, which would bring the object into close contact, have to be defended against, in order to prevent the destruction of the object by the existing hatred. Knight reformulates Freud's "I love him" concept to "I must love him and be loved by him to neutralize my hatred for him, but the nearer I get to him, the more dangerous the relationship becomes for me and for him" (p. 153). Moreover, Knight reduces the problem to a quantitative factor. He believes that the ultimate fate of homosexuality depends on the degree of the intensity of anal sadism aroused and the possibility of its being eroticized by a given individual's ego.

The patient referred to by Knight, although at first in analysis for chronic low-grade depression, ultimately ended up as a hospitalized paranoid schizophrenic. The total picture, with the eventual outcome of gross schizophrenic psychosis, contains many features that Knight's formulation fails to account for. Although his formulation may account for the paranoid constellation, it does not explain why the patient became psychotic. A full-blown delusion can exist only in the absence of the capacity to test reality, and factors other than the homosexual conflict are needed to explain this impairment in reality testing. Here I am referring to the third component of the psychotic process, namely, the specific ego and ego function disturbances.

The role of hostility and aggression, derivatives of the death instinct, and their impact on anal sadism have been underlined by Melanie Klein (1928a, 1932, 1946). Taking as her jumping-off point some of Abraham's ideas on the anal-sadistic phase in libidinal development, she discusses the case of a six-year-old child, Erna, who had many fantasies of being cruelly persecuted by her mother. These fantasies had a paranoid quality (1932, p. 79). Erna viewed everything and everybody around her as a persecutor. She thought she was continually being spied

---

[7]It is interesting to note that, among his many symptoms, Knight's patient suffered from chronic constipation, which he perversely enjoyed. He could work hard with good concentration if he had to move his bowels but postponed it. If he had a bowel movement, he felt empty and impotent in his work (Knight, personal communication, 1962).

upon and experienced numerous effects of such aggression. Klein believes that many of these features were identical to what, in adult paranoiacs, are known as delusions. Moreover, it was in exploring Erna's homosexual tendencies, which were connected to a tremendous hatred of her father, that many of the persecutory fantasies came out. Anal-love desires alternated with fantasies of persecution. In the transference, for instance, she felt that the excreta coming out of the analyst's anus would force their way into hers and injure her. Beneath Erna's homosexual tendencies lay an extraordinarily intense feeling of hatred toward the mother, derived from her early oedipal situation and her oral sadism. This hatred resulted in excessive anxiety.

During the treatment, sadistic fantasies developed which seemed to be related to the envy of the genital and oral gratifications Erna supposed her parents enjoyed during intercourse. This proved to be the deepest foundation of her hatred. She had many fantasies in which she attacked her parents, especially her mother, by means of her excrements. What most deeply underlay her fear of the analyst's feces was the fantasy that she would destroy the mother's inside with her own dangerous and poisonous feces.[8]

Klein (1946) pursues the role of anality and aggression in her study of the early stages of the oedipal conflict. She points out that in the anal-sadistic phase secret methods of attack prevail, such as the use of poisonous and explosive material (excrements representing poisons). In its fantasies the child uses its feces as the persecuting agent against objects, secretly inserting them by a kind of magic into the anus and other bodily apertures of those objects and leaving them there. Because of the multiplicity of incorporated excrements, a multitude of persecutors exists inside its own body, generating the fear of being poisoned. This, according to Klein, is the basis of hypochondriacal fears.[9]

Klein's explanation of paranoia, however, is diffused somewhat by her adherence to the ubiquity of the paranoid position in childhood. She does not, for instance, concern herself with the role of unconscious homosexuality as such in the paranoid constellation. Instead, she emphasizes the anal sadism and projective identification found in the

---

[8] It might be of some interest to mention, at this point, some material from one of my psychotic character patients. She described a nightmare (which, as in many such patients, seemed almost a reality). In it she was suffocating and felt that a mass of feces had engulfed her — the result of her mother's defecating on her.

[9] A psychotic character, in speaking of the aches and pains she had, claimed that these had been caused by a bug which had wandered over her body, defecating and leaving remnants of itself.

paranoid position, along with the primitive ego splits and aggression.

Recently, the dominant role of aggression and hostility in paranoia has been delineated by Blum (1980). In his opinion: "Hostility is a primary problem and not mainly a defense against homosexual impulses. The reverse formulation — that paranoid distrust and hostility defend against repressed homosexual love — is not excluded, [it] is not the exclusive motive of defense but assumes secondary importance" (p. 354). In other words, we now see that it is not only the form of object choice, but the vicissitudes of the mode of gratification and mastery which represent a danger, against which the ego defends itself in the paranoid constellation.

In summary, it can be seen that in attempting to narrow down the features within the homosexual conflict pertinent to paranoia, various authors have focused on the role of anality, first in its erotic aspects, then in its sadistic aspects. Attention to the various meanings of the fecal mass as a. object, the ambivalence toward it, the view of it as a poisonous and dangerous object to be used for attack, as well as the explosive expulsive quality ascribed to bowel movements, bring to the forefront the humiliating sadomasochistic aspects of the unconscious homosexuality in the paranoid constellation. The implicit danger of destroying the object, as well as the anal retaliatory possibilities, shed further light on the homosexual conflict within the structure of paranoid symptomatology.

Admittedly, with some of the contributions emphasizing aggression, we find a denigration of unconscious homosexual conflict as a primary focal point in the paranoid constellation. Other, qualifying factors were introduced and these began to dominate. As we shall see in the next section, with the tendency to look further and further back in psychic development for the understanding of paranoia, the role of unconscious homosexuality as the crucial conflict in this illness was also diminished.

EARLY PREGENITAL FACTORS

In reexamining the Schreber case, White (1961) calls attention to the primitive oral destructive-dependent impulses directed toward a mother figure. He sees the basic defense against such impulses as projection, in which Schreber accused God of being greedy, destructive, and having oral longings for Schreber. Unmanning represented a wish to regress to the period of undifferentiation characteristic of the earliest relationship with mother. Schreber became the fetus as well as the mother carrying the fetus. The father was a repetitive intruder into Schreber's relations with his mother. Ultimately, in White's view, Schreber's oral destructive impulses against the mother aroused the fear that he would destroy her, and since the mother was the world, this would bring the world to an end.

Macalpine and Hunter (1953) also emphasize early pregenital factors in Schreber's symptomatology. They believe his illness can be understood in terms of primitive procreation fantasies. Unmanning permitted him to be a person who could procreate, while the end of the world made for a state of affairs that necessitated procreation. They also relate Schreber's hypochondriasis to pregnancy fantasies. For Macalpine and Hunter, the procreation fantasies were primary — not unconscious homosexuality. Indeed, they contend that Schreber's idea of turning into a woman had little to do with homosexuality. Rather, it represented a confusion in sexual identity. In their opinion, one of the fantasies pathognomonic of schizophrenia is doubt or uncertainty about sexual identity, and this is implied in the ideas of sex change accompanying archaic procreation fantasies. Freud, on the other hand, indicates that Schreber's procreation fantasies were a part of the restitution and reconstruction process, which he sees as the basis for the symptoms of many psychoses. One might well ask: Since procreation fantasies are common to everyone, as Macalpine and Hunter indicate, why do some of these people become paranoid? Moreover, how does this apply to women, in whom procreation is a biological given?

Fairbairn (1956) relates most of Schreber's illness, as well as that of other paranoids, to a horror of the primal scene. Recall that Niederland (1968) describes Schreber's running for office and his appointment to the presidency of the Senate as provocative because they represented an active masculine role, from which there was a flight into illness. Fairbairn, in contrast, believes that the danger lay in the fact that both situations contained the possibility of access to the primal scene. Both suggested being included in the activity of grownups, and thus reactivated rage against the mother for her infidelity. The homosexuality and procreative fantasies served to deny both the primal scene and the hatred of the mother.[10] Fairbairn, like Macalpine and Hunter, relates

[10] It is interesting to note that in the case reported by Knight (1940b) the patient's psychosis was precipitated by the recollection of a memory of an experience at age two and a half. He had walked in on his parents in flagrante delicto, with the father ejaculating on the floor when he jumped out of bed. But Knight's conclusion about the impact of this primal scene event differs somewhat from Fairbairn's, in that he believes it mobilized passive anal wishes in relation to the father.

Schreber's seeming homosexual conflict to confusion over the sexual role.

In sum, with the elaboration of the vicissitudes of the unconscious homosexuality, and the attempt to delineate more specifically those aspects which make for the paranoid constellation, several contributors tended to place the problem farther back in psychic development and to assign unconscious homosexuality a secondary role.

Pseudo-Aspects of Unconscious Homosexuality

Many of the more recent contributions by psychoanalysts view the homosexual features as in a sense pseudo-manifestations of no special significance, representing or even disguising other more fundamental problems (see Federn, 1952; Walters, 1954; Ovesey, 1954, 1955a, 1955b; Grauer, 1955; Sullivan, 1956; Meissner, 1978a; Blum, 1980). Federn (1952), for instance, essentially ignores the role of unconscious homosexuality in the paranoid constellation. Instead, he utilizes his concept of loss of ego cathexis as accounting for most of the symptomatology in the paranoid, as well as in other psychotics.

Grauer (1955), borrowing some of Federn's concepts, challenges the idea of unconscious homosexuality in his critique of Freud's concept of narcissism as a frame of reference for psychosis. To account for the homosexual theme found in some patients, he assumes a universal bisexuality, in which identification with a member of the same sex has to take place for the development of normal sexuality, and identification with the opposite sex is generally latent. If there is a breakdown in ego integration and ego identity, the identification with the opposite sex can no longer be kept latent and has to be defended against. Grauer thus concludes: "What appear then as homosexual tendencies are really released latent tendencies that normally are subordinate to the dominant sexual identification; they are not an expression of a primary homosexual component. Some support for this view is found in the fact that in most homosexual delusions, the content of the delusion indicates a rejection of the homoerotic impulse and a projection of it onto other individuals" (p. 254). I do not quite follow Grauer's reasoning here, however, since I do not see a major difference between "latent identification with the opposite sex" and unconscious homosexuality.

Sullivan (1953, 1956, 1962) also denies that unconscious homosexuality is the focal point for paranoia. Although I intend to focus on Sullivan's views on unconscious homosexuality in the paranoid picture, a few words on his concept of the "paranoid dynamism" seem in order.

To begin with, Sullivan (1956) finds little to differentiate the paranoid from the schizophrenic state and believes that every paranoid has periods of schizophrenic content. Essentially, he sees paranoia as a defense against feelings of inadequacy, inferiority, and unworthiness. These feelings are generated by early experiences of disapproval which leave the future paranoid with an intolerable insecurity. The idea of being persecuted allows the paranoid to shift the basis for feeling insecure. Yet, by doing this, the paranoid is perpetuating the earlier experience of rejection and accusation. Basically, Sullivan's view is that paranoia is culturally determined and evolves during the social periods of life.

Turning to Sullivan's views on the role of unconscious homosexuality in the paranoid dynamism (1956), it is at times difficult to discern whether he is talking of overt or unconscious homosexuality. He remarks, for instance: "But in my simple-minded world, it is a little bit difficult to talk about homosexual conflict where there is no homosexual attachment" (p. 153). He would seem here to be referring to an overt homosexual attachment. In any case, he vehemently rejects homosexuality as a factor in the paranoid dynamism: "Now this wretched business of homosexual interest has gotten itself used as a complete explanation of the paranoid process. I deplore that very deeply" (p. 156).

Sullivan does allow that the male paranoid feels inadequate with women and that men know this. This sense of inferiority as a man would seem to have the implication of unconscious homosexuality. But, to Sullivan, that is secondary. He indicates that the homosexual component of the paranoid dynamism may derive significance from the persistence of a preadolescent security pattern. Indeed, he sees the beginnings of paranoid development in the preadolescent stage of psychic development. If during this period the individual derives some gratification from and a feeling of security in a homosexual relationship, this factor may play a role in subsequent paranoid development; otherwise it does not. Given this attitude toward the unconscious homosexual component in paranoia, it is to be expected that Sullivan takes a strong position against making this a significant aspect of therapy.

Ovesey (1954, 1955a, 1955b) also stresses the social aspects of paranoia, although he develops his ideas along more specifically adaptational lines. He takes the concept of pseudo-homosexuality as a frame of reference for the paranoid mechanism and breaks down anxieties about "homosexuality" into three distinctly separate motivational components: sex, dependency, and power. Only the first component, which seeks sexual gratification as its goal, does he consider truly homosexual.

Although the dependency and power components may use the genitals, they seek other nonsexual goals. In Ovesey's view, it is a failure in social adaptation, resulting in social humiliation, that generates the paranoid mechanism. Thus, he believes that pure power motivation, without any homosexual component, is the constant feature in paranoid phenomena and the essential anxiety is anxiety about survival. The pseudo-homosexual components (power and dependency), the true homosexual motivations, and the survival components are all variables, which can be present or absent.

Ovesey sees certain delusional forms of paranoia as attempts to deny the pseudo-homosexual implications of inadequacy and weakness, to recapture a sense of adequacy. There is an attitude and image of repressed self-pity. Such patients, he contends, turn to homosexuality from a background of weakness and vulnerability, often involving a dominant mother who is close-binding, and possibly even early homosexual experiences. A difficulty in evaluating Ovesey's contribution in this regard arises from his inclusion of cases of overt homosexuality in his material. It is therefore unclear at times whether he is referring to overt or unconscious homosexuality.

From a slightly different angle, Meissner (1978a) also pursues the social and cultural implications of the paranoid process. His thinking is strongly influenced by his sense that "much that had manifested itself to me in the psychotic processes of much more primitive and disturbed patients was also identifiable in relatively healthy and far less maladapted human beings." And he adds: "the basic mechanisms, which play themselves out in distorted and exaggerated forms in the pathology, are in fact the same basic mechanisms endemic to the human developmental process" (p. ix). In this respect, Meissner's perspective shares much with Sullivan's thinking (1956). Meissner specifically points to the impact of social forms of organization on the genesis of paranoia. He claims: "In all the cases we have studied here, an important observation which demands further study and further understanding is that paranoia manifested in the individual patient comes out of a background in the family context in which paranoid elements are identifiable and effectively at work" (p. x).

Meissner suggests that in the development of both the paranoid and the homosexual, the normal process of identity formation, through the reciprocal interaction between the ego and the social organization and processes, is disrupted:

> The negative identity develops as a form of protest and negation of a set of established rules, standards, and values, which are formed by society and enforced by authority figures. The difficulty of maintaining a negative identity in the face of social organizations, regulations, and institutions which suppress the behaviors and norms congruent with the negative identity, leads such individuals to develop rigid ideologies frequently as a means of sustaining the negative identity. The strong rebellion and opposition also involve significant elements of self-negation and self-denial, so that there is a determinant tendency to cling to totalistic ideologies resulting in considerable rigidity and negative conformity. Such a pattern can be identified both in homosexual subjects and in the operation of the paranoid process [p. 21].

Meissner's view would seem to leave unconscious homosexuality only a secondary role in the paranoid process. In pointing to the difficulty in discerning the etiological role of homosexual conflicts, he comments: "homosexuality may be a significant aspect of the symptomatology in all states of schizophrenic regression, rather than specific to paranoia as such" (p. 19). Although he acknowledges the frequency with which the homosexual theme appears in the paranoid, he contends: "it seems more viable to try to understand the paranoid dynamics as related to underlying developmental patterns which may share a common background or foundation with homosexual syndromes" (p. 20).

A view contrary to the social and cultural one has been expressed by Knight (1940b):

> Certainly we are aware of enough environmental influences tending to make homosexuality unacceptable to males in our culture. . . . That these environmental, cultural influences operate as a factor in promoting denial of homosexual wishes cannot be disputed. But it also seems apparent that they are not the crucial factor in enforcing the denial. It is often presumed by the therapist, for example, that if he can by reassurance, re-education and interpretation make the paranoid patient's homosexual wishes more acceptable to him, he could give up the delusions which represent a denial of those wishes. . . . But somehow this sort of therapeutic approach not only does not relieve the patient but often makes him more paranoid than ever [pp. 151–152].

Among other recent contributions challenging the centrality of unconscious homosexuality in paranoia is that by Blum (1980). As indicated above, he views repressed homosexual love as secondary to hostility (which he sees as the primary problem). "Homosexual love," according to Blum, "is of insufficient explanatory value and does not account for the paranoid's stunted and deformed object love. The paranoid is unable to love and to offset or neutralize hatred with love" (pp. 353–354). He maintains that although castration fears and homosexual conflict may precipitate paranoia, this is because any level of psycho-sexual danger may be the form through which more fundamental problems are expressed. In his view, these manifestations are derivative of sadomasochistic beating fantasies.[11] He emphasizes that in the paranoid, we are dealing with a fragile ego structure, in which early infantile narcissism, aggression, and sadomasochism have, as an organizing principle, beating fantasies. (Freud [1919] indicates that these fantasies play a role in character and symptom formation and may play a role in delusional paranoia.)

Blum does admit that beating fantasies alone do not eventuate in paranoia, and it is clear that such fantasies are present in many other conditions (e.g., masochistic perversions, character traits, neuroses). To explain how beating fantasies result in paranoia, then, he has to turn to the fragility of the ego, early infantile narcissism, aggression, ambivalence, and tenuous object constancy and sense of self, with a need to preserve a sadistic and poorly internalized superego. Yet I would question whether beating fantasies per se, without real and actual experiences, eventuate in psychosis of any type. Furthermore, it almost sounds to me as if the derivatives of beating fantasies were brought into the service of dealing with the problems of a fragile ego. In other words, they themselves may be pseudo-manifestations, rather than the central factor in paranoia. As I shall subsequently suggest, it is possible that beating fantasies are a special instance of another more inclusive concept of the underlying conflict in the paranoid constellation.

A whole series of clinical psychiatric studies also explore the validity of the concept of unconscious homosexuality in the paranoid constellation. An excellent survey of such studies has been made by Greenspan and Myers (1961). Many of these studies deal with conscious material, and they emphasize that in female paranoids the persecutory object is of the opposite sex. A frequently quoted study is that by Henrietta Klein and Horowitz (1949). They examined 80 patients (40 males and 40 females) and described their background and clinical pictures. What was most striking in all cases was the extremely disruptive, cruel, and violent childhood background, replete with marital strife. Coupled with this was a very poor adult sexual adjustment, related in many in-

---

[11] Blum's belief here that homosexual conflict is secondary is not too unlike Ovesey's idea of pseudo-homosexuality deriving from the more fundamental struggle over power, submission, autonomy, and independence.

stances to a background of masturbatory guilt. According to the authors, there was little evidence of unconscious homosexuality. Yet most of their data were elicited in the *conscious* sphere and dealt with *overt* manifestations rather than defensive aspects. This limitation leads them to see homosexuality as merely an expression within the sexual area of more generalized problems dealing with failure, blows to pride, etc.

Obviously there is a methodological problem here. Even Greenspan and Myers call attention to this difficulty with most studies: "It is evident that thoughts and feelings concerning homosexuality, incestuous desires, power and dependent struggles and the like would be quite nebulous to the patient and incredibly difficult to establish and verify as fact, especially when we must consider the 'system unconscious.' Because of the nature of the instrument with which we explore a mental illness, that is our intellect, the emergence of a partisan attitude is inevitable" (pp. 24–25). But an even more fundamental defect in such studies, I believe, is the failure to define more critically those aspects of unconscious homosexuality which may eventuate in the paranoid constellation, as I have tried to do above.

UNCONSCIOUS HOMOSEXUALITY IN THE FEMALE PARANOID

Since many psychoanalytic contributions have dealt with studies of the female paranoid, it might be appropriate to direct ourselves to this subject. In one of the earliest cases reported by Freud (1896), the rejected idea which was defended against by the female patient was clearly homosexual in nature. Many of the patients Ferenczi (1911, 1912b) studied in developing his concept of unconscious homosexuality in the paranoid delusional system were female. He reports the case of a woman with delusions of infidelity, who suspected her husband of having a heterosexual affair with the person toward whom she had a homosexual attachment. Ferenczi comments: "This case of delusional jealousy only becomes clear when we assume that it was a question of the projection on to her husband of her pleasure in her own sex" (1912b, p. 169).

Freud (1915a) himself deals directly with this problem. His patient, a 30-year-old unmarried woman living with her mother, had developed a whole system of delusions centering on a man who had some sexual contact with her. Freud was somewhat disturbed at first since this was at variance with his theory that "patients suffering from paranoia are struggling against an intensification of their homosexual trends, a

fact pointing back to a narcissistic object-choice. And a further interpretation had been made; that the persecutor is at bottom someone
whom the patient loves or has loved in the past" (p. 265). However, as
Freud explored further he learned of the patient's attachment to an
older woman in her office, who was clearly a substitute for her mother,
and whom she unjustifiably suspected of having an affair with the same
man with whom she (the patient) had had sexual contact.

A natural question that arises is how the paranoid constellation is
structured in women, vis-à-vis the formulations developed in the various contributions we have looked at. For instance, where do the anal-
sadomasochistic features fit in? Freud, as we have seen, believes that
unconscious homosexuality is the essential conflict area, in women as
well as men. Yet at the time of his formulation, the anal-sadomasochistic relation to the object was not in the forefront of psychoanalytic
thinking on this problem. At any rate, Freud does not write about this
aspect at any great length. Although Melanie Klein (1932) in her description of Erna (see p. 86) highlights the anal-sadistic aspects of
persecution, she somehow circumvents the whole question by finding
the same features in the male and the female, in postulating the paranoid position as the basis for future paranoia. In a sense, this view denigrates the concept of unconscious homosexuality as a frame of reference
for the conflict and makes it unnecessary to differentiate between male
and female paranoids.

I myself have had the opportunity to observe the impact of homosexual conflict in a psychotic female over an extended period (see
Frosch, 1967a). The role of unconscious homosexuality in precipitating
flareups of her psychosis was quite clear. The patient, after an initial
period of disturbance on admission, quieted down and was transferred
to another ward. On her third day on that ward, she became withdrawn, untidy, and mute. She would not leave her bed, even urinating
there. When she did speak, she indicated that her life was in danger,
that she would be killed. She subsequently revealed that another
female patient had kissed her and asked her to live with her. The patient had thought it would be all right to accept this offer, since it would
present a means of getting out of the hospital. Yet it became obvious
from what she said that she had toyed with homosexuality as a defense
against heterosexuality, which she had begun to consider "bad." In a
sense, she retreated from the heterosexual to the homosexual position,
but this could not be maintained, and the disintegration ensued. This
was followed by a period of religious conversion, lasting about three

weeks, during which she walked around with a marked ecstatic and beatific expression on her face. She renounced and denied all sexuality.

It was at this time that she dreamt she was a prostitute (see p. 40). She was quite disturbed by this dream, and after a brief period of remission, there was a flareup of psychotic behavior and she actually became a prostitute for two weeks. This behavior was clearly related to a delusion in which she believed she was being tested to determine whether she was homosexual. She was convinced that the men with whom she was having intercourse were women in disguise. The penises were not real and on occasion she attempted to tear them off. During her subsequent hospitalization, she displayed reactions to both overt and unconscious homosexual preoccupations, against which she was defending herself. She viewed homosexuality as the greatest degradation.

At one point, when this patient was especially attuned to the homosexual climate on the service, she expressed overt sexual fantasies about me and had repeated orgasms (even when she was with me). She dreamt about a woman who she clearly identified in her associations as her mother. Other associations established the provocative effect on her of a homosexual patient on the service. Her intense preoccupation with me, to the point of erotomania, was obviously an attempt to ward off her reaction to this homosexual patient. Although I was not able to clarify to my satisfaction the more specific anal-sadomasochistic features characteristic of the male paranoid, there were some indication of their presence, especially in her extreme hostility and aggression during the height of some of her delusional states.

I should like to describe now in some detail a psychotic character who, during analysis, experienced disintegrative fears in relation to the welling up of homosexual impulses, which were mixed with marked aggression. At one point this patient spoke of a curious incident which took place one day while she was on vacation. One of the women at a party she had attended had looked at her quite intently, concentrating on the lower part of her body. This was rather disconcerting and she found herself anxious to leave the room when this woman was around. She suspected this woman of being a lesbian. In the ensuing days she was disturbed by thoughts of this experience, but brushed them away. One morning she awoke feeling quite panicky. There was an eerie quiet. Some catastrophe seemed imminent. She looked out, saw it was not quite dawn, heard the cock crow and some dogs bark. She remembered that when she was three a tornado had been ushered in by similar circumstances. The patient lay in bed for almost an hour and a half, frightened, perspiring, not quite knowing what to do. She was convinced something terrible was going to happen. She did not know whether to awaken her husband and family, whether to run out of the house, or what. Finally dawn came and she saw that nothing was going to happen, but she felt quite strange throughout the day.

During this and subsequent sessions I raised the question of the relationship between her fear of disaster and the "lesbian" experience. The patient said she had been much more frightened by this woman than she had realized. It was a shattering experience. There was a welling up of fear and she felt she would explode. This self-experience had then been projected as a world destruction fantasy. Later, she turned to her concerns about her own sexual makeup and about lesbian thoughts, questioning her masculinity and femininity.

Whereas I believe that in the male one must look to the patient's relationship with the father for clues to the development of the paranoid constellation, in the female patient one must look to the mother relationship. Hovering around this is the question of early humiliating experiences. In the delusions of my hospitalized psychotic patient described above, there was a recurring feeling of being watched, of being checked for her goodness and badness, etc. Behind this were not only elements from a universal situation (early superego development), but also actual experiences to which she did not have to bring too many fantasies in order to justify her reactions. Even now, when her mother visited her at the hospital, the mother followed the patient into the bathroom, if the mother thought she had been there too long. (The patient knew that her mother had tried to abort her, and in many of her subsequent severe childhood illnesses the patient had blamed her mother.) This intrusive and obsessional mother was an active factor in the patient's psychotic state. Indeed, there was ample evidence that many of the patient's preoccupations concerned the ambivalent relationship to the mother. Her desire to hold onto the mother was expressed in a stereotyped duplication of her mother's gestures.

My other patient, the one who feared a natural disaster, revealed that she had always wondered whether her mother had homosexual tendencies. The mother had openly humiliated the father in front of the patient and called him a little jack rabbit, referring to his sexual inadequacy. Once her mother had dressed up as a man and taken a party around the night spots of Paris, telling them she was a guide and even getting paid for it. According to the patient, the mother was exceedingly forceful and dominating in her relationships with women, and always seemed to have peculiar friends. The patient found the idea that her mother might be a lesbian very frightening and devastating: "She would not be a mother. It is not a mother. There is something so frightening about all this I cannot even talk about it. I do not even want to think about it." The patient then toyed with the idea that her mother might have made sexual advances to her: "Of course this is what I meant by frightening and fearful. I always found that when I lay in bed with her I could not relax. I found myself holding myself very still and there was always something frightening to me about it." Yet the analysis was also full of material pointing to the mother's coldness and aloofness. "When my mother kissed me she would kind of kiss me from a distance and push me away." The only time the mother had actually sheltered and protected her was during the tornado when the patient was three years old. This patient, from time to time during analysis, had fleeting near-psychotic episodes. What was even more obvious was a general paranoid attitude. Yet in her, too, there was very little anal-sadomasochistic material related to these paranoid reactions.

I should like to allude here to a special form of erotomania in women described by Clérambault (see Arieti and Bemporad, 1974). The Clérambault syndrome, or *psychose passionelle*, generally appears in a woman who becomes attached to a prominent figure who hardly knows her, if at all. She, however, interprets everything as a manifestation of this person's love for her.[12] Although the reported cases of *psychose passionelle* do not deal specifically with the unconscious features, they seem to fit Freud's (1911b) famous proposition: "I do not love him — I love her," transposed by the female into "I do not love her — I love him."

In this regard, let me report something that happened a number of years ago, when I was treating a man in his forties for depression. I had the occasion to see his wife quite a number of times in connection with his treatment. She developed a pathological attachment to me, which became quite embarrassing to her husband (as well as to me). She would proclaim my virtues to her husband and rave about me for hours. Although she was not in treatment with me, she did at one point reveal that she constantly dreamt about me. Strangely, these dreams often included women, whose exact role she was unsure of. She

[12] Whether this should be considered a separate syndrome is questioned by Lehman (1975), who argues that *psychose passionelle* is confused with another syndrome (also reported by Clérambault), characterized by feelings of possession.

speculated about my wife and, although she had never met her, described her in extravagantly eulogistic terms, glorifying her looks and intelligence. It was fairly clear that she had developed an attachment to this woman she had never met. When she encountered women on the elevator or in the street near my office, she wondered whether they were my wife and tried to follow them to see if eventually they would meet me. It is not too difficult to conjecture that her attachment to me may have been incidental to the unconscious homosexual feelings she had toward these women.

Paranoia in Overt Homosexuals

Still another question we must ask in discussing the problem of unconscious homosexuality and its relationship to paranoia is: Why do some overt homosexuals become paranoid? Let me remind you of Nunberg's (1938) statement that in overt homosexuals in whom aggression was present, only small quantities of aggression were transformed and turned against the ego (in contrast to the picture in the paranoid). The question of why this happens in some instances and not in others is thus still an open one. Another question that arises is: To what extent may overt homosexuality itself be utilized defensively in certain patients to ward off a psychotic break? In other words, when we see psychosis developing in certain overt homosexuals, are we seeing the failure of a major defensive operation which has borrowed from strong instinctual inclinations?

Rosenfeld (1949), taking Klein's primary paranoid stage of development as his frame of reference, says that increased paranoid anxieties encourage the development of strong "manifest" or "latent" (as he puts it) homosexual tendencies as a defense. When the defensive function of the homosexuality fails, paranoia develops. He holds that underlying paranoid anxieties are frequently found in nonpsychotic overt homosexuals as well. In his opinion, it is the fixation to the early narcissistic level of psychic development, where projective identification operates, that is responsible for the frequent combination of paranoia and homosexuality.[13]

[13] Katan (1950) suggests something similar when he indicates that in the paranoid the unconscious homosexuality represents a retreat from a weak oedipal position and is a valiant attempt to hold onto reality and objects. If this defense fails under the impact of anxiety and danger, there is further regression, possibly to the point of undifferentiation. There was some suggestion of this in the hospitalized psychotic patient I described above who developed world destruction fantasies after she was approached by a homosexual patient and had transiently toyed with the idea of going along with this

An overt homosexual whom I saw in psychoanalytically oriented therapy was, although not psychotic, somewhat grandiosely paranoid and full of outwardly directed aggression. Coupled with this aggression, however, were rather strong feelings of passivity. (I might mention that this man had a particularly cruel and sadistic father.) He complained that on his job he was not getting a decent break in terms of advancement, etc. As a result of treatment, this patient abandoned his overt homosexuality, eventually married, and had a child. I saw him and his wife 20 years later. Although he still had not developed a gross psychosis, he spoke of being discouraged about his job and his whole manner had a marked paranoid flavor. I wondered then whether his overt homosexuality had enabled him to cover up an underlying psychosis.

In a case mentioned to me by a colleague (M. Wolfe, personal communication, 1962), a practicing homosexual was induced to give up his homosexual activities by a priest, who convinced him of the sinfulness of these practices. This man became very depressed, guilt-ridden, and eventually developed a florid paranoid psychosis with ideas of reference, delusions of persecution, and hallucinations. At this point he came to see Wolfe, who felt that the overt homosexuality was a more welcome condition than the psychosis and made a return to homosexuality a goal of therapy. The psychosis did indeed subside with the patient's return to homosexual practices, and he felt less guilt-ridden than before. Years later Wolfe met him at a bar with his boyfriend. He seemed relaxed, and introduced his boyfriend with equanimity. Obviously the issues involved in this case are more complex than such a brief description can suggest. My point is that in his own way Wolfe recognized the defensive nature of the overt homosexuality.

Another colleague, Ira Miller (personal communication, 1963), described an overt homosexual in whom the homosexuality appeared to be a defense against the disintegration fears and self-dissolution characteristic of psychotic anxiety (Frosch, 1967a). This patient revealed the type of reaction to change and uncertainty I have described for the psychotic character (Frosch, 1970). Once, for instance, when Miller

---

proposal (heterosexuality had apparently become dangerous and a source of anxiety for her). But my patient was not an overt homosexual, nor had she, to my knowledge, had any overt homosexual experiences of any sort. On the contrary, as I indicated, she felt homosexuality to be the greatest degradation and humiliation. It should be underlined that both Katan and I are referring here not to overt homosexuality, but rather to defenses against unconscious homosexuality.

shifted the furniture in his office, practically reversing the whole setup, the patient became panic-stricken and confused. He said he felt lost, sobbed, and was unable to lie down on the couch. During the course of the analysis the suggestion was made that his homosexual activities be suspended. He then had a series of dreams associated with an indescribable feeling of terror. While talking about one of these dreams, he became panic-stricken, breaking into profuse and violent sobbing. He was terrified he would become insane and fall apart. After this, he interrupted the analysis. Miller thought that the threatened loss of his homosexuality evoked the panic and disintegrative anxieties (which were psychotic in nature), that the homosexuality enabled him to defend against an underlying psychosis.

The above material suggests that in those instances in which overt homosexuals become psychotic and paranoid, the overt homosexuality may be a defense against an underlying, incipient psychotic process. In other words, in such instances, one would expect to find clinical evidence of the underlying psychotic process, indicating that if the overt homosexuality were abandoned for some reason, a psychotic break might ensue.

A FORMULATION

Let us retrace our thinking a bit and ask what steps lead to the development of the paranoid constellation from an unconscious homosexual conflict. To begin with, the unconscious homosexual feelings (speaking for the moment in instinctual and libidinal terms) may simply be projected. This is not yet persecutory paranoia. At this stage what we may see clinically is a spectrum of reactions to other people who are felt to be homosexuals. But these reactions may have nothing to do with the patient, and may not even refer to a specific person. We obviously need several further steps. At some point a significant and important object must be introduced into the situation, the replica of a significant object from childhood (Waelder's [1951] "return of the denied"). Even so, we still do not have persecutory paranoia. The patient's homosexuality may simply be projected onto this individual with the thought that this individual is a homosexual. Persecutory paranoia requires that the patient be the subject of these homosexual wishes — a passive, not an active, subject.

Why does this homosexual wish not become overt? Why is gratification not sought? Obviously, the wish must be repressed and denied because there is something unbearable about it. It is this quality which turns the positive wish into a negative repulsion and makes the homosexual "partner" a persecutor, the representative of something repulsive. But what exactly is it that is projected — is it the homosexuality, i.e., the libidinal wish, or the defense against it, or both? If we assume the presence of positive homosexual feelings for the object and repulsion or negative feelings as defending against these wishes, it is obviously the latter that are projected and become conscious — namely, the hate part of ambivalence (in the old sense).

Yet we have left unanswered an essential question: What makes the homosexual wish unbearable to the individual? Some authors suggest that it is not the homosexuality per se that is at stake, but allied features growing out of experiential phase-related issues. In this regard, I would like to turn to a reconsideration of the role of anality and aggression.

It is my belief that passive anal wishes have a special meaning for the male paranoid. Can one postulate more than a modicum of passivity in these individuals? This passivity would have to be experienced as dangerous to account for the extensive defensive activities of the ego which are brought into play. In fact, this suggestion is implicit in many of the contributions we have reviewed. Katan (1950), for instance, equates the passivity with castration. But the danger, for psychosis to eventuate, must go beyond that. For the male paranoid, the special meaning of passive anal wishes seems to be colored by many features, including hostility, aggression, and sadism, in addition to fears of degradation and castration. Yet why are the passive anal wishes rejected and not, for instance, expressed in a masochistic perversion? Do the hostility and the sadism evoke retaliatory fears, as has been expostulated by some (the delusional masochism of Bak, 1946)? This explanation, however, leaves me unsatisfied, for it does not really account for why the retaliatory fears become expressed in the persecutory paranoid constellation. My sense is that what lends a special quality to these wishes and makes them unacceptable is their humiliating aspect. One of my patients referred to homosexuality as the worst kind of degradation, as a state of frightening nothingness.

I am inclined to believe that the common genetic denominator in such cases may be actual humiliating experiences at the hands of significant objects of the same sex at crucial stages in psychic development. What makes these experiences especially traumatic is that they are out of phase with the existing stage of ego and libidinal development. They may occur, for instance, at a time when sexual identity has not completely evolved. The actual experiences may dovetail with existing fantasies and lend to these an actuality. They thus reinforce both the wishes and the accompanying feelings of guilt, leaving the conflict unresolved. Whether these experiences are directly sexual or not, they make passivity humiliating, degrading, painful, and possibly catastrophic.

These experiences, then, carry the sense of having been forced upon a helpless victim. Eidelberg (1954, 1959a, 1959b, 1959c) refers to such an experience as a narcissistic mortification. As he puts it: "being forced to accept an order from the object seems reponsible for the sensation of an aggressive pleasure. This sensation of being forced is referred to as a narcissistic mortification" (1954, p. 38). It is "a sudden loss of control over internal or external enemies" (1959b, pp. 274–275). To this is added the element of humiliation and guilt, a humiliation either intended by the perpetrator or experienced as such by the victim as a result of the guilt attached to his own wishful fantasies. In this regard, Eidelberg indicates: "Sometimes an external punishment may lead to self-humiliation under the condition that the individual considers this punishment as something he deserves" (1959b, p. 278). That is, if the punishment fits in with a then-existing fantasy, an act not intended as humiliating may be felt as such. In my opinion, it is these guilt-ridden, humiliating, passive anal-sadistic aspects that make the homosexual wishes unacceptable.

I would suggest that in male patients a particularly cruel and sadistic father may augment the potential for the development of the paranoid constellation. Such a father's sadism and cruelty is not confined to an isolated event, but chronic. Yet his cruelty may become crystallized in the child's mind during a critical phase of psychic development when it lends a particular realness to the child's fantasies. In males the phase most likely to be involved is the anal-sadistic phase, since the father is generally not an oral provider or depriver. For the female child, it is the mother who may be the menacing object, and special humiliating experiences with her may become the core of the paranoid constellation. As I have indicated, in the female paranoid the anal-sadistic component does not appear to be as central as in the male. In both the male and the female, however, the trauma of actual humiliating experiences in early psychic development is incorporated into a dread of unconscious homosexuality. The unconscious homosexuality then becomes the organizing principle for the paranoid constellation.

There is ample evidence for my suggestion in many of the reported cases. Schreber's father, for instance, embodied the cruelty, sadism, and punitive behavior seen in the histories of many paranoid patients (cf. Niederland, 1960; H. Klein and Horowitz, 1949). It is in this light that I would like to reconsider Blum's (1980) attempt to make beating fantasies the linchpin for his concept of paranoia. I believe beating fantasies represent only a special instance of my formulation above. Furthermore, I do not believe that beating fantasies alone will eventuate in the paranoid constellation, without actual and real experiences that dovetail with these fantasies. Blum in fact recognizes the need for realness when he says, "The beating fantasy in my patient was confused with reality because of ego regression and the massive projection of aggression and related repressed impulses" (p. 351). He also recognizes that other factors are necessary for such fantasies to eventuate in the paranoid constellation, let alone paranoid psychosis. He alludes to the fragile personality structure, deficient ego development, failure to negotiate separation-individuation, and impaired object relations. In his patients he found that ego integration, identity, and sexual identity were characteristically unstable. Blum then states: "all levels of psychosexual development and their corresponding danger situations contribute to the transformed fantasy of persecution and punishment" (p. 359). To my mind, the inclusion of *all* these components somehow diffuses his proposition that beating fantasies form the core of paranoia.

By and large, I believe this kind of diffusion through overinclusion occurs in many of the contributions which tend to minimize and denigrate the role of unconscious homosexuality in the formation of the paranoid constellation, particularly in those that try to place the crucial factors further and further back in psychic development. It is a truism that many stages in psychic development contribute to a given clinical picture and that the latter may be overdetermined. But overdetermination does not imply dilution of the organizing role of a particular determining factor. In his own way Schilder (1935) expresses a similar view: "whenever a partial libido prevails, it attracts all events in life; every interest, every emotion becomes connected with that partial desire and with the special organ of it. . . . It is as if there were one deepened canal attracting all the water. We know this principle in physiology, too. Uchtomsky has called it the 'Dominante'" (p. 164).

It should be clear that unconscious homosexuality in general is an attempt at resolution of other conflicts, oedipal or preoedipal. The specific kind of unconscious homosexuality with the features I've described above appears to form the core of the paranoid constellation. However, the presence of the paranoid constellation per se does not indicate psychosis, i.e., a bona fide paranoid delusion and paranoid psychosis, although it contains the ingredients for such a psychosis. What the paranoid constellation provides is the *content*, but it does not determine the *form* in which that content is expressed, i.e., psychosis. In order for a paranoid psychosis to develop, other factors must supplement the paranoid constellation—specifically the components of the psychotic process. There must, for instance, be an impairment of several ego functions vis-à-vis reality, in particular in the capacity to test reality. It is only when the latter impairment is involved that the psychotic aspects of the paranoid constellation become manifest. While the paranoid constellation may lend many ingredients to the clinical picture, such as oversuspiciousness or acute sensitivity to slights, none of these may in and of themselves be psychotic and may, under certain circumstances, even be sociosyntonic.

The sources of the rather severe ego impairment in psychoses will not be explored here, as they will be discussed in later chapters. At this point I should simply like to raise the question whether the factors that play a role in bringing about this impairment may not equally contribute to the evolution of unconscious homosexuality in the paranoid constellation. One might also ask whether the unconscious homosexuality may not contribute to these ego impairments—that is, whether a conflict may not bring about disturbances in reality testing, a view promulgated by Arlow and Brenner (1969), among others.[14] These are not, I should point out, mutually exclusive views.

A CASE OF PARANOID PSYCHOSIS

I should now like to present the case of a chronic paranoid, whom I observed over a number of years. At the time he was first seen, the patient was 61 years old. He came to the emergency room after having been beaten up by some boys. The examining physician thought he seemed somewhat confused, and psychiatric consultation was asked for. What had appeared to be simply confused thinking turned out to be a highly complex delusional system.

Essentially he saw himself as destined for great things in life. He had a mission, but because of interference with certain "basic" physiological functions such as moving his bowels, his whole system had been

[14] Katan (1950), for instance, suggests that in the psychotic, or in the schizophrenic at any rate, there already exists a weakening of the relationship to reality by virtue of the constitutional homosexuality. (Katan subsequently qualifies this by indicating that he no longer feels the homosexuality is constitutional.)

upset and he could not fulfill this mission. Furthermore, he thought that inside him there was some "power" which controlled his behavior and feelings, both negatively and positively. He had not quite reached the stage of being God, but he definitely felt that he had some kind of mission, and one didn't have to search far to find an underlying Messiah delusion. Many people were involved in the plot that prevented him from carrying out his mission. Among these were members of his family, including his dead parents. He retrospectively reconstructed situations and events to integrate people from the past into his developing delusional system. Eventually clear delusions of persecution and grandeur did emerge.

Let us go back a little, however, and look at his idea that his biological functions were being interfered with and his claim: "I could live forever provided I'm allowed to enjoy my physiological health." A key element was a memory from age six or seven. He had wanted to go to the bathroom and the teacher did not permit him to go. He wove this insult into his delusional system; it was part of a plot to interfere with his "constitutional" right to enjoy his physical health. The pupils at school had humiliated him, made fun of him, and also prevented him from exercising this right. Moreover, his parents were not sympathetic about his being so humiliated, and their indifference — "they looked away" — he found humiliating. "When people want to downtrod me and make me nothing," he commented, "they don't look at me" (to Freud, remember, indifference means hate). All this fed into his chronic bowel accumulation.[15] He thought poison gas was formed, which befogged him and prevented him from fulfilling the mission for which he had been born — to lead all humans to better life. We see, clinically, the evolution of his hypochondriacal complaints into somatic delusions, ideas of influence and persecution, grandiose ideas — all somehow interwoven and given some semblance of rational appearance.

At one point the patient referred to an incident that "broke me down" and actually broke into tears. He then asked that nothing of what he was going to relate to me be shown on TV (the session was being videotaped). What he described was an incident that had occurred around the age of seven. His older brother and his friends had manipulated his genitals — "he had like homosexuality with me." The patient

---

[15] It is of interest to note that Schreber, too, had the delusion that people were interfering with his bowel activities. Whenever he wanted to go to the bathroom, someone deliberately occupied it, or made a comment which prevented him from moving his bowels.

remembered crying and escaping into his mother's bed, but he lived in constant dread that this would be repeated. He felt both ashamed and degraded. He then linked his bowel troubles to masturbation: the accumulation of feces exerted pressure on his genitals, stimulating him, but "the genital organ must not be played with." In this way, he conceived of the various interferences with his bowel movements as part of a plot to arouse him sexually and force him to masturbate.

As I indicated above, the humiliating quality of such real experiences has major significance for the paranoid constellation and the impact of unconscious homosexuality. In this patient there were indications of even earlier experiences of a similarly humiliating nature. The later experiences appeared almost as screen memories for the earlier experiences. Moreover, this man's subsequent life was hardly free from experiences in which he was a passive victim. At the age of 18, he claimed, he experienced a murderous assault, which injured him so badly that his chance of recovering his "constitutional physiological rights" was almost totally thwarted. He alluded to terrible things of a humiliating nature which had been done to him during a previous hospitalization. Exactly what these things were or if they indeed took place, I do not know. What was important was his concept of his relation to his environment. He saw himself as the injured victim of a world that did not understand him, that tortured and tormented him externally and internally. In this regard, a particular remark of his is telling:

> They are all able to persecute me and have a leeway and freedom with me because of the power that I have within me. He lets them do what they want. I'm a very nice character and a lovely human being and *maybe they would like to fall in love with me.*

Behind all this man's "torturers" lurked the malevolent figure of his seducer-brother, who he said made the murderous attempt on his life at the age of 18. And not too far behind was the father. But there were mixed feelings toward these torturers. This could be seen in his remarks about an all-good teacher and an all-bad teacher. The good teacher had loved him, praised him, made him feel very proud; the bad one had only criticized and humiliated him in front of others. He insisted that their attitudes to him were "in direct opposition." In his words: "The first teacher always pointed me out to the parents of the other pupils as an exceptional good student. The second teacher, in total contrast, made my life so miserable that I prayed to be dismissed [from school] but tragically for me [this] was never realized." Mixed feelings also appeared in his attitude toward the introjected object in his body, what he called "the power in me."

The finding of feelings of ambivalence toward the beloved object, who then becomes the persecutor, guided Freud in building his conception of the object relationship in the paranoid constellation. In my patient, the struggle to resolve this conflict between love for and hostility toward the object seemed to be an ongoing one. In this regard, we might ask: Were all his experiences of being the victim of assault fortuitous? Were they really accidental? Or were they an integral part of an ongoing conflict and struggle, necessary, if you will, for the preservation of the psyche? In many ways the assaults upon him seemed almost invited. He presented what I would call a victim appearance and almost deliberately exposed himself to these situations. He lent himself to being beaten. Ultimately, his end was tragic — he was found dead in his apartment, the victim of a burglary attempt during which he was murdered.

In sum, my own formulation is that unconscious homosexuality is denied, rejected, and projected onto a replica of a significant childhood object. The subject then becomes the unwilling, persecuted, passive victim. The "persecution" is seen as an anal-sadomasochistic attack, which is felt as degrading and humiliating. Behind this view lie real humiliating experiences at the hands of significant same-sex objects from the past, generally a father figure in the male and a mother figure in the female. These experiences occurred at crucial stages in psychic development, before sexual identity had been established. They were particularly traumatic because they were out of phase with the child's existing stage of ego and libidinal development and tied into the child's fantasies. These experiences, then, make passivity humiliating, degrading, and possibly catastrophic. My point is that although there are contributions from many levels of psychic development to the paranoid picture, it is unconscious homosexuality in this form that is the organizing principle.[16]

[16] Unconscious homosexuality as a defensive outcome of castration anxiety in the male has been amply described. It nonetheless may become the organizing principle underlying many clinical phenomena.

B.
Withdrawal and Restitution

In surveying the impact of the libido theory in the last section, we focused on attempts to define the nature of the conflict and danger. Essentially, without referring to it as such, the contributors were struggling with the first component of the psychotic process (although they did not deal with the fear of disintegration). Here and there we encountered attempts to delineate the mode of dealing with this conflict — the second component of the psychotic process. It is to the earlier roots of this component that we shall now turn our attention. In his report on Schreber, Freud (1911b) refers to "two factors in which we expected from the first to find the distinguishing marks of paranoia, namely, the mechanism by which the symptoms are formed and the mechanism by which repression is brought about" (p. 65). It is within this context that he proposes the concepts of withdrawal and restitution.

Before we examine Freud's ideas, however, it might be appropriate to address ourselves briefly to the terminology used in reference to these concepts. Freud himself uses different terms, such as decathexis and recathexis. Fenichel (1945) speaks of regression and restitution. In so doing, he places neurosis and psychosis on a continuum, although he leaves the question open of what determines the depth of regression. Glover (1939), on the other hand, questions the use of the term "restitution," suggesting that "from the developmental point of view the term 'progression' would be more appropriate" (p. 221). More recently, Pao (1979) has pointed out that while "withdrawal" and "restitution" imply two stages in a psychic process, the symptomatology they produce is by no means distinct and separate. Rather, what we find is an ongoing flux and flow, a continuous back and forth movement, reflecting the interwoven struggle with object relations. Restitutional symptoms, then, are both regressive and progressive in nature as well as in content.

The Initial Concept

Let us now look at Freud's formulation. He relates symptomatology to the various attempts to either withdraw from or restablish contact with the object via the process of restitution and restoration. Specifically, in the Schreber case, Freud explains delusions as an attempt at the reconstitution (restitution) of the relationship to the object. It is true that here the recaptured object relationship is a hostile one, but it is still an object relationship. In brief, he says, repression is accomplished by the withdrawal of libido which is placed in the narcissistic arena. Symptom formation is then via the mechanism of projection, which is utilized in the attempts at restitution. Freud indicates that insofar as paranoia is concerned the fixation point to which repression (withdrawal) takes place is somewhere between narcissism and homosexuality, whereas for schizophrenia it is "autoerotism" (see my remarks on terminology in Chapter 1).

In both dementia praecox and paranoia, then, Freud sees detachment of libido as the main form of repression. The process of repression proper consists in the detachment of libido from people and things that were previously loved. This goes on silently. What forces itself noisily upon our attention is the process of recovery, the attempt to undo the work of repression and bring libido back onto the objects it has abandoned.[17] And here Freud makes another distinction between dementia praecox and paranoia — their different mechanisms for the return of the repressed. In dementia praecox hallucinatory wish fulfillment is the main mechanism, whereas in paranoia the way the object is recovered is primarily by projection.

To account for many variations in the nature of withdrawal and restitution, Freud amplifies several aspects. He is, for instance, concerned with the question of the sequence of withdrawal and restitution. He tries to account for the appearance of some symptoms which, if one step followed another, should not appear the way they do clinically. He says:

> . . . it can be urged that the delusions of persecution (which were directed against Flechsig) unquestionably made their appearance at an

[17] I wonder whether Bleuler's (1911) differentiation between fundamental and accessory symptoms might not be compared to this description of withdrawal and restitution. Just as Freud refers to the manifestations of withdrawal as quiet and the restitutional phenomena as noisy, proclaiming their presence loudly, so does Bleuler depict the fundamental symptoms as silent and frequently overlooked, with the accessory symptoms bringing the patient for psychiatric help.

earlier date than the phantasy of the end of the world; so that what is supposed to have been a return of the repressed actually preceded the repression itself — and this is patent nonsense. . . . We must admit the possibility that a detachment of the libido such as we are discussing might just as easily be a partial one, a drawing back from some single complex, as a general one. A partial detachment should be by far the commoner of the two, and should precede a general one, since to begin with it is only for a partial detachment that the influences of life provide a motive. The process may then stop at the stage of a partial detachment or it may spread to a general one, which will loudly proclaim its presence in the symptoms of megalomania. Thus the detachment of the libido from the figure of Flechsig may, nevertheless, have been what was primary in the case of Schreber; it was immediately followed by the appearance of the delusion, which brought back the libido on to Flechsig again (though with a negative sign to mark the fact that repression had taken place) and thus annulled the work of the repression [1911b, pp. 72–73].

At another point he discusses a very important subject, one to which I will return — the unequal forms of regression. Using ego cathexes (ego interests) and libidinal cathexes as his frame of reference, he states: "It cannot be asserted that a paranoiac, even at the height of the repression, withdraws his interest from the external world completely — as must be considered to occur in certain other kinds of hallucinatory psychosis (such as Meynert's amentia). The paranoiac perceives the world and takes into account any alteration that may happen in it, and the external effect it makes upon him stimulates him to invent explanatory theories (such as Schreber's 'cursorily improvised men'). It, therefore, appears to me far more probable that the paranoiac's altered relation to the world is to be explained entirely or in the main by the loss of his libidinal interest" (p. 75).

In his paper "On Narcissism" (1914a), Freud extends the contributions made in the Schreber case, and deals with Jung's attack on the libido theory. He reemphasizes that whereas in neurotic conditions the withdrawal of libido from external objects is replaced by others in fantasy, in the psychotic:

The libido that has been withdrawn from the external world has been directed to the ego and thus gives rise to an attitude which may be called narcissism. But the megalomania itself is no new creation; on the contrary, it is, as we know, a magnification and plainer manifestation of a condition which had already existed previously. This leads us to look upon the narcissism which arises through the drawing in of object-cathexes as a secondary one, superimposed upon a primary narcissism that is obscured by a number of different influences [p. 75].

Modifications of Freud's Concepts

The use of withdrawal and restitution as a frame of reference for the psychoanalytic understanding of psychosis has undergone change and amplification. Clearly, these concepts do not account for a good deal of psychotic symptomatology, and they have been given varying degrees of emphasis by different authors. Katan (1951), for instance, goes so far as to suggest that all delusional symptoms—be they about the self, the ego, internal reality, or external reality—are restitutive moves in an attempt to re-create a substitute reality. In his opinion, schizophrenics (does this apply to the psychotics?) regress to an undifferentiated state in order to rid themselves of a conflict they cannot master by means of reality. The delusional restitution is an endeavor to master the problem. (It should be noted that Katan himself has admitted [personal communication] that Freud in later years did not share Katan's extreme reliance on the concept of restitution as a frame of reference for symptom formation in psychosis.)

I find Hartmann's (1951) concept of withdrawal and restitution a useful one. He views withdrawal and restitution as a constant, ongoing process, moving in both directions. The whole phenomenon is depicted in terms of cathectic flux—to self, organs, words, object representations, etc. He believes that to speak of the withdrawal of cathexis in schizophrenia is to refer to a withdrawal from the unconscious representations of the object world and not necessarily to a withdrawal from the environment itself. One might, of course, ask whether a withdrawal from the unconscious representation of the object world does not always produce some change in the relationship to the environment.

In a discussion of Hartmann's paper, Nunberg (1951) emphasizes that restitution is an effort at *recovery*. He indicates that there is an intense fear of an overwhelming sense of loneliness with a consequent struggle to regain contact with objects. These objects, however, are the objects of the internal world and of the Oedipus complex. He does not agree that the schizophrenic withdraws libido from the representations of objects. Rather, these are shifted; they are still very much involved, but at a different, earlier level in psychic development.

It is true that we may see intense object *involvement* in psychosis, but this is no longer a true object *relationship*. As Bychowski has indicated (Freedman, 1962, 1964), what we are dealing with here is the persistence or reappearance of old partial and archaic object formations, introjects, which are clung to in a desperate attempt to avoid further regression. Bychowski hypothesizes that the potential psychotic retains object images which have been distorted by early perceptual incapacities, related to the stage of ego development when objects were imperfectly perceived and introjected. In the face of subsequent object loss, the ego is filled with these old objects — with partially introjected objects, distorted objects, shadow objects, incompletely loved and hated objects, etc. These archaic introjects may then be externalized and projected in the psychosis.

Freeman (1973), also using the concepts of withdrawal and restitution, focuses on the fate of the withdrawn libido and the maintenance or loss of self-nonself differentiation as a determinant of differing clinical pictures:

> In psychoses the representations of self are subject to change and their cathexis fluctuates between hypercathexis and decathexis both in the same patient and from patient to patient. In schizophrenia and paranoid psychosis different self-representation systems will be affected. In the former the representations of the bodily self may be subject to derangement while in the latter it may be the representations of the mental self alone which are most affected.... In the schizophrenias and allied states the cathexis of the self-representations results in a pathological narcissism. In severe depressive states there is a withdrawal of drive cathexis from external objects (real persons). Psychoanalytic work with these patients reveals that it is the object representations, past and present, which have become the recipient of this hypercathexis [pp. 6–7].

Freeman then goes on to underline the restitutional impact of projection and identification, arguing that they "not only have a defensive role but they are the means by which the libidinal drive cathexes find their way to objects" (p. 20).

So far we have been looking at amplifications of the concepts of withdrawal and restitution in relation to the psychoses. Yet there are some who reject this as a frame of reference altogether. To Federn (1943), for instance, detachment of object libido (Freud's withdrawal) is not primary but *secondary* to loss of ego cathexis. He sees symptoms such as megalomania and hypochondriasis as deriving from a deficiency in ego cathexis. Delusions and hallucinations result from the loss of ego boundaries. (I might add that the mechanism whereby loss of ego cathexis produces these phenomena is not entirely clear. For instance, I'm not quite sure how this produces megalomania and hypochondriasis — unless Federn is presupposing that loss of ego cathexis reactivates earlier ego states [i.e., narcissism] which contain the ingredients of megalomania and hypochondriasis, a view similar to Bychowski's.)

In more recent years one of the most extensive attacks on the concepts of withdrawal and restitution is that by Arlow and Brenner (1964). They clearly state that neither of these concepts "is warranted today and that neither should be retained as an integral part of the psychoanalytic theory of psychoses" (1969, p. 7). Claiming that these assumptions "are contradicted by clinical observations," they propose to show that "the later concepts of Freud's structural theory, particularly the concepts of conflict, anxiety and defensive regression of ego functions, explain the clinical phenomena of the psychoses better than do the earlier concepts of libidinal decathexis and recathexis" (p. 7).

To my mind, however, Arlow and Brenner's use of the term "withdrawal" is problematic, especially in the examples they present. The word "withdrawal" appears to be used in a generic sense — as a physical pulling away. For instance, they report:

> A psychotic patient, who was in conflict over her angry, sadistic impulses toward her ex-husband, defended herself against those impulses by going into a trance or stuporous state in which she neither moved, nor spoke, nor thought. She behaved as though she must tie herself hand and foot, and even tongue and brain, lest she burst forth in a fury and destroy and devour the object of her wrath. We may say that in our psychotic patient there was a defensively motivated disruption of certain ego functions which are, ordinarily, considerably less affected by inner conflict in normal or neurotic individuals: voluntary motility, external sensory perception, and conscious thought. This disruption resulted in a severe, though temporary withdrawal [sic] from external reality [1964, p. 159].

If Arlow and Brenner are offering this example to demonstrate that "withdrawal" is secondary to disruption of ego functions, that though this patient "withdrew" there was no decathexis of the object, it is somewhat confusing. Physical withdrawal from the environment does not necessarily mean decathexis of the object. A wife, for instance, may quarrel with her husband and in her anger shut herself into another room. She has withdrawn from him physically but has hardly decathected him. A schizophrenic patient, on the other hand, may be in the same room with her husband and even speak to him, and yet decathect him so that he is meaningless to her.

Furthermore, much of the symptomatology Arlow and Brenner use to show that there is no decathexis of the object in psychosis could be viewed by some as manifestations of restitution, since, as Freud points out, withdrawal may proceed quietly and be detected only by subtle symptomatology. Decathexis may manifest itself in a loss of interest in and meaning of the environment. A patient may call his doctor by name, although the latter has no affective significance for him. In other words, the external environment may be meaningless and indifferent to the patient even though he appears oriented. It is this kind of decathexis that I would underline in the withdrawal of schizophrenia. As Hartmann (1956) explains:

> . . . most frequently in schizophrenia it is seen that reality becomes meaningless, reduced to "pure environment," that [these patients] are deprived of the processes which normally give it a place in one's personal world. In this case, we speak of a withdrawal of cathexis from reality (or rather from the presentations of reality), which is certainly a correct description, though probably incomplete. Beyond this, it is likely that specific functions of the ego, which normally account for our world being meaningful also in a personal way, are impaired in the schizophrenic [p. 48].

One might also note again Freud's (1911b) view that withdrawal and restitution attempts may go on simultaneously and that evidence of both may exist. One may, for instance, see delusional formation as evidence of restitution side by side by with decathexis of the object.

Freeman (1970) also questions whether Arlow and Brenner are using the concept of decathexis appropriately. He indicates that they tend to ignore or minimize the economic factor, as well as the fact that a multitude of different clinical conditions are subsumed under the term "psychosis." In his opinion, although there is evidence of object cathexis in psychosis, this is generally weak and fragile. He points out:

> In those cases categorized as catatonic-hebephrenic, for want of a better term, it is possible to find a fragment of the capacity for object relations. Although these patients are withdrawn and unresponsive they are occasionally to be found showing some slight interest in an object. In every case the object tie is based on the wish for satisfaction of some need. It may be for food, cigarettes, the cooperation in some particular aspect of the patient's delusional reality or the wish to get home, if the patient is in a hospital. In all instances the object relationship vanishes once the need is met or if there is a disappointment. The attachments to objects are thus weak and fragile. They are without constancy, being rarely sustained [p. 408].

Restitution to preserve reality is a traditional concept employed to account for psychotic symptomatology. It is, however, I believe, a special instance of adaptation—a regressive adaptation. One could well raise the question whether such restitution is necessarily specific to psychosis. More relevant, I believe, would be to try to designate those restitutive means specific for psychosis, since I do believe that restitution of a sort takes place in neurosis as well. (As a matter of fact, there is some indication of this in Freud's papers on reality, which I shall discuss subsequently.) The various ways in which restitution is achieved are of relevance in differentiating syndromes. Freud himself indicates that hallucinations are the specific way the schizophrenic tries to hold onto the object. Perhaps one also needs to look at the object of the restitutional attempts—that is, not only at the kind of attempts, but also at what the patient is trying to restitute (the internal environment, the object representations, the self in a deeper sense, etc.), and why this restitution is essential.

The question could also be raised whether the idea of withdrawal and restitution is applicable to all types of psychoses, including organic psychoses and depressive psychoses. Or is this process particularly unique for schizophrenia? I have already noted the idea of different levels of withdrawal as a frame of reference for illness. Regression and withdrawal to the deepest levels, to nondifferentiation, to the so-called autoerotic level, to primary identification, are said to produce schizophrenia. (This is the paranoid-schizoid position described by Melanie Klein.) The somewhat higher level, the "narcissistic" level, has been associated with paranoid development. At still higher levels, where object and self exist but in a manifestly ambivalent introjected relationship, we ostensibly find the affective psychoses.

It appears to me that in the broad sense both withdrawal and restitution represent cathectic shifts in the interest of defense. Both seem to be in the service of dealing with a conflict related to a loss or threatened loss of object and self. Various mechanisms may be used to defend against this loss (e.g., projection). Restitution has to take place in the interest of psychic survival, even at the risk of establishing a delusional reality. It is this, I believe, that contributes to the fixity of delusions (Frosch, 1967b).

Bak (1954) addresses himself to the factors that play a role in the regression as well as the restitution. In his opinion: "either through a quantitative factor in the aggressive drive, or through the dysfunction of some specific part of the ego responsible for neutralization, it is the aggressive drive that is instrumental in bringing about the regression" (pp. 130–131). The regression, as he sees it, consists of a dissolving of the object in the self and thus serves to defend against aggression. He assumes that "the ego, in order to avoid the destruction of the object world, has taken a position where the world and the self fall into one unit. In this fusion between the self and the object the operation of aggression has become eliminated" (p. 132). In other words, together with the lack of structural differentiation, there is nondifferentiation of libido and aggression.

Bak describes the basic struggle in schizophrenia as characterized by the need to conserve the ego in the face of an inexplicable, inexpressible anxiety. He believes that this anxiety is a reaction to the danger of ultimately sinking back into a state of impersonality (flowing over into the universe). The schizophrenic struggles against this threat of dissolution. The ego tries to reorient itself, to reestablish itself, to build up a changed existence. Reconstructive attempts are made to arrest the sinking into impersonal existence — "to prevent the dissolution in the collective, and . . . to retain or re-establish the integrity of the personality" (1943, p. 460). It is out of these attempts at differentiation that Bak sees the mannerisms and delusions of grandeur developing. As he puts it: "The threat of the dissolution of the boundaries is met by the ego with attempts to fortify the boundaries by building up an exaggeratedly demarcated personality. Thus the schizophrenic mannerism is the manifestation of the attempted self-cure against the tendency of dissolution of the personality in the group-concept" (p. 460).

Along these lines, it is of interest that Khan (1963) relates multiple clinical manifestations in certain borderline patients to an attempt to cope with an underlying threat of annihilation with consequent disintegration and dissolution. The attempt to ward off dissolution may not always be successful, with some patients remaining at a relatively primitive level, but clinically one may observe all these movements going on almost simultaneously, with a state of continuous flux until some kind of adaptive level is reached. In a sense, what we see clinically, following Freud, are attempts at restoring reality, however distorting these attempts may be. For instance, the intensity with which some psychotics perceive things, such as brilliant color, may be related to their need to hold onto reality, to combat dissolution and loss of self. Indeed, some psychotic and borderline patients who have difficulty holding onto reality may seek out strong sensations, even to the point of inflicting pain on themselves. A schizophrenic circus sword and flame swallower described the need to feel these in his throat and esophagus to the point of pain in order to feel alive. A patient who bit her nails to the point of bleeding, while admitting the masturbatory aspects, claimed she did this to convince herself she was alive. Asch (1971) has reported that some borderline and psychotic wrist-slashers use these acts to establish the existence of their bodies. A patient who engaged in repeated intercourse one night, as many as seven or eight times, said he did so to feel alive.[18]

There is an innate push toward restitution of the object (i.e., the self), not unlike the basic push toward establishing object relations. Both are necessary for emotional survival. Touching on this subject, Freud (1914a) views it from an economic point of view, in terms of libidinal shifts between "ego" (self) and object:

> Here we may even venture to touch on the question of what makes it necessary at all for our mental life to pass beyond the limits of narcissism and to attach the libido to objects. The answer which would follow from our line of thought would once more be that this necessity arises when the cathexis of the ego with libido exceeds a certain amount. A strong egoism is a protection against falling ill, and we are bound to fall ill if, in consequence of frustration, we are unable to love. This follows somewhat on the lines of Heine's picture of the psychogenesis of the Creation: God is imagined as saying: 'Illness was no doubt the final cause of the whole urge to create. By creating, I could recover; by creating, I became healthy' [p. 85].[19]

At some point it becomes clear that what Freud has in mind is not falling ill, but survival.

Katan (1950) relates the origin of attempts at restitution to the forces that compel the infant to develop and the inner impulses that turn the young child toward reality. He refers to Freud's (1923) hypothesis about this compelling force, which I believe is an extension of the ideas expressed above in the paper "On Narcissism." Here, however, Freud proposes that the antithesis between life and death instincts results in the directing of destructive impulses outward to avoid self-destruction. In other words, the conflict between these two forces

[18] A case mentioned to me by Dr. William Frosch involved a man who, fearing total dissolution with the orgasm, had to focus very intently on one part of his wife's body during intercourse—making it become quite sharp and vivid. He felt this would help fend off dissolution. This might also relate to certain borderline and psychotic patients' use of primitive modes of reality testing in which all the sensory modalities are brought into play.

[19] Somewhat similarly, Macfie Campell (1926) says: "Delusion, like fever, is to be looked on as part of nature's attempt at cure, an endeavor to neutralize some disturbing factor, to compensate for some handicap, to reconstruct a working contact with the group, which will still satisfy special needs" (p. 9). (I would like to thank Dr. Donald Burnham for drawing my attention to this quote.)

results in a push toward contact with reality. It is from this outward push, says Katan, that the "attempts at restitution receive nourishment" and create "a new reality by means of delusion." It can thus already be seen that a motivating force for restitution is the deep fear of disintegration and dissolution of self, which I view as the basic danger in the psychotic process (see Chapter 7).

Stereotypies as Restitution

Let us now look more closely at the process of restitution and preservation of the object. As I indicated above, this process manifests itself in many forms. The problem of reestablishing reality, which ultimately means recapturing the object and fending off dissolution of self, is touched on by Jung (1909) in his discussion of stereotypies. Freud quotes Jung as saying that delusions and motor stereotypies are the residues of former object cathexes, clung to with great persistence. Bleuler (1916) and Jung give many examples that illustrate this. Bleuler, for instance, describes a girl who went through the motions of making shoes, the residual of an earlier relationship with a shoemaker. Jung indicates that automatisms (which he relates to stereotypies) derive from a normal developmental phase in which the individual attempted to master a situation by such movements. On the one hand, then, a stereotypy may have its origin in some situation with a significant object; it is continued or revived under the impact of stimulation from the repressed situation (i.e., without the latter being conscious). On the other hand, the patient may currently reactivate older, more primitive magical modes of response, either by virtue of the state to which the ego has regressed, or by virtue of a specific meaning that these modes of expression have for the patient. Actually, both situations may occur. For instance, a regressed ego state may both permit symbolic motor expression and contain the modes of mastery consistent with that earlier phase of ego development.

It is by no means accepted, however, that stereotypies are always involved with the restitution of an object relation. To bring up another point of view, let me briefly review Ferenczi's (1921) remarks. Although his material revolves mainly around tics, he sees no marked distinction between stereotypies and tics. Both, he believes, reflect a hypersensitivity to stimuli and an inability to tolerate stimuli, which create the motive for motor expression. In both conditions there is a deep narcissism, reflected in a damming up of libido in the self, the body, or parts of the body. To defend against this damming up of organ libido, the person uses the tic or stereotypy as a kind of abreaction relieving the accrued stimulation (a kind of discharge phenomenon).

Ferenczi postulates an ego or organ memory system and hypothesizes that when an organ heavily invested with libido is exposed to injury, or some other traumatic situation, the psychic representation of this organ may become a source of accumulated stimulation (very much like an instinctual stimulus) — even after the occasion of the trauma. Motility may then be used in an attempt to relieve this excitation — ergo, the tic or stereotypy.

Ferenczi discusses many ways of dealing with such unbearable stimulation. Yet he runs into trouble. He has to differentiate between tics and stereotypies, on the one hand, and hysterical conversion phenomena and obsessions, on the other. It is here that he emphasizes the position of the object in relation to the symptoms of the latter syndromes. In hysteria, he claims, the memory traces are related to objects and their associative links to different parts of the body, so that in hysterical conversion we are dealing with retention of the object. With tics and stereotypies, however, it is the events surrounding an organ activity itself that are in a sense the memory trace, from which the ensuing psychic alterations flow. Still, the distinction is not clear, for Ferenczi himself speaks of flight and turning against the self in relation to tics and stereotypies — and these suggest some recognition of the external world and an attempt to establish a kind of relationship with it. The fact is that when you examine a given stereotypy after the patient has recovered, you can generally establish the relationship of this stereotypy to some particular group of ideas or objects. This connection may support some of Ferenczi's ideas but it is equally to be understood as object-related.

To illustrate some of these problems, I would like to refer to a patient whose stereotypies could be seen both as attempts to deal with object relations and as representing organ-riddance phenomena. The patient is the one I described in Section A (p. 96) — a 22-year-old woman who had been having numerous delusions, including end-of-the-world delusions, delusions of persecution, feelings of being watched, etc. During one session, I saw her repeating a movement which could best be described as a brushing away with both hands. When I asked her what this was she said, "Nothing," but when I pressed her she said she was brushing away bad thoughts and bad ideas. She indicated that she did not want me to hear these ideas, lest in some way they offend and possibly even hurt me. It was obvious that these ideas were of an aggressive and destructive nature, sometimes involving me. From my knowledge of the case, I knew they were also related to sexual and masturbatory fantasies. In the course of her psychosis, movement of the hands, feet, and other extremities had a sexual significance for her; these were the offending parts of her body.

Without going into too much detail, let me say that there was a gradual transition in this woman's movements from rather overt, easily observable gestures to surreptitious one-handed movements, flicks of the finger, and so on. Then she resorted to all sorts of grimaces, eye and eyelid movements, head turnings. These generally occurred when there were ideas, impulses, or thoughts she wanted to ward off. Eventually even these movements became rather minimal, more what one would call mannerisms, hardly recognizable as related to her original movements. It was obvious all along that these movements represented a controlling force, but they also contained in them features of what was being warded off.

Even these mannerisms began to subside, and the patient became preoccupied with goodness and badness in herself, expressed in terms of ideas and thoughts. She engaged in numerous obsessional-like activities to ward off bad ideas, such as counting and concentrating fervently to divert her mind from these ideas. Yet there were also episodes of quick externalization, with reappearance of the mannerisms and stereotypies. For instance, during our sessions, her eyes might begin to roll around in a frenetic way. After a while she would rationalize this. She once said, "You may think it is because I'm trying to avoid something or pushing something away, the way I used to, but it's not so. It's because I'm not getting enough sleep, and the skin in the eyes becomes hypersensitive and overresponsive to stimuli."

Eventually what had been a delusional system of being tested for goodness and badness began to be internalized, step by step, so that ultimately the construction of an internalized observer on the way to superego formation could be seen developing. It should be mentioned in passing here that as part of her delusional system this woman believed that as a child an observation machine had been implanted in her head. This machine could observe and even control her activities. The patient had a very intrusive mother, who was constantly watching her, following her into the bathroom, etc. There was ample evidence that many of her preoccupations concerned the mother. The ambivalent relationship to the mother contained within it the desire to hold onto and internalize her, which, I believe, also expressed itself in the stereotypies.

During the delusional period, I too had been part of the watching and spying system, but gradually she began to express a need to differentiate herself from me. There were marked attempts to establish her own identity and a struggle against identification, which to her meant engulfment. Yet interestingly enough, the very thing she was struggling against was incorporated. The attempt to establish herself as a separate entity from me contained within it an incorporation of me. For instance, among her many stereotypies was a little gesture of mine, a sort of waving-goodbye gesture, whose source she at first was unable to specify. My point is that this patient's various stereotypies, mannerisms, and other idiosyncratic movements could be seen as object-related in one form or another.

The End-of-the-World Delusion

Let me turn now to another clinical manifestation to which the concepts of withdrawal and restitution have been applied — the end-of-the-world delusion. As Freud (1911b) formulates it: "The patient has withdrawn from the persons in his environment and from the external world generally the libidinal cathexis which he has hitherto directed on to them. Thus everything has become indifferent and irrelevant to him, and has to be explained by means of a secondary rationalization as being 'miracled up, cursorily improvised'. The end of the world is the projection of this internal catastrophe; his subjective world has come to an end since his withdrawal of his love from it" (p. 70).

In highlighting the back and forth movement of libido in terms of the antithesis between ego libido and object libido, Freud comments: "The more the one is employed, the more the other becomes depleted. The highest phase of development of which object-libido is capable is seen in the state of being in love, when the subject seems to give up his own personality in favour of an object-cathexis; while we have the opposite condition in the paranoic's phantasy (or self-perception) of the 'end of the world'" (1914a, p. 76). In a footnote he adds: "There are two mechanisms of this 'end of the world' idea; in the one case, the whole libidinal cathexis flows off to the loved object; in the other, it all flows back into the ego." The implication of all this is that withdrawal of libido from objects, i.e., object representations, eventuates in end-of-the-world fantasies. Yet this is not consonant with what we see clinically.

Freud's explanations here do not seem entirely clear to me, since withdrawal of libido should result in indifference. When he speaks of "internal catastrophe" and says "his subjective world has come to an end," what does he mean? Since libidinal shifts of this sort are postulated as the basis for paranoid or schizophrenic psychoses, why are these conditions not always accompanied by end-of-the-world fantasies?

As we have seen, Freud tries to deal with the seeming inconsistency that Schreber's persecutory delusions appeared earlier than the end-of-the-world delusion by referring to detachment as being more commonly partial and directed against some specific single complex. He says that in the paranoid, even at the height of regression, the ego does not withdraw its interest in the external world completely (see also Hartmann, 1951). Ego functions are still present. The implication is that in paranoia the ego is more intact than in schizophrenia. What Freud does not pursue more definitively at this particular point is what the specific ego functions are that are impaired in psychosis — i.e., reality testing. He does this in 1924.

One of the many questions Freud (1911b) raises is whether withdrawal of libido is sufficient to account for the end-of-the-world fantasy. He indicates that in some way the ego must be involved, and thus opens up the problem of ego functioning and object relations in psychoses. At this point in time, however, let us be clear that Freud is still talking in terms of ego instincts (self-preservation) and sexual instincts (preservation of the species). Ultimately he makes the very important statement that a disturbance in libido can influence disturbances in ego cathexis. (We should not, however, overlook the fact that the converse is possible, that a secondary disturbance of the libidinal processes may be induced by abnormal changes in the ego.) Freud believes that it is probable that processes of this kind constitute the distinctive characteristic of psychosis. Again, we must remember he is using the term "ego" in a different sense. I might also ask: If ego interests are self-preservative, are we not in the area of preservation of self and the psychotic fear of self-dissolution? Perhaps this should be the jumping-off point in discussing the role of the ego in the psychotic process (see Chapter 7).

There have been many studies of the end-of-the-world delusion. Katan (1949), for instance, views Schreber's end-of-the-world delusion as a defense against experiencing the masturbatory genital excitation provoked by Flechsig. This was an earthly pleasure, and he had to abandon it in order to reach God. The only way to do this was to bring the world to an end, to eliminate Flechsig and all others who were constantly stimulating him. When he reached God, the world would be restored. (It is interesting to note that Schreber somehow conceived of himself as surviving the world.) Yet Katan's ideas do not seem sufficient, either in explaining Schreber's delusion or those of others.

From a different perspective, Macalpine and Hunter (1953) see the end-of-the-world delusion as preliminary to procreation and birth fantasies. Spring (1939), on the other hand, considers end-of-the-world fantasies as related to specific destructive wishes which the patient has toward a given individual. These are then dispersed onto the whole world, thereby defending against murderous impulses as well as self-destructive, suicidal ones (a form of self-preservation). Melanie Klein (1946) places this within a somewhat different framework. She sees the splitting of the object as the projection of Schreber's own feeling that his ego was split, and suggests there was a threat of annihilation of one part of the self by the other part. In her words: "The anxieties and fantasies about inner destruction and ego disintegration bound up with this mechanism are projected onto the external world and underlie delusions of destruction" (p. 108). Taking Freud's statement about how disturbances of libidinal process result in the abnormal changes in the ego characteristic of psychosis, she links this to her idea that abnormal changes in the ego derive from excessive splitting in early infancy. She believes that the mechanism of one part of the ego annihilating other parts underlies the world catastrophe fantasy and implies a preponderance of destructive impulses over libido. The ego and internalized objects are felt by the patient to be in bits, and this internal catastrophe both extends to the external world and is projected onto it.[20]

My own feeling is that the actual danger is one of self-dissolution and disintegration, that is, of an ultimate loss of cathexis of the self. Since, to the psychotic, the outside world is not differentiated from the self, the individual fears the destruction of the world because it will bring his own destruction. This idea is embodied in Spring's (1939) paper, but in a somewhat different way. In a sense, my idea is not too different from what Freud implies when he says the end of the world is the projection of internal catastrophe (namely, that the subjective world will come to an end with the patient's withdrawal of love from it). My emphasis, however, is on the fear of loss of cathexis of the self,

[20] One must remember that Klein's paper was published in 1946, after the dual instinct theory had been put forward. Freud, in considering the Schreber case in 1911, had not yet formulated his theories on aggression and thus tended to explain the end-of-the-world delusion more in libidinal terms.

with ultimate disintegration of self and the world.

I should like to return to the patient with stereotypies I described above (pp. 96, 121; see also Frosch, 1967a). Preceding her flagrant psychotic break, this woman was described by her parents as somewhat withdrawn, quiet, preoccupied, and seemingly uninterested in her environment. She seemingly rather suddenly developed the grossly psychotic manifestation that led to her admission. As I pointed out in Section A, after an initial period of disturbance on admission, the patient quieted down and was transferred to another ward. On her third day on that ward, she again became withdrawn and would not leave her bed. For the most part she was mute, but when she did speak, she said she felt that her life was in danger, that she would be killed. This disturbed behavior was followed by a period of religious conversion, lasting about three weeks, during which she renounced all sexuality (see p. 97). Concomitant with her religious preoccupations, the patient became convinced that the world would come to an end on Good Friday, but in the resurrection she would survive. She claimed she would not die, and had actually been sent to the hospital to be prepared emotionally for Judgment Day. She did not feel badly about the rest of the world being destroyed. The megalomania extended to her reliving the agony of Christ, reporting first gum bleeding and then many stigmata. She pointed to little scratches on her body and indicated that these were the bleedings of Christ. After this she concluded she would be resurrected along with other good people on Easter Sunday, and would proceed to enjoy life under the reign of God. Yet it was apparent she was not too sure of this; one could see panic, withdrawal, and fear of disintegration and dissolution side by side with these restitution fantasies. As Good Friday drew close, she became upset, very tense, restless, and sleepless. She openly expressed fears of being cut off from life and wondered if she were two people in one. She described a feeling she said she had had since the age of five: a rubber sheath had surrounded her from waist to knees, with elastic bands connecting her to the outside world. As she grew up, these bands broke one by one. Since then, she felt as if she were in a shell, cut off from the rest of the world.

During this period of confusion before Good Friday, she developed delusions about me and thought I was a priest testing her belief in Jesus and God to determine whether she was worthy of joining the Catholic Church and being saved. She dreamt of being a prostitute and was very perturbed by these dreams, fearing she could not be saved (see Chapter 3). In addition, she was preoccupied with masturbation and had overt homosexual and heterosexual fantasies, many of the latter revolving around me. It was clear that she was caught between a flight from her incestuous fantasies toward homosexuality and a tremendous fear of the latter, which produced even further regressive manifestations of a dedifferentiating nature. The feeling of her own disintegration and fragmentation was projected, so that when she looked out of the window, she saw what seemed to be the beginning of the end of the world — bombs exploding, buildings falling apart, etc.

Over Easter weekend she became very disheveled and confused. She gave away her bathrobe because it was contaminated. There was a flagrant breakthrough of both homosexual and heterosexual ideas, immediately followed by thoughts of hatred of "Negroes and Jews." The fragmentation expressed itself in split good and bad thoughts. The "good" thoughts were that "Negroes and Jews are bad," and the bad thoughts were that "Negroes and Jews are good." As I described earlier, there were good and bad parts to her body as well. Should she let the bad thoughts stay in her mind, she would die of dismemberment. This would begin with an incision of a lipoma on her forehead, and then different parts of her body would be dismembered and distributed to the other patients for the good of humanity. She began to hallucinate openly, claiming that she could hear voices saying "good" and "bad," and that others could read her mind. It was following this, after a period of unusually withdrawn and deteriorated, inappropriate and silly behavior, that the restitutional processes via stereotypies (described above) became most pronounced.

Through my work with this patient, it became clear that an upsurge of instinctual pressures had a disintegrative and fragmenting effect, perceived by her as a threat to survival. She felt herself being taken over by conflicting, uncontrollable forces, which would eventuate in dissolution of self. She tried to ward off this danger by projection. The good and bad hallucinations and the world destruction fantasies represented projections of the warring factions within her and her own feared disintegration. Regressive withdrawal and dedifferentiation were obviously at times defensive, but at the same time they were a source of tremendous anxiety, which generated a push toward reintegration. Splitting into good and bad parts, externalization, internalization, projection, and introjection all existed side by side in her strivings to deal with the dangers, eventuating in withdrawal as well as in a push to reestablish her identity (which was threatened by the withdrawal).

The attempts at reintegration, at reversing the dedifferentiation and reestablishing the psychic structures which had fallen prey to fragmentation, could be observed at various levels. At first this was apparent in the delusions which existed side by side with the ongoing fragmentation. But as the process of reintegration proceeded, higher modes of adaptation became evident.[21] Internalization and attempts at restoring the object and the self could be observed, and the nature of the primary danger began to take on forms consistent with higher levels of psychic development. As I noted above, the sense of being tested as to whether she was good or bad, which at first existed within a very elaborate delusional system, was gradually internalized so that ultimately an internalized observer began to pave the way for superego formation, as well as reintegration of the ego, self, and object.

Another example of the move toward a higher level of psychic development could be seen in the shift of defenses, with obsessive-compulsive modes replacing more delusional ones. These seemed to be concerned with the control of libidinal and aggressive drives as such, rather than with their disintegrative effect. Most interesting was her use of language (see Chapter 3, p. 55). At first, like the typical schizophrenic, she tended to treat words as objects. The words "black" and "green," for instance, were concrete. Gradually she began to use words obsessively to ward off aggressive and sexual impulses. Black and green became "bad." Rituals, counting, and the recitation of the alphabet in various combinations were employed to fend off aggressive ideas which might destroy the object — me or her parents. Every once in a while, questions about the reality of her parents popped into her mind. "I try very hard to push these thoughts away and thinking of my parents as real," she countered. "They are the good part of me. I try to think of good things." The obsessive-compulsive rituals were also used to ward off sexual thoughts about me.

Let me turn now to another interesting attempt to combat dedifferentiation and reestablish her identity, although in a very pathological manner. At first, as she was coming out of her delusional state, she went

[21] The clinical course, however, went through many vicissitudes. There were episodes of externalization with reappearance of the mannerisms, stereotypies, delusions, etc. During one period when she had improved and was permitted to leave the hospital, she visited her old haunts. Transiently her delusions of persecution returned, together with fears of impending disaster. There was also a constant preoccupation with imminent death, fear of loss of control and fear of disintegration. She expressed a complete lack of ability to control her sexual impulses. When she had an orgasm, it would be very disruptive, since it contained within it the possibility of disintegration and impending catastrophe.

through a very intense period of extreme attachment to me. It was an attachment that had all the earmarks of erotomania. She had numerous sexual fantasies and openly declared her love for me, her desire to marry and to have sexual relations with me. All this was accompanied by weeping, exhortations, etc. It reached a peak one night in a kind of cosmic orgastic experience and *unio mystica*. She was lying in bed having fantasies about me and felt her whole body enlarging, so that it merged with me and then with the universe. She felt at one with all around her. This culminated in an orgastic experience in which she was dissolved.

After this experience, she began to withdraw from me and others in the environment. She maintained a "correct and proper" attitude toward me, saying she saw me only because I was her physician and she had to see me. Like a grande dame, she would grant me an interview, frequently keeping me waiting while she finished her toilette. She became quite formal in manner and gait, and spoke in a controlled, stylized, and stilted way. All this was accompanied by massive denial and repression of her sexual feelings and fantasies.

Yet, in spite of the wish to deny her attachment to me, what was incorporated into her whole manner was a fantasy she had expressed during her erotomania — of achieving my love by fulfilling a certain ideal. I was the ideal. She would better her position. She would study medicine, even psychiatry, so that I would not be ashamed of her anywhere. She would be my helpmate, and eventually perhaps I would marry her. Indeed, during this period, she actually began to study very hard, not only to combat her sexual fantasies, but to fulfill her identification with me. As I pointed out above, she even incorporated a little gesture of mine, a kind of waving-goodbye gesture. At the same time there was an element of grandiosity, which underlined her differentness, apartness, even separation from me and others. This was in keeping with a fantasy she had had all along — that she was someone special. (During her grossly psychotic period, she had expressed a typical family romance fantasy in one of her delusions.)

This whole period culminated in her becoming exceedingly negativistic. She would not speak, refused to take medication, and had to be transferred to the disturbed ward. She completely ignored me, and walked away when she saw me come onto the ward. Finally, however, I was able to make contact with her. She said she felt rejected by me because I had not done what she wanted. She had had a fantasy of getting an apartment and living with me even though we were not married. She also confessed that just before her withdrawal she had been flooded with excitement and sexual fantasies about me. Yet she continued to refuse anything I offered, even a cigarette. When she finally did accept one, she said she would have to pay me. She admitted quite openly that much of her behavior was intended to establish her independence from me and to spite me. She objected to my plans to "mold" her.

It became clear that one of the motivating factors in these attempts at separation was her fear of loss of self. Earlier, she had fended off dissolution by her various delusions, some of a grandiose nature (the Christ fantasy). Now she was defending herself by withdrawal from me and negativism. In between, her attempts at integration had taken an outward form of typical neurotic devices used to deal with threatening instinctual impulses, both erotic and aggressive. However, closer examination led me to believe that this was deceptive. The seemingly neurotic compulsive rituals and the obsessional thinking were not at all ego-alien; they were basically attempts to establish and preserve the self and the object at a somewhat higher level than delusional formation. It was clear that whatever functions this patient's various symptoms had, they were necessary for the restitution and preservation of self and object, and hence for psychic survival.

It should be obvious that the idea of restitution of the object and an attempted return to reality in the psychotic is a leitmotiv of psychoanalytic contributions as far back as the 1880s, although this is discussed in the context of the then-existing frames of reference. I shall return to this area later from a different perspective, when I discuss the role of reality and its position in the psychotic process (see Chapter 10).

C.
Projection and Delusional Fixity

Let us go back to a question Freud (1911b) raises in the Schreber case: How is the symptom brought about and what is the role of projection in this process? It should be obvious from the last section that among the restitutional processes, projection plays an important role in the development of the psychotic paranoid constellation.

The subject of projection appears early in the Fliess letters (1887–1902, Drafts M and N, Letters 74 and 75) and in Freud's papers on the neuropsychoses of defense (1894, 1896). Yet it is a subject Freud somehow abandons after 1911; he does not return to it until 1922, and then only briefly.[22] His view is that in projection an internal perception has been suppressed and instead its content, after undergoing a certain distortion, enters consciousness in the form of an external perception. In delusions of persecution, this distortion consists of a transformation of affect. Yet it is important to note that Freud does not see projection as playing the same part in all forms of paranoia. Nor does he limit its appearance to paranoia; it appears in other psychological conditions as well.

If projection is so ubiquitous, what is special about paranoid projection? Is it that a particular phase in psychic development lends a special feature to the content of what is projected and the way in which the projection is carried out? This idea is suggested by Knight (1940b) and Fairbairn (1956), who seem to feel that the anal stage promotes the mechanism of projection by virtue of the expulsive quality of anal activity. Of course, one might ask: Is this not equally true of the spitting out which takes place at an earlier stage? However, at that earlier stage the

[22] In his 1922 paper Freud speaks of the heightened perception that the paranoid patient has of what is going on in the person who is the subject of the projection, i.e., the paranoid's capacity to observe the unconscious of the other person and to shift his own self-observation to a keen awareness of the other person's unconscious.

problem of ambivalence is not as marked. Furthermore, it is doubtful whether food taken in has the same meaning for the individual as the fecal mass, insofar as the latter is considered an inherent part of the self which can be expelled. In some patients, I have found fantasies that the expelled fecal mass continues to represent a lost part of the self, now at large in the universe.[23] Although food may be treated in a similar manner, it has to be taken in before it is considered part of the self and possible to put out again.

To rephrase my question, I would like to ask: What makes for psychotic projection in general and is the kind of projection we see in various psychotic conditions—whether depression, schizophrenia, or paranoia—essentially carried out by the same mechanism? Perhaps we should begin with the definition of projection given in the psychoanalytic glossary:

> Projection is a process whereby a painful impulse or idea is attributed to the external world. The ideas or feelings which the person cannot tolerate in himself may undergo a transformation before they are projected, as in the case of paranoid projections which Freud recognized as being based on unconscious homosexuality. First, the feeling of love is transformed into hatred and then the hatred projected onto the person who was the object of the unacceptable homosexual love. That person is then taken to be the persecutor, and the patient is the object of his hate [Moore and Fine, 1968, p. 30].

This definition, however, does not consider other forms of projection, nor does it relate to the question of what makes the projection psychotic.

It would save us a great deal of trouble if we were to recognize that the term "projection" may be used in several senses. It may be used in a generic sense, as, for instance, to project something into the future. Here its meaning is quite diffuse and we have little use for it psychoanalytically. It may also be used to refer to that particular undifferentiated ego state in which there is no separation between what is inside and outside. What is outside is simply an extension of the self and vice versa. In this sense, projection relates to an ego state in which ego boundaries have expanded to include much that is external. Attitudes, feelings, and sensations derived from the "me" are confusingly extended to what is objectively outside. Even more important, various parts of the self are treated as foreign and external. In addition, the term "projection" may

[23] To this may be added the fantasy of the poisonous quality of the fecal mass, both to the self and others whom it may damage.

also refer to certain processes during the stage in psychic development in which attempts are made to differentiate between the "me" and the "not me."

Projective and introjective techniques are rather important mechanisms in object finding as well as in establishing the self and in the building up of reality. Before the development of a unified body image and unified self, the state of the psyche is such that parts of the self — the body self and the psychic self — may be projected and extrojected. Indeed, the body image and the psychic self are ultimately built up by integrating the various autonomous and hitherto disconnected parts of the self. Such autonomy is even on occasion encouraged in later life. Schilder (1935) talks of the personification of the body parts in children's games and in language. For instance, the fingers and toes are personified in the game "This little piggy went to market." The genitals, both male and female, are frequently given playful, diminutive names, like Johnny, Peter, or little canoe. Freud, with his many intestinal distresses, referred to his bowels as his Conrad. I have mentioned a psychotic character who dissociated himself from his troublesome diarrhea by referring to the offending part of his body as "that son of a bitch" and complaining, "Why doesn't he let me alone?" A child may dissociate from an offending part of the self by saying, "I didn't do it. My hand did it." A patient with hemiplegia as well as an organic psychosis was seen, in what some would refer to as a riddance reflex, trying to push his paralyzed arm out of the bed. But his arm was personified into his son, whom he angrily berated for getting into bed with him: "Get out of here. You're not supposed to be here. Go on, get out of here."

Psychotic Projection

Childlike prototypes of dissociation and denial of unwanted parts of the self lend themselves to the process we call projection. When it appears later in life in these more primitive forms, where the self is no longer unified, it becomes what Katan (1950) calls psychotic projection. I would add that the term "psychotic" is probably not limited to this type of projection, since projection at a higher level may be psychotic if reality testing has been lost. In this latter, defensive type, projection may be viewed as a mechanism to eject (extroject) impulses and stimuli of an unpleasant nature in order to retain the purified pleasure ego, so that everything painful and unpleasant belongs to the outside. All pleasurable experiences have an identity, as do all unpleasurable ones, and this lends a degree of unity to both. In this sense, we can see that when something internal which is unpleasant is perceived as external, the mechanism for doing so derives from that earlier phase described above, where parts of the self are viewed as autonomous and thus potentially external.

Freud (1911b) at first indicates that paranoia really arises from the "misuse" of the mechanism of projection for purposes of defense. Later on, however, he raises the question whether there is anything specific to the mechanism of projection per se that makes for paranoid development. He even speaks subsequently (1922) of normal projection and apparently differentiates between projected jealousy and delusional jealousy, although projection is certainly operative in the latter. Freud seems to make the distinction on the basis of content, indicating that in delusional jealousy we are dealing with a bisexual conflict.

This of course raises the question: What frames of reference are used to differentiate between psychotic and nonpsychotic projection? Katan (1950) speaks of primary and secondary projection. He indicates that a nonpsychotic ego may use secondary projection as a defense, whereas a psychotic ego uses primary projection, by which he means those techniques found in the early, undifferentiated phase of psychic development. In other words, in the psychotic form of projection, there is a regression to the undifferentiated state, and projection is not only defensive, but also a way of dealing with and creating a new reality. It is a sort of regressive adaptation.

Many of Katan's ideas, as well as those expressed above, seem to be related to Tausk's (1919) formulations. Indeed, Tausk's article has always fascinated me. In spite of its obscurity and the difficulty in understanding it, I have always seen it as one of the earliest attempts to delineate some of the primitive ego states that today are of such great interest to many psychoanalysts.[24] It presents a beautiful concept of the earliest stages of psychic development, when the body is evolving from the undifferentiated phase. I should thus like to reemphasize some of Tausk's ideas and apply them to the concept of projection.

Essentially Tausk's thesis is that the influencing machine is a special kind of projection, namely, an organ or body projection, the body correlate of what is seen in the usual paranoid projection. It is essentially the result of a defensive maneuver against the regressive overaccumulation of organ libido, which may reach the point of threatening survival.

---

[24] See, for instance, the paper by Elkisch and Mahler (1959), which develops some of Tausk's ideas.

Contact has to be reestablished with reality and the object, even though at a regressed level. Like Katan, he believes that the mechanism of projection per se, although used defensively here, derives from a very early stage in psychic development, belonging to the primary function of the ego in the process of object finding. He says:

> It would not be too much to say that just as the projection in normal primary development has been successful because the innate narcissistic libido position had to be renounced under the attack of outer stimuli, so also pathological projection takes place because there has developed an accumulation of narcissistic libido analogous to the primary narcissism, though here anachronistic, regressive or fixated but resembling it in character insofar as it isolates the individual from the outer world. Hence, projection of one's own body may be regarded as a defense against the libido position corresponding to the end of foetal existence and the beginning of extra-uterine development [pp. 74–75].

Actually the danger here is the withdrawal of libido from the outer world to the point of threatening survival, as a result of too much primary narcissistic libido. Projection is therefore an attempt at recovery of a relationship with an object, and its prototype lies in one of the earliest forms of establishing such a relationship. In Tausk's words: "We are here dealing with a libido position which is coeval with the beginning of intellectual object finding and which is achieved either by regression or by the persistence of a vestigial phenomenon which has been for years and up to the onset of the illness effectively compensated or concealed.... This period must coincide with the developmental stage of the psyche in which object finding still occurs within the individual's own body, and when the latter is still regarded as part of the outer world" (p. 72).

The projection of one's own body can then be traced back to the developmental stage in which one's own body is the goal of object finding. It is a time when the infant is discovering its body, part by part, as the outer world, and still gropes for its hands and feet as though they were foreign objects. The infant's psyche receives stimuli arising from its own body, but acts upon them as if they were produced by outside objects.

As indicated above, Schilder (1935) discusses how the body image is treated as an outside object during this early stage in development:

> ... the child has in the beginning the same attitude towards the parts of its body as towards strange objects. It watches its arms and legs in motion as it would follow a candle-flame. It looks at the grasping hand as

attentively as at any other foreign action. It observes itself and touches itself in the bath, especially the feet (39th week). It bites its fingers, arms, and toes, so that it screams with pain (409th day). It bangs its own head with violence (41st week). It presses one of its hands firmly with the other on the table like a toy. This interest in observing one's self diminishes with the second year. It is as if the child now knew its body and had no further interest in it [p. 194].

Parenthetically, an interesting manifestation which may derive from this state of the ego appears in projective identification (which I shall discuss in Chapter 8). In this regard, Tausk makes special reference to the symptom that "everyone" knows the patient's thoughts, that the patient's thoughts are not enclosed in his own head but spread throughout the world, occurring simultaneously in the heads of all people. This symptom is part of the phenomenon of transitivism and may be seen in various forms, although it is sometimes not recognized as such. One of the most subtle ways in which it manifests itself is when patients in analysis do not associate freely or present material because they assume you already know what is in their minds. Such patients often begin to speak of people as if you already knew about whom they were talking. In such instances I think we have to assume that we are dealing with a rather early stage in psychic development, related to the stage in which there is a tenuous boundary between self and nonself. I believe that in such patients the ego boundaries are rather fragile. In some instances this way of speaking is used defensively as resistance, to avoid painful subjects.

Some interesting observations can be made in this connection. We might, for example, look at the use of the lie and the development of the secret as important factors in ego formation. I think one has to take due cognizance of the role of the secret in the establishment of ego boundaries and the sense of identity. There are patients who resent very much the request: "Tell me what's on your mind." They want their thoughts for themselves: "These are mine." "It's the only thing I have." One of my patients said to me: "Can't I do anything or think anything without you in some way becoming involved in it?" In effect, these feelings represent a firm attempt to preserve one's identity. In such instances it is sometimes rather important to keep to a minimum "penetration" into the psyche of the individual, especially in terms of withholding transference interpretations until the patient's ego can permit them without threat of loss of identity (see my discussion of psychotic characters, Frosch, 1970).

My point in all this is that in certain conditions we find a type of projection that has as a prototype the most primitive ego state in which object finding originates. It is essentially this type of projection that is seen later on in restitutional attempts at reestablishing contact with the object. And it is this stage which is the prototype for the kind of psychotic projection described by Katan (1950), in which there is a distancing and objectivization of these autonomous parts of the self.

Still, the question of what makes a projection psychotic and delusional remains. Our formulation so far delineates only the regressed ego state facilitating a certain kind of projection seen in psychosis. We must look to the disturbance of other functions involved during this ego state in seeking the essence of psychotic projection. In particular, it appears to me that the role of reality testing has to be considered in defining a projection as psychotic. In such an undifferentiated ego state, reality testing is certainly, to say the least, at a primitive level, if not completely absent. Here a suggestion in Tausk's work may shed some light on our question. As I indicated above, the phenomenon of projection Tausk examines is closely related to primitive modes of establishing object relations and reality contact. Yet at this stage in psychic development the ego functions, such as reality testing, which can establish the reality of a given phenomenon, have not developed. It is this combination, regressively reactivated, that makes a subsequent projection psychotic. As such it is different from projection used as defensive rejection of instinctual or even superego components (although the latter kind may initiate the former).

In psychotic projection, then, we might view the whole problem of the loss and restitution of objects and reality in terms of an archaic and primitive function of projection. One might therefore describe projection in a hierarchical manner and consider it more psychotic the more it approaches the early end of the spectrum. In keeping with this, we should bear in mind that the primitive ego state of the archaic projection prototype deals with phenomena and experiences in a massive way — it is not too selective. Perhaps we could draw an analogy to the functioning of a child's brain. An injury, for instance, to a given area of a child's brain will involve other areas, and this will be reflected in massive defects. In a somewhat similar manner we find the young child responding to situations in a massive and not necessarily goal-directed way, such as reaching for an object with its whole body. This massive type of response characterizes the kind of archaic projection I believe is seen in psychotic projection, which frequently works indiscriminately, with large quantities and qualities, encompassing many aspects of the superego, ego, id, and reality.

Obviously I believe the problem of reality is central to the psychotic process. However, since that will be the focus of a later chapter, I should like to turn now to some other views of psychotic projection. Waelder (1951), for instance, approaches psychotic projection from the framework of denial. He sees the forcible return, in a disguised form, of a denied love object and the feelings for it as essential to psychotic projection. This lends an element of historical truth to the delusion, and results in its resistance to correction, which he believes is the key feature of psychotic projection. Something denied and projected is not yet psychotic. There has to be a return of the denied in a disguised form for the delusion to come into existence. The denial may be directed against an external event or an instinctual drive. It may be accompanied by a claim that supports the denial, i.e., a countercathexis. There then follows a return of the denied in a distorted form. The return of the denied and the various feelings for it are united with the claim, which upholds the denial, and a symptom is formed as a result of compromise formation. Because the denied is essentially based on a return, it is inaccessible to influence; its historical truth makes for the fixity of the delusion. For Waelder, then, projection is a further development of denial; it is a denial with a specific countercathexis, a claim.

Waelder applies his theory to the formulation "I love him / I am a homosexual" and the denial "I do not love him / I am not a homosexual." This is followed by the countercathexis: "Not only do I not love him, but I hate him," and likewise, "Not only am I not a homosexual, but he is a homosexual." (Why is the countercathexis not "I am a Don Juan heterosexual"?) But this is as yet only projection and not real paranoia. Only when there is a return of the denied is the stage set for the paranoid system. The beloved returns with a changed appearance; from a familiar and beloved object, he is changed into a stranger. Waelder proposes an integrated theory at this point, suggesting that in all the various formulations used to explain delusional formation, there is one common factor, namely, the mechanism of denial. He believes that paranoid ideas are as much the result of unsuccessful denial as psychoneurotic symptoms are the result of unsuccessful repression. Essentially, a failure of denial, combined with distortions of the denied, permits the denied to make its appearance, very much as what happens in negation. In sum, what we see in projection is a denial combined with a special countercathexis.

There are many questions that Waelder's paper raises. It is not entirely clear to me, for instance, what has to transpire for the return of the denied to become a delusion of persecution, i.e., for the feelings to turn back on the patient. Obviously, at this particular point the denied love object not only becomes the hated object, but the persecuting one. The formulation becomes "he hates me and persecutes me." This seems to require an additional step, which is not made too clear by Waelder — unless it is that the very strangeness of the returned repressed makes this take on a hostile form. The counterclaim is: "Not only do I not love him, I hate him because he persecutes me." But how is the "I hate him" turned into a delusion of persecution? Waelder does try to answer this question, but it is not clear to me. Of course all this relates to the fact that what is projected is generally, for one reason or the other, intolerable and unacceptable to the patient's psyche (see my earlier discussion, p. 103).

For projection to turn back on the self and eventuate in delusions of persecution, there must be projection and externalization of at least one of the psychic structures (the accuser as personification of the superego), plus the rejected impulses. But, in addition to the rejected impulses, there must be retention of the positive aspect of the wish, i.e., "I love him and want to be loved by him." In all these instances the superego is rather primitive and archaic, consistent with that early phase in psychic development where the ego state permits externalization and personification.[25]

Waelder makes an interesting attempt to differentiate neurotic and psychotic symptoms. He believes that essentially they follow the same pattern, and that the difference is ultimately determined by the nature of the defense mechanism. In both, there is a conflict between an instinctual drive and the ego; in the neurotic, however, there is repression, while in the psychotic there is denial and countercathexis. In the neurotic we see a return of the repressed with compromise formation. In the psychotic, on the other hand, we find a return of the denied with compromise formation, resulting in delusional formation. The differences between pathological productions are determined first by the

[25] I thus feel that Bak's (1946) idea that "paranoia is delusional masochism" should be modified somewhat. The paranoid structure contains as one of its important components, content-wise, projection of masochism. It also contains the projection of the psychic structure involved in effecting the masochism. Moreover, it continues to preserve the position of the subject of this masochism, in relation to the wish for gratification of the rejected impulses. The whole construct has been split, with component parts ascribed to various areas.

nature of the conflict, second by the choice of defense mechanism, third by the choice of countercathexis, and fourth by the conditions under which the warded-off returns. But ultimately, according to Waelder, it is the kind of defense mechanism used that plays the primary role in the choice of illness.

In summary, it should be clear that whether projection is psychotic or not depends on a number of factors. Among these are the content of the projection (i.e., the homosexuality), the state of the ego (the impairment in self-nonself differentiation which facilitates projection), and the disturbances in other ego functions (for instance, reality testing, perception, and modes of mastering tension). Psychotic projection (or perhaps one should confine this to schizophrenic projection) probably has as its prototype the most primitive ego state, where object finding takes place via projective and introjective techniques. That is, the type of projection seen later on, for instance, in restitutional attempts resulting clinically in delusions, is probably genetically related to this earlier, primitive type of projection. While this formulation does not really answer the question of what makes a projection psychotic and delusional, it does portray the ego state facilitating a certain type of projection that one sees in psychosis. Probably the disturbances in crucial ego functions coeval with such an ego state are the determining factors. For instance, it seems to me that the capacity for reality testing has to be considered in establishing a projection as psychotic. In such a regressed ego state, reality testing is certainly, to say the least, at a primitive level, if not lost.

Delusional Fixity

One of the paradigmatic features of the delusion has traditionally been its fixity and the feeling of conviction the patient possesses of its reality (see Frosch, 1967a). Freud (1937) posits that the basis for this fixity and sense of conviction lies in the kernel of historical truth within the content of the delusion. Remember that the sense of conviction of the validity of a reconstruction or recollection is also seen by Freud to lie in its historical truth. The belief attached to delusions derives its strength from a similar reconstruction; we thus have to look for the kernel of truth.

To carry the analogy further, the appearance of unusually distinct fragments in a reconstruction reminds one of the peculiar clarity which sometimes accompanies the development of a systematized delusion. In some instances, in the latter there is even a sharpness in actual perception. Patients will say how clearly they see objects; the sense of sound seems to be heightened (hyperacusis), as do other sensory modalities. One might also speculate whether similar economic factors are not fulfilled when an interpretation is made for the neurotic as when a systematized delusion is "reconstructed" by the psychotic. There is frequently a sudden lightning feeling, a "now I understand" or "I see," in both situations. In a sense, the systematized delusion is the paranoid's own reconstruction. Thus, according to Freud, the element of historical truth lends to the delusion, as it does to the reconstruction, the sense of conviction of its reality.

As early as 1896, Freud brings up the question of the fixity of the delusion and the sense of conviction about its reality. He indicates that a childhood experience lies behind the delusion but the delusion also incorporates the defenses against it. He explains: "In paranoia [in contrast to the obsessional], the self-reproach is repressed in a manner which may be described as *projection*. It is repressed by erecting the defensive symptom of *distrust of other people*." And he goes on to say: "In the delusional idea . . . there is a mnemic content which is almost unaltered and has only been made indefinite through omission. . . . The delusional ideas which have arrived in consciousness by means of a compromise . . . make demands on the thought-activity of the ego until they can be accepted without contradiction. Since they are not themselves open to influence, the ego must adapt itself to them [and out of these evolve] *interpretive delusions* and which end in an *alteration of the ego*" (pp. 184–185).

At this point I would like to interject another question: What is it that distinguishes the fixity of the delusion from other "fixed" ideas? Both Hartmann (1956) and Katan (1960) point out that the incorrectability of an idea is not an exclusively delusional feature. Many ideas which are not psychotic can still not be corrected. Katan indicates that in such instances the beliefs operate in the service of defense of strong denial. In the psychotic, however, the delusions are impervious to logic because the psychotic's reality is not our reality. It is a subjective reality, one which cannot conceivably respond to the rules governing objective reality. Katan further relates the incorrectability of the psychotic's ideas to the loss of the capacity to test reality, which derives from the withdrawal of cathexis of reality. Psychosis, in his opinion, eventuates where denial fails.

The neurotic symptom also seems to have a fixed and compelling quality. I am not referring here to the patient's belief or lack of belief in the symptom. For instance, a man who has a phobia, and is afraid to go out, may reject the reality of the fear and call it very silly; yet he has a feeling of conviction about an impending danger which evokes his anxiety. It is true that neurotics have the capacity to question the reality of their fears. Nonetheless, their reality testing does not seem to relieve them of anxiety in response to an inwardly "real" danger: "I know it's silly, but I'm frightened."

Neurotics, in the construction of their symptoms, borrow copiously from childhood experiences and together with many other factors, build up a kind of fixity in their symptomatology, one which they accept emotionally, if not intellectually. Woven into this tapestry, we may find all sorts of distortions and discrepancies, even a personal myth (Kris, 1956), a kind of secret. We know that in its essence the infantile neurosis, which contributes so largely to neurotic symptomatology, contains elements of historical truth. Does the fixity of neurotic symptomatology, then, to some extent also derive from the kernel of historical truth? Freud (1896) apparently thought so. In a subsequent paper (1937), he says: "Often enough, when a neurotic is led by an anxiety-state to expect the occurrence of some terrible event, he is in fact under the influence of a repressed memory (which is seeking to enter consciousness but cannot become conscious) that something which was at that time terrifying did really happen" (p. 268). At another point he declares: "The cause of this invulnerability of the obsessional idea and its derivatives, is, however, nothing more than its connection with the repressed memory from early childhood. For if we can succeed in making that connection conscious . . . the obsession, too, is resolved" (p. 174).

In the neurotic one finds certain actual experiences that have special significance for the individual. Superimposed on and associated with these actual experiences are many fantasies, images, wishes, and impulses. These experiences may even present themselves as screen memories. A neurotic patient in analysis, for instance, had a recurring childhood memory of an incident at age five. He was playing with a little girl and touching her vagina with a twig. He became very panicky at the thought that he would be found out and that his father would punish him — a rather commonplace experience. This memory kept recurring throughout the many years of analysis. He also had the impression that he had injured the girl's vagina with the twig, and he recalled being quite frightened at this possibility. Gradually, in the course of the analysis, the memory began to present itself with more and more vividness, the color and appearance of the vagina becoming especially vivid. From time to time, one or another fragment would be added, and incidents both before and after this experience were reported. At first they seemed unrelated, but eventually they formed a continuous fabric, in which the incident at age five occupied a focal role.

At one point the patient recounted an event from the age of two and a half. I don't know whether it was true or not, but the setting, the circumstances, and the way in which the patient recounted it suggested that it was. The father, in trying to treat a pimple on the patient's knee, had squeezed it. Infection had set in, necessitating the child's admission to the hospital. Another interesting recollection, antedating the little girl incident, occurring seemingly between the ages of two and four, was of standing in front of a doctor passing black urine. Apparently he had had jaundice, although he did not recall further details. At about age four he remembered playing doctor with a little girl and trying to take her temperature rectally with a cotton spool, which he would smell. This play was interrupted by his mother's coming into the room, and he recalled crawling underneath her skirt. These and other recollections from before, during, and after the vagina incident, containing material with marked castration content, kept reappearing.

The anxiety and panic the patient had at the thought of having harmed the little girl and the punishment he expected at the hands of his father were obviously out of line, since he had made the point that his father never punished him — at least not until adolescence. Yet there was a historical truth, so to speak, in his fear at that time and in his subsequent neurotic symptomatology. The father *had* injured him, although this was utilized in a different context and in conjunction with subsequently developed fantasies. (I am bypassing a discussion of his own hostile fantasies toward the father as a factor in the fear of punishment.)

The patient's current symptomatology was characterized by marked phobias and free-floating anxiety, usually related to a fear of doing some damage in line with his work. He reported the typical morning ruminative state seen in some obsessionals. He would reproach and beat himself unmercifully for something he had done, the consequences of which he anticipated would ultimately lead to his ruin. Analysis revealed this to be the expression of a split in the ego, in which the reproaching, attacking, beating, punitive, and castrating part was his father. The other part, his passive guilty self, was masochistically offered up to the "father," for exculpation and gratification as well as further injury. We can see here the element of historical truth in the patient's symptom. What is missing, however — in contrast to the delusion — is the consistent belief in the reality of the symptom.

As I have said, what the paranoid does in the delusion is also a kind of reconstruction, albeit a corrupt one (also seen in retrospective falsification). To quote Freud: "Just as our construction is only effective because it recovers a fragment of lost experiences, so the delusion owes its convincing power to the element of historical truth" (1937, p. 269). With the delusional patient, however, there is a belief in the reality of the idea, in contrast to the neurotic, who, while reacting intensely to the symptom, realizes that it is a distortion. In the psychotic the historical truth becomes, so to speak, a reality in the here-and-now, indicating a severe defect in ego functioning.

When we examine delusional content, we are at times struck by the rather overt, relatively undistorted or poorly disguised real aspects traceable to childhood. On the other hand, the neurotic patient I described above could not directly relate his extreme anxiety at the expectation of his father's punishing him to actual experiences. His own fantasies were necessary to connect certain events to the vagina incident and expected punishment. Yet my distinction here should not be taken too literally. Certainly fantasies also play a role in delusions. What may be the crucial factor is not only the content of the actual experience, but certain intrapsychic reactions at the time. Lewin (1950) discusses this when he examines the marked feeling of reality the elated manic patient has about current experiences. Lewin suggests that in the manic patient one of the important prototypic situations is the nursing experience. Early preverbal, preideational states are recaptured in the manic and accompanied by a subjective feeling of pleasure in nursing and satiation at the breast. It is the historical fact of having experienced this before that lends a feeling of reality to events experienced by the manic individual. The manic has a feeling of conviction derived from an actual state of the ego during the nursing situation.

Something similar happens in the delusional patient. While the delusional state may be accompanied by alterations in ego states or feelings, these have been experienced at one time and thus lend a feeling of reality to what the individual is currently experiencing. One can even speak of a delusional *déjà vu* experience. (The presence in many psychotics of the feeling that people look very familiar and seem to be actual figures from the past is a case in point.) A psychotic patient, for instance, began to feel very negativistic toward me, expressing this in persecutory feelings. She said she could not understand it, but the feelings of resentment were just like ones she actually had had toward her father. There was a sense of familiarity about the feeling and the relationship with me which at times she found quite disturbing. This became quite pronounced with the flourishing of her delusion, during which my identity was completely distorted.

Another patient, a psychotic character, recounted an experience which had almost delusional qualities. She was at a party and people were paying a great deal of attention to her. Everybody was commenting on her appearance in a complimentary fashion. She felt very uncomfortable and wondered why they did not leave her alone, why they were picking on her. They did not really mean it. She began to feel very peculiar; things around her acquired an unreal, yet familiar, quality. She even felt herself shrink in size. It was the feeling she had had when her mother had criticized her.

I would like to suggest at this point that in the psychotic we see *current* psychic correlates of the primitive modes of ego functioning used in the initial building up and maintenance of reality. The surroundings are related to through primitive introjective and extrojective techniques utilized previously. We find primitive modes of reality testing, very much like the child uses, in the psychotic's use of self-experiences, the body, parental attitudes, etc. (Hartmann, 1950; Frosch, 1966, 1967a). In this regard, let me again point to the heightened perception in the paranoid individual and to the fact that the initiation of many a psychosis is accompanied by hyperperception of stimuli. Freud indicates that the vividness of images in dreams points to the reproduction of an actual childhood situation, and I have suggested something similar for the heightened sense of perception seen in the psychotic (see Chapter 3). I also believe this heightened perception to some extent arises from the current derivatives of a more primitive and vulnerable ego state, during which stimuli could break through the stimulus barrier more easily and were perceived more vividly. Indeed, the impact of excessive external stimulation on the early, highly vulnerable ego, which is incapable of permitting gradual perception and assimilation, has been proposed as a genetic factor in schizophrenia (Bergman and Escalona, 1949). Spitz (1964) also indicates that excessive early stimulation may bring about a severely distorted ego, with subsequent disturbances in the mastery and perception of stimuli.

Silverman (1978) calls attention to the fact that the sensory threshold can change dramatically in paranoid patients. As their illnesses progress, they not only maintain hypervigilance, but also demonstrate photophobia, increased auditory acuity, and unusual temperature sensitivity. Silverman indicates that even on a neurophysiological basis paranoid individuals demonstrate heightened sensitivity. They can pick up subliminal stimulation (exposed at less than four milliseconds), and describe the content accurately, as normal subjects cannot. Sylvan Keiser (personal communication) suggests that such heightened perception may be due to loss of cathexis of the ego functions of hearing or seeing or to a regression of these functions to earlier operating modes, with a failure of secondary process organization of their functions. The vivid acuity is therefore based on direct symbolic translation; for instance, the sharpness in perception of sound may be related to a current derivative of listening to primal scene noise.

My point is that the sense of conviction about the reality of a delusion may relate to the historical truth of certain ego states and functions which are regressively reexperienced during the psychosis. In other words, the sense of conviction of the reality of a delusion may be related not only to the historical truth of the content of the delusion, but to the regressive reappearance of a whole series of associated psychic phenomena coeval with past experiences.

Yet, having said this, we may only understand the feeling of reality about delusion. Why does the delusional hold onto the system with such fixity, and resist, sometimes even violently, attempts to shake it? Even if there is a sense of realness about a delusion, why can it not be corrected by objective data? Supposing, as Waelder (1951) says, it is the return of the denied that lends the sense of conviction to the delusion. Is this enough to account for its fixity? Must we not also ask what the implications are of the return of the denied? Why does it even take place? May it not return to meet the same need that the fixity does? In the same way, in connection with Katan's (1960) suggestion that the imperviousness of the delusion to logic is due to its being built up out of a subjective reality, we may ask why the delusional clings to this subjective reality so tenaciously.

Obviously, just as the neurotic symptom has defensive and protective functions as well as gratifying ones, so must the delusion. Katan (1950) indicates that the very need to build up a subjective reality derives from a need to deny objective reality because of the dangers inherent in the recognition of the latter. He tries, in relation to schizophrenia, to deal with the question of what these dangers are. He believes they derive from an increase of preoedipal feminine (homosexual) strivings. The ego is too weak to cope successfully with castration danger resulting from the urge toward femininity and has to withdraw. The heterosexual urges, compared with this drive toward femininity, are too weak, and the ego can no longer rely on its heterosexual strivings to ward off the conflicting urge. At this point we may witness a desperate attempt by the ego to halt the regressive decline. If this attempt is unsuccessful, an impoverished ego now has to struggle with the upsurging tide of preoedipal feminine wishes. This struggle eventually leads to further ego regression, and finally the ego withdraws the cathexis of the homosexual urge by regressing to the beginning of its development. The undifferentiated state has returned. This ego regression is accompanied by the "loss" of the superego; only primitive forerunners of the superego remain. Katan sees the same danger in paranoia. The distinction he draws is that in paranoia an ego defense appears to have put its stamp on the material, whereas in schizophrenia, id material seems to color the psychotic symptomatology.

Still, we must ask: Is this danger of preoedipal femininity with consequent castration sufficient to necessitate the development of delusions and their fixity? In other words, is it sufficient to account for the way these dangers are met? Even Katan implies that the castration threat itself became overwhelming because the ego was already in a precarious state, making castration have even more dangerous implications. It seems clear that the regressive withdrawal to the undifferentiated state in the schizophrenic is facilitated by some defenses or weaknesses already existing in the ego, which seem to be exploited in the service of defense (see Chapter 10 for more detail).

Let us for the moment return to the psychotic patient described above (p. 96) and review the circumstances which culminated in her hospitalization. Before her admission she had a confused and chaotic mélange of fears that the world would be destroyed by atomic bombs and only a few people would be saved. She felt she was being followed by detectives and that a group of people were interested in her husband and herself because they were intelligent. Her husband had already been accepted by the group so that he became part of the plot, and she had to do something very convincing and drastic in order to be saved and to be accepted by the group. As she explained: "I had to do something terrible and, when I did this, A. [her husband] and the group had to have evidence of it. That is why I committed the adultery and brought a pay check to the man to prove I had been there and I would be admitted." In other words, she indicated a sort of willingness to be blackmailed in order to join the group. It was in this way that she could forestall her destruction.

It was in this state of mind that she went to work on a Saturday when the office was closed, claiming it was Friday and a regular workday. She refused to be convinced otherwise, in spite of facts presented to her to the contrary. She insisted on going to her desk, sorting the mail, etc. Finally, she became rather abusive and vituperative to the superintendent (who had come to the office), and he called the police. It was necessary to restrain her, and she was finally brought into the hospital shouting, screaming, abusive, and assaultive. She quieted down within the next few days, and I saw her when she was relatively calm. When I asked her whether she still thought it had been Friday instead of Saturday, she said no, but brought out numerous facts she felt had contributed to her confusion. There was still some question, however, about whether she did not think she had been right.

Apparently, for many reasons, it had been necessary for it to be Friday. She made a particularly striking statement, however — the essence of which was that to admit the wrongness of her belief would, to her, have raised serious questions about her sanity. Whatever other reasons made it necessary to construct this belief, it had to be true since otherwise she was crazy. Craziness to her meant loss of control, disintegration, and complete negation of self. In a sense, it had to be Friday instead of Saturday to preserve her sanity, her identity, her self from disintegration and dissolution. (I would like to point out that the fear of going crazy, of not being in control of one's thoughts, is also seen in the neurotic. In such cases, however, these fears relate to masturbation, castration, etc., and not to disintegration of self.)

In my patient there was an ever-recurrent interplay of feelings of dissolution and castastrophe (external and internal) with integrative delusional material of varying types. Ultimately, I believe, the danger that is defended against is not only preoedipal femininity and castration, as Katan (1950) says, but disintegration — psychic and emotional death. It is this danger that leads the psychotic individual to the desperate creation of an illogical reality, which is held onto tenaciously. The fixity is engendered by the tremendous fear the individual has of disintegration should he give this up. We must in all this see a desperate struggle against psychic and emotional disintegration, which for the psychotic is very real. I am reminded here of a statement made by Freud: "In every instance the delusional idea is maintained with the same energy with which another, intolerably distressing, idea is fended off from the ego. Thus they love their delusions as they love themselves" (1895a, pp. 211–212).

What I am suggesting is that the extent and the degree of the fixity is a measure of the extent and degree to which that which is fended off threatens the individual's survival. The delusion becomes necessary for the individual to survive; it is narcissistically determined. This lends substance to the restitutional need.

But why is this fear so vivid and real to the psychotic and why does it represent an actual danger? We find ourselves face to face with another aspect of the kernel of historical truth, albeit from a different angle. The threat to survival of self in the psychotic is a very real one, I believe, by virtue of actual survival-threatening experiences in early life, which may literally have meant annihilation. These experiences may become the prototype for subsequent experiences interfering with the development of the ego and its functions, making it difficult to deal later with analogous threats (see my discussion in Chapter 7).

In sum, the delusion derives its fixity and feeling of conviction from many sources. The traditional concept of historical truth applies not only to the content but to the ego state and functions which are reexperienced. Added to this is the fact that holding onto the delusional reality helps the psychotic combat the threat of dissolution and disintegration and facilitates psychic survival. As I just noted, the potential dissolution of the ego and threat to psychic survival are very real for the psychotic because of early survival-threatening experiences. The delusion is one way of dealing with the regressive reoccurrence of this danger of dissolution.

It should be apparent that we have in this section expanded our understanding of several aspects of the psychotic process. We had already looked at various mechanisms resorted to in order to preserve contact with the object and reality. But we have now underlined the basic danger in the psychotic which makes it necessary to maintain this contact, namely, the underlying fear of self-disintegration and dissolution.

D.
Hypochondriasis

I should like to make some comments on the phenomenon of hypochondriasis, certain aspects of which are viewed by some within the
framework of withdrawal and restitution. Although my primary
interest is in the role that hypochondriasis plays in psychosis, it seems
appropriate to elaborate first on how the concept is used psychoanalytically, for the term "hypochondriasis" is blurred by a lack of clear
clinical definition. For instance, grossly delusional somatic complaints has been alluded to as psychotic hypochondriasis where somatic delusions might be a more apt description.

Simply as a clinical observation, somatic complaints and preoccupations, especially in psychotic patients, may sometimes occupy a
very large role in the clinical picture, frequently ushering in a psychotic break. It might therefore be appropriate at this point to honor
a methodological consideration and begin at the descriptive level, discussing the psychiatric and psychoanalytic clinical manifestations of
somatic signs and symptoms, before focusing on the implications for
hypochondriasis and the role of the psychotic process in the latter. I
should first like to list those psychiatric conditions in which somatic
signs and symptoms occupy a large role. I shall then focus on those
which have special psychoanalytic implications for psychosis.

1. Hypochondriasis
2. Somatic delusions
3. Psychiatric syndromes
   a. Depression
   b. Anxiety neurosis
4. Conversion manifestations
   a. Hysterical conversion
   b. Pregenital conversion
   c. Briquet's syndrome

5. Pathoneuroses and pathopsychoses
6. Psychosomatic syndromes and somatization
    a. Organ neuroses
    b. Organ psychoses
7. Malingering—Munchausen syndrome
8. Organicity

Let us turn to the concept "hypochondriasis." In order to be consistent, we shall start with a desciptive definition. The usual dictionary definition indicates that hypochondriasis entails a marked anxiety about one's own health, with conjuring up of imaginary ailments. Hinsie and Campbell's *Psychiatric Dictionary* (1970) defines hypochondriasis as "morbid attention to the details of body functioning and/or exaggeration of any symptom, no matter how insignificant. Although hypochondriasis may appear in the form of a specific neurosis, it may also occur in association with such disorders as anxiety neurosis, obsessive-compulsive neurosis, and most often with the initial states of any psychosis. The hypochondriacal patient is typically self-centered, seclusive, and sometimes almost monomaniacal in his attention to his body; his major environmental contacts are somatically colored" (p. 363). In this condition there is an absence of morphological or functional disturbance, and in spite of extensive workup there does not appear to be any demonstrable evidence of organic factors.

The hypochondriac lives with his body in a highly constricted way, in terms of both his personality and his social life. To word it somewhat differently, in hypochondriasis we are concerned with a narcissistic libido shifted from the self as a whole (narcissism) to an organic bodily function. In contrast, in hysterical conversion there are actual functional disturbances. A relation with a love object is involved and the organ or organ function, via identification, symbolism, or fantasy, is the area within which the libidinal relationship is worked out. Vomiting, for instance, may be a general expression of tension or anxiety, in hysteria it may be a symbol for either a wish for or a rejection of pregnancy. Although pregenital conversions are conversion phenomena in the true sense of the word (psychic phenomena expressed somatically), they are genetically, dynamically, and phenomenologically different (even though they present functional disturbances without demonstrable organic pathology). They are generally viewed as deriving from conflicts much earlier in psychic development and are reflected in personality features deriving from these earlier developmental stages.

Terminological Confusion

When we approach hypochondriasis, we find, as I indicated above, a maze of terminological confusion. The term "hypochondriasis," for instance, is used by Freud to express what is ordinarily today, I believe, in most instances called a somatic delusion. This confusion is encountered in many of the psychoanalytic contributions. We must further differentiate the syndrome "hypochondriasis," as an actual neurosis, from the many other conditions in which hypochondriasis may manifest itself.

An unusual preoccupation with one's health, focused on one or several organs, may or may not be hypochondriacal in the true dynamic and genetic sense. The cancerophobic patient, for instance, may have an unusual concern about every little somatic manifestation and see in a little pimple a potential life threat. Although such a preoccupation, more fittingly associated with a kind of free-floating anxiety, may fulfill the broad descriptive definition of hypochondriasis, this is not the case dynamically and genetically. Such "hypochondriacal" manifestations show basic hysterical mechanisms. Here we do not see actual functional disturbances as in conversion hysteria; nonetheless, in such cases the organs may assume a symbolic meaning. The symptoms are object-related and thus under the impact of the neurotic process. In contrast are those organic preoccupations that are narcissistic and under the impact of the psychotic process. From the descriptive angle, the extreme weakness of a patient who felt depleted after he had a bowel movement, or after masturbation, could have been viewed as hypochondriacal, perhaps even neurasthenic, in the old sense. Yet it was a manifestation of his underlying disintegrative anxiety.

My point is that one has to examine somatic manifestations very carefully within the context of dynamic and genetic formulations, before designating them truly hypochondriacal. We must, for instance, understand the underlying meaning of a disease symptom which presents itself as a phobia. One patient with a severe case of syphilophobia would wrap his penis in cotton batting and would always carry reams of toilet paper and Kleenex with him, lest he have to use a public toilet. He would practically coat the toilet seat and bowl to prevent any contact with his penis. Many of the formulations made were related to castration anxiety. This was valid up to a point. The real underlying anxiety was that if this penis became infected, it would rot and fall off, and then his whole body would fall apart and disintegrate. A psychotic disintegration fear lay behind his somatic "phobia."

Still another patient, much concerned about body disintegration, especially in relation to her intestinal tract, had numerous somatic pre-occupations, which took bizarre forms. For instance, she viewed her feces as cement which kept her intestines bound together. She feared having a bowel movement and losing this cement, and constipation was a constant preoccupation. One must in such instances evaluate how close the somatic organ preoccupation borders on the delusional and involves impairment of ego functions such as reality testing. In this patient, although the symptoms derived from attempts to deal with the disintegrative fears of the psychotic, she was still able to test reality. The manifestations had not as yet evolved into somatic delusions. She could recognize the bizarreness of her preoccupations and be embarrassed that her mind went in such directions.

Hypochondriasis is viewed by some as a transitional state between reactions of a hysterical nature and those of a delusional, clearly psychotic one. This confusion is exemplified, for instance, in Ferenczi's report (1919) on a case of "hysterical hypochondriasis," in which the patient's somatic complaints clearly had symbolic meaning and were related to an identification with an insane father as well as a paralyzed child. Ferenczi was aware of the confusion in combining these two concepts: "We are dealing here with a mixture of purely hypochondriacal and hysterical symptoms, and at the beginning of the analysis the clinical picture of the illness merged into schizophrenia, while towards the end it showed indi-cations, however slight, of paranoia. . . . It seems as though the same stagnation of organ libido — according to the patient's sexual constitution — can have either a purely hypochondriacal or conversion hysteria 'superstructure'" (pp. 123–124). I believe that this patient would more accurately have been designated as a case of hysterical psychosis.

A similar patient was seen by me in psychoanalytically oriented psychotherapy. A 26-year-old married but childless female presented herself with multiple somatic complaints. Among these were constipa-tion and peculiar sensations in her face, which she felt was thinning out. The facial bones were shifting, and the fatty tissue was being redis-tributed. She also had sensations in her vagina, as if she were about to have her period. She related some of these to dietary ideas, saying that the food she was eating was not being digested and therefore contrib-uted to the changes in the fatty tissue. She was quite demonstrative and dramatic, weeping at her fate. Yet this patient did not strike me as schizophrenic. She seemed to be object-related and claimed she had always had friends. Although she had stuck rather close to home, she had liked to go out on dates and had had numerous dates before she married. As a matter of fact, she met her husband at a resort. She did admit, however, that her sex life with him was not satisfactory.

In the course of psychotherapy a whole delusional system connected with pregnancy emerged, involving her wish for a child and her extreme distress at not having one. When I inquired what her concept of pregnancy was, it turned out that all the many sensations she experienced were ones she had read or heard about in conversations with women, as associated with pregnancy. The facial appearance she claimed she had was that of a pregnant woman. It became clear to me that whatever else this woman suffered from, part of the somatic symptomatology was a wishful pregnancy fantasy being fulfilled in an admittedly bizarre fashion.[26]

As we explored the pregnancy fantasy, the delusional system subsided. She ultimately adopted a baby and had no subsequent psychiatric reactions. The obvious wish-fulfilling somatic delusions would, I believe, have been designated by some as hypochondriasis, perhaps with the qualifier, "psychotic." But it is clear that in this case, which I refer to as a hysterical psychosis, the somatic complaints did not have the deeper psychodynamic significance that a true psychotic hypochondriasis has.

The case of the Wolf Man highlights many of the terminological and conceptual problems related to hypochondriasis. The Wolf Man's whole history, both past and recent, was full of somatic manifestations and complaints. At the age of 13 he had a nasal catarrah — the model, according to Brunswick (1928), for his future illnesses. Blemishes covered his face. He was teased by other children and became very sensitive about his nose. Throughout his life he was pursued by illness. Some of these were bona fide illnesses, such as the gonorrhea at age 17½. Some were allegedly "inflicted" upon him by others. Still other symptoms were not clinically demonstrable but nonetheless torture to him. His nose, his mouth, his teeth were affected, and some of this resulted from supposed injuries at the hands of dermatologists and dentists.

The Wolf Man had a great propensity for somatic identifications,

[26] Let me add a clinical comment related to a person's preoccupation with different features of the body. The sensitivity that one's nose is too large or too small may be based realistically on a somewhat large or small nose. The reaction may be somewhat exaggerated. However, the belief that one's nose is growing large and actually changing in size is psychotic. My patient's belief that her facial bones were shifting was patently psychotic.

almost to the point of completely taking over the other person's symptomatology. Many of his somatic complaints were related to somatic difficulties of his mother, his sister, or Freud.[27] For instance, in November
1923, at age 36, he noticed a black wart on his mother's nose and remarked that his mother had become somewhat hypochondriacal, afraid
of dust and infection. It is interesting to note that his wife also had
warts on her nose and he thought how terrible it would be if he himself
had a wart on his nose. Then, at the beginning of 1924, he began to
have trouble with his teeth, with small pustules on his gums. It is not
clear from Brunswick's report whether he had two teeth extracted in
1924, or in 1921. (If it was 1924, one must consider an identification
with Freud's illness.) At any rate, it was a Dr. Wolf who extracted the
teeth, and he predicted the patient would soon lose all of his teeth
because of his bite.

In his work at about this time the Wolf Man was transferred to the
office of a rather gruff superior. In February 1924, marked troublesome
symptoms appeared. He began to have queer thoughts about his nose.
As indicated above, at puberty he had had a nasal catarrah, with sores
on his nose and lips. Salves had been prescribed for treatment by the
same doctor who later treated his gonorrhea. During his analysis with
Freud, the patient had been treated by Professor X., with whom he
was not entirely satisfied. Nonetheless, he felt it was lucky that he had a
nose without a blemish.

Brunswick emphasizes the psychotic aspects of the Wolf Man's
hypochondriacal complaints, referring to his symptoms as a hypochondriacal type of paranoia. This is in keeping with her belief that true
hypochondriasis is not a neurosis but belongs more to the psychoses.
Strictly speaking, many of the Wolf Man's complaints did assume the
form of somatic delusions. In this type of hypochondriasis there is characteristically an exclusive preoccupation with one organ, which is
either injured or diseased. The hypochondriacal ideas in such instances
may cloak ideas of persecution and are thus defensive in nature. The
psychosis, although presenting itself with hypochondriacal symptoms,
is really persecutory. For instance, in analyzying one of the Wolf Man's
dreams, Brunswick establishes that he held Freud as the unnamed one
responsible for all the misguided somatic treatments he had had, and

---

[27] Ruth Mack Brunswick had severe sinusitis and rhinitis when I knew her in 1938.
I have often wondered whether she had this condition at the time of the Wolf Man's
analysis with her and whether some of his complaints may have been related to her
condition.

thus responsible for his multiform diseases.

Brunswick also indicates that in blaming Professor X. the Wolf Man himself had constructed the persecutory situation. He pushed Professor X. into the various treatments, which resulted in the various, sometimes imagined, somatic manifestations of which he complained. This tendency was already manifest at puberty, when he had used more medicine than was prescribed and thus had aggravated his skin condition. The Wolf Man himself was constantly demanding and promoting bad treatment on the part of his doctors. Distrust was a prime characteristic of treatment (an indication of the future paranoid).

The marked masochism in the Wolf Man's character structure has been explored by others. But also important is why, in this instance, a hypochondriacal delusional system arose. One can say that his experiences with Freud had something to do with his symptomatology, in the sense that Freud's illness and the Wolf Man's death wishes against Freud necessitated self-punishment. Still, this does not quite clarify — why psychosis?

How should one categorize the Wolf Man's somatic symptoms? His propensity for taking on others' symptoms suggests a hysterical mechanism. Yet the evolving clinical condition was at times grossly psychotic. When such symptoms develop into somatic delusions, as they did with the Wolf Man, there is obviously a loss in reality testing, a severe disturbance in an important ego function. In a sense, libidinally he appeared to have advanced to a higher developmental stage while his ego showed defects deriving from an earlier stage in psychic development — ergo the propensity for loss of reality testing. It thus appears that his subsequent psychosis is consistent with the genetic and dynamic features I have described as typical for a hysterical psychosis. Yet I do think overall he was essentially a psychotic character (Frosch, 1964), under which diagnosis much of the total clinical picture could be subsumed. The designation of his somatic manifestations as hypochondriasis highlights the terminological and methodological problems I described above.[28]

[28] The development of somatic manifestations via identification is strikingly demonstrated in the couvade syndrome. The husband, in relation to his wife's pregnancy, develops many somatic manifestations associated with childbearing. Trethowan (1972) reports that 20–25 % of the males in his study developed symptoms such as nausea and vomiting, alterations of appetite, indigestion, heartburn, abdominal pain, abdominal swelling, tooth problems and labor pains. Although in most instances these manifestations appeared to be hysterical in nature, in some cases they assumed psychotic proportions, becoming somatic delusions. Passive-feminine identifications, hostility toward the childbearing partner, and envy of her capacity to give birth have been formulated as unconscious factors in the couvade syndrome.

Toward a Theory of Hypochondriasis

As I indicated in our discussion of withdrawal and restitution, it is within this framework that Freud discusses hypochondriasis. He explains: "The hypochondriac withdraws both interest and libido — the latter specially markedly — from the objects of the external world and concentrates both of them upon the organ that is engaging his attention" (1914a, p. 83). On the other hand, hyponchondriasis has been viewed not only as a manifestation of withdrawal, but also as a restitutional attempt on the way back to reality, in which the body and its organs are seized upon as objects.

Freud describes three groups of symptoms arising from partial withdrawals proceeding step by step, rather than total withdrawal. First, we see what remains of the normal state in a clinical picture. Second, we see what arises from the detachment of libido from its object (resulting in megalomania and hypochondria). Finally, we see a group of symptoms representing restoration or attempts at restoration, in which the libido is once more attached to the object. Hypochondria, according to Freud, may be a step on the way toward achieving object relations in the same way that words are treated as objects in schizophrenia and come to represent a phase or step in the restitutional process, as well as the withdrawal process (see Chapter 3).

One of the most dramatic presentations of somatic symptomatology, viewed from the perspective of libido theory, is Nunberg's (1920) report on a catatonic patient. This patient developed a psychosis following an attempt to rape his sister. I shall cite only the somatic manifestations (which underwent many changes). Before the psychotic episode, the patient was intensely concerned with his body. He tried to perfect himself through exercise and wanted to become strong. In this he did not succeed. Soon all sorts of somatic manifestations appeared — burning sensations in his back, muscle aches, the belief he had a hole in his stomach, etc. Nunberg refers to these as hypochondriacal sensations. The patient then tried to regenerate and strengthen his body by influencing the process of "combustion," which he ascribed to breathing. Breathing exercises would restore his health.[29]

---

[29] I have alluded to the excessive preoccupation of some individuals with bodybuilding. Behind this effort may lie hypochondriacal preoccupations, sometimes conscious. In the ileitis patient I described above (p. 80), body and health preoccupations long antedated the psychotic break after the "assault" on his body. It is interesting that already in 1932 Glover called attention to the role of excessive health concerns in dealing with deep psychotic anxieties. He remarked: "Perhaps the most impressive exam-

None of this was successful. The patient felt himself disintegrating. It was in this state that he attempted to rape his sister with the grandiose idea of propagating mankind. (Note that the psychotic fear of self-disintegration brings in its wake attempts to ward it off — a point I shall return to later.) According to Nunberg, there were many libidinal shifts, which brought about various organ gratifications and over-cathexes in an attempt to ward off disintegration. These were all restitutional attempts. In his opinion, "even preceding the hypochondriasis the idea of self-renewal was an experience of the struggle to free the ego of the dammed-up libido" (p. 51). "On the whole," Nunberg postulates, "the delusional system was an attempt to cathect anew the objects of the outside world with the overflow of narcissistic libido. Since apparently the path of the once retracted libido is no longer passable, the regressive way is continued until the point is reached where parts of one's own body or organs represent themselves to the ego as objects. . . . The endeavor to regain the objects is realized through the body" (p. 14).

It is clear that Nunberg tries to explain much of the symptomatology in terms of the pleasure-unpleasure principle, namely, getting rid of the accumulation of libido. Yet, at the same time, he weaves this in with the state of the ego, with the potential dissolution of the ego (self?) and the fears connected to this possibility. The push from excessive narcissism toward the object, which may be a result of accumulation of unpleasure, is something Freud himself touches on. I believe, however, that one must also consider whether overcathexis of organs may increase the possibility of disintegration and dissolution of self. This basic fear of the psychotic may thereby be activated, with desperate attempts to combat self-destruction. In other words, the various delusions are responses to this basic fear, as I described in the section on delusional fixity above.

There is by no means agreement about the applicability of the concepts of withdrawal and restitution to hypochondriasis. Many offer other frames of reference within which to view this phenomenon. For

ple is that organized 'health movement,' which seeks to canonize anxiety reactions as part of a praiseworthy hygienic system. It is not simply that our advertisement columns encourage intestinal hypochondria by the terrifying caption 'Constipation,' or that we are exhorted to purify the blood, to kill flies, to wear soft collars, expand the chest and breathe pure air, use carbolic soap or drink hot water: the fact is we are encouraged to invest every round of waking activity with a typical neurotic or psychotic anxiety charge" (1932a, p. 237). In his view, "some 'modern' health movements are in many respects manifestations of psychotic reaction" (p. 246).

instance, Macalpine and Hunter (1953), in their critique of Freud's concept, suggest that he neglects how Schreber's hypochondriacal manifestations relate to procreation fantasies. They indicate that Schreber's hypochondriacal symptoms express primitive, pregenital procreation fantasies in the form of body hallucinations, and indeed see all of his symptomatology in these terms.

Here one must make some reference to Melanie Klein's contributions (e.g., 1946). According to her, the somatic complaints in hypochondriasis are essentially a variant of introjected objects, whereby the various parts of the body represent introjected objects that cause discomfort and difficulty. One of my patients spoke of a bug depositing bowel movements in different parts of her body. These gave her pains in her joints, muscles, etc. — wherever the deposits were. Still another patient spoke of the war going on inside her. This "battle" brought on severe abdominal pains and she had to visit her doctor frequently. She localized the war in her pelvic region, more specifically where she felt her uterus was. Soon she converted this into a machine, which would attack her body and provoke all sorts of symptoms — insomnia, headache, pains, ataxia, dropsy, etc.

A special facet of Klein's concept is discussed by Rosenfeld (1958, 1964a). He views chronic hypochondriasis as a defensive function, a variant of projective identification. Its main defense seems directed against the confusional stage which is often of a schizophrenic nature. He states:

> I would like to emphasize that chronic hypochondriasis cannot be considered only as a regressive condition, but as a defence against a confusional state. The ego seems unable to work through the confusional state in the mental apparatus. It projects the confusional state, including the internal objects and parts of the self, like sadism, onto external objects, which are instantly reintrojected into the body and body organs. In this way the ego succeeds in splitting off the confusional state from the mental sphere and converting it into hypochondriacal symptoms. Sadistic impulses, in particular oral sadistic envy, which is responsible for the confusional state, influence constantly the patient's relation to external and internal objects and are an important factor in hypochondriasis [1958, p. 124].

I might add that this is not an unusual explanation for clinical conditions in Kleinian terms; it is not, in my opinion, particularly specific to hypochondriasis.

From a different perspective, Fenichel (1945) refers to hypochondriasis as an organ neurosis whose physiological factor is still unknown. He says: "It may be assumed that certain psychogenic factors, namely, a state of being dammed up and a narcissistic withdrawal, or rather a readiness to react to the stage of being dammed up with narcissistic withdrawal, create organic changes which then in turn give rise to hypochondriacal sensations" (p. 261). He points out that two situations have to be distinguished: organic processes may heighten the tension in certain organs, resulting in painful sensations, or a withdrawal of object cathexis may change the mental economics, so that libido normally connected with ideas of objects now invests the organs. In other words, an intrapsychic object representation becomes an intrapsychic organ representation.

With this in mind, I would like to look at Ferenczi's (1916–1917) study of the relationship between organicity and psychic reactions to neurotic illness. He sees many of the dynamic features in what he calls the pathoneuroses as essentially similar to those encountered in hypochondriasis, and describes them as libidinal shifts to already diseased organs. (One must bear in mind that both Freud and Ferenczi thought that in hypochondriasis there are nondemonstrable organic changes.) It is Ferenczi's idea (and Freud credits him for this) that in organic illness there is an increase in narcissism, with a concentration of all "egoistic" as well as libidinal interests in the ego. According to Ferenczi, a bodily illness or an injury can "quite well result in regression to so-called traumatic narcissism and to its erotic variance." Thus, superimposed on an organic illness may be many reactions. Ferenczi uses the term "disease neuroses" or "pathoneuroses" for those conditions in which neuroses supervene after organic illness or injury. Libido which has been withdrawn from the outer world is directed not toward the whole ego but chiefly toward the diseased or injured organ, causing a local increase of libido and evoking symptoms related to this increase. Actually what is involved here is a genitalization and heightened eroticization of an organ, which to begin with contained narcissistic elements and the capacity for erotogenicity.

Essentially what Ferenczi suggests is the superimposition of various psychological reactions on an injured organ. Some of these may assume the form of hysteria, whereby the injured organ takes on a symbolic psychological elaboration. Others may appear as simple, almost actual-neurosis-like reactions, where the accumulation of libido in a given organ results in tension. Still others may produce pathopsychotic-like rather than pathoneurotic-like reactions, and come under Ferenczi's heading of narcissistic neuroses. Ferenczi is not too clear about all this, but these implications are subsequently developed by Meng (1934) in more detail.

The concept of pathopsychosis is developed by Ferenczi in his paper on general paresis (Ferenczi and Hollós, 1922). He makes the point that disease of "or damage to the erotogenic zones can lead to severe psychotic illnesses," what he calls "pathopsychoses." (I believe he uses the term "pathopsychoses" here for the first time; earlier he referred to them as neuroses of the narcissistic type.) Ferenczi then applies this concept to general paresis, which he views as a kind of cerebral pathoneurosis (although from his description I think he means a cerebral pathopsychosis). He takes as his jumping-off point the idea that just as the genital becomes the leading erotogenic zone, so does the brain become the central organ of ego functions and the organ for the control and distribution of external stimuli. He discusses the symptomatology of paresis in terms of various stages, beginning with neurasthenic and hypochondriacal complaints and depression, followed by manic excitement, the formation of paranoid delusions, and terminal dementia. What we see in general paresis is the destruction, one by one, of all the hitherto successfully accomplished identifications, the sum total of which signifies the attainment of the patient's ego ideal.

Perhaps one of the most significant contributions in helping us theoretically understand the phenomenon of hypochondriasis is Tausk's paper on the influencing machine (1919), which I discussed above. In one way or another many of the ideas which appear later in Ferenczi's and Meng's contributions are embodied in Tausk's concept of an organ representation system, derived from earlier phases in psychic development. Remember that in this system the different parts of the body somehow have an autonomous and independent existence and are viewed as objects. Regression to this particular stage might account for various clinical manifestations, from simple peculiar sensations on the way to being used symbolically or hysterically, to the perception of organs as objects with a certain degree of animism, as we see in some psychotics. In applying his concept to hypochondriasis, Tausk postulates:

> Whenever there occurs an inflexible organic narcissism in a given organ as a site of predilection, there may also occur a consciousness of organ relations and organic functions which in normal life are relegated to an unconscious and vegetative role. Analogously, objects cathected by psychic narcissism and object love come to consciousness wherever the cathexis has reached a sufficient degree of strength. This influx of libido

directs attention to the organ and provides the consciousness of a transformation of the organ or its function, i.e., a feeling of estrangement.
This is the mechanism described by Freud as hypochondria. This influx
of libido is followed by a turning away of the ego from the organ pathologically charged with libido or from its functions, that is, by estrangement. This is to be considered a defensive measure against the anxiety
associated with hypochondria. The feeling of estrangement is a defense
against libidinal cathexis. The estrangement is a denial of pathological
cathexis [p. 78].

In hypochondriasis, then, there is too much investment in the organs
and there may be a projection, leading to somatic delusions of the paranoid type.

Schilder (1951) pursues a similar theme, following Freud's concept
of hypochondriasis as libidinal overcathexis of organs. "In every case of
hypochondriasis," he claims, "much too much of attention, of libido, is
concentrated upon one's own body. The environment, although clearly
perceived, holds no interest for the patient, neither the experienced nor
the non-experienced elements of the environment" (p. 27). Schilder
lends support to Tausk's concept of objectivization of organs in commenting on the self-observation and self-scrutiny characteristic of such
patients, through which process the organs are objectivized and thus
made closer to the outer world. To scrutinize an organ hypochondria-
cally means to externalize it to a greater or lesser extent. Schilder adds
that introspection represents an attempt, on the part of a more highly
developed element of the personality, to rid itself of some uncomfortable content by objectifying it. This is not unlike both Ferenczi's and
Tausk's views that an overaccumulation of libidinal demands may be
released through symptoms and projection to externalization.

Schilder goes on to ask what it is that is "felt" by the earliest organ
when something takes place on or in its "body." Where is it "perceived"?
In his view: "This subjective experiencing must certainly possess
something of the qualities of a 'perception,' since we must bring the
concept of 'feeling' into closest relation with that of a 'body.' The concept 'body' already presupposes, however, the correlated concept of
'environment.' The concept 'body' is quite without meaning without
the concept 'environment'" (pp. 29).[30] Again we are dealing here with

---

[30] Pötzl, in a fascinating hypothesis cited by Tausk (1919), suggests that the awareness of sensations and perceptions may be related to the phylogenetic development of
various organ systems, which were previously accompanied by certain sensations.

the postulation of an organ memory system, existing at the deepest level, which I suppose encompasses engrams of experiences at this level involving organs.

Here I would like to recall Ferenczi's proposal that in an oversensitive person of narcissistic constitution the injury of a part of the body heavily charged with libido results in a deposit of instinctive stimulation in the ego memory system (or organ memory system). From this, unpleasurable excitation flows to internal perception (the organ representation) even after all consequences of the external injury have disappeared. Ferenczi indicates that in some organs there may be an increase in tension, not in the organ as such, but in its psychic representation, creating the so-called organ memories, by virtue of the trauma or some other factor. As a result, there is a need for discharge just as an instinctual drive may push toward discharge. In hypochondriasis, then, the involved organ becomes regressively charged and is a source of stimulation and preoccupation.

The concept of an organ memory system is, I believe, very much related to Tausk's concept of the body ego. Such organ memories may therefore be regressively activated by many circumstances, traumatic or otherwise. More important, significant organ memories may be borrowed in the service of some psychic needs. For instance, these organ memories may lend themselves to fending off disintegrative fears by facilitating the objectivization of organs, and ultimately even their externalization in the form of somatic delusions or harmful introjects.

Fenichel (1945) also suggests the concept of organ memories. He remarks that "an individual's own body and its organs are represented intrapsychically by a sense of memories of sensations and their interrelations." I believe such organ memories become a part of the body image (an idea suggested by Schilder). Tausk speaks of a libido toneness, which in a sense holds the organism together. There is an unconscious organic narcissism which guarantees the ultimate unity and functioning of the organism. The fragmentation of this unity is one of the consequences of overcathexis of any one or several body organs or functions. The body image may be represented in the psyche in a hierarchy from its most primitive fragmented form, to its most advanced unified level. The most primitive is part of the deepest unconscious and may be reactivated in schizophrenics and psychotics.

Although it is not my intention to examine psychosomatic manifestations in any great detail, I shall briefly sketch in some perspectives on the role of the psychotic process in some of these conditions. Macalpine

(1952) considers psychosomatic symptoms to be rudimentary and partly expressed emotions, not a defense against conflict. In this respect, the structure of the symptom is dynamically similar to that of a psychotic symptom. It represents an attempt on the patient's part to experience his emotions fully in the face of poorly tolerated anxiety. The anxiety underlying psychosomatic conditions is of a primitive, disruptive type — the result of inadequate discharge and, consequently, of overstimulation of the primitive body-mind unit. These patients, like psychotics, suffer from an excess of anxiety from which they cannot defend themselves. Indeed, Macalpine's view resembles Meng's concept of organ psychosis.

Meng (1934) emphasizes the psychotic substratum in psychosomatic diseases such as anorexia nervosa, asthma, and various skin disorders (see also Meng and Stern, 1955; Stokvis, 1952). In his view, somatization occurs as a substitute for resolution of a conflict, which under other circumstances might produce psychotic-like episodes. Instead of the ego, the organ representation in the body-image schema is affected by the psychotic process. Organic illness may constitute a protective wall, behind which the ego appears to remain intact. Massive somatization, however, is often a defense against the threat of psychosis. The primary disturbance in such "organ psychoses" is found in the body image, probably the result of disturbances of the body-image schema in early childhood.[31] It is clear that Meng sees severe ego disturbances as antedating the psychosomatic illness, which masks and represses an underlying psychotic potential. If this repression fails as a result of some loss or traumatic experience, psychosis may ensue.

Essentially what I think is involved in the organ psychoses is that the psychotic process is expressed through the organs. Similarly, in the organ neuroses the expression is via neurotic processes. The organ psychoses are characterized by rather primitive states of psychic development, in which the various organs are treated in pre-object-related terms. Meng points out that many of his patients presented features frequently observed in psychoses. The somatic illness was actually substituted for the psychotic one. In other words, the somatic phenomena may serve to ward off psychosis; if they were not present, then psychosis would be present.

Somatization occurs as a substitute for a conflict whose resolution under other circumstances would produce psychotic-like episodes. In-

[31] M. Sperling (1955) also concentrates on the pregenital component in reports of several cases where there was an unconscious identification with a psychotic mother.

stead of the ego, the organ representation is affected by the psychosis. One is reminded of Schur's (1955) concept that somatization processes are very primitive ones and represent regressive defenses. Although massive somatization is often a defense against the threat of psychosis, I would say that in all of these cases there is evidence of ego defects independent of the somatization. Essentially all these patients with organ psychoses already manifested severe disturbances of the ego and body image in early childhood.

Brunswick (1928), in her discussion of this subject, seems to feel that all hypochondriacal complaints are psychotic. She does not define what she means by hypochondriasis, so it is difficult to tell. But I would certainly go along with the idea that somatization of one sort or another may be the last step or one of the steps just before a psychotic break. It is a primitive type of psychic process and, as I pointed out above, may sometimes be defensive in nature. When the defensive process fails, we have the possibility of disintegration and to ward this off the restitutional aspects of hypochondriasis may come into being. As I indicated above, Rosenfeld (1964a) looks upon hypochondriasis as a defensive means for resolving the confusional state of psychosis, and this illustrates my point. So long as hypochondriasis exists, the confusional state subsides. If this breaks down, you may have a confusional psychotic state accompanied by the anxiety related to potential disintegration.

The relationship between hypochondriasis and paranoia is emphasized by Freud. It might be recalled that in discussing the Schreber case, he remarks: "I shall not consider any theory of paranoia trustworthy unless it also covers the hypochondriacal symptoms by which that disorder is almost invariably accompanied. It seems to me that hypochondria stands in the same relation to paranoia as anxiety neurosis does to hysteria" (1911b, p. 56). He says that the relationship of hypochondria to "paraphrenia" is dependent on ego libido, and that hypochondriacal anxiety, coming from ego libido, is the counterpart to neurotic anxiety coming from object libido.[32]

Freud then broadens his discussion somewhat, examining the relationship between symptomatic hypochondriasis and psychosis in general. An important element in this is of course the question of the role of

[32] It is difficult to understand what Freud means. In suggesting that hypochondriasis occupies the same position in relation to paranoia that anxiety neurosis does to hysteria (within the framework of his earlier formulation about anxiety), does he mean that anxiety is converted into symptoms of hysteria whereas hypochondria may be converted into symptoms of paranoia? At this stage he is apparently still under the influence of the hypothesis that anxiety is converted into hysterical symptoms.

the somatic delusion. As a basis for comparison, we might take the case of the Wolf Man, especially during his contacts with Brunswick, and Nunberg's (1921) schizophrenic patient, whose somatic complaints assumed all the bizarre elements that we see in the full-blown schizophrenic psychotic. For that matter, the bizarre somatic phenomena Schreber showed could also be compared with the type of somatic manifestation found in the Wolf Man.

There is no doubt that clinically and dynamically the Wolf Man's symptoms and the way these manifested themselves reflected a higher level of psychic development, one at which object relations still seemed to play an important role within the somatic symptomatology. The element of identification, for instance, seemed to play a large role. In this sense, the somatic manifestations were almost hysterical in nature, but there was one great difference. At some particular point, the Wolf Man's symptomatology evolved into what Ferenczi would call a pathopsychosis or hysterical hypochondriasis — or what I would call a hysterical psychosis. Actual or imagined symptoms were related to a specific act either done to the patient by himself or by others, as a result of his manipulations. All the circumstances surrounding these symptoms were incorporated into his delusional system. Dynamically, insofar as ego functions are concerned, this is obviously at a much more primitive level than the true hysterical conversion symptom. The somatic symptoms seemed to fulfill needs and gratifications deriving from much earlier levels of psychic development than we see in hysteria.

As I have indicated, the Wolf Man's tendency to turn to organ systems is seen throughout his life, almost from the earliest periods. At the age of three months he had a life-threatening illness, which may have brought in its wake severe ego impairments as well as persistence of the then-existing organ autonomy (see Frosch, 1967b). The body image must have been impaired rather early, enhancing psychotic–like somatization as a characteristic reaction. As we have seen, hysterical mechanisms combined with a proclivity for primitive somatization tendencies lent the Wolf Man's symptomatology features resembling hysterical psychosis. I do wish to reemphasize, though, that in his overall character structure he resembled a psychotic character, a diagnosis which can embody all these manifestations.

Nunberg's patient and Schreber were even more primitive. In such cases, I believe the level of psychic regression is to that stage where the whole ego structure (if one can even speak of it in those terms) appears to be a body ego. As I have pointed out, this is the stage of the earliest beginnings of ego development, when the various body parts assume an independent, autonomous role, serving as objects — even foreign objects — and representing the world and reality for the patient.

I would like to add some comments on this highly complex area. In general, I would say that somatic complaints within the psychiatric and psychoanalytic sphere require one economic condition — a hypercathexis or an investment of libido, for whatever reason, in organs, organ functions, or the mental representations of these areas as well as the "organ memories." This assumption does not yet indicate what kind of symptomatology will ensue, since the economic condition per se simply creates a setting in which it is possible for certain psychological elaborations to take place. For instance, what may ensue may be a heightened awareness of the existence of these organs, possibly a hyperperception of them. A piece of food between the teeth may bring in its wake a hypercathexis and hyperperception of this area.

Just as with heightened awareness of external stimuli, heightened awareness of internal stimuli may reflect a change in the state of the ego characteristic of earlier phases in psychic development. It is of interest here that Freud suggests that when we see something exceedingly clearly in dreams this has some basis in a childhood experience which was actual and real. In this sense, the heightened perception of internal stimuli may indeed reflect earlier ego states in psychic development. I have previously referred to the clarity with which something on the outside is perceived (encountered in some delusional and psychotic developments) as equally reflecting earlier ego states (see p. 145). The withdrawal of libido from the external world, the gradual investment of libido in the body, and the concentration of libido on various experiences in connection with the organs involved point in the direction of a primitive state. But it would be hard to say how the symptomatology will unfold if at all. For instance, directly or indirectly this economic condition may lead to symbolization of the various organ systems.

The question may be raised here whether there is a hypercathexis because of a preceding symbolization of an organ, or if the particular symbolization comes after the hypercathexis. As I noted in discussing the Wolf Man, somatic manifestations may have symbolic meaning by virtue of identification (see p. 156). The identification may bring in its wake hypercathexis of the involved organs. On the other hand, symbolization may arise when a specific system was in use at the time the emotionally charged and subsequently repressed situation transpired, as with Anna O. In still another case, symbolization may result from displacement from organ to organ, or from displacement from below upward. The hypercathexis may follow or occur simultaneously with the symbolization.

In my opinion, two situations may make somatic symptoms psychotic even though the mechanism through which the somatic manifestations arise appears to be hysterical. In the first set of circumstances, we see the impact of ego defects derived from earlier stages in psychic development, when ego functions such as reality testing have not yet evolved or may be impaired. We may see evidence of such impairments antedating the somatization. In the second instance, we find that the level of psychic development at which organs assume an autonomous and independent role is regressively reactivated. The organ almost becomes the external world itself or a part of the external world, as is the case with organs in earlier psychic development. Actually the two situations may be coeval developmentally. Organ autonomy may be accompanied by various disturbances in reality, reality testing, etc., which may result in a psychotic state. In a sense the organs become objects and the actual representation of reality in the more primitive sense. This is viewed by some as a restitutional attempt to hold onto reality, the objects in reality being the various organs. The coeval lack of development of appropriate ego functions makes effective reality testing impossible and the resulting condition is psychosis.

I think that true hypochondriasis may serve the function of restitution as well as the function of defense. In the former situation the organs have assumed the original autonomous form they had in early psychic development. It is in this setting that psychotic symptomatology, i.e., somatic delusions, may develop. The autonomy of the organs may evolve into personifications. They may actually assume, for the patient, the form of a human being, or become an introjected object. One of my patients personified her uterus into an evil force within her which controlled and influenced her behavior. Another had a being within him, shaped like his heart, which unmercifully criticized and flayed him and then forgave him.

Naturally, as I indicated above, one has to view all of this on a spectrum, and one will not see this as clearly and as sharply delineated as I have portrayed it here. Yet the tendency to view parts of the body as external may be seen in many patients, even those who are not psychotic. For instance, one of my psychotic character patients, mentioned earlier, became very angry at his rectum during a bout of diarrhea and spoke of "that son of a bitch who would not let me alone." At the time this transpired, he was not psychotic. But this patient revealed throughout a kind of oblivious disregard for his health, exposing himself to all kinds of situations with a fantasy of omnipotence that nothing could happen to him. When a part of his body became impaired (for instance, he developed gonorrhea at one point), his resentment toward that part of the body for having let him down and threatening his omnipotence was almost as if a foreign and alien force had dared to attack him.

The personification of body parts may lend itself to communication. This is especially true in the schizophrenic patient who, as Freud (1915d) points out, communicates with his body and even speaks in body language. Freud emphasizes the organ speech or hypochondriacal speech in such cases, in which references to body organs or innervations are given prominence. He cites as an example of organ speech a woman who, after a quarrel with her lover, complained that her eyes were not right. They were twisted. She said of her lover that she could not understand him at all; he looked different every time; he was a hypocrite, an eye-twister (*Augenverdreher* — deceiver). He had twisted her eyes, and they were not her eyes anymore. Now she saw the world with different eyes. I have already mentioned Nunberg's (1920) patient who used body functions for communication — for instance, using his bowel movements to pay off debts.

This brings me to the role of the soma in fantasies of omnipotence and the consequence of threats to this omnipotence. Basically, I think that a patient excessively concerned with health and exercise, as Nunberg's patient was, may already be aware of possible ego disintegration, a threat to the grandiosity associated with the extreme narcissism in such patients. The health preoccupations, then, are an attempt to stave off this threat; they are at first defensive in nature. The next step in the breakdown is hypochondriasis, as was seen in Nunberg's case. The organs acquire regressive autonomy and are seized on to hold onto reality, to prevent self- and world disintegration. This may evolve into somatic delusions.

I would like to reemphasize a point. In the potentially psychotic individual, when we see hypochondriacal complaints coming into the picture, we find behind this the fear of total self-disintegration and dissolution, which I believe is the underlying fear of the potentially psychotic. The desperate, primitive way in which such a patient seizes on the various organs to combat this threat is indicative more of a psychotic than a neurotic type of illness. I have often wondered whether one could not make some kind of analogy, dynamically, between some instances of hysteria and organ neurosis, and hypochondriasis and organ psychosis. I would stress again that in the latter two we are at a much more primitive level, close to that stage in psychic development where organs have an autonomous existence, permitting them to be used as objects.

Yet, given all this, the question still presents itself: When does a somatic preoccupation become a somatic delusion and psychotic? Again, I have to indicate that one cannot limit this to the economic factor, namely, the libidinal shifts and the accumulation of libido in the organs (which becomes painful, necessitating rejection). All of this may be true, but there also have to be certain ego changes for delusions to occur. The fragile ego of the potential psychotic cannot tolerate the overaccumulation of libido, and the disturbances in the ego functions concerned with reality allow delusional formation.

We may summarize the role of hypochondriasis, insofar as its relationship to psychosis is concerned, by saying we have to view this on a spectrum. The point along the spectrum is determined by the level of psychic development, the purpose of the hypochondriasis, the person's relationship to reality, the role of symbolism, and the impact of narcissistic needs. What makes for somatic delusional development is the persistence of or regression to that stage in psychic development where body organs and somatic sensations have a certain autonomy and represent reality. This, along with the persistence of primitive ego functions, especially defects in reality testing, establishes the soil out of which somatic delusions grow. It should be borne in mind that this delusional system will at times have a defensive function, to stave off disintegration and dissolution of the self, as well as a restitutional function. I should like to underline one additional aspect. In those instances in which hypochondriasis comes under the influence of the psychotic process, body-image disturbances have usually been present all along. A lack of integration of body parts lends itself to treating organs as autonomous, augmenting the potential for future psychotic development.

I have in this chapter discussed various manifestations of withdrawal and restitution. Although at first the thinking on these evolved essentially within the framework of libido theory, it soon became apparent that wider understanding required a more systematized theory of aggression, especially sadism. The impact of the dual instinct theory, with its emphasis on the death instinct, was not spelled out in this chapter, although obviously it influenced many of the contributions in these areas. It is to this concept and its impact on the psychotic process that we shall now turn our attention.

5.
The Dual Instinct Theory

The application of the concept of the death instinct to the psychotic process has the same limitations that its application has in general to other psychic phenomena. Even suicide, as we shall see, has not been explored explicitly with the death instinct as the main frame of reference. Although Federn (1952) figures as an adherent of the death instinct, he himself admits that *mortido*, as he calls it, cannot do justice to all observable phenomena. On the other hand, in discussing the death instinct in relation to mental pain, he explains: "The second kind of mental pain has no pleasurable counterpoise; it is produced in the individual himself by the destructive forces which are turned outward as hostility, aggression, and destruction, and inward as auto-destruction. It was Freud's conviction that all these kinds of destruction are due to one and the same principle, the death instinct. I join his opinion, and have termed *mortido* the energy produced by the death instinct" (p. 271).

I should like at this point to review the impact of the dual instinct theory on certain considerations about the psychotic process. As we saw in Chapter 4, the dual instinct theory, with its special emphasis on the derivatives of hostility and aggression, has broadened the understanding of unconscious homosexuality as a factor in psychosis, especially in paranoia. Some authors, for instance, have attempted to relate the sadistic element of anality to unconscious homosexuality as specific for paranoid development. Others have focused on anal-sadistic components without unconscious homosexuality, and still others on aggression as such, especially in relation to schizophrenia. Another consideration, which I shall take up later in this chapter, is the role of hatred, hostility, and aggression in the psychotic affective disorders.

A.
Contributions on Hostility
and Aggression

I would like to turn now specifically to the contributions on aggression and the anal-sadistic components of this aggression, an aspect I treated at some length in Chapter 4. You may recall that Stärcke (1920) discusses ambivalence toward the fecal mass as a factor in the development of delusions of persecution. As I also pointed out above, Melanie Klein takes as her jumping-off point some of Abraham's concepts about the anal-sadistic phase in libidinal development. She rather early ascribes an important role to sadism in her concept of paranoia, making sadism one of the fixation points. She points to excessive sadomasochistic forces which cannot be dealt with by the ego except by projection. Objects therefore become highly threatening, and a source of intense anxiety is established, leading to a break with reality. As Klein explains it:

> The fixation point for paranoia is, I think, this period of the phase of maximal sadism in which the child's attacks upon the interior of its mother's body, and the penis it imagines to be there, are carried out by means of poisonous and dangerous excreta, and delusions of reference and persecution spring from the anxiety situations attached to these attacks. . . . According to my view, the child's fear of its introjected objects urges it to displace that fear into the external world. In doing this, it takes its organs, objects, feces, and all manner of things as well as its internalized objects, and equates them with its external objects; and it also distributes its fear of its external object over a great number of objects by equating one with another [1932, p. 207].

In other words, Klein sees the role of aggression and hostility as expanding with the projection of the inner introjects, distributing the persecutory ideas over many objects. She believes "the child's sadistic fantasies about the interior of his mother's body lay down for him a fundamental relation to the external world and to reality" (p. 208). With projection, this moves into the realm of developing object relations.

Underlying the sadism is the death instinct, and Klein proposes that "the primary cause of anxiety is the fear of annihilation, of death, arising from the working of the death instinct within." It is her belief that "fantasies operate from the outset, as do the instincts, and are the mental expression of the activity of both the life and the death instincts. Because the perpetual interaction between the life and death instincts and the conflict arising from their antithesis (fusion and defusion) govern mental life, there is in the unconscious an ever-changing flow of interacting events, of fluctuating emotions and anxieties" (p. 51).

The importance of the death instinct for Klein is apparent in her emphasis on the destructive drives that have to be dealt with at various stages of psychic development. She sees ego splits as bringing about a defusion between destructive impulses over libidinal impulses, which accounts for the aggression and hostility in the paranoid, and equally for world destruction delusions. Remember that Freud views world destruction fantasies as deriving from a projection of the withdrawal of cathexis from the object. Klein (1946), on the other hand, pictures world disintegration delusions as a projection of the warring components within the ego, destructive versus libidinal.[1]

Certainly Melanie Klein and her followers have been the main psychoanalytic contributors to apply aspects of the dual instinct theory to an understanding of the psychotic process. Yet there are several other writers whose work touches on this area — at least in the consideration of the role of aggression. Although these authors are not really working within the framework of dual instinct theory per se, I would like to mention some of their remarks here.

Fromm-Reichmann (1950b), for instance, considers schizophrenic symptomatology as an expression of anxiety as well as of defenses against it. In her opinion, the central core of schizophrenic anxiety lies in the patient's fear of the manifestations of his hostility, his own disapproval of it, and the anticipated disapproval of significant people in the present and past. Coming closer brings great danger that hostility will be aroused. (This is not unlike Knight's [1940b] view described in

---

[1] For my own views on the import of world destruction fantasies, see Chapter 4, Section C, as well as my later discussion of the fear of self-disintegration in Chapter 7. As I indicated in Chapter 3, world destruction dreams may be either a reflection of ego disintegration, in which case the onset of a psychosis may be considered likely, or they may represent the ego's reaction to instinctual drives directed against the outside and the self. In the latter case, we are at a much higher level in psychic development, and the basic psychotic fear of loss of self is not the area of conflict.

Chapter 4.) Fantasies of the end of the world, according to Fromm-Reichmann, express the schizophrenic's anxiety about being destroyed in retaliation for destructive magic thoughts and acts.

From a different perspective, Hartmann (1953) makes a defect in the neutralization of aggression one of his focal points in discussing schizophrenia. He believes that because neutralized aggression is needed for countercathexis, there is an incapacity for countercathexis, which leads to many serious disruptions in other ego functions, affecting reality testing as well as the development of object relations. These defects in turn contribute to defects in the capacity to neutralize aggression. Hartmann sees deficiencies of primary autonomous ego functions (which contribute to the defect in the capacity to neutralize) as the hereditary core in schizophrenia, as well as other factors, such as bisexuality. Among several questions raised by his valuable contribution is whether defects in the capacity to neutralize aggression don't play an important role in other conditions as well, i.e., the so-called impulse-ridden character, without eventuating in psychosis. One must also ask: Is this concept applicable to psychosis in general or only to schizophrenia?

I have already mentioned Bak's (1946) description of paranoia as delusional masochism and his view of delusions of persecution as projected sadism. In another paper (1954), he broadens his examination of the role of aggression. Taking as his jumping-off point Hartmann's concept of the defect in neutralization of aggression, Bak articulates a difference between neurosis and psychosis. In neurosis, he indicates, there is an unsuccessful defense against libido whereas in psychosis the unsuccessful defense is primarily against aggression. The liberation of aggressive drives brings in its wake the threat and the fear of destruction of both the object and the self (which has become the object). Many of the symptoms in the schizophrenic patient revolve around attempted defense against aggression, including withdrawal, projection, and regression of the ego, sometimes to the point of undifferentiation.

In a way, what we are concerned with here is delineation of what I believe to be the danger most feared in psychosis — namely, dissolution and disintegration of self. The threat of this may even be instigated by defensive ego reactions to tremendous aggression. For instance, one might view dedifferentiation as a defensive maneuver by the schizophrenic in the attempt to avoid intense emotional charging of the object. By permitting some dilution and diffusion of impulses, dedifferentiation would make it possible to deal with and even to control them and so ensure survival. On the other hand, Jacobson (personal communication) contends: "The most essential reason for the patient's fear of complete annihilation is not the drive deneutralization but the surplus amount of sheer aggression. Dedifferentiation in the psychotic is so anxiety-provoking because of the intensity of sheer destructive forces which precludes the reestablishment of self-object boundaries."

In line with Jacobson's comments, I might mention a patient I have described elsewhere in great detail (Frosch, 1967a). At one point she began to talk about her hatred and aggression. She indicated that her whole problem was tremendous overall hatred. All her life she had been rather sensitive to people's remarks, and she related this to her own hatred and aggression, which she felt could not help but be expressed toward her by others. In this way she pointed to projection of her hostility, anger, and aggression. She concluded, "I am very touchy, sensitive and full of hatred. That's my psychosis, I guess."

The upsurge of drives (both aggressive and libidinal) is felt by the psychotic as self-disintegrative. But it should be borne in mind that object-directed destructive drives are equally devastating for the patient, for the wiping out of self-nonself differentiation means that destruction of the object is destruction of self. In other words, the confusion between self and object brings with it the danger that destruction of the object means psychic death for the patient. These patients' fears of their destructive impulses lead them to be terrified that they may destroy the therapist. And in doing so, because of lack of differentiation, they themselves will be destroyed. Indeed, one of my psychotic characters came in one day and said, "Thank God you're alive. I killed you so many times over the weekend. I was frightened. How could I go on without you? It's like without me."

It is necessary for the therapist to help the patient overcome the fear of facing these destructive impulses. At the same time the therapist must show that he is not afraid of them and will survive the patient's destructive impulses, thus presenting himself as the indestructible object. By showing the "destroyer" that the destructive drives will not destroy the object on whom he is dependent for survival, the therapist encourages the patient to face up to and not fear these impulses. Ultimately the patient comes to realize that these wishes will not translate into reality. As Giovacchini describes it:

> Patients with characterological and schizophrenic disorders frequently look around to see if the analyst is still alive. They are often very sensitive to what seems to be a rejection and abandonment by the analyst, but analysis reveals they are also concerned about having killed the analyst.

They are frightened that the analyst will not be able to survive their projection. Insofar as the analyst is able to survive the projection, he is
"stronger" than the dangerous introjects. What had previously been self-
destructive impulses, because of the transference projection, are now
destructive impulses towards the analyst. They are manifested as negative transference. The patient gains considerable security in that he no
longer feels as threatened and, since the analyst is not destroyed, the patient no longer believes that his hostility is overwhelming and uncontrollable [Boyer and Giovacchini, 1967, pp. 330–331].

In summary, aside from Federn's and Melanie Klein's assumption
of the relationship of the death instinct to aggression and hostility in
psychotic manifestations, few contributors appear to deal directly with
this aspect of aggression. Insofar as the psychotic process is concerned,
inherent in the role of aggression is its impact on the self and the object
(whose destruction is also self-destructive). In particular, an examination of the role of sadism, the fate of the object, and the various
methods of dealing with object loss (such as introjection) has expanded
our understanding of the psychotic affective disorders, and it is to this
area that I shall now turn.

B.
The Psychotic Affective Disorders

Terminology

Although I shall confine my discussion to the role of the psychotic process in the affective disorders, a few remarks on terminology seem in order. The term "affect" has been used as a class name for feeling, emotion, or mood (Hinsie and Campbell, 1970). The psychoanalytic glossary (Moore and Fine, 1968) does not define "emotion" and simply refers to affects as "subjectively experienced feeling states." Jacobson (1971) remarks that there is no reason why psychoanalysts should not use the term "emotion" interchangeably with "affect" to designate the whole complex of psychological and physiological manifestations of pleasurable or unpleasurable feeling states. In this regard, Rapaport (1942) says: "the word emotion is sometimes used to designate a phenomenon, and sometimes the dynamics underlying a phenomenon of any single 'emotion' such as fear or rage; the expression 'emotion' refers to a phenomenon, but in a psychotic disease the expression 'emotion' refers to the dynamics and etiology of the disorder" (p. 11). Here I think Rapaport is using the term "emotion" in its broadest sense, as an "emotional" illness. It thus involves drives and their derivatives, conflict and affects, etc. He does not opt for any new terminology but deals with emotions as a process, with psychological and physiological manifestations.

When we come to the term "mood," we have even more difficulty. As Jacobson explains: "Moods seem to represent, as it were, a cross-section through the entire state of the ego, lending a particular uniform coloring to all its manifestations for a longer or shorter period of time. Since they do not relate to a specific content or object, but find expression in specific qualities attached to all feelings, thoughts or actions, they may indeed be called a barometer of the ego state" (1971, p. 68). Obviously the term is very broad.

We also encounter difficulty in discussing disturbances of affect, since traditional psychiatric texts often do not include many disturbances of affect under the "affective disorders." Even *DSM–III* (American Psychiatric Association, 1981) appears to be restricted by this line of thinking, primarily because of the attempt to delineate clinical syndromes in which common identifiable features are the frames of reference. For instance, prominent among the affects is anxiety. Yet a clinical syndrome such as "anxiety neurosis" is not included under affect disorders.

A slightly different problem occurs with the syndrome of depression. We find a spectrum of depressions, both clinically and dynamically, including reactive depression, neurotic depression, psychotic depression, mourning, grief, and melancholia. Depression may also be manifest in schizophrenia and organic illness. Bibring (1953), for one, tries to cut across all types of depression and proposes common denominators, ostensibly encompassing normal, neurotic, and psychotic depressions. He defines depression as "an ego-psychological phenomenon, a 'state of the ego,' an affective state" (p. 21).[2] Yet such a broad-based definition has its limitations. The 1977 symposium on "Depression and Other Painful Affects" at the meetings of the International Psycho-Analytical Association (Prego-Silva, 1978), for instance, contributed little to the understanding of *psychotic* depression.

Even if we restrict our discussion to manic-depressive illness, we may have a problem, since the manifestations of the manic and depressive aspects of the illness may not be psychotic — they may not fulfill our criteria for psychosis. For instance, in a typical cyclothymic disorder we may not be dealing with psychosis. To give an example: For many years I treated a patient with classical mood swings of an appreciable nature. When the depressive aspects were manifest, she quite realistically evaluated these: "There it goes again, that darned depression. I don't feel like getting up again." She described her withdrawal from her family, her lack of interest and drive, and the constant desire to stay in bed. Yet she would add, "I know it will pass, and hope it won't last as long as the last time." These episodes were interspersed with marked moods of elation, which would unquestionably be designated as

[2] A similar view of mania is offered by Bibring: "Though elation frequently occurs as a compensatory reaction to states of anxiety as well as to states of depression, it nevertheless has to be considered as a basic (independent) state of mind in the ego's inventory of responses to internal or external stimuli. In contrast to depression, elation is the expression of an actual or imaginary fulfillment of the person's narcissistic aspirations" (p. 35).

"manic." Nevertheless, although this patient had a classical manic-depressive illness, she was not, in my opinion, psychotic. Her reality testing and other ego functions were not grossly impaired.

Contributions from Libido Theory

Having looked at the terminological difficulties, I would like to turn now to the psychoanalytic literature on the psychotic affective disorders, especially the manic-depressive psychoses. Libido theory plays a large role in the earlier contributions that lend understanding to the psychotic affective disorders, although later contributions rely heavily on other frames of reference in addition to libido theory. Among the earliest contributors using the framework of libido theory was Abraham (1911, 1916, 1924). Freud's *Mourning and Melancholia* (1917b) was of course the seminal contribution, with the ideas of introjection and psychotic identification being elaborated upon by subsequent contributors, especially Jacobson (1953, 1954a, 1964, 1967, 1971).[3]

There is much in Abraham's early contributions that presages later developments in psychoanalysis. This is especially true of his remarks on ambivalence in the obsessional and the depressive. He draws many analogies between the two, but differentiates the depressive's hatred as resulting in a type of projection: "they hate me because I am cursed with inborn defects—so I am unhappy, and depressed" (1911, p. 145). Unconscious sadistic wishes, which completely overpower the positive libidinal tendencies of the depressive, become a source of guilt. Masochism is a natural derivative of the sadism, and the depressive draws pleasure from his own suffering. Abraham's views on mania, however, are not as thoroughly articulated at this point. He emphasizes the failure of repression and the breaking through of love and hate, with regression to infantile modes of gratification. These ideas are developed further in another contribution (1916), in which Abraham indicates that the ambivalence and narcissism of the manic-depressive patient described in the first paper have an oral-erotic root. One finds in some of what Abraham says about manics hints of Lewin's (1950) subsequent contribution on elation.

Freud's *Mourning and Melancholia* (1917b) is an elaboration and extension of ideas expressed in his paper "On Narcissism" (1914a). Its major contribution lies in its definition of the identification that is

[3] See also Melanie Klein (1934, 1940), Rado (1928, 1951), Lewin (1950), Bibring (1953), and Freeman (1973).

unique for the melancholic.[4] Freud incorporates Abraham's idea of oral and cannibalistic components in this process of identification in which the ego incorporates the object into itself by devouring it. As Freud explains it:

> An object-choice, an attachment of the libido to a particular person, had at one time existed; then, owing to a real slight or disappointment coming from this loved person, the object-relationship was shattered. The result was not the normal one of a withdrawal of the libido from this object and a displacement of it on to a new one, but something different, for whose coming-about, various conditions seem to be necessary. The object-cathexis proved to have little power of resistance and was brought to an end. But the free libido was not displaced on to another object; it was withdrawn into the ego. There, however, it was not employed in any unspecified way, but served to establish an identification of the ego with the abandoned object. Thus the shadow of the object fell upon the ego, and the latter could henceforth be judged by a special agency, as though it were an object, the forsaken object. In this way an object-loss was transformed into an ego-loss and the conflict between the ego and the loved person into a cleavage between the critical activity of the ego and the ego as altered by identification [pp. 248–249].

What Freud is really talking about here is introjection.[5] The self-accusation is really directed against this introjected object.

> If one listens patiently to a melancholic's many and various self-accusations, one cannot in the end avoid the impression that often the most violent of them are hardly at all applicable to the patient himself, but that with insignificant modifications they do fit someone else, someone whom the patient loves or has loved or should love. Every time one examines the facts this conjecture is confirmed. So we find the key to the clinical picture; we perceive that the self-reproaches are reproaches against a loved object which have been shifted away from it on to the patient's own ego [p. 248].

Freud views the nature of the object choice to begin with as narcissistic and thus the process of withdrawal is to narcissism. In mania, the ego has recovered from the loss of the object and the accumulation of cathexis which was bound in the melancholia now becomes free, accounting for some of the symptomatology. In Freud's words: "In mania, the ego must have got over the loss of the object (or its mourning over the loss, or perhaps the object itself), and thereupon, the whole

---

[4] There is some difficulty in correlating Freud's contribution with those of later authors since he does not use the term "self" but speaks of the ego.

[5] The relationship of introjection and identification will be discussed in Chapter 8.

quota of anticathexis which the painful suffering of melancholia had drawn to itself from the ego and 'bound' will have become available. Moreover, the manic subject plainly demonstrates his liberation from the object which was the cause of his suffering, by seeking like a ravenously hungry man for new object-cathexes" (p. 255). Later (1921), in examining the shift from melancholia to mania in the bipolar cyclothymic disorders, Freud expands on this:

> . . . the misery of the melancholic is the expression of a sharp conflict between the two agencies of his ego, a conflict in which the ideal, in an excess of sensitiveness, relentlessly exhibits its condemnation of the ego in delusions of inferiority and in self-depreciation. . . . [In contrast] in cases of mania the ego and the ego ideal have fused together, so that the person, in a mood of triumph and self-satisfaction, disturbed by no self-criticism can enjoy the abolition of his inhibitions, his feelings of consideration for others, and his self-reproaches [p. 132].

In his 1924 paper Abraham examines Freud's contribution on melancholia. He adds several observations regarding the libidinal development of the melancholic, pointing to the prominence of oral sadism in this condition. There are foreshadowings of the Kleinian view in his reference to the oral-destructive and cannibalistic devouring of the loved object, with these impulses being turned against the self via the superego. Abraham also emphasizes the vulnerability of the melancholic to object loss because of pronounced narcissism. Rickman (1928) provides a clear summary of Abraham's views:

> (1) Constitutional increase of oral erotism. (2) Specific fixation of libido at the oral stage of libido organization. (3) Severe injury to the child's narcissism (weaning is often traumatic — psychically — in these cases) so that they suffer from a sense of desertion. (4) Imperfect attainment of the phallic stage of libido organization with a distortion of the Oedipus situation, disappointment at this stage causing a regression to the oral-sadistic stage, hence a permanent association of love relationships and destructive-oral impulses. These factors lie dormant until in later life there comes (5) A frustration in object-relationships (insofar as these have formed) or a wound to narcissism, or anything which by weakening the ego incapacitates it in its permanent task of repression. Between attacks melancholics do not attain full object-love; though the tendency to incorporate the object and destroy it is in abeyance, ambivalence and a measure of hostility remain [p. 114].

The Theme of Loss

The theme of loss of some sort seems to be common to many psycho-analytic contributions on the affective disorders. Something or someone has been lost. It may be an object in reality, or something in relation to the object (e.g., loss of love, disillusionment, loss of a belief or ideal, loss of approval).[6] Or it may even be a physiological loss, leading to a sense of emptiness and depletion. Indeed, the role of direct organic factors in producing the phenomenon "depression" has been accentuated in the current psychopharmacological treatment of depression. Still, I would wonder whether the sense of depletion as a result of biological factors may represent a loss, and contribute to the drop in self-esteem so frequently seen in depression (especially in old age). This sense of loss may bring in its wake many other psychological manifestations related to the meaning of loss and earlier loss experiences. My thoughts about the sense of loss created by biological factors are reflected in Freud's (1917b) statement: "These considerations bring up the question whether a loss in the ego irrespectively of the object — a purely narcissistic blow to the ego — may not suffice to produce the picture of melancholia and whether an impoverishment of ego-libido directly due to toxins may not be able to produce certain forms of the disease" (p. 253). Jacobson (1953) summarizes all these possible variations of loss: "Increase or inhibition of libidinous or aggressive discharges, a libidinous impoverishment or enrichment of the self from outside or inside, from somatic, psychosomatic, or psychological sources may reduce or increase the libidinous or aggressive cathexis of the self-representations and lead to fluctuations of self-esteem and corresponding vacillations, that is, to depressed or elated states" (pp. 59–60).

The reaction to loss, such as a drop in self-esteem, anger, or hatred, is dependent on many factors, including narcissistic vulnerability. Crucial to some forms of severe depression is the feeling the person has about the role he played in this loss (e.g., actively contributing to it or not doing anything to prevent it). Several questions arise. If there is, for instance, a feeling that hatred and anger played a role in bringing the loss about, to what extent does this contribute to the guilt we see in some forms of depression, especially psychotic depression? What is the stage of superego development and does a punitive, harsh superego contribute to the self-accusation one sees in true melancholia? How does this eventuate in mania? Is the denial directed against the hatred,

---

[6] The fear of loss of the love object and its role in Melanie Klein's depressive position will be discussed in Chapter 11.

with the feeling of responsibility in contributing to the loss, and consequent feeling of guilt, redirected externally in the manic phase? We may see this in the form of paranoid accusations in some manic patients. The word "they" begins to replace the word "I." The failure to deny and to redirect such feelings outwardly may bring suicide in its wake.

The fear of loss of the love object through the child's own destructive drives plays a role in what Melanie Klein designates as the "depressive position," which follows the paranoid-schizoid position. The child comes to fear destruction and possible loss of the love object. Ordinarily, ultimately the goal is to establish a stable, good, unified internal object through integration of all the various part-object components. Yet a problem arises. If the infant's destructive drives are aimed at the good object, with the fear that hatred and aggression may be stronger than love, there ensues a fear of the loss of the good object (the good breast). It is therefore important for future development that a predominantly positive object relationship be established prior to loss of the first breast-object. The infant must in some way come to terms with a real object loss during the weaning period, and this is the basis for the depressive position.

Both the paranoid-schizoid position and the depressive position are key concepts in Kleinian thinking about future psychotic development. Klein describes the pathology that may eventuate if the individual is incapable of overcoming the infantile depressive position as follows:

> Failure to do so may result in depressive illness, mania or paranoia. I pointed out one or two other methods by which the ego attempts to escape from the sufferings connected with the depressive position, namely either the flight to internal good objects (which may lead to severe psychosis) or the flight to external good objects (with the possible outcome of neurosis). There are, however, many ways, based on obsessional, manic and paranoid defences, varying from individual to individual in their relative proportion, which in my experience all serve the same purpose, that is, to enable the individual to escape from the sufferings connected with the depressive position. . . . The ego uses various ways of dealing with paranoid fears (which will be the stronger the more hatred is reinforced). For instance, the internal 'bad' objects are manically subjugated, immobilized and at the same time denied, as well as strongly projected into the external world [1940, p. 336].

She also contrasts pathological depression (melancholia?) with normal mourning and relates the outcome to negotiation of the depressive position:

In normal mourning, as well as in abnormal mourning and in manic-depressive states, the infantile depressive position is reactivated. The complex feelings, phantasies and anxieties included under this term are of a nature which justifies my contention that the child in his early development goes through a transitory manic-depressive state as well as a state of mourning, which become modified by the infantile neurosis. . . . [Thus] the manic-depressive and the person who fails in the work of mourning, though their defences may differ widely from each other, have this in common, that they have been unable in early childhood to establish their internal 'good' objects and to feel secure in their inner world. They have never really overcome the infantile depressive position [pp. 336–337].

A specific type of disruption (loss) in relation to the object is seen by Rado (1928) as initiating the process of melancholia. He describes melancholics as highly narcissistic individuals, in whom the slightest rejection or fancied rejection results in a drop in self-esteem. The process of melancholia is an attempt to repair this loss of self-esteem and to bring back the relationship to the object by a withdrawal from the real world, and the problem is thrashed out intrapsychically. The "program" used follows the prototype of infantile feelings of guilt, atonement, and forgiveness. Guilt derives from the ambivalence and hostility toward the object, with its possible destruction. Atonement is achieved by the ego taking itself as a weak, hateful object and placing the superego in the role of parents whose forgiveness has to be sought by abject behavior. We find here a double identification: the ego as bad parent and the superego as the good one. Ultimately forgiveness may be achieved through fusion with the superego—the prototype of earlier situations. Alimentary orgasm and intoxication are achieved. This is mania.[7] Rado also indicates that in recovery the obsessive state keeps the object from being hurt or destroyed by ambivalence.

Jacobson's Contributions

In more recent years some of the most significant contributions on psychotic depression have been made by Jacobson (1953, 1971). Interest-

[7] One finds in Rado's formulation of mania many similarities to Lewin's concepts (1950, 1952, 1954). As I indicated in Chapter 4, Lewin sees mania as recapturing subjective feelings of pleasure in nursing and satiation at the breast. It is the historical fact of having experienced this before that lends a feeling of reality to events experienced by the manic, and the elated individual. Lewin also interprets some of the classic symptoms of mania as if they were dream elements (see Chapter 3). One might also compare Bibring's (1953) view of mania (see p. 178n).

ingly enough, she lays emphasis on the somatic substrate in much of depressive symptomatology:

> Valuable diagnostic criteria may be gained by focusing on the psychosomatic, "endogenous" features in the questionable syndrome. I refer not only to the symptoms that impressed even Freud as having somatic rather than psychological origin: the insomnia, the anorexia, the amenorrhea, the loss of weight, the metabolic disturbances, or the frequent gastrointestinal or cardiovascular psychosomatic symptoms. What I wish to emphasize especially are the psychosomatic features in the depressive retardation. True cyclothymics will experience their slowing up quite differently from the way depressive neurotics experience their inhibitions. Cyclothymics seem to be aware that there is a somatic quality to this phenomenon [1953, p. 51].

Nonetheless, various clinical manifestations of the depressive are to be understood psychologically. For Jacobson: "The central psychological problem in depression appears to be the narcissistic breakdown of the depressed person: his loss of self-esteem, or, to put it more broadly, his feelings of impoverishment, helplessness, weakness, and inferiority; or, in the melancholic type, of moral worthlessness and even sinfulness" (p. 53).

In offering a frame of reference for these features, Jacobson emphasizes a number of factors:

> . . . the concept of self-representations, and its importance for an understanding of the depressive type of identification; the cathectic fluctuations and shifts from self- to object representations and the reverse, and the fusions with each other; the struggle of the manic-depressive to maintain and recover his position of participation in the power of his love-object; the defense function of the patient's clinging to the real, outside love-object during the depressed period; and, finally, the melancholic symptom formation as an expression of his last failing attempts at restitution of a powerful love-object in the superego [p. 82].

She presents a patient to illustrate the cathectic flow of libidinal and aggressive drives back and forth between self and object, with either overevaluation or underevaluation. The patient feels himself or the object (or both) worthless, via aggressivization. There are then attempts at restitution by turning to the real object world for support. Toward the therapist, he behaves in an extremely submissive, masochistic, and even sadistic way. The insatiable demands cannot be met. He may endow the therapist with primitive sadistic and omnipotent qualities. If this fails, he may retreat from the object world and a psychotic melancholia may develop.

Like Klein (1940) and Lewin (1950), Jacobson highlights the role of denial in supporting manic-depressive symptomatology. As she explains it:

> The manic-depressive has to protect himself by strong pathological safe-guards, essentially by the denial mechanisms so beautifully described by Lewin (1950). He can maintain a lasting libidinous overcathexis of the love-object image only by constant efforts at denial of his own intrinsic value and of the weaknesses of the real love-object, and an equally illusory under- or overestimation of himself. If he meets with disappointment or failure, the denial mechanisms will either break down or have to be so fortified that the patient may go into a manic state, which — in contradistinction to schizophrenic feelings of grandeur — represents, I believe, a state of lasting participation of the self in the imagined omnipotence of the love-object [p. 73].

In this regard, let me add that in *psychotic* denial I believe it is still necessary to consider the loss of reality testing. Dorpat (1977), addressing himself to this issue, says:

> Because of its interference with reality testing, denial has an especially disruptive effect on the inhibition automatism. Denial reactions adversely affect the subject's recognition and acceptance of losses or frustrating events, and they may also diminish the subject's awareness of his helplessness and hopelessness about altering painful realities. The subject may deny the unpleasurable feeling, the event, or both. The unconscious fantasy content of denial defenses in such contexts may be paraphrased in this schematic formulation: 'It is not true that I am helpless and hopeless about such-and-such a situation; rather, I am able to attain my aim in this or that way.' In the above formula a negation of the subject's powerlessness is followed by an affirmation of his capacities. The negating and defensive content of denial is often buttressed by compensatory gratifying fantasies which emphasize the subject's real or imagined abilities. Such conscious or unconscious fantasies may be acted out in psychopathic, compulsive, or hypomanic forms of hyperactivity [p. 17].

Ginsberg (1979) comments: "mania does not end depression, it interrupts it. It attempts to restructure the psychic conflict, predominantly through the use of denial. Mania is not an 'up' it is another attempt at an 'out.' It attempts to deny not only the ideas of reality but more importantly the emotional aspects of reality. It represents a further regression utilizing denial" (p. 8).

We might well ask here whether the level of regression distinguishes the psychotic affective disorders. In a general way it is clear that they are genetically at a higher stage in psychic development than the schizophrenias. Jacobson (1953) makes this point:

> Possibly it is the depth of regression that determines the development of a manic-depressive or a schizophrenic psychosis. Manic-depressives seem to have reached a higher level in the differentiation and integration of the psychic systems, to begin with. Consequently, the acute regressive process during their episodes does not go so far as in schizophrenics. Usually, it does not lead to a complete disintegration of the personality, but it is reversible. It stops at a point that still allows a rather complete recovery. Bleuler has described as a characteristic difference between the schizophrenic and the manic-depressive that the fears of the first refer to disasters occurring at the present time, those of the latter to future catastrophes. I believe that this difference is an expression of the metapsychological distinction that in the schizophrenic the object- and self-representations, in the system ego, break down actually to the point of dissolution, whereas the manic-depressive only feels threatened. His anxieties may be severe, but they are not true states of panic. His delusions in manic or melancholic states show characteristic differences from schizophrenic delusions, which, I believe, prove this point. As to the suicide of the melancholic, we may remember, Freud . . . said that the love-object is shown to be more powerful than the self. I may venture to add that in the suicidal act the self, too, regains a feeling of power and achieves a final, though fatal, victory [pp. 65–66].

Ambivalence and Helplessness

It is clear from much of the above that a leitmotif in psychotic depression involves ambivalence, hatred, and aggression. To Glover (1932b), it is the interplay between the hated introjected object and the way it is reacted to by the ego that is crucial in melancholia. As he puts it, in melancholia hate rages against hate. In his usual elegant fashion, Glover explains: "Introjection is essentially a mechanism for dealing with lost or disappearing objects. The more the ego is threatened with loss, the greater the hate; the greater the hate, the greater the projected hate; the greater the projected hate, the more dangerous the world of objects; the more dangerous the world of objects, the more poisonous the effect of introjection" (p. 177).

Bibring (1953), however, qualifies the role of hatred, assigning it different roles in different depressions. In reviewing contributions to the subject of depression, he says:

> According to one approach there exist at least two types of depression which differ clinically as well as theoretically; the first type (called sim-

ple, essential, endogenous, mild, blank, etc.) is represented on the one hand by the uncomplicated grief reaction (Freud), on the other hand by the depression primarily due to exhaustion of the "ego energy," for whatever reasons, and in whatever ways this may come about. The second (severe or melancholic) type is characterized by the familiar etiological syndrome: narcissistic injury, oral mechanisms of recovery, such as identification via incorporation and the concomitant turning of the aggression from the object against the self. According to the second approach, a loss of self-esteem is common to all types of depression. Consequently the clinical differences (ranging from simple sadness to the severe forms of melancholia) are explained by additional predominantly oral-aggressive etiological mechanisms which are employed in the course of the struggle for readjustment [p. 20].

At another point he summarizes: "In brief, simple depression results from exhaustion of ego libido due to an unsolvable conflict (the 'ego' is 'empty') whereas melancholic depression is due to self-hatred as a consequence of an extensive loss of self-esteem through rejection" (p. 19). Yet, overall, Bibring gives hatred a secondary place. Essentially he views depression as deriving from a tension within the ego itself, "from an inner-systemic 'conflict.'" Any intersystemic conflict, such as with the superego, is secondarily developed. Nor does he believe that orality and aggression are primary. He insists that: "basic depression represents a *state of the ego* whose main characteristics are a decrease of self-esteem, a more or less intense state of helplessness, a more or less intensive and extensive inhibition of functions, and a more or less intensely felt particular emotion; in other words, depression represents an affective state, which indicates the state of the ego in terms of helplessness and inhibition of functions" (p. 23; my italics). And he adds: "what has been described as the basic mechanism of depression, the ego's shocking awareness of its helplessness in regard to its aspirations, is assumed to represent the core of normal, neurotic and probably also psychotic depression. . . . This state is later on regressively reactivated whenever situations arise which resemble the primary shock condition, i.e., when for external or internal reasons those particular functions which serve the fulfillment of the important aspiration prove to be inadequate" (p. 39).[8]

As indicated above, Bibring's formulation tends to subsume all types of depression and much of what he describes clinically does not seem to apply to *psychotic* depression, which is essentially our concern

___

[8] Much of what Bibring describes as bringing about this state of helplessness can be compared to Eidelberg's narcissistic mortification (1954, 1959a).

here. To clarify my point, I would like to cite a patient's differentiation between "sadness" and "depression":

> Sadness is different from depression. You're not separated. You are sad about something, someone. It transforms, but objects do not become separated. It has beauty; it is a thoughtful feeling. It is everybody's sadness. Everyone has it. Most of all — it is not hate; it is not fear, or anger, or separation. It is longing.
>
> Depression puts you outside of life and makes you feel different. You are isolated and separated from everyone. Depression is anger, hatred. You stand alone with yourself but unable even to give to yourself what you want. When I visit you I can tell how I'm going to be in treatment, before I get to you, by the way I feel about your car when I pass by. It is your object. It is you and it looks reassuring and important to me and most of all real — like it does when I'm not depressed and I know you will reach me. I guess that is my depression. It is fear, separation, doom and deprivation. I am then an outcast and I am angry. Am I isolated because I killed everyone or do I kill them because they isolate me? On Sunday you are dead. I'm separated from you. You don't exist. It's depression — isolation — hatred and fear."

Dorpat (1977), following Bibring, also denigrates the role of anger, hatred, and aggression. He views helplessness and hopelessness as derivatives of the depressive affect, which he describes as a primary affect. Reactions to an actual or expected traumatic situation are also seen as derivative. Essentially depressive affect is viewed as serving both adaptive and defensive purposes (e.g., inhibition of action).[9] Again, I would say that little in this picture applies to psychotic depression, beyond its general statement of the spectrum from signal depressive affect to the uncontrolled affect characterizing psychotic depression.

Observations on Suicide

At this point I would like to make some observations on the relation of depression to suicide. Although every depressive should be con-

---

[9] I might add a note to Dorpat's view of inhibition of action as a defensive component of depression. The depressed patient's tendency to withdraw and become inactive may be an adaptive response to whatever it is that lies at the core of the illness. Inhibition of action may prevent the external expression of hostility and hatred and minimize action that would facilitate the expression of these toward the self. Thus, activity programs or exhortations toward activity may be counterproductive. Such activities may mobilize aggression before the patient is able to deal with it effectively and to channel it appropriately externally. The aggression may then turn on the self. It is this, I believe, that accounts for the suicides in some patients who seem to be improving and are prematurely discharged.

sidered a potential suicide, there is no doubt that some kinds of depressives are more likely to suicide. On the other hand, some suicides may not even be depressively based (for instance, suicide as a symbolic act with the goal of eternal life). Freeman (1959) refers to suicide in the hebephrenic, in contrast to the depressive, as not reflecting superego activity but rather a kind of symbolic or riddance phenomenon.

I should like, in this context, to make some comments on the suicide cache. The patient tries to accumulate all types of medication secretly (although frequently the secret is not too successfully kept). This act would appear to represent a preparation for future suicide. But it contains within it a certain grandiosity — in the patient's wish to control his own destiny: "I will determine when and how I will die." This and other aspects are beautifully described by Goethe (1795):

> We had long treated him, morally and physically, as our best consideration dictated; in some degree the plan was efficacious; but the fear of death continued powerful in him, and he would not lay aside his beard and cloak. For the rest, however, he appeared to take more interest in external things than formerly; and both his songs and his conceptions seemed to be approaching nearer life. A strange letter from the clergyman, as you already know, called me from you. I arrived: I found our patient altogether changed; he had voluntarily given up his beard; he had let his locks be cut into a customary form; he asked for common clothes; he seemed to have all at once become another man. Though curious to penetrate the reason of this sudden alteration, we did not risk inquiring of himself: at last we accidentally discovered it. A glass of laudanum was missing from the parson's private laboratory: we thought it right to institute a strict inquiry; every one endeavored to ward off suspicion and the sharpest quarrels rose among the inmates of the house. At last this man appeared before us, and admitted that he had the laudanum; we asked if he had swallowed any of it. 'No,' said he, 'but it is to this that I owe the recovery of my reason. It is at your choice to take the vial from me, and to drive me back, inevitably, to my former state. The feeling, that it was desirable to see the pains of life terminated by death, first put me on the way of cure: before long the thought of terminating them by voluntary death arose in me, and with this intention I took the glass of poison. The possibility of casting off my load of griefs forever gave me strength to bear them; and thus have I, ever since this talisman came into my possession, forced myself back into life by a contiguity with death. Be not anxious lest I use the drug, but resolve, as men acquainted with the human heart, by granting me an independence of life, to make me properly and wholesomely dependent on it.' After mature consideration, we determined not to meddle further with him;

and he now carries with him, in a firm little ground-glass vial, this poison, of which he has so strangely made an antidote [pp. 555–556].[10]

Sometimes the secret cache does eventuate in suicide. (The patient Goethe describes did commit suicide, although not with his vial of poison.) Yet what underlies the suicide cache syndrome is the grandiosity and sense of omnipotence. We might compare this to the wish for rescue seen in some suicides (see Abraham, 1922; Sterba, 1946). Karl Menninger (1933) comments that one who wishes to kill himself does not wish to die. He lists several components of suicide: (1) the wish to kill, (2) the wish to be killed, (3) the wish to die, and (4) an unfulfilled wish to be rescued.

Jensen and Petty (1958) find the prototype for some suicides in the mother-child situation, specifically in an early abandonment by the mother. The suicide attempt and the rescue represent a restitution of this early abandonment. The appeal for help in the suicide attempt is associated with the fantasy of being rescued and the wish not to die. Generally the chosen rescuer represents someone upon whom originally a great deal of hostility and aggression were projected, and whom the suicide unconsciously holds responsible for his impending death.

These dynamics could be seen in a patient who fed a baby she was taking care of barbiturates. When the baby's mother frantically expressed her concern over her child's condition, the patient was gratified. The mother should not have left her child, but her concern really showed that she cared for the baby. So it was with the patient's own suicide attempts. She knew she would not ultimately die. It was a test situation of her mother's love for her, which she had always doubted. She generally contrived to make her suicide attempts when the mother was in the vicinity. This person who was the object of her hostility would rescue her, and by this rescue would show that she cared. The attempt to poison the child she was babysitting for was clearly an acting out of an identification with the seemingly abandoned child.

I would like to add some comments here on the sociological and cultural aspects of suicide and how these relate to the psychological aspects. We somehow seem to associate suicide with certain cultures (e.g., Scandinavian). The facts are that a few years ago the highest suicide rate was in West Berlin and Hungary, not in Scandinavia.[11]

[10] I am indebted to Dr. Walter Bennett for calling this reference to my attention.
[11] Interestingly, Hendin (1969), who had earlier studied suicide in Scandinavia, found that in New York suicide was twice as frequent among black men aged 20 to 35 as it was among white men of the same age.

Certain symbolic kinds of suicide are also associated with particular cultures. Among these are Kari Kiri — the culmination of a feeling of shame and failure — or various acts of protest such as self-immolation, ostensibly to arouse guilt in others. One might cite, for instance, the military tactics of the ancient Chinese, who would line up a group of soldiers and have them commit suicide opposite the enemy. The enemy would be filled with guilt and demoralized. Then they would be attacked successfully, by a back-up group of Chinese soldiers.

The current high rate of suicide among adolescents has led to the belief that this is a recent problem, which is not the case. This problem was the subject of a symposium on suicide in 1910, held by the Vienna Psychoanalytic Society. Friedman (1967) quite appropriately indicates that many of the views expressed at that meeting were in keeping with the then-prevailing knowledge. (The meeting preceded Freud's *Mourning and Melancholia* [1917b] and his dual instinct theory, which highlighted the relation between suicide and aggression.) It was pointed out at the time that epidemics of suicide among young people had existed for almost three centuries, and it was emphasized by one observer, Professor Oppenheim, that "Suicide in youth was a social phenomenon which stretched much further back in history than the public grasped." That the problem of adolescent suicide is still with us is attested to by recent newspaper reports. For instance, in Germany it was projected that in 1978 there would be about 500 adolescent suicides (*New York Times*, December 9, 1978).

Through the years there have been many attempts to explain suicide, ranging from the sociological to the depth-psychological ones of classical analysts. One of the best-known sociological explanations is that of Durkheim (1897), who postulates two fundamental cultural tendencies that create the conditions for social suicide. There is the tendency to integrate members of a group into a whole, and the tendency to regulate their feelings and behavior. Durkheim believes that any overintensification or weakening of these tendencies results in a "suicide-genetic current." The intensity of this social current determines the "suicide rate" of a given society or group.

I should now like to return to the role of hatred and hostility in suicide.[12] Although a marked drop in self-esteem may eventuate in suicide

----

[12] I am not going to discuss letting oneself die, or other indirect forms of what is most likely suicide, but I would like to mention Bibring's (1953) comment: "Finally there is a decisive difference between the 'ego killing itself' and the 'ego letting itself die.' Only in the first case is aggression involved. Giving up the struggle because one is

and the social climate may well be a factor, the presence of hatred in depression always carries the possibility that this hatred may be turned against the self. At the conference on adolescent suicide in 1910, Stekel remarkēd: "No one kills himself who did not want to kill another, or at least wish death to another" (Friedman, 1967, p. 347). Freud (1917b) comments: "We have long known... that no neurotic harbours thoughts of suicide which he has not turned back upon himself from murderous impulses against others" (p. 252). Freud goes on to underline the element of hatred and anger in depression that may eventuate in suicide:

> It is this sadism alone that solves the riddle of the tendency to suicide which makes melancholia so interesting and so dangerous.... The analysis of melancholia now shows that the ego can kill itself only if, owing to the return of the object-cathexis, it can treat itself as an object, if it is able to direct against itself the hostility which relates to an object and which represents the ego's original reaction to objects in the external world [p. 252].

The question of suicide is pursued by Freud (1923) in his discussion of the role of the superego:

> If we turn to melancholia first, we find that the excessively strong super-ego which has obtained a hold upon consciousness rages against the ego with merciless violence, as if it had taken possession of the whole of the sadism available in the person concerned. Following our view of sadism, we should say that the destructive component had entrenched itself in the super-ego and turned against the ego. What is now holding sway in the super-ego is, as it were, a pure culture of the death instinct, and in fact it often enough succeeds in driving the ego into death, if the latter does not fend off its tyrant in time by the change round into mania [p. 53].

He adds:

> ... the ego gives itself up because it feels itself hated and persecuted by the super-ego, instead of loved. To the ego, therefore, living means the same as being loved — being loved by the super-ego, which here again appears as the representative of the id. The super-ego fulfills the same function of protecting and saving, that was fulfilled in earlier days by the father and later by Providence or Destiny. But, when the ego finds itself in an excessive real danger which it believes itself unable to over-

---

tired and feels helpless is not identical with self-destruction." Engel and Schmale's (1967) concept of giving up and giving in seems to have much in common with Bibring's idea of depression in which the ego lets itself die.

come by its own strength, it is bound to draw the same conclusion. It sees itself deserted by all protecting forces and lets itself die [p. 58].

Schilder's direct question to a patient — "Did you ever try to kill yourself?" — points to the deeper significance of suicide. Even when the sociological factors appear most prominent, there is anger and hatred turned on the self, as Hendin (1969) emphasizes. Hendin calls attention to the fact that black suicide reached a peak at the same time as black homicide did. He also makes the interesting observation that the suicide rate has decreased sharply in times of war, again raising the question about the relationship to hostility and killing.

In studying suicide among blacks in relation to difficulties with the law, Hendin underlines the feeling of impotence in dealing with arbitrary authority. I think this is related to narcissistic mortification and the feeling of humiliation. But Hendin contends that this simply reinforces an underlying guilt relating to these black men's own rage, violence, and murderous impulses. Let me quote Hendin: "If so much of the black man's behaviour, including the riots in which he burns his own community, still seems self-destructive, in the black man's attempt to cope with frustration and rage, his feelings of impotence and self-hatred often cause his own anger to turn against himself. They see living itself as an act of violence and regard death as the only way to control their rage" (p. 147).[13]

I have by no means exhausted the many conditions in which suicide may occur. Among these are histrionic, melodramatic suicide attempts; suicides by impulse-ridden characters (e.g., wrist-slashing) and by alcoholics (e.g., alcoholic hallucinosis); suicide in cases of organic delirium; and many others. Suicide is a final common pathway reached through many routes. My focus has been on its occurrence in relation to depression.

[13] There are cultures in which violence is the main mode of communication and survival. I had occasion to set up a program for mental health aides in a community mental health center located in one of the most deprived black and Hispanic areas in the country. At some point a shooting took place between two of the mental health aides, deriving from some dispute over money. In talking to one of the participants, I learned that this was the only way he knew to deal with what he felt was an injustice and humiliation. When I asked him why he had joined the program, he indicated he wanted to better himself, so as to achieve some upward mobility on both the economic and social scales. I pointed out to him that on higher levels there were other forms of communication than violence, and that is what he had come to learn in the program. Violence in such a setting was counterproductive. (Obviously I did not use such language.) After several interviews he seemed to grasp what I was telling him and gradually he did move along in an upward direction successfully.

It should be clear that in psychotic depression several factors tend to run like a red thread through the picture. The first of these is loss. The second is a reaction of hatred and anger to this loss, and the third, a feeling of guilt at one's culpability in contributing to this loss in some way. I have indicated that the hatred and aggression may be primary. We can understand the pathological resolution of the conflict into mania as a blurring of the distinction among the various psychic structures, making possible the redirection of these forces to the outside rather than to the self.

Various aspects of the psychotic process, which I shall discuss in more detail in Part III, are present in the psychotic affective disorders. Disintegrative fears, for instance, may be seen in gross depressive somatic delusions, such as "my body is rotting away" or "my brain is turning to water." Defenses such as psychotic denial and introjection are also present. Distortions of the position of the ego vis-à-vis reality bring in their wake distortion of the self and the object, as well as intersystemic conflicts between the ego and the superego. Crucial to the impairment of ego functions in psychotic depression is the loss of reality testing. All this adds up to the psychotic state in the depressive and the manic. It should be added that in these regards the structural model of the mind has expanded our understanding of the psychotic affective disorders. We shall now turn to a more detailed look at this model.

6.
The Structural Model
of the Mind

The structural model of the mind as a frame of reference for understanding the psychotic process was already used by Freud in many earlier contributions. I have discussed at length the concepts of withdrawal and restitution and the dual instinct theory as they relate to the psychotic process. Inherent in this discussion was the question of the fate of the self and the object — and the nature of the object is clearly related to reality.

Although I shall subsequently direct myself more extensively to the role of reality in the psychotic process, I should like to point out here that Freud dealt with this facet throughout his writings (see 1894, 1896, 1911a, 1911b, 1914b, 1920, 1923). These ideas come to a head in his 1924 papers, in which he places the conflict in neurosis between the ego and the id and in psychosis between the ego and the external world (reality): "neurosis is the result of a conflict between the ego and its id, whereas psychosis is the analogous outcome of a similar disturbance in the relations between the ego and the external world" (1924b, p. 149). Specifically, the concept of narcissistic neurosis is modified somewhat to represent only melancholia (i.e., a conflict between the ego and the superego), whereas transference neurosis represents a conflict between the ego and the id, and psychosis one between the ego and the outer world (see Chapter 10).

To begin to understand the view of the psychotic process given within the framework of the structural model, I would like to cite Hartmann's (1953) remarks on the close relationship between the role of differentiation in self and object development and differentiation of the psychic structures from each other. By and large there is agreement that dedifferentiation between and among the psychic structures is responsible for much of the symptomatology in psychosis — both ego-id dedifferentiation and ego-superego dedifferentiation. As Jacobson (1971) points out: "psychotics retransform not only functional psychic units but whole functional systems, such as the (ego-) id or the superego (-ego) into omnipotent object or self images which, insofar as they are dangerous or frightening, are attacked and eradicated" (p. 131).

I think there is agreement that in psychosis, as part of this structural dedifferentiation, there is a relative closeness of the various functions of the ego to the id. Ego functions begin to operate on the model of the id. They lack organization and lose the capacity for delay and discharge. Cathexes become highly mobile, with primary process taking the place of normal ego processes. The marked contamination of both primary and secondary autonomous ego functions certainly makes for severe impairment of the ego's position vis-à-vis reality in all spheres.

Psychotic patients show a frightening propensity for dipping deep into the unconscious and coming up at times with relatively undistorted id-derived material, hitherto repressed. The result is frequently a replacement of reality by fantasy, with a dominant invasion of primary process into many ego functions, affecting thought, feeling, and behavior. The regressive propensities can be seen in the rather primitive, pregenital manifestation of their instinctual drives, frequently reflected in a marked ambivalent reaction toward objects.

The lack of differentiation between and among the psychic structures also has an impact on affects. Jacobson (1971) points out that superego regression, or defective superego structure, may, by virtue of a loss of the superego's signal function, result in a tendency to rapid or extreme pathological mood swings, or to a lowering or rising of the mood level. There is, moreover, an inability to delineate affects clearly. Eissler (1953) indicates that ordinarily, in the course of normal psychic development, certain defense mechanisms arise from congealed emotions, which have been tamed by the ego from instinctual drives. In the schizophrenic the ego lacks such defensive structure, which should ordinarily establish a relative independence of the psychic apparatus from emotions. This lack leads to the state in which emotions and ego cannot be distinguished and seem identical. One of my psychotic character patients revealed something seen in many psychotics — an inability to differentiate among her various affects. She did not know whether what she was feeling was love, hatred, anger, or fear, or whether these feelings were a true reflection of herself.

As I indicated above, the lack of structural differentiation affects the position of the superego. In Jacobson's (1953) view, the dedifferentiation between the psychic structures is closely related to the lack of separation in self- and object representations. Referring to the impact on the superego, she says:

> The superego will not be a firmly integrated system. It will be personified, unstable in its functions, and will tend either to assume excessive control of the ego or to disintegrate, dissolve, and merge with object and self-representations. It will be easily reprojected on the outside world. The superego, the object and self-representations will be prone to a regressive fragmentation, to a splitting up again into primitive early images and, on the other hand, to fusions with one another [p. 62].

Superego development has generally been associated with resolution of the Oedipus complex. There is therefore a need to account for the manifestations of the more regressive type of superego generally seen in psychosis. Zetzel (1953) asks whether it is not possible that in depressive illness regression takes place to the now generally accepted precursors of the definitive superego—the introjections and identifications of the pregenital period. Melanie Klein (1928a, 1928b) assumes an archaic pregenital existence of the superego, consistent with her view that oedipal fantasies appear in the early months of life. In the schizophrenic, she believes there is usually a primitive archaic superego, often with a mixture of persecutory and depressive features, the origins of which go back to the first years of life.

In psychotic patients the superego has not achieved that degree of depersonification characteristic of mature development. One encounters regressive and archaic precursors with an alien quality and a marked tendency toward externalization and projection. The superego is at the same time lacunae-riddled. Concomitant with impulsive break-throughs, we find hypercritical and harsh reactions, possibly leading to disproportionate guilt and depression. Along these lines, Wexler (1951a) views defective superego formation as fundamental to schizophrenia. He believes that an archaic, harsh, destructive superego overwhelms the ego, ultimately leading to the ego's fragmentation and a disruption of ego functions.

The attempt to delineate those areas in psychosis which are definitive is obviously influenced by the existing frames of reference. With expanding knowledge, it becomes clear that many frames of reference need to be considered. Certainly lack of harmony between and among the various psychic structures brings in its wake much of what we see in psychotic symptomatology. Yet much remains to be examined. I find

Hartmann's (1953) comments pertinent here: "What has become known of the development of early object relationship, ego-id relationship, defenses, reality testing, constitutes a vast reservoir of data which today we consider essential to any systematic approach to psychosis" (p. 178).

Let us see if in an attempt at synthesis we can delineate some of the areas brought out by our discussion thus far. Most of the questions can be subsumed under the following:

1. Can we clarify what we mean by reality?

2. Why is it so essential for reality to be retained? What is the danger, the threat that requires such severe measures — namely, the changing of existing reality?

3. Is there anything specific to the nature of the conflict in psychosis, different from that in neurosis, which might require such drastic means?

4. What are the specific techniques for dealing with this conflict?

5. What ego functions are involved in maintaining the denial that permits and supports such a degree of reality alteration? Can we see in these disturbed ego functions anything specific to psychosis?

As I have already indicated, these questions can be summarized:

1. Is there a conflict or danger specifically and uniquely associated with the psychotic process in contrast to the neurotic?

2. Are there modes of defense or operations in response to the particular danger that characterize the psychotic process?

3. Are there unique ego functions or ego impairments that are more characteristic for the psychotic process than for the neurotic?

These three questions outline what I see as the essential components of the psychotic process. It is to their more specific aspects that we shall now direct our attention.

PART III

THE
PSYCHOTIC
PROCESS

7.
The Nature of the Danger
and the Conflict

The first question I shall explore is whether there is a conflict or danger uniquely associated with the psychotic process, as opposed to the neurotic one. As I indicated above, Freud (1924a, 1924b) is not too specific about the nature of the danger in reality, but rather focuses on the way psychotic patients react to a painful reality. Jacobson (1967) indicates that Freud does not consider the particular instinctual and narcissistic conflicts preceding and inducing the psychotic break with reality. In my opinion, the problem of danger must be viewed hierarchically. The meaning of the danger and possibly the modes of coping with it are phase-related. Freud himself clearly demonstrates this in his discussion of anxiety (1926). Within the stages of psychic development, these phase-related dangers assume forms that refer to the level of object relations, the stage of ego and reality development, as well as instinctual demands.

Basic Anxiety

No matter which way one looks at it, the relation between anxiety and its biological function cannot be ignored. Anxiety is, after all, intimately tied up with the autonomic nervous system, which we might say represents a final common pathway for situations requiring an outlet or release—danger being one of these. At certain stages of life, conditions may prevail that evoke an automatic reflex response which has a utilitarian value at the time. Birth seems to be such a situation. Crying, the respiratory response, the temperature regulatory apparatus, the gastro-intestinal movements, the cardiac responses—all seem to be set into play to meet an emergency situation, a threat to survival at the most primitive level.

While such a response comes into play reflexively, automatically, perhaps as an expression of discharge to accumulated tension, it has utilitarian value. It is not difficult to visualize a newborn infant in recurrent states of tension, evoked by biological needs. Outward manifestations of this tension, such as discharge reactions with crying and kicking, have all the appearance of discomfort. The tension is experienced passively and most likely for some time nonideationally. After a while we might assume that at the deepest levels of the psyche a sense of helplessness and of inability to cope with the accumulating tension develops. This feeling of helplessness and inability to cope with an overwhelming situation constitutes a dangerous situation, and provokes an automatic reflex response, reflected in crying, kicking, etc. To some extent, this is a basic type of traumatic situation.

As time goes on a more conscious awareness of helplessness and the accompanying physiological responses may enter into play. Whether one should call this anxiety is debatable. It has an amorphous, all-pervading, nonspecific quality. One could perhaps more correctly look at this as a prototype of a reaction to a danger situation, as a precursor to anxiety. I will refer to it as *basic anxiety*. In later life this basic anxiety may automatically come into play in every danger situation, although generally appropriate action will take over and this prototypic reaction will remain in the background. If it does come into the foreground and dominate the picture, it is pathological, for its original purposeful role no longer exists.

I think that in most primitive states, disagreeable tensions related to lack of need gratification are perceived nonideationally at the biological level. When actual biological threats to survival are involved, such as a life-threatening illness, the danger may also be perceived nonideationally. In time these percepts come to have psychic representation; they are the prototype for what is experienced as survival-threatening. The psychotic — who is pressured by unneutralized and deneutralized instinctual drives, whose ego is weak to begin with, and whose hold on reality is already tenuous — may experience an identity of perception of current threats and dangers with the early survival-threatening experiences of infancy.[1] What may be particularly significant is not so much the actual experiences from infancy but their impact on the developing and still vulnerable ego structures. These may remain in a somewhat diffuse and fragmented state, or at best a poorly integrated

---

[1] One should also note the "kernel of historical truth," which supports the feeling of reality of analogous subsequent traumatic states.

state, highly susceptible to dedifferentiation in the face of subsequent "danger" experiences.

This basic anxiety, which evolves as a response to the sensed possibility of disintegration and dissolution of self, is what I believe we encounter in the psychotic process. Ultimately it revolves around the issue of survival. Its psychic representation is fear of disintegration and dissolution of self, i.e., psychic and emotional death. Because of the amorphous, all-pervasive quality of this fear, the adult psychotic patient finds it difficult to articulate. Frequently when such patients are asked to describe their anxiety they are unable to do so: "I just don't know what to say." This anxiety may be accompanied by restlessness and even a kind of pan-anxiety. Some of my patients have spoken of an eternal nothingness, going on forever. Since there is no limitation in time or space to this nothingness, it is overwhelmingly frightening. As one patient put it: it is not quite death or dying. It is disappearing, being completely engulfed, dissolving — nothingness.

A number of authors have referred to this kind of anxiety. Sullivan (1956) describes the schizophrenic's terror as "an almost unceasing fear of becoming an exceedingly unpleasant form of nothingness by collapse of the self system" (p. 318). Waelder (1960) indicates: "there also seems to exist in psychoses anxiety of an intensity and intolerability not encountered to any comparable degree in normal life or in the neuroses, a mega-anxiety as it were" (p. 206). Melanie Klein (1946) points to a primordial anxiety with the death instinct as its source, while Winnicott (1970) speaks of annihilation anxiety. He says that a patient suffering from such anxiety cannot take survival for granted and relates psychotic anxiety developmentally to disturbances in the earliest mothering care of the infant.[2]

Jacobson (1967) specifically differentiates psychotic danger and anxiety from that found in the neurotic. She explains: "Whereas the central fear of the neurotic is castration fear, the psychotic is afraid of an impending dissolution of the psychic structure — involving a partial or total breakdown of object and self representations and resulting in a withdrawal from the external world to the point of manifest psychotic symptom formation" (p. 13). In further clarifying her distinction, Jacobson states:

[2] Basic and primitive anxiety, it should be noted, may be present in other conditions. For instance, I believe it characterizes the catastrophic reaction in severe organic syndromes.

> At this point I only want to stress that, in contrast to neurotic patients, psychotics tend to use the external world for the purpose of preventing a dissolution of their ego and superego structures and a regressive dedifferentiation and disintegration that would threaten them with a manifest psychotic breakdown. For this reason they may not hold on, or even cling, to the external world, but try to change it, to create one that will suit their special needs, and to reject and deny those aspects that are of no use to them [p. 19].

For the neurotic, the external object generally retains its identity as an object. In the psychotic, however, differentiation is tenuous and may in gross decompensation be lost.

Another picture of the psychotic danger emerges from Mahler's (1968) description of children who are vulnerable to stress, with the fear of disintegrating, fragmenting, and falling apart. Such "organismic distress," Mahler suggests, may be the forerunner of anxiety proper. The neurobiological patternings are thrown out of kilter by organismic distress, and somatic memory traces are established which may amalgamate with later experiences.[3] In discussing symbiotic child psychosis, Mahler points out that previous traumas predispose the child to react drastically to changes. She observes: "His [the child's] anxiety reactions are so intense and so diffuse that they are reminiscent of the organismic distress of early infancy" (p. 73). In other words, somatic memory traces of organismic distress may create a heightened predisposition to anxiety in the psychotic, so that when confronted by a situation which should evoke ordinary anxiety, he experiences organismic panic. It appears to me that the feeling that such situations cannot be mastered, with the fear of consequent disintegration, is basic to this panic. Freud (1926) distinguishes between automatic (id) and signal (ego) anxiety and postulates that the ego's helplessness in the face of excitations it cannot deal with evokes automatic or id anxiety. This is not too dissimilar from the basic anxiety experienced in the psychotic.

Pao (1979) uses the term "organismic panic," explaining that "when conflicts are reactivated, schizophrenics do not experience anxiety as it is familiar to the average human being; they experience organismic panic" (p. 218). Organismic panic is related to the collapse of psychic structure, with a refusion of self- and object images and an inability to sustain a realistic concept of self. Although Pao compares his concept to Greenacre's and Mahler's concept of organismic distress, he also differ-

[3] This is not unlike the organ memory system described by Ferenczi (1916–1917) and Tausk (1919).

entiates it: "The term organismic distress, as used by Greenacre and Mahler, emphasizes more the physiological than the psychological aspect of the matter, whereas the term 'organismic panic' refers to psychological experience — the experience of the ego, even though the ego has developed defectively" (p. 220). With this in mind, Pao describes organismic panic as "attended by a shocklike reaction in which the ego's integrative function is temporarily paralyzed" (p. 221). He equates this view with the concept of internal catastrophe. In his opinion, organismic panic takes place when the psyche senses a link between earlier organismic distress situations and the present threat of ego-disorganizing experiences.

At this point I should perhaps clarify that I do not believe basic anxiety is necessarily related to conflict. The fear of disintegration, of falling apart, of being overwhelmed by forces one cannot control, may be defect-derived. I use the term "conflict" in the more restricted sense, to denote an opposition of forces that has not been resolved. Defects may predispose to conflict. With the term "defect" I am in most instances referring to an ego defect or relative ego insufficiency. This defect may appear in the face of unusually strong drives or an unusually strong and archaic superego — all of these may coincide. In this sense, then, basic anxiety is not too dissimilar from traumatic anxiety.

Fear of Disintegration and Fragmentation

The danger of disintegration and self-dissolution may be expressed in fears of fragmentation, of breaking into bits and pieces. Melanie Klein (1946) describes the fragmentation of parts of the object via oral-sadistic and cannibalistic attacks on the breast and nipple, which fragment these and leave them in bits. Through projective identification, the infant too feels itself in fragments and bits. One of my patients had severe body-image distortions with an omnipresent feeling of not being together. The threat of any illness threw him into panic lest he become fragmented and fall apart. Another patient described her body as a mosaic or, at times, a flagstone terrace. The various parts of her body were joined to each other in the same way flagstones are by cement. She felt that under the impact of powerful emotions she would fall apart.

The potential for disintegration and fragmentation makes such patients unable to cope with the pressure of strong instinctual drives. Waelder (1960) refers to the "fear of the intensity of one's own instinctual drives, i.e., the fear of being overwhelmed by uncontrollable forces and thus disintegrating as it were, as a person" (p. 161). The welling up of seemingly uncontrollable aggressive forces thus represents a particular danger for the psychotic. Waelder relates the psychotic's anxiety to a direct fear of disintegration, independent of the fear of outside punishment. It is not simply that there is a fear of retaliation, as may occur in the neurotic (i.e., the obsessional). The danger is that the self will disintegrate in the face of powerful forces it cannot assimilate. The same holds true for any strong emotional experience. It represents a threat to the fragile sense of self.

A borderline patient was sitting on a couch opposite a person who was saying things that enraged her. I thought at first she was holding onto the couch to control her destructive impulses against her adversary. Actually, it turned out that this was to prevent herself from falling apart. With her mounting rage, she suddenly felt as if her body were a mosaic made up of thousands of little pieces which would spring apart if she let go of the couch. During analysis, with the welling up of homosexual impulses, this patient experienced intense disintegrative anxiety, with world destruction perceptions. Another patient spoke of a bug inside her, which she said was her anger. It was limitless, without extremities, and it could swell up and encompass her completely, enveloping and destroying her. This patient did not express a fear of retaliation; her fear was that she would be consumed by her anger. The fear of disintegration related not only to aggressive drives, but to libidinal ones as well.

The psychotic's fear of self-disintegration may be projected in the form of world disintegration dreams or delusions (see Chapter 4, Section B). That is, world disintegration manifestations may reflect an internal awareness of disintegration, splitting, and fragmentation, which has been externalized. In one of my psychotic patients it became very clear that any upsurge of instinctual forces had a disintegrative and fragmenting effect so that they were perceived as a threat to survival. She felt herself being taken over by conflicting, uncontrollable forces, which would eventuate in a dissolution of self. She tried to ward off this danger by projection, in the form of world destruction hallucinations and delusions. Looking out the window, she saw what she felt was the beginning of the end of the world—bombs, explosions, buildings falling apart. The conflicting and warring factions within herself were also projected and incorporated into this doomsday picture.

In the analysis of these patients with disintegrative anxiety, body-image distortions and their accompanying psychic correlates are prominent. The sense of a unified body image is highly impaired. Federn (1932) refers to "an enduring feeling and knowledge that our ego is continuous and persistent despite interruptions by sleep or unconsciousness" (p. 61). He refers to a somatic and psychic feeling, experienced as one. In psychotic fragmentation and splitting, however, the various somatic and psychic components may be experienced individually. Thus, Winnicott (1970) points to the disruption of the continuity of being in severely disturbed patients. One might also cite Jacobson's (1964) remarks about the objective and subjective aspects of identity. In her opinion, it is the subjective aspect, the *sense* of identity that is markedly impaired in these patients.

The psychobiological prototype for disintegration relates to very early stages in development, before the unified body image and psychic self have developed. Yet, in discussing the potential for regression to this early stage, Schilder (1935) emphasizes that the potential for body disintegration exists side by side with the potential for cohesion. As he explains:

> One would like to say that we lose the unity of our body only under special pathological conditions; but we also have to remember how much the feeling of our body varies under normal conditions. When we touch an object with a stick we feel with the end of the stick. We feel that clothes eventually become a part of ourselves. We build the picture of our body again and again. . . . There are forces of hatred scattering the picture of our own body and forces of love putting it together [p. 166].

Schilder then points out that even though "the unit is. . . in continual danger of losing some of its parts," one never fully loses these parts:

> What has once been part of the body does not lose this quality completely. The bowel movement also separates the faeces only physically from the body, psychologically they remain a part of ourselves. We are dealing with a spreading of the body image into the world. Finger-nails, everything which comes out of the mouth and nose, hair which has been cut off, always remain in some psychological relation to the body. The organization of the body-image is a very flexible one [p. 188].[4]

With these ideas in mind, Schilder elaborates on the pathological manifestations of "a general fear about the integrity of the body," or

[4] I wonder whether this is a variant, in a nonpsychotic sense, of self-nonself dedifferentiation. There is no separateness. As such, could this be the soil in which projective identification develops?

what he calls "a general dismembering motive and fear" (p. 190). This dismembering motive, he contends, "plays an important part" in psychosis and is quite marked in alcoholic hallucinosis. The patient hears vivid voices, generally two people talking to each other about dismembering and mutilating the patient. Although these remarks usually refer to the genitals, they may also relate to other body parts. In the desire to escape this fate, the patient may attempt suicide. Interestingly enough, Schilder found that often the suicide attempt itself involved clear self-mutilation. For instance, one patient slashed his throat.

The dismembering motive can be directly related to other aspects of psychic fragmentation in the psychotic. The patient with world disintegration fears I described above (see p. 127), split her thoughts into good and bad thoughts. There were good and bad parts to her body as well. If she allowed bad thoughts to stay in her mind, this would result in her death by dismemberment, and gradually the different parts of her body would be distributed to the other patients for the good of humanity.

The disintegrative effects of projected hatred are brought out in Schilder's (1935) report of a patient who had marked sadistic impulses to tear others apart. Yet this patient also feared her own disintegration. As Schilder points out: "It is, however, remarkable that this sadism directed against others also affects her own body. She does not feel a tendency to hurt herself, but she feels her body falling to pieces. . . . The patient is dismembered under the influence of her own sadistic tendencies against the outside world and against herself. At the same time there are parts of her in the outside world, and she projects herself into the outside world" (p. 164).[5]

The sense of disintegration and loss of unity is graphically described by the patient: "I am completely in pieces, there is no ground under the feet when you are not on the earth. . . . When I am melting I have no

[5] To me, this sounds like what Melanie Klein refers to as projective identification. The impulses are pushed onto others and experienced in the self. One might also note again how self-nonself dedifferentiation brings in its wake fear of self-disintegration through destruction of the object. Campion's (1981) report on eight schizophrenic men who had committed matricide is of interest here. Several of these men had experienced sensations of disintegration, expressed in the form of somatic delusions. The cause was projected onto the mother, and she was seen as physically and emotionally destroying them. One mother was accused of destroying her son's viscera and mind, another of destroying his physical well-being and his separate identity. In some instances these feelings were supported by the mother's dominating behavior and her seeming attempt to enforce symbiosis. An overwhelming fear of disintegration led to the murderous attack on the mother.

hands, I go into a doorway. . . . In the doorway I can gather together the pieces of my body" (p. 159). It is almost as if a structured situation were necessary to ward off disintegration. Schilder's patient goes on: "When the anxiety in the street catches me I do not feel anything, then I hurt myself with my nails in order to feel myself" (p. 159). She describes what one of my own patients did; she bit her nails to feel her identity. A wrist-slasher I examined described the whole experience of cutting her wrists and seeing her blood as the need to feel herself, her body, as really being there.

Another viewpoint is articulated by Schwartz (1978), who de-emphasizes the regressive aspects of the disorganizing and fragmenting experience of the schizophrenic. Instead, he cites "new (to that person) phenomena which are a regular part of that schizophrenic episode of regression" (p. 79). By "new," Schwartz means experiences not "seen as previously existing organizations of growth in that person's developmental processes." And he states: "Nor does fragmentation, for example, seem describable as a defensive regressive return to an earlier level of developmental adaptation" (pp. 79–80). Yet, as I have indicated, the earliest stages in psychic development do present just such fragmentation of the self, which has to be ultimately integrated into a unified body and psychic self. I believe what Schwartz questions is whether this is at that time defensive in any way (cf. Melanie Klein's [1946] views of this stage of psychic development).[6]

Dedifferentiation

The possibility of dedifferentiation and self-object fusion is crucial to the basic anxiety of the psychotic. As Modell (1968) points out: "when there is intense fear of merging with a 'bad' object the subject may fear a loss of identity, a dread of being influenced, and ultimately may fear complete annihilation" (p. 37). Schur (1955) also sees this as a crucial problem. He remarks: "The simultaneous tendency for refusion of self and object representation and for vagueness of self boundaries constitutes the greatest threat to the maintenance of reality, to females as well as males. In the schizophrenic the defense against this most

---

[6] Actually when we speak of regression, we speak of two aspects — form and content. These are translated into the language of more recent levels of psychic development. The regression consists of modes of dealing with problems which have been translated at many levels in line with what has subsequently transpired in psychic development. The latter may nonetheless be influenced by primary process.

primitive identification can only result in feeble, repetitious and futile attempts to find the restitution of an external object" (pp. 150–151). In a similar vein, Loewald (1951) speaks of primary identity, i.e., union with the mother, as the source of the deepest dread: "the original unity and identity, undifferentiated and unstructured, of the psychic apparatus and environment, is as much of a danger for the ego as the demand of the 'paternal castration threat' to give it up altogether" (p. 15).

Yet, at the same time that the fear of disintegration and dedifferentiation feeds the basic anxiety of the psychotic, there is nonetheless a resort to regressive self-nonself diffusion in the interest of defense. What Bak (1943) calls "flowing over" does permit some dilution of the impulses, making it possible to deal with and perhaps even to control them and thus ensure survival. It is during the stage of unconditional omnipotence that one's survival seems under one's own control. Blurring of ego boundaries and dedifferentiation may be a step toward recapturing the breast, making the nourishing object a part of the self. Yet this is not an unmixed gain for the psychotic, as there is also the danger of being engulfed by the object. Dedifferentiation turns out to be an illusion and the basic fear of disintegration may then drive the psychotic in the direction of restitution.[7] Still, deteriorated psychotics may abandon themselves to this psychic death, as the back wards of many an institution testify.

The whole question of withdrawal and restitution in relation to psychotic dedifferentiation is an issue I discussed earlier in detail (see Chapter 4, Section B).[8] At this point let me again comment on Bak's (1943) concept of "flowing over." He believes that the schizophrenic's anxiety is a reaction to a sinking back into a state of impersonality, with a concomitant push toward restitution and reconstruction in an attempt to arrest this sinking back. He maintains that "the concept of

[7] Some authors have attempted to describe many of the psychotic's actual clinical manifestations in terms of attempts to deal with the basic anxiety related to the fear of disintegration and dedifferentiation. Rosen (1950), who believes that the basic anxiety in the schizophrenic is a reaction to life-threatening deprivation, suggests that a good deal of the patient's symptomatology can be understood as the result of attempts to ward off such life-threatening deprivations by conjuring up life-saving gratifications.

[8] In a penetrating study Thomas Frosch (1974) describes William Blake's intense preoccupation with the problem of disintegration and restitution. Blake takes as his model, the myth of Creation, from the fall from Paradise to the ultimate restoration. The Fall is accompanied by a fragmentation and disintegration of the five senses and the restitution is achieved by unified perception, through the synthesis of the five senses. This process is a fundamental motif in Blake's poetry and art, as Frosch demonstrates.

decomposition results only from the isolated observations of the ego; if, however, we take into consideration the relation between the ego and the outer world, resulting from decomposition, it then becomes obvious that this relation is marked by the over-flowing of the personality into the outer world. There is a mechanism of self-cure which tends to prevent the dissolution and attempts to retain or reestablish the integrity of the personality" (p. 460). He indicates that the threat of dissolution of boundaries may be met by the ego with attempts to fortify these boundaries by building up an exaggeratedly demarcated personality.

From a different perspective, Freeman (1959) also suggests that in the severely regressed patient, such as the schizophrenic, one finds an attempt to regain, by whatever means, the sense of identity and the spatiotemporal orientation of normality. Anna Freud (1952) emphasizes that in some instances negativistic states may be used to ward off disintegration of the ego. As she explains it:

> . . . passive surrender to the love-object may signify a return from object-love proper to its forerunner in the emotional development of the infant, i.e., primary identification with the love-object. This is a regressive step which implies a threat to the intactness of the ego, i.e., a loss of personal characteristics which are merged with the characteristics of the love-object. The individual fears this regression in terms of dissolution of the personality, loss of sanity, and defends himself against it by a complete rejection of all objects (negativism) [p. 265].

The fear of dissolution is met with in some patients not only by negativism but also by massive denial and the development of delusions, stereotypies, and various mannerisms. I have already described in considerable detail a patient who used all these modes in her attempt to differentiate and reestablish a self (see pp. 96, 121, 126). Let me simply recall to mind a few points here, indicative of the recurrent interplay of feelings of dissolution and catastrophe with restitutive delusional material. Remember that the patient's feelings of disintegration were followed by a period of religious conversion. She was convinced that the world would end on Good Friday, but in the Resurrection she would survive. It was apparent, however, that she was not too sure of the latter point. One could see her panic, her fear of disintegration and dissolution, side by side with her restitution fantasies. Throughout the clinical course she was preoccupied with imminent death, fear of loss of control, and fear of disintegration. In my work with her it became clear that whatever the function of her various symptoms — the delusions, the stereotypies, the mannerisms, the negativism — they were brought into the service of combating the basic anxiety deriving from the threat to preservation of self and object. As such, they were essential for psychic survival.

Even though regressive dedifferentiation may be resorted to defensively by the psychotic, it still represents a danger. The psychotic finds the blurring of ego boundaries frightening and disturbing. One of Jacobson's (1954a) patients clearly expressed this fear: "Do you know the difference between closeness, likeness, sameness and oneness? Close is close, as with you; when you are like the other, but he is still he and you are you; but oneness is not two, it is one, that's horrible, horrible — don't get too close, get away from the couch, I don't want to be you" (p. 251).

A psychotic patient of mine, when somewhat better, discussed this problem of loss of self in connection with her acting. She mentioned that, according to certain schools of acting, it was important to "lose yourself and come as close as possible to being the person you are trying to portray." But she added that you have to keep a little bit of yourself on this side; you have to retain a part of your own self — "otherwise you become psychotic like I was." Although she was constantly on guard against this eventuality, on one occasion her efforts failed and she made a bizarre suicide attempt, which had many of the features of the current role she was playing. This resemblance was recognized by the director, who spoke to me about it. He indicated how frightening at times it was to see how long it took the patient to come back to herself. In a typically schizophrenic *pars pro toto* way, she once put some white powder on her face and became the nurse, a role she was supposed to play.

Even changes in the external environment may disrupt the body image, indicating the problem of preserving identity. One patient, for instance, became quite upset when I moved my office. She had already formed an image of herself in relation to my office. She knew who she was, who my office was, etc. The new office was, first of all, too big, and she felt somehow engulfed by it. She was not quite sure of who or where she was in relation to it. This tendency toward anthropomorphism and identification with the nonhuman environment, so commonly seen in psychotics, also surfaced when this patient moved from one apartment to another. Again, she knew who she was in the old place, but somehow could not identify herself in the new one and even found it threatening at times. She felt guilty and visited her old apartment to make up for having abandoned it. In a sense, this was a mutual consolation for their common loneliness. Yet she also felt quite anxious about her inability to separate herself from the old apartment.

Why should dedifferentiation be so anxiety-provoking? It is the possibility that dedifferentiation might eventuate in total loss and dissolution of self that makes it so frightening to the psychotic or borderline psychotic. This threat may be especially frightening because the possibility of reversal is minimal. In the normal person and in the neurotic, the blurring of ego boundaries and dedifferentiation may be tolerated in the belief that ultimately ego boundaries can be reestablished intact. It resembles regression in the service of the ego (or under ego control), as there is always the awareness of enough capacity for ego integration to reverse dedifferentiation. In the psychotic, however, since the chance of reversal is less, the process of dedifferentiation may really eventuate in dissolution of the self. Thus, in the psychotic, dedifferentiation is a real danger.

While we can only guess at some of the reasons why dissolution of self is so frightening, it should be clear that this is one of the deep fears in the psychotic. When she had improved somewhat, the psychotic patient described above said that the problem in schizophrenia was overwhelming and paralyzing fear. As I have already mentioned, she could not articulate what this fear was—it was not quite death or just dying; it was disappearing, nothingness, being completely engulfed and dissolving.

The psychotic's basic fear of dissolution makes unneutralized or deneutralized instinctual demands a more devastating problem than in the neurotic. Whether we postulate innate or acquired quantitative differences in drive strength, a weak or weakened ego, or disturbances in the ego function of neutralization (Hartmann, 1953), instinctual demands, exerting themselves on a weak ego, bring into focus the problem of possible disintegration and dissolution of self. Homosexual fears, for instance, are reinforced in the potential psychotic by the underlying disintegrative anxiety—loss of control would bring in its wake the underlying disintegrative anxiety.[9] I referred in Chapter 4 (p. 97) to a patient who, with the upsurge of homosexual feelings, developed world disintegration fantasies. She feared the welling up of forces she could not control and being overwhelmed by these wishes. The feared fragmentation was projected in a hallucination of natural disaster, which

[9] Katan (1950) discusses the psychotic's gradual retreat from a dangerous reality, through various stages in psychic development, to the ultimate point of dedifferentiation. He believes the basic danger to be the preoedipal feminine homosexual strivings, with which a weak ego was unable to cope.

contained not only aggressive impulses but also the wish for, and fear of, union with the mother.

In the psychotic, dedifferentiation or a developmental lack in differentiation makes it possible for the various parts of the psychic structure, reality, objects, etc., to fuse, so that self and object become one. As Fenichel (1937) states so well, the ego and the self are part of reality. Inevitably then, loss of the object means possible dissolution of self. That is, the psychotic views loss of control as eventuating in being overwhelmed and engulfed by instinctual drives, ultimately resulting in destruction of reality and self. Again, the danger of disintegration and dissolution, the threat to survival of the self, appear very real to the psychotic. External frustrations and deprivations may trigger off this basic, primitive fear and, by projection, come to represent the internal threat.

The underlying danger the psychotic defends against is thus psychic and emotional death. It is this threat to survival that leads the psychotic to the desperate means of creating an illogical reality, to which he holds on tenaciously. Delusional fixity is enforced by the tremendous fear of disintegration should the delusion be given up.[10] Moreover, we should note again the kernel of historical truth that makes the threat to survival a real one for the psychotic. As I discussed above, there were in all likelihood real survival-threatening experiences in the early life of the psychotic patient, which may literally have meant annihilation. Identity of perception brings in its wake attempts to ward off dissolution and to preserve psychic survival. All the manifestations we see as pathological are in the interests of preservation of self.

Rosenfeld (1950) describes how the confusion in the psychotic subsides with the beginning of the delusion. The delusion almost seems to have an integrative, unifying effect on identity. I have already mentioned the feeling of clarity and the diminution in anxiety (or at least the changes in its quality) with which the onset of an organized delusion may be accompanied. Moreover, the systematized delusion, itself a product of synthesis, may, if successfully walled off, facilitate the re-integration and functioning of the rest of the personality at a higher level, with good reality testing. Schreber, for instance, returned to the community with his delusional system well-established but was able to

---

[10] I should note again that it is hardly likely that the return of the denied, as postulated by Waelder (1951), accounts for the fixity of the delusion. At most, it accounts in part for the means whereby the delusion is developed (just as the return of the repressed does).

discuss world affairs and legal problems intelligently, with complete clarity. His brief for his appeal is a model of clarity (Schreber, 1900).

Having said all this, there is still the question of whether the threat to psychic survival is the basic danger for all kinds of psychoses, or whether it is most particular for schizophrenia. This is hard for me to answer. Basically, I am inclined to believe that the fear of disintegration and dissolution is present in all psychoses (I have alluded to it in discussing the psychotic affective disorders, as well as the catastrophic reactions in organic brain disease). The differing clinical manifestations depend on the extent to which this fear becomes conscious, the ways in which the psyche attempts to deal with this threat, and on the success or failure of these attempts. The outcome, of course, will be determined genetically by the level of psychic development.

Finally, it should be evident from the discussion so far that the nature of the relationship to the object and the latter's preservation are very much involved in the danger to the psychotic. The object is reality. The psychotic needs the object for survival, yet dedifferentiation and merging with the object is both desired and feared. The fear of dissolution and loss of self is closely related through projective identification with the object. We have discussed the need to combat this fear. Let us turn now to a more specific examination of some of the defenses employed by the psychotic in this attempt.

8.
The Nature of Defense

The second question I proposed in examining the psychotic process was: Are there any characteristic modes of defense in response to a given conflict that differ in psychosis as opposed to neurosis? As indicated in the last chapter, many of the psychotic's maneuvers derive from attempts to deal with intense anxiety over possible loss of the object, as well as the self, and to ward off that loss. Yet these maneuvers may in themselves be a source of anxiety, as in the use of dedifferentiation to deal with aggression. Such manifestations are generally associated with particular stages in psychic development and are presumed, when used subsequently, to be defensive. Yet they may equally reflect preexisting defects in a fragile ego, which are borrowed in the service of defense.

Melanie Klein (1946) suggests that certain manifestations encountered in childhood may not only be prototypes for psychotic defenses but may even actually be psychotic defenses, resorted to during early stages in psychic development to deal with conflicts not too dissimilar from those encountered in adulthood. Jacobson (1971) differs with Klein in this regard. She does not believe, for instance, that the adult patient's projective identification, observable either in the transference or acted out by the patient with objects in his environment, is a repetition of early infantile projective and introjective processes. In her view, this is to be understood as a later defensive process. As such, early processes cannot be observed in the transference.

Although Arlow and Brenner (1964) contend that the defenses of psychotic patients differ in many respects from those of nonpsychotics, they nonetheless suggest that there is no sharp dividing line between psychotics and nonpsychotics in this respect, since these defenses are against the emergence of anxiety connected with inner conflict. It is, however, my view that the nature of the danger and conflict, as well as the source of anxiety, is of some significance in determining the nature of the defense in the psychotic. Moreover, as will become evident in my later discussion (see especially Chapter 15), much of what takes place in psychosis reflects an interplay between defect and defense.

It has been generally accepted by psychoanalysts that neurosis is generated by a conflict between forces, out of which evolves a compromise containing elements of both forces. The processes instituted revolve around the pressure from instinctual demands at a relatively higher level in psychic development and the way in which the ego can best deal with these. Repression, displacement, reaction formation, and conversion are some of the observed higher-level defensive operations in these cases. In contrast, Jacobson (1971) points out: "In psychotics repression and other more normal defense mechanisms fail and are replaced by archaic processes.... When a patient hates and tries to kill and eradicate either his id or his superego in toto, this is, in my opinion, a characteristically psychotic type of defense" (p. 133).

In the psychotic, preservation of self and object is the main frame of reference. One encounters regressive dedifferentiation, introjective-projective techniques, projective identification, fragmentation, splitting, massive denial, and severe ego defects (loss of reality testing). Jacobson (1971) indicates: "Isolation, denial, introjection, and projection, instead of being used for the purpose of instinctual defense are in the psychotic utilized for 'loss and restitution' processes." She points to "the tendency of latent or ambulatory psychotics to externalize their conflicts, to act out, and to employ external objects and reality as an aid for their failing defenses" (p. 133). Again, however, I should add that the very defenses resorted to may lead to danger, in that they contain within them the possibility of loss of self (e.g., through regressive dedifferentiation).

I should like now to select for more extensive discussion some of these primitive defenses, such as splitting, denial, identification, introjection, and projective identification. I have already discussed psychotic projection at some length (see Chapter 4, Section C).

A.
Splitting and Fragmentation

Kernberg (1967, 1976a) argues that splitting is the essential defensive operation in the borderline personality organization, underlying all other defensive operations. I believe, however, it is important to differentiate splitting and fragmentation, both as stages in psychic development and as defensive operations. I view fragmentation as a very primitive stage in psychic development, preceding even the formation of part-self and part-object images. It is a precursor to splitting. Splitting comes into play at a higher level of psychic development, although it still occurs at a stage where part-self and part-object images have not been integrated and synthesized. In my view, splitting in the borderline patient is the correlate of fragmentation in the psychotic.

Many facets of splitting and fragmentation are evident in both borderline and psychotic patients and bring in their wake bizarre body-image fantasies in the borderline and delusions in the psychotic (see Tausk, 1919). I have referred to a psychotic character who felt that his head was not securely fastened to his neck, and grew his beard quite long so that it might help to keep his body intact. This patient also revealed a primitive defense mechanism, namely, splitting off and rejecting parts of his body when they became ill. Another patient with a psychotic organic brain syndrome tried to split off and personify his hemiplegic side.

Such splitting may also be resorted to at times to preserve the object. One patient, for instance, was able to split me into various parts so that she could destroy some of these parts and still preserve me and thus herself. It was easier to express her anger at me by directing it against one part. If she killed only that part, I could go on living. It would be terrible if she destroyed me, yet she had to express her hatred.

Although such manifestations often appear as fantasies in borderline patients, they may assume a feeling of reality during analysis of such patients, with decompensation into psychosis. (In the psychotic, as we have seen, body-image distortions frequently become part of the content of the patient's delusions.) That such severe psychotic-like regressive manifestations do arise during analysis of borderline patients was the subject of a panel discussion (see Weinshel, 1966; Frosch, 1967a, 1967b). In these patients dedifferentiation, fragmentation, and splitting may eventuate in psychotic symptomatology, although this is generally of a transient nature. Some believe that these phenomena are inherent in the analysis of borderline patients.

B.
Denial

I should like to turn now to the mechanism of denial, which is so prevalent in the psychotic process. Our understanding of denial as a mechanism in the psychotic process is complicated by the way the term is used and the fact that, as a phenomenon, denial is not necessarily psychotic. Nor can it be said that denial alone is responsible for psychotic manifestations. Denial, for instance, is an ever-present concomitant of the sense of conviction of delusional material (see Chapter 4). The delusion requires denial of facts which may be contrary to the delusion, as well as denial of certain inner experiences. Yet, as I have already pointed out, certain changes in ego functions vis-à-vis reality must also exist to maintain the delusion.

Freud deals with the mechanism of denial rather early (1894, Section 3), and later clearly implicates its use in psychosis (1911b, 1924a, 1924b). Near the end of his paper "Neurosis and Psychosis" (1924b), he makes a rather interesting observation, one which he subsequently expands (1927, 1938, 1940). He remarks: "it will be possible for the ego to avoid a rupture in any direction by deforming itself, by submitting to encroachments on its own unity and even perhaps by effecting a cleavage or division of itself. In this way the inconsistencies, eccentricities and follies of men would appear in a similar light to their sexual perversions, through the acceptance of which they spare themselves repressions" (pp. 152–153). He then raises the question of which mechanism, analogous to repression, facilitates the ego's detachment from the external world, and indicates that this has something to do with the withdrawal of the cathexis sent out by the ego. It seems to me that Freud is dealing here with the mechanism of denial, although he does not spell it out as such.

Later, in 1925, Freud turns to the problem of differentiating denial from repression and negation. He sees negation as a way of taking cognizance of that which might have been repressed. In a way, this is how the delusion finds its way into consciousness: the delusion represents a denial of an unconscious idea. "I love him," for instance, comes into consciousness in a distorted, negative way. However, in true negation alternatives are considered, whereas this is not so in the delusion. Negation, then, reflects a higher level of psychic development, in which the potential for judgment is already present. Denial is a more primitive mechanism.

Indeed, in discussing the question of negation and reality testing, Ferenczi (1926) looks at negation as a stage between denial and repression, as a kind of transition phase between ignoring and accepting reality. In the psychotic, we find complete denial. In the normal, we find acceptance of painful reality as something one has to live with. One cannot continue to deny painful reality into maturity. That is, the capacity to test reality and the building up of reality derive from the experiencing of pain and frustration, and the making of compromises, in terms of accepting something less unpleasant for something even more unpleasant. It is obvious that the early ego cannot tolerate pain; thus, unpleasant ideas must be ejected, and denial serves as an exceedingly important factor in this process of preserving the self. The mature ego, on the other hand, has to abandon the defensive denial of objects and experiences that cause pain, and ultimately incorporate them into the ego.

In his 1938 paper, Freud examines the split in the ego that facilitates one form of denial. He also discusses disavowal, disowning, negation, and denial, especially in relation to children's reaction to the difference between the sexes. Here, the question of terminology comes up. What is the relationship, for instance, among negation, disavowal, denial, rejection, and repression? Freud applies the term "repression" to defenses against internal instinctual demands, whereas "disavowal" or "denial" is used to refer to a defense against claims of external reality. This distinction is reiterated by Anna Freud, although Lewin, Waelder, and Jacobson disagree.

An interesting point is made in Freud's paper, to which I shall return repeatedly. In order to maintain denial of reality, namely, external reality (although this may apply to internal reality as well), a loss of reality testing has to be present. If reality testing is retained, the individual cannot maintain denial. I think this is a very crucial point, and it is one which Anna Freud (1936) also stresses. She indicates that the child's use of denial in fantasy, word, and act, if resorted to in the adult,

suggests psychosis. Anna Freud underlines what I indicated above —
that the ego's use of denial under ordinary circumstances is inconsistent
with another function, namely, the capacity to test reality. The ego's
mature relationship to reality is stronger than that of the infantile ego,
so that in the normal adult, fantasy and reality are distinguished. As
Anna Freud comments: "We do not as yet know precisely what takes
place in the adult ego when it chooses delusional gratification and renounces the function of reality testing. It severs itself from the outside
world, and entirely ceases to register external stimuli" (p. 88). She then
goes on to emphasize that denial is directed against the external world
(reality), while repression is directed against instinctual life.

Freud (1927) points out that the fetishist's denial in many ways is
not too different from that seen in psychotics. However, there is a major
difference — namely, the fetishist does not contradict his perceptions
and hallucinate a penis where there is none.[1] What he does do is to
displace from one area to another area in the woman, giving to the
displaced area the value of the original one, which he hoped was there
to begin with. In other words, there is no maintained reality distortion
of perception, for such a distortion of perception cannot be maintained
in the face of reality testing.

Freud pursues this question further in the *Outline* (1940), where he
states that in testing reality we have to fall back on perceptions but reality will always contain unknowable elements. We therefore endeavor to
increase the efficiency of our sense organs with "artificial aids." We
have, he claims, two mental attitudes, one which takes account of
reality and another which, under the influence of the instincts, tries to
detach the ego from reality. These mental attitudes exist side by side,
and the outcome depends on the relative strength of one over the other.
As Freud explains: "In all psychoses there is a split in the ego but this
also applies to the neuroses, so ultimately it depends upon which wins
out and whichever wins out depends upon the retention of perceptual
capacities (an ego function) and the capacity to test reality depending
upon these perceptions" (p. 202).

Freud (1922) indicates that delusions exist ready-made in the unconscious, side by side with other ideas, *before* their manifest outbreak.
Yet, if we take the fetishist, he does not have the courage to assert that
he actually sees a penis there. He takes the fetish to represent the penis.

[1] In the neurotic or the fetishist, the split is between a conscious and an unconscious perception and the denial is unconscious. Certainly the fetishist in his conscious
functioning does not deny the existence of the vagina as such.

This is *not* true of the psychotic. Again, let me quote Freud (1940): "The infantile ego under domination of the external world disposes of undesirable and instinctual demands by means of what are called repressions. We can now supplement this by a further assertion. During the same period of life the ego often enough finds itself in the position of warding off some claims from the external world which it feels as painful, and this is effected by denying the perception that brings to knowledge such a demand on the part of reality" (pp. 203–204). What is implicit is that there are two contrary attitudes, producing a split in the ego. Whichever attitude dominates will determine the clinical picture.

Clearly, there is a relation of splitting to denial here, a point discussed by Kernberg (1975a) with regard to borderline patients. He suggests that an "emotionally independent area of consciousness" is split off and denied. The denial then reinforces the splitting by disavowing any relationship to that which has been split off. Kernberg goes on to stipulate that in borderline patients denial may "manifest itself only as simple disregard for a sector of their subjective experience or for a sector of the external world" (p. 32). Whether Kernberg views this specific experience as psychotic is not clear. He does, however, allude to the loss of reality testing in some forms of denial, which would obviously make this psychotic. He also differentiates denial from negation, which he sees as a higher level of denial, linked with repression and quite close to isolation. After further discussing denial in mania and depression, he concludes: "Denial then is a broad group of defensive operations, and probably related at its higher level to the mechanism of isolation and other higher level defenses against affects (detachment, denial in fantasy, denial in word and act) and at its lower level, to splitting" (p. 33).

While Freud emphasizes that denial is directed against reality and the external world, Lewin (1950) contends that denial may operate in both ways, just like repression. Denial may oppose the intellectual recognition of a fact (percept), or it may oppose the felt impact of this external fact on the psyche. In saying this, Lewin is not disagreeing with the idea that denial disclaims the external world and repression disclaims the instincts. His point is that there can be repression of an idea (the representation of an instinct), repression of the affect charge, and *also* repression of the anxiety generated by this charge when the ego perceives it as a danger. Denial, in his opinion, may assist or replace repression in this regard: "When the instinct representations have become conscious and have made a claim on the ego to be accepted as reality, denial makes its appearance." In other words, he believes that denial may operate in different ways, just like repression. It may oppose the intellectual recognition of a fact, or it may oppose the feeling or meaning and impact of the external fact. An important point that Lewin makes here is that the ego state which maintains denial can be related to the purified ego state and that denial is a function of the pleasure ego. With the other defenses (i.e., projection and identification), denial is thus a derivative of an early type of ego organization. It is this particular ego state — the pleasure ego — that rules in elated states, and its appearance in the adult indicates a regression to this stage of development.

Jacobson (1957, 1971) can be seen as supporting Lewin, since in general she views denial as a primitive, archaic mechanism directed against both external and internal reality. In her opinion, it may precede repression, or it may reinforce and assist repression subsequently. The two may collaborate, with denial of internal and external reality as an auxiliary defense, playing a large role in certain kinds of perceptual distortions to support repression. Denial of instinctual drives may be facilitated by the ability to externalize these, and in this sense denial may support repression when the latter fails. By and large, however, it operates in a more massive manner than repression and within the framework of earlier ego states, which tend to treat internal and external reality equivalently in a concretistic manner (with deneutralized energy).[2] In differentiating psychotic from neurotic denial, she indicates:

> . . . the neurotic ego that uses such defenses has only partly regressed to a stage where internal psychic reality, though clearly distinguished from external reality, is still treated in the same concretistic manner. Although neurotic denial may involve processes of disconnection, isolation, and collective joining of psychic elements, which turn them into quasi-concrete, imagelike units, the latter *do not lose the quality of being psychic in nature.* The line of *demarcation between internal and external reality is maintained,* even in view of such introjections and projections. . . .
>
> In psychotics, however, the pathological process leads to a real fragmentation, a splitting, a concretization, and externalization of psychic manifestations, to the point of lending them truly concrete qualities.

[2] I wonder whether in repression the instinctual drive is not somehow accepted as a part of the self, with the individual trying to deal with it and master it via repression. In psychotic denial, on the other hand, that which is denied is cast off from the self either in its entirety or in the main. An effort is made to dissociate and separate the self from the denied completely, and quite consciously.

Consequently we find an equation between what is abstract and psychic and what is concrete and physical in nature [1971, pp. 133–134; my italics].

The concretization described by Jacobson is literal and actual with concomitant reality distortions. By and large she believes that in the neurotic, denial and repression may be brought into the service of instinctual defense, whereas in the psychotic denial deals with the problem of loss and restitution, operating with marked drive regression, mainly massive deneutralization of aggression. She sees the ego state from a certain stage in development as the prototype for denial. The regression is to a concretistic infantile stage where the child, although aware of the difference between the internal and external world, between self and object, still treated them both in the same manner.[3]

Jacobson's view of denial and repression is shared by Freeman (1973), although he takes object loss as the main frame of reference:

Denial is common in schizophrenia and mania but it is quite unlike the denial found in the neuroses. It ignores reality testing and in this respect can be compared to the forms of denial which occur in childhood. The denial which is encountered in the psychoses is essentially a decathexis of object and realistic self-representations. This decathexis may affect real external objects whose identity the patient denies. Such denial is no different from the decathexis which leads to the kind of "repression" which has already been referred to as occurring in schizophrenia. Both "repression" and denial in psychoses thus consist of a decathexis of self- and object representations. These mechanisms are associated with a loss of the anticathexis (repression proper) which (ordinarily) prevents the emergence into consciousness of drive derivatives and the primary process [p. 22].

To clarify the distinction I would draw between neurotic and psychotic denial, let me begin by describing the neurotic denial found in hysterical sensory distortions. Here an unconscious, id-derived impulse is translated into an external experience, which is then blotted out, or denied. This denial facilitates the maintenance of repression. In this regard, I should like to refer to some unpublished experiments conducted by myself and Dr. William Frosch many years ago with nonpsychotic individuals. Pictures were flashed at varying speeds on a tachistoscope, and the subjects were asked to relate what they saw. One of

[3] At a Kris Study Group in 1958 Rubinfine suggested that hallucinatory wish fulfillment is a prototype for denial. Although I believe that denial already assumes the existence of a "me" and a "not me," it is possible that prototypes of denial may be found in a stage of development where the "me" and the "not me" have not been established.

the pictures was of a large male genital. In several instances it was not identified as such (one subject, for instance, described it as a protruding tongue). Such misperceptions persisted even when the picture was exposed for several minutes. Ultimately, however, these subjects could no longer deny the image — otherwise they would have been psychotic. It seemed clear that the actual perception had been registered but was kept repressed in the unconscious. When the time factor was increased radically, this repression had to be supported by denial, and a significantly altered image was reported.[4]

To illustrate further how perceptual denial in the neurotic process reinforces repression, I would like to present some material from the analysis of a neurotic patient. This patient, a woman in her early forties, often went through periods of silence during the analysis, apparently related to various four-letter words which she was afraid would pop out if she let her thoughts flow freely. Whenever I urged her to express the thoughts in her mind, she would reply, "As soon as you say that, these words come into my mind and I can't say it. I don't know what you'll think of me. Oh, I know that you're familiar with them, but I don't like for you to hear me say them." It took quite a long time before she was able to mention any of these words. One of the words was "shit." She recounted that as an adolescent she would frequently go to the bathroom, close the door, and yell out loud all the expletives she knew. She reported this with a great deal of embarrassment, discomfort, restlessness, and blushing. Quite some time elapsed before this could be explored further and understood. It became clear that in her adolescence, play with obscene words was part of her masturbatory experience.

Some time later, during a session after I had moved to a new office, this patient mentioned various superstitions — thoughts she did not like to voice for fear they would come true. She hated to think of her husband's illness and his possible death. If she let herself think about it, it might come true. Soon after this, we ran into a familiar block, and the patient said, "There are those words again. I simply can't say them." Finally, with some urging and a great show of embarrassment, she began to shout, "Fuck, fuckin' bastard, shit, so there." This was accompanied by considerable restlessness. After yelling these words out loud a number of times, she said to me, "I dare you to say them. Go ahead, I

[4] That such perceptions are stored in the unconscious was demonstrated by Fisher (1953), who conducted similar experiments and then was able to demonstrate that the repressed and denied remained as day residues in subsequent dreams.

dare you to say them." Later, at the end of the session, the patient got up and said, "I must look at your books." She walked over, took a quick look at the books on my desk, and left.

In the next session she made no reference to this behavior, or to the expletives she had given vent to. During the following session, however, an opportunity presented itself to bring up the patient's going over to look at my books. She said she had wanted to know what kind of books were on my desk. There had been no books on my desk in the previous office, but she had already made a number of visits to my new office during which time there were books on the desk, and she hadn't commented on them. When I asked her what the books were she had seen, she claimed she hadn't really noticed. She did mention a medical directory, but in general just said she felt reassured for some reason. When questioned why, she replied, "Well, they were the sort of books, like the medical directory, the sort of books which were innocuous." She was apparently relieved that I did not have any books one might expect an analyst to have, namely, books about abnormal things. I pointed out that although she had gone to look at the books, she did not really see, for she had missed some obviously analytic books. At my request, she got up and looked again. Once more she expressed relief that none of the books dealt with analysis, although one book actually had my name and the word "psychoanalysis" on it in very bright colors. In listing the various books she had seen, she deliberately omitted this one.

Again, I asked her to get up and look. To her astonishment, she read the title of the book, but she did not see my name and had to be directed to this element. She seemed quite amazed that she had blotted out both the title of the book and my name. I then brought her back to her yelling in the previous session, and her daring me to repeat her words. It became clear that, among other things, this was an invitation to sexual play. Looking at the books, then, was a way of saying, "Well, if you don't want to participate with me in this sexual play, I'm going to look and see anyway." But she was afraid to look and really see, since this represented a taboo situation. If I had sexual books on my desk, and thus was familiar with sex, the threat to her defenses would be greater. This was corroborated when the patient indicated that she had initially panicked at the thought that I might repeat her expletives. I, too, would be degraded, like her, and she would think less of me. But also it would mean that I was a sexual being, and thus her defenses against her own sexual fantasies would be lessened.

The patient came into the next session feeling pretty good, referring to a sense of warmth. Further material was brought out indicating her attempt to dissociate me from anything sexual and not wanting me to be a sexual being. (It was during this session that she stated that she had been quite frightened when she had dared me to use the expletives — on the one hand, wanting me to, and on the other, being afraid of what might happen.)

The analyst as a sexual being represented a danger to her. She indicated that she had many sexual fantasies, and then recounted a dream in which her husband died and she subsequently married me. Clearly, the superstitious ideas she had discussed earlier were related to this fantasy. There was also a relation to sexual fantasies about her father which were connected with the masturbatory activities, expletives, etc. Once this began to be mobilized within the transference, a rather primitive defense had to be called upon — namely, denial. It was supported by a marked but specific perceptual difficulty. Had this persisted when she was forced to confront reality, it would have represented a severe break with reality, as is seen in psychotic denial.

In contrast to denial in the neurotic, denial in the psychotic is much more concrete. It is in the service of self-preservation and restitution and is accompanied by loss of reality testing. A clear example involves a patient I saw many years ago who had multiple sclerosis. He believed the neurologists were mistaken — as neurologists they did not know much about psychiatry, and it was obvious that he was suffering from hysteria. In his persistent denial of a serious physical illness in the face of obvious evidence to the contrary, this man could be viewed as psychotic.

Schilder (1935) discusses organic cases of hemiplegia with denial of the diseased parts and even of the whole body's existence. In a dramatic example of this, a man with a hemiplegia was seen repeatedly trying to throw his arm and leg out of the bed, yelling all the time: "Get out of here. What are you doing here? You don't belong here." Sometimes he would call these parts by the name of his son, whom he then upbraided for creeping into bed with him. Although it was not possible to examine this man in depth immediately after the hemiplegia, before his attempts to get rid of the diseased parts, it is not at all unlikely that these parts were not felt as real and that a state of depersonalization preceded the riddance attempts. In contrast to the more classical neurotic type of depersonalization, this went on to denial, to rejection of the diseased part, and ultimately to objectivization and externalization of it totally, accompanied by a loss in reality testing.

   Jacobson (1954a) discusses the effect of early traumatic experiences which, she indicates, may result in a tendency to use archaic mechanisms of identification. She questions to what degree traumatic exposure to frightening perceptions, particularly during the preoedipal phase, may create a special propensity for denial. Many of her patients had suddenly perceived something terrifying during childhood. Of course, such an experience would have a dramatic effect in general on ego development, so that denial is only one aspect of the distorted ego development.

   I should like to refer here to a patient I described above (p. 97), in whom denial was a prominent factor in analysis. In this patient, in contrast to the neurotic, denial was brought into the service of preserving the object. The patient had marked difficulties in preserving self-nonself differentiation. Orgasm, for instance, would result in a feeling of disintegration and loss of self. She experienced states of depersonalization and feelings that her body was fragmenting. During analysis there were repeated perceptual distortions. Nonetheless, by and large, she functioned reasonably well.

   From time to time she brought up a memory which referred to an incident at age three, or a little bit later. At first I thought this dealt exclusively with primal scene material. Although it was also brought into the service of primal scene material, it turned out to involve a scene of violence, in which her father had tried to murder her mother, and her mother had attempted suicide. Many things about this were completely unclear to the patient. All she remembered at first was awakening at night and seeing rain coming in through the cracks in the wall. Gradually this picture was filled in so that she recalled not only awakening and seeing the rain, but also being frightened and, finally, hearing shouting and screaming and seeing something terribly frightening but not quite knowing what it was. It is interesting that the rain coming in through the cracks remained for years the most vivid recollection and served as a screen memory. This whole experience was coeval with the tornado which had threatened her whole environment. But what had been most frightening was the possible loss of her mother in the scene of violence between the parents. With the loss of her mother, her whole world would disintegrate.

   Throughout many years of analysis, this patient had the opportunity to learn what had actually happened, but she did not take the trouble to establish the facts. It was not until she had worked through a great many anxieties related to her own aggression and hostility toward the mother, her own murderous impulses, that she finally took steps to ascertain what had transpired. Only then did she learn that the scene had to do with some extra-marital accusations (which I shall not detail here). Essentially I want to make the point that this patient's amnestic problems served to deny certain exceedingly traumatic experiences which threatened preservation of self and object. She also showed a rather concretistic literal-mindedness and difficulty in abstraction that went far beyond the mechanism of denial. I cannot help but feel that denial was only one facet of a whole series of ego disturbances resulting from this patient's repetitive traumatic experiences with a rather sadistic mother (who, I think, was in many ways somewhat psychotic). Perhaps the denial itself could only exist in the face of these disturbances in ego functioning.

In psychotics there is a real fragmentation, an actual concretization, so that what's outside actually becomes the inside and vice versa. Abstract and psychic become concrete and physical. The need to deny unacceptable thoughts and ideas led one patient to concretize a "bug" which wouldn't let her sleep, dominated her, and dictated rules of behavior. The bug assumed different appearances — sometimes dressing bizarrely. At times the bug was her childhood, with she herself harrying her mother. At times it had an almost hallucinatory and delusional vividness, but there was always enough reality testing to permit her to place this phenomenon in perspective. She went through all sorts of maneuvers to get rid of the bug. Once she saw a dead cockroach in my bathroom and became convinced that this was her bug and that I had removed it from her. She became depressed, felt low and lonely, and missed it, as if she had been emptied of something. It became very clear that the bug was an object toward which she had positive feelings. Later the bug reappeared, although not as strong and as powerful as before. She became panicky, however, lest it resume its previous dominance over her life.

At the appropriate time I began quite firmly to treat the bug as her own thoughts. She fought this desperately — cried, attacked me, tried to blot me out by not looking at me. She was obviously frightened and claimed I was removing the possibility of her getting better, for how does one renounce one's own thoughts? So long as she had an "it" to deal with, it was possible that "it" would go away. There then ensued a period during which I was quite firm and refused to let her use the word "it" in reference to her thoughts. This was a productive, if stormy, period.

After we had finally established that she would have to accept these as her own thoughts, she developed rather classical-appearing obsessive-compulsive rituals. Their significance in terms of retaining contact with reality was particularly clear in her bedtime rituals. The patient would repeat certain touching compulsions a given number of times — arranging her pillow, etc. At first these appeared only in the service of warding off "bad thoughts" revolving around masturbation and aggression. Upon exploration, it was ascertained that the various objects she touched were bits of herself which she had to quiet down and bring together before she could go to sleep. But it was even more complex. I learned that she fantasied she was her mother putting her (the patient) to sleep as a child. At the same time, the objects were bits of her mother, whom she was trying to quiet down.

The concretization of denied parts of the self is evident in many psychotics' delusional systems. The very process of projection must be preceded by a denial of a thought or an impulse, which is then concretized into a persecuting object. Waelder (1951), however, points out that denial and projection are not enough to make for a psychotic delusion; something else is required. In psychotic projection, there is a disguised return of the person, the love for whom the patient has denied and perhaps projected. The return of the denied object and the feelings for it is what lends the element of historical truth to the delusion and hence its resistance to correction (see Chapter 4, Section C).

The point has been made that, whereas denial may contribute to the incorrectability of beliefs, this does not make the belief psychotic in nature. Hartmann (1956) emphasizes, as does Katan (1960), that the incorrectability of an idea is not exclusively a delusional feature. Many ideas that are not psychotic still cannot be corrected. Katan indicates that in such instances the beliefs operate in the service of defense, supported by strong denial. In the psychotic, however, the delusions are impervious to logic because the psychotic's reality is not our reality. It is a subjective reality, one which cannot conceivably respond to the rules governing objective reality. Katan further relates the incorrectability of delusional beliefs to the loss of the capacity to test reality, which derives from the withdrawal of cathexis of reality. In his opinion, psychosis eventuates when denial fails.

It appears to me that coeval with the kind of regression which has to be present for psychotic denial to operate, there must also be certain disturbances in other ego functions. Specifically, I mean the various alterations in the ego's relation to reality, feelings of reality, and reality testing, all of which contribute strongly to producing those clinical manifestations generally designated as psychotic. It is certainly clear that in order to maintain persistent denial of external reality a loss in reality testing has to be present. As I indicated, Freud (1940) points out that in the fetishist there is no maintained distortion of perception. A distortion in perception cannot be maintained in the face of preserved reality testing. It is also obvious that perceptual distortions play a role in maintaining denial as well as deficient reality testing. (I shall discuss in more detail later the role of perception in the psychotic process.)

C.
Incorporation, Introjection, and Identification

I should like now to examine the role of incorporation, introjection, and identification in the psychotic process. Before doing so, it will be necessary to clarify the meaning of these concepts. Several authors have pointed to inconsistencies in the use of these terms and have attempted to delineate similarities and differences (Fuchs, 1937; Knight, 1940a; Freeman, 1959; Schafer, 1968). These inconsistencies are not clarified by the definitions in the psychoanalytic glossary (Moore and Fine, 1968):

IDENTIFICATION: An automatic, unconscious mental process whereby an individual becomes like another person in one or several aspects. It is a natural accompaniment of maturation and mental development and aids in the learning process (including the learning of speech and language), as well as in the acquisition of interests, ideals, mannerisms, etc. An individual's adaptive and defensive reaction patterns are often attributable to identification with either loved and admired persons, or feared ones. By means of identification with a needed person an individual can often provide for himself the satisfaction of the needs desired from that person. Separation from a loved person becomes more tolerable as a result of identification with him.

For identification to occur, sufficient psychic development must have taken place for the individual to distinguish himself from others in his environment. Such differentiation of self and object representations normally occurs in early childhood [p. 50].

INTROJECTION: Originally used synonymously with the term *identification*. Recently it has been differentiated from identification and employed in two different contexts:
1. The assimilation of the object-representation into the self-representation whenever the boundaries between the self and object representations are indistinct. The individual then becomes confused in regard to his separateness and even his identity.

236

2. The child's taking into himself as a psychic phenomenon the object's (usually parent's) demands as if they were his own, so that he reacts in the same way whether or not the object is present. The child does not copy the object as he would if he identified with it. The regulating, forbidding and rewarding aspects of the *superego* are formed by the introjection of parental directions, admonitions and rewards [p. 58].

INCORPORATION: A special form of *introjection*, a taking into the mind of the attributes of another person, which follows the model of the bodily function of oral ingestion and swallowing. It is the primary mechanism in *identification*... the process whereby change in individuality is accomplished through becoming like someone (or something) else. Identification accomplished via incorporation implies change by fantasied oral consumption of an *object* (person), as indicated by cannibalistic wishes in dreams and associations. The mechanism is encountered in *psychoses, impulse disorders*, severe oral characters, and in less neurotic individuals during states of severe *regression* in analysis. Although it has some import for psychological understanding (being one way of mentally assimilating interpretations), it is a hazardous basis for mental stability since such incorporative identificatory mechanisms may malfunction or break down easily [p. 52].

Clearly such definitions suffer from methodololgical inaccuracy and considerable overlap. It might, for instance, be simpler to use the term "incorporation" in its generic sense (i.e., to include something into the self or the self-representation), and then to describe the processes via which this is accomplished (e.g., oral incorporation), rather than assume that incorporation is always oral. Indeed, Fenichel (1931) views incorporation as occurring in many forms—anal, epidermal, respiratory, ocular, etc.

Such terminological difficulties run throughout the literature. Fuchs (1937), for instance, uses the term "introjection" to describe an instinctive incorporation into the mind and views it as an "eating-up" process resulting in identification. Schilder (1976) speaks of identification as a form of introjection in which the other person becomes incorporated into one's personality. According to Knight (1940a), introjection is an unconscious inclusion of an object or part of an object into the ego of the subject. It involves previous projections onto the object of the subject's own unconscious tendencies.[5] Knight differentiates identifica-

⎯⎯⎯

[5] It should be noted that Knight uses "projection" in its standard dynamic, defensive sense, whereby the subject attributes his own unacceptable tendencies to an object and then perceives them as tendencies possessed by the object. He thus does not take into account the kind of projective process which is coeval with self-nonself dedifferentiation (see Tausk, 1919; Katan, 1950).

tion from introjection by indicating that identification is not a mechanism but a resultant phenomenon, which may eventuate from many processes. He states: "Identification is an accomplished fact not an act, and may result from several different mechanisms acting separately or together. It may occur by displacement or substitution (with possible projection and introjection also) when we identify one object with another object (misidentification); it may occur mainly by projection as in the case of 'altruistic surrender'; it may result mainly from introjection; but in most instances, perhaps, complex interaction of both projection and introjection will have operated to produce the identification" (p. 341). Clearly he sees introjection as one of the preliminary steps to identification. Without using the term, he describes projective introjection as playing a role in many processes resulting in identification, for instance, "altruistic surrender," falling in love, and transference patterns.

A highly restricted definition, at variance with traditional views, is given by White (1963). Using his concept of effectance, he sharply distinguishes identification and introjection as two different phenomena:

> The latter [introjection] then moves back chronologically to the oral stage, carrying with it the connotation of an emotional tie in some such form as a wish for union and merging with the mother. This leaves identification as an imitative process which comes to its first peak during the phallic stage and continues to influence development in the manner described by Erikson. . . . The two things are psychologically very different. Introjection, if it is not literally modelled on oral incorporation, at least must signify an attempted restoration of the total nursing situation with its feeling of closeness, a relatively passive state not characterized by feelings of efficacy. Identification happens actively in the interests of competence, its chief reward being an increased sense of competence [p. 191].

Rapaport (1951), focusing on the development of object relations, claims: "when reality obliges [the person] to give up these objects, they are not given up intrapsychically: in fact, their intrapsychic existence only then really begins, since their memory-trace instead of their perception is then drive-cathected." It is this process he conceptualizes as introjection. According to Rapaport, these "introjected objects constitute major sub-organizations within the developing memory-organization," and it is these organizations resulting from introjection that he conceptualizes as identification. He concludes: "Introjection and identification thus enable us to take over, as our own, the feelings and reactions of other people, and later their thoughts also, both those directed specifically towards us and those more general" (pp. 724–725).

Schafer (1968) distinguishes introjection and identification as different forms of internalization. In his opinion, "introjection should be used to refer to one kind of internalization only, namely, the processes whereby object representations are constituted as introjects or are changed into them.... Identification refers to modifying the subjective self or behavior, or both, in order to increase one's resemblance to an object taken as a model; it does not refer, as introjection does, to carrying on certain purely internal relations with an object represented as such (the introject)" (p. 16).

The confusion in terminology is compounded by varying viewpoints regarding the sequential relationship between these two processes. Does introjection, for instance, have to precede identification? Sandler (1960) tends to see introjection as a necessary step on the way to identification. He claims that during regression there may be a decomposition of identification into introjects and that in psychosis some introjects established early in life have never evolved into identifications. Schafer offers a modification of this view in saying: "identifications may be built out of introjects and so they may regressively decompose into introjects too, but it is not clear that all identifications must be built in this way" (1968, p. 20). He rejects the use of the term "introjection" as "a synonym for identification or internalization [or] as the basic mechanism of identification or internalization" (p. 20). Kernberg (1976a), in contrast, delineates a hierarchical internalization process. In his view, ego integration proceeds from early primitive introjections, through coalescence of these introjections into identifications, to ultimate ego identity. As he explains: "Introjections, identifications, bring about psychic precipitates or structures for which we will use exactly the same term as for the respective mechanism. Introjection, for example, will be considered to be both a process of the psychic apparatus and, as a result of that process, a structure" (p. 25).[6]

The confusion in the terms "incorporation," "introjection," and

---

[6] I should like to emphasize, as I did above, that in discussing the identification that takes place in melancholia, Freud (1917b) is really talking of introjection of the lost object. I should like to refer briefly here to the concept of psychotic identification, which will be discussed in more detail later. Jacobson (1971) uses self-object dedifferentiation as the frame of reference to discuss psychotic identification in both the manic-depressive and schizophrenic. In the former, the regressive process does not go all the way to the earliest state of total dedifferentiation, as it does in schizophrenia.

"identification" has to some extent developed historically from attempts to integrate later knowledge by using language and concepts more in keeping with earlier knowledge. An example, as I indicated above, may be the use of the term and concept "incorporation." My own view is that all of these processes (incorporation, introjection, identification) are part of the overall process of internalization—a view shared by Schafer (1968). Internalization then refers to the process of setting up internal psychic structures, derived from an interplay with external objects. More precisely, it is a shift from the object representation to inclusion in the self-representation.

Via this process, introjections (introjects) are created, and they may be almost anything deriving from the object representation, which in a sense has been abandoned or gone lost but whose retention is essential for the organism. Such introjects may be set up in the psyche in relatively unchanged form in early developmental stages and during these stages they may, under certain conditions, be ejected or "extrajected" (Weiss, 1947), or projected. Or such introjects may persist into later life, representing a potential for "extrajection," or more often psychosis. In the course of normal development and maturation, perhaps with the formation of other introjects, they become integrated into a homogeneous aspect of the psyche, losing (so to speak) their independent and autonomous operation so that ultimately they are not identifiable in their original form. It is then that one may speak of identification, which, by virtue of its integrated state, can under ordinary circumstances no longer be ejected, certainly not in any way resembling its original form.

The counterpart to introjection may thus be projection or "extrajection" (Weiss, 1947). We appear to have no equivalent or counterpart in our psychoanalytic language for identification. (I have never heard the term "disidentify" used to imply this process, and perhaps this is for good reason in light of my above discussion.) The true introject is still to some extent isolated from the rest of the ego and somewhat alien. There is still some separation of the introject from the core self and, especially in the psychotic, some awareness of distance. In melancholia and in schizophrenia, however, this is not clearly delineated because of some degree of fusion of self and introject. Yet the latter is not true identification. Stability of the ego requires that that which is incorporated and introjected eventually become an integral part of the ego, and be integrated into it in a harmonious fashion. Kernberg (1975a) speaks of "non-metabolized," early pathological internalized object relations (p.

34). This, in a sense, is equivalent to my own differentiation of an introject from a true identification. For identification to occur, there are certain prerequisites: the development of an ego apparatus separate enough from its object, with appropriate inner and outer boundaries to perceive (not necessarily consciously) the qualities of the other.

Let me draw a crude analogy between the introject and the food bolus, which has not yet been digested or metabolized and can be regurgitated. The regurgitate still has some recognizable feature identifying what was taken in. So it is with psychic introjects; they may remain in the psyche but are perceived as introjects, or they may be ejected in the form of persecuting delusions, influencing machines, etc., not too unlike their original source. To continue with the analogy, once the bolus is digested, it enters the blood stream and is metabolized. Ultimately it becomes part of the body chemistry and structure. Its external sources are no longer recognizable. The substance becomes part of the warp and woof of the body, albeit analysis may enable us to reconstruct its sources. So, too, I believe with identification we may reconstruct that with which the organism has identified and from which it has in a sense evolved. But true identification is homogeneous with the psyche.

Rapoport (1944), Isaacs (1946), Bender (1952, 1954), and others point to the persistence of certain childhood introjects as almost pathognomonic for schizophrenia. According to these authors, all children have imaginary companions and introjected objects in the course of development. Indeed, as Bender remarks, "Fantasied companions compensate for deficiencies in the child's emotional experience and are one of the constructive factors in personality formation. Hallucinations, too, often serve a similar function" (1954, p. 89). These authors describe a spectrum of clinical cases, ranging from the psychoneurotic to the schizophrenic. They maintain that the pathology was determined by the persistence of introjects into adulthood and by their quality. "As we turned from the psychoses and approached the neuroses," Bender explains, "we found instead of the bizarre, primitive and unrealistic fantasy objects of the former, fantasy objects which were more conditioned by actual experiences and which were more related to the external parent" (p. 90).

A patient of mine (described in Chapter 4, Section A) believed there was a "power" within him which had a form and controlled his behavior, both negatively and positively. He had difficulty locating this "entity" in his body, but he gave it shape and form: "Sometimes it's shaped like an orange, sometimes like a Russian potato, like a head, like a tumor, a cancer. One time I began to think maybe it was my heart." He also mentioned that this power talked to him in a loud voice. When I asked if I could hear him, he replied: "If he talks in a low tone there is a way to use a microphone, to put it on a part of my body and if someone puts an earphone to his ear he could listen to what he says." I then asked: "Does anyone else hear him?" The patient responded: "I'm trying to find that out. Everything sounds crazy, but sometimes he acts like a third person. When I'm talking to someone else, he talks in a certain way."

As I described in Chapter 4, this patient had been subjected to what he felt were humiliating experiences during his childhood. He had developed delusions of persecution and believed the "power" in his body was in league with all his torturers. It was not too difficult to imagine all the figures ultimately introjected as this "power." Particularly evident in his relation to this power were feelings of ambivalence related to his father. This patient's ongoing struggle between love and hate for the object had ultimately been internalized in the form of a concrete, discrete introject.

Parenthetically, I might observe that there were indications suggesting that he himself was the introject residing in his body. This use of introjects is suggested in a delightful example given by Rapoport (1944), who describes an 11-year-old child with many introjected objects. One day this boy ripped apart a small rag doll, which to him represented various fantasy objects, and removed the stuffing. He then attempted to climb in it himself, feet first. Although Rapoport does not go into the implications of introjected objects for womb fantasies, this has been suggested in some patients I have observed.

D.
Projective Identification

It is appropriate here to select for more detailed discussion the controversial concept of projective identification, originally suggested by Melanie Klein (1946), I shall begin with the views of Klein and her followers, who see projective identification as a process fundamental to the development of object relations. It should be emphasized that in the Kleinian view projective identification is present at all stages of early psychic development, and it is its vicissitudes that result in one or the other clinical condition. According to Klein, projection "originates from the deflection of the death instinct outwards and. . . helps the ego in overcoming anxiety by ridding it of danger and badness" (1946, p. 101). In this way, self-destruction is avoided. Moreover, Klein goes on: "Much of the hatred against parts of the self is now directed towards the mother. This leads to a particular kind of identification which establishes the prototype of an aggressive object relation. Also, since the projection derives from the infant's impulse to harm or to control the mother, he feels her to be a persecutor. In psychotic disorders this identification of an object with the hated parts of the self contributes to the intensity of the hatred directed against other people" (p. 102).

It is to this process that Klein applies the term "projective identification." A portion of what is projected remains, contributing to the infantile superego (to which are also added the previously externalized destructive forces via introjection). The back and forth movements of these forces bring in their wake extremes of destructiveness, expressed directly externally by the subject, as well as indirectly as fantasied retaliations by the object. As Klein explains: "the projection of a predominantly hostile inner world which is ruled by persecutory fears leads to the introjection — a taking back — of a hostile external world. Vice versa, the introjection of a distorted and hostile external world reinforces the projection of a hostile inner world" (p. 103). Further, it is not only the

243

bad parts of the self that may be expelled and projected but also the good parts of the self.

As is so often the case, it is the poet, the philosopher, the writer, who perceptively illuminates such significant psychological factors in human relationships. We might see the impact of projective identification in Meyrinck's (1972) description of intense hatred of the father: "No one can hate anything as deeply as I do unless it is a part of himself. . . . Sometimes I think it is more than a coincidence that I am consumptive and spit blood; it's my body probably, revolting against everything that pertains to him [the father] and refuting it with loathing" (pp. 127–128).

Summarizing Klein's view, Rosenfeld (1970) stipulates:

'Projective identification' relates first of all to a splitting process of the early ego where either good or bad parts of the self are split off from the ego and are as a further step projected in love or hatred into external objects which leads to fusion and identification of the projected parts of the self with the external objects. There are important paranoid anxieties related to these processes, as the objects filled with aggressive parts of the self become persecuting, and are experienced by the patient as threatening to retaliate by forcing themselves and the bad parts of the self which they contain, back again into the ego. Melanie Klein gives the name 'projective identification' both to the processes of ego splitting and the 'narcissistic' object relations created by the projection of parts of the self into objects [pp. 1–2].

Bion defines projective identification as follows:

. . . parts of the ego are projected into the object, causing this object to be experienced as controlled by the projected parts and imbued with their qualities. This mechanism, active from the beginning of life, may have various functions: of relieving the ego of bad parts; of preserving good parts by protecting them from a bad internal world; of attacking and destroying the object; etc. One of the consequences of this process is that, by projecting the bad parts (including fantasies and bad feelings) into a good breast (an understanding object), the infant will be able — insofar as his development allows — to reintroject the same parts in a more tolerable form, once they have been modified by the thought (reverie) of the object. . . . there is a form of pathological projective identification, which takes place in certain psychotic illnesses or which is used by the psychotic personality where there is a predominance of envy and greed. In this case, the splitting of parts of the ego is so severe that it results in a multiplicity of minute fragments which are violently projected into the object. These fragments, which are expelled by pathological projective identification, create a reality populated by bizarre objects and which becomes increasingly painful and persecuting [Grinberg et al., 1977, p. 29].

Bion adds a special dimension to the process of projective identification in which the projected bad parts are modified and then reintrojected in this attenuated form. As he explains it: "An evacuation of the bad breast into the real external breast takes place through a realistic projective identification. The mother, with her capacity for reverie, transforms the unpleasant sensations linked to the 'bad breast' and provides relief for the infant who then reintrojects the unmitigated and modified emotional experience, i.e., reintrojects an alpha-function, a nonsensual aspect of the mother's love" (p. 57). He refers to this, as the container-contained model: that which is projected is "contained" by the object (the container). It is modified and made less dangerous. Because it is less dangerous, when it is reintrojected by the subject, it can be mastered more easily.

To some, projective identification is a process applicable to the development of all object relations; to others, it is highly restricted, limited to psychotic manifestations. Pacheco (1980), for instance, assumes that all patients have a "free" area, a neurotic area, and a psychotic area. In the latter two projective identification plays a role, but to varying degrees. Still, since all patients have these areas, it follows that projective identification plays a role in all patients. Ogden's (1979) use of the concept is also quite broad. He views it as a type of defense, a mode of communication, a primitive form of object relations, as well as a pathway for psychological change.

Although Schilder (1976) does not explicitly refer to "projective identification," many of the manifestations he describes appear to represent aspects of this phenomenon. For example, he says: "For the paranoiac, the dismembered object is basically another multiplicity of persecutors, since every piece turns a persecutor. The object is reduced to many dangerous pieces, which are only appreciated as belonging to the inside of the body, like feces. The persecutors are due to the introjection of a partial object" (pp. 58–59). I referred in Chapter 7 to one of Schilder's patients who wished to tear others to pieces and at the same time felt herself falling into pieces. A part of her projected destructive impulse was reintrojected and supported that portion of the destructive impulse she had retained. Schilder broadens this idea in describing the fear of losing parts of the body, pointing out that one never loses the parts (see p. 210). What has once been part of the body never completely loses this quality. It may be projected, but it remains in some psychological relation to the body.

In Chapter 4, I mentioned that we can see this in the concept of the skybalum as the persecutor (Van Ophuijsen, 1920; Stärcke, 1920) – an idea suggestive of projective identification. The relation of the skybalum to projective identification is especially clear if one views it in terms of something that is part of you, in your body, and that remains part of you even if expelled from your body. Because the hardened, painful fecal mass is a part of the person, when the person reacts to it by projecting it onto an external persecutor, the persecutor becomes part of the self – a bad self. Even if the mass is expelled, it is not lost, but returns in the form of the anal persecutor, who can attack, at times in the very area from which it came. In this way, anal persecution fantasies can be viewed as a special form of projective identification.

Before proceeding to a discussion of projective identification in the psychotic process, I should like to comment on the terms used. It appears to me that the term "projection" here refers to that stage in psychic development where self-nonself differentiation is not yet clear, where what exists internally and externally is not clearly defined. It is similar to what Katan (1950) refers to as psychotic projection, but not entirely so. The word "identification" is, however, a bit misleading. We are in this process speaking of introjection and even Klein repeatedly uses this term. These introjects are not metabolized into the psychic structure as an integral part, as in true identification, but remain more or less discrete and can be externalized again, as occurs in the psychotic process. I therefore believe that if we are going to accept Klein's concept at all, we must more strictly speak of *projective introjection.*

Self-Nonself Dedifferentiation

Let me now turn to the state of self-nonself dedifferentiation which coexists with projective introjection, as I prefer to call it. There is some question whether a state of total fusion between self and object is necessary for projective introjection to take place. Jacobson (1954a), discussing psychotic identification, speaks of the diffuse boundaries between self and object and the resultant fusion between the two. She views this state as facilitating primitive introjective or projective identifications, evolving out of fantasies of incorporation, devouring, invading, or being devoured by the object. Jacobson sees the adult psychotic's projective identification as an attempt to split off and project onto a suitable external object those parts of the self which were unacceptable to the adult ego. The external object would then represent the patient's "bad self."

Rosenfeld (1970) contends that projective identification "is not identical with symbiosis. For projective identification to take place some temporary differentiation of 'me' and 'not me' is essential. Symbiosis, however, is used by Mahler to describe a state of undifferentiation, of fusion with the mother, in which the 'I' is not yet differentiated from the 'not I.'" Yet, while Rosenfeld believes that for projective introjection to take place some degree of differentiation is necessary, he also uses the concepts of fusion and projective identification interchangeably and argues that excessive projective identification obliterates differentiation of self and object. On the other hand, earlier he says:

> Identification is an important factor in narcissistic object relations. It may take place by introjection or by projection. When the object is omnipotently incorporated, the self becomes so identified with the incorporated object that all separate identity or any boundary between self and object is denied. In projective identification parts of the self omnipotently enter an object, for example the mother, to take over certain qualities which would be experienced as desirable, and therefore claim to be the object or part-object. Identification by introjection and projection usually occurs simultaneously. In narcissistic object relations, defenses against any recognition of separateness between self and object play a predominant part. Awareness of separation would lead to feelings of dependence on an object and therefore to anxiety [1964b, pp. 170–171].

Freeman (1959), focusing on self-nonself differentiation, views introjection, projection, and identification as defensive mechanisms in the nonpsychotic. According to him, the use of introjection and projection as defense implies the presence of a boundary and some degree of ego functioning. In psychosis, however, the ego which initiates defense is defective; thus projection and introjection really reflect loss of ego boundaries and self-nonself dedifferentiation. To Freeman, then, projective identification as a clinical phenomenon is really nothing more than lack of self-nonself differentiation.[7]

Underlining self-nonself dedifferentiation in the projective-introjective process, Kernberg (1975a) claims: "projective identification is

---

[7]Schilder (1976) also relates what might be called projective identification (see above) to self-nonself dedifferentiation, which facilitate the flux, back and forth, between projection and introjection.

characterized by the lack of differentiation between self and object in that particular area, by continuing to experience the impulse as well as the fear of that impulse while the projection is active, and by the need to control the external object" (p. 31). He continues:

> ... projective identification may be considered an early form of the mechanism of projection. In terms of structural aspects of the ego, projective identification differs from projection in that the impulse projected onto an external object does not appear as something alien and distant from the ego because the connection of the self with that projected impulse still continues, and thus the self empathizes with the object. The anxiety which provoked the projection of the impulse onto an object in the first place, now becomes fear of that object, accompanied by the need to control the object in order to prevent it from attacking the self when under the influence of that impulse. A consequence or parallel development of the operation of the mechanism of projective identification is the *blurring of the limits between the self and the object* (a loss of ego boundaries) since part of the projected impulse is still recognized within the ego, and thus self and object fuse in a rather chaotic way [p. 56; my italics].

Meissner (1980) suggests that since self-nonself dedifferentiation underlies projective identification (introjection), this concept is applicable only to psychosis. Here Meissner touches on what has troubled many regarding Klein's concepts. Klein refers to the infantile state during which projective identification exists, coeval with lack of self-nonself differentiation, in psychosis language (i.e., the paranoid-schizoid position). When this state reappears in adulthood, whether by regression or fixation, it may then appropriately be viewed as psychotic. Yet even Klein views only excessive projective identification as leading to psychosis. She sees it as leading to major confusion between self and object. In this sense, she views projective identification as leading to self-nonself dedifferentiation, rather than the latter being the psychic state in which projective identification develops. Obviously, there is by no means unanimity on whether projective identification (introjection) is merely another aspect of self-nonself dedifferentiation or is a psychic state coeval with this process.

Impact on the Object

Floating around many of the discussions on projective identification (introjection) is the question of the impact on the object, onto whom the projection takes place. Opinions vary considerably. There are those who view projective introjection as a fantasy in the subject, with the interaction taking place between the self-representation and the object representation. Meissner (1980) emphasizes this view and claims: "the Kleinian discussion of object relation is cast, not in the language of real relationship, but rather in the instinctively derived language of fantasies about objects and their relation to the subject" (p. 48).

Ogden (1979), on the other hand, maintains that the object projected onto experiences pressure to think, feel, and act in accord with the projection. This then is metabolized in the object, processed and reinternalized by the projector. In this sense, Ogden sees projective identification as a mode of communication (in the sense of making the other person feel what one is feeling), and as a transitional form of object relations. Yet Ogden is not quite consistent for he defines projective identification "as a group of fantasies and accompanying object relations having to do with the ridding of the self of unwanted aspects of the self; the depositing of those unwanted 'parts' into another person, and finally, with the recovery of a modified version of what was extended."

Searles (1963) leaves no ambiguity on this subject. He unquestionably belongs to those who believe that the projectee must have a feeling of participation. As projective introjection is played out in therapy, the therapist must feel involved in the process. This of course is not without implications for therapy. The extent to which the therapist not only accepts and "contains" that which has been projected, but also feels and experiences this projection, is not without import. This experience becomes very much a part of the therapeutic process and is even essential as part of a feeling of participation with the patient in therapy.

It is not entirely clear what kind of patients Ogden is dealing with. Searles is obviously dealing with grossly psychotic patients. I somehow have the impression that Ogden views this as a phenomenon in all analyses. The view that severe regressive states occur in all analyses, with fragmentation, as well as phenomena akin to projective identification taking place, was expressed by several participants in a panel on severe regressive states during analysis (Weinshel, 1966; Frosch 1967a, 1967b).

As I see it, in the psychotic the whole process is experienced both internally and externally, so that ultimately real external objects may become involved. The patient reacts to the external object as literally possessing what has been projected and his behavior toward that object is influenced accordingly. This behavior may instigate behavior and reactions on the part of the object, which may in turn communicate to the patient the validity of his belief that what has been projected exists in the object. When this transpires in the therapeutic interaction, the therapist may become a sort of transitional object, helping the patient deal with the bad part of himself. (I shall later deal with the subject of the therapist as transitional object in the treatment of psychotic character disorders.)

Although I am primarily concerned with projective introjection as it relates to the psychotic process, I would like to raise some questions about the overall applicability of this concept. Can we see it as a process along a spectrum of object relations, ranging from the nonpsychotic to the grossly psychotic? Let us take a not uncommon transference manifestation found in analyses of nonpsychotic patients and not infrequently analytic trainees. The patient overidealizes the analyst by projecting onto the analyst his own narcissistic identification (introjection) with an overidealized parental figure or surrogate (Frosch, 1959). He then identifies with (reintrojects) this overidealization and begins to make analytic interpretations wherever he goes. He tends to analyze people he comes in contact with, much to their discomfort. In this process there is no loss of self-nonself differentiation. We might view this as a kind of projective identification (introjection), although I doubt whether Kleinians would accept it as such.

Clinical Material

I should like to describe a patient's reaction to my telling her that we were going to terminate and that coeval with this termination, I was giving up my private practice. She became quite panicky and angry. How could I give up treating patients who need me? Why was I so selfish, thinking of my own interests, depriving the world of my services? I would be punished. I would become sick if I did not work at my profession. She then described the nature of my sickness. I would develop all sorts of bowel problems—constipation, hemorrhoids, bleeding. My whole gastrointestinal system would disintegrate, become cancerous, and I would vomit. I would not be able to sleep and would consequently be tense and anxious.

When I pointed out that all these had been her symptoms, she quite readily acknowledged this. When I also pointed out that this was a way of holding onto me, she indicated that her symptoms would now return, although perhaps not with as much power. She would be able to control these fears and dangerous forces in herself.

Why, I asked her, did my also having them help her? It became clear that through our common experience she would not lose me. Furthermore, she knew from previous experience that I did not disintegrate when she tried to destroy me (in fantasy). It was this very inde-structibility that reassured her and enabled her to deal with her own hatreds and hostilities, both self- and object-directed. In other words, she would ultimately master and control these forces through introject-ing this part of me as well. This healthy component from me would become part of her self. In a way she was speaking of an ultimate iden-tification. I might say parenthetically that much of this had been experi-enced with her mother, with one major difference. The mother actually acted in keeping with the patient's fantasies, whereas I did not. There was a part of me she could use as a transitional object to work out her ultimate separation from me. This patient, a psychotic character, re-tained her capacity to test reality — although at times this was quite fra-gile. All of the above occurred with a basic recognition that these were her fantasies and fears and had little basis in reality. She was able to keep the boundaries between me and herself clearly defined. Much in this patient reminded me of Bion's (1967) view of the container and the contained. As a result of being contained, what is projected can be modified, attenuated, and neutralized, and then safely reintrojected. To Bion, this process reinforces the relationship between child and mother.

A similar process could be seen in a more seriously disturbed patient reported by F. Nakhla (personal communication, 1980). This woman dreamt that an aunt murdered her sister (another aunt). She had on previous occasions described her aunt as crazy, with murderous im-pulses. That murderous impulses had been felt by the patient toward her own sister was pointed out by the therapist. The patient reacted to this observation with anxiety, fearing she was going to pieces and was seriously ill. In the dream, the therapist had been trying to comfort her (as was the case in reality), but he was also sick, even though he reassured the patient that both he and she were not seriously ill. Nakhla felt that when the murderous feelings she had projected onto the aunt were reintrojected, the patient again felt they were destroying her. In the dream she tried to project her disintegrative fears onto the therapist. There was a projection of the patient's destructive impulses as well as her mutilated self onto the therapist. This was reexperienced in herself with resultant annihilation anxiety. These impulses, how-ever, having been so to speak contained, neutralized, and modified in the therapist, could now be introjected and ultimately mastered.

I should like to move on to more obviously psychotic manifestations of this process. Many of these clinical manifestations reflect self-nonself dedifferentiation. An example is transitivism, when the patient feels within himself phenomena which are going on in another person, such as genital sensations or aggressive feelings. He may, in his delusional system, then ascribe these as being evoked in him by that person. Another example may be mutism, which may result from the idea that there is no need to speak since self and object are one—undifferentiated. As one patient said to me, "We don't have to speak because you hear what I hear; you think what I think."

I believe that variations of the influencing machine reflect projective-introjective mechanisms. One patient imagined that a highly complicated outside apparatus was capable of experiencing certain sensations felt by him at the same time. He described a mechanical body (a duplicate of himself) which could lie right next to his bed, and which was under the influence of still another machine, located in a radio station. This machine broadcast waves affecting various parts of this phantom body, which corresponded to parts of his own body. He therefore felt the same sensations.

Another patient described an influencing machine which evolved from feelings of being hyponotized by a given individual. The patient felt parts of her body moving independently: "I wouldn't know how my hand had got there. I know that I would want to turn on the hot water faucet but I see my hand turning on the cold water faucet." She found herself falling out of bed, dropping objects, all influenced by this external apparatus. Actually, at this stage she had begun to place the influencing apparatus inside herself, referring to it as some kind of object or machine inside her. At times, then, she objectivized it externally, and at other times she was willing to accept it as part of herself. She described it as a churning evil. The uterus and the genitals were clearly the focus and source of the churning. However, transitional components were already evident, since she spoke of forces outside of herself as related to this churning. She projected this whole (evil) process and then reintrojected it.

A more obvious manifestation was seen in a man who complained of all sorts of peculiar sensations in his heart, including pain, irregular heart beats, and dizziness. He tried to ward these off by, in some way, affecting his wife's heart. He had, to begin with, felt that his wife's heart disease had many peculiar qualities. Whether she had any in reality I do not know. She had the power to affect other people's hearts through her heart disease—whether through emanations of rays or other forces, he wasn't quite sure. She had succeeded with her first husband and he had died. He himself felt that his own heart ailment was being aggravated by this process. He tried through his own emanations to ward off the wife's rays, but was not too successful. As the anniversary of her first husband's death approached, he became more and more apprehensive. He felt the power of her heart attacking him vigorously. When his countermoves did not quite succeed, he killed her.

Summary

We have seen that the concepts of introjection, identification, and incorporation are frequently used interchangeably and in an overlapping fashion. I maintain that they are all manifestations of internalization. Introjects differ from identifications in still retaining a degree of separateness and autonomy in the self-representation. Identifications, in contrast, are woven into the warp and woof of the self-representation, no longer discrete. Whereas introjection is a process, identification is an end-product, which may result from this process.

The concept of projective identification, or projective introjection as I choose to call it, derives from an early infantile stage in psychic development which is viewed by Klein in terms of psychosis — essentially the paranoid position. A major problem with Klein's concepts relates to her speculative formulation of the infant's fantasies during this stage (see Chapter 11). There is less of a problem in applying this concept to adult psychosis. One is much more comfortable clinically with the concept of projective introjection in adult psychoses. But even here I am not quite sure whether, to explain all these clinical phenomena, one has to fall back on a concept like projective introjection. Much of what we see, especially in psychosis, could be understood as deriving from states of dedifferentiation, where self-nonself fusion exists. Indeed, all the psychotic phenomena I described above could be understood within this framework. Therefore, although perhaps for different reasons, I agree with Meissner (1980), who says:

> . . . the difficulties inherent in the concept of projective identification are particularly methodological in nature, and result from the mixing or confusion of fantasy and process, of metaphor and mechanism, and result in failures in the differentiation of levels and forms of psychic organization and functioning. Consequently, I would urge that the term be abandoned as contributing more confusion than clarification to psychoanalytic thinking and that, in its place, more specific formulations

regarding the interactions and relationships of forms of externalization and internalization be employed [p. 65].

The process described by Klein as projective identification, if considered at all, should more accurately be called projective introjection. As I indicated, however, I believe it is essentially one manifestation, among others, of loss of self-nonself differentiation.

We have in this chapter looked at some of the techniques the psychotic resorts to in dealing with the basic danger of self-disintegration and dissolution. These are coeval with certain ego states and are related to specific ego disturbances, which now require examination.

9.
The State of the Ego
and Its Functions

I should like to turn now to the third question I proposed in examining the psychotic process: Are there ego or ego function impairments specifically characteristic of the psychotic process? In discussing the nature of the conflict and the nature of the ego's defensive operations, we have already been dealing with the state of the ego and its functions. All of these areas are closely related. I have pointed out that the nature of the danger and the source of anxiety are not without some significance in the choice of defense. Similarly, the response to the danger, and even the very perception of danger, will be affected by altered ego states and defects in ego functions. As we shall see, however, there is considerable difference of opinion on whether these ego defects are primary or secondary, defensive or adaptive, etc.

In the Schreber case (1911b), Freud was already fully aware that the ego and its role in the psychotic process would have to come in for more study. Somewhere along the line we find that he mentions that side by side with the libidinal disturbances, we must search for the characteristic ego disturbances that make for psychosis. This already presages future preoccupations, so that near the end of this paper he makes a very important observation about the mutual influences of ego and id, implying that possibly ego defects would be the area to study in the psychoses. He alludes to this observation in a letter to Ferenczi a few years later (1913) by saying: "I have always thought that sexual physiol ogy lies behind actual neuroses just as ego psychology lies behind paraphrenia."

A.
The State of the Ego

Before discussing this subject, we should note the many ambiguities in the term "ego." The ego has been conceptualized as a unified, tightly knit psychic structure, with defined boundaries—part of the tripartite structure of the psyche. It has also been conceptualized to include certain functions used in dealing with mental conflict—the so-called ego defense mechanisms. With the development of psychoanalytic ego psychology, it has been further conceptualized as a body of functions sharing certain identifiable features (such as being guided by secondary process) and functioning in a sense coherently and cohesively, so as to lend themselves a quality of unification (the functions are usually associated with each other). These ego functions in one way or the other mediate between the demands of the id, the superego, and reality. The seeming unity of ego functions is, however, belied by the fact that not all ego functions develop or even function equally, as we shall see below.

Federn's (1952) concept of the ego varies somewhat from that of other authors. Central to his contribution is the concept of the ego as a dynamic entity, with the ego boundary as its perceptual sense organ in relation to both external and internal reality. It plays an essential role in discriminating real from unreal. Variations in the cathexis of ego boundary produce a myriad of symptoms: "An object is sensed as real . . . when its impressions impinge upon a well-cathected ego boundary. The weakening of the inner ego boundary is responsible for delusions and hallucinations" (p. 13). Referring to schizophrenia, Federn states: "The loss of ego boundary cathexis thus results in the following: (1) Impairment of distinguishability of thought and object, (2) Falsified reality of thought, (3) Falsified certainty of judgment and conclusion, (4) A generalized false certainty as to the quality of acts" (p. 235). Waelder (1960) summarizes Federn's concepts:

Federn's concept of the ego is not that of a problem-solving agency but rather that of the seat of sensations; it encompasses a person's feelings about himself, in relation to himself (in situations of inner conflict and in self-observation) as well as in relation to the outside world. Federn correlated the various phenomena of "ego feeling" to processes of libidinal or destructive cathexis. His concept of the ego is related to, though not identical with, the "self" — a term widely used in philosophy for reflective activities in which man takes himself as an object, and introduced into psychoanalysis by Hartmann [p. 186].

I shall return to these concepts when I discuss the blurring of ego boundaries in the psychotic process. At this point I would like to take up the last point in Waelder's remarks — his indication of some ambiguity in the distinction between "ego" and "self." This confusion is especially evident in discussion of ego boundaries and self-nonself differentiation, particularly insofar as the ego's relationship with the object and reality is concerned. Jacobson (1964) is well aware of this problem:

We appear to be on the horns of a dilemma which, as we shall see, is mainly the result of terminological confusions. They refer to the ambiguous use of the term ego; i.e., to the lack of distinction between the ego, which represents a structural mental system; the self, which I defined above; and the self representations. Hartmann (1950), who called attention to this point, suggested the use of the latter term (analogous to object representations) for the unconscious, preconscious, and conscious endopsychic representations of the bodily and mental self in the system ego. I have worked with this concept for years, because I have found it indispensable for investigation of psychotic disorders. . . . The meaning of the concepts of the self and self representations, as distinct from that of the ego, becomes clear when we remember that the establishment of the system ego sets in with the discovery of the object world and the growing distinction between it and one's own physical and mental self [pp. 18–19].

She later adds:

By a realistic image of the self we mean, first of all, one that correctly mirrors the state and the characteristics, the potentialities and abilities, the assets and the limits of our bodily and mental self: on the one hand, of our appearance, our anatomy, and our physiology; on the other hand, of our ego, our conscious and preconscious feelings and thoughts, wishes, impulses, and attitudes, of our physical and mental functions and behavior. Since ego ideal and superego are part of our mental self, such an image must also correctly depict our preconscious and conscious ideals and scales of value, and the effectiveness — or ineffectiveness — of our self-critical functions. To the extent to which, at any level, the id communicates with the ego or finds access to it, the id, too, is naturally represented in the image of the self [pp. 22–23].

The position of the ego in relation to the self, is not too clear. Is the ego as a system incorporated within the self or is the self incorporated within the ego? In any case, for Jacobson, the self-representation seems to grow out of actions of the ego and its functions. From this viewpoint, when we speak of processes such as projection and introjection, we are dealing with endopsychic processes involving shifts between the self- and object representations. Dedifferentiation, then, involves these endopsychic structures. Nonetheless, this may extend to involve material external reality, e.g., in some delusions which involve distortions of the substance of material reality.

Despite the many difficulties and confusions, there is heuristic value in retaining the concept of the ego as a unitary entity, with characteristic qualities and functions. The concept of ego boundaries is also quite appropriate, although I would not take it as literally as Federn does. Adding Jacobson's all-inclusive concept of the self-representation, we could say that self-nonself dedifferentiation may proceed at different levels and in different areas of the psychic structure. For instance, certain portions of the self may be involved, with others relatively uninvolved. Certain ego functions may be affected and others not. It may concern the bodily self and yet preserve relatively sharp delineation in other areas of the self-representation. Or dedifferentiation between the ego and the other psychic structures may be involved, an important factor in the psychotic process.

An important factor in the healthy relationship with reality, for instance, is the existence of consistent, clearly defined ego boundaries with adequately developed differentiation from reality (see Freud, 1930, pp. 66–68). Yet even here perhaps one should more accurately speak of self-boundaries. Ordinarily, in the sense I am using the term "ego boundaries" here, we are dealing with self- and object representations, as well as the representation of reality. Cathectic shifts take place between the representations. It should also be borne in mind that when we speak of differentiation, this involves processes that refer to the establishment of the psychic structures.

The whole question of self-nonself dedifferentiation insofar as it concerns the ego's relation to objects will be discussed later (see Chapter 10). At this point it suffices to underline that such dedifferentiation brings with it diffusion and looseness of "ego boundaries" insofar as reality is concerned, thus playing a large role in contributing to the pathology of psychosis. The genetic factors related to lack of self-non-self differentiation also relate to a lack of differentiation of the ego and its functions. This relationship is clear when we know how closely intertwined the development of ego, self, reality, and the object are. One aspect of this is ably expressed by Fenichel (1937):

> In any case, "arising of the ego," and "arising of reality" are identical.
> . . . It is thus that in describing the nature of schizophrenia, for instance,
> we can just as well say that the organism "has broken with reality" as
> that "the ego is disrupted"; or we can just as well say that the schizo-
> phrenic has regressed to the time "before ego differentiation began." We
> are two persons inasmuch as we experience ourselves in contrast to
> others. Owing to this relation of the ego to reality, it is only a difference
> in terminology whether we speak of "stages in the development of the
> ego" or of "stages in the development of the sense of reality" [p. 29].

The active role of the ego and its functions in the building up of reality is further clarified by Hartmann's (1956) contribution. For instance, the establishment of reality is especially facilitated by reality testing. Hartmann points out that a child confirming the existence of an object by means of reality testing has now added to his world of reality. It is equally important to note that the ego needs and uses reality testing for its own survival.

Among the many questions raised by Freud's 1924 papers is: Why do some individuals appear to be able to deal with "painful reality" and others not? Here we are immediately confronted with the concepts of ego strength and ego weakness. Weiss (1952), reflecting Federn's viewpoint, cautions: "When speaking of ego strength and weakness, one should indicate which specific ego functions are impaired. True, there are cases of a general ego weakness which leads to complete disintegration of the ego in all its functions. But in most cases some ego functions are strong while others are weak" (p. 19).

The question of using ego strength and weakness as a framework for defining mental health and illness is a broad one, which I shall not go into in detail here (see Frosch, 1978). Some have stressed the importance of social and cultural variables in defining emotional health and illness, but this emphasis has its limitations (see Chapter 14). At this point I would simply like to underline several other frames of reference, in addition to the cultural, which must be evaluated in determining ego strength and weakness, as well as emotional health and illness. Among these are: (1) the ego's position vis-à-vis the external and internal environment; (2) the extent to which the person is functioning up to capacity in most areas; (3) the person's physical and emotional-subjective well-being; (4) the level of response to stress and strain, as well as habitual modes of mastery; (5) the capacity to permit and reverse regression and dedifferentiation; and finally, (6) the capacity of the ego's organizing function to establish a harmonious balance between and among the various psychic structures. These frames of reference are offered as no more than that — with full awareness that it is still at times exceedingly difficult to draw a sharp line between ego strength and ego weakness, let alone emotional health and emotional illness.

Turning to psychosis, we need to go beyond the question of whether we are dealing with a weak and ineffective ego. We need to ask: Wherein does this weakness lie and why is it of such a nature as to eventuate in psychosis? Hartmann (1953), in addressing this question, asks whether there is anything inherently defective in the ego and its functions. Should such weakness be related to the strength of the id, the nature of the particular conflict, the nature of reality, etc.? Or is there anything in the ego and its functions that leads to specific responses resulting in psychotic symptomatology? Some of these questions have already been looked at in our discussion of withdrawal and restitution (Chapter 4, Section B). These questions have also been addressed by a discussion group on the nature of the psychotic process (Freedman, 1962, 1964). Many of the participants viewed the weakness in the psychotic ego as related to: (1) instability in the ego's capacity for defense, (2) a marked vulnerability to stress, (3) fragmentation of the ego, (4) poor resistance to aggression, (5) a tendency to dedifferentiation, (6) difficulty in reversing such dedifferentiation and reestablishing identity, and (7) disturbances in the ego and in object relations.

Growing out of these defects are many clinical manifestations reflecting regressed ego states. These include disordered states of consciousness such as hypnoid, twilight, or dream states; oceanic feelings; cosmic identity; feelings of unreality; depersonalization; estrangement; and Isakower phenomena, as well as feelings of dissolution. They may be accompanied by mild to severe disturbances in identity, such as identity diffusion or severe body-image disturbances. Freud (1930) graphically describes such pathological manifestations:

> Pathology has made us acquainted with a great number of states in which the boundary lines between the ego and the external world become uncertain or in which they are actually drawn incorrectly. There

are cases in which parts of a person's own body, even portions of his own mental life — his perceptions, thoughts and feelings — appear alien to him and as not belonging to his ego; there are other cases in which he ascribes to the external world things that clearly originate in his own ego and that ought to be acknowledged by it. Thus even the feeling of our own ego is subject to disturbances and the boundaries of the ego are not constant [p. 66].

To understand the ego disturbances, we need to be aware of the diffuseness of ego boundaries, of self-nonself boundaries, which makes it difficult for the psychotic to differentiate the inner and outer worlds. As I discussed in Chapter 3, Section A, psychotic patients frequently have difficulty separating dream from reality. I described a patient who rushed into the emergency room convinced that he had killed his brother-in-law. It turned out it was a dream.

Blurring of ego boundaries, with self-nonself dedifferentiation, may be coupled with a tendency toward anthropomorphism, as well as identification with the nonhuman environment. Diffuse boundaries facilitate merging and fusion, which may ultimately be carried to a state of cosmic identity. Such extreme fusion is apparent in the following interchange with a 22-year-old male patient:

> Contact with another person is quite direct. There is total communication right down to the heartbeat. Right down to every slight movement on total response.
> *Do you have a oneness with the other person?*
> Completely, totally. I become everything I experience to a point where it ultimately resolves into a state of considering myself the universe. I can open myself completely. My mind withdraws from anything that is directly dangerous to my body. I'm totally conscious of the flow between myself and all other energy changes.
> *Do you become the universe?*
> If I take it all the way, I become the universe. It means my sense of identity is expanded and there is no longer a me.

Another patient, who "became" the universe, would stand rigidly in a catatonic state lest any movement create chaos and disruption in the world. Clearly in this way he could also control the turmoil and chaos within him.

Solitude may facilitate the blurring of ego boundaries and self-nonself confusion, to the point of cosmic identity. Melville (1851) provides a poetic description of this state:

. . . but lulled into such an opium-like listlessness of vacant, unconscious reverie is this absent-minded youth by the blending cadence of waves with thoughts, that at last he loses his identity; takes the mystic ocean at his feet for the visible image of that deep, blue, bottomless soul, pervading mankind and nature; and every strange, half-seen, gliding, beautiful thing that eludes him; every dimly-discovered, uprising fin of some undiscernible form, seems to him the embodiment of those elusive thoughts that only people the soul by continually flitting through it. In this enchanted mood, thy spirit ebbs away to whence it came; becomes diffused through time and space; like Cranmer's sprinkled Pantheistic ashes, forming at last a part of every shore the round globe over. . . . There is no life in thee, now, except that rocking life imparted by a gentle rolling ship; by her, borrowed from the sea; by the sea, from the inscrutable tides of God [pp. 168–169].[1]

Freud (1930) portrays the origins of oceanic feelings or cosmic identity in drawing an analogy between the process of self-nonself differentiation and the ego's incorporation of the pleasurable and ejection of the unpleasurable:

> In this way, then, the ego detaches itself from the external world. Or, to put it more correctly, originally the ego includes everything, later it separates off an external world from itself. Our present ego-feeling is, therefore, only a shrunken residue of a much more inclusive—indeed, an all-embracing—feeling which corresponded to a more intimate bond between the ego and the world about it. If we may assume that there are many people in whose mental life this primary ego-feeling has persisted to a greater or less degree, it would exist in them side by side with the narrower and more sharply demarcated ego-feeling of maturity, like a kind of counterpart to it. In that case, the ideational contents appropriate to it would be precisely those of limitlessness and of a bond with the universe [pp. 67–68].

Any discussion of the blurring of ego boundaries requires some further consideration of Federn's (1952) concepts. As I indicated above, although the use of terms allies Federn with those who view ego disturbances as fundamental to understanding the psychoses, it is essential to recognize that Federn's view of the ego and its role has a special meaning, unique to him. As we have seen, Federn views the ego as a sensing organ, a subjective experience, and equates the ego with the actual sensation of one's own ego, which he calls "ego feeling." He takes

---

[1] My thanks to Dr. James P. Frosch for calling my attention to this paragraph. It is also of interest that primary-process thinking was manifest in an experimentally established situation of isolation (Holt and Goldberger, 1959).

the position that one's own ego is actually felt. In his opinion, altera-tions in this ego feeling account for much of pathological symptoma-tology.

It is important to note that, in contrast to more traditional views, Federn believes the impairment of the ego and its functions in psy-choses is due not to an enrichment of ego cathexis at the expense of ob-ject libido, but to an impoverishment of ego cathexis. Hallucinations and delusions do not constitute unsuccessful attempts to establish an emotional rapport with the external world, but indicate lesions of the ego itself (a breakdown in the sense of reality). Delusions and hallucina-tions manifest themselves prior to, and independently of, the ego's loss of interest in the external world; they are due to a lack of cathexis at the ego boundaries, making for a fusion of false and actual reality. This fusion, however, is only one of the reasons for the impairment in the patient's thinking. Deficiency of ego cathexis also deprives the patient of the ability to use an important tool — controlled conceptual thinking.[2]

Des Lauriers (1962) shares Federn's view that the loss of cathexis at the ego boundaries accounts for much of the pathology in psychoses:

> To the extent that a human being lacks sufficient narcissistic cathexis of his bodily boundaries, he does not possess the necessary psychological structures to experience himself as a reality separated and differentiated from others. Such a situation is dramatically illustrated in the schizo-phrenic condition. He is essentially an individual who has lost the capacity to experience himself as real, separated, and differentiated from others, because of a severe diminution of narcissistic cathexis of his bodily boun-daries [p. 51].

To summarize what is characteristic of the psychotic ego, I would like to refer again to the views expressed at the discussion group on the nature of the psychotic process (Freedman, 1962, 1964). In the eyes of some, it may be more appropriate to say that in psychosis, insofar as ego states are concerned, what we have is a decathexis of an adult ego state and a recathexis of earlier ego states (a view that, in my opinion, allows us to understand the "historical truth" of delusions (see Frosch, [1967b]). Underlining what may be more specific to the psychotic ego, Bychowski (Freedman, 1964) indicates that primitive introjects and primitive defense mechanisms form the core of the psychotic ego.

[2] Federn's concept of impoverishment of ego cathexis in the psychotic influenced his approach to therapy. With the manic, for instance, he stressed ego support with efforts to help the patient conserve mental energy. I shall discuss this treatment ap-proach in more detail in Chapter 18.

Others see a kind of fragility in the ego, with a tendency toward regression and dedifferentiation, as one of the critical elements in psychotic psychic development. Again, the question arises: Is this dedifferentiation in the service of defense or a direct consequence of the defective ego? The potential for dedifferentiation and the consequent undifferentiated state of the ego, in relation not only to reality (the object) but also to other psychic structures, are linked by many to defects in ego functions.[3] To some, these defects are crucial in facilitating dedifferentiation; to others, they are the result of this process. This difference of opinion on whether the lapses in ego functioning represent unwelcome defects or merely modes of defense against anxiety generated by conflict — the defect-defense controversy — will be discussed in more detail in Chapter 15. At this point I should like to turn to an examination of the nature of the ego functions in the psychotic process.

[3] The concept of identity diffusion is used to designate this state. In psychosis identity diffusion permeates the organism at all levels — intrastructurally, interstructurally, as well as in terms of the ego's position vis-à-vis reality. Identity diffusion should be differentiated from identity confusion, which is more what we encounter in neurotic disturbances in identity, where self-nonself differentiation is preserved.

B.
The Nature of the
Ego Functions

As I pointed out in the last section, the ego is conceptualized by some as a body of unified functions guided by secondary process. Generally, ego functioning is coherent and cohesive, yet not all ego functions develop or function equally—a phenomenon that is especially observable in conditions under the impact of the psychotic process. A similar inequality may hold for ego development in relation to libido development. One may find regressive ego function impairments existing side by side with libidinal attachments that preserve a relationship with the object at a higher level. My point is that this cannot be perceived as all or none—progressive *or* regressive. There are unequal forms of progression and regression in ego and libido development. Inhibition in some areas may exist alongside progression in others.

Glover (1939) takes the stand that while libido regression may exist side by side with higher levels of ego functioning, the reverse is not true. Yet I wonder if the picture of hysterical psychosis might not illustrate the opposite. As I indicated in Chapter 4, Section D, in hysterical psychosis the libidinal relationship to the object seems to be preserved at a relatively high level, while the ego operates at relatively primitive levels, with ego functions more related to earlier phases in psychic development.

It is of interest that Beres (1956), in studying the essential features of schizophrenia, uses as his frame of reference an examination of the following ego functions: (1) relation to reality, (2) regulation and control of instinctual drives, (3) object relations, (4) thought processes, (5) defense functions of the ego, (6) autonomous functions of the ego, and (7) the synthetic function of the ego. It is in the deviation of these functions that Beres believes much of schizophrenic symptomatology can be understood. Whether similar deviations are important in other psychoses, however, is not made clear.

In looking at the nature of the ego functions in the psychotic process, I should again make clear that the nature of the conflict, the ego's defenses, altered ego states, and defects in ego functions are all very closely related. We have seen that there are differences of opinion on the existence of disturbances in these areas, as well as on the meaning and nature of these disturbances. It is here that we encounter questions about the specificity of ego function defects in schizophrenia and other psychotic conditions, as well as the question of whether these ego defects are primary or secondary, defensive or adaptive, etc. (I shall address these questions more extensively in discussing the defect-defense controversy in Chapter 15 and in presenting an integration of the views on neurosis and psychosis in Chapter 17).

At this point I would like to look briefly at Arlow and Brenner's (1964) view. They maintain that regressive alterations of ego functioning serve to defend against the emergence of anxiety connected with inner psychic conflict. In their view, the break with reality described by Freud is not a result of withdrawal of cathexis but a byproduct of the ego's attempts at defense:

> . . . the great majority of the alterations in ego and superego functions which characterize the psychoses are part of the individual's defensive efforts in situations of inner conflict and are motivated by a need to avoid the emergence of anxiety, just as is the case in normal and neurotic conflicts. In the psychoses, the defensive alterations in ego functions are often so extensive as to disrupt the patient's relationship with the world about him to a serious degree [p. 157].

Essentially, then, Arlow and Brenner see the same overall mechanism operative in both neurosis and psychosis and view the differences merely as a matter of degree. The differences they point to in the psychoses are: "1) a greater degree of instinctual regression or infantilism; 2) a greater prominence of manifestations of the instinctual drive of aggression and of conflicts over such manifestations; and 3) more severe and more widespread abnormalities in various ego and superego functions" (p. 153).

The view that the ego functions and modes of defense are more regressive and primitive in psychosis than in neurosis has been by and large accepted in psychoanalytic circles. Jacobson (1957, 1964), for instance, discusses the levels of regression quite extensively. Glover (1939) also emphasizes the depth of regression in differentiating between neurosis and psychosis. He says: "libido regression activates more primitive modes of infantile sexual impulses; similarly the ego reactions awakened belong to an early period when ego-synthesis is very weak and dissociation the rule. These factors lead to a more or less complete rupture with reality" (p. 130).

In the psychotic process, there seems to be a continuous invasion of ego functions by id derivatives. The ego's incapacity or deficiency in neutralization results in its being invaded by instinctual drives, libidinal and aggressive, untamed, unneutralized, or deneutralized. Id derivatives come to dominate the ego's adaptation in all areas, with the primary process serving as the guiding principle, affecting thinking, feeling, and behavior. Obviously, as Hartmann (1953) discusses, this whole process affects many ego functions. Thus, the ego's incapacity for neutralization will affect its countercathectic functioning, so that material from the unconscious permeates consciousness in a persistent manner. Yet whether these manifestations may be viewed only as defensive, as Arlow and Brenner suggest, is open to question.

Several questions are raised by Arlow and Brenner's formulations, but I shall allude to only two aspects here. Arlow and Brenner speak of *more* primitive and infantilized defenses and ego functions, seemingly in quantitative terms. Is there not a point at which the more or less regressive character of defense mechanisms and ego functions produce qualitative differences? Are those ego functions which are regressively employed already defective to begin with? It is furthermore unclear what determines the choice of these more regressive modes. These and many other points need to be clarified (see Chapter 15).

My own perspective, it should be clear, is that the defects in ego functions are a key element in the psychotic process. In particular, I would underline the impairments vis-à-vis reality. It is to various aspects of this problem that we shall now turn.

10.
The Ego's Position
vis-à-vis Reality

My selection of the ego's position vis-à-vis reality as a frame of reference for the psychotic process is not arbitrary. I have been guided by time-honored traditional approaches in classical contributions, especially Freud's. In previous communications (e.g., Frosch, 1964, 1976), I have proposed as the main frames of reference the state and position of the ego and its functions as these relate to the external and internal environment. I have suggested evaluating the ego and its functions vis-à-vis reality, object relations, and the other psychic structures. Obviously, separating these areas is a highly artificial procedure. Moreover, there is a close genetic interrelationship among these areas — among the ego and its functions, the id, the superego, object relations, etc. I have already cited Fenichel's (1937) remarks in this regard (see p. 259). Hartmann (1952) and Anna Freud (1952) equally emphasize that to separate these various areas is highly artificial. Their interdependence and mutual influence are thus taken for granted. They are merely taken apart here to facilitate examination, with full cognizance of their intricate and subtle interweaving at all levels.

We have seen that the whole movement toward restitution of the object and an attempted return to reality is a leitmotif in psychoanalytic contributions as far back as the 1880s, although this is discussed within then-existing frames of reference. Ultimately, the problem of re-establishing and restituting reality means recapturing the object and has to do with fending off dissolution and disintegration of the self. Certainly, the roles of reality and of the love object are central concerns in Freud's thinking, as can be seen in his "Two Principles" paper (1911a). It is, however, in the two 1924 papers that he crystallizes his thinking about the role of reality in the psychotic process. His later work (1933, 1940) reaffirms the essential contributions of these papers.

269

Let us briefly retrace the thinking which leads to these papers (see also Chapter 2). Already in 1894 and 1896, Freud discusses psychosis as evolving out of a denial of and break with a painful reality. The cornerstone for his concept of the role reality plays in psychotic symptom formation is laid in the Schreber report (1911b), within the framework of withdrawal and restitution.[1] It is clear that the concept of restitution rests on the assumption of the important role that loss of reality and the object play for the psychotic. The restitution may relate to an actual loss of the object, or the need to ward off a threatened loss, especially if there has been a previous trauma or frustration, accompanied by partial withdrawal. There may even be a valiant attempt to rush into reality (Jacobson, 1967), as is sometimes seen in certain forms of acting out to preserve identity (Angel, 1965). In any case, what is clear at this point is the close relationship between the concept of reality and the love object, which adds significantly to the meaning of reality loss to the patient.

In his paper "Types of Onset of Neuroses" (1912a), Freud is concerned with the role of the ego's relationship to reality in symptom formation and, by implication, the ego's relationship to objects. In this paper and a subsequent one (1914b), he comes more and more to grips with the whole question of the position of the ego vis-à-vis reality, as well as the fate of libidinal drives and object relations, in the choice of illness. Freud expands on the role of frustration in the development of illness, something to which he had alluded previously. He discusses several possibilities and variations. In certain cases, there is an external frustration when some object is withdrawn without a substitute to take its place. The result is the damming up of libido, and this, combined with the dispositional factor, brings illness. (By "dispositional," Freud means not only constitutional factors, but also libidinal fixations resulting from developmental experience.) The libido withdrawal results in a turning away from reality and a seeking out of fantasies which are impervious to reality testing. The tendency to slip further back creates conflicts because of the demands of present-day reality. This conflict is resolved by the formation of symptoms which bring the individual back to reality, again via substitute gratification.

The reference in these papers is to neurosis, but I believe what Freud describes generally illustrates a kind of restitutional attempt via symptoms to maintain a relationship with the object, i.e., reality.

---

[1] Nunberg (1920) expands on Freud's ideas in following the vicissitudes of a patient's withdrawal from and attempts to regain reality (see Chapter 4, p. 158).

Although Freud does not actually come to grips with the problems of psychosis here, there is nevertheless a hint that in certain cases frustration of extreme narcissistic demands may eventuate in psychosis. There is also a suggestion that ego weakness may, with relatively minor reality frustration, contribute to major and severe symptom formation.

A decade of fertility follows these papers, with Freud clarifying his metapsychology, advancing his structural model in *The Ego and the Id* (1923), and ultimately applying this model to the psychoses (1924a, 1924b). The latter two papers have served as a frame of reference for many subsequent discussions on the psychotic process and are particularly germane to our examination of the ego's position vis-à-vis reality. The break with and denial of a painful reality that Freud (1894, 1896) originally postulated for psychosis is now examined within the framework of the structural model and with regard for the position of the object in this reality. In the first paper (1924b), he points out that in "transference neuroses" (as he still calls them), the ego defends itself against an unbearable impulse by repression. There is then a return of the repressed (that is, a failure of defense) with a compromise, resulting in symptom formation. In this instance, the ego sides with reality, although providing for some degree of id gratification (the neurotic process). In psychosis, however, it is the force of the id that dominates, and the outer world is "either not perceived or the perception remains without effect." (This is essentially what he says in Section 3 of the first paper on defense neuropsychoses.)

In the psychotic state, then, we see the mechanism of denial at work. Current and fresh perceptions are denied. Equally noteworthy is that the importance of the existing inner world is also denied. The ego creates for itself a new inner and outer world in keeping with the demands of the id.[2] Freud points out that the motive behind this maneuver lies in the frustration of a wish by reality. (Note the connection to his [1912a] paper.) Freud subsequently modifies this, however, to say that overwhelming id demands, as well as painful and frustrating reality, or the combination of both, may be the precipitating factors in psychosis. In the *New Introductory Lectures* (1933), for instance, he indicates that in psychosis the turning away from reality is brought about either because the repressed unconscious is too strong, overwhelming the conscious attempt to cling to reality, or because reality has become

[2] Retrospective falsification must involve some alteration of the internal world residues (memories) of objects and perceptions, probably in keeping with the current alterations of the external and internal worlds.

so unbearably painful that the threatened ego, in a despairing gesture (of opposition), throws itself into the arms of the unconscious impulses. In a sense this adds up to a relative insufficiency of ego strength at a given point.

In any case, in the 1924 papers, Freud points to the marked attempt, if somewhat unsuccessful, to repair the rift between the ego and reality. These attempts at repair are what we see as symptoms. In other words, he suggests a reparative or restitutive concept of symptom formation in psychosis. He also discusses the role of splitting and denial in this process (see Chapter 8, Section B).

Yet Freud admits to a difficulty in his concept, in that other illnesses besides psychosis show problems with the outer world, as well as distortions in the relationship with (outer) reality. He says: "every neurosis disturbs the patient's relation to reality in some way . . . it serves him as a means of withdrawing from reality, and . . . in its severe forms, it actually signifies a flight from real life" (1924a, p. 183). With this point in mind, he elaborates on the difference between neurosis and psychosis: "We can understand the seeming difficulty [namely, that both show disturbances in relation to reality] somewhat better if we viewed both processes, that is neurosis and psychosis, as taking place in several steps. In both of them what we see finally in the clinical picture is already a later stage in a whole series of events, which go on before the final process is reached, the final process being seen by us as the symptoms" (p. 186).

What, then, are the underlying "events" in neurosis? According to Freud, there are at first id-derived demands; the ego at the behest of reality represses these. At this stage there is no alteration in the relationship with reality. Very little, actually nothing, is seen, as the ego attempts to obey reality. But then there is a failure of defense, with a return of the repressed. This failure may be occasioned by many things — an increase in id demands, factors that weaken the ego, or some reality situation. At any rate, with the return of the repressed, a compromise is reached, bringing in its wake some interference with the patient's life situation. Perhaps this could best be illustrated by a phobia, or amnesia, where there is obviously some disturbance in the patient's relationship to outer reality. What we see at the end in neurosis is in a certain sense a modification of the relationship with reality, a flight from reality, or an ignoring of it.

Now, what do we find in psychosis? Freud suggests that there is a painful frustration in reality, and a withdrawal from and denial of reality. This withdrawal is in the interests of the id. Already at the start, then, with this withdrawal, a disturbance with the outer world, a break with reality occurs. (There may even be some outward manifestations.) It is at this very beginning of the illness that Freud sees justification for his statement that in psychosis the conflict is between the ego and reality, and in neurosis between the ego and the id. The next step is something like a return of the repressed, or Waelder's (1951) "return of the denied," by virtue of increasing reality demands. A compromise has to be struck, and there are attempts to repair the rent between the ego and reality—attempts, which faulty though they are, try to preserve contact with reality, just as the neurotic symptom tries to gratify some needs of the id.

In psychosis the contact with reality is established on another footing, namely, by distorting the existing reality and creating a new one. In the second step, the ego tries to "make up" with reality, to meet it, but fails to do so satisfactorily. In contrast, in neurosis the ego tries to make up with the id, and does so via a compromise. According to Freud, the second step in both neurosis and psychosis is induced by a tendency to deal with the id's struggle for power. Again, I would point out that the second step in neurosis entails a return of the repressed, while in psychosis it involves a return of the denied, which may concern reality as well as id-derived demands. In both, then, there is a kind of failure of defense (see Waelder, 1951).

In summary, in neurosis a part of reality is avoided and in psychosis it is remodeled. In psychosis the need to meet the demands of reality almost acquires the strength of an instinctual demand. Reality makes a claim and exerts pressure on the ego. Reality tries to undo the denial, just as the id tries to undo the repression. If these efforts fail, a compromise must be reached. Essentially Freud says that the neurotic does not deny the existence of reality but tries to ignore it. The psychotic, on the other hand, denies reality and tries to substitute something else for it. It is true that Freud admits that neurosis in a sense also creates a new reality, but this is internally in the form of fantasies. The fantasies latch themselves onto reality and contaminate it, but they do not alter it in a material sense.

By no means is there general agreement on the picture described above. Even if we grant the disturbances in the sphere of reality and object relations, as well as the severe impairments in certain ego functions, we must ask whether these are *primary* disturbances, unique for psychosis. As I indicated in Chapter 9, Federn (1952) takes exception to the concept of withdrawal from and restitution of reality as a useful frame of reference, placing emphasis instead on loss of cathexis of ego boundaries. In his opinion, the loss of reality is the consequence, not the cause, of the basic psychotic deficiency, and he even sees it as part of the self-healing process of psychosis. I have also mentioned Arlow and Brenner's (1964, 1969) stance that the alterations in relation with reality are byproducts of ego defects, which themselves result from regressive ego alterations in the service of defense.

Macalpine and Hunter (1956) state: "Patients grossly out of touch with reality and obviously alienated are now called psychotic instead of mad, while those thought to be in contact with reality are diagnosed as neurotics and considered essentially sane" (p. 134). To their minds, "The pitfalls of placing so much importance on reality sense for the purpose of distinguishing neurotics from psychotics. . . are clearly demonstrated in Schreber's case. . . his reality sense was so little impaired at the time of his appeal that he took an almost decisive part in the proceedings in court himself" (1955, p. 408). Knight (1954), although not as emphatic, believes that one of the criteria leading to diagnostic errors in borderline cases is the concept of a "break with reality," as this is usually thought of in gross terms, manifest only in full-fledged psychosis. Instead, he suggests: "The break with reality, which is an ego alteration, must be thought of not as a sudden and unexpected snapping, as of a twig, but as the gradual bending as well, which preceded the snapping" (p. 99).

On the other hand, Des Lauriers (1962) takes reality as the essential frame of reference for childhood schizophrenia: "In childhood schizophrenia I saw a structural deficiency, in personality development, which left the child incapable of experiencing reality in a meaningful and goal-oriented way. . . . He was incapable of establishing stable reality relationships, because he lacked whatever was necessary for a reality experience to take place" (p. 7).

But even if we place the emphasis on reality, several other questions remain to be dealt with. In reading Freud's contributions, as well as those of others, one tends to become somewhat confused by what is meant by reality, the outer world, the inner world, etc. Nowhere do we find a clear definition. Nor does Freud define too clearly, in 1924, the inner and outer world needs. Moreover, although Freud speaks of a painful reality situation that necessitates withdrawal, it is not too clear what this painful situation is or why it is painful. (I might mention that in his 1924 papers Freud is not too specific about the nature of the danger, and the case examples he gives do not focus the problem on any specific kind of danger in reality, but rather on the way these individuals reacted to a "painful" reality.)

When we come to the painful reality situation, are we dealing with quantitative or qualitative factors? Is there anything specific about the reality that makes it so painful and threatening as to eventuate in a withdrawal leading to psychosis? Is there anything specific to the danger that plays a role in the severe alterations of ego functions so characteristic of psychosis?

Freud indicates that "the outcome of all such situations will depend on economic considerations — on the relative magnitude of the trends which are struggling with one another" (1924b, p. 152). Yet the reactions to a painful reality vary greatly, leading Hartmann (1953) and many others to focus on disturbances in the ego and its functions as taletelling in determining the ego's response to danger. Hartmann claims that "conflict with reality can, as to its causative impact, only be evaluated in relating outer frustration not only to instinctual but also to the ego aspects of the situation" (p. 179). At another point he says:

> If frustrations, and particularly narcissistic injuries, which would be of minor importance if occurring to other individuals, are frequently capable of inducing a detachment of libido and precipitating a schizophrenic process, this is essentially due to the deficiency or to the lack of stabilized power of object relations and certain ego functions. The vulnerability of the schizophrenic ego to frustrations from without indicates that its relations to reality must have been damaged. The schizophrenic ego cannot deal with those frustrations in the way they are usually dealt with because. . . its faculties of defense and of neutralization are impaired [p. 187].

I shall not at this point enter into an extensive discussion of the provocative contributions cited above. There seems, however, to be a reasonable consensus on at least the *existence* of disturbances in the ego's position vis-à-vis reality. I have already indicated that the differences in emphasis depend to a large extent on the importance given to one disturbance versus another, and on whether the ego defects are considered primary or secondary, defensive or adaptive, etc. The issue becomes even more complicated if one considers that while primary ego defects may make it difficult for reality contact to be maintained in the face of stress, they may at the same time be employed defensively, for adaptive purposes.

As we have seen, in both neurosis and psychosis there are alterations in the relationship to reality. Thus, in my opinion, there must be a rather important additional factor, which differentiates between the two. I am not sure that Freud spells this out too specifically, although in discussing denial he alludes to it (1925a, 1927). What I would say is that the alteration in the neurotic relationship with reality (e.g., flight) takes place *with the preservation of the capacity to test reality.* This is certainly not the case in psychosis, where one must presume some severe impairment of this ego function. Reality testing must be lost in order for such a severe alteration of reality to take place, for such a marked denial to be maintained. How else can we account for the extreme degree to which fantasy (the inner world) invades and retains its position in the outer world?

In previous contributions (Frosch, 1964, 1966, 1970), I have indicated that the term "break with reality" is too broad a frame of reference for establishing the presence of psychosis. With the development of a psychoanalytic ego psychology, it has become possible to examine the specific ego operations involved in such a disturbance with reality (see, for instance, Beres's [1956] list cited in Chapter 9). I myself believe that when one speaks of a break with reality, one should designate the specific area involved. Is this break reflected in the relationship with reality, the feeling of reality, or the capacity to test reality? Clearly, many other ego functions are involved in these three areas; moreover, all three are themselves interrelated. Lability in the first two areas, for instance, points to a rather tenuous hold on reality and thus affects the capacity to test reality. Yet these two areas may be impaired with a reasonable retention of the capacity to test reality. The psychotic patient may show disturbances in all these areas, but, to my mind, what is crucial to the establishment of psychosis is the loss of the capacity to test reality. Before we look at this criterion, however, we need to understand what is meant by the concept of reality and how reality is built up.

A.
The Concept of Reality

What do psychoanalysts mean when they refer to "reality"? One of the most definitive papers on this subject is by Hartmann (1956). He points out that there is an objective reality which can be validated by certain methods. Intersubjectivity plays a role in this validation, with the opinions and reactions of others to a given phenomenon taken into consideration as objective data. Yet there is also a conventional or socialized knowledge, which is intersubjectively accepted without validation. Elaborating on this idea, I would suggest that the external world (external reality) consists of a material objective reality, which stimulates the sense organs, and a nonmaterial reality (e.g., conventional and socialized knowledge). It *also* consists of the mental representation of these, the so-called object representations.

Turning to internal reality, Hartmann says: "In speaking here of 'inner reality' I am referring to the fact that in a sense all mental functions, tendencies, contents are 'real.' Fantasy activity also is real, though not realistic.[3] That is, to recognize that a fantasy is, as a mental act, real, does not mean that its contents reproduce reality" (p. 50). The internal world (internal reality) — and I am proposing this in a rather broad sense — includes, on the psychic side, memories, fantasies, impulses, desires, affects, thoughts, the body image, identity, self-representations, etc. It *also*, in my opinion, includes the correlate of material objective reality — material internal reality, namely, various somatic phenomena (which may be derived from explicable processes or even inexplicable ones). These include somatic sensations of various sorts, such as pain, spasms, heart rhythm, etc. Admittedly, these are not generally included in the concept of the internal world, which has traditionally been construed as psychic. The mental representations of these phenomena are the ones frequently involved in psychic processes.

[3] I suggest that this could contribute to the sense of conviction about something which is not realistic.

A rather intriguing view of reality is offered by Kafka (1977). As he sees it: "Our 'realities' depend on the time grid of perception, but I visualize not only different sizes of the holes in the grid, but also different shapes and different textures of the mesh. Different meshes, to carry the analogy further, permit the passage, so to speak, of different ego states from earlier and later developmental phases, various ego states in which object representations have different qualities" (p. 155).

Perhaps to underline the rather artificial separation of the various components which go to make up reality, it might be well to spend a few moments on genetic considerations in the development of reality. In doing so, it will become clear how interrelated reality development is with the object, as well as how the relationship with reality, feelings of reality, and reality testing are interwoven developmentally and operationally. In considering this subject, we might wonder how various developmentally phase-appropriate ego functions subsequently manifest themselves in the psychotic process.[4] It is obvious that reality assumes different forms at various stages in psychic development and that such realities are phase-related and appropriate. As Glover (1939) puts it: "In the clinical sense a child has a sense of reality that is just as adequate to its conditions of existence as the reality sense of the normal adult is adequate to his condition" (p. 280). Yet when the child's reality is the sole frame of reference for the adult, it is out-of-phase and inappropriate. It is viewed as psychotic.

The Building of Reality

Let us turn, then, to a survey of contributions on the development of reality, with an eye to those aspects that have the most direct relevance for an understanding of the psychotic process. To begin with, I would like to suggest a rereading of Ferenczi's (1913) contribution, which attests to the intertwining of developing object relations and the ego's position vis-à-vis reality. Both his and Freud's contributions emphasize the close relationship between ego (self), object, and reality. We can say that in the early stages of psychic development, the self and the love object are reality. Thus, genetically, retention of reality means retention of the object and involves survival of the self as well. It is from this perspective that Glover (1932b) refers to reality as the need-gratifying ob-

---

[4] I would like to make clear that I am referring here to prototypic processes (form), which may subsequently be used in the service of psychic needs, rather than to the specific content of earlier, phase-related ego functions.

ject: "From the psychiatric point of view, adult reality sense represents the capacity to maintain psychic contact with the object in or through which post-infantile modified instincts are or can be gratified. This world of objects includes all substitutions or replacement of primary unmodified objects" (p. 179).

As we shall see, certain stages in the development of object relations are crucial to the building up of reality. Interference with the unfolding of these stages will have an impact on the concept of reality, the relationship with reality, the feeling of reality, reality testing, etc. In particular, appropriate resolution of separation-individuation is coeval with the building up of reality. Along the way, the child needs an appropriate experience with transitional objects and phenomena, the intermediate area where subjective fantasy and reality overlap. Disruptions during these periods bring in their wake disturbances in the relation to reality and objects — disturbances not infrequently seen in the psychotic or the psychotic character, such as lack of object constancy and reality constancy. But I shall return to this subject later.

It should be pointed out that one of the ways the child learns about reality is through the relation to its own body (see Schilder, 1935). Yet even more important is the child's relation to significant early objects. The distinction between parts of one's own body and external objects is not yet formed during the earliest stages of psychic development. Thus, the role of the object becomes crucial in learning about reality and establishing frames of reference for reality testing. Hartmann (1956) clearly states: "The dependence upon the object, as is well known, becomes an essential factor in the human child's learning about reality. It is responsible also for typical or individual distortions of the picture of reality which the child develops. . . . A 'realistic' object can be of great assistance to the child in discriminating fantasy and reality" (pp. 42–43).

I should also like to point out that the child's psychic reality is to begin with taken from the parent's psychic reality. As Hartmann indicates: "pleasure premiums are in store for the child who conforms to the demands of reality and of socialization; but they are equally available if this conforming means the acceptance by the child of erroneous and biased views which the parents hold of reality" (p. 43). Moreover, Hartmann points out: "The child is constantly confronted with value judgments which cannot be validated objectively but which are presented to him as statements of fact. 'This is good' and 'that is bad' are often presented to him in the same way as 'this is red' and 'that is green'. Such presentations also become part of socialized reality" (p. 44).

External objects present themselves as models for reality testing and contribute significantly to the development of this ego function. A parent who says to a child, "Always do what you feel is right not what you think is right, or what is right for society" is devising not only a concept of reality for the child, but modes of testing reality. The kind of knowledge of reality the parents impart may interfere with reality testing. Durrell in *Mountolive* (1958) says: "Distortion of reality means distortion of the parents too, and the appearance of the parents and what they stand for."

Modell (1968) emphasizes the need for a "good object" in building reality and establishing reality testing: "In order to accept the separateness of an external object, something of the external world must have been brought into the ego, that is, an identification must have occurred with protective, loving, parental objects" (p. 102). Modell presupposes that the inborn autonomous ego functions involved in the structuring of reality are not impaired in borderline patients and schizophrenics. It is the subsequent ones involved in the organization of reality that are affected, and these are dependent on good mothering. He claims: "Autonomous structures will be impaired if there is an absence of the maternal environment; this more plastic organ for the structuring of reality will be impaired if there is failure of the maternal environment" (p. 88).

White (1963), in contrast, focuses on the interplay between constitutional deficiencies in the child and the mother's response to them. The former, he suggests, "seriously frustrate maternal competence and thus evolve some some of the excessive compensations that have been described in 'schizophrenogenic' mothers" (p. 189).

The role of renunciation and frustration in the building up of reality, the reality principle, and reality testing is by now accepted (see Weisman's 1958 review). The building up of reality and reality testing require the abandonment of the pleasure principle, or instinctual gratification. There must be an acceptance of what is painful and unpleasant, and of loss as part of reality. As Freud (1911a) points out: "A new principle of mental functioning was thus introduced; what was presented in the mind was no longer what was agreeable but what was real, even if it happened to be disagreeable" (p. 219). Ferenczi (1926), speaking of the incorporation of the unpleasant into one's concept of reality, indicates that the mature person takes into consideration, and into the ego, the existence of painful and frustrating aspects of reality.

Pursuing this theme, Jacobson (1964) clearly summarizes the beneficial effects of certain frustrating experiences:

The total effect of [the child's] disheartening experiences is a "disillusionment" (*Enttäuschung*, the German term for disappointment), which normally has a beneficial, double influence. Promoting the child's testing of external and of his own internal reality, it assists him... in gradually relinquishing his illusions, i.e., his magic fantasies about his love objects and himself. At the same time, however, it is the main incentive for the child's increasing idealization of his parents, because it stimulates the development of strong, reactive libidinal strivings. In general, if the hostility released by such experiences can be sufficiently absorbed and utilized by the ego, the function of reality testing profits greatly. Critical and self-critical functions are stimulated, the realistic perceptions of the world and of the self expand and sharpen, and the ability of the ego to tone down illusory concepts and expectations becomes reinforced in turn [p. 106].

Modell (1968) underlines the link between the object and reality, and claims that "the acceptance of painful reality rests upon the same ego structures that permit the acceptance of the separateness of objects" (p. 88). He relates this to reality testing, which requires the capacity for delay.

In addition, the expectation and anticipation of future gratification are important ingredients in building up reality and the ego functions related to reality. The role of expectation in the development of reality has been discussed by Benedek (1938). She describes how reality is built up out of both gratification and frustration. It is the early experience of gratification that helps to develop the person's confidence and positive anticipation that instinctual needs will be gratified by an object, i.e., reality, and this in turn helps to establish object and reality constancy. Benedek's clear description is worth citing at length:

... the child sucks playfully on the breast and plays with its hands. The libidinal satisfaction keeps the child awake and being awake enables it to perceive the environment beyond the immediate satisfaction of the need. With the experience of repeated gratification... the infant does not show its hunger with an immediate cry but follows with concentrated gaze the preparation for feeding. Thus the child has learned to wait.... The ego, which forms itself by these acts of perception, establishes its relationship to the environment; this relationship is based on confidence that the instinctual need will be satisfied really and pleasurably. The first recognition of the mother as a part of the outer world is induced by the certainty that the mother equals breast and will return to

the ego, that the mother will be within reach for gratification of the instinctual need. This confidence is a stage of object relationship which
precedes the positive object love. . . . This step levels the way from the
stage of primitive omnipotence and the reality of the object world [pp.
262–263].[5]

Repeated frustration without ultimate gratification results, in
Benedek's opinion, in impairment of ego development. She points out
that "confidence is essential in protecting the ego against object loss,"
and she believes that this also encourages reality adaptation.

Hartmann (1956) explains that the willingness to tolerate mounting
frustration, in anticipation of future gratification, paves the way for the
development of the reality principle. "This clearly presupposes two
other ego functions of the greatest importance — postponement and anticipation" (p. 32). With the acquisition of the function of anticipation,
Hartmann indicates: "What one could call the pleasure-unpleasure
balance. . . will now include, beyond the consideration of the present,
also the consideration of the future. The child in his development. . .
learns to anticipate the interaction of inner and outer reality" (p. 51).

Whereas frustration leads to the search for substitute gratification,
clearly at some point gratification is necessary to further the building up
of reality. One would expect that whatever disturbances in object relations one finds in the genesis of psychoses, one will also find some disturbance in positive anticipation, that is, in confidence in the reality of
expected gratification. The danger of the outer world as a threat from
which the psychotic withdraws is related to the fear of frustration, as
Freud indicates. But the danger also arises from a failure in the development of positive anticipation. In the paranoid psychotic, for instance,
positive anticipation is clearly impaired. The paranoid anticipates danger and frustration, not gratification. Glover (1932b) has called attention to the similarity between childhood phobic formations and subsequent paranoid reactions to the environment. This raises the question
whether one of the precursors of childhood phobias lies in the failure of
positive integration of confidence and lack of fear. This failure would
enhance negative anticipation — anticipation of frustration, danger,
and fear.

[5] In a previous communication (Frosch, 1966), I discussed at length the development of anticipation and the capacity for delay. It is this capacity for delay that facilitates the building up of reality and the ability to carry out many functions related to
reality, such as reality testing, as will be discussed in Section D of this chapter.

Reality Constancy

Anticipation, predictability, perception, reality testing, and other ego functions are facilitated by reality constancy. It enables the ego functions concerned with the environment to operate at a mature level. It combats regressive modes of operation and yet, under appropriate circumstances, permits the ego to tolerate regression. In this way it contributes to ego autonomy and ego strength. Clearly, defective reality constancy will play a large role in the psychotic process. At this point, then, it seems appropriate to detail the concept of reality constancy, which I reported on in 1966.

Reality constancy is a psychic structure that arises in conjunction with the establishment of stabilized internal representations of the environment. It evolves out of a concatenation of environmental experiences, memories, perceptions, ideas — deriving from cathected relationships with the human and nonhuman environment. Its existence is reflected in the autonomous operation of the ego functions concerned with the environment, for instance, those involved in the contact with reality, the feeling of reality, and the testing of reality. Reality constancy lends to these functions a stability and continuity which enable the individual to preserve his identity and to tolerate alterations and changes in the environment, without psychic disruptions or adaptational dysfunction.

Genetically, reality constancy is, in the earliest stages of its development, intimately interwoven with the development of object constancy, and to a considerable extent evolves out of the latter. McDevitt (1965) points out that a fruitful way to look at the matter is to think of both object constancy and reality constancy slowly developing as a consequence of the multiple interactions between the infant (with its maturing drives and autonomous ego functions) and the environment (both animate and inanimate). A consistent positive relationship with the libidinal object (the mother) is crucial in this step-by-step acquisition of both object constancy and reality constancy.

Disturbances in development of object constancy may interfere with development of reality constancy. For instance, traumatic experiences at the hands of the love object may interfere with drive neutralization, and as a consequence, there may be a pervasion of the nonhuman environment with unneutralized drive energy. This in turn may interfere with the internalization and building up of stable representations of the environment, thus affecting reality constancy. Nonetheless,

I believe it is important to note that some of the disturbances in the ego functions concerned with reality may derive from environmental experiences not directly related to the love object. I would further stress that reality constancy is not identical with object constancy. Nor do I believe there is a one-to-one correspondence between the development of object constancy and that of reality constancy. The operation of reality constancy ultimately achieves an autonomy, which has its own special qualities. Subsequent development, in my opinion, makes it pertinent, and heuristically valid, to view reality constancy as a more encompassing structure than object constancy, and it may ultimately even include the latter.

In the building up of reality, through the interactions of the organism with the human and nonhuman environments, there is a developmental course moving toward reality constancy just as there are lines of development in the evolution of object constancy (A. Freud, 1963, 1965). It is, however, a developmental course influenced by stimuli and experiences deriving from phenomena other than the love object. In early development, reality is generally interpreted in terms of the self experience. However, ultimately this exclusive dependence on the self experience has to be abandoned if reality adaptation is to develop independent of instinctual needs. In the building up of reality, forces ultimately deriving from the environment other than the self and the love object assert themselves to augment the overall process of internalization, which eventually results in the stable representation of reality. A mature capacity for environmental adaptation makes it imperative that reality evolve beyond the self and the love object as the frame of reference.

All this becomes clear when we evaluate the influence of stimuli on psychic development. It has been pointed out that not only deprivation of stimulation but also overstimulation can produce severe distortions in psychic development (Greenacre, 1941, 1952, 1954; Bergman and Escalona, 1949; Spitz, 1964; Shengold, 1967). As Greenacre (1954) indicates, "when very prolonged, severe stimulation or when multiplicity of simultaneous stimulations occurs which results in a flooding of the organism with excitation, then all channels of discharge are utilized and there may be a state of confusion, with loss of specificity of response to stimulus which is repeated later in life in states of stress" (p. 225).

Shengold (1967) views overstimulation as a traumatic experience which is ego-destructive. He cites the early stimulation derived from the feeding experience, in which the idea of being eaten by oneself, or eating oneself, is projected onto the breast as the biting object. He sees this as the prototype for later overstimulating experiences of a sexual or other nature, at the hands of significant objects, with the later experiences regressively reactivating the earlier one. This reactivation brings in its wake danger, to which the individual may react with denial, lying, etc. It represents the prototype for ego disintegration and dissolution as a result of overstimulation.

Perhaps the crucial factor is not so much insufficient stimulation or overstimulation, as non-phase-related and inappropriate stimuli. Greenacre (1952) summarizes this view:

> It appears that in evaluating the effect of trauma in the young developing organism, it is important to consider not only the maturational phase at which the trauma occurs, whether the specific nature of the trauma is one which tends to reinforce the libidinization of the dominant phase or to reinstate an already developed phase, either by direct stimulation or by encouraging regression for adequate satisfaction; but further whether the specific nature of the stimulating trauma calls for a response in accordance with a phase which is close to maturity or as yet quite immature. In addition to the specific nature of the trauma in terms of its relation to the timetable of libidinal development, the severity and the duration of traumatic conditions are most important in shaping the results [pp. 294–295].

This aspect of the problem — the impact that traumata have on psychic development — served as a focus for discussion at the Arden House meetings, at which Anna Freud (1954) and Greenacre (1954) again underlined the importance of relating the traumatizing effect of stimulation to the developmental phase. Goldfarb (1963) has suggested that "the so-called hypersensitive child is one who is living in a family environment which is specifically hyperstimulating for *him* and beyond *his* capacity to cope with perceptually" (p. 54).

In contrast to the emphasis on the negative effects of chronic overstimulation is Ferenczi's (1913) concept of the impact of traumatizing experiences in facilitating the development of new faculties:

> It is more remarkable that in the identification, the working of a second mechanism can be observed, a mechanism of the existence of which I, for one, have had but little knowledge. I mean the sudden, surprising rise of new faculties after a trauma, like a miracle that occurs upon the wave of a magic wand, or like that of the fakirs who are said to raise from a tiny seed, before our very eyes, a plant, leaves and flowers. Great need, and more especially mortal anxiety, seem to possess the power to

waken up suddenly and to put into operation latent dispositions which, uncathected, waited in deepest quietude for their development [pp. 164–165].

What I wish to emphasize is that there are stages in psychic development in which restriction of stimulation by the environment is appropriate and that certain kinds of stimuli may be phase-related. In other stages, more active and different kinds of stimulation may be needed for furthering psychic development. It is the dysphasic nature of the stimulation, as well as other experiences surrounding it, which may be crucial. The child may experience painful external and internal stimuli which are quieted by the ministrations of the mother, so that mothering tends to reduce the intensity of stimulation and facilitates the maturational development of the stimulus barrier. This is especially true at the time of access of the aggressive instincts. As Benjamin (1961) succinctly points out: "We have reason to hypothesize from our own small sample within the range of so-called normal mother-child relationships that the absence of adequate tension reduction during this 'critical period' has important results in helping to create an increased predisposition to anxiety" (p. 27).

On the other hand, the child's reactions to the environment in the process of need gratification amply indicate that there seems to be a reaching out for and seeking out of these experiences and stimuli, in addition to a responsiveness to them. At a certain stage this reaching out goes beyond need gratification — for instance, playful movements in response to sound, reaching out for the presented rattle after feeding, etc. This environment-directed seeking out reflects the active role the ego plays in the building up of reality and ultimately in contributing to reality constancy. Indeed, White (1963), with his concept of "effectance," goes so far as to say:

> The objective stable world is thus best conceived of as a construction based upon action. Knowledge about the environment is knowledge of the probable consequences of action. It is a system of readiness for action which can properly be conceived of as patterns of facilitation and inhibition in the nervous system. This is the form in which reality leaves its record, and instinctual drives are governed by it — become bound by it — because they have to use the nervous system as their means of expression, complete with its acquired facilitations and inhibitions. There is no need to assume that cathexis plays any necessary part at all in knowledge of reality [p. 188].

Certainly many of the stimuli impinging on the child are derived from other than the maternal object. In the earliest psychic stages it is probable that all stimuli, even those derived from the nonhuman environment, fall within the global experience of the infant-mother relationship. They become associated with the mother and are encompassed in the early memory traces of the latter and in representations of the love object. As such, they play a role in the development of object constancy. However, this is different in later stages of psychic development. With the gradual development of differentiation of self from external reality, there begins to evolve a capacity to discriminate between the quality and the source of stimuli, and a capacity to differentiate an experience as deriving from the love object and other human objects, as well as from the nonhuman environment.

Although not referring to reality constancy as such, Goldfarb (1963) alludes to its development as follows: "In the process of evolving a clear differentiation of the whole self from the whole environment, it is clear that there must be a consciousness of the environment as a constant source of stimulation, shifting and yet permanent and continuous in time and space" (pp. 51–52). He refers to schizophrenic children in whom deviant motility did not permit this constancy to develop and says, "The most obvious result of such environmental kaleidoscopic inconstancy is the above-mentioned disorientation with regard to the crucial concepts of time, place and person. Clinical manifestations of the disorientation to the outer world are manifold. What is most significant is the impact of such confusion on the child, an impact which includes a sense of environmental fluidity, temporariness, and unfamiliarity, whether in reference to things or humans. Objects are not conceived as unitary and permanent, particularly if they are absent from direct sensory contact" (p. 52).

Just as separation and individuation, self and nonself discrimination are essential for the development of object constancy (Hartmann, Kris, and Loewenstein, 1946; Mahler, 1963), so too are the capacity to differentiate self from the environment essential in facilitating the development of reality constancy. The latter in turn ultimately supports the preservation of differentiation between the self and the environment. Reality constancy appears and grows to the accompaniment of separation and individuation, the development of the reality principle, and concurrently with environmental differentiation.

Reality constancy is within the domain governed by the reality principle, and even contributes to its operation. Just as the development of the reality principle depends on the evolution of ego functions concerned with reality, so too is it related to the development of reality constancy, which is itself an expression of the operation of the reality principle. Schur (1965) suggests that reality constancy is the more or less permanent result of the functioning of reality testing (as well as other ego functions concerned with reality), extended over a prolonged period of maturation and development, under the dominance of the reality principle.

ANIMISM

In many borderline and psychotic patients this environmental differentiation has not fully developed, and the nonhuman environment is still instinctualized and animistic. The symbolic meaning of the inanimate and nonhuman environment takes on pathogenic anthropomorphic dimensions with the defective reality constancy seen in these patients. The environment has not acquired its full reality significance and is frequently alive for such patients.

It is of interest that in discussing the reality world of the child, Glover (1939) points to the animism that permeates this world: "Thus the bars of the cot against which the infant strikes itself may be a number of malignant mothers whom he attacks and who at the same instant strike him back. His thumb may be a mother-god to be alternately sucked and bitten or a father-god to be adored; a piece of tinkling glass may promise him ecstatic communion with the cosmos. Later, every recognisable object in the nursery is alive and according to his mood menacing or friendly. His inside in possessed of demons or sometimes of angels" (p. 31).

In previous communications (Frosch, 1959, 1964, 1970), I have discussed the clinical manifestations of animism in a number of patients. During an especially phobic period, for instance, one female patient said, "You know, Dr. Frosch, everything around me is alive — the lamp, the book, the pillow, everything." These objects were all capable of feeling and of having affect. At one point, the patient indicated that if things around her were alive, she too could feel and be alive.

This patient recounted how her mother touched objects: "My mother just loved objects. They are, like, alive for her. She speaks about them: 'Look how sad this object looks — isn't it beautiful? You should not neglect it. Turn it around and let it breathe a little.' She never treats me this way. She will look at a saucer and say it is beautiful. The cup on the saucer is like a man and a woman, but it is not like me; a cup can't screw a saucer. I can screw and I am different." From this, she came to her own attempts to animate objects. It was clear that in doing so she hoped to establish a relationship with her mother.

Renee (Sechehaye, 1956a) describes the aliveness of her nonhuman surroundings: "Suddenly 'the thing' sprang up. The stone jar, decorated with blue flowers, was there facing me, defying me with its presence, with its existence. To conquer my fear I looked away. My eyes met a chair, then a table; they were alive, too, asserting their presence. I attempted to escape their hold by calling out their names" (p. 35). Things to her became more real than people.

There are many situations in which such animism may occur in the adult. A person in a state of isolation may, in addition to hallucinating, experience the whole environment as animated. Andreyev (1925) describes a man who was isolated in a prison cell, condemned to death. He appeared to enter into a depersonalized state, and as he did so all in the cell became animated:

> He was in the situation of a man who, left alone in a house at night, should see all things become animate, move, and assume over him an unlimited power, suddenly the wardrobe, the chair, the sofa, the writing table would sit in judgment upon him. He would cry out, call for help, and move from room to room; and the things would speak to each other in their own tongue; and then the wardrobe, the chair, the sofa, and the writing table would start to hand him, the other things looking on [pp. 405–406].

In a television show I watched recently a woman was making the final rounds in a house from which the family was moving. She began to feel terrified that the house, in its anger at being abandoned, would avenge itself upon her. The walls, doors, windows, floors — all began to assume a threatening stance. She no longer had the house keys and was supposed to exit through the open garage doors and then close them. Suddenly the garage doors began to descend and, before she could do anything, the garage was closed. The door leading into the house could not be opened. She felt she was doomed to perish as punishment for abandoning the house.

Loewenstein (1965) suggests that a well-developed reality constancy could be characterized in terms of emancipation from animistic or anthropomorphic reactions to inanimate or nonhuman reality. It is not necessary, however, to assume that maximum independence is always optimal. Writers, poets, and painters, for instance, may need to preserve remnants of a somewhat anthropomorphic view of nonhuman nature. It is possible that for some descriptive biologists the same may be true. In contrast, in other people, remoteness from an animistic view of nature may go beyond the usual. They like to think of and understand nature in terms of abstract concepts, removed as far as possible from an experiential approach to nature. None of these various approaches to nature should be considered as pervading the whole personality; for instance, a theoretical physicist may possess a very animistic approach to some aspects of reality, while an artist may have perfectly well-developed reality constancy.

FURTHER IMPAIRMENTS OF REALITY CONSTANCY

It is important in the process of differentiation between self and environment that the ego functions concerned with the latter develop so that they may operate in a relatively conflict-free manner and with relatively neutral energy, thus facilitating the mastery of environmental experiences. In the same way that ambivalence toward the object impedes the development of object constancy, so does ambivalence in the relationship to the environment interfere with the development of reality constancy. In a sense the development of reality constancy is supported by the neutralization of energy used by those ego functions concerned with environmental mastery, and subsequently reality constancy also facilitates the preservation of this neutralized energy.

Patients under the impact of the psychotic process show an inability to tolerate changes in the human and nonhuman environment, as well as difficulty in receptivity and adaptation to new experience. This limitation is related to defects in the establishment of both object and reality constancy. One of my psychotic character patients was quite uncomfortable in new and unfamiliar settings. She had difficulty orienting herself in such situations and restricted her field of operations, devoting herself with almost obsessive fixity to familiar housekeeping tasks rather than embarking on new, more venturesome enterprises. Yet the same difficulty also appeared in relation to certain familiar experiences. Although she made the same trip on the subway innumerable times, she had to reorient herself each time as though it were the first.

Spitz and Wolf (1949), in discussing this problem, indicate: "It is the original experience with the libidinal object which creates an expectancy pattern. Where that is lacking each single object will have to be approached as an experiment, as an adventure, and as a peril" (p. 110). I would say that this is equally true in meeting new environmental experiences when there is deficient development of reality constancy. The latter facilitates, for instance, the transition from the analytic situation to reality. Patients with defective reality constancy have repeated difficulty in reorienting themselves to the external environment after an analytic session. They also have difficulty in preserving their identity in relation to physical changes in the office.

Similar reactions may be experienced in relation to the changing appearance of the analyst. Freedman (1964) has presented a situation in which he believed psychotic transference reactions developed. During a vacation he grew a beard and, on his return to practice, he observed the effect of his changed visage on the transference situation. All his patients noticed the beard and reacted to it in some way, but the effect on the transference situation differed considerably. Disturbed reactions were especially evident in borderline patients, who were in some instances quite markedly shaken and upset. Freedman suggests that his neurotic patients, in whom the ego functions concerned with reality were preserved, could deal with their fantasies about the analyst and recognized the analyst as a separate being. This, however, was not always true of his borderline and psychotic patients.

The psychotic process disrupts the stability of internalized images of the external environment achieved with reality constancy. Reality representation is no longer fused or correlated with material reality. To correlate the two, these patients need constant reaffirmation by material reality. In many instances, they can hold onto material reality quite well, but the hold on representations is insecure. I have described a patient who had considerable difficulty buying clothes for her children when they were not physically present (Frosch, 1964). She could not visualize how big they were, whether they were thin or fat, etc. She also had difficulty buying things for the house, such as curtains, because she was never quite sure what the house really looked like when she was not in it. This is one of the consequences of tenuous reality constancy, and it brings into play regressive modes of relating to reality.

Clearly, many areas overlap in the concept of reality. This is especially true when we consider the genetic factors, which highlight the close interrelationship between ego, self, object, and reality. Genetic considerations also encompass the relationship with reality, the sense of reality, reality testing, and the relation with the object — all of which will be discussed in more detail in the forthcoming sections.

B.
The Relationship with Reality and the Object

I have repeatedly called attention to the overlap of the areas under discussion. Nowhere is this more apparent than in a consideration of the relationship with reality and the love object. As I pointed out above, in the early stages of psychic development the self and the love object *are* reality, so that genetically, retention of reality signifies retention of the object and touches on survival of the self. Although I believe there is heuristic value in teasing these areas apart for discussion, let me stress again the importance of keeping in mind the intertwining of the different aspects of reality.

The Relationship with Reality

The relationship with reality involves one's capacity to perceive the external and internal world and the appropriateness of one's relationship to them. Disturbances in the ego's relationship with reality may manifest themselves in perceptual distortions.[6] Rubinfine (Freedman, 1962, 1964) believes that in all psychoses, whether schizophrenic, organic, or depressive, there is a primary and constitutional disturbance in perceptual consciousness. The defect in this ego function retards and interferes with the development of the boundary between self and nonself because it interferes with the registration of information from the outside world, as well as from the inside world. He postulates that there may be an inherent defect in psychotics which predisposes them to loss of sensory intake from the outer world. This loss contributes to the blurring of ego boundaries as well as to distorted perception of reality.

Goldfarb (1963) describes "an active cognitive process intermediate between percept and action which stores the multitude of diverse and disparate percepts in the form of essences, regularities, universals, con-

[6] Perception is one of the many ego functions involved in the relationship with reality, and it is interwoven with the development of reality constancy.

stants, and predictables." "On this basis," he says, "the ego is able to formulate suitable representations of the environment and plans for
managing it" (p. 59). In Goldfarb's opinion, the building up of the
"constancy" and "universality" of the environment is facilitated by distance perception — i.e., by visual and auditory cues. This is not possible
with proximal receptors. Yet while the capacity for discriminatory perception facilitates the development of object constancy and reality constancy, it is also dependent on the existence of these structures, at least
in elementary form.

Mahler (1960) has indicated that early traumatic experiences may
contribute to failure in the perceptual-integrative capacity of the ego.
This defect potentiates dedifferentiation to the point where the primary
discrimination between animate and inanimate is lost. In essence,
Mahler looks on dehumanization and reanimation as a regressive adaptation, when the ego's perceptual-integrative capacity fails. Yet it is the
latter defect that facilitates reanimation of the nonhuman environment. I also wonder what role defects in the development of reality
constancy play in facilitating dedifferentiation (see my discussion of
animism in the last section).

Perceptual distortions may occur in relation to internal as well as
external reality. Various somatic sensations, for instance, may reflect
such a distortion. A patient may become acutely aware of his heart
beat, breathing, peristaltic action, etc., and this may assume bizarre
proportions, to the point of somatic delusions and introjected objects.
As I have noted elsewhere, one patient felt pulsating sensations in her
uterine area, and these ultimately became a being who exerted great
power over her actions.

An interesting form of perceptual distortion in the psychotic or
potentially psychotic is heightened perception, in which sensory stimuli
are experienced very vividly. External objects assume particularly clear
outlines; colors stand out sharply. A heightened awareness of somatic
processes may even be incorporated into a delusional system (see
above). The same may hold true for thoughts. Clinically, we are familiar with the heightened perception and the sense of apprehension in the
paranoid (see, for instance, my discussion of Silverman's 1978 remarks
in Chapter 4, p. 145). There is an extreme sensitivity to loud voices of
any type, as well as a tendency to hypercathect external stimuli. Indeed, the initiation of many a psychosis is accompanied by such hyperperception of stimuli.

Elaborating on Freud's idea that the vividness of images in dreams points to the reproduction of an actual childhood situation, I have proposed something similar for the heightened perception seen in the psychotic (Frosch, 1967a). To some extent, the vivid perception in the psychotic may also be due to current derivatives of more primitive and vulnerable ego states, during which stimuli could break through the stimulus barrier more easily and be perceived more vividly. In particular, the alertness and heightened responsiveness of the paranoid to stimuli may relate to a period in psychic development when anxieties about the outside world provoked not only a withdrawal but a sharpened defensive interest in it.[7]

In children, animistic fears of the outside world may manifest themselves as phobias and other allied anxieties. Glover (1939) suggests: "When the mechanisms governing these reactions are identified it will be found that they are in many respects similar to those observed in paranoid states. Most significant in this respect are the primary phobias of infancy, e.g., of being alone (subject to danger), of darkness, noise, food, and of strange objects" (pp. 232–233). Glover considers these responses as deriving from projection of internal pain and overexcitation. But the heightened responsiveness to stimuli which goes with such phobias is highly suggestive of those ego disturbances in primitive states described by Bergman and Escalona (1949). In the adult paranoid this appears as an exquisite capacity to sense the finer nuances of external situations. The antennae are sharply attuned to stimuli, which may then be woven into the psychotic system.

An interesting question presents itself concerning the stage in the perceptual process at which distortion takes place. A patient hearing a car backfire says it is a rifle shot which has killed a relative. Is there already some disturbance at the level of sensing and registering the external stimulus, or is the external stimulus sensed correctly, only to be distorted later in the perceptual chainwork, and if so, where? Are we perhaps dealing with an impairment in the discriminating ability of the stimulus-sensing organ, which facilitates the substitution of one stimulus for another in the service of the patient's needs? It is not unlike the problem of the working over of the day residue in dreams. At which stage in the process, from the experiencing of the day residue to the dream, does the dream formation take shape?

There is ample evidence to indicate that even in instances of seem-

---

[7]Sylvan Keisser (personal communication) suggests that the heightened perception is due to a regression of the ego function of perception (hearing and seeing) to earlier modes which were less discriminating or selective.

ing nonperception accurate registration has been made, even though this registration may have been subjected to subsequent symbolic distortion (Fisher, 1953). Hartmann and Betlheim (1924), in their work on perceptual distortion in Korsakow's psychosis, found that the stimulus had been registered as well as retained, even though it was distorted in the patient's confabulations. Such material would reemerge even after surprisingly long intervals. To quote the authors: "It seems to be significant that we found no correlation between registration disturbance and confabulatory tendency. It is justifiable to assume that impairment of registration tends to facilitate the emergence of subjective material which in turn may render the retention of external impressions difficult; nevertheless these disorders seem to run two rather independent courses" (pp. 363–364).

It is still, however, unclear at what point in the chain of events the distortion takes place. Nor is there any concrete evidence that in the nonorganic psychotic there is any impairment of the actual sensing and registration of stimuli, although this is suggested in the dedifferentiation of the perceptual experiences in the organic psychosis. In the nonorganic patient, the backfiring of a car may be sensed as accurately as any loud noise. The dedifferentiation in the psychotic process may take place subsequent to registration and facilitate the emergence of subjective material, very much as impairment of registration in the organic may do. Yet here Freeman (1973) contrasts perception in the organic and nonorganic patient. He points out that in organic psychoses perception can be severely disturbed and yet object constancy can be retained. This is not true, however, in the nonorganic psychoses, where object representations periodically lose their cathexis.

McGhie (1966), in his psychological studies of schizophrenics, points to defects in attention, immediate memory, and perception. Clinically, this may lead to manifestations such as distractibility, lack of attentive capacity, and faulty concentration. George Klein (1959) emphasizes that other processes than repression may block awareness of stimuli. A wide array of nonexperienced contents may be subjected to perceptual maneuvers and different states of consciousness, aside from repression, which may operate to keep such nonexperienced contents out of the sphere of awareness. Cancro (1976, 1979a, 1979b) also emphasizes attention defects as of major significance. He claims: "The regulation of attention can explain the psychology of the cardinal symptoms of schizophrenia, including the disorders of cognition, affect, and object relations. Attention is the psychologic construct that is hypothesized as the regulator of information flow in the nervous system, particularly the distribution between inner and outer sources of stimuli" (1976, p. 92).

I have referred already (p. 228) to a study in which marked perceptual distortions took place in a tachistoscopic exposure of sexual material. The nature of the material seemed to produce a degree of regressive dedifferentiation in the sensing experience, which facilitated denial and symbolic distortion, resulting in perceptual distortion.[8] Such dedifferentiation, as a defense or as a byproduct of a defective ego, would seem to have special significance for the psychotic.

As noted above, dedifferentiation — one of the characteristic mechanisms in the psychotic process — is related by Mahler (1960) to a failure in the ego's perceptual-integrative capacity. The ego "is eventually relegated to become the passive victim of the defused, rapidly deneutralized instinctual forces. . . [and] in this regressed state the impulse is experienced as a compelling command which continually threatens the disintegrating ego from within. . . . Stimuli reaching the rapidly fragmenting ego from the living object world are much more complex, and seem to be much more dangerous." In trying to ward off the impact of stimuli, the ego resorts to psychotic mechanisms such as massive denial, condensation, and dedifferentiation. Mahler goes on to say: "Complex stimuli, particularly those demanding social emotional responses, are massively denied, autistically hallucinated away, so that ego-regression may not halt before a level of perceptual dedifferentiation at which primal discrimination between living and inanimate is lost" (p. 549). She sees as common to all psychotics, a blurring or failure of perceptual discrimination of the social and the human object world from the inanimate environment. There is a consequent deanimation of the human object, with concomitant animation of the inanimate environment. In this process of dehumanization, there is also devitalization of the patient's own body feelings.

Implicit in the above discussion is the idea of a failure in the stimulus barrier, which, with maturation, should have evolved to deal with unwanted internal and external stimuli. The concept of the stimulus barrier as a means of protection and defense against impingement of

[8] As I have discussed on previous occasions (Frosch, 1967a), there are suggestions that the psychotic process brings into being ego functions coeval with earlier phases of psychic development. I have also suggested that insofar as perception is concerned, this nondiscrimination of external stimuli — so characteristic of early sensory development — is reinstated, thus facilitating distortion.

both internal and external stimuli on the nervous system was formulated rather early by Freud. Physiologically, its immature, early state is reflected in the Moro response in infants to loud noises or sudden disruptions of equilibrium. Lustman (1956) in fact reports marked variation in the infant's response to stimuli applied to various parts of the body.

The gradual development of the physiological stimulus barrier goes hand in hand with that of the psychological one. The latter incorporates multiple ego functions, such as the capacity for reality testing, evaluation, judgment, anticipation, and delay, among others. All of these not only facilitate the mastery of stimuli but also defensively control the impact on the psychic apparatus. Indeed, Silverman (1978) proposes that the development of defenses, and methods of coping with stress, is phase-related to the development of the stimulus barrier.

In early development, then, coeval with the lack of self-nonself differentiation, there is an absence of the capacity for perceptual discrimination of stimuli, which makes it difficult to distinguish dangerous from nondangerous stimuli. The development of this capacity seems to be multiply determined, depending not only on psychological factors such as the development of self-nonself differentiation and related ego functions, but also on biological and cultural variables. It has, for instance, been found that the capacity to discriminate stimuli is lost in monkeys when parts of the temporal lobe are removed (Klüver and Bucy, 1937), suggesting a physiological correlate. From a different angle, studies on pain perception indicate that such perception differs from person to person and from culture to culture. As Melzak (1973) points out, although there is a uniform sensation threshold, attention, suggestion, cultural background, and early childhood experiences all play a role in pain perception. These factors that apply to pain perception may apply to other perceptual experiences, either in over- or underperception or in the attaching of some significance to perception. Moreover, many psychological variables may intervene between stimulus registration and perception, producing a high degree of variability between the two.

The interrelationship between biological and psychological factors in perceptual experiences of the psychotic may be indicated by biochemical studies of the role of catecholamine receptors as well as endorphin and enkaphalin receptors. Work by Rosengarten and Friedhoff (1979) suggests that in the earliest stages of development there is a lack of differentiation in receptors, leading to stimulus confusion and thus response confusion. It is striking that this state is coeval with lack of self-nonself differentiation, making it difficult for the early psychic organism to interpret the location and meaning of sensory experiences of all types. Probably, both biologically and psychologically, this state has an impact on the stimulus barrier, facilitating excessive impingement on the psychic apparatus or the opposite. If this state persists or is regressively reactivated, it may lend itself to various interpretations by the patient in the light of existing conflicts and dangers, be they derivatives of aggressive or erotic drives or, as in the psychotic, danger of self-dissolution and threat to survival.

In the psychotic process we see a reactivation of an archaic stimulus barrier with a psychologically low threshold. The causes may be endopsychic, neurochemical, or exogenous in origin. It is interesting that Silver (1981) reports that children with central nervous system dysfunctions are unable to manage stimuli, and are overwhelmed by such stimuli as a result of a lowered stimulus barrier. The anxiety these children develop resembles the basic anxiety I described in Chapter 7.

The clinical implications of the impact of stimuli on an early, highly vulnerable ego, which is incapable of permitting gradual perception and assimilation, have been discussed by Bergman and Escalona (1949), among others (see p. 284). They propose that this is a genetic factor in schizophrenia. Based on a study of several children they considered psychotic, they suggest that constitutional defects in the stimulus barrier made the children highly sensitive to stimuli. In an effort to defend against this, there was a premature development of ego functions which apparently collapsed after a while. In their opinion, "the infant who is not sufficiently protected from stimuli either because of a 'thin protective barrier', or because of the failure of maternal protection, may have to resort for such protection to premature formation of an ego. When this premature ego breaks down, possibly as a consequence of a trauma, the psychotic manifestations are thought to set in" (p. 347). Bergman and Escalona are, however, very careful to caution against considering unusual sensitivities in children as indications of future psychosis. Unfortunately there was no follow-up study on these children or others.

Whether such findings should be looked upon as causative or as concomitant findings in a potentially psychotic individual is of course open to discussion. Still, the impact of excessive stimuli on the as yet vulnerable ego of the infant is considered highly contributory to severe ego ruptures. The early experience of being intruded on and penetrated may, for instance, contribute to continued disruption in the development of ego boundaries, impaired self-nonself differentiation, and other distortions in ego (self) experiences vis-à-vis reality, with accompanying ego states regressively reexperienced in the psychotic patient. These ego defects may of course be borrowed in the service of many needs and fantasies.

The impact of all the above disturbances in the ego's relationship with reality clearly involve the nature and level of object relations. As I have emphasized several times, object relations are intertwined with all the areas we have been discussing (e.g., the nature of the conflict and danger confronting the psychotic). I would now like to elaborate on some specific aspects of object relations and how they affect the relationship with reality.

THE RELATIONSHIP WITH THE OBJECT

Throughout the discourse thus far I have made repeated reference to the position of the object, which I have indicated is really an integral part of the relationship with reality. Yet even the heading here is ambiguous, since to a large extent we are concerned with the position of the *self* vis-à-vis the object, as well as with the role of the ego and its functions in this relationship.[9] What will become clear is that I view self-nonself disturbances as an outgrowth of disturbances in the ego and its functions vis-à-vis reality, including the relationship with reality.

I should also note that in discussing the role of the object in the psychotic process, I do not intend to survey the spate of contributions to object relations theory. Object relations theory suffers from the variety of ways in which the concept of object relations is defined (see Kanzer, 1979). In more traditional theories, the concept is tied in with psychosexual development, with emphasis on the drive-centered development of object relations. Object relations are seen as offering a means for libidinal drive gratification. In contrast are those theories in which libidinal drives are depicted as fulfilling a primary need for object relations. I shall return to this subject subsequently. Let me simply state at this point that to the extent that contributions from object relations theory have some relevance to my focus on the psychotic process, I shall try to evaluate such contributions.

In discussing the position of the object, we have to differentiate be-

[9] Again, what is required is a somewhat clearer delineation between the terms "ego" and "self," a distinction not too frequently observed in the psychoanalytic literature (see p. 257). Winnicott, Federn, and many others use the terms interchangeably.

tween the need for the object, the fear of its loss, the struggle to retain it, and the disturbances in ego functions that make the hold on the object a rather tenuous one. We need to evaluate those ego functions which have contributed to making the object relationship what it is, and those which influence the struggle for retention. To put this somewhat differently, we must look at both those impaired ego functions which affect disintegration of the object relationship, as well as those which facilitate subsequent restitution. Impaired ego functions make the possibility of loss greater in the psychotic (or potentially psychotic) and the possibility of restitution or reintegration less.

THE GENETIC ASPECTS

I have already discussed some of the genetic features in the development of object and reality constancy (see Section A), and will now expand on this subject. An understanding of these aspects is important as the psychotic process regressively reactivates the early level of object relations, bringing with it the ego functions coeval with that early level. It may even be that in the potential psychotic, inherent defects in those ego functions which go into the building up of reality and object relations make for fixation to this mode of relating to reality and the object.

Object relations evolve as a differentiating process from the mother-infant dual unity. Mahler (1968) describes, as a first step, the development of libidinal cathexes proceeding from the internal organs (the viscera in particular), toward the periphery, the rest of the body self (see also Schilder, 1935; Federn, 1952). This step is part of a process leading to the building up of a body image and a self-image. As this process evolves into a relationship with the object, the love object is at first a need-satisfying part-object; only later is the object viewed as a whole person, independent of need gratification. It is at this later stage that object constancy begins to evolve, accompanied by self-object differentiation and the consolidation of a sense of separateness and individual identity.[10] This process is partially facilitated by identification with the object.

I have already noted how many writers use instinct theory and the idea of libidinal gratification and frustration as the frames of reference in establishing the intimate relationship between the self, the object, and reality. Libidinal shifts are held to be the most tale-telling in the

[10] Modell points out that "those individuals who have the capacity to accept the separateness of objects are those who have a distinct, at least in part, beloved sense of self" (1968, p. 59). This enables one to accept limitations.

building up of reality. To Glover (1932b), as we have seen, reality is the need-gratifying object. In other words, the object is the world of the infant, and its retention is most essential for survival. As Modell (1968) says: "if we consider the early development of the mind, we know that for the young child the mother and the environment are indeed synonymous" (p. 8). Indeed, I doubt whether there would be much disagreement with the concept that in the early stages of psychic development the self and object are reality and that the retention of reality really means, genetically, the retention of the relationship to the object and involves survival of the self as well.

In the hierarchy of reality development, need-gratifying aspects are supplemented by frustrating, painful, and unpleasant aspects (see p. 280). Actually Freud's very concept of reality is related to the father, with the castration threat becoming a representation of reality. Loewald (1951) widens the scope by postulating two pairs of relationships, both ambivalent, toward the parents, these influence the meaning of reality and the relationship with the object. Toward the mother, there is a positive libidinal attachment growing out of the primary narcissistic attachment, but there is also a negative, defensive relationship based on a primitive fear of being sucked back into the maternal womb. Toward the father, there is a negative, defensive relationship based on the threat of castration, but there is also a positive one based on identification, which is used as a defense in an alliance with the father against the fear of being swallowed up by the womb.

Adding an additional perspective, Hartmann (1956) remarks:

> I just want to note the obvious truth, that a child's attitudes towards reality and conceptions of reality pass through several stages of relations to the objects which leave their imprint on them. Both mother and father play a dominant role in the vicissitudes of the child's relation to reality, but I think that the concepts of both reality and the reality principle as presented by Freud are of a far more general nature. The child's concepts of reality can be followed through the vicissitudes of object relations and conflicts [p. 34].

But Hartmann believes that it goes beyond this and that there are inherent ego apparatuses which are the precursors of reality and play an important role in its establishment (e.g., delay, anticipation, objectivization, differentiation).

As I indicated earlier, White (1963) tends to minimize the impact of instinct-gratifying or frustrating objects in the development of reality. He sees the child's actions as not simply instinct-motivated but also as "responsible for important learning about the ways in which reality can and cannot be influenced. The reality principle is broadly based in action, and action is broadly based not only in instinctual energies but also in the exploratory and manipulative tendencies that spring from the independent ego energies here called effectance. Instinctual frustration provides but one of several inducements to shape behavior in accord with realistic considerations" (pp. 47–48). Like Hartmann, he believes that autonomous and conflict-free ego energies are directly involved in building up reality, and that these will encompass the inanimate world quite actively, apart from the aims of food, sex, or avoidance of pain. He seems therefore to reject the whole concept of libidinal cathexis as playing a necessary part in the knowledge of reality, and attacks the concept of the mother as being the center for the development of and testing of reality. As a matter of fact, he suggests that inanimate objects are more conducive to the development of object constancy than the less reliable and more variable maternal objects.

Des Lauriers (1962) is quite at variance with White, for he makes the mother and the instinctual drives the focus for the development of reality. According to him, the libidinal needs are most active in building up and maintaining reality. Reality therefore grows out of need-gratifying situations and objects. In addition, Des Lauriers reemphasizes what is commonly accepted, that differentiation of self from nonself is most crucial in the development of reality: "Thus the primary model of reality, in the psychological experience of reality, achieved through the development of the ego, can be seen, with reference to the developing subject as the ego feeling of his bodily boundaries, and with reference to the formation of an object, as the ego's awareness of the bodily limits of the mother" (pp. 29–30).

Modell (1968) also emphasizes the role of the mother in the development of object relations. In his opinion, "psychic development requires a specific form of identification that depends upon the actual experience of 'good enough' parental care. Historical reconstruction does not permit us to date precisely when this identification has occurred; it is a period prior to the development of the definitive superego, that is, prior to the ages of three to five" (p. 56). He later refers to the impact of a failure in this identification, saying that "a failure in the 'holding environment' leads to a failure of identification. Such a failure has momentous effects. It leads to the persistence of 'untamed' instinctual demands, a relative inability to tolerate frustration, an inability to tolerate the limitations of loved objects. Such an intolerance is displaced upon the world at large and is experienced as an inability to accept the pain and frustration of reality" (pp. 86–87).

Without entering into this controversy over the import of libidinal gratification in detail, let me say that, in my opinion, White oversimplifies the problem at the cost of throwing out the baby with the bathwater. There is no doubt that much of what White reports is observationally verifiable (he leans heavily on Piaget's findings). However, a good deal of confusion arises from his equation of the word "external" with the adult's concept of the "not me." Nothing that he points out appears to me to negate the important role of the maternal object in providing libidinal (instinct) gratification and frustration, and thus serving as a model and central factor in all aspects of reality. It is this role that leads to an interweaving of reality, reality testing, discrimination of self, and the whole area of object relations. That autonomous ego functions and the built-in ego apparatus for carrying out reality-related activities are actively engaged in this process is, I think, most plausible. But prototypically, these are brought into the service of instinct-initiated needs, even though the later derivatives and representations of these activities may be mainly in the service of mastering the environment, using mainly, if you will, "neutral" ego energies.[11]

It should be pointed out that a child who meets a need for gratification, by means of an action, may not as yet have evolved a concept that this gratification derives from the external environment. The source of the gratification is unknown at the early stages in psychic development. Such gratification could very well be in the service of relieving some vague kinesthetic sensations, as the result of neurogenic processes which not only facilitate the child's actions, but even initiate them. In other words, bodily sensations of some sort may require action or movement, and may in turn be gratified by the child's actions. Such sensations may even contribute to the building up of the body image and sense of identity. The source of the means of gratification, during the stage of unconditional omnipotence, may even be viewed as deriving from the self, vague as this entity may be.

Certainly there seems to be a relationship between neurological development and facilitation of behavior. The sensations accompanying neurological development (e.g., myelinization) may be a motivat-

---

[11] I suggested to Hartmann many years ago that one ought to differentiate inherent *neutral* energies from those which derive from the neutralization of instinctual drives. Only the latter should be referred to as neutral*ized* energies. Hartmann seemed to agree.

ing force toward action. Such sensations, biologically derived, may be construed as unpleasurable and the ensuing action may be in the service of the pleasure-pain principle. Essentially actions which are not in themselves directly tension-reducing, but which affect the environment in some way that favors tension reduction, may even be in the service of the reality principle. The psychotic process may reactivate such earlier concepts of reality and the object, as well as modes of dealing with needs, in a manner consonant with those earlier concepts. But one does not have to go as far as Glover does in postulating that all later objects and reality are essentially displacements of earlier libidinally cathected ones. Nor does one have to go as far as White does in rejecting the role of the mother and libidinal needs in the building up of reality.

Hartmann's (1953) survey of the genetic factors in object relations seems quite relevant at this point. He describes two stages of development in object relations in terms of the relation to the need-satisfying object and in terms of the achievement of object constancy. He points out that in the early stages of self-object development the self is still nothing but a prolongation of the child's activity. Later, with some differentiation between the object and the self, the child makes distinctions between the activity and the object toward which the activity is directed. This later stage brings out an aspect of objectivization (an ego contribution to the development of object relations), and from now on there is a difference between the cathexis of an object-directed ego function and the cathexis of an object representation. Hartmann indicates that the disturbance in schizophrenia does not permit this objectivization and degree of differentiation, so that together with self-object dedifferentiation or lack of differentiation, one sees cathexis of activities involving need-gratifying objects and lack of object constancy.

Hartmann's (1952, 1953) interest in delineating the impaired ego functions in schizophrenia leads him to state that full object relations require, as one contribution from the ego, some degree of neutralization of libidinal and aggressive energy to secure constancy of the object independent of the need situation. He claims:

> It is very likely that distorted object relations are one predisposing agent in the development of schizophrenia. They have to be considered from the point of view of aggression as well as libido and also as to the mutual influences of ego and id — one decisive factor on the side of the ego, being the level of neutralization. In schizophrenia this level is lowered as shown in the defenses, in reality testing, and contact with reality. This dedifferentiation of the ego also means that the more differentiated form

of object relations (and for that matter objectivization) can no longer be maintained. In their place we find incomplete demarcation or fusion of self and object, and lack of differentiation also between ego and id. We know that in the development of the child, self-object and ego-id differentiation run parallel [1953, p. 191].

Transitional Objects

It is inevitable that early disturbances in object relations have an impact on subsequent developmental stages, affecting development of a mature sense of self and object. There is no doubt that various stages in the separation-individuation process are impaired (see the discussion of Mahler's contributions in Chapter 12). For instance, the positive development of a transitional object on the way to mature object relations will be affected. Modell (1968) has described at length the therapeutic implications of defective transitional object relations in his borderline patients. He summarizes the concept of the transitional object as follows:

> ... the transitional object is a substitute for the actual environment, a substitute that creates the illusion of encapsulating the subject from the dangers of the environment. The transitional object is not a hallucination — it is an object that does exist "in the environment," separate from the self, but only partially so. It is given form and structure, that is, it is created by the needs of the self. The relationship of the subject to the object is fundamentally ambivalent; the qualities of the object are magical and hence there is an illusion of connectedness between the self and the object. The relation of the subject to the object is primarily exploitive, the subject feels no concern for the needs of the object and cannot acknowledge that the object possesses his own separateness and individuality. The transitional object relationship is dyadic — it admits no others [p. 40].

Modell, however, broadens the concept of the transitional object by equating it with part-objects and symbiotic objects. He thus diffuses this most useful concept beyond its original intent, at times adding considerable confusion. For instance, he says: "Object relations based on a transitional mode acknowledge the existence of an object outside the self, but its separateness from the self is denied by magical illusion. . . . Although the object is created by the subject, it is still an object; it is something which the self requires for its safety" (p. 109).

Modell keeps emphasizing the protective quality of the transitional object. I believe, on the other hand, that compensation for loss is the important factor in the development of the transitional object. A five-year-old child, for instance, looked on her transitional object, a doll, as a little sister. She had none in reality, and lavished on this doll the love and attention she yearned to have. Through an identification with both the doll and her mother, she found gratification in this transitional object. The specific object was supplemented by numerous imaginary companions, all of them sisters.

In some of my psychotic and psychotic character patients, there has either been an absence of a transitional object or some interference with this stage in the development of object relations. A 32-year-old female patient, for example, revealed some interference in the full development of a transitional object. Although she had had some stuffed toys, her mother had never let her take any of them to bed. For years, as an adult, she had a little dog which she took to bed with her regularly. "I love that animal more than anyone else," she explained. She would cuddle and hug it and keep the dog very close to her in bed. Her life had been characterized by repetitive failures in her interpersonal relations, with both men and women. She would try in a sense to have them fulfill her need for a transitional object. No one was really perceived by her as a person with autonomous needs of his own. Relationships with others only had meaning in terms of her own self. Invariably these relationships would collapse, but she always attributed this to the other person's disappointing her in some way.

Object Constancy

In discussing the development of object relations, it is obvious that the ultimate outcome should be the development of object constancy. Defective object constancy is an integral part of the psychotic process, very much as defective reality constancy is (see Section A of this chapter). Yet, although both are usually impaired in the psychotic process, it is possible in some instances for object constancy to remain reasonably intact while reality constancy is defective, or vice versa (Frosch, 1966). It is thus appropriate to clarify the concept of object constancy.

Anna Freud (1963, 1965) traces the development of object constancy from the earliest periods of biological unity between infant and mother to its firm establishment. For this, as many writers have emphasized, consistency in the behavior opf the primary love object is necessary; it facilitates the formation of an object representation which can remain constant in time and space and consistent with itself in spite of subsequent alterations and changes in the object relations of the developing individual (Spitz and Wolf, 1949). When these features characterize object representation, we have object constancy. Its establishment facilitates the tolerance of temporary separation from the love object, as well as the ability to tolerate ambivalence toward the love object without fear of the impact of such ambivalence on the latter (A. Freud, 1965).

It should be made clear that the psychoanalytic concept of object constancy is not to be confused with the concept of the "stable object" in academic psychology. The latter evolves out of external perceptual experiences and does not take into sufficient account important intrapsychic and interpsychic processes. The development of object constancy proceeds under the impact, not only of external stimuli, but also of those derived from the internal environment. Furthermore, the nature of the energy and the extent to which cathectic flux plays a role in the development of object constancy are not taken into sufficient account by academic psychologists, some of whose views derive from Piaget's contributions. As Hartmann (1952) indicates: "This constancy probably presupposes on the side of the ego a certain degree of neutralization of aggressive as well as libidinal energy... and on the other hand it might well be that it promotes neutralization. That is, 'satisfactory object relation' can only be assessed if we also consider what it means in terms of ego development" (p. 163). It is perhaps because he does not take these factors into consideration that Robert White (1963), as pointed out above, has made the assumption that inanimate objects are more important than the maternal object in the development of stable object relations.

In animals the impact of strong emotional experiences and arousal in relation to objects during so-called critical periods has been cited by Scott (1962) as tale-telling in the development of strong and lasting attachments to such objects. Punishment, for instance, did not inhibit the formation of a social bond. Observations in humans are somewhat analogous. But close as it is, this type of relationship does not necessarily mean that object constancy has been established.

The patient I described in Chapter 4 (p. 97) had a physically close but extremely ambivalent contact with a very sadistic, cruel, and from what I could tell almost psychotic mother. At the age of 43, the patient was incapable of tolerating separation, while changes in object contact provoked anxiety. The unresolved ambivalence did not permit the development of object constancy in spite of the continuous, but highly charged, physical contact with the mother.

An interesting illustration of the fact that continuous physical pres-

ence is not the determining factor in the development of object constancy
is provided by William Niederland (Freedman, 1964). He describes the
experiences of a patient who, as a child, was forced by Nazi persecution
to live in secrecy with his parents in a very small room in the home of
some benefactors. The ever-present possibility of discovery and the
constant attempts of the parents to prevent the child from making noise
which might betray their presence contributed to disturbances in the
development of object and reality constancy, in spite of the continued
actual presence of the parents in what was a limited and constricted,
seemingly "unchanging" physical environment.

It must therefore be reemphasized that the continuous physical
presence of an object does not itself result in the development of constancy. The reciprocal interaction between ego functions and object
makes it clear that the psychoanalytic concept of object constancy goes
far beyond strictly sensorial perceptual experiences in relation to physically "stable" objects, and that the totality of psychic operations contributes a great deal to the development of object constancy. Many of
these considerations prove relevant to the concept of reality constancy
discussed above.

Primitive and Infantile Object Relations

In many of the contributions on defective object relations, we find
the leitmotif of self-nonself dedifferentiation and self-object fusion (see
pp. 261–263). Obviously, in keeping with primitivization of object
relations, the ego boundaries are diffuse and differentiation is not developed. Since it is in this diffusion of ego boundaries that the relation between the self and the object takes the form seen in psychosis, it might be
appropriate to define more clearly certain concepts such as primitive,
infantile, and part-object relations. These terms are used to refer to
many types of early relationships, including autoerotism, primary narcissism, primary identification, and even symbiotic and transitional object relationships.

A major problem in drawing conclusions about the infant's view is
that when we talk of the infant's relationship with reality, it is *we* who
are observing it. We are the ones defining what reality is and what the
object is. It is because this is not borne in mind that mistaken frames of
reference come into being. Let us take, for example, the concept of
part-object. Glover (1958) indicates that the term "part-object" can be
legitimately used as a descriptive term only when the subject already
recognizes the complete object, and Modell (1968) supports this view.

Yet this term is still used with the observer as the frame of reference; the nipple, which to the observer is a part-object, may be the whole object to the infant.

To deal with this dilemma, I suggest that we differentiate between primitive and infantile object relations. In the latter, no matter how early in psychic development, there is already a differentiation between self and nonself. This differentiation may be between part-self and part-object, but it is a differentiation nonetheless. In primitive object relations, this differentiation is nonexistent. Primitivization of object relations, or lack of progression from archaic object relations, is traditionally associated with psychosis. The degree or level of such primitivization in extreme instances is at pre-object levels of undifferentiated psychic development, that is, primary narcissism.

We must bear in mind that such primitive object relations may form a symptomatic spectrum from autistic relationships to cosmic identity and oceanic feelings. Furthermore, there may be a progression in some aspects of object relations and not in others. But keeping these reservations in mind, one can accept as a workable hypothesis that in psychosis the nature and level of object relations are generally primitive rather than infantile. This, as will be seen, may result in severe identity disturbances (e.g., identity diffusion), for there is no sense of self at this stage. If, in the psychotic or potential psychotic, a sense of self does exist, it is poorly organized and unstable. Its loose integration makes for potential fragmentation.

I should again like to make the point that nothing I am describing is all or none; everything exists side by side. Many, such as Otto Will, G. Bychowski, Philip Seitz, and Kurt Eissler (Freedman, 1962, 1964) take the position that there is no such thing as complete loss of object relations. Bychowski indicates that the psychotic clings to old partial and archaic objects, to avoid sinking back to primary narcissism.

In using the concept of primary narcissism in relation to a psychotic state, I am not referring to the concept that led Freud to call psychosis a narcissistic neurosis. I have already alluded to the terminological confusion around the concept of narcissism in Chapter 1. Let me repeat Glover's (1932b) comments: "A narcissistic organization could be postulated in all psychoses without any indication of the stage of the ego structure to which any one psychosis regressed" (p. 161). Hartmann (1953), as I indicated earlier, also has many reservations about the unqualified use of the concept of narcissism. He believes that in itself it does not account for the difference between cathexis of the self-image

and ego functions, which distinction he sees as relevant in psychosis. I
would agree that the term "narcissism" is too broad as a frame of
reference within which to consider the psychoses, unless one designates
at which level the narcissistic disturbance is involved. Modell (1968) has
put it nicely: "The term 'narcissism' as a descriptive adjective is indispensable; it has become part of our everyday language. However, as
a basic concept it is. . . too complex and covers too many different kinds
of phenomena to be fully serviceable" (p. 9).

   There is no doubt that the lack of differentiation which exists in the
state of primary narcissism is the setting in which psychosis is manifested. I should therefore like to elaborate on this aspect of the dedifferentiation that runs like a red thread through all manifestations of the
psychotic process, whether in gross psychosis or in severe psychotic
character disorders. Dedifferentiation may occur at all levels — in its
primitive form, where there is a total absence of differentiation between self and object; at somewhat higher levels, in symbiotic relationships; or even in marked transitional object relationships, in which this
boundary, although present, is murky with frequent overlap of self and
object.

   I have on a previous occasion (Frosch, 1967a) discussed the danger
to the psychotic of dedifferentiation, i.e., the equation of object loss and
dissolution of self (see also Chapter 7). This danger is enhanced by the
tenuous boundary between self and nonself in the psychotic and psy-
chosis-prone individual. Whoever works with psychotics is constantly
struck by the confusion between self and object, with the underlying
omnipresent danger of dissolution of self and of self-nonself fusion.
Whatever may be true of normative development, it is clear that this is
the problem in these patients, whether by virtue of inherent defects,
developmental experiences, or inhibitions of ego functions. The primitive level of differentiation appears to bring with it the possibility of
engulfment and absorption by the object, with the ultimate danger of
disappearance of self and fusion with the nonself.

   In Chapter 7, I described the basic anxiety associated with the possibility of self-object fusion. Underlining the need for differentiation in
the preservation of reality and ultimately the self, Des Lauriers (1962)
says:

> . . . it would appear that in the development of the ego, striving to define
> itself and separate from itself an outside world, the greatest pain, the
> deepest source of fear or anxiety would be the loss of reality, that is, psy-
> chological death as far as the ego is concerned. . . . The experience of

reality varies as the individual develops and as more and more functions are organically available to him; but the conditions of the reality experience never vary; on these conditions, the separation and differentiation of the ego, through the definition of its physical and psychological boundaries, depends the very existence, psychologically speaking, of the individual [pp. 37, 40].

Pao (1979) points out that in the acute phase of schizophrenia the patient cannot distinguish what is inside him from what is outside. Self and object are not differentiated. In one of Pao's patients, the source of anxiety at the oedipal period was the possibility of "reemerging" and being reengulfed. It was this fear, rather than genital-generated anxiety, that was reenacted in the transference. Freeman (1973), describing these manifestations in the chronic schizophrenic, comments:

> Clinical observation indicates that while the self is the principal recipient of libidinal cathexis, merging occurs with objects. . . . This merging is . . . a primitive kind of identification analogous to the primary identification postulated as an early developmental phase in object relations. Anna Freud believes that borderline children ". . . are constantly on the border between object cathexis and identification and [she] describes how they revert to identification with the object and that this may lead to a merging with the object" [p. 317].

Although Kernberg (1976a) emphasizes splitting between and among various early introjections (see Chapter 8), he does say that in psychosis this is further complicated by fusion between the self and object introjections. He admits:

> It is possible that in psychotic reactions the main common psychopathological factor (in addition to persistence of splitting mechanisms) is the lack of differentiation between self and object images in the earliest stages of ego development or a regressive fusion of those early self and object images under the impact of pathogenic factors. . . . Lack of differentiation of self and object images in the earliest introjections interferes with the differentiation between self and object and therefore with the delineation of ego boundaries [p. 50].

Kernberg (1975a) underlines the distinction between his borderline personalities and psychosis in this way:

> Vicious circles involving projection of aggression and reintrojection of aggressively determined object and self images are probably a major factor in the development of both psychosis and borderline personality organization. In the psychoses their main effect is regressive refusion of self and object images; in the case of the borderline personality organiza-

tion, what predominates is not refusion between self and object images, but an intensification and pathological fixation of splitting processes. . . . Psychotic patients have a severe lack of ego development, with mostly undifferentiated self and object images and concomitant lack of development of ego boundaries [pp. 27, 39].

Early pathological splitting threatens the integration of the ego, as well as the ego's future capacity to function as a whole. This failure of integration of the early introjections via identification, together with fusion and lack of differentiation, characterizes the psychotic process (see also my discussion in Chapter 8).[12]

Kohut (1971) distinguishes his narcissistic personalities from the psychotic or borderline patients as "not [being] seriously threatened by the possibility of an irreversible disintegration of the archaic self or the narcissistically cathected archaic object" (p. 4). He suggests:

[It would be] fruitful to examine the psychopathology of the psychoses — in harmony with the assumption that narcissism follows an independent line of development — in the light of tracing their regression along a partly different path which leads through the following way stations: a) the disintegration of higher forms of narcissism; b) the regression to archaic narcissistic positions; c) the breakdown of the archaic narcissistic positions (including the loss of the narcissistically cathected archaic objects), thus the fragmentation of self and archaic self-objects; and d) the secondary (restitutive) resurrection of the archaic self and of the archaic narcissistic objects in a manifestly psychotic form [p. 6].

Jacobson (1953, 1954a, 1954b, 1964, 1971) uses the degree of dedifferentiation as a frame of reference for discussing psychotic identification in both the manic-depressive and the schizophrenic:

In manic-depressives the regressive processes are different from those found in schizophrenia; they do not proceed as far and do not result in a return to the early symbiotic state of "total identifications." They may result in fusions of bad or good love-object images with the self image and with the superego and eventually lead to a severe pathological conflict — of harmony — between the superego and the self representations. In schizophrenics the ego and superego systems deteriorate to a much more dangerous extent. The pathological identifications are the expres-

----

[12] Any attempt to separate the danger and anxiety generated by self-nonself dedifferentiation from coeval ego function defects is an artificial one. The level of object relations in psychosis brings with it ego functions coeval with that level of object relations. It may even be that to begin with one may find inherent defects in those ego functions which go into building up of reality and object relations, thus facilitating dedifferentiation.

sion of alternating introjective and projective processes that lead to a more or less total merging between these self and object images within the deteriorating ego-id. The manic-depressive treats himself as if he were the love object, whereas the schizophrenic behaves as if he believes himself to be the object [1971, p. 262].

Clearly, one common denominator characteristic for the psychotic process is self-nonself dedifferentiation and the possibility of self-object fusion (in various degrees). It is also increasingly clear that preservation of reality and the object are essential to self-preservation. Be that as it may, we find that in the psychotic reality is very much bound up with the self and the object. Reality is the object and the self as they were in the earliest stage of psychic development. Many consider the fate and position of the object the crucial feature in establishing the existence of psychosis. In the psychotic, dedifferentiation, or the developmental lack of complete differentiation, makes it possible for the various parts of the psychic structure, reality, object, etc., to fuse. At the very least, the borders are tenuous. The loss of reality thus includes loss of organization of the ego (self), as well as loss of the object.

I have already discussed how disruptions in certain developmental stages bring in their wake defective object and reality constancy. These defects create an ever-present danger of disintegration of both self and object as well as reality. The clinical manifestations of this are illustrated by the patient I described in Chapter 4 (p. 97). The patient had numerous fantasies of world disintegration. Exploration revealed the close relationship between poorly developed object constancy and the world disintegration fantasy. Moreover, the destructive hostility brought in its wake the possibility of her own disintegration because of self-nonself confusion. Her very world, so to speak, would disintegrate with the destruction of the love object. The world destruction fantasy was also related to faulty development of reality constancy, which derived in part from her actual experience of a natural disaster at age three. She had actually seen the environment disintegrate around her. Buildings collapsing, people dead and dying, the whole physical environment in chaos—all had a tremendous traumatic impact on her. Later, with the upsurge of her own aggression and hostility, this experience served as a model for projection (her world disintegration fantasies).

This patient's background was replete with shifting environments, human and nonhuman. She had lived in so many different places that in a good portion of the analysis she could only recall them when they were equated with certain significant events: "Oh, that was when I lived on X Street." Or a particularly unpleasant color might be associated with a given place. Her adult life, because of the nature of her job, was also characterized by transience and inconsistency. In the course of her analysis, she frequently had feelings of unreality, depersonalization, and uncertainty about her environment as well as her own identity. Her dreams frequently involved world destruction and disintegration. For example, she had a marked flight phobia, and whenever she had to fly, she would have recurring dreams of world destruction, storms, etc. There were marked feelings of inadequacy, as well as an actual inability to cope with and master ordinary environmental situations, such as orienting herself while traveling. Any sharp dividing line between this patient's poor object constancy and defective reality constancy would be difficult to establish. Nonetheless, the impact of an ever-changing or highly charged environment in bringing about poor reality constancy should not be minimized.

In Chapter 4, I also described an experience the patient had which mobilized unconscious homosexual feelings related to her mother, whom she suspected of being a lesbian. This latter suspicion had a devastating effect on her. With the welling up of the homosexual feelings and the wish to be with the mother, the natural catastrophe reappeared — in a most shattering way — in a hallucinatory form. On the one hand, the patient wished to be closer to, to merge with her mother. Yet this was accompanied by a tremendous dread, bringing in its wake the fear of overwhelming natural forces which she could not control. She feared that she would disintegrate and disappear, just as the universe would. The hostility and ambivalence toward the mother contained the possibility of destruction of the mother. It brought in its wake the possibility of her own disintegration because of the self-nonself confusion. Automatically her very world would disintegrate. Again, I would like to point to the close relationship between this patient's poor object constancy and defective reality constancy, and the way the sense of her own dissolution became intertwined with disintegrating surroundings.

As I have already mentioned (p. 264n), one of the most common manifestations of self-nonself dedifferentiation is identity diffusion. One of my patients, who showed a propensity to dedifferentiate and fuse with the environment, became very disturbed when both she and her daughter wore pink dresses. The common color led to a fusion of herself with her child so that there was one pink object. She became very confused as to who she was and who her child was, making her very anxious and frightened. On another occasion, while feeding her baby, she became very angry with it. She did not like the fact that it was having so much pleasure. The sense of its pleasure was so real that she felt her own body changing, her lips smacking; she was almost merged with the child as a child. Although obviously aggressive and engulfing wishes were present in these feelings, what was terribly frightening to her was the sense of losing herself and her identity.

In connection with this, I would like to allude to some remarks a psychotic character made about her symbiotic relationship and deeper fusion with her mother. "Even if I died, I would still be with her. I would be in her thoughts. We would never be separated," she explained. Subsequently she added, "I didn't want to be born. Why was I? It was nice in there. After I was with my mother so long, I didn't want to change. I don't like changes. I don't like to move. Is that why I don't like to go away from home? When I'm inside, no one looks at me or criticizes me; all my wants are taken care of. I'm with my mother." Yet there was something frightening about this and she felt very uncomfortable. She felt no sense of self, and could not tell whether she was she or her mother. This patient mentioned a fantasy which to her represented the greatest danger of all. She would be walking in the street; suddenly she would fall into a hole, say, a manhole, and would continue to fall until she reached the center of the earth. Then she would burn up and disappear.

Extreme diffusion in identity, with blurring of clear-cut boundaries, not only between self and nonself, but even within the self-representation and the psychic structures, was illustrated by a psychotic patient who announced that she was God. "Why are you God?" I asked. "Because I can make the world go on and stop it. Because I got God in me and I've gotta go out in the world and fight it. 'Cause I'm a man." At one point, after she had been quite unresponsive, she said, "Youse can hear what I hear. What goes on in my head goes on in yours. I can read it in everybody's head." When I asked if this was why she didn't speak at times, she replied, "Yes."

I have previously discussed the question of why dedifferentiation and blurring of ego boundaries with loss of self should be so disturbing to the psychotic (see Chapter 7). One might ask: Is it that for psychic survival some degree of differentiation is necessary? Freud (1914a) hints at this in his paper on narcissism. Is it that once differentiation has to some extent been established, dedifferentiation has other implications and may be experienced differently? The problem of survival takes on a different form when some degree of differentiation has taken place. This brings with it an awareness of dependence on objects, as well as the possibility that basic survival needs may not be met. Reality (the object) becomes essential for survival, and this is conceived at first in primitive terms.

Dedifferentiation with fusion of self and object brings with it the possibility of unconditional omnipotence and assurance of automatic gratification of needs, by means of absorbing the object into the self. But it may also bring with it the possibility of engulfment and absorption by the object, with the ultimate disappearance of self. Those who work with borderline patients encounter this in many forms, one of which is the patients' marked fear of identification with the analyst lest they lose their "identity."

From all the contributions we have looked at, whatever the differences in their perspectives, it is clear that, as Mahler (1968) indicates, "Psychotic object relationships whether with human beings or otherwise are . . . restitution attempts of a rudimentary or fragmented ego, which serves the purpose of survival. No organism can live in a vacuum and no human being can live in an objectless state" (p. 65).

C.
The Sense of Reality

The next area to be considered in discussing the ego's position vis-à-vis reality is the sense of reality. When we talk about the sense of reality, we are concerned with the sensation and feeling of outer and inner reality experienced by the individual. Ordinarily there is a feeling that what is going on around and within one is real. Disturbances in the sense of reality are often connected to the disturbances in self-object differentiation I have just described. As I indicated, it is often difficult to distinguish between impairments in the relationship with reality, the sense of reality, and reality testing. Where one area begins and the other lets off is frequently hard to tell. Obviously we are concerned with an impairment of ego functions involved in all these areas. Heightening and lessening in perceptual strength, for instance, may be accompanied by feelings of realness or lack of realness. Yet, despite the overlap, one area may be more morbidly impaired than the other, and the dynamic, economic, and genetic factors involved may be at different levels. Thus, some differentiation seems warranted.

Ferenczi's classic paper "Stages in Development of the Sense of Reality" (1913) is one of the earliest contributions on the hierarchic development of reality. His term "sense of reality" encompasses a broad area, including many of the features I have tried to tease apart in discussing the ego's position vis-à-vis reality. At times he uses the term in relation to perceptual phenomena, pointing to the role of the sense organs in building up reality; at other times he uses it to connote the feeling tone of reality. My own opinion is that the term "sense of reality" should be used in a more limited sense to connote the feeling of reality.

Numerous attempts have been made to differentiate the feeling of reality from other ego functions related to reality (see, for example, Federn, 1952; Weiss, 1950b; Weisman, 1958; Glover, 1932c; Modell, 1968). Yet considerable confusion still exists, with the terms "sense of reality," "reality sense," "sensing of reality," "sensation of reality," and "feeling of reality" frequently used interchangeably. Some authors have attempted to relate reality sense to reality testing. Glover (1932c), for instance, says: "Reality sense is a faculty the existence of which we infer by examining the processes of reality testing" (p. 216). His concept of reality sense, however, differs from that of Weisman, who tends to view reality sense as implying sensation and feeling, as well as from Weiss's and Federn's ideas.

Since the feeling of reality is very much involved with the sense of self, it seems quite pertinent to cite Federn's (1952) concept of ego feeling at this point. Clearly, in view of the genesis of the ego and reality, the "realness" of reality must be intimately linked to the "realness" of the ego. Federn's contribution on "ego feeling" is therefore most relevant, if somewhat controversial in the minds of some. As I indicated earlier (p. 256), he sees the cathexis of ego boundaries as a precondition both for differentiating ego from non-ego (self from nonself) and for the feeling of reality. For the latter, there must be a penetration of ego boundaries, which is what lends a feeling of realness to perceptions.[13]

In contrast to Glover, Federn does not believe that the sense of reality rests on the function of reality testing. In his opinion, "An object is sensed as real without the aid of any reality testing when it is not only excluded from the ego but also when its impressions impinge upon a well-cathected ego" (1952, p. 13). Insofar as this applies to the hallucinations and delusions of psychotic patients, as well as the dreams of healthy people, these consist of mental products which are sensed as external realities independent of any reality testing. Certainly, to the psychotic patient, his hallucinations have a feeling of reality. In contrast to Federn's view, however, I believe that to a large extent a precondition for this experience is the loss of the capacity to test reality.

Federn (1928) takes the position:

> . . . we possess therefore, quite apart from Freud's reality test, according to which the outer world is recognized in its independence of the ego by means of search and comparison, a permanent evidential feeling of the outer world which originates in the fact that impressions from the outer world pass a corporal ego boundary charged with a particular quality of sensation and corporal ego feeling. . . . The normal person with a completely healthy ego . . . possesses uninterrupted his full feeling for cor-

[13] Nunberg (1922), in speaking of self-observation in depersonalization, alludes to a similar factor, when there is a refusal to accept perception as real: "In depersonalization the ego perceives but the reality of the perception is somehow not acknowledged by another part of the ego" (p. 135).

poral boundaries which permanently and unobtrusively demarcate the outer world [p. 405].

A caution is in order here. The validity of Federn's concept of the sense of reality rests to a large extent on his use of ego cathexis as a frame of reference. Further, some terminological blurring has arisen since the concepts of the self and self-representation were introduced, subsequent to Federn's contributions.

In closing my discussion of the terminological variations, I would like to cite Weisman (1958), who quite clearly relates reality sense to the feeling of conviction that something is real. He indicates: "The sense of reality acts on the whole experience, rather than on any of its parts. It is immediate, forcing us to believe beyond dispute. The reality sense is more apparent in the fact of an entire emotional experience than in the rigors of logical thinking. It requires no more proof than do artistic creations and dreams" (p. 236). Further on, he says: "Intuition is emphasized here as a process which vividly conveys a sense of reality to the structure of perceptual and conceptual information. It endows experience with conviction rather than truth, with the feeling of reality, rather than with final reality value" (p. 239).

I shall discuss ramifications of these points later on. At present I wish simply to underline the need to preserve the term "sense of reality" to distinguish reality feeling.

Depersonalization

Clearly, the feeling of the realness of both the external and internal world strongly depends on perception, and will be influenced in one direction or the other by disturbances in this ego function. This is not to deny that many other factors are involved. A nonpsychotic patient suffering from depersonalization may describe a limb as feeling disembodied, not real, devoid of sensation, not solid. At the same time, when directly questioned, he may use his senses to perceive that the arm is his, that it really is not lacking circulation, and say, "Yes, I know it's so, but it *feels* like it doesn't belong to me." In a sense he doesn't give full credence to his perceptions. Even here he is driven to renounce a part of himself, although he still possesses that judgment related to the ego function of reality testing.

Obviously, in cases of depersonalization and feelings of unreality, multiple functions need to be evaluated, especially when these experiences assume psychotic proportions. Before I concentrate on the role of the psychotic process in these phenomena, however, it might be appropriate to clarify certain general concepts. The term "depersonalization" is used to describe altered states of consciousness affecting the feeling of reality, and it encompasses many clinical conditions. To many authors, the term "depersonalization" includes feelings of unreality about both one's own self and the outside world. Nunberg (1922), for instance, views both feelings of unreality and depersonalization as part of the same process, which he relates to a withdrawal of libido: "it is hardly possible to draw a sharp line of demarcation between the two, for wherever estrangement of the external world appears, an estrangement from the ego sets in" (p. 60). For him, "Depersonalization is a state of illness in which the world and all that is perceived appears changed and strange to the perceiving ego. . . the subject's own body appears changed and strange" (1955, p. 134). Many other authors use the term "depersonalization" in this broad sense (e.g., Schilder, 1935, 1942, 1951; Federn, 1949; Oberndorf, 1934, 1935, 1939).

Under a stricter definition, "depersonalization" is used for that self-observation in which parts (or all) of the self, physical and mental, are not felt as solid or real although they are perceived and recognized as belonging to the self. In the usual type of depersonalization, the patient is aware of the feeling, complains about it, and may say, "I feel like a zombie. I hear my voice, and I know it is my voice yet it seems not like me. I see my hand moving. I know it is my hand and yet it doesn't feel part of me." This disembodied feeling and sense of detachment may also apply to one's inner world, i.e., one's thought processes.

The feeling is analogous to the feeling of estrangement from the outer world which accompanies feelings of unreality. The latter, in the stricter sense, applies to the external world, both material and non-material, neither of which may feel substantive or real. Some use the term "derealization" for this phenomenon, to distinguish it from depersonalization. In both instances, it is important to note that the capacity to test reality is maintained. If it is lost, the phenomena assume a different meaning and we are dealing with full-fledged psychosis.

In the psychotic, disturbances of the sense of reality may manifest themselves in many forms, all accompanied by loss of reality testing. For instance, there may be marked alterations of states of consciousness, with feelings of unreality and depersonalization accompanied by gross body-image disturbances and self-nonself differentiation. (The sense of self is obviously markedly impaired.) Things may look and feel unreal to the point where ultimately they are viewed as different and changed. For instance, in the Capgras phenomenon, "the illusion of doubles," a person, usually a relative, is misidentified as someone else, usually a double of the relative, and may be viewed as an imposter. These delusions may be accompanied by alterations in the feeling of reality, as Vogel (1974) points out in discussing such a patient: "Understandably, the patient must change her emotional world and the person or persons of high significance to her" (p. 924).

Alterations in reality may, in the psychotic extension of depersonalization, be carried to the point where the whole world appears strange and the end-of-the-world delusion may evolve. There may also be alterations in the self and the internal world. Body-feeling alterations may first be manifest as hypochondriasis and evolve into somatic delusions, or the self may be misidentified and the individual may view himself as another (appersonation). The delusion that the patient is the second Christ is one manifestation. One patient, after his brother died, became the lost brother, both physically and mentally. He even assumed his name. Obviously, in such instances, we have long since left neurotic changes in the sense of reality and entered into psychosis, where the capacity to test reality is lost.

Let me try to clarify a bit further the place of depersonalization in the psychotic process. In Federn's (1949) opinion, "Depersonalization as disrupture of the cathexis unit of the ego, belongs nosologically as well as clinically to the group of schizophrenic psychosis" (p. 258). But he adds that the move from depersonalization to schizophrenia does not always take place. Nunberg (1955) views the strangeness of the world in depersonalization as similar to the "end of the world" in schizophrenia, but in schizophrenia the objects are either lost or about to be lost. As I have just indicated, a careful examination of the manifestations resulting from alterations in feelings of reality in the psychotic will reveal many of the features of the psychotic process, such as underlying fears of self-disintegration and blurring of self-boundaries, as well as attempts to deal with this by objectivization, externalization, extrojection, introjection, and denial. But, above all, one finds a loss of the capacity to test reality.

As an example, I should like to describe a 22-year-old psychotic character, who for two years had feelings of weakness. His body did not feel strong and he became easily depleted with exertion. Although all medical workups were normal, there was some suspicion that this condition may have followed an infectious mononucleosis. Still, there were many indications of marked emotional factors playing a role in this condition. From time to time, this man would experience what he called "hyperventilation" — a feeling of lightheadedness. His head would feel as if it were floating away and his body would feel kind of empty. As I explored this, it became clear that these states arose in connection with marked feelings of rage and hostility toward his parents, especially his mother. Closer examination of the symptoms revealed a definite feeling of tension, which would mount to the point of explosion. Then the "hyperventilation" would ensue. This state was really a feeling of disintegration, with the accompanying disintegration anxiety so characteristic of the psychotic process. The anxiety lest he disintegrate was very real to him, but it did not persist and he was generally able to reverse the feeling. My point is that while the lightheadedness carried features of depersonalization, more basically it represented aspects typical of the psychotic process (i.e., the sense of disintegration and self-dissolution). It was at times taken almost to the point of gross psychosis, but could be reversed before reaching that point. When he was unable to reverse this, parts of the self were disowned and disavowed and even viewed as enemies.

In this regard, I might refer again to the patient with hemiplegia who disowned and rejected the diseased part of his body, which he had personified as his son (see p. 231). As I pointed out, a state of depersonalization related to this body part probably preceded his riddance attempt.

On the other hand, the dissociated part may be viewed as foreign but remain as an introject. I have already described (p. 241) a man with an introjected body which controlled his life, and had an impact on his physiological functions, primarily his bowel activities. He saw his bowel functioning as essential to his life, and the difficulties in this area were externalized into a persecuting delusional system. He also converted this into the feeling of having a foreign body inside himself, which produced all sorts of feelings, such as fuzziness, unclear thinking, dizziness. These were phenomena he associated with inability to get rid of one's feces. Another patient described many peculiar body sensations, essentially localized in the lower part of her abdomen. She eventually identified this area as her uterus, which would produce alterations in feelings such as confusion, instability, and dizziness. Eventually the patient depicted this as a machine inside of her, controlling her life.

In the early stages, the manifestations just described were accompanied by alterations in the sense of reality, such as feelings of unreality

and depersonalization. This then proceeded to the psychotic manifestations. In all of these patients, there were severe body-image distortions
and attempts to dissociate an undesirable part of the self. Although this
mechanism appears in neurotic depersonalization, in the psychotic, the
psychotic process determines the course of these attempts. The psychotic state itself is accompanied by a feeling of realness and a sense of conviction about delusions, which replace the unease and discomfort of the
feelings of unreality and depersonalization. A psychotic character, for
instance, was troubled by marked feelings of unreality. From time to
time she would have psychotic breaks, during which she had gross
delusions and hallucinations. Although the feelings of unreality were
still present, they were now understood as part of a delusional system of
persecution, against which she directed her efforts.

Heightened Perception

In contrast to the feeling of unreality, I have already indicated that it is
not uncommon in certain conditions for the psychotic to experience
sensations quite vividly. This phenomenon will frequently be accompanied by a heightening of the feeling of reality, involving both the external and internal environment. Nunberg (1955) comments: "the heightened self-observation, which increases with narcissism and withdrawal
of libido, brings with it a heightened awareness of new sensations and
their reality" (pp. 135–136).

Under ordinary circumstances, one is intrinsically aware of a body
unity and rhythm, of an integration in the operations of internal reality. There is a sense of the body's predictability and automatic awareness of the interrelatedness of body sensations, body functions, and
body parts. We take for granted that a sensation in the bowels relates to
evacuation, that the heart is beating, the lungs breathing. Goldfarb
(1963) has called attention to the difficulty schizophrenic children have
in "consciously recognizing and assigning meaning and predictability to
inner body processes, even when these are rhythmically recurrent and
daily in occurrence" (p. 50).

Reality constancy is a factor in awareness of the unity of internal
processes, and disturbances in reality constancy may be reflected in un-
duly heightened perception of ordinary body operations, as well as in a
lessening in the feeling of reality about one's body parts (as seen in
depersonalization). All these sensations may be quite vivid and, in the

psychotic, may ultimately be incorporated into a delusional system in the form of somatic delusions, ideas of influence, introjected objects, etc. The onset of the delusion may be accompanied by a flash reaction —light bursts on the patient and the realness of his belief overwhelms him. This flash reaction may be accompanied by heightened awareness of internal and external sensations. External objects at times assume a sharper outline. Internally, there is a heightened awareness of the various somatic processes, and even of psychic ones (thoughts may almost assume structure).

In contributing to a feeling of reality, the heightened perception may play a large role in the sense of conviction that accompanies psychotic beliefs (see Frosch, 1967a, 1977a; Weisman, 1958). It should be noted, however, that a feeling of realness and sense of conviction does not always accompany such heightened perception. Hypomanic patients, for instance, may on occasion retain some degree of reality testing. They will describe these experiences of heightened perception as uncomfortable and view them with suspicion. Similarly, it has been found in research on various hallucinogenic drugs such as LSD that not infrequently the individual retains the capacity to test reality. He is able to evaluate accuracy of the heightened perceptual phenomena, and the sense of conviction of their reality is absent.

Lewin (1950) examines the marked feeling of reality that the elated and manic patient may have about current experiences. As pointed out above (p. 144), he reemphasizes what is well known, that an affective reliving and reexperiencing lends the sense of conviction to a reconstruction. The manic, in Lewin's opinion, has a feeling of conviction about current reality because the happy mood derives from an actual ego state during the early nursing situation. Similarly, the sense of conviction and feeling of the reality of a delusion may relate to the historical truth not only of the delusional content but also of certain ego states and functions from the past which are regressively reexperienced during the psychosis (see Chapter 4, Section C).

The relationship between the sense of conviction and the feeling of reality has been stressed by many—sometimes to the extent of denigrating the role of reality testing in maintaining the sense of conviction. Weiss (1950a) suggests that once individuals have a feeling of realness about something, they abandon any attempt to test reality to support their feeling of conviction: "the sense of reality often defies reality testing." At another point he says: "Once the ego boundary is established in regard to any particular component, it is no longer necessary for the individual to test reality in that connection" (p. 47).

Self-Observation

Let me return to the feeling of unreality. In many contributions on the subject of depersonalization, the phenomenon of self-observation is viewed as an essential component. It is a manifestation of a split in the ego, which may take many forms. Schilder (1951) refers to ongoing splits in the self, eventuating in a scrutinizing self and a scrutinized self. What is scrutinized may be the body or mentation. Self-observation refers to taking cognizance of one's sensations; it is an inwardly directed observation. Closely associated with introspection, self-observation brings in its wake alterations in reality, which some authors view as a result of withdrawal of libido onto the self. Yet it must be remembered that the phenomenon of self-observation ranges widely, from the reality-adapted to the extremely pathological.

En passant, one is struck by aspects of self-observation in the tremendous preoccupation with health sweeping the country, from running to body exercise of the most minute, specific, muscle-directed kind. There are all kinds of machines to support this self-observation, even pulse-counting machines. Although Schilder (1951) suggests that this type of self-scrutiny should be differentiated from true self-observation, which signifies the turning of one's attention to one's own sensations, I believe the two phenomena overlap. In the current self-preoccupation, one even hears of an ignoring of the outside world accompanied by altered states of consciousness, as in the "high" described by some runners. At times the self-absorption may focus on a given part of the body to the exclusion of the rest of the body. In this whole phenomenon, it is as though in taking care of the body people have objectified it as some *thing* to be cared for.[14]

This kind of self-preoccupation is beautifully described by Henry James (1881), who discusses the reaction of one of his characters when he developed tuberculosis and had to devote himself extensively to self-care:

> He had to give up work and apply, to the letter, the sorry injunction to take care of himself. At first he slighted the task; it appeared to him it

[14] In some instances, especially in borderline or potentially psychotic patients, such preoccupations may mask hypochondriasis or even deep-seated body-image concerns of a psychotic nature, such as fears of disintegration (see p. 157n). I mentioned Nunberg's patient, who was intensely concerned with his body before the psychotic episode. He indulged in all sorts of special breathing exercises to strengthen his body and ward off disintegration. Within this context, I should also like to call attention to those patients who seek strong stimuli and sensations in order to affirm their reality.

was not himself in the least he was taking care of, but an uninteresting and uninterested person with whom he had nothing in common. This person, however, improved on acquaintance, and Ralph grew at least to have a certain grudging tolerance, even an undemonstrative respect, for him. Misfortune makes strange bedfellows, and our young man, feeling that he had something at stake in the matter — it usually struck him as his reputation for ordinary wit — devoted to his graceless charge an amount of attention of which note was duly taken and which had at least the effect of keeping the poor fellow alive [p. 44].

Intense concentration on one's own sensations is the leitmotif of many sex-training procedures. This concentration on specific sensations may, however, become an end in itself, at the cost of missing out on the total loss of self which accompanies the orgasm of psychic potency. (The latter phenomenon is known to prostitutes, who arrange for a "creeper" to come into the room and empty the contents of the client's trousers at the height of the orgasm.)

Creativity also brings with it a withdrawal from reality through introspection and self-observation (of ideas), and this may bring about alterations in the feeling of outside reality, so that the latter seems vague and dreamlike. The caricature of this is the absent-minded professor. Although this may be somewhat different from scrutiny of one's own sensations, I do feel that the same mechanism underlies both.

The self-scrutiny and self-observation one observes in hypochondriasis is, as Schilder (1951) points out, a form of objectivization and externalization, as are the above phenomena. In hypochondriasis, externalization from the self may assume the form of an introject or projection, leading in the latter case to somatic delusions. A bodily organ that is painful attracts self-observation. This painful organ has to be rejected as a part of the self. Hypochondriasis and depersonalization are closely related since self-observation and self-scrutiny are prominent in both. In both phenomena, according to some, there is a withdrawal of libido with an overcathexis of bodily organs, accompanied by alteration in reality. As Schilder puts it: "In every case of hypochondriasis much too much of attention, of libido is concentrated upon one's own body. The environment, although clearly perceived, holds no interest for the patient, neither the experienced nor the nonexperienced elements of the environment" (1951, p. 27). There is heightened self-observation, with an extreme awareness of the organs and their functioning. According to Nunberg (1922), this heightened awareness may be due to an accumulation of libido. It may well be a prelude to somatic delusions. In the schizophrenic, self-observation is quite marked: "Subjectivity has assumed the character of an object" (Nunberg, 1922, p. 26).

The prototype for self-observation is seen by Schilder (1951) in the child's watching the various activities of its body as though these were foreign and strange objects.[15] He emphasizes the voyeuristic and sado-masochistic components of self-observation. Like others, he points to the identifications which lay the groundwork for self-observation (1942, 1951), indicating that both self-observation and introspection are conditioned by the ego ideal. In his view:

> In self observation we see ourselves with the eyes of others. We take the others into ourselves as ego ideals and superegos and continue to observe ourselves with the eyes of others. . . . Most of the depersonalization cases excel at least in one respect. In the majority of cases the individual has been admired much by the parents for his intellectual and physical gifts. A great amount of admiration and erotic interest is spent upon the child. The child expects that this erotic inflow will be continuous [1942, pp. 188, 196].

Dissatisfaction inevitably ensues. Ultimately by identification with the parents, self-observation takes the place of observation by others:

> The individual will at first be able to admire his body as well as his thinking. Since such detachment from the love objects cannot remain satisfactory the self-adulation will be followed by hypochondriac signs, a denial of vision in the sphere of perception as well as in the sphere of representation and to the loss of relation to other persons is now added the loss of relation to one's self. Depersonalization is the neurosis of the good-looking and intelligent who want too much admiration. It is one step beyond social neurosis [pp. 196–197].

In Oberndorf's cases (1934, 1935, 1939), as we shall see, one of the

[15] In psychosis, especially in schizophrenia, the body image may be fragmented into its various components so that separate components and functions appear to have the autonomy of the earliest stage in psychic development. But a similar body autonomy appears in old age, where through a regression brought on by the organic changes of aging, the various body components and functions achieve a kind of independence. This is beautifully described by Arnold Bennett (1910): "He seemed to be so fully occupied all the time in conducting those physical operations which we perform without thinking of them, that each in his case became a feat. He balanced himself on his legs with conscious craft; he directed carefully his shaking and gnarled hand to his beard in order to stroke it. When he collected his thoughts into a sentence and uttered it in his weak, quavering voice, he did something wonderful; he listened closely, as though to an imperfectly acquired foreign language; and when he was not otherwise employed, he gave attention to the serious business of breathing. . . . He had grown down into a child again, but Providence had not provided him with a nurse" (pp. 234–235).

parents rejected the child and came to be viewed negatively by the child. The internal representation of this set the stage for clashing identifications.

Genetic and Dynamic Considerations

It might be appropriate at this point to discuss further some of the contributions on the dynamic and genetic factors in depersonalization, to see how these differ in neurotic and psychotic manifestations. As we have seen, Nunberg's (1922, 1955) formulations are essentially within the framework of the libido theory. Aggression is not alluded to as a main factor. Depersonalization is essentially related to loss, which is frequently equated with castration. In Nunberg's opinion, the withdrawal of libido from both the external world and the self is, in depersonalization, accompanied by retention of the unconscious object. In schizophrenia, however, even this is lost; there is a further regression to the earliest ego states and the loss is replaced by psychotic productions. In contrast, in true depersonalization, the loss is not replaced, and the patient feels and complains of this loss in reality and in the self; it is a narcissistic injury. There is no gratification from the symptoms. Nunberg explains: "the schizophrenic hypochondriac suffers from a surplus of organ libido, the depersonalized patient from a lack" (1922, p. 67). Unlike schizophrenics, depersonalized patients do not regress to infantile narcissism (primary narcissism), but merely complain of losing their feelings, their ego. There is, however, a heightened perception of loss. Since in depersonalization the ego is weakened,[16] fantasies may come up which are ordinarily repressed, and reappear as symptoms. In this way, depersonalization is a precursor of fantasy. Moreover, detachment of libido is a regular mechanism in the initial phase of regression. The ultimate course depends on the degree of regression.

In summary, Nunberg indicates that states of depersonalization "are based on a libido detachment; the actual ego perceives the inability to gratify the libidinal strivings; the loss of the libido is felt as a narcissistic injury; the ego-ideal cannot find fulfillment in its ego, having broken off relations to it. Hence a derangement of self-feeling sets in" (p. 74). Although Nunberg sees a detachment of the libido in both the

---

[16] This is not too unlike Federn's (1949) views, which I discussed above. He views depersonalization as an ego disease. There is a loss of cathexis of the ego, which he refers to as "ego atony." It is a subjective experience of a disruption in one's ego. Fatigue, exhaustion, intoxication, or emotional excitement can interfere with regular ego cathexis so that the core of the ego is deprived of libido.

narcissistic and the transference neuroses, he differentiates the two: "In the former, even if the detachment is only partial, it affects the unconscious objects, whereas in the latter case only the real conscious objects are affected. In either case the ego is weakened, facilitating intrusion of unconscious fantasies into consciousness" (p. 74). His formulation here is not too unlike Jacobson's (1959) description of the breakthrough of regressive drives in the psychotic derivative of depersonalization.

I have the feeling that when Nunberg talks of the ego ideal severing its relationship with the ego, he implies that the superego forbids the ego (self) to feel. In a sense, depersonalization is a form of denial imposed by the superego. Also implicit in much of what Nunberg says is the idea of an underlying fluidity of self-nonself boundaries, which would account for depersonalization and the lack of feeling of external reality. They are both part of the same process. This connection becomes quite manifest in those psychotic states of unreality and depersonalization in which blurring of self-nonself boundaries facilitates the psychotic development of these phenomena.

The idea that a split in the ego results from a clash of identifications in which one becomes unacceptable and that this underlies depersonalization is suggested by both Oberndorf (1934, 1939) and Jacobson (1959), although with differing emphases. Oberndorf focuses on a clash in those identifications which ordinarily go to make up the superego. He lists four factors that eventuate in depersonalization as a solution to this clash:

> 1) parental identifications where a certain characteristic of one parent continues to be considered by the patient unconsciously as specific to the sex of that parent; 2) erotization of thinking and its excessive cathexis as characterized in such identifications. During this process there is a withdrawal of libido from the more vital human occurrences in the environment and from the body itself. It is invested in other activity, primarily thinking, either in form of abstractions or in fantasy; 3) identification of thinking as a characteristic of the parent of the opposite sex, most often this occurs in the female child who regards "thinking" as a masculine characteristic (of her father); 4) through repression, because of the resulting conflict the patient attempts to rid himself of that portion of the superego which, as he grows older, he comes to consider as incongruous with and therefore harmful to his biological role in life [pp. 137–138].

The resolution of the clashing identifications is achieved through a denial of feeling—depersonalization.

Jacobson (1959), on the other hand, emphasizes a clash between incompatible components of the ego as the setting in which depersonalization takes place. She points out that depersonalization or its analog develops in psychosis, where a sudden regression allows invasion into the ego of hitherto repressed drive diffusion and pregenital drives. These are perceived by the patient as foreign, undesirable invaders. She also reports on Nazi war prisoners who developed depersonalization at the sudden loss of their old self-image in the face of the imposed image, in which they were viewed as criminals. A part of them accepted this view. The ego split then facilitated an aggressive disavowal of this criminal self. This split in the ego is a defense, in which a detached, intact portion regards the unacceptable part as though it were emotionally or physically dead or gone. In other words, Jacobson regards depersonalization in such instances as a defense of the ego involving a detaching and disavowing of the "diseased" part (very much like what Schilder described above). Yet, in my opinion, this is valid only so long as there is a portion of the ego which is relatively intact. In Jacobson's formulation, in order for psychotic depersonalization to take place, the intact portion of the ego must be inoperative, necessitating more dramatic steps. As I indicated above, in psychosis, the distancing may be carried through by objectivization and externalization to delusional proportions, facilitated by loss of reality testing.

To these well-known contributions, I would like to add some considerations. I believe that the disturbances in the development of reality constancy which I discussed in Section A of this chapter may facilitate feelings of unreality. As I pointed out, it is generally accepted that renunciation and frustration play an important role in the building up of reality and reality testing. Jacobson (1964) speaks of the impact of "disheartening" experiences in promoting the child's testing of external and internal reality (see p. 281). Painful and unpleasant experiences have to be considered, mastered, accepted, and incorporated into the representation of reality. Ultimately this contributes to the establishment of reality constancy, which in turn facilitates the acceptance and the recognition of unpleasant ideas and experiences as part of the environment, as well as the need to "reckon with it," as Ferenczi (1926, p. 378) puts it. In this "reckoning," reality constancy plays an important role. It enables the ego to deal with unpleasant reality, rather than to deny it, for instance, by taking refuge in psychosis.

I would also like to reemphasize that the expectation and the experience of gratification are important ingredients in the building up of reality, the ego functions concerned with reality, and thus in the development of reality constancy. Freud (1900) alludes to the role of the experience of satisfaction in the building up of reality (p. 566). Hartmann, Kris, and Loewenstein (1946) also suggest the important role that drive gratification plays in facilitating self-nonself differentiation, as well as the development of object constancy and the ego function of anticipation. For anticipation to operate effectively in the service of the reality principle, there must be a reasonable expectation of gratification, an expectation that must have been fulfilled at some time. As I indicated earlier (p. 281), Benedek (1938) in particular underlines the importance of gratification in the building up of reality, maintaining that physiological satisfactions facilitate periods of preoccupation with the environment and that this widens the horizons of reality. The development of confidence and positive anticipation, in her opinion, occurs through gratification rather than frustration. Repeated frustration without ultimate gratification, or the anxiety generated by undue delay, results in impairment of ego development.

The expectation that a given set of circumstances, or an object, may within time gratify one's needs makes one willing to accept its reality. If an external source of need gratification does not fulfill its function, in time, after repeated disappointments of anticipation, it is no longer considered a part of reality. If a child is repeatedly offered a toy, reaches out for it, but is not permitted to get it, he will after a while give up trying to reach for it. He may simply lie and look at the toy, or even become apathetic and unresponsive to the stimulus. Although one can assume the object is still acting as a stimulus on the sense organs, it is not accepted as a bona fide stimulus, containing within it the expectation and anticipation of gratification and mastery. Even if this external object later becomes available, it may be regarded as unreal because the element of expectation and anticipation has atrophied.

The tornado patient I described above (pp. 97, 313) developed periods of detachment during analysis. On closer examination, these detached phases assumed aspects of depersonalization and feelings of unreality. Frequently there were perceptual distortions of the treatment situation and the room itself was seen to take on a different form. This patient's life experiences showed a repetitive cycle: she would quite unrealistically glorify and exaggerate the attractiveness of a given person or situation; inevitably disillusionment, rage, depression, and detachment followed. The withdrawal and depersonalization not only related to a denial and repression of the rage, but represented an identification with a near-psychotic mother, who had had what appeared to be depressive withdrawals. The mother repeatedly frustrated and disappointed her child with aloofness and traumatic rejections (to which the patient frequently alluded). The patient described her mother as being "out of this world" and, without relating the two, she spoke of her detached feelings as having an out-of-this-world quality. She also showed lack of trust in her environment and a general feeling of cynicism and hopelessness about people's intentions. They were "really playing a game; didn't really mean it; it was not for real," etc. As I mentioned earlier, once, when she went to a party and was complimented on her appearance, she began to feel very uncomfortable; things around her acquired an unreal yet familiar quality. This was the feeling she had had about her mother, who would on rare occasions say something complimentary, but who had more often betrayed and disappointed her.

The patient frequently experienced feelings of unreality and depersonalization after the failure of a project she had undertaken. Her initial enthusiasm was followed by disillusionment. She indicated this was not unlike earlier experiences, when she "lived in a dream world," rather than coping with and mastering environmental situations, such as work at school. She was incapable of sustained effort and would become discouraged very easily. As I pointed out above, this patient, at an early age, had been exposed to a real environmental disaster, in which the world around her actually fell apart. Moreover, her whole life had been characterized by transience. The external environment could not be depended upon, just like her mother. She could not count on physical structures being where she thought they should be, etc. Reality constancy was impaired. For some time following the traumatic early experience, nothing seemed quite solid or real. She could not be sure of things; in fact, her memories of this period and even of recent events were quite vague.

Another patient described how everything had appeared unreal at a party she had gone to with her husband. The people were not clearly defined. She became terribly frightened, fearing she was losing her hold on reality. In talking about this, she mentioned feeling a little guilty because her mother was staying at her house and she had not prepared anything to eat for her before going to the party, or at least what she had prepared were just hamburgers. Somehow she felt she should have been with her mother, feeding her, instead of at the party. Again, she spoke of the fear of losing reality; possibly she would then lose her mother. At one point, she indicated, she had asked her husband for a drink; for some reason, he had paid no attention and she did not get it. It was at this point that the feelings of unreality had become quite marked, and she had panicked. In describing this, she again spoke of losing her mother. The denial of gratification and frustration were clearly related to the feeling of unreality. Yet, as in the previous patient, it was not only a denial of rage and murderous impulses that played a role in the depersonalization and feeling of unreality. As the material unfolded, it became very clear that disappointment and lack of gratification led her to feel that the object was frustrating and depriving, that she could expect nothing from it. She felt guilty when she could not feed her mother, in the same way that she had felt rejected when her mother had disappointed her. Throughout my work with this patient, material relating to her extreme expectation and anticipation of gratification from the mother and the disappointment in this, accompanied by feelings of unreality, pointed to the important role that lack of anticipation of gratification and loss play in the feelings of unreality.

With these cases in mind, I wonder whether feelings of unreality may, in some instances, derive from a prototypic feeling related to recurrent frustration and disappointment of the anticipation of wish gratification, or to unsuccessful attempts at mastery of environmental experiences. Experiences with the nonhuman environment may also contribute to such feelings. The repeated disappointments and loss may result in a disbelief in the reality of a need-gratifying object or situation, even when this ultimately presents itself. In other words, there is a refusal to accept the reality of the perceived situation, a lack of belief in one's perceptions. The feelings of unreality may in such instances ward off the pain of disillusionment which was previously experienced. My point is that in addition to the many other factors playing a role in feelings of unreality, in some cases the function of anticipation may be impaired, and that in such instances reality constancy is impaired. These considerations underline the importance of need gratification in widening the scope of the child's world of reality and in establishing reality constancy.

I have already indicated that in many psychotics and psychotic characters there is a need for reality contact and excessive stimulation to preserve a feeling of reality and a feeling of self. This is especially true if reality constancy is impaired. When reality constancy is not established, the person resorts to earlier modes of testing reality. For instance, support from the object may be needed to confirm reality, or earlier sensory modalities may be used. During analysis, these patients with faulty reality constancy need the continuous perception of their surroundings to maintain contact and to ward off feelings of the unreality of both the external and internal worlds. They may become quite anxious when placed on the couch, especially during earlier stages of treatment. Actually, in later stages of treatment, even with patients with fairly severely regressed ego states, I have found I can work with these patients on the couch, provided I allow ample opportunity for perceptual contact with their surroundings. I am reminded of the stage before object and reality constancy have developed, when the child is unable to tolerate the nighttime separation (A. Freud, 1952, 1965). The need for the light to be on, the repeated requests for the rereading of a story, the endless calls for a drink of water — all operate in the interest of nullifying separation both from the love object and reality.

The need to preserve contact with reality will, in some adults with tenuous object and reality constancy, lead to their clinging to transitional objects and phenomena (Winnicott, 1953). An illustration of this is a man who at night turns on the radio, ostensibly to hear the news. He falls asleep with the sound of the radio droning in his ears and turns it off only much later, while still practically asleep. Such a person cannot permit himself the degree of regression required to fall asleep; he must preserve some tie to the environment via a "transitional object" — the radio.[17] In such instances we see the result of deficient development of object and reality constancy, which may bring in its wake feelings of unreality and depersonalization.

As we have seen, alterations in the feelings of reality may occur in numerous conditions. Under the impact of the psychotic process, feelings of unreality and depersonalization, or even hyperperception, may evolve into delusions of world and self-destruction, somatic delusions, extreme body-image disturbances, etc. More careful examination of psychotic symtomatology, however, reveals certain distinguishing features. In such instances the anxiety is related to an underlying fear of self-disintegration and to the blurring of self–nonself boundaries. There are severe disturbances in object relations, which in many instances develop following loss. In addition, the defensive operations resorted to are consonant with what I have described for the psychotic process, i.e., massive denial, externalization, extrojection, or even introjection. We encounter splitting in the ego and between and among the psychic structures. Above all, we find the loss of the capacity to test reality — which brings us to an examination of this most important ego function.

---

[17] Whether this is a true transitional object or not depends on the degree to which the person views it as a part of the self.

D.
Reality Testing

It should be clear by now that I believe that the presence of psychosis to a large extent hinges on the loss of the capacity to test reality. What we are dealing with in this ego function is a person's capacity to evaluate appropriately the reality of phenomena going on around and within him. One may need a basis for comparison, and the baseline an individual uses to test reality may be difficult to establish. It may well involve the previous level of the individual's relationship with and feeling of reality. Furthermore, testing reality relates to the existing attitudes of others in a given culture, and thus one must take into consideration conventional or socialized knowledge of reality. With these qualifications in mind, we may nonetheless say that the capacity to test reality involves the ability to arrive at a logical conclusion from a series of observable phenomena. If the individual is consistently unable to reach such a conclusion when presented with objective data, the capacity to test reality is impaired.

Obviously the nature of the danger and the modes of dealing with this danger are important in psychosis, but, to my mind, reality testing is the ultimate criterion. Its loss is psychosis. Its presence doesn't mean that psychopathology, even severe psychopathology doesn't exist. But the person who retains a consistent capacity to test reality is not psychotic. From this viewpoint, an individual may have disturbances in the relationship to reality and in the feeling of reality and still not be psychotic, as I have indicated may be the case with psychotic characters in the nonpsychotic phase (Frosch, 1970).

A qualification must be added. I must reiterate that the separation I am making is in many respects an artificial one. For how can we talk of reality testing without taking into consideration those ego functions, such as perception, which enter into the other two areas, namely, the reality relationship and the feeling of reality? As Weisman (1958) points out, not only does the reality sense influence reality testing, but

reality testing also modifies the direction and degree of libidinal attachment, the latter being very important to the reality sense. Indeed, he
indicates that there is such a degree of interweaving and overlap as we
move up the scale in psychic development that analysts may be severely
criticized for seeming to sacrifice the facts as they exist, in the interest of
clarifying a concept.

This interweaving has in fact been emphasized by many authors,
including Freud (1921, 1923), Ferenczi (1926), and Hartmann (1956),
who stress that the very building up of reality is facilitated by reality
testing. To quote Hartmann again: "A child confirming the existence of
an object by means of reality testing has now added to his world of reality" (p. 43). The dependence of reality testing on other ego functions is
also looked at, although from a different angle, by Kubie (1953). He
sees the disturbance in reality testing as secondary to a more basic disturbance in symbolization. This disturbance brings about disruption in
perception, conception, language, symbol formation, etc.

Nonetheless, as I indicated in the previous sections, I believe there is
sufficient methodological justification for teasing apart the relationship
with reality, the feeling of reality, and reality testing. In studying reality testing, it is relevant to try to evaluate the individual's reactions to
phenomena discussed in the first two areas. We must try to distinguish
between the presence of a certain phenomenon, for instance, a distortion of perception, and the patient's reaction to it. It is conceivable that
a hallucination, a severe distortion in perception, may not be accompanied by a loss in the capacity to test reality. The patient's ability to
recognize this for what it is, i.e., a distortion, would reveal the preservation of an important capacity, that of testing reality. One sees this in
hypnagogic and hypnapompic phenomena, where an individual may
momentarily be carried away by what appears to be the reality of an
experience, but may then be able to evaluate this distortion as internally derived in the face of observable phenomena.

Several authors in fact lend support to my contention that the
capacity to test reality is crucial in establishing whether a person is psychotic or not. Glover (1939), for instance, emphasizes "reality-proving"
as the main frame of reference in establishing psychosis: "By far the
most reliable indication of psychotic disorder is disturbance of the function of reality-proving" (p. 242). Kernberg (1976a), in describing the
lower level of organization in the borderline patient, includes all the
features of psychosis with one difference — retention of the capacity to
test reality:

The differential diagnosis between patients with borderline personalities and those with psychoses centers on the persistence of reality testing in the former and its loss in the latter. This difference depends, in turn, on the differentiation between self and object representations and its derived delimitation of ego boundaries; these are present in the lower level of organization of character pathology, lost or absent in the psychoses [p. 148].

The presence or absence of reality testing as a criterion for psychosis is also used by Freeman (1973):

It can be said that reality testing has only partially returned when the positive symptoms of a psychosis (delusions, hallucinations, catatonic signs) disappear. The complete return of reality testing can only be presumed to have occurred when the patient acknowledges that he has been ill, is aware of the fact that he no longer enjoys capacities which were present prior to the illness and has some recollection of the experiences of the illness. When these criteria are fulfilled the patient may be considered to have passed from the psychotic phase of the illness and to have the potential for a complete remission [p. 207].

The manner in which the loss of reality testing serves as a common denominator is clearly demonstrated in Freeman's attempt to differentiate among various psychotic pictures, based on the extent to which the self is differentiated from the object and the extent to which "the patient retains the capacity to see himself as a distinct entity vis-à-vis other entities" (p. 199). Using this frame of reference, he defines a range extending from those clinical syndromes in which there is a loss of the boundary between the self and the nonself to those psychoses in which the distinction between self and the object is relatively secure, despite marked disturbance in ego functions. Yet all these the clinical pictures reflect a basic defect in reality testing. What Freeman points out is that this function may be disturbed even when the self and object are differentiated.

In this regard, it is of interest to recall Glover's (1939) use of the point at which reality testing breaks down to differentiate between manic-depressive illness and schizophrenia:

In the case of manic-depression... the first step in clinical classification and in treatment is to discover the location of the pathogenic introjection (the so-called 'new object in the ego' or, alternatively in the 'superego'). It is at this point in the depressive process that the patient's sense of reality-proving becomes faulty and first gives rise to characteristically psychotic thought or behaviour. In the case of schizophrenia more extensive investigations are necessary. It is not possible to establish one point at which reality-proving breaks down. Not only are the fixation points in any one case multilocular but these points vary in the different (so-called) sub-groups of schizophrenia. This means in effect that we must discover in each case the 'general fixation level' of the ego as well as of the infantile instincts. In other words it can be assumed that the final infantile level of ego development in the schizophrenic constitutes a base line, regression to which will, given an excess of excitation, disrupt the faculty of reality-proving [pp. 220–221].

Genetic and Dynamic Considerations

Glover's remarks here lead into an issue to which I would now like to turn. What, we need to ask, are the genetic and dynamic factors that contribute to the development of reality testing, or its ultimate impairment?

Freud addresses the problem of reality testing in a number of papers dealing with the concept of reality, beginning with the *Project* (1895b) and continuing in multiple publications thereafter (1900, 1911a, 1911b, 1915a, 1915b, 1917a, 1921, 1923, 1924a, 1924b, 1925a).[18] It should be noted, however, that although the problem of distinguishing reality from fantasy already occupies Freud's thinking in the *Project*, he does not actually use the term "reality testing" until 1911. Essentially throughout his various papers, he tries to define the ego functions involved in reality testing. One such function of reality testing is to distinguish between an idea (a presentation) and a perception, between what is external and what is internal (Freud means physically internal). "What is unreal, merely a presentation, and subjective is only internal," he explains, "what is real is also there outside" (1925a, p. 237).

According to Freud, secondary process plays a role in the mechanism of delay, thereby facilitating reality testing. This function of delay and inhibition also allows for control of impulsive action (see Frosch, 1977b). In any case, in reality testing, delay and judgment are used to establish the psychically internal or external location of a phenomenon.

Freud also suggests that muscular action may be used to facilitate reality testing: "The capacity to distinguish between internal and external according to muscular action must be examined. A perception

---

[18] An extensive survey of Freud's developing thinking in this area has been made by Dansky (1970). There is also an excellent historical survey of Freud's writing in relation to reality testing, and the shifts in his thinking, in the Editor's note to the metapsychological supplement on dreams (1917a).

which is made to disappear by an action is recognized as reality. Where such an action makes no difference, a perception originates within the subject's own body, and is not real" (1915b, p. 119). This of course is a rather primitive way of testing reality, one which may be resorted to regressively.

I should note at this point that Freud's muscle movement idea is taken up by White (1963) in his emphasis on effectance and action in the building up of reality. He indicates that the importance of his concept of effectance "lies in its suggestion that apart from instincts the human organism is still a restless creature, constantly directing itself toward its surroundings and learning through experience the effects that can be produced upon the environment — the kind of relations that can be sustained with it. [This] energy leads to exploring and testing reality" (pp. 180–181).

On the other hand, Federn (1952) questions the muscle action frame of reference for reality testing:

> ... this primitive testing through movement is a means for the first orientation in the establishment of ego boundaries. . . . Once the dynamically efficient ego boundaries are established, this primitive form of reality testing loses its function of orientation. What is sensed as real can no longer be reversed by any reality testing or reasoning. . . . The individual has, very early, given up using movements as a means of discriminating between "real" and "imagined." In further development reality testing becomes much more complex and serves the purpose of obtaining knowledge of realities. Remembering and learning are the basic functions at the service of reality testing. . . Psychotic individuals sense the contents of their delusions and hallucinations as real because they arise from mental stimuli which actually entered consciousness without obtaining ego investment, not because of a defective reality testing [pp. 13–14].

But let me return to Freud. As indicated above, he proposes that a certain amount of delay has to exist for reality testing to occur. He also points to the need for a certain hypercathexis of perception (attention). As Strachey explains in a note to Freud's (1911a) paper: "The aim of inhibition is to give time for indications of reality to arrive from the perceptual apparatus, but the ego is also responsible for directing cathexis of attention on to the external world, without which the indications of reality could not be observed" (p. 220).

Freud (1925a) formulates another concept which is rather interesting, although at times difficult to follow. It is now no longer a question of whether what has been perceived should be taken into the ego or not, but of whether something which is in the ego as a presentation can be rediscovered in perception as well. Freud makes an intriguing statement: "It is not only important whether a thing possesses a good attribute and so deserves to be taken into his ego, but also whether it is there in the external world so that he can get hold of it whenever he needs it" (p. 237). In a sense this statement, that it is not simply important whether a thing possesses a good attribute, moves away from the early pleasure ego as the sole frame of reference for taking something in or excluding it (see my discussion on p. 280). The first immediate aim of reality testing is therefore not to find an object in real perception which corresponds to the presented one, but we do at times try to find such an object to convince ourselves that it is still there. Freud also indicates that a precondition for the setting up of reality testing is that objects shall have been lost which once brought satisfaction. (Ultimately the object to be refound, according to Lewin [1950], is the mother's breast.)

In discussing these ideas, Rapaport (1951) says, "Freud apparently refers to the distinction between verification of the existence of the reference of a memory image in reality (rediscovery) and the successful search for a reality reference of an invention of creative imagination (discovery)" (p. 346). Yet there is still some question in my mind as to what Freud means. Does Freud mean that one has to have learned something about an object, or to have had some kind of an experience with an object, in order to test the reality of a subsequent object? It is probably true that reality testing involves some previous experience with an object, or something similar enough to the object, so that a representation is established which can then subsequently be matched with a real material object and used to test its reality. For instance, if we want to convince ourselves about the reality of a tree, is it necessary for us to have seen a tree before? Or do we bring to bear certain ego functions and experiences from the past to find (or refind) an object in the outside world? We are dealing here with the role of past experiences of realized anticipation. Perhaps when one tests the reality of a tree one reasserts the capacity to find again an outside object in the world (although not necessarily the tree as such), as a result of previously having been able to do so. As such, the role of realized anticipation in reality testing is significant.[19]

[19] When Freud states that a precondition for the setting up of reality testing is that objects shall have been lost which once brought satisfaction, I think this too refers to realized anticipation. I have already discussed the role of anticipation of gratification

Hartmann (1956) expands on Freud's concepts in saying: "When Freud speaks about reality testing he usually means the capacity to distinguish between ideas and perception. In a broader sense reality testing also refers to the ability to discern subjective and objective elements in our judgments on reality. The former we expect to function rather reliably in normal adult persons; the learning of the latter is an unending process" (p. 43). He emphasizes the significance of testing the within, in addition to testing the without; that is, he distinguishes inner reality testing from outer reality testing. He points out that in the neurotic, interference with the testing of inner reality is in the foreground. In psychosis, however, the basic properties of outer reality testing break down.

Kubie (1953) also maintains that reality testing differs in the neurotic and psychotic, agreeing with Hartmann that in the former inner reality testing is impaired, and in the latter the impairment is in outer reality testing. Kubie goes on to differentiate between neurotic and psychotic processes in terms of the site of the symbolic disturbance, whether it is at the introceptive or extroceptive end, the "I" or "not I" end of the "symbolic hammock." I suppose that this would depend on which component of inner reality we are talking about. I would also like to add that inner reality testing may be severely impaired in the psychotic, leading to distortions in evaluating disturbances, for instance, in the sense or feeling of reality. This may be seen, as I pointed out above, in the hyperperception of somatic functions such as breathing, the heartbeat, etc. Defective inner reality testing may evolve into somatic delusions, the presence of introjected objects, and may involve the thought processes as well. Yet wherever the disturbance is — in the inner or outer world — one of the important measuring rods is ultimately the capacity to test reality.

What I would stress at this point is that we need to take into consideration the hierarchical development of both the concept of reality and modes of reality testing. As we have seen, Freud repeatedly emphasizes the role of specific ego functions in making a distinction between an idea (a presentation) and a perception, between what is exter-

---

in building up reality and reality constancy (see p. 281). This factor obviously enters into reality testing as well. The previous mastery of an environmental experience and the successful employment of the ego functions involved in doing so achieve representation. Among other factors, we are dealing with past experiences in realized or fulfilled anticipation as an important factor in the building up of reality constancy. The representations of such experiences bring about the development of reality constancy, which ultimately makes possible good reality testing.

nal and psychically internal as the essential early function of reality testing. The use of muscular activity, body sensations, etc., represents an early mode of reality testing, which gradually gives way to internalized, higher-level modes, involving delay, judgment, thinking, memory, etc. Hurvich (1970) outlines the various factors involved in the more mature layers of reality testing, noting: "What has been described in the literature as reality testing includes at least the functions and processes of attention, perception, memory, secondary-process thinking, delay of discharge, judgment and reflective awareness." He continues: "later writers have included the acquiring of knowledge of realities through learning, and drawing logical conclusions from perceptions and memories." Moreover, "in addition to inner-outer distinction," he includes, "the overlapping components of accuracy of perception and accuracy of inner reality testing" (pp. 309–310).

Hartmann (1953) provides some clarification in distinguishing the different layers and aspects of reality testing which may be damaged in pathology:

> The basic layer would be the one most often referred to by Freud: the capacity to distinguish perceptions from ideas (presentations); its impairment is also one side of that fusion of inner and outer world we see nowhere clearer than in schizophrenia. Another one appears in what I described in briefly discussing one characteristic of schizophrenic delusions. In the cases I had in mind, perception is unchanged, but the meaning of the perception is radically altered. A further aspect of reality testing, of a more general nature, may be described as the correction, or elimination, of subjective elements in judgments meant to be objective — delusions can be described as a special case of its pathology, which, however, covers a much wider field of phenomena. The basic layers of outer reality testing break down only in psychosis; superficial layers may be interfered with also in neurotic and normal persons. Actually, as mental phenomena are no less "real" than the outer world (though we often refer to the latter only in speaking of "reality"), it might prove useful to broaden the concept of reality testing to include testing of the within besides testing of the without. Every neurosis adulterates insight into inner reality; and reality testing of the inside is never perfect even in the normal person (with the exception, maybe, of the ideal case of a "fully analyzed" person — if there is such a human being). In schematically contrasting what in a given situation a neurotic and a psychotic would do, Freud says: the neurotic represses the instinctual demand, while the psychotic denies outer reality. In this case, we could say that with the neurotic, testing of inner, with the psychotic, testing of outer reality, is interfered with [p. 192].

In talking about a regression to earlier ego states and the use of early modes of reality testing, I would note that an individual, once having experienced certain modes of reality testing, will try to borrow copiously from them. This is especially the case in the psychotic, who will borrow from regressive modes in testing reality. Yet more advanced modes of reality testing may coexist. I do not believe, as Weiss (1952) says, that the psychotic patient makes no effort to test his delusion. Actually I doubt there can be a regression to a time before reality testing arose. Reality and reality testing exist at all times, in a phase-related manner. What we may find is an unevenness, with progression and regression, so that reality testing may be seen functioning effectively in some areas, and not in others.

Actually the delusional patient who tries to convince you of the reality of his beliefs may, up to a certain point, accept mature modes of reality testing. If you ask a delusional patient why he thinks people want to kill him, he brings to bear a number of seemingly logical observations. Even though certain deductions, conclusions, and connections may be fallacious, the delusional patient frequently uses conventions of reality testing in an attempt to give coherence to a situation and try to convince you of his beliefs. One might even go so far as to say that many advanced ego functions, such as reasoning, are used in the service of unreal situations. Psychotics' use of more advanced modes of reality testing, in the interest of supporting distorted conceptual formation, depends to a large extent on the extent to which they have retained these functions and on the degree to which these modes are necessary to lend coherence and integration to the psychotic material.

I have also called attention to the integrative effect of the systematized delusion (see Frosch, 1967a). By binding the anxiety, the delusion allows many of the patient's cognitive functions to operate. The systematized delusion also appears to have an integrative and unifying effect in facilitating the maintenance of identity. Indeed, if successfully walled off, the systematized delusion, which is itself a product of synthesis, may facilitate the reintegration and functioning of the rest of the personality at a higher level, with seemingly good reality testing. Schilder (1933) says: "When we deal with systematic delusions of a paranoid type, we have to reckon with the synthetic power of the ego and the superego, which try to unite the products of regression into some adaptation to reality" (p. 11). I am reminded of a psychotic patient who walled off his delusional system and was able to finish two years at law school. When I met him at that time, I asked him about his delusional system. He smiled and said that he wouldn't talk about it to people because they thought he was joking, or they looked at him "kind of funny."

The fact is that almost anybody can transiently suspend or lose the capacity to test reality, even though to begin with this capacity shows no basic defect in its structure. One certainly knows that certain neurotics, under the impact of anxiety or some strong affect, may temporarily show impaired reality testing, so much so that it may seriously interfere with making proper business decisions, etc. At the same time they may retain their capacity to test reality in other areas. But remaining for the moment in the domain of psychosis, one can, as I have just pointed out, observe inconsistencies even in these conditions. The well-known case of Schreber is illustrative. Even during the time when his ability to test reality was seriously impaired, insofar as his delusional system was concerned, he was able to apply reality testing to objective data which did not involve him personally (i.e., to write legal opinions, etc.). This is a repeated clinical observation.

All this argues very strongly for the contention that there are irregular developmental movements, with facets of ego functioning moving ahead and others lagging behind (see my discussion on p. 265). Such discrepancies may occur within the sphere of reality testing, since it is composed of subsidiary ego functions which may not develop uniformly. The same is true of the disparity in libidinal and ego development. Recall, in this regard, my earlier remarks on the so-called hysterical psychosis. I am of the opinion that in this case a libidinal conflict at a relatively high level of development is being dealt with by ego functions at a relatively low level of psychic development. The patient deals with a wish-fulfilling (or wish-denying) fantasy derived from a higher stage of libidinal development with modes and techniques that belong to a more primitive level. Interestingly, frequently such patients are able to recover and show relatively good insight and reality testing in relation to material which had been obviously psychotic. Does this too suggest higher levels in ego development that had transiently regressed? These questions need to be examined more closely.

What enters into reality testing is probably a highly complex series of ego functions. The capacity to test reality in the mature adult derives from and depends on certain primary autonomous ego functions such as learning, judgment, perception, attention, delay, synthesis, etc. These are usually derived from conflict-free spheres of the ego. When they are interfered with or impaired, however, there may be problems in reality testing. As Freeman (1973) points out:

Reality testing is dependent upon drive representations which have secondary-process qualities. Once these are lost and replaced by drives having the characteristics of the primary process, reality testing will be held in abeyance. The intrusion of the primary process into ego functioning is in part a consequence of the return of drive cathexis to the self, following upon the operation of projection and total identification. Cognition, speech, thinking, perception, memory, is influenced by condensation, displacement and the tendency toward the hallucinatory revival of memories [p. 11].

In addition to defects in subsidiary ego functions which contribute to defective reality testing, the loss of reality testing may be borrowed in the service of defense and to support other ego functions. Let me elaborate. To deny a specific situation to such an extent as to negate its existence, requires an extreme alteration in reality. Let us say a patient has lost her father and as part of her psychosis has a delusion that her father is not lost, that she hears him speaking. Obviously this involves a certain degree of loss of reality testing. Is this loss in reality testing resorted to defensively to support another defensive operation, i.e., denial? Or do we have to assume that there is already some impairment in the ego functions which go into this patient's capacity to test reality? If this is the case, this would then facilitate the borrowing of defective reality testing, which would in turn facilitate psychotic denial.

The borrowing of ego functions to support other ego functions in the service of defense may be further illustrated by the role of perception in reality testing, as well as the impact of the latter on perception (which is interwoven with the very development of reality constancy and reality testing). As Goldfarb (1963) indicates, there is a mutual dependency between discriminatory perception and object and reality constancy (see my discussion on p. 293). At this point let me recall my remarks on the change in the sensory threshold in the paranoid, which results in an unusual capacity to pick up stimuli. The fact is that even in situations not involved in the delusional system, the paranoid shows a heightened capacity to perceive stimuli. What is the nature of the energy involved; is it neutral or neutralized energy? Can deneutralized energy, i.e., aggression, contaminate perception of nonconflictual material and yet be subject to appropriate reality testing? At the same time one must ask whether unimpaired perception and feelings of reality may nonetheless be distorted by virtue of some impairment of the ego functions involved in reality testing. The latter may well be the case in some paranoid conditions where actual physiological perception seems to be intact, yet at some point along the line to thought formation there is a distortion in evaluating the perception. In the interest of supporting a delusional system, the patient may perceive quite accurately and yet arrive at an erroneous observation.

Let me reiterate: Many psychotics will accept the so-called adult, normal mode of testing reality and still come up with a false conclusion. This may not simply involve perception alone, but even up to a point, a mode of reasoning. Again, the delusional patient may even try "rationally" to convince you of the validity of his convictions; yet at some point the seemingly logical train of ideas leads to a false conclusion. This is especially true of the more highly organized psychotics and less true of deteriorated schizophrenics, who may show little interest in trying to convince others of the validity of their psychotic ideation.[20] On the other hand, as indicated above, the paranoid is exquisitely aware of perceptual experiences, sometimes distorting them and at other times even reaching out to find them and weave them into support of his delusional system.

It is clear that distortions in perception may be brought into the service of supporting faulty reality testing. It is also clear that accurate perception may be contaminated by faulty reality testing. An interesting area is opened when one examines a related question: Can reality testing, or modes of reality testing, be brought into the service of supporting psychotic ideation? Arlow and Brenner (1964, 1969, 1970) view the loss of reality testing as defense not as defect. As such, they believe it serves the function of dealing with anxiety in the psychotic. (I shall discuss their point of view in more detail in Chapter 15.)

It is relevant to note that areas involved in other aspects of the psychotic process are equally important for the functioning of good reality testing. The same genetic factors that contribute to the psychotic process affect the development of impaired reality testing. For instance, impaired object relations, so crucial in psychosis, also play a role in impaired reality testing and in the faulty development of other ego functions involved in reality testing.

I have already discussed at great length the role of the object in the development of reality and reality testing (see Section B of this

---

[20] This is exemplified by the story of the patient who had the delusion he was dead. The doctor, in an attempt to convince him otherwise, cut into his skin deeply so that the patient bled profusely. The doctor called his attention to this, indicating that his own eyes should convince the patient that he was not dead. To this the patient replied that all the doctor had proved was that the dead could bleed!

chapter). Modell (1968) points out that "the sense of identity is essential for the testing of reality" (p. 46). What he means is the sense of self as separate from the nonself. In other words, self-nonself differentiation must exist for reality testing to take place. As I mentioned earlier, external objects, especially the parents, present themselves as models for the modes of reality testing. The child is constantly confronted with value judgments which have an impact on its reality testing, even persisting into later life.

I would also like to recall the role of the need-frustrating and need-gratifying object in the development of reality, which proceeds hand in hand with the development of reality testing (see p. 300 ff.). This frame of reference is perhaps best exemplified by Glover (1932c) who stipulates: "Efficient reality testing, for any subject who has passed the age of puberty, is the capacity to retain psychic contact with the objects that promote gratification of instinct, including here both modified and residual infantile impulse" (p. 217). At another point, he says:

> . . . it is not within the scope of metapsychology to give a definition of 'absolute reality.' In spite of this, we are able to attach a precise significance to the term 'reality testing.' The metapsychological definition of 'reality testing' is based on the view that the ego is a sampling apparatus as well as an organ for reducing instinctual excitation. Reality testing then, from the medical psychologists' point of view, is the capacity to maintain psychic contact with the objects which promote gratification of the modified impulses of adult life. And adult normality is a state in which infantile 'psychotic' views concerning the external world have been so reduced that they do not interfere with possibilities of adult gratification; in other words, it is a state in which the psychotic estimate of the object world coincides with an objective estimate in two main respects, (a) the amount of love that can be satisfied and (b) the amount of danger to the ego that is present [1932a, p. 246].

Glover repeatedly emphasizes this view. In a subsequent contribution (1939), he expands:

> . . . as has been seen, this disturbance is a measure of the degree of abandonment of objects. We are therefore in a position to indicate the function of reality-proving in terms of the relation of the ego to the objects of its instincts. The faculty of reality-proving can be defined as the capacity of the ego to apprehend the relation of its conscious instinctual urges to the objects of the instincts in question, irrespective of whether these urges have been, are or will be either frustrated or gratified. . . . The psychotic may be defined as a person who to a greater or lesser degree refuses to conform to this painful standard, and who at the same time

substitutes for it a subjective (originally unconscious) measure of reality, clinically recognizable in delusions and hallucinations [p. 242].

Clearly, according to Glover, the genetic development of reality testing is very much tied up with the object as a source of instinctual gratification. He summarizes: "In the long run of course, the definition of reality testing must be in the simplest terms of instincts and their objects" (1939, p. 219).

White (1963), as I have indicated several times, would take exception to Glover's view. In White's opinion, it is action derived from independent ego energies, not instinct-motivated ones, that is responsible for learning about the ways in which reality can and cannot be influenced and tested. He sees instinctual frustration as providing but one of several inducements to shape behavior in accord with realistic considerations. Here I would disagree. To my mind, the prototype for reality exploration is instinct-derived. I believe that it is activity *in relation to* instinctual gratification that provides the model for subsequent activity. For instance, sucking to ease the tension created by hunger becomes an activity which may subsequently be brought into the service of exploration, play, etc. The pattern which originally produced gratification may be the one relied on for later activities. The child may suck his thumb to ease tension in a general way, with the idea that since sucking eased tension before (by getting milk), it may prevent tension if the child does it now. That is, the early technique of obtaining pleasure or easing tension may serve as the model for future activities, in the attempt to recapture pleasure or ease tension in some way.

Is it possible, then, that the original ego function and pattern established for the purpose of instinctual gratification may, without postulating deneutralization, be brought into the service of other ego activities to provide other gratification? White states it somewhat differently: "The reality principle can be said to replace the pleasure principle to the extent that actions are interpolated which are not themselves directly need-reducing but which affect the environment in some way that favors need reduction" (p. 47). If some action is required for reality testing, the question has to be raised whether those ego functions which are involved in carrying out this action are intact, or interfered with, or whether they are to begin with impaired, and whether this in itself does not have some impact on reality testing, even though primarily these actions may not be involved in reality testing. I have discussed this question above (p. 345).

The question of where the seat of reality testing is has also been a subject of extensive discussion. Freud (1900, 1917a) at first adds reality testing to the other functions of the ego, i.e., censorship and repression. He then places it in the ego ideal (1921), only to return it again to the ego (1923). Still later, he makes some comments which seem to ascribe some role in reality testing to the superego (1936). Balint (1941) reemphasizes the important role that the superego plays in reality testing, as do Hartmann and Loewenstein (1962). Nunberg (1951) states: "Conscious perception of the ego must be sanctioned by the superego in order to acquire qualities of full uncontested reality. This assumption should be helpful in understanding why. . . changes in the patient's superego also enchance the reality testing faculty of the ego" (p. 8).

As was pointed out above, Hartmann (1956) indicates that the ways in which the data of inner reality are integrated, the image of the child's own self and its evaluation, are codetermined by the parents in their roles as models or as prohibiting agents. It finds its clearest expression in the formation of the superego, which includes some degree of narrowing or distorting of the child's knowledge of inner reality. Hartmann points out that the superego influences the testing of outer reality and may even add to the motivation for objectivity in terms of setting up certain standards for truthfulness, intellectual honesty, etc. In other words, there is interference with objective cognizance of the world not only by instinctual needs, but also by ego and superego functions. Earlier stages of development in reality testing utilize the self-experiences, somatic and psychic, as well as the parental attitudes.

Stein (1966) emphasizes the importance of self-observation as an essential element in the process of reality testing and for the evaluation of reality. He indicates the differences of opinion concerning the structure responsible for reality testing and specifically questions the assignment of self-observation to the ego by Hartmann, Kris, and Loewenstein (1946). He believes that the superego, as well as the ego, plays a crucial role in the development and functioning of reality testing, that the principle of multiple function applies.

I'm inclined to believe that certainly the genesis of reality testing, as well as the picture in regressed states, is very much under the influence of the superego and ego ideal. Since, as pointed out above, reality testing is under the influence of the early significant objects in the environment, the ego ideal and early superego would seem to play a very large role in the developing techniques of reality testing. Intersubjective acceptance without validation plays an important role at that age, and the child needs the parent's external support of the parent in its developing attempts at testing reality. Only later does reality testing become an internalized function of the ego, although it is still most likely under the influence, more or less, of the earlier ego ideal and superego.

As it develops, reality testing requires the diminution of those influences which originally played a role in shaping it. The earlier modes of testing reality must give way to more autonomous ones for mature functioning to be achieved. As Jacobson (1964) points out, the establishment of reality and of object and self-representations depends to a large extent on the maturation of perceptive functions, i.e., on reality testing at the expense of the projective and introjective mechanisms more characteristic of earlier modes of reality testing. In the course of psychic development, reality testing becomes more and more internalized. Jacobson explains: "during the oedipal phase reality testing gains more and more. . . and promotes the child's distinction between his wishful imagery and more or less realistic representations of the object world and of his actual as well as his potential self. Thus processes develop which advance under the influence of beginning superego development, but, above all, of ego maturation, of improving reality testing and self awareness, and of expanding functional ego activities" (p. 91).

All this goes hand in hand with the evolution of reality constancy, which is correlated with the stabilization of internalized images of the external environment and its qualities, and which constitutes a more reliable frame of reference for reality testing. It is clear that the more advanced the modes of reality testing are, the more firmly reality constancy is established, and vice versa. To reiterate: the capacity to test reality in the mature adult derives from and depends on certain primary autonomous ego functions. These are interwoven with the development of reality constancy, as well as with its operations. The hierarchical development of reality constancy goes hand in hand with the hierarchical development of these ego functions, and this will have an impact on the function of reality testing.

The impact of constitutional deficiencies on the subsequent development of reality constancy and reality testing warrants consideration. Modell (1968) presupposes that the inborn, genetically determined autonomous ego functions involved in the structuring of reality and thus reality testing are not impaired in borderline patients and schizophrenics. It is the subsequent ones involved in the organization of reality, which are dependent on good mothering, that are affected. White (1963), however, takes exception to such a view by emphasizing the interplay between constitutional deficiencies in the child and the mother's response to them. Such constitutional deficiencies "seriously frustrate maternal competence and thus evolve some of the excessive compensations that have been described in 'schizophrenogenic' mothers" (p. 189).

A related question is: To what extent does reality testing depend on other ego functions which, to begin with, may be biologically affected? For instance, is the capacity for hyperperception, seen in some instances, biologically determined? If it is, does it then interfere in the course of psychic development with those ego functions which enter into what later on becomes the highly complex functions of reality testing, as well as in the structure of reality?

A biological basis for early modes of reality testing can be found in Klüver and Bucy's (1937) work with monkeys. When extensive portions of the temporal lobes and limbic systems were removed, the monkeys developed "psychic blindness," among other manifestations. There was a need to examine objects visually, tactilely, and orally. Almost all objects were smelled and mouthed. Of course one does not know if the monkeys did this to test the reality of objects, but it is the way very young children test reality and build up a concept of reality. These early modes of reality testing are coeval with the biological stage in development in which the biological base for internalization and reality constancy has not yet taken over. The physiological mechanism for reality testing exists at several levels, including the cortical and temporal lobe levels, as well as the amygdoloid complex, hippocampus, etc. If these areas are removed, regressive forms of reality testing (tactile, visual, olfactory) reappear. There is also an inability to differentiate between dangerous and nondangerous objects. This regression has also been observed in humans following injuries and illnesses in which these areas are affected.

In addition to constitutional and biological factors, we must consider the impact of early traumatic experiences on those ego functions which are incorporated into reality testing. I have already discussed the impact of real traumatic experiences on ego development in the psychotic, and at that point I mentioned Spitz's (1964) discussion of the effects of overstimulation (see Section A of this chapter). Here I would also cite recent studies on isolation which show concomitant perceptual distortions, in many instances bringing disturbances in reality testing to the point of psychosis.

I have also described how early modes of reality testing, as well as the processes leading to self-awareness, use body sensations and activities such as touching, tasting, and smelling, as well as introjective-projective techniques, etc. Frequently the outer world has to be especially vivid to emphasize reality. A curious phenomenon in one of my patients illustrates related disturbances in the relationship with reality, as well as a special form of reality testing. My patient suffered from anosmia, which dated from as far back as he could remember. He could discern certain strong odors, such as that of gasoline. His perception of strong body odors was almost tactile. The air felt heavy, or somehow different. He was also able to perceive odors at special times, for instance, when he had satisfactory sexual relations for the first time.

The use of this anosmia to distort and deny certain aspects of reality was illustrated by his fantasy that people did not exist and objects were not real unless they had an odor. He himself made sure of his existence by not bathing for weeks and even months at a time. As a result, he smelled to others and thus was real to them. If others did not smell to him, however, he could deny their existence. I shall refer only tangentially to this patient's need to deny the perception and body odors of his mother, as well as his many fantasies regarding the function of the nose. I should simply like to underline the inordinate use of a sensory modality to test reality.

The extent to which reality testing is influenced by intrasubjective acceptance of reality without validation, especially in relation to significant objects, was also illustrated by this patient. During the early stages of analysis, my role was that of a tester of reality to support his own not yet clearly developed technique for testing reality. Repeatedly, during the early stages, I was called on to validate his own rather tenuous efforts. I practically had to teach him the criteria for testing reality. This patient did not trust his own perception. Once, while lying on the couch, he saw the lights dim. He became anxious and needed my confirmation that the lights had in fact dimmed.

The contribution of the superego and the ego ideal to reality testing was clearly indicated by my patient. Although he feared engulfment by what he thought were my values, he repeatedly sought them. The goodness or badness of things played a very important role in testing reality, and invariably his concept of what my reaction would be strongly influenced his acceptance or rejection of something (which meant its reality or unreality). Although he still looked to external sources for support, his internalized capacity for reality testing increased as the analysis proceeded. Apparently, then, primitive modes of reality testing will persist if there is any interference with maturation in this area of ego functioning.

Let me reemphasize a few points here. As we have seen, an organized sense of self and identity, with differentiation, is essential to facilitate mature reality testing. It is clear that the love object (first the mother, later joined by the father) plays a large role in this process and in the development of reality constancy and reality testing. Although the development of reality and object constancy is facilitated by the internalization of those ego functions which are part of their development, these structures equally facilitate the internalization of those features which go into mature reality testing. The capacity for reversibility, for instance, is facilitated by reality constancy, as well as object constancy. The psychotic character, in contrast to the grossly psychotic patient, has to some extent advanced sufficiently in psychic development to be able to retain, albeit precariously, some of those features which facilitate reversibility.

Many factors impinging on the developing organism contribute greatly to the evolution of this process. I have already indicated the inherent strength of the push toward maturation, toward individuation and differentiation, which facilitates progression and combats regression and dedifferentiation. The capacity to reverse regression also derives from identification with objects, who play a significant role in the development of reality testing. It should be clear that the child needs the external support of the parents in its developing attempts at testing reality. It is only later that reality testing becomes an internalized function of the ego, although still most likely under the influence of the earlier ego ideal and superego (especially in those instances in which maturation is interfered with).

From our discussion of the genetic factors in reality testing, it becomes clear what the sources of disturbances in reality testing may be in the psychotic process. Interference with the internalization of reality testing, as well as with the development of object and especially reality constancy, will contribute to the persistence of early modes of testing reality. These patients do not quite learn to trust their own perceptions and need constant external affirmation. The archaic superego frequently continues to exert its influence on the ego in reality testing and contributes to the persistence of primitive modes of reality testing. As we have seen, early modes of reality testing are tied up with the body; the child uses its somatic self-experience to test reality, through touch, taste, smell, use of the muscle apparatus, etc. Similarly, regressive modes of reality testing in the psychotic frequently involve the use of the senses to make direct physical contact. The psychotic may seek strong external and internal stimulation to confirm reality (see Frosch, 1966, 1967a, 1970).

Where poor reality constancy exists, trust in one's own perceptions is impaired, requiring reinforcement by strong external stimuli or constant external reaffirmation. In such instances, parental images continue to exert an active influence on the ego in reality testing. This is especially true when the symbiotic mother-child relationship has been prolonged and the process of internalizing reality testing has been frustrated. The differentiation that facilitates internalization is lacking, with the symbiotic mother continually testing reality for the child. In subsequent development, the independent capacity for reality testing is lacking.

The psychotic's use of the object to test reality and to affirm reality has been pointed out by Burnham (Freedman, 1962, 1964). He uses the term "heteronomy" to designate the condition where the mother acts for the child. There is evidence that in schizophrenic cases heteronomy has been prolonged. The mother imposes definitions of the child's condition rather than letting the child determine his own state of affairs and then ratifying the child's definition, which has been arrived at by his own active inquiry. A common example of this is the mother who tells her child when he is hungry. Another example is a mother who was annoyed when her child rattled a piece of paper and told him he was trying to bother her by doing this. The intent to bother the mother was not part of the child's motivation in rattling the paper. Burnham describes an obsessive schizophrenic patient who complained when there was no thermometer on the wall of the office. Without a thermometer he did not know whether to keep his coat on or take it off. His mother had always told him when it was hot or cold. Similarly, Bychowski (Freedman, 1962, 1964) describes a patient with fluctuating hallucinations who wanted his mother to spend the night in a hotel room with him so she could tell him whether the voices he was hearing were real or not. The patient needed an external object to make up for his inability to distinguish outside from inside. One should be mindful here of Rubinfine's contention that there is a constitutional defect in perception in the schizophrenic (Freedman, 1962, 1964).

The defects discussed are reinforced not only by lack of self-nonself differentiation, but also by the concomitant lack of differentiation between the psychic structures. The latter has a decided impact on the capacity to test reality. As I have indicated, there is by and large agreement that dedifferentiation between and among the psychic structures is responsible for much of the symptomatology in psychosis. In this one may point to not only ego-id dedifferentiation, but also ego-superego dedifferentiation. I think there is agreement that in psychosis there is a marked structural dedifferentiation with a relative closeness of the various functions of the ego to the id. The primary process is the dominating influence on many spheres of ego functioning, affecting thinking, feeling, and behavior. These defects unquestionably have a severe impact on the capacity to test reality. But there is equally, as I have indicated, an invasion of archaic superego influences on the ego and its functions, which severely impairs reality testing. And it is the sustained impairment of the reality testing that is crucial for psychosis.

I have, throughout Part III, extensively examined the various components of the psychotic process — the nature of the danger and the conflict, the modes of defense used to deal with this conflict, and the impact on the ego and its functions, especially reality testing (whose impairment is crucial to evaluate in establishing psychosis). Many authors, as I pointed out, have in one way or another dealt with one or the other aspect of the psychotic process, although not spelling this out as such. Some of these contributors are in agreement and others in disagreement with the formulations I have proposed. In particular, I would like to look at the views of Melanie Klein, Fairbairn, and their followers; Mahler; and Sullivan and his followers. Although their contributions have been discussed when appropriate in the preceding chapters, I intend now to elaborate on certain points.

PART IV

FURTHER
CONTRIBUTIONS

11.
Melanie Klein, Fairbairn, and Derivative Contributions

I should like to review several contributions on those early stages in psychic development which, it is claimed, play a significant role in subsequent psychotic development. Much of our earlier understanding of the genetic factors in psychoses was derived from reconstruction in work with adult patients. More recently, attempts have been made by psychoanalysts to study grossly psychotic children, as well as more normal children, and thus shed light on those factors in child development which could potentiate psychotic development.

Foremost among the early contributors were Melanie Klein and her followers. Anyone who has worked with psychotic patients cannot help but be impressed by their observations. Yet seminal as these contributions have been, much has also been controversial (see the critiques by Glover, 1945; Bibring, 1947; Zetzel, 1953; Jacobson, 1953, 1971; and Kernberg, 1969).[1]

In reviewing the contributions of Klein and her followers, I shall concentrate mainly on those features relevant to the psychotic process (see also my remarks in Chapters 4 and 5). To begin with, however, some mention of her overall frames of reference is necessary (see also Klein's own concise summary [1952]). The Kleinian perspective on psychic development is intimately intertwined with psychotic terminology and concepts. According to Klein, as a result of painful oral frustration, the earliest oral libidinal needs become quickly linked with oral sadism, which augments the death instinct. The infant's feeling of helplessness in the face of mounting rage and fear of its destructive impulses

---

Dr. Fayek Nakhla was most helpful in the preparation of this chapter.

[1] In his extensive survey of the ego-psychological critiques of Kleinians, Kernberg (1969) indicates that several Kleinians, Rosenfeld in particular, have modified their views, bringing them closer to the ego-psychological approaches of other analysts. Rosenfeld gave me a similar impression (personal communication, 1972).

mobilize projection of the tension and hatred, with a subsequent merging with the disappointing and hostile object. Dangerous impulses and substances, such as excrements, are expelled from the self onto the mother. Through this expulsion, the mother comes to be viewed as the bad self, since she contains these ejected dangerous substances. These projected bad parts of the self may be reintrojected, leading to feelings of inner persecution. The same process applies to the good parts of the self, with the result of overdependence on the now good object, which is loved as a representation of the self. In the absence of good mothering, then, the ego is constantly beset with anxiety.[2] Internal dangers are exchanged for external ones.

This stage in psychic development is characterized by terrifying, aggressive sadistic and masochistic fantasies concerning the relationship between the parents, the inside of the mother's body, and the infant's own internal situation. In keeping with wholesale introjective-projective processes, it is referred to as the paranoid-schizoid position (see p. 87). Actually Klein refers to these processes as projective identification, a concept I discussed extensively in Chapter 8. As I indicated there, projective identification is a mechanism whereby the infant takes on and identifies with an envied role or function of the object. At the same time the infant projects unwanted parts of the self onto the object, causing the latter to be identified with the bad parts of the self. These are then reintrojected. As Waelder (1960) indicates, "In Melanie Klein's theory all these factors have their place: the intensity of self-destructive forces, the immaturity of the ego that cannot deal with them except by projection, the paroxysmal anxiety, aroused by objects who therefore appear as highly threatening, and the break with reality" (p. 207). It is the failure to work through the paranoid-schizoid position that may result in adult schizophrenic and paranoid mechanisms, with projective identification the mechanism used to deal with (and create) conflict.

As I discussed above (p. 183), the paranoid-schizoid position is followed by the depressive position. At this stage there should be integration of the good and bad part-objects into the whole mother object. The fear of destroying the object invokes the possible loss of the good object and the good breast, with consequent guilt, mourning, severe depression, and anxiety. It is thus important that a positive object relationship be established before the real loss of the first object during weaning. The infant's coming to terms with this dilemma is the basis

[2] Much in this resembles Kohut's (1971, 1977) concept of the selfobject, as well as his views on the lack of an empathic mother.

for the "depression position." Klein proposes that the child goes through a depressive episode during this period and future pathology ensues if this is not resolved.

The thinking of the British object relations theorists, as Sutherland (1980) calls Balint, Winnicott, Fairbairn and Guntrip, in many ways parallels that of Klein. Both Fairbairn and Klein, for instance, reacted independently to Abraham's work (Padel, 1977). These theorists elaborated many of their concepts in work with "schizoid" personalities, and thus their ideas might be seen as having special relevance for an understanding of the psychotic process.

In Chapter 10, Section B, I discussed at length the various viewpoints on early object relations development. As I indicated, there is quite a dichotomy in views. Some take recourse to instinct theory and emphasize libidinal gratification and frustration as the frames of reference in the development of object relations. The object is at first a need-gratifying object, and only in later stages does the need for the object as object, independent of need gratification, evolve. In contrast are the views of the British School. It is appropriate here to begin by referring to Fairbairn's views.

Fairbairn (1946, 1954, 1963) explicitly rejects Freud's instinct theory as a frame of reference for the evolution of object relations. Instead, he offers a theory of the personality conceived in terms of primary object relations. Libido is used in the service of object-seeking, contrasting with the view that sees the object as gratifying libidinal needs. Fairbairn proposes object relations as the primary motivation in psychic development, rather than "erotic" sensations, which require gratification. He therefore postulates object-seeking activity from the earliest periods in life. In this respect he differs from Klein, who emphasizes the infant's oral libidinal sucking needs as primary. Klein's view is that with frustration, gratification needs become coupled with oral-sadistic destructive and devouring drives (augmenting the preexisting death drive), and it is this that colors the relation with the object.

Kernberg (1980) indicates his agreement with Sutherland, and implicitly Fairbairn, that we never see pure drives but always object relations under the impact of drive derivatives.[3] As I have already indi-

[3] Choisy (1961) docs not direct herself specifically to object relations theory. In a sense, she writes with a religious frame of reference. Nonetheless, in her discussion of prostitution, she seems to adhere to the concept that libidinal needs are in the service of object relations (which is the primary need). The sexual drive itself facilitates object relations. The participants are objects seeking an object relationship.

cated, my own view is that libidinal and aggressive drives are biological givens activated by experiences and thus developing derivative manifestations. The newborn's response to stress and tension seems clearly generated by biological needs, which result in yelling, screaming, kicking — all manifestations of the impact of a pure drive, unrelated to an object. In my opinion, then, it is only subsequent drive derivatives that can be viewed in terms of object relations. Indeed, the very word "derivatives" suggests this.

Let us return to Fairbairn's concepts. Out of the various affects related to gratifying and rejecting experiences with the object, Fairbairn suggests that specific positions and internalizations evolve as defensive measures against rejecting, but later also against "stimulating and exciting," objects and experiences. These are related to specific components of the ego,[4] and the ego's defenses are geared to the qualities of the object. A conscious and preconscious ego (self?) develops which relates to a conscious and preconscious "idealized" object. Unconscious ego segments (self segments?) also develop — an anti-libidinal ego related to an anti-libidinal prohibitive object, and a libidinal ego related to an exciting and gratifying "libidinal object."

All of these ego and object structures, invested with energy, should in the course of normal development ultimately fuse into unified, mature ego and object structures. Each developmental stage has an impact on successive development of self-object relations. This is not unlike Klein's concept of "activating systems," whereby preceding stages activate and are incorporated into subsequent stages in psychic development.

The earliest state is viewed by Fairbairn as a splitting in the interest of defense, and he refers to this as the "schizoid position" (a term Klein added to her own "paranoid position" to arrive at the "paranoid-schizoid position"). This schizoid position is followed by a depressive position, related to separation anxiety (again, note the similarity to Klein). Fairbairn indicates that as a result of excessive splitting, what remains in the schizoid personality is an impoverished central ego which relates to an "ideal ego," shorn of the split-off frustrating and exciting aspects. Fairbairn draws an analogy between the emotionally superficial attitude of the schizoid and the "impoverished" dissociative state of the hysteric. I do not believe, however, that this is a valid anal-

[4] There is a problem with the concept of the ego in the British School's thinking. They tend to interchange the concept "ego" with the concept "self," or what we now call the "self-representation." One is never sure how the word "ego" is being used.

ogy either clinically or psychodynamically. I think Fairbairn's concept of splitting is not differentiated adequately from the process of fragmentation (see Chapter 8), and this leads to the assumption of a close relationship between hysterical dissociative states and schizophrenia. In the former, the dissociative states are still unitary complexes, operating coherently within the framework of that dissociative state. They are object-related. Indeed, this was one of Freud's and Abraham's earliest distinctions between hysteria and dementia praecox. In schizophrenic fragmentation, object-relatedness is lacking.

It should be pointed out that the various infantile positions postulated by Fairbairn are endopsychic. For normal development, the schizoid and depressive positions must be successfully surmounted. In the adult schizoid personality, this negotiation either hasn't effectively transpired or else there is regression which reactivates the schizoid or depressive position.

Fairbairn sees the earliest form of anxiety as separation anxiety, which is reactivated with subsequent frustration by the love object. Yet his concept of the danger in the schizoid position entails ego fragmentation, and loss of the sense of oneness. This is not unlike what I have designated as "basic anxiety," a fear of ultimate dissolution and disintegration of the self. In the depressive position, the loss of the love object, destroyed by one's own aggression, becomes the greatest danger. Fairbairn suggests that the child fantasizes that its own badness evoked the frustration and attack from the good object. Somehow, however, the potential guilt deriving from this does not seem to be considered. In his formulation, Fairbairn again denies the primacy of the source of aggression, i.e, its instinctual, biological basis.

Fairbairn's formulations imply that subsequent experiences of a frustrating nature in the external world evoke the "basic anxiety" and lead the schizoid personality to withdraw into his internal world. These experiences may also reactivate the depressive position. What determines which position is reactivated is the nature of the anxiety and whether, to begin with, these positions were pathologically marked in childhood. Fairbairn thus presumes that the child's experiences can be equated with the adult's experiences, i.e., that the schizoid and depressive positions find their equivalent in adult schizophrenic and depressive psychoses, as well as psychotic anxieties, which may take many forms.

Along these lines, one might mention Grotstein (1977), who borrows extensively from Klein, Fairbairn, Bion, and others in presenting his views on the primacy of object relations in psychic development. He presumes an active infantile psychology from the beginning of extra-uterine life. For him, it is the evolution of internal objects and their ulti-mate fate that is tale-telling for pathological development: "Each period of development will be the ongoing serial of the self in struggle and in harmony with transformation of these internal objects" (p. 422). He postulates an "infantile psychosis as an organizing framework for all normal and pathological development." All this is reminiscent of Klein's (1940) view that "each successive stage of development unfolds as an as-similation of the previous stages and is directly and indirectly modified by them." One finds in these thoughts reverberations of Klein's concept of "activation" as a factor in the continuity of psychic development.

In addition to postulating various psychotic positions, both Fair-bairn and Klein believe that unconscious knowledge is innate and oper-ates from the beginning of psychic development. This premise allows many psychic structures and conflicts traditionally ascribed to later stages in development to be present quite early (e.g., the Oedipus com-plex, penis envy, the superego). It is not always clear, with Fairbairn or Klein, whether what is going on during these periods is totally endopsy-chic, without external clinical manifestations which could be desig-nated as psychotic at that time. One is troubled by the inability to observe directly at that age the phenomena they describe. There is a great deal of reliance on reconstruction and theoretical formulations of endopsychic fantasies, some of which is based on work with adults only. The application of these terms to earlier stages in psychic development carries some degree of adultomorphizing, which may or may not have validity. For instance, to use phenomena from later psychotic pictures that demonstrate introjective-projective manifestations to postulate stages in psychic development where these manifestations are said to be present as phase-related phenomena, and then to call them schizoid, paranoid, or depressive, with the implication that these later psychotic states are duplications of the earlier ones, may be open to question methodologically. Hartmann and Kris (1945) have cautioned against the use of just such a genetic fallacy.

Zetzel (1953) also sees the designation of "schizoid," "paranoid," and "depressive" positions as prototypes for later psychotic states as unwar-ranted. She points to the "considerable step between recognizing and interpreting specific unconscious material and constructing a theoret-ical reconstruction with far-reaching implications" (pp. 114–115). Ad-dressing herself specifically to the depressive position, she says: "It is, in short, particularly important to ascertain whether, in talking of 'the infantile depressive position,' [Klein] is comparing the infant with the adult melancholic or with the normal mourner. In my opinion, some of the objections to her conception arise from a misunderstanding of this crucial point. Granted that there are accepted resemblances between mourning and melancholia, the crucial differences between them must always be borne in mind! Mourning, however painful, is, no matter how much its dynamic unconscious structure resembles that of patho-genic illness, a normal human experience which few of us escape" (p. 104). Later, Zetzel adds: "Finally with regard to the concept of 'the depressive position,' I feel that more than anything else, the term is unfortunate, since it seems to imply more far-reaching implications of infantile psychosis than is in fact the case" (p. 112).

Yet it should be noted that Glover (1932b) repeatedly refers to early stages in psychic development as unequivocally psychotic. He assumes that psychosis is a state that characterizes childhood and refers to this state as "normal psychosis." In his opinion, "Every child in the first year of life is *from the adult psychiatric point of view* in a state of pan-psychosis, always acute and very largely hallucinatory. . . . So we term them the normal reactions of a child, even when they are plainly of a psychotic pattern" (pp. 239, 240; my italics). He qualifies this some-what by saying, "Unless the child comes to terms with reality, he remains in a true psychotic state of anxiety. Exaggerated manifestations of this anxiety are entitled to be called the 'clinical psychoses' of childhood as distinct from the 'normal psychoses' of childhood" (1932a, p. 179).

Despite the many similarities to Klein's viewpoints, Fairbairn, as I have indicated, rejects primary aggression and ergo the death instinct (a concept vital to Klein). Klein (1946), although acknowledging simi-larities to Fairbairn, highlights certain areas of disagreement:

I disagree—to mention first the most basic issues—with his revision of the theory of mental structure and instincts. I also disagree with his view that to begin with only the bad object is internalized—a view which seems to me to contribute to the important differences between us regarding the development of object relations as well as ego develop-ment. For I hold that the introjected good breast forms a vital part of the ego, exerts from the beginning a fundamental influence on the process of ego development and affects both ego structure and object relations. I also dissent from Fairbairn's view that 'the great problem of the schizoid individual is how to love without destroying by love, whereas the great problem of the depressive individual is how to love without destroying by hate' (cf. Fairbairn, 1941, p. 271). This conclusion is in line not only with his rejecting the concept of primary instincts but also with his underrating of the role which aggression and hatred play from the beginning of life. As a result of this approach, he does not give enough weight to the importance of early anxiety and conflict and their dynamic effects on development [p. 100].

A leading disciple of Fairbairn and Winnicott is Guntrip (1961, 1969), who also underlines "schizoid phenomena." He sees schizoid individuals as suffering from a massive withdrawal from external relationships in response to a total failure in early mothering. This lack results in a flight back to the internal world and its objects in the search for security; there is extreme anxiety about possible loss of self due to the lack of anybody who could make it possible to hold the self together. In these individuals, Guntrip (1969) believes:

> ... the underlying, unconscious strata of their personalities are on the pre-moral level of infantile fear, ego weakness, and flight from life. ... Mental illness springs specifically from the ravages of early fear and basic weakness of the ego, with consequent inability to cope with life in any other way than a dangerous state of anxiety. ... The core of psychological distress is simply elementary fear ... fear carrying with it the feeling of weakness and inability to cope with life; fear possessing the psyche to such an extent that ego experience cannot get started [pp. 10–13].

He adds:

> In pathological anxiety the danger situation is an internal one, ultimately the fear of ego-breakdown, past fears having so determined the development of the personality structure that they both infect new object relationships, and also operate in an internal fantasy life, undermining the personality both inside and out. ... The infant cannot take literal flight, and can only take flight in a mental sense, into an attempt to create and possess an hallucinated or fantasied safety in a purely psychic world which is part of his own experience, an inner world split off from the realities of everyday living. ... Since, however, anxiety situations cannot be kept out of even this private inner world, it precipitates a final split in the infantile ego which permits a most secret hidden core of the self to regress completely into what is probably an unconscious hallucinated reproduction of the intrauterine condition [pp. 87–88].

Yet this withdrawal, this defense, is in and of itself a great source of danger. "Of all the ultimate terrors," he comments, "my clinical experience suggests that the last and worst is the one that is set up precisely by too drastic use of this defence by self-isolation, namely, the feeling of being 'a psyche in a vacuum,' out of all touch, out of all relationship, empty of all experience, and so to speak, collapsing in on itself, lost in a sense of complete unreality, and unable to be an 'ego'" (p. 238).

The anxiety, the basic terror that Guntrip describes, the threat to existence and possible loss of self, is a concept shared by others, although described in different terms, such as disintegrative anxiety or annihilation anxiety. Nor is it dissimilar from the fear of dissolution and disintegration of self I described above as the basic danger in the psychotic process (see Chapter 7).

Sutherland (1980), in his succinct survey of the British Object Relations School, points out that although there are many areas of agreement with Melanie Klein, in their view she minimizes the role of the external object in her emphasis on the endopsychic features. It is in a defect in relation to the external object, essentially the mother or the mothering object, that the British Object Relations School finds the trigger for pathological processes. All these theorists underline the failure in the infant-mother relationship due to a lack of fit between the infant's needs and the mother's response. Balint's "basic fault" is referred to by the others with different terminology, such as the absence of "good mothering" or a defect in "maternal empathy" or lack of a "good-enough mother." Yet I'm not sure this phenomenon is only observable in schizoid patients since defective mothering appears to be the leitmotif in many other contributions.[5] (The therapeutic implications of this viewpoint will be discussed in Chapter 18.)

As I indicated earlier, anyone who has worked with severely ill patients, especially psychotic ones, cannot help being impressed by this group of contributors. Nonetheless, there is much that is troublesome. In their observations deriving from their work with such patients, there appears to be an extrapolation to cover other forms of psychopathology, and even normal human behavior, without specificity as to what eventuates in which development. As I shall discuss in Chapter 13, a similar methodological generalizing characterizes the contributions of the Interpersonal School, as well as those of Karen Horney. From work with schizophrenics, the Interpersonal School postulates basic concepts and applies these to neuroses. Similarly, Horney's concepts of the neurotic personality are applied to the psychoses without the rich clinical, or even established, theoretical frames of reference to support this. The British Object Relations School assumes that the major neurotic syndromes simply reflect different ways of dealing with the conflicts of the

---

[5] Kohut's concepts, for instance, rely a great deal on this defect as responsible for narcissistic personality disorders.

schizoid and depressive positions. The positions are viewed as configurations of object relations, anxiety, and defenses, which are maintained through life. Movement may be from one position to the other, depending on whether the depressive position or the schizoid position is predominant.

Pao (1979) points out that the broadness of Fairbairn's approach does not help to explain more specific symptomatology. Sutherland (1980) has pointed to the same flaw in Balint's contributions, remarking: "Balint... while giving us clinical data on the existence of the phase and how it manifested itself plus its damaging ramification, did not take its conceptualizations further, nor did he suggest how it linked with future conflict" (p. 851).[6] While Balint's and Winnicott's views offer a broad frame of reference for psychic development, the actual application to specific clinical diagnostic categories can only be understood within these broad categories. For instance, which features of Balint's and Winnicott's work can help us to understand the *difference* between obsessive-compulsives and hysterics, or phobics? All of them would appear to have some basic fault or defect in maternal empathy. But what in this defect specifically leads to the one or the other clinical picture? I suspect that neither Balint nor Winnicott would feel that this is important to establish. They deal with fundamental defects. The same may be said, although perhaps to a lesser extent, of Fairbairn and Guntrip. In the case of Guntrip, the link to future conflict is essentially for schizoid personalities and less so for neurosis or the usual character disorders. Nonetheless, he does indicate that what he calls basic terror, and the defenses he sees as dealing with this terror, may eventuate not only in schizophrenia, but also in manic-depressive states and neuroses. But Guntrip's application of this concept is most thoroughly explored in "schizoid personalities." It seems to me that the schizoid personality and the schizoid position, as defined by the object relationists, appear to have little to do with the clinical psychoses known as schizophrenia.

The object relationists formulate many of the features which constitute the psychotic process as I have described it. Although they use different terms, the components I have delineated are recognizable, namely, the nature of the danger, the nature of the defenses, and the state of the ego. They do not, however, it seems to me, stress that impairment of ego functions — in particular, of reality testing — which

---

[6] Somewhat similar is Padel's (1977) criticism of Klein as "a most unsystematic and imprecise writer... [who] had a difficulty in producing something formed and whole" (p. 27).

makes for clinical psychosis. Indeed, the latter is not dealt with in depth. Perhaps this is because they did not work extensively with gross psychotics but mainly with severe character disorders with "schizoid" features (although Guntrip presumably worked in psychiatric hospitals).

I have the impression that in their work with such severe character disorders, the patients were made to fit into a Procrustean bed, consisting of that impairment in personality which to these theorists characterizes the early stage in psychic development they designate the schizoid position. Because some of the mechanisms used by the infant at that stage, for instance, projective-introjective techniques, resemble those seen in the adult "schizoid" individual, they apply the same psychiatric terminology to this early stage. They therefore imply that what is a stage in early psychic development, what is phase-related and appropriate at that stage, is psychotic.

Insofar as the validity of the basic object relations theory is concerned, I should like to say that there seems to me to be a tortured quality to differentiating the infant's needs as primarily object-related or primarily instinct-gratifying. As Hartmann (1939a) indicates: "We should not assume, from the fact that the child and the environment interact from the outset, that the child is from the beginning psychologically directed toward the object as an object" (p. 52). The child's feeling of security lies in the feeling of sureness that its biological and life-serving needs will be met (Ferenczi's "unconditional omnipotence"). How else would these needs be met other than through an object? It is questionable, however, whether in the earliest stages of psychic development this is perceived as such by the organism, Klein and Fairbairn notwithstanding. What makes the child restless and tense and uneasy is the mounting tension generated by biological needs which become linked with an object who holds, cuddles, and warms it. Eventually the two become inextricably interwoven. It may be that the object is eventually sought for, in and of itself, but I doubt if this is the case at the beginning. No matter how much you cuddle and hold the child, sooner or later you have to feed it. It is in subsequent phases of the infant-mother relationship that the need for "good mothering" independent of need gratification assumes dominance. This, I believe, is similar to Mahler's perspective, to which I shall now turn.

12.
Childhood Psychosis and Mahler's Contribution

Given the criticisms of Melanie Klein's and Fairbairn's ideas, it is relevant to spend some time with those psychoanalytic contributors who have studied not only psychic development in children but psychoses in children. In 1959 a symposium on "Psychotic Object Relationships," focusing on psychotic children, was held at the meetings of the International Psycho-Analytical Association (the papers were published in 1960). Among those participating were Lebovici, Diatkine, Mahler, and De Souza. These authors focus on special facets related to distortions in the mother-child relationship, either viewed within the framework of self-nonself confusion, perceptual ego defects conducive to lack of differentiation, or Kleinian projective identification. In spite of the seemingly different frames of reference, a common denominator appears to be the existence of primitive ego levels and primitive object relations. Lebovici (1960), for instance, reports on the analysis of a mother and nine-and-one-half-year-old child, in which severe regressive manifestations, in the form of projective identification and fusion with the analyst, were present. He highlights the severely regressive sadomasochistic oral-impulsive characteristics of the highly disturbed mother, and the impact on the child of her behavior in gratifying her impulses.

Diatkine (1960) presents a child who until the age of five manifested autistic behavior. Objects were meaningless to him. Diatkine does not refer to this stage as psychotic object relations. Yet in children similar to this patient, he describes the "meaningless world of precociously psychotic children who, far from isolating themselves, display both interest in and affection for others, but with a total lack of differentiation em-

---

Dr. Isidor Bernstein was most helpful in putting Mahler's work in perspective.

bracing their parents, strangers, objects, the furniture, etc. This lack of discrimination, in spite of a normal motor-perceptive development, has an identical significance" (p. 545). In his patient there was a shift from this objectless state to an object-related period at the age of five, and Diatkine now refers to this as the child's psychotic object relations. He believes that this child's seemingly autistic behavior had behind it an anxiety caused by the fear of fragmentation. This fear became more openly expressed when the child reached the stage where his body image assumed some degree of unity and the process of identification was initiated. These advances made the possibility of fragmentation more threatening. It was then that oral projective-identification manifestations appeared, which Diatkine views as the manifestation of a psychotic object relationship.

I have already alluded to Mahler's (1960) contribution (see p. 296). Essentially she says that in the psychotic child and adult, there is a failure of the ego's perceptual-integrative function, so that the ego is unable to discriminate stimuli. It is thus exposed to an onslaught of stimuli against which it tries to defend itself by massive denial, condensation, and dedifferentiation. The latter is resorted to to dehumanize the very threatening human environment, and in doing so the person may animate the inanimate. Inanimate objects may become "alive," and possibly threatening, but not as threatening as the human environment.

De Souza (1960), within a strictly Kleinian frame of reference, presents a two-and-one-half-year-old child who, he indicates, had a depressive reaction to loss. She was unable to deal with this depressive reaction and regressed to the paranoid-schizoid position. De Souza conducted therapy along Kleinian lines, interpreting in play therapy the introjective-projective techniques directed against the actual play objects, the furniture in the room, and the therapist. He viewed these as directed against her parents as well as her own inside. The patient also destroyed verbal thoughts in herself, projecting this onto the therapist and rejecting all his verbalizations and interpretations. De Souza points out that "annihilation of the object that goes with the annihilation of parts of the self is a psychotic type of object-relationship. With splitting and projective identification, it shows the psychotic paradox of an ego which, not being well integrated, in the same process of defence, attacks some of its own functions in order to prevent something coming into perception that already existed internally" (pp. 557–558).

Thomas (1966) has applied Anna Freud's diagnostic profile in a study of self- and object representation in four institutionalized psychotic children, aged seven to ten years, all of whom showed primitive instinctual behavior and uneven ego development. They presented unusual or bizarre behavior, speech disturbances reflecting confusion of thought, and disordered relations to people. Thomas's findings suggest an arrest in development at the most primitive ego levels, before structuralization. There were signs of self-nonself confusion and fears of merger and dissolution. These children made some advances during therapy. Nevertheless, these advances "still seemed to be carried out in the face of a severe arrest in the area of self and object relationships, in which for long periods, feeling states were in abeyance or defended against and in which preoccupation with the inanimate was an unusual feature. When for internal reasons, these defensive activities failed, there appeared a trend toward animistic thinking with the denial of differences between child and adult" (p. 579).

Freeman (1973) sees many descriptive similarities between adult and childhood psychoses:

> The phenomena which have been described show that childhood psychoses resembles most closely those adult states where an extensive dissolution has affected mental life. Thus the most striking similarities have been found in psychoses of acute onset and in cases of chronic schizophrenia characterized by withdrawal, disinterest, lack of affect, negativism and catatonic signs. There are fewer resemblances when the childhood states are compared with cases of paranoid psychosis where cognition still operates at an advanced level and where there are complex delusions. Delusions are rudimentary or nonexistent in the chronic patient and in the psychotic child. In both they are confined to omnipotent fantasies and to isolated persecutory ideas which may be attached to anyone in the immediate environment [p. 313].

In both, he believes the danger of object loss and the fear of the consequences of merging with the object are of major significance. He goes so far as to postulate that adult schizophrenia grows out of a childhood psychosis: "The question which springs to mind is whether the adult schizophrenic, in his childhood, sustained a mental disturbance similar in form, if not in intensity, to childhood psychosis. The assumption would have to be made that instead of a permanent or semi-permanent developmental arrest having taken place, the libido and ego continued their maturation with later achievements in interpersonal relationships and cognition concealing the earlier pathological state" (pp. 321–322).

Foremost among the contributors to the understanding of childhood psychosis is Mahler. In order to understand Mahler's view of psychoses in children, it is important to examine her frames of reference for psychic development. Mahler (1960, 1968) applies the term "normal autism" to the first weeks of life, when the infant is in a state of primitive hallucinatory disorientation in which need satisfaction belongs to its own omnipotent autistic orbit. "From the second month on, dim awareness of the need-satisfying object marks the beginning of the phase of normal symbiosis, in which the infant behaves and functions as though he and his mother were an omnipotent system — a dual unity within one common boundary" (1968, p. 8). During the symbiotic phase the infant is absolutely dependent on the symbiotic partner; the "I" is not separated from the "not I." According to Mahler:

> The essential feature of symbiosis is hallucinatory or delusional, somato-psychic omnipotent fusion with the representation of the mother and, in particular, the delusion of a common boundary of the two actually and physically separate individuals. This is the mechanism to which the ego regresses in cases of the most severe disturbance of individuation and psychotic disorganization, which I have described as "symbiotic child psychosis" [p. 9].[1]

Toward the end of the third month, the precursors of the body image and "core self" begin to evolve. As Mahler points out:

> The infant's inner sensations form the *core* of the self. They seem to remain the central, the crystallization point of the "feeling of self," around which a "sense of identity" will become established. The sensoriperceptive organ — the "peripheral rind of the ego" as Freud called it — contributes mainly to the self's demarcation from the object world. The two kinds of intrapsychic structures together form the framework for self-orientation [p. 11].[2]

With the third month, the symbiotic phase begins to crystallize. The object begins to be perceived as an unspecific need-satisfying part-object, with the gradual beginning of an ego in the child. By the time the fifth month has arrived the infant has achieved a specific symbiotic relationship with his mother. The height of symbiosis is four to five months.

The ensuing months up to two years and beyond represent the important steps toward separation and individuation. This is a process with several subphases. The infant begins to be aware of stimuli ema-

---

[1] Many features of this state are analogous to Klein's and Fairbairn's paranoid-schizoid position, but Mahler doesn't relate to the Kleinian deeper instinctual interplay between mother and infant, nor does she deal with the extreme sadism and death drives as extensively as Klein does.

[2] This is not too unlike what later on becomes what Federn calls "ego-feeling."

nating outside the the mother, which brings with it outward-directed attention, and "hatching" begins. There is a widening of the symbiotic orbit with, however, constant checking back to the mother's facial gestalt. Out of this the infant develops a "permanent alert sensorium." If this proceeds smoothly, the transition from the symbiotic orbit can take place without traumatic consequences. This "checking back" and comparing require, of course, an available stable frame of reference—the mother. If this stage doesn't proceed smoothly, one may find the potential ingredients for distrust in one's own perceptions so that reaffirmation of the reality of a perception is required from an external object.

During the practicing period, which begins toward the end of the first year and culminates at about 18 months, the toddler practices separation and return and develops a sense of sharing in his mother's magical powers. "But," according to Mahler, "even at the height of the second subphase of individuation—during the practicing period— neither the differentiated self representations nor the object representations seem to be integrated as yet into a whole self representation or a whole libidinal object representation" (p. 18).

The 16- to 18-month period is a nodal point in development. It is Mahler's opinion, which I share, that disturbances during this period may contribute to the interference in the development of reality constancy. The child ventures out, but also checks back. It utilizes its own developing autonomous functions, but in venturing into the world it needs support and reaffirmation from the mother. If she is unrealiable, unpredictable, unstable, anxiety-ridden, or hostile, there is no reliable frame of reference for checking back. There is a lack of a frame of reference for perceiving the world outside of the mother. In such cases, self-confidence and self-feeling are shaky and new experiences of separate functioning are thereby interfered with. These are the ingredients of the defective reality constancy seen in the psychotic process.

The practicing period gradually evolves into the rapprochement subphase, during which the developing child wishes the mother to share its newly acquired skills and experiences. Individuation and internalization move apace and true identification with the parents evolves. Ultimately object constancy develops. Mahler (1971) discusses problems during the rapprochement subphase that presage borderline pathology. Deficiencies of integration and internalization leave residues which may later manifest themselves in borderline phenomena. There are marked alternations between extreme coercive and desperate clinging behavior. This derives from more than optimal splitting into good and bad objects.

In contrast to the unsuccessful resolution of the rapprochement phase, which may lead to borderline phenomena, Mahler views the unsuccessful working through of still earlier phases, such as the symbiotic phase, as eventuating in specific forms of psychopathology, contributing to the psychotic process. As she puts it:

> This phase of extrauterine evolution, the symbiotic relationship, is either gravely distorted or missing in infantile psychosis, and it is this that represents, to my way of understanding it, the core disturbance in infantile as well as adolescent and adult psychosis.
>
> The core disturbance in infantile psychosis is therefore, as I see it, a deficiency or a defect in the child's intrapsychic utilization of the mothering partner during the symbiotic phase, and his subsequent inability to internalize the representation of the mothering object for polarization. Without this, differentiation of the self from symbiotic fusion and confusion with the part object does not occur. In short, faulty or absent individuation lies at the core of infantile psychosis. In other words: the psychotic infant seems to lack or fails to acquire in earliest extrauterine life the capacity to perceive and thus to use the mothering agent for maintenance of his homeostasis; nor can he later release her [1968, pp. 32–33].

Differing from the British Object Relations School, Mahler views the newborn's waking life as centering around attempts to reduce tension. Good and bad revolve around tension-reducing and tension-creating or non-tension-reducing stimuli, with alteration of the good and bad to the self and nonself. The infant has to become acquainted with reality via its mother. The psychotic child is unable to use the mother to achieve this. Mahler views this as primary to the etiology of psychosis. She suggests that this defect is constitutional, inborn, probably hereditary or possibly acquired in the first few days or weeks of life. In terms of the resultant psychopathology, she states:

> The two main mechanisms which the psychotic child uses, in different combinations and admixtures, are essentially autistic and symbiotic — deanimation, dedifferentiation, devitalization, and fusion and defusion. These can be called neither defense mechanisms nor adaptive mechanisms in the sense in which these terms are used with any other group of children, normal or neurotic. For that reason, I would prefer to call them *maintenance mechanisms* [p. 52].

As I pointed out above, Mahler indicates that early traumatic experiences may contribute to a failure in the perceptual-integrative capacity of the ego. This defect will potentiate dedifferentiation to the point where primary discrimination between living and inanimate is lost. In essence, Mahler looks on dehumanization and reanimation as a regressive adaptation when the ego's perceptual-integrative capacity fails. Yet it is the latter defect which facilitates the reanimation of the nonhuman environment. I also wonder what role defects in the development of reality constancy play in facilitating this dedifferentiation. Mahler remarks:

> The phenomenon that is more or less overtly common to all psychotics is the blurring, if not complete failure, of distinction, of affective discrimination between the social, the human object world and the inanimate environment. In some cases, we find only a lack of or very tenuous emotional contact, phenomena of estrangement, complaints of derealization. In cases of acute severe psychotic breakdown, however, we find deanimation of the human object world with concomitant animation of the inanimate environment [pp. 53–54].

> I was able to observe a most striking inability, on the part of the psychotic child, even to see the human object in the outside world, let alone to interact with him as with another separate human entity. This often seemed to be the most conspicuous, indeed the cardinal feature of childhood psychosis [p. 3].

Permeating this situation is a kind of tension referred to by Mahler as organismic distress (see Chapter 7). She refers to the physiological state of high tension experienced early in life and relates this to an accumulation of physiological needs without gratification. As I noted earlier, Pao (1979) uses the term "organismic panic" for the response to considerable chronic organismic distress early in life. Such distress may be experienced either because of defective biological givens, or because of the lack of an empathic mother (see also Kohut, 1971). In schizophrenia, according to Pao, the somatic memory of organismic distress creates a predisposition to anxiety, which is so heightened that when the person meets a situation that should evoke only ordinary anxiety, he experiences organismic panic. I would add that the inability to master such situations and the feeling of being overwhelmed by them produce a fear of disintegration and falling apart, which is basic to experiencing such anxiety.

Mahler's direct studies of psychoses in children are based on patients older than the earliest few months, the period for which most of the Kleinian endopsychic postulates were reconstructed. Apparently the clinical manifestations were more crystallized and visible, with many similarities to adult psychosis. Still, clarification is needed on how similar the clinical manifestations in adult psychoses are to the observable manifestations in children. Moreover, the same question could be raised here as was raised in connection with the formulations of Klein and Fairbairn: What were the specific clinical manifestations in the young infants designated as psychosis? Such clarification would lend more validity to the prototype for future psychotic clinical syndromes.

As was pointed out above, Freeman (1973), in his profile survey, maintains that with some minor difference the observable data are quite similar in schizophrenic children and adults, although less so in the delusional paranoid picture. He and others (Thomas, 1966) find in these children the basic conflicts, dangers, and anxieties which have been described as typifying adult psychoses. Self-nonself confusion, with the prevalence of merging; fear of self-dissolution, and the tremendous anxiety associated with the fear of disintegration and annihilation — all were quite prevalent (cf. Chapter 7). In discussing this anxiety, Freeman says: "The thought content associated with the anxiety was found to consist of fears of bodily disintegration, fear of loss of personal characteristics and fear of loss of control over sexual and aggressive impulses" (p. 312). I have made the point, and it appears to be confirmed, that the fear of such impulses is not due to a fear of condemnation or punishment but a fear that the strength of these impulses will overwhelm the patient and will lead to disintegration of self, with the resultant molecular fragmentation which may encompass the body image, language, ego function, affects, etc. This holds true for any strong emotional experience.

In sum, it appears fairly clear in that in the view of many there is a distinct relationship and similarity between childhood and adult psychoses. Although not denigrating the impact of early developmental experiences on subsequent psychic development, the Interpersonal School tends to deemphasize this in their concepts. I shall now turn to an examination of their concepts.

13.
The Interpersonal School

Just as in using the term the "English School," one has in mind Melanie Klein, Fairbairn, and their followers, so when one alludes to the "Washington School," it is Sullivan and his followers — Fromm-Reichmann, Will, Thompson, Searles, and others — one thinks of. Although they evolved a theoretical frame of reference as a basis for the understanding of human behavior in general, their essential contribution has been to the understanding and the treatment of psychoses, particularly schizophrenia. A good deal of their early work was done with very sick, hospitalized psychotic patients at Sheppard and Enoch Pratt Hospital and at Chestnut Lodge. Indeed, the main interest and contribution of the Interpersonal School might be described as therapeutic, although it has an underlying theoretical orientation.

Basic to their concepts is the idea that there is no fundamental difference between the normal and the pathological. Modes of expression of anxiety in the healthy and in the mentally ill are essentially the same. This is cogently stated by Fromm-Reichmann (1950a): "It is my belief that the problems and emotional difficulties of mental patients, neurotics or psychotics, are, in principle, rather similar to one another and also to the emotional difficulties in living from which we all suffer at times. Should these difficulties become so great that a person is unable to resolve them without help, thereby feeling the need for assistance, he may become a mental patient in need of psychotherapy" (p. xi). She adds that essential to treatment is the psychiatrist's recognition that the patient's difficulties in living are not too different from his own. The mentally disturbed patient shares with the healthy person a "two-sidedness of motivation," as well as many modes of expression reflecting means of alleviating anxiety. Fromm-Reichmann expands her analogy between the two by comparing the dreams of the healthy with psychosis. They are viewed as transitory psychotic states through which we all pass (see Chapter 3).

Although I shall focus on those contributions specifically related to the psychotic process, some general survey of the frames of reference used is indicated. The perspective on psychic development is cogently formulated by Will (1961). He indicates that psychic development reside:

> . . . in the insecurity of the young human in the primary relationship with the one who cares for him and teaches him, with varying degrees of distortion, something of the culture in which he is to live. In his dependence upon another, he develops the need and ability to receive and to give tenderness and love, thus becoming inextricably bound — with anxiety, doubt, and fear, sorrow and delight — to the community of men. When this beginning is marked by the apprehension of losing the security-providing person, the bases of what is later known as anxiety are formed, and certain complexities of behavior — detachment, dissociation, sublimation, and withdrawal — are evolved in the service of altering the dynamics of the interpersonal situation in such a way that its necessary continuance is seemingly assured and some semblance of the increasingly important sentiment of security is maintained [p. 74].

It is, in other words, dependency on and the fear of loss of the love object that is the frame of reference — not unlike the viewpoints of Klein, Fairbairn, Mahler, and Winnicott, to whose work Will refers.

As I have already indicated, Sullivan (1953, 1956, 1962) differentiates between biological satisfaction needs, and cultural or security needs. It is when the latter, interpersonal security needs are not met that anxiety is generated. This anxiety triggers the "self-dynamism," as Sullivan calls it. He describes three self-images: a "good me," which is free of anxiety; a "bad me," with lots of anxiety; and a "not me," with extreme anxiety, terror, and dread. The "not me" appears to have much in common with the basic anxiety I described in Chapter 7 and with the organismic or primordial anxiety others have described. The "not me" also resembles the loss of self, loss of identity, and disintegration of the self pinpointed by others. It is the "not me" which is the state of the schizophrenic, according to Sullivan.

"Self-dynamisms" are evolved and organized to avoid or minimize anxiety. They undergo changes in various developmental phases as well as in pathological states. All sorts of security operations are developed to safeguard the functioning of the self-system. Such operations are called into play to deal with the schizophrenic's self-disintegration fears, the terror of possible self-dissolution, which Sullivan refers to as nothingness. In the background of the future schizophrenic, the source for the infant's "not me" experience is the anxiety-ridden mother. The anxiety derives from strivings which were incompatible with the environmental standards of significant people in childhood and thus aroused the fear of disapproval.

Sullivan finds little to differentiate the paranoid from the schizophrenic state. As indicated in Chapter 4, Section A, in my discussion of the role of unconscious homosexuality in the paranoid constellation, Sullivan categorically rejects this view of paranoia. Essentially, to him, paranoia is a defense against feelings of inadequacy and unworthiness evoked by an early life replete with disapprovals. In other words, paranoia is culturally determined, evolving during the early social periods of life.

Fromm-Reichmann (1950b) believes that all anxieties share "a cultural common element, namely, the dread of loss of love from significant people in the childhood scene" (p. 37). In the schizophrenic, she says:

> . . . secondary anxiety is developed by the patient at the prospect that he will realize his own retaliative hostility, which he abhors. Coming closer means greater danger that this hostility will be aroused, that the other person will notice it and that disapproval by others and further self-disapproval will take place. . . . The schizophrenic's magic regressive hostility, the fear of the manifestations of his actual hostility, his own disapproval of it, and the anticipated disapproval of significant people in the present and the past constitute the central core of anxiety. Schizophrenic symptomatology should be dynamically understood as the expression of this anxiety and as a defense against it [pp. 38–39].

In the dynamics of schizophrenia, Fromm-Reichmann (1959) sees:

> . . . narcissistic regression. . . producing withdrawal, the overrating of positive skills and negative powers, difficulty in dealing with hatred and potential violence, and the severe judgment of negative character traits, due to the narcissistic self-conception. Being a severe judge, the narcissistic schizophrenic patient fears his hostile impulses, fleeing into a self-imposed state of psychical and emotional paralysis. The schizophrenic patient fears closeness. . . . The schizophrenic patient also feels the need to be guided; however, his hunger for love and dependence is counteracted by the wish for independence [p. 418].

Will (1961) suggests that in the schizophrenic a fear of loss is established early, along with deficiencies in self and identification, eventuating in patterns of behavior which are "ineffective in enabling the person to follow the fundamental course of human maturation toward both greater autonomy and self-identity and a sense of unity with his kind" (p. 74). It is through the interplay of physiological maturation and social learning that an integral concept of self should develop. In contrast:

> In the schizophrenic reaction, the self-image, poorly organized and differentiated, reflecting comprehended and clarified symbols, and dependent upon dissociation of major integrative systems with the support of such devices as obsessional substitution, selective inattention, sublimation, and physical incapacitation, is disrupted. The result is a sense of personal chaos of which there is urgent need for resolution [p. 75].

Will, then, sees the schizophrenic picture as characterized by "uncertainty regarding self-identity; misidentification of others; instability of 'ego boundaries'; feelings of 'depersonalization'; self-disorganization; regression; denial; control by an 'influencing machine'; delusions and hallucinations; paranoid phenomena of grandiosity and projection; rage; habit deterioration and withdrawal; and stereotypy and poverty of thinking" (p. 77).

As one surveys the crucial concepts on the psychotic's fears, anxieties, and terror, it becomes clear that these are not too dissimilar from the basic anxiety I have postulated for the psychotic process. However, the initiating factors that produce this anxiety carry a somewhat different emphasis. In my view, the deeper, early biological factors create the prototype for subsequent anxieties initiated by traumatic cultural experiences.

It is also clear that the Interpersonal School's basic theoretical frames of reference are applicable to both neurosis and psychosis, although the contributions to the understanding of the psychoses receive greater prominence. I have mentioned their belief that normal and pathological problems are not too dissimilar. They give less emphasis to disturbances in ego functioning, such as reality testing, which I believe are crucial in psychosis.

Much about these concepts appears to be a reformulation, with different emphasis and terminology, of the idea of phase-related ego and self-development coeval with methods of coping with stress consistent with these phases in development. Yet the impact of early developmental features is not emphasized, at least in therapy, as the main frame of reference.

The technical considerations arising from the perspective of the Interpersonal School will be discussed in Chapter 18. Basic to their therapeutic process is the concept of the participant observer. The therapist participates in the patient's experiences and not infrequently invites the patient to share the therapist's experiences. As Fromm-Reichmann (1950a) indicates: "it is the interpersonal exchange between the patient and the psychiatrist as a participant observer which carries the possibility of therapeutically valid interpersonal investigation and formulation" (p. xiv).

PART V

SPECIAL
CONSIDERATIONS

14.
Etiology

Many of the contributions I have discussed touch on the question of etiology. As we have seen, the emphases vary, ranging from constitutional factors, both biological and psychological; to early developmental experiences, encompassing various types of tale-telling traumata, both physiological and psychological; to the impact of present-day forces on the personality, encompassing the role of social and cultural factors, as well as somatic factors.

It might be appropriate to define what I mean by these terms. The term "constitutional" is used here in the broad sense, as encompassing all the potentials for development psychologically and physiologically that an individual has at the time of birth. In this broad sense, the term covers both hereditary factors (inborn and genetic) and intrauterine and birth experiences (which are generally not included as constitutional factors). It should be emphasized that these built-in potentials and givens interact with life experiences, both early developmental experiences and later life experiences, whether physiological or psychological, or both.

Present-day forces and current stress may, in my opinion, facilitate the development of psychotic behavior by interacting with the constitutional potentials and the early developmental experiences, which have already lent psychotic potential to the personality. Particular phases in the life cycle, such as puberty, menopause, and old age, may create settings in which psychotic potential may come to expression. In addition, extraneous traumas, illness, or emotional experiences (especially object loss) may precipitate a psychotic breakdown.

The differences in opinion on etiology often arise from an exclusive emphasis on one factor or another, with resultant variations in prediction, prognosis, therapeutic implications, etc. It is probable, however, that it is the interplay of all the factors that makes any given picture develop. Let us conceptualize this in terms of maldevelopment and malfunctions in the three areas I have cited: (1) constitutional poten-

387

tial, (2) early developmental experiences, and (3) present-day forces impinging on the personality. Malfunctions in these areas do not necessarily lead to psychopathology. A person born with poor intellectual endowment may still function reasonably well, if subsequent experiential factors in development are good. This may or may not be the case if there is reasonably good constitutional endowment but very traumatic early developmental experiences. Let us say, the mother dies at childbirth, the father cannot care for the child and it is boarded out with many disruptive changes. It would require exceptional freedom from traumatic present-day forces and stress for such an individual to avoid a pathological outcome. On the other hand, let us take good constitutional and developmental factors but exposure to highly traumatic present-day forces and stress. With combat casualties, for instance, it has been found that some, after a few days' rest away from the battlefront, lose their symptoms and can return to combat. Others require more prolonged care, with psychotherapy of varying depth, before they can return to combat. An irreducible minimum, however, have to be discharged. The latter show long-standing disturbances of varying degrees, in some instances going back as far as birth and usually involving family psychopathology. The ones who respond with rest and removal from the scene of combat are analogous to people in toxic states who recover once the toxin is removed. In other words, the prognosis with good constitutional and developmental factors and traumatic present-day factors is good. It is, however, clear that the interplay of all these forces will be the determinant in the nature of psychopathology, its prognosis, and its responsiveness to psychotherapy.

Insofar as schizophrenia is concerned, Pao (1979) indicates: "The knowledge accumulated in the last few decades from early developmental studies of normal and deviant infants strongly suggests that neither nature nor nurture alone can lead to schizophrenia. Rather, the interaction of the two in the very early phase of the infant's life results in certain experiences that later evolve into the multifarious symptoms of the schizophrenic illness" (p. 143).

Recent contributions on the role of biochemical factors in mental illness, as well as studies of monozygotic twins, have provided strong statistical evidence for the operation of genetic factors in psychoses in about 50% of the cases reported. Although the concordance is high, these studies do not preclude the importance of environmental factors in the remaining 50%. Moreover, several criticisms have been voiced about these studies. Lidz and his co-workers (1965) severely question the methodology. Cancro (1979b), after reviewing the hereditary component in schizophrenia and critiquing the twin studies, says: "The very fact that different gene-environment combinations can produce the phenotype or phenotypes which are necessary but not sufficient for the schizophrenic syndrome means that there are multiple etiologic pathways through which this syndrome can develop.... The search for a single etiology is unlikely to be productive and that there is neither a single environment nor a particular genetic constellation which is schizophrenogenic" (pp. 148–149).

Bellak (1958) uses Beres's (1956) list of ego functions in discussing the etiological factors that bring about schizophrenic deviations. He views schizophrenia "as a syndrome characterized by a final common path of disturbances of the ego, with a primary etiology of chemogenic, histogenic, genogenic, of psychotic nature and a combination thereof, different in each individual case, but probably identifiable as clusters in subgroups" (p. 61).

The contributions from psychoanalysis, especially classical psychoanalysis, generally look to the impact of early developmental experiences, although they do not ignore constitutional and social factors as considerations. While it is far beyond the province of this contribution to do full justice to this subject, which almost warrants a separate study, a consideration of some of the more commonly held views is appropriate.

Constitutional Factors

Freud repeatedly acknowledges the significance of constitutional factors. In 1937, for instance, he remarks that we have to recognize that the peculiarities of the ego one detects in resistances may be not only acquired in defense conflicts but (also) determined by heredity. Hartmann (1939a) also emphasizes constitutional factors in psychic development, stating that "the human individual possesses at his birth an as yet unexplored inventory of mental dispositions, comprising constitutional factors important in ego development" (p. 50).

It should be noted that many of the psychoanalytic contributions on constitutional factors are based on reconstructive hypotheses, which are difficult to evaluate. Other contributions stem from longitudinal studies, such as Freeman's (1973) application of Anna Freud's profile to the psychoses, Fries's studies of archaic ego types (1977b) and her concept of congenital activity types (1937; Fries and Woolf, 1953); and

Mahler's (1968) work with psychotic children. Still other studies are based on direct observations from birth and soon thereafter. It should be kept in mind, however, that we tend to fall back on constitutional factors in the absence of knowledge of the extrauterine factors that may play a role.

As a frame of reference in considering constitutional psychological factors, we might use Hartmann's (1950) concept of undifferentiated id and ego potentials or Glover's (1939) idea of ego nuclei that ultimately mature but may be constitutionally impaired. Arlow and Brenner (1964) also point to constitutional factors in suggesting that the ego's inability to fend off anxiety resulting from danger connected with intrapsychic conflict may arise from a constitutional inadequacy in the ego.

I have already discussed (pp. 284 ff, 296 ff) the many factors playing a role in the establishment of the stimulus barrier. Furst (1978) surveys the literature on the role of constitutional factors in establishing the stimulus barrier, as well as the subsequent environmental factors affecting the stimulus barrier in the developing neonate. He correlates these factors with the impact of stimuli in traumatic situations and subsequent psychopathology. In his opinion, there is "impressive evidence for the existence of an innate mechanism which serves not only to protect against strong or noxious stimuli, but also to regulate intake to achieve an optimal level of stimulation" (p. 346). Neonates show constitutional differences in their responses to stimuli, and stimuli affect the neonate's level of consciousness, the state of tension or arousal. All this adds up to the indication that "reactivity to stimuli is determined by innate autonomic mechanisms, and that constitutional variations in reactivity are present and demonstrable in the first days of life" (p. 347). "In effect," Furst concludes, "neonatal and sleep-dream studies provide evidence for the existence of an innate biologic mechanism which serves as the basic defense against excessive stimuli from within or without" (p. 348). Although, with development, the innate stimulus barrier moves into the background, it continues to serve as the basic defense against overwhelming stimuli.

As I indicated above, it is probably a combination of factors that makes for psychopathology, and much of the psychoanalytic writing on constitutional variables reflects this perspective. Fenichel (1945), for instance, in his attempts to delineate the etiology of psychotic states, or what he calls "malignant narcissism," comments:

> It must be admitted that as yet nothing specific is known concerning either constitutional factors or personal experiences that determine the malignant narcissistic fixation.... It may be assumed that unknown

organic factors determine or contribute to the malignant depth of the regression. Perhaps the typical infantile anamnesis of schizophrenia reflects less a single trauma in very early life than a series of general impediments in all vital activities, especially in those activities directed toward objects. Most probably the actual cases represent different combinations of these three possibilities: organic disposition, early traumata, and manifold impediments [p. 442].

We have seen that Hartmann (1953) views a defect in the ego's capacity for neutralization as basic to schizophrenia. He indicates that this inherent defect has a wide impact on the development of object relations and on many of the essential ego functions which appear to be affected in psychosis. Bak (1939), although greatly influenced by Imre Herman's emphasis on the effects of the object's warmth or coldness, its nearness or distance, etc., also cites constitutional ego defects as playing a role in the development of object relations and contributing to the development of psychosis. Similarly, Mahler (1968) stresses the significance of constitutional factors in the impairment of object relations. In discussing the nature-nurture controversy, she observes:

Looking at autistic and symbiotic psychotic children, one cannot help but feel that the primary etiology of psychosis in children, the psychotic child's primary defect in being able to utilize (to perceive) the catalyzing mothering agent for homeostatis, is inborn, constitutional, and probably hereditary, or else acquired very early in the very first days or weeks of extrauterine life. In other words, there seems to be a predispositional deficiency [pp. 47–48].

She emphasizes that in the absence of such predetermined constitutional factors, traumatic experiences must be quite profound to produce psychosis, if at all.

In the same vein, Jacobson (1971) says:

Infantile environmental factors certainly may have a paramount pathogenic or predisposing influence on the development of psychoses, and disturbing current experiences may provoke the final psychotic break. But few psychiatrists doubt that psychoses are based on endogenous, as yet unknown, physiological processes. . . . The assumption that psychosis, in contradistinction to psychoneurosis, represents not only a mental but an unknown psychosomatic process is well founded [p. 104].

Although at times failing to recognize that much is left to be explained and understood about human behavior beyond underlying biological factors, some have given considerable weight to Freud's remarks in his paper "On Narcissism":

... all our provisional ideas in psychology will presumably, some day, be based on an organic substructure. This makes it probable that it is special substances and chemical processes which perform the operations of sexuality and provide for the extension of individual life into that of the species. We are taking this probability into account in replacing the special chemical substances by special psychical forces. I try, in general, to keep psychology clear from everything that is different in nature from it, even biological lines of thought. For that reason, I should like, at this point, expressly to admit that the hypothesis of separate ego-instincts and sexual instincts (that is to say, the libido theory) rests scarcely at all upon a psychological basis, but derives its principal support from biology [1914a, pp. 78–79].

Certainly, many psychoanalysts have emphasized the significance of constitutional and organic factors in psychopathology. There are others, however, who deemphasize these factors. Janet's (1906) comments provide an amusing footnote to this controversy. Referring to the respectability lent to a formulation of psychiatric phenomena by physiological terminology, he observes:

... one can make, nowadays, a so-called physiological definition at smaller cost. It is enough to take the most commonplace psychological definitions and replace their terms with words vaguely borrowed from the language of anatomy and the current physiological hypotheses. Instead of saying, 'The function of language is separated from the personality,' one will proudly say, 'The centre of speech has no longer any communication with the higher centres of association.' Instead of saying, 'The mental synthesis appears to be diminished,' one will say, 'The higher centre of association is benumbed,' and the feat will be done.
... I again observe to you that I consider the pretended physiological definitions as mere translations of the psychological ideas [pp. 322–323].

On a more serious note, let me cite Hartmann's (1939a) position on this question: "Psychology and biology are for us simply two different directions of work, two points of view, two methods of investigation and two sets of concepts" (p. 34). He does not believe that the two are antithetical. On the contrary, he says:

We reject the customary form of this question: What is biological and what is psychological in the developmental process? We ask instead: What part of it is congenital, what maturational, and what environmentally determined? What physiological and what psychological changes take place in it? Our psychological method encompasses more than just the processes of mental development. Precisely because the psychological is a part of the biological, under certain conditions our

method sheds light on physiological developments, particularly on those
pertaining to instinctual drives [pp. 34–35].

In some limited way I have tried here and there in this volume to
follow Freud and others in accepting our biological givens and interweaving these with psychoanalytic concepts of the psychotic process.
Yet instead of looking on Freud's biological roots as a strength, some
critics have denigrated these as limitations. The denial of biology has as
a correlate the idea of being able to control one's destiny. Some, like
Brenner (1980), have gone so far as to suggest that in our psychoanalytic
work biology has no relevance. Perhaps in terms of specific technique
biology may not be our area of expertise, but to deny its role in some of
our patients' problems is to deny to psychoanalysis its place as a meaningful contribution to the understanding of human behavior. Rather,
what we should try to see is how and to what extent these biological
givens interrelate with our psychoanalytic concepts.

As an example, we might take the various stages in physiological development, especially puberty. The advent, for instance, of seminal
discharge, with the possibility of the consummation of the sexual act,
and the occurrence of nocturnal emissions may have a significant impact on psychic development. This is especially true of the borderline
patient and the potentially psychotic. We need to understand the multiple meanings of nocturnal emissions, which are not infrequently associated with psychotic reactions, and to use this understanding in psychoanalytic therapy. The guilt that some adolescents feel with the first
nocturnal emission, the idea that this may have been caused by some
forbidden act of their own (i.e., masturbation), illustrates, rather
superficially it is true, such an interweaving of the psychological with
the biological.

The whole field of psychosomatic medicine requires an acceptance
of the biological factors to lend understanding to our psychoanalytic
work with such patients. We need to consider the impact of organic
disease in understanding and dealing with its clinical and psychological
consequences. In this regard, one might cite Ferenczi and Hollós's
(1922) study of general paresis. Or perhaps a more mundane phenomenon: the impact of a common illness on a very successful, active busi-
nessman. I know of one such man who committed suicide after a coro-
nary attack. This body-oriented person could not tolerate what he felt
were the limitations imposed on him as a result of this experience. The
blow to his narcissism, and the loss he experienced as a result of this

physiological assault, produced a severe depression, which was more than he could bear.

Let us take the loss in physiological capabilities that accompanies the aging process. We who have contributed so much on the role of loss in depression should be able to relate this to our work with aging patients. I have referred above (p. 182) to the way physiological loss may bring in its wake the same sense of emptiness and depletion found in psychotic depression. As I indicated, both Freud (1917b) and Jacobson (1953) refer to ego impoverishment as a result of physiological factors, which then results in depression. I have in some instances seen this accompanied not only by a drop in self-esteem but also by guilt. This guilt derives from a feeling of: What did I do to bring this on? Did I do it deliberately, or what did I not do that could conceivably have avoided it? Even more significant is the question of who is being destroyed or hurt by this physical limitation. All these features appeared in a 79-year-old man who was being treated for depression by psychoanalytically oriented psychotherapy.

I would like to underline my point: If we presume to be a psychology of human behavior, we would be derelict to ignore biology, or even more, not to take the biological givens into consideration in our psychoanalytic *verstand* and work.

Early Developmental Experiences

The constitutional factors mesh and interact with early developmental experiences that may contribute to possible future psychotic development. In Chapter 7, I discussed in some detail the factors in the first few months of life that lay the groundwork for the development of "basic anxiety," which I see as the prototype for the future psychotic's reaction to danger. As I indicated, the impact of early survival-threatening experiences on the developing and still unformed ego structure contributes significantly to the fragility of the ego in the potential psychotic. Mahler (1968) indicates that the neurobiological patternings are thrown out of kilter by organismic distress and that the created memory traces may amalgamate with later experiences. These memory traces may create a predisposition to anxiety, which is heightened in the psychotic.

I have repeatedly called attention to the basic danger and fear in the psychotic, the threat of dissolution and disintegration of self. I have elsewhere (Frosch, 1967a) discussed at length why I believe this threat to survival is so real to the psychotic. My contention is that the realness of this threat derives from actual survival-threatening experiences in the early life of these patients — experiences which may literally have threatened annihilation. These experiences may be reinforced by subsequent ones, also carrying the danger of annihilation. Moreover, these early experiences interfere with the development of the ego and its functions, making it difficult to deal subsequently with analogous threats. One might of course also postulate that innate ego defects enhance the likelihood that frustration and deprivation will be experienced as survival-threatening (see Rosen, 1950). At any rate, the psychic representations of these prototypic, actual early experiences are very meaningful to the psychotic. Identity of perception makes subsequent danger a real threat to survival, in terms of disintegration and dissolution.

William Niederland (personal communication, 1962) refers to the many traumatic experiences in Schreber's early life, which were subsequently incorporated into his delusional system: "Sometimes, in fact, one has the impression that there exists a sort of one-to-one relationship between the pathogenic event and the later emergence of this event in the delusional formation, as I could show in Schreber's system of delusional 'miracles.'" More generally he comments: "It seems that the more severely disturbed and more primitive ego state of the psychotic lends itself to the psychic 'environment' of the concrete nature of the event."

Pao (1979) speaks of "basic experiential disturbances," shaped by the interaction of nature and nurture. A basic experiential disturbance has an impact on the developing personality; it then interacts with other environmental experiences to produce another, new basic experiential disturbance, and so on. Pao envisions a form of epigenesis in which new basic experiential disturbances continually evolve out of the interplay between the preceding disturbance and the environment. Clarifying this idea, he mentions that "a libido-aggression imbalance or a disturbed perceptual registration may tend to intensify an exaggerated predisposition to panic; repeatedly experienced panic may interfere with the development of the sense of self-cohesion; inadequate affective responses may heighten aggression. As each disturbance is intensified, schizophrenia may eventuate" (p. 160).

Whether such basic experiential disturbances will be so severe as to eventuate in psychosis depends on many factors. It depends on the nature of the trauma as well as its intensity, the age of the child, the stage of ego development, and the ego's capacity to deal with, master, and metabolize traumatic experiences. It also depends on the extent to which those ego functions which will support the innate stimulus barrier have successfuly developed. In this regard, one might point to Fries's (1977b) discussion of the "archaic egos" of her borderline and psychotic patients. She refers to traumatic experiences in the first six to eight weeks of life which contain the potential for psychotic development. It is during this preverbal period that something analogous to imprinting takes place, of actual physical or psychic life-threatening experiences. Unified ego development has not yet taken place, so that early ego function development will be seriously impaired, including the development of those functions which play a role in self-nonself differentiation, reality testing, etc.

In other words, when these early experiences transpire will determine to what extent a given stage of ego development will be interfered with. The earlier the age, the greater the potential for psychotic development. If, for instance, traumatic experiences occurred after a given ego function had developed, its loss may be utilized more defensively and exploration with interpretation may be effective. If, however, the trauma occurred before the ego function developed, we are dealing with a defect, and it is questionable whether the damage can be undone by such techniques. Furthermore, what may be particularly significant is not so much the actual experience, but its impact on the developing and still unformed and vulnerable ego structure. The ego may remain in a somewhat fragmented state or at best a poorly integrated one, highly vulnerable and easily subject to dedifferentiation.

I have already extensively discussed the role of the stimulus barrier and the impact of under- and overstimulation on psychic development (pp. 284 ff, 296 ff). The reader is urged to review this material, which is of particular relevance to understanding the etiology of psychosis. In my earlier discussion, I described the concept of the stimulus barrier as a means of protection and defense against both internal and external impingement of stimuli on the nervous system. I have also indicated (p. 390) that there is evidence of an innate constitutional mechanism that regulates the intake of stimuli — protecting against both over- and understimulation. This constitutional mechanism eventually evolves into and is supported by many psychological factors and ego functions which facilitate the regulation of stimulus perceptions and their metabolism. In addition, cultural factors, such as parental attitudes toward reactions to stimuli, affect the development of discriminatory stimulus perception. Benjamin (1965, 1972), for one, reports on the phase-related changes in the stimulus barrier during the course of development, as it moves from a passive to an active stimulus barrier.

As we have seen, defects in the stimulus barrier, either biological or psychological, interfere with the development of perceptual discrimination. There may, for instance, be an inability to differentiate dangerous from nondangerous stimuli, or to discriminate between and among affects. Silverman (1978), in addition to others (Hartmann, 1950; Spitz, 1957) has suggested using the stimulus barrier as a frame of reference for the phase-related development of defenses and the management of stress. He indicates that not only may the stimulus barrier itself be seen as the prototype of defense, but also that a dysfunction of the stimulus barrier itself, in terms of either a pathologically low or pathologically high barrier, sets the stage for future psychopathology within the elaboration of defense. Silverman puts forward the concept of "defense demands" in the neonate. If, because of various neurophysiological and possibly neurochemical deficiency states, the infant has not developed the capacity to meet these "defense demands," it will suffer, from birth on, repetitive and chronic trauma.

I have already pointed out that the impact of excessive stimulation on the highly vulnerable ego, which is incapable of permitting gradual perception and assimilation, has been suggested as a genetic factor in schizophrenia (Bergman and Escalona, 1949). Spitz (1964) specifically discusses how the impact of excessive stimulation on a highly immature ego brings about a severely distorted ego, whose subsequent mastery and perception of stimuli may be markedly disturbed. Greenacre (1952) further describes how the flooding of the organism with excitation may result in a state of confusion with loss of specificity in response to stimuli.

Several participants in a discussion group on the nature of the psychotic process (Freedman, 1962, 1964) hold similar views. Rubinfine, for instance, suggests that unregulated excessive inner and outer stimulation and the need to defend against it in earliest infancy have a great deal to do with the pathological development of the organ of consciousness, which he believes is impaired in later psychosis. Eissler proposes that a lack of differentiation in affects is to some extent contributed to by deficiencies in the barrier to internal and external stimulation. The patient is overwhelmed by all sorts of stimuli, cannot differentiate between and among them, and consequently experiences a sense of disintegration and panic.

Among genetic considerations, one must give weight to the impact, not only of deprivation or of excessive stimulation but also to out-of-phase stimulation. Indeed, as I have indicated, the crucial factor is not so much insufficient stimulation or overstimulation as non-phase-related and inappropriate stimulation. It is equally important to evaluate whether the time at which a given experience transpires is a "critical period" in development (Scott, 1962). It is also of some crucial significance to what extent traumatic experiences interlace with fantasies and wishes existing at that time (see Chapter 4, Section A).

In Chapter 11, I discussed the studies of disruptions in early self-object relationships made by contributors from the various object relations schools of thought. The lack of a proper fit between the infant's needs and the mother's responses has been a frequent frame of reference. I would say that in such instances there is a lack of match between the child's inherent capacity for an average expectable environment and whatever that environment may be. Where there is such a mismatch there is a mutual interplay of forces stemming from the child and from the mothering object that severely disrupts early psychic development.

As I pointed out above, Modell (1968) focuses on defects arising out of failures in the maternal environment, leading to developmental arrests. Specifically, he believes that the failure of the "holding environment" may lead to an impairment of autonomous structures, resulting in a persistence of untamed instinctual demands with an inability to tolerate frustration and to accept the pain and frustration of reality. Looking at borderline and schizophrenic patients, Modell indicates that the development of many ego functions concerned with reality is dependent on good mothering. Ego function development, object relations development, self-object differentiation, the appropriate libido-aggression balance, all of these are disrupted by poor mothering. This lays the groundwork for manifestation at an early age of severe anxiety and other disruptive reactions, which, like a feedback mechanism, further contribute to the mismatch between the infant and environment. The infant's consequent image of the environment and the mother's image of the infant follow both of them in the course of the child's development and, through perceptual identity, trigger reactions later on. The resultant clinical picture will vary depending on the nature of the attempts to deal with these disruptions. From very early on, the infant may resort to extreme means, calling into play, for instance, what Mahler (1968) terms "maintenance mechanisms." There may be marked withdrawal and dedifferentiation, wiping out of self-nonself boundaries, deanimation, etc. — all ingredients of the psychotic process.

Social and Cultural Variables

I should like to turn my attention now to an examination of the impact of social and cultural factors on the psychotic process. The whole question of the role of cultural variables has been somewhat muddied by Rosenhan's (1973) project. In this study several people, purportedly normal, presented themselves for admission to various hospitals and were diagnosed as psychotic. Rosenhan observes that the salient characteristics that lead to diagnoses reside not simply in the patients themselves, but more tellingly in the environment and contexts in which observers find them. He indicates that what is viewed as normal in one culture may be seen as quite aberrant in another. Ultimately, therefore, he believes that psychiatric diagnoses are in the minds of the observers and are not valid summaries of the individual's characteristics (see my discussion on p. 259).

The problem presented by someone who was severely emotionally disturbed used to be relatively simple: If an individual was declared flagrantly "psychotic," this ultimately led to hospitalization. Although many currently view such "psychotic" manifestations as decompensations or failures of adaptation, there are others for whom they represent a unique kind of adaptation, which should not necessarily be defined as pathological at all. Not only is it argued that such individuals should not be confined, but the question is raised whether they are even "psychotic." R. D. Laing, for instance, tries to make a case for a crazy world, from which the individual quite appropriately tries to protect himself through behavior which is viewed by others, not understandingly, as sick. To people like Thomas Szasz, hospitalization reflects the societal scotoma around mental illness, and thus ultimately reflects a failure in society.

It is clear that the attitude of society toward emotional illnesses, and even toward physical illness, is exceedingly important. The need and capacity to tolerate illnesses in certain cultures may, for instance, mean that such individuals will not seek help. People live with all kinds of physical and emotional problems, which in certain cultures are not even necessarily viewed as pathological, or in need of help. This does not make these individuals any the less ill.

It is not at all without some degree of relevance to evaluate how the majority in a given culture respond to certain phenomena, nor is it irrelevant to evaluate how frequent or widespread a given phenomenon is in a specific culture. Yet I question whether using this as the sole frame of reference to establish health or illness is appropriate. Normality and complete reality adaptation are not completely identical. I do not want to get involved here in a discussion of cross-cultural psychological phenomena, which have been extensively explored by many anthropologists. Nonetheless, I would like to raise the question of whether, regardless of what the culture is, there are not basic psychiatric givens — givens that exist across cultures and transcend specific cultures. Are there manifestations that should be viewed as pathological regardless of what the culture is? While this question is a highly complex one and really outside my area of competence, I would like to make the point that the fact that a phenomenon is widespread does not make it normal or healthy. It makes it common, and it may certainly influence how the given culture responds to this phenomenon, whether it is receptive to it and provides appropriate social receptacles.

All of these considerations apply to the manifestations of psychosis.[1] There are settings in which such manifestations are not viewed as pathological and may even be quite sociosyntonic. For instance, the "formal thought disorder" considered so pathognomonic for schizophrenia will generally be reflected in a peculiar use of language (see Chapter 3, Section B). Yet such "oddities" may in certain cultures be viewed as a special gift and the individual is described as able to speak in "tongues." Thus, the phenomenon may not be viewed as idiosyncratic in that culture. But it may nonetheless be a formal thought disorder. If schizophrenia is not viewed as idiosyncratic in a given culture, it does not make it any the less schizophrenia.

Certain forms of psychopathology may not only be syntonic within a given culture and setting, but may even be adaptive, enabling an individual to survive in a given setting. As Hartmann (1939b) comments: "the nature of the environment may be such that the pathological development of the psyche offers a more satisfactory solution than the normal one." Glover (1932a) remarks that under certain circumstances "normality may be a form of madness which goes unrecognized because it happens to be a good adaptation to reality" (p. 248). The degree of social compliance in certain behaviors and symptomatology may make these syntonic with a given setting. For instance, in a general medical workup of executives of a corporation, one man, who was highly successful, recounted with some concern what would unquestionably be viewed as paranoid trends. He was especially concerned

---

[1] It should be noted that I am not referring here to primary-process manifestations *in the service of the ego*. These are not psychotic.

because his father had been grossly psychotic. He feared that his paranoid trends presaged his own breakdown and was quite anxious and depressed about them. He was especially sensitive to remarks and attitudes which he felt conveyed veiled threats, and, truth to tell, in the setting in which he worked they may very well, on occasion, have done so. Yet he himself recognized that at times his "antennae" were a bit too sensitive and that he was picking up things because of his own exaggerated degree of sensitivity. It should be added that it was these very paranoid tendencies that enabled him to be on the alert for bona fide threats to his position; they helped him to survive in this "jungle," as he called it. Thus, we might refer to this phenomenon as sociosyntonic psychopathology.

Another example that comes to mind is a type of individual who seems to fulfill many of the criteria which would lead us to call him a psychopath. Such individuals are highly narcissistic, egocentric, frequently grandiose and manipulative. They lack that capacity for appropriate guilt or anxiety which ordinarily derives from a healthy superego. They also lack the capacity for meaningful human relationships, although they are frequently glib and articulate. These very features may blend into and be syntonic with a given setting, even making it possible for such individuals to function successfully in this setting. They could then be described as sociosyntonic psychopaths. In particular, in certain political settings such psychopaths may achieve such a degree of sociosyntonicity as to be highly successful. Gilbert (1948), who studied Hermann Goering at the Nuremberg trials, describes him as a ruthless psychopath in a psychopathic government. A well-known Nazi said: "Goering is a brutal egotist who doesn't give a damn about Germany as long as he can amount to something." The thin line that separates such an individual from social and political success and criminality was perceptively recognized by Goering's mother, who predicted, when he was a child: "Hermann will either be a great man or a great criminal." Gilbert suggests that Goering's suicide represented the achievement of the supreme goal of his lifelong fantasy: to get his picture into the German history books — either as "a great man or a great criminal" (the interpretation depending on the culture's values). It is easy to see how Goering, with all his psychopathic traits, could have been successful in the political climate of Nazi Germany, which set a premium on such traits. But this in no way minimizes the fact that these traits were psychopathic. It is equally obvious that the social and cultural frame of reference may lend itself to political purposes in deciding who is or is not emotionally sick.

It is clear to me that the widespread existence of a phenomenon does not necessarily, in and of itself, make it normal or healthy. Nor does the existence of certain phenomena in given cultures which are receptive to them make these phenomena normal or healthy. It is my own belief that we need to differentiate between intrinsic pathology in the more restrictive sense, if it exists, and the behavior resulting from such pathology, which may or may not be consonant with a given society and culture. The rule of the majority or the social or cultural frame of reference by itself does not seem a satisfactory one to define normality or abnormality, health or illness. At most, in my opinion, this frame of reference relates to the social attitude toward, the culture's receptivity or lack of receptivity to, such pathological behavior. It does not define health or illness in any intrinsic sense.

In Chapter 13, I called attention to the Interpersonal School's emphasis on the impact of cultural factors and the here-and-now at all levels. Lidz et al. (1965) and others have highlighted the role of the family structure in both the etiology and maintenance of a psychotic structure. I have elsewhere reported on the impact of a deprived community on impulse-ridden behavior (Frosch, 1977b). In a similar vein, Marcus (1974) discusses Engels's description of the degradation experienced by the working class in Manchester at the time of the Industrial Revolution and its role in impulse-ridden behavior:

> What Engels has seen in that the counterpart of the deprivations, instabilities, degradations and depression of the working-class life he knows, is its tendency to be impulse-ridden. This has always been the classical diagnosis of the culture of poverty; it remains so today. It consists of behavior and attitudes that are generally regarded as "nonadaptive." In addition to drunkenness, Engels discusses the other classical components of this syndrome: impulsive and promiscuous sexuality, general improvidence, lack of foresight, inability to plan for the future, insufficient internalization of disciplines, regularities and normative controls, and adaptive inflexibilities. . . . The behavior in question is short-term and consummatory, and Engels includes among it certain kinds of theft and even suicide [p. 210].

Whether cultural factors of this type have an impact on psychotic development is an oft-debated question. Knight (1940b), as I indicated in Chapter 4, Section A, takes exception to the role of such environmental influences in the development of the paranoid constellation. In recent years, while working in a psychiatric setting in a highly deprived community, I had the opportunity of studying various psychiatric conditions, in both hospitalized and ambulatory patients. I had the definite impression that these were in no way different, clinically or psychodynamically, from psychotic states in which economic or cultural forces did not appear to be significant. Those factors in the deprived community essentially operated as a precipitant in individuals already predisposed to psychosis. In their illnesses these patients still had the same basic anxieties, wishes, and defenses found in patients from other levels of society. It is true that in some instances cultural factors fed into the psychotic systems. For instance, the possibility of being mugged and raped was a pervasive source of anxiety. One 58-year-old woman with considerable anxiety reported repeatedly hearing the voices of young boys talking about raping her and commiting all types of violence upon her. Although she did not elaborate specifically, she implied that this violent action would be degrading. Yet it was clear that these "voices" were hallucinations involving incestuous fantasies related to her 18-year-old son, who had died some years previously.

In the main, psychoanalytic contributions in this area have considered present-day forces more as precipitants than as "causes" of psychotic development. Often these factors are seen as having some underlying relationship to earlier factors in psychic development, not infrequently with regard to object loss. This is not to say that present-day factors are underestimated. One cannot help but recall Freud's (1937) comment that whether patients who are seemingly helped in their suffering by psychoanalysis decompensated again in the future will depend on how kindly fate treats them.

Psychoanalytic studies of traumatic experiences of a social nature (such as war), or of cases in which some intervening organic illness has eventuated in psychotic symptomatology, tend to view the impact of these experiences within the framework of the *person* involved, rather than attaching exclusive importance to the role of the particular trauma in psychotic development. The reader might recall in this regard my discussion of the ileitis patient who developed a paranoid psychosis following surgery (see p. 80). I have also seen similar paranoid psychotic reactions after accidents. The anxiety in these instances assumed extreme proportions, to the point of fears of self-disintegration and self-dissolution (the basic anxiety of psychotics). In such instances, the underlying features of the psychotic process were operative long before the traumatic experience.

I should also call attention again to the impact of and interrelationship between various stages in physiological development and emotional illness. One thinks, for instance, of the depressive reactions accompanying menstruation, menopause, and aging. Jacobson (1971) has pointed out how fluctuations in libidinous and aggressive discharge resulting from physiological factors may lead to depressed or elated states.

Let me close this chapter with an overall comment. Although one might have the impression from reading the above that there is a wide diversity of opinion among psychoanalysts about the etiological factors in psychoses, there is nonetheless a certain perspective that is shared. The impact of severe traumatic experiences in the earliest stages of psychic development is one area upon which there seems to be a general consensus.

15.
The Defect-Defense
Controversy

Having just discussed the various viewpoints on etiology, it may be appropriate at this point to pause and return to a consideration of whether conflict plays the primary role in the psychotic process. This question was posed in Chapter 9, but warrants repetition here. Is it at all necessary to evolve a concept of psychosis that is primarily related to the need to deal with a conflict? Is it possible that disturbances in ego functions per se represent the central core in psychosis and that conflict is a secondary development of these disturbances? Is the supposed increase in the potential for conflict in psychosis merely the reflection of ineffective ego functions?

That the latter is the true state of affairs is implied by Hartmann (1953), as well as in Federn (1952). Des Lauriers (1962) says:

> . . . it seems to me that the hypothesis of deficiencies in primary autonomous factors in the ego contributing to the vulnerability of defense and of neutralization (and other ego functions) and this representing one etiological factor in schizophrenia, is very likely to be true. It is this state of affairs which may predispose and lay the groundwork to the kind of conflict . . . situation so characteristic of schizophrenia [p. 46].

It might be mentioned that there are others who have addressed this issue, although from different points of view. White (1963), for instance, postulates independent ego energies, existing from the very beginning, which are brought into the service of ego functions. He focuses on this factor as actively involved in reality building, reality testing, etc. It is the defect in the development of these independent ego functions that eventuates in the deficiencies seen in psychotics.

Since object loss has been emphasized as a major factor, we might ask: Does the capacity for establishing object relations already reflect some disturbance in the ego or psychic structure of the potential psychotic? Does this defect then facilitate the impact of object loss more readily in the potential psychotic than in the nonpsychotic? In other words, does perhaps the fragility of the ego reflected in blurring of self-nonself differentiation potentiate such object loss? As I indicated in Chapter 9, the potential for dedifferentiation and the resultant undifferentiated state of the ego in relation not only to reality (i.e., the object) but also to the other psychic structures has been linked by many to defects in ego functions. To some, these defects are crucial in facilitating dedifferentiation; to others they are a resultant of this process. To some, they are unwelcome deficiencies; to others, but modes of defense against anxiety generated by conflict.

The controversy between the defect and defense points of view has been highlighted by Arlow and Brenner (1964, 1969) and their contributions served as a basis for discussion at a meeting of the International Psycho-Analytical Association in 1970. As I have already indicated (see p. 266), they insist that the regressive alteration of ego functioning serves as a defense against anxiety connected with inner psychic conflict. They believe this is essentially the same in neurosis; they see no sharp dividing line between psychotic and nonpsychotic in this respect. It is the primitive aspects of these ego alterations they point to as the differentiating factor: "In psychoses, particularly in schizophrenia, the defensive alterations and ego functions are often so primitive as to disrupt the patient's relationship with the world about him to a serious degree" (1969, p. 15).

They view the end-of-the-world experience, for instance, as a projection of aggression, and see decathexis of internal object representations as a defense to protect the object from the patient's own aggressive impulses.

The essential thrust of Arlow and Brenner's contributions is that under the impact of intrapsychic conflict there is a regressive alteration of ego functioning which produces the psychotic symptomatology. Perceptual distortions, for instance, are primarily defensive and not defect-generated:

> We suggest that delusions and hallucinations may be explained as follows within the conceptual framework of the structural theory. In either case a fantasy has resulted from the patient's inner conflict, whether that conflict is over instinctual wishes, self-punitive demands, or both. Whatever other defensive mechanisms may be involved in the formation of the fantasy, e.g., repression, projection, denial, etc., there is among the ego's defenses a regressive alteration of reality testing. The

ego's ability to distinguish between external reality and the particular fantasy in question is impaired in order to avoid or minimize the development of anxiety [1969, p. 10].

They do say at another point that the defenses psychotic patients employ are different in many respects from those employed by nonpsychotic individuals. They speak of more primitive, infantile defenses and ego functions in the psychotic, but it is not too clear what determines the choice of the more primitive modes if, as they contend, the conflict is essentially the same in neurosis and psychosis.

There are many contributors, however, who do hold to the view of primary defects in ego functions as crucial in the psychotic process. As indicated above, Des Lauriers (1962) suggests that deficiencies in primary autonomous ego functions predispose and lay the groundwork for the conflict characteristic of schizophrenia. White (1963) supports a similar view, although what he emphasizes is the impaired development of those ego functions which facilitate reality testing, and thus the failure of that essential function.

I have also called attention to Hartmann's (1953) concept of defects in the schizophrenic's capacity for neutralization. Bak (Freedman, 1962, 1964) is equally a defect proponent, viewing changes in the ego as primary, and contending that it is these primary defects that secondarily make overt hitherto latent conflicts. He suggests that the withdrawal that takes place during the psychotic process may not be related to conflict at all, but to disturbances of the ego. Nor does he believe that this ego defect is necessarily the result of earlier conflict. For instance, a disturbance of the ego function of integration or thinking could be affected primarily and only secondarily appear as conflict.

Kohut (1977) implicitly allies himself with the defect school when he says: "I call a structure defensive when its sole or predominant function is the covering over of the primary defect in the self. I call a structure compensatory when, rather than merely covering a defect in the self, it compensates for this defect" (p. 3).

Will (Freedman, 1962, 1964), in addressing the question of whether an instinctual conflict or a conflict with reality is essential for the development of psychosis, suggests an alternative possibility. He indicates that the psychotic conflict may emerge due to processes in the ego which make previous conflict solutions impossible. He adds that disturbances in ego functions may lead to conflicts with reality.

Wexler (1971) focuses the issue, in stating: "It may be necessary to

clarify our thinking in order to differentiate more sharply between conflict disorders and deficiency disorders" (p. 98). He himself leans in the
direction of viewing many of the clinical manifestations of schizophrenia as defect-derived. Such a perspective, he indicates, carries implications for therapy. For instance, he says: "Inhibiting free association and
directing the patient's attention cathexes to reality objects serves the
reconstruction process far better, provided, of course, one is convinced
that the nature of the illness lies more in the direction of ego deficiency
than in the realm of conflicting impulses and ideas, however rich these
may also be in the clinical picture" (p. 96).

The impact of developmental variables in all this is taken up by
Aronson (1974). In addition to the failure of the mother to provide the
means of mastering stress, the infant, he suggests, may have a defect in
the genetically determined tendency to internalize. This is not unlike a
defect in the inherent ego functions that enable one to deal with an
average expectable environment. One might also cite Pao's (1979) distinction between two types of deficiencies, one which exists before the
"internal catastrophe," and one which follows. He calls the former the
genetic deficiency and the latter the functional deficiency. Yet he adds
that the impact of such defects does not preclude the interpretation of
defenses and resistances in the treatment of schizophrenics.

London (1973) joins the defect-defense controversy with a special
frame of reference. He refers to *unitary* and *specific* theories insofar as
these apply to schizophrenia, although he draws wider implications for
psychoanalytic theory. The unitary theory uses the intrapsychic conflict
and defense compromise of neurosis as a frame of reference for schizophrenia. The specific theory proposes a unique and specific defect in
the capacity to organize and sustain mental representations. London
uses the latter term in a broad sense, to encompass object and self-
representations, as well as representations of instinctual drives,
defenses, affects, anxiety, space and time. In a sense, he implies, as does
Aronson, a defect in the capacity for internalization. Yet he believes
these defects may be utilized in the service of defense, a process I have
also proposed.

Grotstein (1977) specifically offers a "reconciliation" of the defect-
defense dilemma. As he puts it:

> [The defect proponents] hold that the schizophrenic has a defective ego
> from the start and that this defect may be due either to an inborn error
> or may be due to sufficiently bad early object relations. This defect of
> ego development is characterized by an inability to hold onto internal

object representations and to perform other ego functions.... The analysts who hold this position emphasize the primacy of the economic principle and feel that the "ego-defect" is a manifestation of a defective narcissistic cathexis of objects (and of representations in general) [p. 404].

On the other hand:

[The conflict and defense proponents] hold that the psychopathology of schizophrenia can be explained, as are the neuroses, on the basis of a dynamic conflict between an instinctual drive component and the defense against it. Signal anxiety in the ego is seen as the instigator of the defence.... Most of the symptomatology can be seen as regressions of reality-testing resulting from a defensive withdrawal at the instigation of anxiety as the signal [p. 450].

Grotstein attempts to reconcile these differences by offering a different frame of reference for viewing the psychoses and schizophrenia:

The "conflict" school and the "ego defect" school are then reconciled by a unified theory of psychoanalysis which emphasizes the interrelations between narcissism, infantile psychosis and infant development. Thus a quantitatively significant fixation in early infancy may confirm the "ego defect" point of view, and a qualitatively serious regression could confirm the "conflict" point of view. In short both are correct; they erred largely in terms of their generalizations and in the mutual exclusiveness of their definitions [p. 450].[1]

Other attempts have been made to reconcile this controversy. Jacobson (Freedman, 1962, 1964) remarks:

[It is] difficult to separate the factors of conflict, disturbed ego function, disturbed object relationship to mother, instinctual development, and so forth. It is difficult to say which is primary and which is secondary. For example, if we were investigating a case, we might find that the development of reality testing and perception were brought about by difficulties in the early object relationships. It might be a mother who would restrain the child or deprive the child of perception. It might be a mother who puts the baby with herself and doesn't want him to grow up so that the motor functions, perception functions and other important ego functions are developed in the dream world of this important object relationship. There would necessarily be a simultaneous development

---

[1] In his attempt at a unified concept, Grotstein leans heavily on Melanie Klein and Fairbairn. At one point he says: "I have tentatively hinted at a psychoanalytic theory which is based upon the infantile 'psychosis' as the progenitor of psychosis, narcissistic disorders and the neuroses, in order to enfranchise the infantile psychotic positions and the narcissism under which they serve, as the most important determinants of personality development" (p. 450).

of conflict between the child and his mother with much aggression piling up within the restrained child.

Bychowski (Freedman, 1962, 1964) calls on Freud's concept of the complemental series in considering this question. He explains: "Certain ego functions may be damaged at such an early age that they never develop properly. If this happens then life itself is traumatic. There need be no important events, no loss of objects; psychosis must occur in any event. If the ego functions are not so badly damaged or not at such a crucial age, then the events are of much greater importance."

I myself have tried to demonstrate the interrelationship of the disturbances in ego functions with the danger and conflict. However, my viewpoint differs from that of Arlow and Brenner, since I believe that the nature of the danger in the psychotic is radically different from that in the neurotic (see Chapter 7). Yet I do not believe that the defect and defense concepts are mutually exclusive. Earlier I proposed that defects may be borrowed in the service of defense (see p. 345). If I may use a banal analogy, a man who is deaf may use his deafness to avoid relating to or hearing things he does not want to hear. It is clear that in some instances breaking away from reality, dedifferentiation, loss of reality testing, etc., may be special modes of defense and a regressive adaptation. But such modes of defense are facilitated by defects or weaknesses already existing in the ego, which seem to be exploited in the service of defense.

One of my patients perceived her ego splits and multiple identifications almost as a physical fragmentation. After extensive exploration of this, she realized she had probably felt this way all her life. It suddenly occurred to her that she also had a peculiar feeling of waiting for something to happen; she then realized that she had been waiting all her life to be "put together." By way of a bit of teleological reasoning, she saw this as lying behind her fragmentation: "If I'm in a thousand pieces, I can be put together again." Yet she feared being whole: "If I'm whole, I would detest myself—at least fragmented I can live with myself and not hate myself." Without going into detail, I should mention that the mother and subsequently the father played a prominent role in this fragmentation.

During the course of a long analysis, this patient experienced repeated episodes of what she described as "detachment," which took the form of depersonalization and depression. These episodes reflected the reappearance in the analysis of regressive ego states which contained both an identification with the mother and a need to withdraw from and fend off a very painful environment. To a large extent, many of my patient's regressive dedifferentiated states arose for defensive purposes, but her potential for entering into these states rather easily in situations of stress bespoke a predisposition toward this psychotic-like defense, which depended on preexisting ego defects.

In the psychotic, we see reestablished the current psychic correlates of those particular modes of ego functioning which the primitive ego utilized in building up and maintaining reality. These primitive modes of ego functioning are revived, I must emphasize again, in terms of their *current* psychic correlates. The surroundings are related to by primitive introjective and extrojective techniques, and primitive modes of reality testing, very much like those the child uses, are frequently evident (see p. 352, as well as Hartmann, 1950; Frosch, 1966, 1970).

Again, one might postulate that innate developmental defects may be conducive to experiencing frustration and deprivation as survival-threatening (see Rosen, 1950). At any rate, the psychic representations of these prototypic, actual early experiences are very meaningful to the psychotic and identity of perception makes the subsequent danger a real threat to survival, via self-disintegration and dissolution. I have indicated that Hartmann (1953) points to deficiencies in primary autonomous features of the ego as contributing to the vulnerability of defenses, and representing one of the etiological factors in schizophrenia. It may therefore be that the impact of traumatic experiences on such a vulnerable ego is tale-telling, that they are perceived as annihilating and survival-threatening. The ego and self may be left in a somewhat fragmented state, or at best poorly integrated and highly vulnerable to dedifferentiation. Even Arlow and Brenner (1969) appear to support this view:

> According to our view, the changes in ego functioning result from the inability of the ego to fend off anxiety resulting from the dangers connected with intrapsychic conflict. The ego may be unable to do this for many reasons and many theories have been advanced to account for this. The ego may be *constitutionally inadequate*. It may have been *impaired* early in childhood, in the first few months of life, perhaps, by repeated traumata, the early object ties may have been extremely pathological, etc. . . . Such *conditions of ego vulnerability may facilitate ego regression* in a manner similar to the way in which instinctual fixation may lead to instinctual regression [pp. 10–11; my italics].

Does this not refer to a defect, i.e., an ego vulnerability, as a result of constitutional factors or developmental trauma?

16.
Adaptation

The ego's attempts at adaptation reflect the various defects I have been describing. It should be clear that the psychoanalytic concept of adaptation is a broad one, and is not to be equated with conformity. Freud, in his many contributions dealing with the ego's position vis-à-vis reality, is obviously dealing with the psyche's attempts at adaptation, although he does not spell it out in these terms. It is Hartmann's (1939a) seminal contribution that specifically defines the meaning and role of adaptation in the psyche's operation.

Adaptation relates to the mastery of reality, both external and internal. The apparatuses used to facilitate adaptation exist even before birth — prepared to deal with what Hartmann calls the average expectable environment. In the course of development, these apparatuses mature. When they fit in with an average expectable environment, we may expect adaptation at a healthy level, thus facilitating productivity, an ability to enjoy life, and an undisturbed mental equilibrium. Hartmann points out: "The degree of adaptation can only be determined with reference to environmental situations (average expectable — i.e., typical — situations, or on the average not expectable — i.e., atypical situations)" (p. 23).

It may well be that an individual inherently has all the seeds and potential for adequate ego function development and under ordinary circumstances should be able to master both internal and external reality. Yet the reality itself may not fit in with such developed ego functions. This state of affairs results in psychopathology — which in itself is a form of adaptation, although not at the level of a good fit between ego functions and the environment which was expected to relate to these functions. In Hartmann's view: "the question is whether, and to what extent, a certain course of development can count on average expectable stimulations (environmental releasers) and whether and to what

413

extent, and in what direction, it will be deflected by environmental influences of a different sort" (p. 35). On the other hand, the tools and apparatuses for dealing with such an environment may be defective to begin with, thereby engendering a lack of fit. Psychotic development, with a reality-dystonic state, may ensue. In any case, growing out of these basic disturbances are a multiplicity of symptoms and the disturbances in the internal and environmental adaptations found in the psychotic. I would like to emphasize, for instance, that patients' inability to see themselves appropriately in relation to reality is frequently reflected in bizarrely distorted attitudes toward their responsibilities within a given culture, as well as in bizarre deviations in social amenities.

It would be appropriate at this point to review a traditional concept concerning adaptation, namely, autoplastic and alloplastic adaptation. Perhaps the earliest attempt to make a differentiation of this sort can be seen in Freud's attempt to distinguish between auto- and alloerotism (see p. 29). Ferenczi (1919) describes autoplastic adaptation as achieved by modification of one's own body while alloplastic adaptation is achieved by a modification of the outer world. Later (1930), he refers to autoplastic adaptation as being achieved by means of an alteration in the organism itself while in alloplastic adaptation there is an attempt by flight and defense to achieve an alteration in the environment. Glover (1925) explains it this way:

> Instinct tension being a tension from within, modification can conceivably take place within the individual (e.g., in meeting sexual need by autoerotic discharge). This is the autoplastic method, to use the phrase coined and adopted by Ferenczi and Freud. But as the ego develops, instinct tension has come to be bound up with outer objects. Hence effective discharge involves modification of environment. This is the alloplastic as opposed to the autoplastic method. Now modification of external environment implies a sound reality sense, and effective displacement; but even if these are not sound or effective, it is still possible to deal with tension through environment by giving up reality, and projecting on to environment an emergency reality. This is the psychotic method. The neurotic has, however, in effect an unimpaired "sense of reality testing," as can be seen by contrasting the subjective attitudes of patients to a phobia and to a delusion respectively [p. 57].

It is traditionally accepted that in psychosis we see an alloplastic modification of psychic and material reality, accompanied by a severe disturbance in the capacity to test reality. There is a denial of reality and replacement by a new reality built out of autistic productions.

Even material external reality is distorted. As I have already stressed, such a severe disturbance of the ego's relationship to reality can only be maintained when the capacity to test reality is disturbed. While the outcome may be an ego-syntonic adaptation, it is a reality-dystonic one.

In neurosis we see alterations in inner reality. Although the life of the neurotic vis-à-vis the external environment may be affected, we certainly do not see the wholesale replacement of material reality we do in psychosis. We see alterations in psychic reality and thus symbolic distortions, but at no time does reality lose its material meaning. Autoplasticity reflects an attempt to deal with the ego's disturbance in the relationship to reality by working out the problem within oneself. Although this has repercussions in both internal and external adaptation, the relationship to material reality is preserved. Money is money even though it may symbolically represent feces. What results may be an ego-dystonic adaptation with, however, a reality-syntonic one.

It is relevant at this point to reemphasize the difference between the alloplastic adaptation found in character disorders and that seen in psychosis. In psychosis, there is a replacement of reality by a new reality, while in character disorders, reality is not so much replaced as used by the patient in the service of his own needs, whether defensively or for direct instinctual gratification. In the neurotic character disorder, reality may be symbolically distorted, but at no time does its lose its "real" material meaning. The antisocial character and the impulse-ridden character, on the other hand, do not symbolize but will utilize the environment directly to gratify their impulses. In other cases, patients with character disorders may try to deny reality or minimize its influence by ignoring it, but they will not for any consistent period replace it, as psychotics do, by their own autistic productions. Some, such as the antisocial character, may rebel against authority because it may act as a restraint to the gratification of impulses. Or the neurotic character may rebel because authority symbolically represents the father. To the psychotic, however, authority as such may not exist. The psychotic substitutes for it his own omnipotent self or some other object, derived from his autistic fantasies.

Thus we see that one of the essential features in alloplastic adaptation, insofar as psychosis is concerned, is the preservation or loss of the capacity to test reality. In the alloplasticity of some character disorders the capacity to test reality may wear thin under certain circumstances, but it is never really lost. The adaptation that results depends on the nature of the character disorder. In the neurotic character disorder it may at some point be both ego- and reality-dystonic with no loss in reality testing. It is at this point that therapy is frequently sought. In the antisocial and impulse-ridden characters we may have an ego-syntonic yet reality-dystonic adaptation not too unlike the psychotic, but reality testing (although at times minimal and somewhat impaired) is not basically lost.

The definition, however, becomes confused by the lack of clarity regarding the use of the word "environment," internal and external. This was discussed in some detail in relation to the concept of reality (see p. 277). In general, when we speak of reality, we refer not only to material reality but to the psychic representation of reality. Similarly, when we speak of the internal world, we refer to a material and psychic internal reality. Is the alteration of the latter, then, an auto- or alloplastic adaptation? Should the term "alloplastic" be applied only to external material adaptation? A delusion that involves the external world but doesn't result in any activity on the part of the patient vis-à-vis the external world is still an alloplastic modification. This view is consistent with the concept of the psychic representation of reality as being the object for cathectic movements of energy, such as withdrawal or investment.

Freud (1924a) unquestionably envisions this as an alloplastic adaptation when he speaks of the psychotic denying reality and trying to substitute something else for it: "In a psychosis the remodeling of reality is effected by means of the residues in the mind of former relations and reality" (p. 185). He indicates that the remodeling of psychic reality brings with it the need to create perceptions in keeping with this remodeling. On the other hand, a somatic delusion secretly nurtured by a patient without any noticeable attempt to modify material reality may not be viewed as an alloplastic adaptation, since, in the broad sense, it is within the self-representation that the change takes place. I therefore lean in the direction of using the term "alloplastic" to relate to the psychic representation of external reality, but am by no means satisfied that this answers the question.

The problem in using "auto-" or "alloplasticity" as a frame of reference is actually pointed out by Hartmann (1956), who suggests that there is a third alternative to these two forms of adaptation, namely, finding a new environment. This possibility was already suggested by Ferenczi (1919, 1930). Yet could this not be considered a special kind of flight from reality? It also raises the question of social receptivity to psychotic conditions. As I indicated in Chapter 14, I do not believe that too much emphasis should be placed on this factor in evaluating whether a patient is psychotic. That there are social climates receptive to psychotic symptomatology is quite clear from cross-cultural studies. The medicine man may reveal many of the features alluded to above which are considered as essential to the psychotic process, and yet these very features may be acceptable in the social setting in which he exists. The epileptic is a sacred creature of God in some cultures. As Hartmann (1939a) says, "individual propensities which amount to disturbances of adaptation in one social group or locus may fulfill a socially essential function in another" (p. 32). I have referred to this as sociosyntonic psychopathology.

The other side of the question is the extent to which psychotic structures may be retained relatively intact with seemingly good adaptation to material reality. This is best exemplified by Schreber's asymptotic state after his second illness (see above p. 216). He returned to the community with his psychotic structure essentially intact, although willing to defer much of its content to future happenings. He did, however, show evidence of active hallucinations, and from time to time, the bellowing, which had been prominent during his hospitalization, reappeared. Nonetheless, he was on the whole able to converse and function at external reality levels quite well. I have also described a patient who retained intact a systematized delusional system and yet was able to complete two years of law school (see p. 343).

It is clear that in both Schreber and my patient a very important aspect of reality contact was at play. In areas outside their delusional systems the ability for some degree of reality testing was present, as well as many other ego functions which enabled them to reach an asymptotic state. Their delusional systems, in other words, did not interfere with their making a reality-syntonic adaptation. Furthermore, there must have been some desire and need for reality contact. The deteriorated schizophrenic who has abandoned herself to her hallucinations and delusions, to self-gratification, is not concerned with reality, nor does she make much of an effort to be concerned about how others react to her or what they think. The delusional patient may make strong efforts to convince the world of the validity of his delusions, or he may preserve his delusions by not speaking about them or acting on them.

What is it that facilitates this latter adaptation? For some time, as I pointed out above, it has been clear that in some instances the systematized delusion has a reality-adaptive value in terms of its integrative and unifying effect on the establishment of identity (see Bak, 1943; Frosch,

1967a; Rosenfeld, 1950). Frequently we can clinically observe the psychotic's anxiety and confusion subside or shift in character with the development of a systematized delusion. As I stated earlier, the systematized delusion, itself a product of synthesis, may, if successfully walled off, facilitate the reintegration and functioning of the rest of the personality at a high level, with the preservation of reality testing in many areas. Yet one often finds that the confusion and anxiety recur when the systematized delusion no longer suffices to bring about the binding of the danger.

I have also pointed out that the onset of a delusion may be accompanied by a flash of sudden clarity, which may even extend to the perceptual sphere, so that objects and colors stand out sharply, with an accompanying feeling of realness (see Frosch, 1977a). In examining several factors that play a role in this experience, I have come to the conclusion that such alterations of ego states and functions are regressions to earlier phases of psychic development (see pp. 144, 324; see also Frosch, 1967a, 1977a). In addition, I have described the intensity of perception as a way of holding onto reality, to combat dissolution and loss of self.

With all the qualifications discussed above, I believe that we may say that in psychosis we see an alloplastic modification of psychic and material reality, accompanied by a severe disturbance in the capacity to test reality. There may be a denial and replacement of reality by a new one built out of autistic productions, resulting in distortions of external material reality. The usual outcome is an ego-syntonic adaptation but a reality-dystonic one.

17.
An Integration of Views on
Neurosis and Psychosis

At the risk of repetition, I would like to summarize some thoughts on the differences between neurosis and psychosis (see also Frosch, 1981a). As I suggested in Chapter 1, an important question is which frame of reference one should use. Glover (1932b) also makes this point:

> Can we subdivide the main psychoses and neuroses in accordance with ego-object relations? Can we roughly separate out groups characterized by limitation of object relations, by regression to an old ego-system, by processes of introjection, tendencies to retire to primary (hallucinatory) identification? On the other hand, can we distinguish conditions in which the relationship to the external world is distorted or vitiated in some important respect, in which the mechanism of projection is constantly exploited, in which environment is used as an unrealistic defence against ego excitation? Finally, can we, using the reality sense test, subdivide these two main groups sharply, so that the psychoses will fall into a different category from the neuroses? [pp. 180–181].

As we have seen, there are those who view all emotional disturbances on a spectrum, with some even viewing the psychotic as not essentially different from the normal (Fromm-Reichmann, 1950a; Meissner, 1978b). Here we encounter many questions regarding the definition of normality (see pp. 259, 399; see also Frosch, 1978; Sachs, 1977). While I do not wish to go into this subject in great detail, I would like to refer again to the questions raised by Rosenhan's (1973) article. A frequent concern is whether the frames of reference we have to distinguish normal from abnormal are adequate. Rosenhan asks whether we can even do so, and whether it is of any value to do so. He wonders if the frames of reference we have for making a psychiatric diagnosis may not be influenced by extraneous factors, not inherent in the patient. Can we ultimately distinguish normal from abnormal, sane from insane, deviant from nondeviant, emotional health from emotional illness?

In questioning the validity of these terms, Rosenhan suggests that our notion of normality and abnormality may not be quite as clear-cut as people believe.

Inherent in all these questions is an implied criticism of the medical model as an approach to understanding human behavior. It is felt that this model has traditionally used pathology as the jumping-off point for understanding human behavior, as well as for defining the role of the mental health professional. The same criticism is made of classical Freudian psychoanalysis, i.e., that it does not provide a normative frame of reference for human behavior.

Simply put, do we, as psychoanalysts, have any clear frames of reference to distinguish normal from abnormal, emotional health from emotional illness, let alone neurosis from psychosis? The question is a troublesome one—especially when we consider the complications raised by those who relate concepts of emotional health to changing variables such as culture, the era in which we are living, the age of the individual, the fluidity of the environment, the receptivity or the tolerance of an environment to certain deviant behavior, etc. (see Chapter 14). As I have pointed out, certain cultures show a receptivity toward violent behavior (see Frosch, 1977b) and there may be overwhelming social factors which make such behavior understandable. How, then, do we define such behavior?

The use of symptoms as the frame of reference in attempting to differentiate normal from abnormal is not always satisfactory. For instance, fundamental disturbances, such as character disorders, may exist without discretely delineated symptoms. As Hartmann (1939b) has said, "So long as we make freedom from symptoms . . . the criterion of mental health, it is comparatively easy in practice to arrive at a decision—freedom from symptoms, however, is not enough for health."

The question of whether there is any fundamental difference between normal and abnormal is an underlying one, but I would like to focus at this point on the question of whether there are any basic differences between neurotic and psychotic processes, and the clinical entities deriving from these processes. Even if we accept that there are differences, we must ask: Are these differences qualitative or quantitative? As we have seen, there is by no means agreement on this question. Knight (1953), for instance, is critical of the criteria for separating neurosis from psychosis, the two clinical syndromes eventuating from these processes. He takes issue with the emphasis on a "break with reality"; the assumption that "neurosis is neurosis, psychosis is psychosis"; and the use of stages in libidinal development as a frame of reference in making the diagnosis. On the contrary, Knight contends that when there is a break with reality we are already in an advanced stage. With regard to the second misconception, that neurosis and psychosis are mutually exclusive, he argues that both psychotic and neurotic mechanisms may develop in the same individual and that this is the crux of the problem in many borderline cases. Turning to levels of development as a frame of reference, he says: "reliance on the ladder of psychosexual development with a line of reality testing drawn between the two anal substages has resulted in many blunders in diagnosis, especially in the failure to perceive the psychosis underlying a hysterical, phobic or obsessive-compulsive clinical picture" (p. 99).[1]

Here again, I think that we must remember that contributions are made by many levels of development in dealing with a problem. The crucial question is: What is the basic danger or conflict the individual is trying to deal with and what is his rock-bottom way of dealing with it? Does the person show traces of more primitive ways of dealing with this problem? Essentially Knight is not too far removed from my viewpoint when he points out that hysteric, phobic, obsessive, and compulsive devices may represent holding operations, while major portions of the ego have regressed far behind these in varying degrees of disorder. What is essential to determine is the organizing principle for any given syndrome, with the understanding that many subsidiary features may be incorporated into the given syndrome (see p. 105).

As I have already discussed in some detail, Arlow and Brenner (1964) view neurosis and psychosis on a continuum, as part of one process, differing only in degree. To reiterate: they argue that there is no sharp dividing line between the two conditions, that both involve defenses against the emergence of anxiety connected with inner psychic conflict. Although they admit that the defenses psychotic patients employ are different in many respects from those employed by nonpsychotics, they contend that this difference is essentially a quantitative one. What they point to is the *extent* of instinctual regression, the *degree of intensity* of the conflict over aggressive impulses, and the *severity* of disturbances in ego and superego functioning in psychosis as compared with neurosis.[2]

[1] However, as I pointed out above, frequently on closer examination these seemingly neurotic manifestations contain many features of the psychotic process.

[2] As I discussed above, Freeman (1970) believes that Arlow and Brenner ignore the economic factors, and he claims that they "appear confused in their images of the concept of decathexis" (p. 411).

Glover (1939) also takes a quantitative view. He points out that "it is the particular method of dealing with quantitatively excessive endopsychic conflict that lends their characteristic features to the psychoneuroses and to the psychoses. The ego-organisation, defect of which is responsible for the psychoses, is much more primitive than that responsible for the psycho-neuroses. And we would accordingly expect functional disturbance of the mental apparatus to be much more obvious in the psychoses than in the psycho-neuroses, as indeed it is" (p. 186).

On the other hand, there are those who draw qualitative distinctions. Kernberg (1975a), for instance, delineates his concept of psychosis in drawing a distinction between his borderline patients and psychotics. In both, he sees projected and reintrojected, "aggressively determined" object and self-images as major factors. Yet he distinguishes the regressive refusion of self- and object images in psychotics from the pathological splitting of these images in borderline patients. Differentiation between self- and object images seems better preserved in the borderline personality. Extending this, Kernberg suggests that in neurosis we are dealing with qualitative differences from a much higher level in psychic development.[3]

Freeman (1970), in addition to examining the fate of the object, focuses on the impact of the breakthrough of drive representations and the different ways this is dealt with in neurosis and psychosis. He points out:

> There are similarities in the initial stages consisting of efforts at repression. These fail, but the failure in psychoses is on a much more massive scale. There is the irruption of repressed drive-representations which have a primary-process quality.[4] From this point on the mechanisms are entirely different. In neurosis the repressed contents are dealt with by means which hold the drive-derivatives back from direct expression, simultaneously giving them a partial outlet in the symptoms. In psychosis projection and hallucination alter the aim and object of the drive-representations which have emerged from repression. The cathexis of these representations allows for their becoming a new (psychotic) reality for the patient — the phase of recathexis [p. 414].

As I have indicated on the preceding pages, many contributors agree that the lack of differentiation between self- and object images is

---

[3] Kohut (1971) also proposes qualitative differences in stating that patients with narcissistic personality disorders, unlike psychotic and borderline patients, are not threatened by the possibility of an irreversible disintegration of self- and object images. Although he does not concern himself primarily with psychoses, he clearly views the psychoses as a subject for study along different lines from Arlow and Brenner.

[4] For a discussion of the impact of the primary process on ego functioning, see p. 267.

an important criterion in differentiating psychosis from neurosis. To cite Kernberg again: "It is possible that in psychotic reactions the main common psychopathological factor (in addition to persistence of splitting mechanisms) is the lack of differentiation between self- and object images in the earliest stages of ego development or a regressive fusion of those early self- and object images under the impact of pathogenic factors" (1976a, p. 50). Bak (1943) proposes that there may even be a constitutional defect in the capacity to form object relations. As we saw in Chapter 12, Mahler (1968) also relates the psychotic process to an early disturbance in object relations. She relates psychotic manifestations in children to early stages in psychic development, in which self and object are not yet clearly delineated. Hartmann's (1953) remarks seem to encapsulate this point of view: "It is very likely that distorted object relations are one predisposing agent in the development of schizophrenia. Dedifferentiation of the ego also means that the more differentiated form of object relations and for that matter objectivization can no longer be maintained. In their place we find incomplete demarcation and fusion of self and object, and lack of differentiation also between ego and id. We know that in the development of the child, self-object and ego-id differentiation run parallel" (p. 191).[5]

Hartmann's statement brings us to another consideration — the question of unique disturbances in ego functioning, which I treated in detail in Chapters 9 and 10. At this point I would like to return to Glover's (1939) differentiation between psychosis and neurosis. Despite the quantitative emphasis mentioned earlier, Glover does suggest certain qualitative differences — differences that, from the more current perspective of ego psychology, we would relate to disruptions in ego functioning. In an earlier paper (1932b), Glover points out: "The potential psychotic is one who has come to precarious terms with reality, with a narrow margin of effective repression and who is therefore at the mercy of any severe frustration either actual or the result of internal (libido) changes" (p. 179). Because the potential psychotic so symbolizes the external environment, Glover indicates, precipitating factors may have a much more devastating effect, since they may carry special significance for him. Moreover, the potential psychotic, according to

[5] One should also recall Jacobson's (1971) use of self-nonself differentiation to discuss psychotic identification in both the manic-depressive and the schizophrenic. She points out that in manic-depressive illness the regressive processes do not reach the extreme point of self–nonself and ego-superego dedifferentiation they do in schizophrenia. The manic-depressive treats himself as if he were the object, whereas the schizophrenic becomes the object.

Glover and others, seldom succeeds in establishing stable relations with real objects, and thus the regression to narcissism is much more profound than in the neurotic. This regression brings in its wake a marked rupture with reality. The attempts at restitution tend to focus on those points where the patient is actually suffering the greatest disturbance of instinctual equilibrium, and he is, as a result, most vulnerable at these points. Although Glover notes that reparative attempts are present in both the neurotic and psychotic, he draws a distinction:

> In the case of the psychotic, although the technique of symptom formation is the same, the ego regression that accompanies the libido regression is itself responsible for pathological disturbances of function which appear as 'symptoms' and which in the case of schizophrenia and melancholia affect the greater part of the ego. . . . All this can be made more comprehensible if we say that in the psychotic case the ego-regression to its fixation point, unlike the libido regression of the psychoneurotic, does not remain unconscious. It obtains expression in thought, feeling and action [1939, pp. 130–131].

Writing at a later date, after the advent of ego psychology, Jacobson (1953, 1964, 1971), looks more closely at the ego disturbances, as well as at the extensive disruptions in the inter- and intrasystemic structure and object relations. In the psychotic, she believes, we see not only instinctual regression, but also a severe regressive process involving the whole personality organization. In her opinion, these patients are predisposed to such a total regressive process by arrested, defective ego and superego development, as well as by a lack of lasting cathexis of object and self-representations and firm ego and superego identifications. The demarcation between self- and object representations breaks down in the psychotic and leads to a split into archaic self- and object images as well as a fusion of self- and object representations. The inevitable consequence is a loss of self-boundaries. It is this fusion of self and object that results in a loss of identity. According to Jacobson, new units are formed through the merging of regressive self- and object images with remnants of realistic and more mature self- and object images.[6]

Jacobson does not believe that such threats to identity are predominant in neurosis. However, I believe there is a different kind of threat in neurosis, in contrast to psychosis. It is not a disintegration of identity or disruption of unity that is feared, as in the psychotic. Rather, I would

[6] In a way this is conceptualizing within the structural model what had previously been referred to as regression to the autoerotic stage, primary narcissism, and primary identification.

say, what we find is identity confusion, not identity diffusion. Neurotics, in spite of identity confusion, still retain a unified and nonfragmented self. The problem is knowing who and what they are, not the fear of falling apart and disintegrating.

Jacobson also differentiates the psychotic's tendency to react to conflicts with the object world, not by ego defenses against unacceptable strivings, but by withdrawal of cathexis. She believes a deneutralization of instincts unleashes a furious struggle for supremacy between libidinal and destructive forces. Ego functions and emotional relationships with real objects deteriorate, with misinterpretations of and inadequate responses to the object world. The psychotic mechanisms then aim at the maintenance and/or restitution of object and self-representations. The psychotic at first attempts to save himself by support from without—by a strengthening of his perceptual and motor functions, by "looking for emotional and ideational stimulants from the outside world. If this effort fails, he will retreat from the object world. Regressively revived, primitive object- and self-images, which have found their way to consciousness will merge and join with remnants of realistic concepts to form new units. In this way, delusional object- and self-representations will be built up, in disregard of reality, and will be reprojected on the outside world" (1953, p. 64).

Let me now clarify my own perspective, with attention to the three aspects I have highlighted in the psychotic process—the nature of the danger, the nature of the defenses, and the state of the ego and its functions. In the neurotic process, I believe, the source of anxiety stems from a much higher level in psychic development than in the psychotic. We are dealing here with an instinctual conflict, with an ego structure and ego functions sufficiently developed to cope with the threatening danger (be it separation, loss of love, castration, or superego punishment). The regressive fear of disintegration of self and reality is not the focal danger as it is in the psychotic process; even if it does appear, it does not dominate the picture. Instead, the main focus seems to be on the problem of handling the instinctual demands per se. That is, the neurotic is concerned with higher-level psychosexual demands rather than primitive survival needs, as is the case with the psychotic.

In neurosis, self-preservation is taken for granted in view of the relatively strong ego and the nature of the danger involved. The degree of differentiation between self and nonself facilitates the capacity to maintain contact with reality and the object. Moreover, the neurotic is struggling with human relationships at a much higher level than the psychotic. Will they love me? Will they hate me? If I show my anger and hostility, will I be rejected? These are among the recurring concerns of the neurotic.

In contrast, I consider the anxiety in the psychotic process to be what I have called "basic anxiety." At first it is present at a nonideational, biological level and ultimately revolves around the problem of survival. The psychic representations of this fear are those of the disintegration and dissolution of self, i.e., psychic and emotional death. In the earliest stage of psychic development, this may be experienced as a sense of helplessness in the face of accumulating tension or other overwhelming situations with which the organism is unable to cope and thus constitute a danger. The anxiety has an amorphous, all-pervasive, nonspecific quality and may arise subsequently in relation to other danger situations. For the psychotic, as I have indicated, the threat of dedifferentiation, with eventual self-disintegration, is very real and may be especially frightening because the possibility of reversal is minimal. That is, since the chance of reversal is less in the psychotic, dedifferentiation may really eventuate in dissolution of self, making it an ever-present and real danger.

Let us turn to the nature of the defenses, or modes of reacting to the danger. It is generally accepted that the neurotic process involves a conflict between opposing forces, out of which a compromise evolves, containing elements of both forces. Just as the pressure of instinctual demands comes from a relatively higher level in psychic development, so does the manner in which the ego deals with these demands. Repression, displacement, reaction formation, and conversion are among the generally observed defensive operations in the neurotic process. In the psychotic process, however, where preservation and survival of self and object are the focal point, one more commonly sees regressive dedifferentiation, introjective-projective techniques, projective identification, fragmentation, splitting, massive denial, etc. Severe ego disturbances (loss of reality testing) may be brought into the service of the need to preserve the object by creating a substitute for the lost object. Yet the very defenses resorted to may heighten danger, in that they contain within them the possibility of loss of self (e.g., through regressive dedifferentiation).

We now come to the third question: Are there unique distortions or impairments of the ego and ego functions in the psychotic process, in contrast to the neurotic process? As I pointed out above, in the neurotic process we are dealing with an ego structure and functions sufficiently differentiated to cope with the threatening dangers. Contact with reality and the object is maintained. While the external world may be symbolically distorted, it is not perceptually distorted. For the neurotic, an individual may represent the father but is not physically seen as the father, as may be the case in the psychotic. The ego may undergo autoplastic distortions, but they are perceived as internally, not externally, derived.

With the psychotic process, however, one finds a gamut of regressed ego states, expressed in disordered states of consciousness and including oceanic feelings, cosmic identity, feelings of unreality, depersonalization, estrangement, as well as feelings of dissolution. In understanding these ego disturbances, we need to be aware of the diffuse ego boundaries which make it difficult for the psychotic to differentiate reality from the inner psychic world. The blurring of ego boundaries, involving self-nonself dedifferentiation, is coupled with a tendency toward anthropomorphism and merging with the nonhuman environment. All of this points to a disturbance in the relationship with reality.

In looking at the state of the ego and its functions in the psychotic process, I have chosen as my main frame of reference the position of the ego vis-à-vis the external and internal environment. This essentially concerns reality, object, and the other psychic structures. In terms of the relationship with reality, the psychotic patient is unable to see himself appropriately in reality. There may be bizarre attitudes about social responsibilities, as well as gross deviations in social amenities. This generally reflects an alloplastic modification of psychic and material reality, accompanied by a denial of reality and replacement by a new reality built out of autistic productions. The result may be a literal distortion of external material reality — a severe disturbance of the ego's relationship to reality which can only be maintained when the capacity to test reality is lost. The usual outcome is an ego-syntonic adaptation, but a reality-dystonic one. Disturbances in the ego's relationship with reality may also manifest themselves in perceptual distortions, such as hallucinations and illusions. In addition, disturbances in the sense of reality will affect the sense of the real. There may be feelings of unreality, or depersonalization, accompanied by marked body-image disturbances and feelings of estrangement.

Clearly, the ego's relationship with reality involves the nature and level of object relations. As I pointed out above, the diffuse ego boundaries make it difficult at times for the psychotic to distinguish between self and nonself, as well as between human and nonhuman objects (a difficulty that contributes to the underlying fear and danger in the psychotic process). Primitivization of object relations or regression to (or nonprogression from) archaic object relations is an underlying potential in the psychotic process. In extreme instances, such primitivization may reach pre-object levels of undifferentiated psychic development, that is, primary narcissism.

In evaluating the ego's position regarding reality, all areas have to be considered. However, I believe that, in any given condition, the existence of clinical psychosis hinges to a large degree on the loss or retention of the capacity to test reality. As I have indicated, in studying the capacity to test reality, it is relevant to evaluate disturbances in the relationship with reality and the sense of reality. One must try to delineate between the presence of such phenomena as a distortion of perception or a feeling of depersonalization and the patient's evaluation of them. It is conceivable that a hallucination, which represents a gross distortion in perception, may not be accompanied by a loss in the capacity to test reality — the patient may be able to recognize the phenomenon for what it is, that is, as internally derived.

As we have seen, interference with the internalization of reality testing as well as with the development of object and especially reality constancy will contribute to the persistence of earlier modes of testing reality, which frequently manifest themselves in psychotic patients. Such patients have not quite learned to trust their own perceptions and need constant external affirmation. The superego and parental images continue to exert influence on the ego in reality testing. As in the young child, direct sensory contact (touching, tasting, smelling, etc.) may be used to test reality in the psychotic process. The psychotic often explicitly seeks external and internal stimulation to confirm reality.

Finally, I should remind the reader of the dedifferentiation between and among the psychic structures that many authors see as responsible for symptomatology deriving from the psychotic process. There seems to be a continuous invasion of ego functions by libidinal and aggressive id derivatives, which come to dominate the ego's adaptation in all areas. The primary process exerts its influence on many spheres of ego functioning, affecting thinking, feeling, and behavior. Such regressive preoccupations can be seen in the pregenital and primitive manifestations of the instinctual drives which are frequently reflected in a marked ambivalent attitude toward objects.

The lack of differentiation also affects the position of the superego. In such patients, the superego has not achieved that degree of depersonification characteristic of mature development. One encounters regressive and archaic precursors with an alien quality and a marked tendency toward externalization and projection. The superego is also lacunae-riddled. Concomitant with impulsive breakthroughs, we find hypercritical and harsh reactions, with the possibility of disproportionate guilt and depression as a reaction.

To quickly summarize: In my opinion, the common denominators of the psychotic process, differentiating it from the neurotic one, include the basic anxiety; self-object dedifferentiation; the dominance of primary process in all psychic operations, with a preponderant aggressive breakthrough; regressive defenses; and the impairment of the ego functions concerned with reality, especially reality testing.

PART VI

THERAPEUTIC
CONSIDERATIONS

18.
Approaches to the Psychoanalytic Treatment of Psychoses

As I pointed out in the Prologue, Freud took the position that the psychotic's ego is such that a therapeutic alliance and an appropriate transference cannot be established. As late as the *Outline* (1940), he reaffirmed this position. Yet he continued to see some psychotic patients to the end. This view that psychotics cannot be worked with analytically has obviously not been shared by many, as the number of contributions on this subject referred to in this book should indicate. I have already amply demonstrated the ongoing interest not only in theory, but in the therapeutic implications of some of the theoretical frames of reference. In this chapter I would like to elaborate on some aspects of these therapeutic considerations.

It is not my intention to detail the specific technical maneuvers used in treating all the various clinical manifestations deriving from the psychotic process. The multiplicity of these would warrant a book in itself — if we even knew how to deal with all the varying clinical pictures. These pictures range from the deteriorated long-term schizophrenic, to psychotics who are able to adapt at a functional level, to psychotic characters constantly teetering on the border of psychosis and from time to time tipping over into overt psychosis, to psychotic characters who appear to have made a sociosyntonic adaptation enabling them to function, if ever so tenuously, without psychotic decompensation. Rather than examine each of these pictures, I propose to see what psychoanalysis has to offer generally in the therapy of those derivatives of the psychotic process that lend themselves to its technical approach.

It should be clear that I take a strong position about the role that psychoanalysis has played and continues to play in our understanding of the psychotic process. To what extent an understanding of this process can be translated into meaningful therapy and, moreover, a psychoanalytic one may be challenged. Opinions range from Freud's position

433

that these conditions are beyond our therapeutic reach to those who believe that psychoanalytic treatment is useful even with chronic, grossly
psychotic patients. But most problematic, perhaps, are those patients
who find their way to the psychoanalyst's office. It is they who place a
burden on the analyst in deciding on treatment, and we find ourselves
enmeshed in the ongoing debate about the distinction between dynamic
psychotherapy, psychoanalytically oriented psychotherapy, and traditional psychoanalysis. There is hardly a meeting of the various psychoanalytic organizations where this discussion does not occur, whether in
a panel, workshop, or presentation.

At a recent meeting of the International Psycho-Analytical Association, for instance, several sessions were devoted to this topic. Orgel's
(1979) succinct presentation ably summarizes the dilemmas posed by
the differing opinions. At one end of the spectrum we find Sandler's
view that training institutes should confine themselves to analytic training in the traditional sense. As Orgel indicates, Sandler's remarks reflect
the concern within some institutes that "elements of psychodynamic
psychotherapy these days tend to resemble those of psychoanalysis in
form and orientation." Furthermore, according to Sandler, the application of the "widening scope" to different kinds of patients, and the
modifications introduced by such analysts as Heinz Kohut in the U.S.
and the British Object Relations School, have made for substantial
departures from what is accepted as "standard" analytic practice.
Sandler complains of the frequency and ease with which psychoanalysts adapt themselves to "special circumstances" and to "nonclassical
patients," and call everything they do "analysis." To the contrary, it is
his conviction that it is only a "rather conservative extension of psychoanalytic training which gradually equips the analyst best to work flex-
ibly and comfortably with a variety of patients." Kernberg, on the other
hand, believes that clear distinctions can be made, and can be systematized within three basic principles applicable to *all* psychoanalytic
psychotherapies, including analysis. He emphasizes "the value to the
analytic beginner of the theory and technique of psychotherapy properly taught, in order to enhance the development of these *same* desirable attributes."

Despite the disapproving voices, I believe we need to examine the
role of psychoanalysis vis-à-vis conditions stemming from the psychotic process. Clearly, in this I am accepting a widened scope for psychoanalysis, if only to promote understanding of these conditions
within a psychoanalytic framework, whether or not we speak of "stan-

dard" psychoanalytic treatment procedures. That so many analysts have accepted the widening scope of psychoanalysis, or at least entered into the discussion, makes clarification all the more necessary. We need to do this if for no other purpose than to define frames of reference for serious students and others whose psychoanalytic education requires such frames of reference.

It is of some interest to note in this regard how the optimistic view of the reversibility of schizophrenia by psychoanalysis and the more pessimistic view that psychoanalysis has little to offer such an illness, so heavily leaden with hereditary factors, have influenced the therapeutic approach of analysts. At one end we find Boyer, who treated schizophrenic patients in his office using the couch (Boyer and Giovacchini, 1967). At the other are those who emphasize the need to operate within the patient's limitations and thus use mostly supportive techniques. In between are a host of analysts who combine a bit from both extremes. As I sifted through these various approaches, what became clear was that the nature of the patient selected for treatment played a large role in the different viewpoints. Boyer, for instance, excluded deteriorated, back-ward patients. Others, such as the Chestnut Lodge group, worked with markedly disturbed patients within a hospital setting. They nonetheless felt that they operated within a psychoanalytic orientation, albeit different from the traditional one.

At the meeting of the International Psycho-Analytical Association in 1979, referred to above, Nuñez took the position that psychoanalytic treatment is not indicated for psychosis, especially since the advent of the psychotropic drugs. In his work with a hospitalized psychotic population in Brazil, Nuñez found that psychotropic medication appeared to be the treatment of choice with such patients. On the other hand, he claimed he saw these patients psychotherapeutically at least once a week and used the Kleinian view of projective identification as a frame of reference for this treatment. It was not clear to what extent the improvement he noted in some patients was attributable to this psychotherapy, as opposed to the medication.

If I were to be consistent with the theme of this book, I would have to consider the components of the psychotic process and how the various therapeutic approaches deal with them. I would, for instance, need to look at how the psychotic's basic anxiety is dealt with and examine what role the various coping mechanisms play in the therapeutic process. I would, furthermore, have to relate to the impact of the psychotic process on the ego and its functions and how the therapeutic process affects disturbances in these areas. Yet it would be difficult within such a clearly defined and almost mechanistic frame of reference to discuss the therapeutic process. Nonetheless, I believe that as we examine the various approaches, it will be seen that in a way we are dealing with these aspects of the psychotic process, although perhaps from a slightly modified perspective.

Indeed, in a rather crude way, attempts have been made to categorize the various therapeutic approaches according to which psychic structure is used as a frame of reference. There are those who relate to id derivatives very directly, either verbally or through action. They deal in primary-process terms with the breakthrough of unconscious drives as well as with the patient's libidinal wishes. Others use an approach that in one way or another is ego-directed. They may attempt to give direct support to the ego or emphasize support or interpretation of defenses. Still others employ technical approaches that are superego-directed, concerning themselves with the harsh archaic superego they believe is found in many psychotics and which at certain stages warrants support and interpretation. Yet all of these approaches, whether intentionally or not, overlap, so that to categorize them solely in this manner is not entirely correct.

The Primary-Process Approach

With the caution just noted in mind, I would like to turn to several contributors who emphasize the primary process in their work. As I have indicated, the kind of approach may well, to a large extent, depend on the type of patient being treated, as well as the stage of the illness. Eissler (1951) divides the treatment of schizophrenia into two phases. In the first phase, the therapeutic approach emphasizes primary process as the guiding principle. In the second phase, secondary process becomes the frame of reference in treatment. These two phases correspond to the stages of the illness. In the acute stage, the symptoms are more or less ego-syntonic, and the ego acts in accordance with the symptoms, so that the patient cannot participate in active therapeutic work. In the stage of relative clinical muteness, the ego is partly free of and partly affected by the symptoms; the patient may in fact ignore or deny the symptoms.

When Eissler talks of beginning by creating a climate of primary process, he is really talking about meeting the patient's needs rather than making interpretations. He seeks to organize the primary process in the patients' environment, avoiding as much as possible subjecting them to approaches which require secondary-process thinking. The latter would be meaningless to them at this stage. In addition, Eissler tries to minimize the patients' exposure to direct or indirect manifestations of hostility from the environment. It is his contention, or at least suggestion, that it is this use of primary process as a therapeutic tool, that is the common denominator in all the techniques that have succeeded in halting the acute stage of schizophrenia. He specifically indicates that the content of interpretations given during this phase is of secondary importance, if of any. Ultimately, however, he believes that the criteria for "cure" are (1) insight into the nature of the acute disorder and (2) that feelings of automation and loss of personality are no longer present.

Those who use the primary process as the guiding frame of reference frequently accept this process as a means of relating to the patient. They may do this not only through interpretation but through actual behavior. Even some of the older and ostensibly more traditional analysts, those who worked in institutions of one sort or another with psychotic patients, suggest this approach. Nunberg (1920, 1921), in his brilliant report on the course of a catatonic patient, describes the clinical manifestations within the framework of libido theory and primary-process operations. It is clear that he was very much involved in treating his patient at this level.

One might also cite Simmel (1927, 1929, 1937), who established a sanitorium in Berlin (Schloss Tegel), where he worked "psychoanalytically" with very ill patients. He also arranged with a nearby psychiatric institution (which had a closed ward for psychotics) to treat these patients psychoanalytically (Deri and Brunswick, 1964). Hollós (1928), in a book which he sent to Freud, describes his psychoanalytic work with hospitalized psychotics.

It seems in this early work that in some instances, especially in the acute phase, what Eissler (1951) calls a primary-process climate was established. The analyst involved himself extensively in the world of the psychotic, seeing to it that the patient's libidinal needs were met and even actively taking over the management of the patient's affairs (as Eissler describes for one of his patients). No interpretations were given.

In a similar vein, Federn (1943) describes how at certain stages of "analytic treatment" he would provide such overall care through a helper: "No psychoanalysis of psychotics can be carried through without skillful assistance. The patient should be aided and protected; he should not be left to himself and his tribulations outside of the analytical hours. . . . Without such a harbour of libidinous relief psychoses are not cured" (p. 120). Gertrude Schwing (1940), one of Federn's most devoted disciples, also reports on the caretaking aspects of her work with severely ill psychotics in the hospital and even in her own home. She sees her "mothering" approach as meeting the libidinal needs of the patient. Yet I must note that this approach was not solely id-directed. As Federn (1943) points out, the analyst also fortified the ego "by protection, transference, identification and last but not least, insight into the patient's terrors and inner turmoils" (p. 134).

Common to the work of many who operate within a primary-process approach is an acceptance of the patient's psychosis and an attempt in one way or another to relate to the patient in the language of the psychosis. Sechehaye (1956b) suggests doing this with what she calls "symbolic realization." After years of work she realized that she could best make contact with her patients by resorting to a kind of primary-process play technique, which essentially used transitional objects to facilitate the working out of aggression, hostility, love, hate, and gratification. For instance, she used apples at a certain stage in the treatment to convey the idea of breast and milk. The milk or the breast could not be given directly, it had to be the apple. Similarly, a doll might be used to represent the patient at a given stage of development. What Sechehaye stresses is that each stage has to be lived through again before the patient can make contact with reality, with an object in reality. Such contact represents at a more mature stage what the symbolic object represented at an earlier stage.

Among the leading exponents of the primary-process approach in recent years are Rosen and Searles. Rosen (1947, 1962), in what he calls "direct analysis," involves himself physically with the patient — feeding, bathing, holding, and cuddling the patient when he believes this activity will remedy a childhood lack or fulfill the patient's wish. At the same time he makes deep id interpretations, talking with the patient in the "language of the unconscious," unmasking symbols and symptoms. Eissler (1951) contends that Rosen's allegedly dramatic results with this primary-process approach only occurred during the acute phase. Others have questioned whether sustained improvement was really achieved.

From a different angle, Searles seeks to understand the patient's experiences through reverberations in himself, and then takes steps to communicate this shared experience through words or action. In a dramatic paper (1959), he describes the wish to drive the other person crazy as an inherent part of everyone's personality, more prominent in some than in others. He then points to aspects of the therapeutic situation that reproduce the early mother-child relationship. What he underlines is the mutual wish and need in the patient and the therapist to preserve a symbiotic relationship, that is, a "crazy relationship." He believes this relationship should be encouraged. In this paper, Searles's own intensive involvement with patients and his use of his own subjective experiences (e.g., feelings of disintegration) stand out. Indeed, he contends that such experiences are essential in work with psychotic patients. (It should be noted that much of Searles's work seems to be with severely psychotic, hospitalized patients.)

Rosenfeld (personal communication, 1972) also stresses how analyzing his own countertransference reactions enables him to understand his psychotic patients. If he feels unusually confused, in working it through, he realizes it is the result of something the patient is doing. He then shares this with the patient. This is not unlike Searles's description of the attempts of the patient to drive the therapist crazy.

Little (1958, 1960, 1981) describes something similar in her work with psychotic patients, as well as other types of patients who apparently cannot benefit from transference interpretations. These patients do not constitute a clearly defined group. They include people suffering from character disorders, sexual perversions, psychosomatic and psychopathic conditions. Yet certain characteristics are found in their analyses: (1) ordinary dream analysis does not work; (2) acting out is violent, or violence appears negatively as passivity; (3) they are dependent on someone else to carry out many ego functions; (4) there is neither real separation nor fusion, and relationships become a *folie-à-deux*, with the analytic relationship understood in these terms; (5) there is an insatiable need for love and affection; and (6) the mother herself seems to have been infantile. In therapy these patients try to establish a total identity with the analyst, a state of undifferentiation from the analyst. To this state, Little applies the term "basic unity" — "nothing exists apart from anything else." It is a delusional transference.

As Little (1981) sees it: "The analyst's task, then, is to enable the patient to suspend the defensive functioning of his own ego, to let the analyst function for him, and let happen what happens, the analyst being in charge and looking after things, otherwise chaos develops. This process can come about through this same basic unity, for the patient feels 'What you want is what I want, since you are me and I am you'" (p. 89). She adds that "the analyst must accept fully the basic unity, being

at once indistinguishable, psychically, from the patient, and still preserving his identity" (p. 90).

According to Little, this experience is founded on certain factual
realities; it is the psychic representation of these memories. She views
these patients as "people who cannot in any circumstances take survival
for granted. There exist in their unconscious memories, experiences of
something which we must really regard as annihilation; in many cases
there has been in early infancy some actual threat to life — illness of the
infant or mother, hostility in the environment, etc." (p. 109).[1]

In dealing with psychotic anxieties or patients with actual psychotic
illness, Little believes that a more direct contact with the analyst is necessary. Not unlike Searles, she sees the work as involving the analyst's
feelings about the patient, with the analyst sometimes even supplying
feelings the patient is unable to find in himself. She, too, suggests that
no real change can take place in the absence of such reactions on the
part of the analyst. As she describes the treatment situation:

> . . . very primitive emotions are suddenly aroused in him [the analyst],
> often leaving him no time for conscious thought before he has to speak or
> act. . . . He may sometimes have to use body activity and movement.
> . . . He may have to allow his feelings to be plainly seen. . . . There are
> times when nothing can reach a patient but a direct expression of what
> the analyst is feeling at that instant. . . . Ordinary interpretative tech-
> nique forms the main part of the analysis; it cannot be superseded or
> replaced, but it can be supplemented in the ways I have indicated, to
> make the ego accessible to interpretation. The technique needs to be
> flexible, with free use of imagination (and flexibility does not mean slop-
> piness, any more than rigidity means strength). The fundamentals of
> analysis must be observed, and the analyst's own analysis must be con-
> tinued, actively, throughout [pp. 86–87].

Despite her remark about interpretation, her technique essentially has
all the ingredients of an id-directed, primary-process approach. At
another point she says:

> Where ordinary conditions are not enough, some adaptation may be
> needed to make analysis possible, such as hospitalization, the analyst
> visiting the patient, altering his room or his timetable, interviewing
> relatives, etc. . . . Those who look after the patient (in factual reality)
> become psychically not only extensions of the analyst but identical with

[1] This is similar to what I described in Chapter 7 — namely, that in the background
of the potential psychotic there are real traumatic experiences which threatened
psychic survival.

him. . . . In areas where the patient cannot use inference, analogy, symbolization, or deductive thinking, realities that are actual, concrete, and bodily are used in order to show the unreality in fact of the delusional ideas. . . . I am speaking here of such things as answering questions, touching or being touched by the patient, or using objects as if they were the things they represent, 'symbolic realization,' as described by Mme. Sechehaye. . . , or direct use of the analyst's own emotions. . . . The outcome of the analysis of a transference psychosis is that the analysand finds and retains a psychic unity with the analyst, while establishing a true separateness from and independence of him [pp. 117–119].

I have the impression that many of those working in this area almost believe that at a certain stage of treatment, not challenging the patient's primary-process way of thinking, feeling, and behaving gives the patient a feeling of authenticity and a sense of identity. This serves as a base for establishing a relationship and for subsequent work in bringing the patient ultimately to reality.

There is much that one may question about the methodology and theoretical premises of many who work within this framework. They are all, in a sense, seemingly undoing a lack in the early lives of these patients. This borders on the corrective emotional experience. Sechehaye (1956a), for instance, points to the extreme deprivation her patient had experienced as a child at the hands of a very sadistic father and a cold, rejecting mother. In her opinion, since this experience was at a preverbal level, it had to be related to preverbally. Little even suggests that prenatal and early postnatal experiences may have to be dealt with, obviously preverbally.

At a somewhat different level and with many more refinements, Kohut and the British Object Relations School also take the lack of an early empathic relationship between mother and child as the frame of reference for their therapeutic approach. What is common to all of them is the basic assumption that defects in the early infant-mother relationship have an impact on ego development and that this early relationship has to be reexperienced and worked through in the transference relationship. Yet the methods of working through the problem vary considerably. Unlike the Kleinians, for instance, the British Object Relations School suggest that interpretation is not enough and that a real relationship with the patient is essential. In characterizing the therapeutic approach of the British Object Relations School, Sutherland (1980) stresses: "they all placed the therapeutic task as paramount. They refused to adhere rigidly to the method when they felt this might lose the patient. Any parameters introduced were not such as would preclude further understanding. To many their work would be described as analytical psychotherapy rather than analysis. . . . Analytical psychotherapy does not necessarily mean the unconscious is no longer being explored" (p. 805).

Borrowing much from this school of thought, Guntrip (1969) sets his therapeutic goal in relation to "the persistence of a fear-ridden and withdrawn (or regressed) infantile self in the depths of the unconscious, and even the fact of unrealized potentialities of personality that have never been evoked." In his opinion: "The rebirth and regrowth of the lost living heart of the personality is the ultimate problem psychotherapy now seeks to solve" (p. 12). A major source of resistance to psychotherapy, he claims, is "the extreme tenacity of our libidinal attachments to parents, whatever they are like. This state of affairs is perpetuated by repression in the unconscious inner world, where they remain as subtly all-pervasive bad figures generating a restrictive, oppressive, persecutory, inhibiting family environment in which the child cannot find his real self, yet from which he has no means of escape" (p. 344).

In his approach to the therapy of the psychotic, Guntrip leans heavily on Fairbairn's and Winnicott's concepts of the transference relationship, both positive and negative, as occupying a central role. He agrees with Winnicott's criticism of the analyst who deals with primitive mental mechanisms by interpreting projections and introjections, paranoid anxieties, etc., and says that this is research analysis. The patient's needs in terms of infantile dependence are overlooked. His own personal and professional experience with Fairbairn led him to accept the view that the nearer adult analysis came to child analysis, the better the result would be. He underlines, as a source of resistance to analysis, how "the adult in the patient finds it so disturbing and humiliating to go back to having to experience himself on the level of a child with another adult" (p. 314). He then describes reliving a patient's childhood in sessions "from bottle feeding to games on the floor (tearing up paper and flinging it around, drawing, plasticene modelling in which the whole family were stamped on and destroyed) to the ultimate embarking on friendships with men, with me as a father to whom she could talk freely without moralistic criticism" (p. 314).

In a way one might compare Guntrip's emphasis on the need to "respect and to be concerned about the other person's reality in himself and apart from oneself" to the Interpersonal School's approach to the psychotic patient. This attitude leads to a personal involvement of the therapist in the patient's life. Guntrip cites Winnicott:

> In our *therapeutic* work over and over again we become involved with a patient; we pass through a phase in which we are vulnerable (as the mother is) because of our involvement; we are identified with the child who is temporarily dependent on us to an alarming degree; we watch the shedding of the child's false self or false selves; we see the beginning of a true self, a true self with an ego that is strong because like the mother with her infant we have been able to give ego support. . . . My thesis is that what we do in therapy is to attempt to imitate the natural process that character- izes the behaviour of any mother of her own infant [p. 361].

He extends this view from the treatment of severely regressed patients to the treatment of lesser degrees of illness:

> The therapist has no choice but to be deeply involved with the patient, who is at last compelled to give up the futile struggle to keep going on the adult level, and relapses willy nilly into the depths of infantile terror, iso- lation, and the evaporation of his ego into a feeling of nothingness. He must keep as constant and close contact with him as is humanly possible, especially if the patient's human environment is not as supportive as one might wish. He must see the patient through into the ultimate accept- ance of a therapeutic regression from which he must be mentally nursed to a rebirth and regrowth of a real self. The therapist is utterly indispen- sable to him at that stage [pp. 361–362].

Guntrip cites the need for the therapist to be available by whatever means are possible. Telephone contact is used when no other contact is possible, to offset the patient's feeling of aloneness and abandonment. Visiting the patient or involving himself in the care of the patient out- side of the office is viewed by Guntrip as part of the attempt to deal with the mother-infant relationship, and ultimately to help the patient outgrow the need for dependency. Yet such personal involvement with patients does *not* mean sharing with them the therapist's innermost thoughts and feelings or facts about the therapist's personal life. "What does concern the patient, and it is the only thing about the therapist that does really concern him, however much other things may crop up accidentally or incidentally, is whether the therapist as a real human being has a genuine capacity to value, care about, understand, see, and treat the patient as a person in his own right" (p. 350).

It should be added that side by side with the reality involvement, Guntrip advocates an attempt to understand and help the patient understand the basic psychological problems which play such an im-

portant role in the patient's needs, fears, and anxieties. "Psychotherapeutic success depends ultimately not on theory, and not on a stereotyped technique, but on the individual therapist's ability to understand
intuitively and accurately this particular patient, and to sense what is
truly this patient's problem (p. 316).

TRANSFERENCE VICISSITUDES

All of the above relates to a specific kind of patient-therapist relationship found in psychotic or psychotic-like patients. Valenstein (1981)
reemphasizes the view that a true transference is not established with
borderline and psychotic patients. However, he does say that they form
a kind of transference relationship which is "predominantly dyadic,
centering on security and nurturant needs with misperceptions and
misconstructions of self-object discrimination." He characterizes this as
a "developmental neurosis" due to developmental traumas and deficits
occurring very early in life.

Such "transferences" have been designated in many different ways.
The terms "transference psychosis," and "delusional transference" have
been applied to the appearance of psychotic and psychotic-like phenomena during analysis. According to some, these phenomena must be
clearly distinguished from a psychotic transference, namely, transference manifestations in which the patient simply extends his psychotic
system to include the analyst. On the other hand, Rosenfeld (1952) and
Searles (1963) describe patients who show psychotic manifestations
during treatment as an extension of an already-existing psychosis, or as
a recrudescence of a previous psychosis. When these patients extend
this psychotic system to include the analyst, Rosenfeld and Searles call
the reactions "transference psychosis."

To a large extent the choice of terminology depends on how one defines transference. Giovacchini (Boyer and Giovacchini, 1967) broadens
the concept considerably in dealing with transference manifestations in
the psychotic and indicates that there are transference elements in all
behavior. He believes that schizophrenics' archaic images consist of
part-object introjects. During treatment they not only project these
onto the analyst, but also externalize them on others. Giovacchini considers even these latter externalizations as part of the transference
manifestations.

If, however, one defines transference in a more restricted way — as a
phenomenon newly reevoked in the analysis, with special features of its
own, and not merely an extension of the patient's ongoing patterns of

behavior — one cannot truly speak of the reactions described by Rosenfeld and Searles as transference psychosis. To be consistent, we must limit the term "transference psychosis" to a new phenomenon, arising in the treatment and containing within it the core of the patient's problem, very much as the transference neurosis does. A natural corollary of this concept would then be the idea of an infantile psychosis. Indeed, within the narrower definition, a number of analysts look at psychotic reactions during analysis as variants of a transference psychosis containing within it derivatives of an infantile psychosis. Holzman and Ekstein (1959), for instance, see transitory, psychotic-like ego regression as a special form of repetition of infantile situations occurring in patients particularly prone to identity diffusion. They believe that by such repetition the patient tells the therapist how he coped with a difficult situation in the recent past; the patient "repeats an earlier dynamically similar problem and presents his modes of solving it." Reider (1957) suggests that psychotic reactions within the transference may occur either as reenactments of a childhood psychosis or as an identification with a psychotic object. Both are experienced within the framework of the transference.

Obviously, if one assumes that there are phase-related developmental stages in which such "psychotic" states are present, then the occurrence of these states later on, during therapy, will necessarily be viewed as a reenactment of an infantile psychosis. In this sense, it seems natural for Klein and her followers, with their idea of a paranoid-schizoid position in psychic development, to view features from this stage appearing during therapy of adults as a transference psychosis in the more restricted sense. Similarly, given Little's concept of "basic unity," which contains within it all the features of the earliest, undifferentiated state of psychic development, what she calls "delusional transference" in therapy would be viewed as a transference psychosis in the more literal sense. Jacobson (1957) comments: "If one adheres to the conviction that during the first months of life the infant passes through a period called 'the paranoid-schizoid position,' which is followed by the 'depressive position,' he must also assume that delusional psychotic symptoms will inevitably revolve around the therapist, and regard every psychotic reaction as an expression of true transference phenomena derived from the infantile past" (pp. 62–63).

Freeman, Cameron and McGhie (1966) indicate that therapists like Rosenfeld (1952), Bion (1957), and Searles (1959) tend to view psychotic manifestation as true derivatives of infantile psychotic manifestations. However, whether the latter are developmental in nature (and reflect the state of the psyche at that period of development) or whether they represent a specific psychotic state, the content of which is reactivated in the transference, is hard to say. Only in the latter case would we be speaking of a transference psychosis in the strict sense. As I pointed out above, Grotstein (1977) seems to think this.

In other words, to use the concept of an infantile psychosis that is reenacted in the transference as a transference psychosis in the more restricted sense, such an infantile psychosis should have a form other than some phase-related "position." It should arise during psychic development, and in and of itself represent a regression to an earlier and more primitive stage in psychic development. It may, for instance, arise in reaction to a danger and overwhelming anxiety in childhood. This danger calls into play certain more regressive ego states, which would be consonant with the development of a childhood psychosis. It is then, according to some, that we may correctly speak of an infantile psychosis. The subsequent reenactment of this truly psychotic content and ego state would be consistent with what is called a true "transference psychosis."

Such a definition of infantile psychosis, however, is questioned by Mahler (1968). Although she indicates that psychotic disturbances in children may be related to various stages in psychic development, she makes it quite clear that "the intrapsychic situation in the psychotic child does not involve a regression to *any known phase* of development" (p. 55). Instead, she believes these pathological states, "whether they are predominantly autistic or symbiotic syndromes, represent grave distortions that take place by way of a pathological intrapsychic process" (pp. 54–55).

One may also wonder about the relationship of adult psychoses to childhood psychoses. Should one take the position, as Klein and her followers do, that adult psychoses have a counterpart in infantile psychoses? Freeman (1973) in his comparison of adult and childhood psychosis, seems to think so. He believes that beyond the developmental deficits seen in adult schizophrenics, we may find fleeting psychotic episodes during childhood. Anna Freud, in her introduction to Freeman's book, supports this view: "the prehistory of every schizophrenic patient may include not only the developmental weaknesses and failures which promote breakdowns and regressions in later life, but actual transitory episodes of psychotic functioning which during infantile life have gone unnoticed" (p. ix).

In Chapter 4, I called attention to what may have been a true transference psychosis in the Wolf Man (see also Frosch, 1966). It may be recalled that, some time after he left Freud, the Wolf Man developed a whole series of somatic complaints and preoccupations revolving around his nose and teeth, which led him to many doctors. At times these ideas assumed almost delusional proportions. In his analysis with Ruth Mack Brunswick (1928), she began to attack his grandiosity. In response to this technical move, the Wolf Man began to act most abnormally. He talked wildly, seemed cut off from reality, developed a gross delusional system, and threatened to shoot both Freud and Brunswick. Brunswick suggests that the destruction of his grandiose ideas brought this persecutory note to the fore, and she raises the question whether the megalomania was not part of a defense cloaking his unconscious homosexuality.

Harnik (1930, 1931), in his comments on Brunswick's analysis of the outbreak as well as the resolution of the psychosis, points to the many indications that as a child the Wolf Man had had a psychotic reaction following the famous wolf dream. This had all the features of a paranoid reaction. He was irritable, had temper tantrums, was suspicious, did not trust anyone, and could not bear to have people look at him. Based on these symptoms, Harnik sees the paranoid psychosis the Wolf Man developed in relation to Brunswick as a regressive repetition of a conflict from early childhood which was reactivated in the analysis. In his opinion, this childhood psychosis represented a regression to an even earlier period in psychic development, and it was this condition which was reactivated in the transference psychosis with Brunswick. Without specifically stating it, he obviously views a transference psychosis as containing within it the ingredients of a childhood psychosis.

The question of defining a transference psychosis is complicated by the fact that many of the psychotic reactions arising during analysis are characterized by some loss of differentiation between self and analyst and confusion of the latter with significant early objects, recalling features of early psychic development. Bychowski (Freedman, 1962, 1964) refers to the psychotic core in borderline patients. In his opinion, when a patient with a psychotic core is in analysis and the defenses are stripped away, a transient psychosis may be precipitated and the archaic object relations are seen. In such instances the analyst, who is endowed with fantasied attributes, is frequently confused with the real, threatening parent. Many see this as a psychotic transference relationship. As Nacht (1958) puts it: "The neurotic reacts as if his father had been a bad father and as if his analyst serves as substitute for the bad father, but if he has really had a monstrous father or an abominable mother, interpretations of this kind have no place. The patient unconsciously carried in him the presence of hateful and terrifying objects; the therapist is not likened to a bad object, he is for him a renewal of the bad object" (p. 272).

Along these lines, Hammet (1961) reports the treatment of a patient who developed a "delusional transference," in the course of which the patient ceased to know his therapist in a real way and literally mistook him for his dreaded father. In other words, the transference became indistinguishable from reality. Little (1981) also describes such reactions as "delusional tranferences." Distinguishing this from neurotic reactions, she says: "But a neurotic can recognize the analyst as a real person, who for the time being symbolizes, or 'stands in' for his parents, either as they actually were, or as he experienced them in his childhood, and he is accessible to verbal interpretation of the transference. Where the transference is delusional there is no such 'stand-in' or 'as-if' quality about it. To such a patient the analyst is, in an absolute way, with a quality of 'authenticity,' both the idealized parents and their opposites, or rather, the parents deified and diabolized, and also himself (the patient) deified and diabolized, for the analyst is assumed absolutely to be magical" (p. 83).[2]

As I discussed above (p. 292), the ego function of perception is severely impaired in the psychotic, and this facilitates misidentification of the other person (e.g., the Capgras syndrome). This defect makes it possible to implement the need to see the analyst as the parent. As Freeman (1973) explains:

> Reality testing breaks down with the appearance of misidentifications and false perceptions and must therefore be regarded as depending, to some extent at least, on the quality of the drive derivatives which invest the object representations. The degree to which object representations are invested with drive derivatives of secondary process type will reflect the presence and strength of the remaining healthy mental functions (the nonpsychotic part of the personality). . . . Whether the treatment will continue and reach a favorable outcome will depend on whether or not the nonpsychotic part retains its integrity. This is lost whenever the libidinal drive derivatives are affected by regression, thereby regaining their instinctual quality. When this happens cognition falls under the

[2] At a future date I will report on the role of the therapist as a transitional object in the treatment of psychotic characters, as well as of the work of others who for technical reasons feel it appropriate to accept the patients reacting to them as real parental objects.

influence of the primary process and the cathexes invest object and fantasy representations with the development of a delusional reality. This penetrates the therapeutic relationship and frequently destroys it [p. 11].

Inevitably we must question the relationship of such phenomena to the analytic process itself. The analytic process, with the development of the transference, may bring about new and deeper regressive tendencies. To some (e.g., Peto, 1967), the very process of analysis brings about decompositions and fragmentations which, although related to the transference, do not necessarily contain the structure of a childhood psychosis. Such regressive transference manifestations may even assume psychotic-like proportions, as we often find in the analysis of borderline patients (see Weinshel, 1966; Frosch, 1967b).

Because the transference psychosis arises during analysis, it carries particular therapeutic implications, a point underscored by Little (1981). As I indicated above, Little describes how in the "delusional transference" the analyst becomes an absolute representation of the parents, "deified and diabolized," with magical powers. The main mechanisms of this delusional transference are splitting, denial, isolation, projection, and introjection. According to Little, the inaccessibility of the ego to transference interpretations seems to entail a failure of integration of psyche and soma. The transference delusion conceals a state which the patient both needs and is fearful of achieving. In it there is no sense of person, only an undifferentiated psyche-soma, experienced as chaos. Reaching this state means becoming, for the moment, only a rage, a scream, wholly dependent on the analyst. If the delusion is disturbed, recognition of reality is experienced almost as an "orgasm of pain," a moment of frenzy and real danger, which may take suicidal form or result in a maniacal attack on the analyst.

Like many who share this concept, Little assumes that this state has to be reached in the course of analysis "so that the unreality of these identities can be recognized." Successful analysis depends on breaking up the delusional transference. "To do this, reality must be presented undeniably and inescapably so that contact with it cannot be refused, and in such ways that the patient does not have to use either inference or deductive thinking" (p. 85). To resolve the transference, patients have to be enabled to bring their love and hate for one person together, to find both good and bad aspects of the analyst, their parents, and themselves as human beings, and to know the difference between imagined and objective reality.

In Little's view, when movement is toward the analyst, contact is made with a person who is separate, thus creating a new situation in which the delusion cannot be maintained. Recovery begins as the primary identification breaks up, secondary identification becomes possible, and the ability to accept the consequences of an event emerges. In such cases, the analyst's ego function must be maximal, his object function minimal. The analyst's instinctual impulses must be used fully and directly, and he must be capable of showing his feelings. Special techniques used for delusional transference make the ego accessible to the usual interpretive techniques, while the fundamentals of analysis are still observed, including the continuation of the analyst's own analysis.

Rosenfeld's (1952, 1965) therapeutic approach also leans heavily on use of the "transference psychosis." Although he is very much influenced by the Kleinian viewpoint, it is difficult to tell whether he views the "transference psychosis" as analogous to the transference neurosis, with an infantile psychosis analogous to an infantile neurosis. It is clear, however,that when he talks of the transference psychosis, it is within the framework of Klein's projective identification. It is manifestations of the projective identification within the transference that are repeatedly dealt with via verbal interpretations. Rosenfeld describes the treatment of a schizophrenic patient in whom one of the dominant sources of anxiety seemed to be the fear of losing himself within the analyst, or symbolically within the analyst's room. The fear that the analyst would leave him was also dominant because he felt he would thereby lose both the object and himself.

Although Rosenfeld insists that his treatment retains the essential features of psychoanalysis, there are many modifications. Very early in treatment, he gives his psychotic patients what he calls transference interpretations, which focus on the patients' introjective and projective identifications with the therapist. Much like Guntrip (1969), Rosenfeld maintains that there are certain parallels between the psychoanalytic approach to acute schizophrenics and the analysis of small children. In both instances, the patients are not expected to lie on the couch, their words as well as their play and gestures are used, and cooperation between patient and analyst is desirable. Yet in both cases, Rosenfeld believes the basic rule of psychoanalysis should be retained and the use of nonanalytic means, such as advice or reassurance, is not only unnecessary but even detrimental to the analysis.

In contrast to Rosenfeld's verbal approach to the "transference psychosis," Searles (1959, 1963) deals with both his and his patient's reactions in a less directly interpretive manner. He conceives of the transference "as being in the nature basically of a relatedness to the therapist as a mother figure from whom the patient has never as yet become deeply differentiated" (1963, p. 273). He believes that the patient needs this symbiotic relationship and he provides it, using silence to encourage the therapeutic symbiosis. On one occasion he describes how in this silence he and his patient sat and listened to each other's borborygmi.

Searles defines transference psychosis as any type of transference that distorts or prevents a relatedness between the patient and therapist as two separate, alive, human and sane beings. He then cites four varieties of transference psychoses. In the first kind, the patient has not yet built up part-object relationships, an image of self and mother as separate objects, and the therapist feels unrelated to the patient. Searles compares this to the autistic phase of childhood. In the second category of transference psychoses, clear relatedness has been established between patient and therapist, and thus the therapist no longer feels unrelated to the patient. Yet the relatedness is a deeply ambivalent one, with a fear of annihilation accompanying the patient's wish to join with the therapist. The therapist is deeply involved with the patient, feeling and sensing the patient's confusion, even feeling the threat of annihilation and questioning his own sanity. The third category includes those transference psychoses in which the patient's psychosis represents an effort to complement the therapist's personality or to help the therapist become established as a separate and whole person. The fourth variety takes place with deeply and chronically confused patients who in childhood were accustomed to their parents doing their thinking for them and are ambivalently trying to perpetuate this symbiotic relationship.

All the above authors view what they are doing as psychoanalysis. Whatever the terms used, the goal of these approaches is to achieve some reintegration of the psyche. Even the so-called primary-process approach hopes, through achieving some kind of patient-therapist communication, to establish a therapeutic alliance, and through this to achieve some degree of synthesis. My point in saying this is that in turning to what are seen as ego-directed therapies, it should be clear that other approaches also relate to the position of the ego. One may direct oneself explicitly to the state of the ego, as Federn does, or look at the ego's position vis-à-vis the other psychic structures, as in so-called id-directed or superego-directed approaches. Or one may concern oneself with the various ego functions, defensive or otherwise. In all this, as I pointed out above, there is a great deal of overlap.

Ego-Directed Approaches

Federn's use of the term "ego," as we have seen, diverges somewhat from the usual definition. His perspective is that psychosis is due to a decreased ego cathexis, while neurosis leaves the ego cathexis itself intact or increased and only disturbs various functions of a still intact ego. In line with this, he proposes certain treatment principles which are, in the main, ego-supporting and encourage repression. He believes that this approach will help patients conserve energy. Expanding on this idea, he explains:

> Psychotic patients are helped by being made to recognize that it is their ego that has fallen ill and needs treatment. A broad mental hygiene program is needed in which all specialists in the field must participate to make it effective, because the ego diseases start at the beginning of the ego, i.e., at birth. A "cure" of psychosis may be limited to achieving but restricted social, sexual and economical functioning. The deficiency of the cathexes calls for never-ending protection from overstrain, regardless of whether it is of internal origin in the form of exaggerated sexual demands or of external origin in the form of stress or pain [1943, p. 5].

It is the decrease of strain, either through change of reality or through narrowing of the ego boundaries, that enables the ego to recover from the state of defeat it experiences in psychosis.

In his work with schizophrenics, Federn takes the position that they can be worked with analytically, but that the treatment may require some modifications. In dealing with the patient's unconscious and resistances, he claims, one must proceed in a way opposite to that adopted in the analysis of neurotic patients. He eschews dealing with negative transference manifestations, and utilizes positive transference to support the ego. Complete sincerity toward the patient is imperative; under no circumstances should the patient be deceived. In addition, the patient should be helped to solve current life problems through the aid, not only of the therapist, but also of family members and a disciplined environment. No treatment of psychotics can be successful, in Federn's opinion, without a skilled female helper, a mother or sister figure. If a psychotic patient develops a mother transference with a male therapist, this confuses the patient because he is unable to distinguish this feeling from a homosexual one.

According to Federn (1943), the general features which should be considered in any psychoanalytic treatment are: "Establishment of positive transference; interruption of treatment when transference becomes negative; provision of the feminine helper; lasting psychoanalytical postpsychotic mental help and supervision; settling of the sexual problem. These general rules are not just instructions which, when followed, facilitate the psychoanalysis of a patient. They are, as I said, conditions for the treatment. In severe cases they are indispensable; in milder cases they shorten the treatment" (p. 122).

Federn's technique, especially in its emphasis on the family's cooperation and the use of a female helper in the role of mother or sister, has much in common with child therapy. Federn even considers play therapy a possibility. He also notes: "In view of the regression to early ego-states, in the advanced cases use of oral gratifications is most helpful. In view of the probability of organic factors in many psychoses, organic therapy, even on an experimental basis, may be applied concomitantly with psychotherapy" (pp. 6–7).

Federn does not use the couch since he believes the associations will be schizophrenic in nature. In his opinion:

> In psychosis, one slows down and even tries to stop such spontaneous delivery of still unconscious mental complexes, because one does not want to face an increase of the psychotic disorganization until the ego has been re-established within its normal boundaries, sufficiently invested with mental cathexis to stand the dynamic forces of the unconscious. . . . In neuroses, the goal is to replace the rule of the id by the rule of the ego. In psychoses, the goal is the same, but before it can be attained many functions which have abnormally entered into the conscious ego have to be re-repressed and must return to the id. In psychoses the psychoanalytical use of transference is more limited, but is of even greater value than usual. The antithesis is this: In neurotics, transference is used to make repressed material free; in psychotics, to make free material repressed. . . . The problem arises of deciding whether to try to lead the patient back to normality or to use his psychic state to make him cope with his deepest desires, images, conflicts, fears and terrors [pp. 140, 149].

In most instances it is clear that Federn opts for re-repression. A positive transference should be utilized and not disrupted by psychoanalysis. He opposes dealing with the negative transference. This is a position to which Fromm-Reichmann (1959) takes exception since she believes the patient's hostility must be faced by the patient and the therapist. Federn instead supports the positive transference; he sees to it, for instance, that oral needs are gratified; providing cigarettes, sweets, etc. Nonetheless, Federn, in contrast to Fairbairn, Guntrip, and others, believes one should be careful to keep one's distance from the patient.

A somewhat different frame of reference is apparent in the ego-directed approach of the Interpersonal School. As I indicated in Chapter 13, their therapeutic approach is greatly influenced by the belief that the problems of emotionally disturbed patients are not too dissimilar from those which we all suffer from at times. In line with this, the therapist must respect the psychiatric patient. Moreover, the Interpersonal School sees the therapist as an active participant observer in the therapeutic process, with emphasis on the interpersonal exchange between patient and therapist. Out of all this arise certain technical considerations, which Fromm-Reichmann (1950a) summarizes:

> ... the clarification of a patient's difficulties with his fellow-men through observation and investigation of the vicissitudes of the mutual interrelationship between doctor and patient; the encouragement of recall of forgotten memories; the investigation and scrutiny of the anxiety connected with such recall, including the patient's resistance against this recall, and his security operations with the psychiatrist who tries to effect it. It is in the light of these memories and of the patient's and doctor's interpersonal experiences with each other that the patient's communications are interpreted with regard to their unconscious genetic and dynamic implication. . . . It is not only the wording per se (i.e., the interpretive give-and-take) which relieves the patient but also the discharge of affect plus insight gained by the patient. The non-verbal interplay experienced between patient and doctor which accompanies verbalized interchange also plays an integral part in all intensive psychotherapy [p. xix].

Sullivan (1956), however, does not stress insight. Instead, he focuses on the reoganization of the disintegrated personality. He believes there is a large proportion of recovered schizophrenics with a reasonably unified personality, seemingly well-adapted socially, without the generally accepted evidence of insight. In this respect he is not too far from Federn, who in stressing re-repression also underlines the need to avoid further probing after the patient has made what he calls a "recovery." Sullivan emphasizes the patient's current significant interpersonal relations which have ties to the past. Although in the main Sullivan is quite optimistic about recovery, he shows pessimism about a certain group of patients, in whom he believes there is an organic factor, hereditarily determined.

The goal of establishing the patient's sense of identity leads the therapist to deal with the lack of differentiation so frequently seen, especially in schizophrenia. Taking Sullivan's interpersonal theories, Brody (1961) relates the thinking on self-nonself differentiation to the various positions of the therapeutic relationship, with respect to the phase of psychic development from which the conflicts derive. Indeed, this particular area seems to be the focus of interest of therapists like Will, Fromm-Reichmann, Searles, and others. Among other things, they relate the question of differentiation of self from nonself to the concept of identity. In many ways, the ultimate reversal of dedifferentiation and establishment of identity became the goal of therapy.[3]

The problem of self-object dedifferentiation, as well as the special kind of introjections the psychotic resorts to, is also viewed by Jacobson (1967, 1971) as a crucial frame of reference in the therapy of the psychotic. She makes this her focal point in therapy, indicating that attention to defenses and resistances should be superseded by evaluation of disturbances in the self and identity. The psychotic desperately tries to hold onto reality in many different ways. Jacobson directs herself to supporting such attempts as well as to facilitating the reintegration of self. Although she observed hospitalized schizophrenics in florid psychotic states, her essential therapeutic experience with psychotic patients was with manic-depressives, ambulatory schizophrenics, and patients during periods of remission from a psychotic episode. According to her, "they usually need many years of analysis with slow, patient, consistent work in the area of ego and superego functioning, with great attention to their particular methods of defense and to the affective responses in which these defenses find special expression" (1971, p. 235). She describes what she considers the characteristic treatment phases as: "the initial, spurious transference success; the ensuing period of hidden, negative transference with corresponding negative therapeutic reactions, i.e., waxing and more severe states of depression; the stage of dangerous, introjective defenses and narcissistic retreat; and the end phase of gradual, constructive and conflict solution" (p. 287).

Jacobson stresses how the analyst becomes the "central love object" for some of these patients and how they need to cling to the external ob-

---

[3] I should like to make a personal comment on my contact with some of the therapists at Chestnut Lodge, where I spent a few days. In speaking with Dexter Bullard, Sr., about results he rather cynically, I thought, said: "The usual one third, one third, one third." I believe he was being a bit modest since he was talking of treating severely ill patients who were in the main hospitalized. None, at that time at any rate, were treated with shock treatment or neuroleptics.

ject world: "In some patients, [the love object] may alternately be close
and distant, dependent and autistic, touchingly clinging and frankly
aggressive, cold and shallow and intensely demanding" (1967, p. 50).
There is an inconsistency, and they ascribe rapidly changing roles to the
person to whom they attach themselves. With regard to the treatment
of ambulatory schizophrenics, she says: "If we understand their defensive devices and the different roles in which they cast us, we can, at least
during certain critical periods of our therapeutic work, lend ourselves
to assuming these roles. I believe that some therapists who work with
psychotics intuitively respond to their patients in this way. This explains the amazing transference successes that under these circumstances can be achieved with psychotics" (p. 56). She illustrates her
point with a case example. Although conducting "genuine psychoanalysis," she explains, "I permitted this patient to 'use' me in the ways and
roles that he needed. I adapted my emotional attitudes and behavior to
his wishes, either for warmth and closeness or for more distance. I let
him 'borrow' my superego and ego; regard and treat me as his bad id
and his illness; project his guilt, his faults, and weaknesses onto me; or
turn me into the ideal of saintliness he needed" (p. 57).

During such periods she avoids deeper interpretations. Yet she does
not believe that this approach warrants the development of the kind of
interrelationship that Searles advocates. As she puts it:

> . . . although I admire the frankness with which he discusses his own
> countertransference manifestations, I must admit that I consider coun-
> tertransference problems a private matter. Except in very general terms,
> their open discussion and public exhibition do not seem to me to be par-
> ticularly useful. Such problems must be recognized and controlled in
> one's self-analysis or, if this does not work out, by re-analysis. . . . I
> believe that if the therapist permits himself to establish a parent-child
> relationship with the patient, which includes not only feelings of fond-
> ness and affection but even parental incestuous desires; and if at a cer-
> tain stage of the treatment the therapist regresses along with the patient
> to a mutually symbiotic dependency — then the therapist will find him-
> self in dangerous situations which, in my opinion, are of no therapeutic
> value [pp. 60, 62].

Obviously, the type of patient, as well as the stage of the illness, will
determine whether the classical analytic approach will be adhered to or
whether modifications of various types will be instituted. As we have
seen, Boyer essentially opts for a classical analytic approach with some
modifications (Boyer and Giovacchini, 1967). He reports on the office

treatment of patients, many of whom had been hospitalized previously and had received general psychiatric care, although he excluded chronically regressed "back-ward" patients. After a few initial vis-à-vis interviews, Boyer uses the couch. He refers to the initial period of treatment as the "noisy phase." During this phase he is active, in one way or another making his presence felt. As Boyer explains it: "When a person lies down on the couch, his contacts with the therapist are diminished abruptly and he maintains contact primarily through hearing. Thus, the attitudes of the analyst, as reflected in his words, voice tones, and other sounds, assume great importance, and cannot be disguised" (p. 178). He restricts his activities to observation and interpretation, encouraging "controlled regression" which facilitates the development of a psychotic regression. He then opts for continuing with the patients after the psychosis has subsided, and the "transference psychosis" has been succeeded by a "transference neurosis."

Arlow and Brenner (1964, 1970), consistent with their position that the processes in neurosis and psychosis are basically the same, deal with the defenses against anxiety via interpretation, in a manner resembling standard psychoanalytic technique. Reporting on a psychotic patient who, in defending against her angry impulses toward her husband, went into a trance or stuporous state, they suggest: "One could say to her, in effect, 'The fact that you have to paralyze your mind and body so completely when you're angry at your husband indicates that you're very afraid of becoming openly angry at him. You seem to be afraid of what you'd think, and of what you'd do. It's important to try to find out what wishes or ideas you're so afraid of, and why they frighten you so, i.e., what you think will happen if you think or wish them.'" In this way, they claim, "Analyst and patient were... led to explore the motives of the patient's defense as well as its historical (infantile) determinants" (1964, pp. 160–161). Ostensibly this approach is not too different from traditional analysis of neurotics. Yet the overall technical implications of Arlow and Brenner's concept of psychosis are difficult to evaluate since the impact of the interpretations and the ultimate course of treatment in the cases presented are not discussed (see also my criticisms on p. 266).

Superego-Directed Approaches

Dealing with the archaic superego of the psychotic, especially the schizophrenic, is considered essential by many analysts, as we have already seen in Jacobson's remarks above. Rosenfeld (1952), using a Kleinian frame of reference, points out that in all schizophrenics there is a particularly severe superego of a persecutory nature. He believes that these patients continuously have to put their superego into the analyst. The analyst must interpret this situation until these patients are gradually able to accept both their love and hate and their superego as belonging to themselves.

Although also recognizing the existence of a harsh, archaic superego, Wexler (1951a, 1951b, 1971) relies less on interpretation. He discusses the need to ally oneself with the harsh, primitive superego of the schizophrenic. Drawing on his experience with a female schizophrenic patient, Wexler describes how, after several months of going along with the patient's psychosis, her delusions and hallucinations, he shifted his approach. He began to agree with her exaggerated moral scruples, with her condemnation of sexual activities and temptations, and her insistence on avoiding sexual thoughts. Indeed, he actively forbade and physically restrained her exhibitions of force and sexual provocations, following each episode with peace-making and affection.[4] Wexler asserts that such an active alliance, which enables the patient to control the violence of instinctual impulses, may serve as the core for internalizing a more civilized superego and lead to the formation of sounder object relations in the schizophrenic.

According to Wexler, schizophrenics are tremendously frightened of the power of instinctual drives, and a relaxed atmosphere may induce free expression of these frightening forces. His assumption is that a primitive, archaic, and devastatingly punitive superego plays an important role, along with the pressing instinctual demands, in producing schizophrenic disorganization. Because the ego is inaccessible, therapy must be directed either to the id or the superego. Present data seem to indicate that the schizophrenic ego can frequently be strengthened by the therapist's determined assumption of superego roles, a conclusion consistent with psychoanalytic understanding of the importance of the superego in the development of a sense of reality.

I am reminded of a patient I treated very early in my career, when my lack of understanding of these points led to an error in therapy. The patient was a 16-year-old female, bright and attractive. Among her many psychotic symptoms, she had the belief that her masturbatory activity was literally retarding her physical development. She indicated

[4] In a sense, this is not unlike Federn's re-repression technique.

that a sign of this immaturity was that the aureole on her breasts were unusually large, in proportion to the breasts, just as in childhood. In a somewhat offhand manner, attempting to reassure her, I minimized the harmful effects of masturbation. She appeared to be reassured. A short while later, however, I received a frightened call from her father, who was a physician. Could I come to see his child? She was in a terrible state and they couldn't handle her.

I went to the house. When I walked into the room, there was my patient huddled in a corner, dirty and disheveled, her hair wildly strewn over her face. But what struck me most was the look on her face — a mixture of anger, almost hatred, and fright. As I came near her, she pulled further and further away. She said not a word. Finally, with the help of her father, we got her on a bed.

At that time I was still using intravenous sodium amytal for mute and resistant patients. I had no sooner injected about one cc. than the patient burst forth, "It's all your fault." I was taken aback, since the image I had of my treatment of this patient was one of kindness, gentleness, and forbearance. Essentially what she said was, "Here I was struggling with the bad part of me and you came along and took sides with the bad part until it won out. I couldn't stand it." Her guilt had become overwhelming. She was telling me in her own words that her id-derived impulses were frightening and that her ego was being overwhelmed and her superego couldn't support the ego in controlling these impulses. Instead of my supporting her archaic superego, I had sided with the id, making it even more difficult for her to control what her archaic superego said were forbidden gratifications. I admitted to the patient that I had misunderstood her and promised to help her by supporting her efforts to control the bad part of herself. This had a most salutary effect. The treatment became more structured and I took a more forceful approach. Gradually we were able to move into more insight-achieving treatment.

More recently, in a teaching exercise, I had the chance to bring up the need of psychotic patients for more structure and authoritative restraint to enable them to cope with the disintegrative effects of the breakthrough of powerful libidinal and aggressive drives. I came into the conference room of the ward and noticed a six-inch-blade knife on a chair. Preceding our conference some of the patients had had a meeting. I suggested to the staff that the room be made available to the same patients for another meeting and, if possible, they should occupy the same chairs. It was soon clear which patient had deliberately left the knife on the chair. In the ensuing discussion, he said he had begun to pocket the knife when the policy of checking patients for harmful implements was discontinued. He said it was the staff's fault. They were derelict in their duty to protect the patients from each other, but even more so from themselves. The patients were here because they couldn't do it themselves; they needed the help of the staff. In this sense the staff had failed. My point is that it is through psychoanalytic *verstand* that we come to know how to establish even the appropriate milieu therapy. Obviously one has to temper authority with understanding in order to establish the kind of relationship that lays the groundwork for a therapeutic alliance, which then makes insight therapy possible with appropriate patients.

Considerations in the Choice of Therapy

Whether one or the other therapeutic approach will be successful depends on many factors. The broad spectrum of psychotic patients, for instance, makes it quite difficult to pinpoint a single effective therapeutic approach. In an attempt to clarify the treatment issues, Pao (1979) and his colleagues at Chestnut Lodge have classified schizophrenic patients into four groups, with development and self-cohesion as the frames of reference. In Group I, there is generally no marked pathology of a schizoid nature in the mothering person. "The patient's history reveals near-adequate development and functioning, including satisfactory sublimatory activities, until the late teens." It is at this point, "with the final steps of the second separation-individuation process, [that] the patient develops acute symptoms" (p. 22). In discussing the treatment of such patients, Pao says: "In the early phase of treatment. . . I introduce parameters. For instance, before I am sure that the patient can tolerate certain degrees of separation, I prefer to talk to him in a face-to-face position. I keep my interpretations at a level that seems not too abstract for the patient. As much as I try to think a step ahead of the patient, I am always a step behind him. I see to it that he understands whatever we talk about. If possible, I refrain from pointing out his pattern of interaction with me until we have had an opportunity to establish beyond doubt that that pattern is as active with others as it is with me" (p. 318).

In the Group II patient, there is generally a more disturbed infancy and childhood than in the Group I patient, and the parents are often quite disturbed themselves. Although latency is uneventful, there is "a definite lag in each phase of development." Symptoms appear in mid-adolescence, with the reemergence of old conflicts. According to Pao, "Psychoanalytically oriented intensive psychotherapy can be useful in improving [the patient's] outlook and should be recommended" (p. 24). He also recommends that the parents be involved in the treatment.

The Group III patient, on the other hand, "has had a very disturbed infancy and childhood... [and] shows distinctly defective ego functioning, noticeable from the early developmental phases on.... The family members... are usually quite disturbed" (pp. 25–26). These patients are usually withdrawn and quiet and can often be treated in the office for quite some time, but hospitalization is generally preferable.

Finally, there is the Group IV patient, who "may have begun as a schizophrenic-I, -II, or -III. After repeated hospitalizations and/or prolonged periods of confinement in an institution, however, he can no longer be designated as still belonging to the subgroup to which he was originally assigned. Being sick for many years seems to have robbed him of hope. He is now in utter despair, and resigned to sickness as a way of life" (p. 26). These are hospital-treated patients in whom the therapeutic alliance is quite fragile.

Interestingly, later in his book, when he focuses on treatment, Pao no longer takes the four groups as his frames of reference but considers whether the patient is in an acute, subacute, or chronic phase. In the acute phase, he believes one has to be concerned with the patient's lack of a sense of self-continuity, or its fluidity. The patient is in extreme terror and must be given relief. At first, then, Pao avoids interpretation. The patient is encouraged to talk — mainly to make contact. In the subacute phase, Pao stresses: "(1) helping the patient not to settle for the closure of a pathological viewpoint about himself and his object world, and (2) helping the patient to conceptualize that a symptom is a symptom, that it is related to his experience of anxiety or lack of sense of well-being, and that his anxiety or lack of well-being is rectifiable in the context of his object relations" (p. 393). With regard to the chronic phase, Pao indicates that "the patient's distorted views about himself and his object world, organized since the recent break with reality, have become solidified and are not easily modified." In this phase "the therapeutic team must make a concerted effort first to help the patient make known his wishes and then to help him fulfill them if that is possible" (p. 412), as the patient will generally not do so spontaneously.

It becomes clear that in evaluating different therapeutic approaches to the psychotic, one must look not only at the therapist's theoretical orientation, but also at the kind of patient, the stage of illness, the setting in which the therapy takes place, and the goals that have been set. Equally significant is the extent to which a therapist is willing and able to work with severely ill patients. This consideration brings us to the question of the personality of those working with patients suffering from various manifestations derived from the psychotic process.

There have been several attempts to study the personalities of psychotherapists working with severely disturbed patients. In some instances, rating scales were used, and an attempt was made to correlate the personality of the therapist with the success, or failure, of psychotherapy. James Frosch and Gunderson (1982), in surveying these studies, point out their limitations. Although cognizant of the methodological difficulties, they raise several questions they believe need to be asked: "How many years has the therapist been practicing? What fraction of the therapist's time has been spent doing psychotherapy? What fraction of the psychotherapy hours have been devoted to the treatment of patients like the subjects under study? How does he feel about working with this particular patient group? How desirable does he consider such psychotherapy? And, finally, what sort of track record of success or failure has he had in working with such patients?" (p. 6). In other words, the authors see the therapist's experience, as well as his theoretical orientation, as essential to any such evaluative effort. They also highlight the need to establish a working alliance between the therapist and the research team, and suggest means of doing so.

Fromm-Reichmann (1948), as we have seen, particularly emphasizes how the personality of the psychiatrists may affect work with psychotics. She recommends that "the therapist be trained in recognizing and controlling his own dissociated feelings and motivations and in overcoming his own insecurity, previous to working with schizophrenic patients. Many failures in the treatment of schizophrenics, due to the therapist's failure in handling his and the patient's mutual interpersonal problems adequately, could then be avoided" (p. 179). In a similar vein, Anna Freud (1954), although narrowing the scope of psychoanalytic treatment, at some point raises the question of how necessary it is in working with borderline patients to realize "that analyst and patient are also two real people of equal adult status and [in] a real formal relationship to each other."

The personality and vulnerability of the therapist are especially important considerations for those who take the primary process as a frame of reference. Eissler (1952) describes some of the necessary features in the personality of the therapist who uses this approach. To be successful in treating the acute phase, the therapist must believe in his own omnipotence, be intensely interested, have command of the whole gamut of emotionality at the level of the primary process, be unconcerned about the time spent, and be unable to accept failure. Such a person will, by implication, easily elicit primary processes and thus will succeed far better than someone whose effect on others depends on the content of verbalizations.

The therapist's personality inevitably relates to the role that the therapist fulfills for the patient. In stressing how the analyst becomes the "central love object" for some patients, particularly severely depressed ones, Jacobson (1954b) discusses how she permits these patients to use her in the ways and roles they need. She emphasizes that the therapist working with depressed patients should not be detached but rather warm by temperament. Schizophrenics, who at times need warmth and closeness and at times the opposite, may require a more distanced stance and a certain amount of strictness and discipline. (The latter is consistent with the archaic superego these patients have.) Yet, as we have seen, in contrast to Searles and others, Jacobson (1967) places limits on the therapist's revelation of his own feelings. It is also fairly clear that although she becomes quite active at certain points, here, too, there are limits. At one point she asks: "Can we avoid or do we promote such results by gratifying the patients' needs, first for stimulation of their vanishing libidinous resources, then again for an either punitive or forgiving superego figure?"

During pronounced depressive periods, she believes that therapists must be patient listeners and yet inject themselves into the situation to show their interest, especially when patients are withdrawn in their daily life. "There must be a continuous empathic tie between the analyst and his depressive patients. We must be very careful not to let empty silences grow or not to talk too long, too rapidly and too emphatically, that is, never give too much or too little" (p. 604). In addition, there must be sufficient spontaneity and flexibility to adjust to varying mood levels, with warm understanding and, especially, unwavering respect. Jacobson also discusses the analyst's spontaneous reactions both in terms of anger and positive feelings. She says that the most precarious point is the patient's temporary need for the analyst's show of power. The analyst must be prepared to respond with either a spontaneous gesture of kindness or even a brief expression of anger to carry the patient over particularly dangerous depressive stages.

Addressing himself to this issue, Des Lauriers (1962) advises:

> . . . the therapist must establish himself as the most important intruding
> factor in the life of the schizophrenic. . . . All the energies of the
> therapist must be geared to establishing, maintaining, or encouraging
> and developing "contact" between the patient and himself. The word
> "contact" is used here in its broadest sense: it includes physical, sensual,
> intellectual, affective, emotional, conative and motoric contact between
> the patient and the therapist [p. 63].

Such intensive involvement makes it imperative that those working
with psychotic patients be particularly motivated to do so. A number of
years ago I attempted to ascertain what factors led psychoanalysts to
work with psychotic patients. I contacted a number of analysts who
were extensively involved in work with psychotics, as well as many who
seemed to avoid such work. Several were quite frank in revealing significant psychopathology in their family background, as well as in themselves personally, as motivating factors in their work with psychotics.
Others gave a variety of reasons, not overtly related to personality problems. Several who did not work with psychotics indicated that such
work was not within the province of psychoanalysis. Freud, it will be
recalled, openly expressed his aversion to working with psychotics. Still
others, who accepted that this work was within the province of psychoanalysis, felt that they were personally unsuited for such work.[5]

Eissler (1952) has particularly called attention to the role of the
therapist's background in work with psychotic patients. He explains:
"It is inescapable that childhood fantasies are activated in those who
are dealing with schizophrenics in the acute phase. I believe that the
content of the early childhood fantasy, the kind and intensity of its
cathexis, are among the factors which decide whether a psychiatrist
develops the skill of successfully treating the acute phase" (p. 136). A
similar point is made by Hoedemaker (1967). He describes reactions
similar to those of Searles, in referring to a patient who deluged him
with a "cacophony from the past": "Such outpourings have driven me

[5] I recall a discussion with Ernst Kris, in which he recounted the experiences of a
prominent analyst who seemed to enjoy working with very sick patients. This analyst
had described how one of his patients went into what appeared to be a catatonic state
during a session. The analyst bent over the patient and mumbled some incantations,
accompanied by hand movements, and the patient responded. Kris said that he did
not doubt the purported effectiveness of this maneuver, but "I would have felt very
foolish in doing it."

close to despair and appeared at times to threaten my psychic organization, with the impulse to drive her from my office in a rage. . . . Is it not possible that our failures or the length of treatment with any particular schizophrenic patient are due often to the vulnerability of the therapist to the trauma of the psychotic transference upon him?" (pp. 192–193).

A troublesome question is what it is that helps such patients, and how closely this ties in with the personality of the therapist. The allegedly good results that Gertrude Schwing, for instance, achieved with very sick patients make one wonder what exactly it was in what she did that led to these results. What is the relationship between what one does and what happens? I do not question results, but rather wonder what in what was done had a direct bearing on the results. I recall an incident during the analysis of a patient when I made what I thought was a brilliant interpretation. I was mistakenly reassured in the correctness of my interpretation by an improvement in the patient's condition (generally not a reliable indicator of the correctness of an interpretation). I subsequently learned that the patient had not heard a word of what I had said. What she found gratifying was to hear the sound of my voice, which she felt was an infrequent occurrence during treatment sessions. It became clear that the sound of my voice also had many other implications for her. I had given her something.

Coming back to the question of the technique used in treating these very sick patients: Is this a technique that can be imparted to others? Is it teachable as a body of knowledge? Can anyone who is trained employ this technique? Or is a special kind of charismatic personality necessary — someone who not only uses this technique, but also imparts something by virtue of his personality that meets the needs of very sick patients?

Eissler (1952), in commenting on Schwing's work, says:

> Like a medieval saint, she released the schizophrenics from their strait-jackets, and patients who had just been howling immediately quieted down when she turned toward them. There is no doubt that some personalities have the distinguished quality of spreading a richly structured background atmosphere. Without saying or doing much they will create, by virtue of their mere appearance, a large number of associations in their partners. The effect they have on others always goes beyond what they directly say or do. It concerns a nonanalytic problem, namely what it is that in a person is responsible for an effect which is close to fascination, on others [p. 165].

We also need to ask: What is the nature of the analytic treatment of psychotic patients? Are the various modifications which Jacobson and others have introduced to be viewed as analysis, or are these modifications of analytic technique that take the work out of the framework of analysis? Some, such as Sandler, Glover, Anna Freud, and others, argue that such techniques no longer fall within the province of psychoanalysis. Others emphasize that if one approaches a patient as an analyst, with an analytic attitude, if one uses an analytic way of thinking and deals with situations in the treatment within an analytic frame of reference, then this is part and parcel of the procedure. According to some, to make a fine differentiation, to say, "At this point I am analyzing and at this point I am not; now I am functioning as an analyst, and now as a psychotherapist," is an arbitrary statement, which carries formalism to an extreme degree. These analysts suggest that their technique with these patients is an analytic one whether they sit them up or lie them down, whether they respond to them and provide something for them or not.

My question here touches on the role of psychoanalytic parameters, in Eissler's sense, and the definition of modifications and interventions, especially in the treatment of borderline patients. To give an example: A very depressed psychotic character, who was in psychoanalytic therapy, improved after I had prescribed medication. I subsequently learned that she had not taken the medication. This was subjected to analysis. I had not thought of my giving her the medication as a true analytic parameter, for I was simply trying to lift her out of her depression. As such, it was an intervention. Yet it ultimately became subtly incorporated and dealt with as an analytic parameter.

I myself lean somewhat toward the view of those who believe that the treatment of severely disturbed patients falls within the province of psychoanalysis. My own experience runs the gamut from working with markedly psychotic, hospitalized patients to seeing ambulatory psychotics in the office. Mostly I have been involved with psychotic reactions in psychotic characters during analysis or intensive psychoanalytically oriented psychotherapy. Yet, even with the grossly psychotic, hospitalized patient, my therapeutic approach has varied as the patient's condition fluctuated.

Let me once again refer to the psychotic patient I described in Chapter 4 (see p. 96). During this woman's acute delusional period, my goal was to try to establish a therapeutic relationship, and to try to understand what was going on. I saw the patient not only every day but several times a day. The staff reemphasized that I was the one to take care of her and that they were there to help me. Availability was a key factor; the patient knew that when she was most frightened and terrified I would be there. If, for some reason, I could not be there, someone working with me would be. At night, on several occasions, the staff put the patient on the phone to talk with me, although at the height of one of her delusional states, when I was the enemy, this took on a delusional aspect (she felt she was being tested).

During the florid delusional phase there were intermittent flashes of reality, during which times I could make contact with the patient at a different level. I would very actively try to get hold of the healthy part of her ego and deal with some of the delusions in an interpretive manner. For instance, she went through a period where she made many overt sexual advances to me, throwing off her clothes and inviting me to embrace her. I dealt with this quite firmly while trying, at the same time, not to let her feel that she was not good enough. During one of her rational periods she said to me, "You know, I can love you; it doesn't always have to be transference." I dealt with this in a realistic manner, pointing out the impossibility of such a relationship. She felt rejected and became hostile. I then indicated how with this reaction she could view me as the enemy, as she did during the delusion, but it was really her own sexual impulses and drives that she viewed as her enemy and this was their projection onto me. She then expressed the idea that all that was going on around her was a test situation to determine whether she was bad or good. I linked this to the fact that she felt at one point that her father was not her real father but part of an overall plot to test her for goodness or badness. I could only do this, however, during a quiescent period when I was able to reach a rational part of the ego. These periods increased with frequency and I was able to work more and more within a psychoanalytic atmosphere.

The importance of availability as a fulcrum in work with such patients could be illustrated with another patient, a psychotic character who had made a rather severe suicide attempt during a period of decompensation, and was brought to a municipal hospital in a catatonic state. I went to see her and arranged for her to be transferred to the hospital to which I was attached. I was worried about her and came in to see her on Saturday. When I subsequently came in to see her on Monday, she came running up to me and said, "The nurses said you came in on Saturday just to see me. Dr. Frosch never comes in on Saturday. Is that true?" When I confirmed this, she threw her arms around me and kissed me. Knowing my patient, I suspected there was more to the embrace than gratitude. I asked what she had thought when she embraced me. She hesitated, and I said it for her: "You felt your breasts pushing up against me and wondered if I could feel them and if I would become sexually excited." She blushed and admitted this was so. I took this occasion to weave this in with her psychotic symtomatology, and she showed considerable understanding. I am sure that my involvement in taking care of her, and my permitting her gleam of gratitude, also enabled me to deal with her psychotic behavior in an interpretive manner during her more rational periods.

It should be clear that, especially during the acute phase, most of the therapists I have mentioned operate within the patient's psychotic state. With few exceptions, they do not try to attack the delusional system through interpretations. Yet it is psychoanalytic understanding of the nature of the psychotic process in all its components that enables one to grasp and respond meaningfully to the patient, at whatever stage of the illness, whether acute or more chronic. With this understanding, decisions can be made about the feasibility of management and treatment programs. Clearly, while many of the therapeutic approaches described above deviate considerably from classical psychoanalysis, psychoanalytic theory and concepts enrich the technique used in working with severely disturbed patients. In the view of many, this is an area in which psychoanalysts should be involved.

Epilogue

What should one make of the welter of psychoanalytic contributions to the subject of psychosis? I would like to refer to what may strike one as a pessimistic note — to a remark made by Waelder (1960) after he had surveyed several contributions:

> . . . there are objections to seeing in any one of these factors the basic disturbance of *schizophrenic* psychoses. . . . All these aspects are probably relevant for psychosis but we are not sure how they all hang together, whether they all need to be present in every case, whether one of them represents the original disease process from which the others follow, or whether they are not only the psychologically unconnected debris of organic destruction. There are many clues but few secure results [pp. 207–208; my italics].

Freeman et al. (1966) acknowledge some decline of interest on the part of *psychiatrists* in the psychoanalytic contributions to the understanding of the psychoses. This, however, is not the case in the field of psychoanalysis itself, where the contributions to this area are continually abundant. Freeman et al. point out: "It is incumbent upon psychoanalysis to demonstrate how the theories and methods of psychoanalysis can be fruitfully employed in both research and therapy" (p. 2). They suggest that psychoanalysis offers a technique whereby a unique contact can be made with the patient. When this contact has been achieved, it will facilitate access to the patient's deepest subjective experiences. They add: "Psychoanalysis has a second contribution to make in providing the investigator with a theory of mental illness that is closely integrated with its general theory of mental functioning. Psychoanalysis, apart from its therapeutic aspects, offers a developmental theory of mind with an emphasis upon the emergence of differentiated mental activity from a matrix of primitive, syncretic mental processes" (p. 3).

As we examine the literature, we see that many are struggling with the same problem, albeit from different angles, and that there are many areas of agreement. Many of the criticisms one author makes of another seem to derive from a difference in the frame of reference used. In this context, I might say that as one reads the various contributions on psychosis and specifically schizophrenia, it is sometimes difficult to escape the feeling that although different terms are used, they in themselves do not add more knowledge or understanding, and that essentially they refer to the same thing. It is clear that the contributors use the language of a time-related frame of reference or, still more, the knowledge available at a given time. For instance, if we read the word "self" rather than "ego," would some of Freud's earlier contributions come closer to current theories? Would the same be true if we viewed Federn's concept of ego cathexis in terms of cathexis of the self? And taking it a step further, when we talk of primary narcissism, regression to the autoerotic state, loss of self-nonself differentiation, loss of ego boundaries, etc., are we not talking of the same psychic state? Or are we talking of coexisting, coeval psychic states, which should nonetheless be viewed as different?

How can one even speak of object relations theory as so fundamental and so separate from libido theory, or drive theory, or need theory, or whatever terms one chooses? Giving priority to one over the other is presumed to have some impact on our explanations of clinical manifestations, as well as on therapeutic frames of reference, but in actual practice I doubt if this is the case. "Good mothering" or empathy devoid of need gratification is an artificial formulation to fulfill a Procrustean need of a given theory. To separate the need for the object, for love, for empathy from instinct gratification is equally artificial.

I should like to address myself here to a methodological consideration, to which I have already alluded (see p. 105). In the attempt to broaden the scope of our understanding of specific phenomena, there has been an increasing tendency to elaborate on many features in psychic development as being central to the etiology and understanding of such phenomena. This has, for instance, brought in its wake many contributions on preoedipal and pregenital factors as crucial to clinical manifestations. Inevitably, such factors are present in everyone, since they are part and parcel of psychic development. Yet let us take, for example, certain instances in which the Oedipus complex, as the focus for a given syndrome, has been challenged because of the emphasis on earlier, preoedipal features. This debate bypasses a rather important consideration — namely, what is the organizing principle, under which rubric all these features could be subsumed and seen as contributory? It is this organizing principle that should tie together the multiple features and provide a frame of reference for the understanding of any given clinical phenomenon.

I believe that if one stands back a little to view the various opinions a bit more kaleidoscopically, one cannot escape the feeling that there is some common direction to these trends. Throughout the volume I have tried to see how the seemingly diverse contributions fit into the frames of reference I have suggested for studying the psychotic process — the nature of the danger, the methods of coping with this danger, and the specific impairments of the ego and its functions. Within these frames of reference, there appear to be two recurring themes in most of the contributions, which suggest common denominators in the psychoses. The first of these concerns phenomena related to the fate of the object and the need to preserve the love object and the self. There is a deep basic anxiety deriving from the fear of dissolution of self, accompanying self-nonself dedifferentiation. This seems to be the leitmotif in many psychoanalytic contributions to the understanding of the psychotic, and it is the frame of reference underlying many contributions on genetic and therapeutic considerations. The second theme relates to defects in ego functions, especially reality testing. Both of these areas are examined within the framework of levels of regression.

Admittedly, the problem of loss of self-nonself differentiation is most evident in contributions dealing with schizophrenia, although it is dealt with in other syndromes. Interestingly enough, Freud's phase of autoerotism and primary identification can be compared to that stage in object relations or, if you will, lack of object relations, that many more recent authors describe in the schizophrenic, albeit with varying frames of reference.

While not dealt with as widely as self-nonself dedifferentiation, it is almost self-evident that loss of reality testing means psychosis, regardless of the nature of the psychosis. It appears to represent a clear common denominator in all psychoses. Severe disturbances in self-nonself differentiation, both developmentally and in their manifestations, are coeval with severe disturbances in ego functions, among them reality testing. I should, however, reiterate that there may be severe impairment in object relations, with clinical evidence of perceptual disturbances and many other impairments, and yet reality testing may be preserved, however tenuously (see Frosch, 1970). In such cases, as I have indicated, the patient ought not to be considered *clinically* psychotic, although we are still dealing with a psychotic process.

The implications of object loss and ego function defects were examined within the context of subsequent developments in psychoanalytic thinking, or a particular contributor's views, and among the controversies generated was that between the defect and the conflict-defense schools. I have the impression that those analysts who are working with ambulatory and less sick psychotic patients may be inclined to focus on the conflict-defense aspects, which stand out more clearly in such patients. Those who work with hospitalized or severely disturbed psychotics, on the other hand, may be impressed by the defect components of the illness.

It also seems to me that the emphasis different authors give to one or the other feature may be partially occasioned by the varied pictures the psychotic presents. We see inhibition and regression in development as well as progression, differentiation side by side with dedifferentiation, regressive alterations of ego states and functions along with relatively unimpaired ones. One may also view the different psychoses in terms of unequal regression and progression in various parts of the psyche. It has been maintained, for instance, that in the paranoid and psychotic-affective disorders, one sees evidence of much higher levels of psychic development than in the deteriorated schizophrenic. The presence of an object relationship has been pointed out, as well as the fact that certain ego functions are relatively better preserved in these conditions than in schizophrenia. Some look upon these variations as representing different levels of regression or progression in development of the individual psychic structures, or even of components within these structures. In other words, as unequal manifestations of regression and progression of "id," ego, and superego. It has been suggested that the ego is relatively preserved in the paranoid and that it is the regression of the superego to a more primitive and archaic level that is unique for this condition. Others see certain ego functions relatively well preserved side by side with primitive ones.

These observations raise many challenging and important questions about the factors responsible for differences in progression and regression. What are the genetic factors that play a role in such differences? Constitutional factors, in the form of basic defects in ego potentials (which have a subsequent impact on psychic development), as well as the disruption in the development of autonomous ego functions engendered by early trauma, have been viewed by some as especially significant (see Chapter 14). Are there traumatic circumstances which can affect one set of ego functions while preserving others? Related to this is the question of the role of actual traumatic experiences in the development of psychic disturbances — a question that has recently received renewed interest. To what extent do actual, out-of-phase disruptive experiences lead not only to conflict-oriented fixations but to disruptions in the development of important ego functions, thus creating a setting for psychotic as opposed to neurotic development?

How can we continue to study these questions psychoanalytically? In addition to the interesting work being contributed by child analysts and longitudinal studies, such as Freeman's application of Anna Freud's profile to psychoses, I believe a fruitful area will be the continued study of borderline patients, with whom so many psychoanalysts are concerned today. Perhaps a productive area for exploration would be not why some people are psychotic, but why so many are not. Why is the borderline personality and psychotic character generally not grossly psychotic? Why is it that some such patients decompensate into psychosis and others do not? Further exploration of severe regressive states occurring during psychoanalysis may also be helpful. If there is such a phenomenon as a true *transference psychosis*, what are the circumstances that bring it about? Is it possible that it contains the ingredients of an infantile psychosis and may thus shed light on some of the genetic and dynamic factors in psychosis?

Psychoanalysis could contribute an attitude and a theory of mental illness, which could then be integrated with the work of research psychologists into a general theory of mental functioning, thus facilitating studies of the psychoses. In this regard, Freeman et al. (1966) point out:

> The psycho-analyst confines himself to the consulting-room and hoards away the rich clinical material which he obtains from his patients. He has not, in spite of the example of Schilder and others, recognized the value of discussing his data with colleagues in other psychiatric disciplines. This tendency is gradually being reversed. . . . Today psychoanalysis takes full cognizance of the developments which are taking place in experimental and genetic psychology, the more so because many of the findings and concepts are in line with the basic theories of psychoanalysis. . . . Such data must be available to the psycho-analytic investigator because in the psychoses it is the formal aspect of mental activity — particularly of cognition — which is disturbed [pp. 5, 12].

There are psychoanalysts, psychoanalytically trained psychologists, neurologists, and microbiologists who have been able to bridge the gap between disciplines and thus enrich psychoanalytic thinking about the psychoses.[1] We are familiar with Freud's concept of levels of regression and its relationship to Hughlings Jackson's concepts of the stratification between lower and higher levels of neurological functioning. Schilder's contributions on the body image cut across many lines — biological, psychological, social, and cultural — and in doing so borrow from and contribute extensively to psychoanalytic thinking. A challenge today would be the integration of biological studies of psychotics with basic psychoanalytic thinking. I have already called attention to the many psychoanalysts, from Freud on, who have suggested a basic somatic component in the psychoses. Jacobson (1971), in calling attention to the interrelationship of organic and psychological factors in the psychoses, says:

> This hypothesis, first of all, will act as an incentive to a sound collaboration of physiological, biological, and psychological research on the problem of psychosis. And, regarding the psychological aspects, which are our subject matter, I believe, indeed, that we can make an inroad into the psychology of psychoses only by studying the specific predisposition to these disorders and the specific structure of the psychotic conflict, defenses, and the restitution mechanisms [p. 104].

In Chapter 5, I discussed whether a sense of depletion resulting from biological factors may represent a sense of loss, and thus contribute to the drop in self-esteem so frequently seen in depression, bringing in its wake the many other psychological manifestations related to the meaning of loss and earlier loss experiences. Similar thoughts are suggested by Freud's (1917b) question about "whether an impoverishment of ego-libido directly due to toxins may not be able to produce certain forms of the disease" (p. 253). Jacobson's (1971) remarks on this subject are quite relevant:

> We may well speculate that the underlying psychosomatic processes in psychoses result in a reduction and exhaustion, or else in an insufficient reproduction, of libidinous drives, which enforces a reversal of the neutralization process and changes the absolute proportion between libido and aggression in favor of the latter. . . . Whatever sets it going, this struggle may lead eventually to a fatal libidinous impoverishment, an accumulation of sheer aggression, and a dispersion of the defused instincts in the whole self. I suspect that the "endogenous" psychosomatic

---

[1] One thinks of the contributions from the Research Center for Mental Health of New York University by David Rapaport, Robert Holt, George Klein, Leo Goldberger, and others, as well as the work of David Shakow, Philip Holzman, and still others.

phenomena in psychosis, arise with the development of such a state [pp. 228–229].

On the other hand, Waelder (1960) wonders:

> Even if the etiology of the psychoses should be proved to be mainly organic, it does not follow that each psychotic manifestation is a direct outgrowth or organic destruction of malfunctioning; some psychotic manifestations would be just that, but others could be the psychological consequences of the former. One possible relationship between organic and psychological factors could well be this: schizophrenic psychoses could be the product of understandable psychological processes not unlike those that occur in the formation of the neuroses, with the difference that, through organic destruction or malfunctioning, one factor in the chain of events — as, e.g., the libidinal attachment, or the destructiveness, or the power of self-control, or the anxiety — may be substantially changed in intensity, with completely different outcome [p. 204].

I might add that the innate defects may be in those ego functions involved in the building up of the capacity for object relations or, as Hartmann points out, in the capacity for neutralization as well as those ego functions concerned with reality. Waelder adds that "allowance must be made both for cultural impact and imminent trends, so an intricate web of relationships in brain and mind seems to require the study of both organic conditions and psychic processes in the psychoses" (p. 205).

Fisher (1966), in reporting his REM studies on dreams, also takes up the question of the integration of disciplines. He emphasizes that psychoanalytic theories can lead us to hypotheses about the workings of the central nervous system, and neurophysiological findings can have an impact on our views of psychic functioning. He quotes Miller (1965), whose lines seem an appropriate closing to our subject:

> One mystery alone remains
> Of my beloved's sleep:
> We've solved the movement of her eyes
> And why they do repeat;
> We know what brings her breath in sighs;
> We've tracked her EEG,
> The haunting doubt that still remains
> Is does she dream of me?

In the same way, we might ask: If the paranoid hallucinates, why are the voices calling him such bad names and making such derogatory remarks? Psychoanalysis tries to answer questions such as these.

APPENDIX
The Pimp Fantasy

In Chapter 4, I mentioned the role of unconscious homosexuality in the pimp fantasy (see p. 70). I should like to elaborate on this manifestation. As I stated earlier, the male may, either in fantasy or actual activity, use the female to make contact with another male. In my opinion, the woman is used as a sacrificial object to ward off attack from the male. At the same time, through her, indirect sexual contact is made with the male. In this process there is an identification with the woman.

For instance, during sexual relations, the husband of a patient would require her to relate stories in which she would meet somebody, be picked up, and have an affair. She would have to tell him all the details of the experience. He found this very exciting. She, on the other hand, used to find it burdensome and had to force herself to make up stories to please her husband. It is of interest that this patient never alluded to the "homosexuality" in her husband except during manic episodes (see my remarks on p. 70).

A 38-year-old married male patient, who was quite openly promiscuous, not only kept his wife informed of his affairs, but also urged her to have affairs, at the same time professing his love for her. When I pursued this with him, he admitted he wanted his wife to describe these proposed affairs — how she felt, what the man did, how he reacted, etc. The fantasy played a large role in his own lovemaking, and even talking about it excited him. His wife quite judiciously did not accede to his request. Interestingly, the patient also told his father about his promiscuity and enjoyed giving him the full details. According to the patient, his father seemed to enjoy these confidences, and he often wondered if this excited the father sexually.

A similar phenomenon is sometimes encountered in the analysis of male patients who recount their sexual exploits in detail. Behind this is a fantasy of arousing the analyst and in this way sharing the sexual experience. I shall describe such a patient below.

The wish to share one's female partner with another man is illustrated by Cervantes's (1605) story of the extreme attachment of two men who swore eternal friendship. One of them fell in love with a woman and married her, protesting that this would make no difference in their relationship. His friend was a bit more realistic, but the three did form a very close friendship. At some point, the husband felt it necessary to test his wife's loyalty and love, and urged his friend to make advances to her. Initially he refused, but the husband was insistent. The friend decided to lie to him and simply told him that his wife had rejected his advances. Eventually, however, the friend did indeed become interested in the wife and she reciprocated his love. The husband, although ignorant of the actual affair, continued to be interested in the details of the supposed test. It is not too difficult to recognize in this story the intense interest and attachment the husband had for his friend, as well as the latent meaning of offering his wife to his friend.

It appears that this theme, in one form or another, antedates Cervantes's story. Candaules, a king of ancient Sardis, was allegedly so enamored of his wife that he wanted others to share his passion for her beauty. He induced his favorite bodyguard, Gyges, to see her naked when she came in to the king. After much protestation at sharing his master's love for his mistress, he agreed, but was observed stealing out of the room by the queen before anything happened. It all ended badly for Candaules (see Herodotus, 450 B.C.).

One patient, during analysis, repeatedly described to me all the physical attributes of his mistress. He also discussed her every move during intercourse, how exciting she was. At some point he admitted to a recurrent fantasy that I would meet his mistress and make a pass at her. He began to speak of his jealousy, but I called attention to his multiple descriptions of her sexual virtues. I pointed out that with all the seductive details he had practically invited me to have an affair with his mistress. My comment evoked many protests but also some anxiety. What soon became clear was that these descriptions represented a way of getting close to me sexually but at the same time avoiding direct contact. By offering me his mistress, he was warding off his homosexual wishes for me and fears of sexual attack by me. Yet he was also gratifying those wishes indirectly through our "shared" experience with the same object. In a way, as I pointed out to him, he would have had his penis in the same place that I did. This wish had come up before, indirectly, in a dream (see Frosch, 1977a).

A recurrent theme in this man's analysis was the infidelity of the women in his life. His first marriage had ended in divorce, ostensibly because of his wife's extramarital affairs. Yet he had practically invited her to have these affairs. When he went off to war, he indicated to her that since he was not going to be around to watch her, she could do as she pleased. An almost parallel situation had arisen in his current marriage. Moreover, he suspected his mistress of sleeping with other men and questioned her repeatedly, wanting to know all the details, in spite of her denials. He himself took special delight in having affairs either with married women or women known to be promiscuous. While he was critical of these women, he wanted to know the details of their other affairs.

Frequently this patient alluded to the infidelity of his father, who had had multiple extramarital affairs, from one of which he had contracted gonorrhea. (The patient, with his own pecadillos, had also contracted gonorrhea.) At some point he brought up a business trip with an old friend of his. They were sleeping in the same room and he was suddenly struck by the thought: What would he do if his friend made homosexual advances to him, or something along that line? He then remembered lying in bed with his father as a child and thinking he could feel his father's erect penis pressing against his back — a rather uncomfortable sensation. It seemed clear that this patient's unconscious homosexuality was reflected in the multiple instances in which he used women to make contact with another male. It is significant that, although not grossly delusional, he showed an ongoing distrust of others which bordered on the delusional. He also had many fantasies of anal assault, both fearing and wishing this.

On a different note, it is of interest that Hartmann (1922) describes the onset of depersonalization in a man after he developed the obsession of imagining his wife having intercourse with another man. The onset of this obsession was followed by his inability to imagine this scene — or anything at all. The depersonalization started with this rejection of his voyeurism.

Eidelberg (1961) has described what he sees as the widespread existence of rape fantasies and dreams in men and women, and I have encountered these in some patients. One of my patients fantasied herself being subjected to a sexual line-up in which she was violated rectally by one man after another. In real life, however, she did not permit her husband any sort of deviation. Another patient masturbated with the fantasy of having an enema, with the water taken in causing extreme pain. When I asked her if she had ever given herself enemas in this manner, she looked at me incredulously and said, "Dr. Frosch you don't understand; I would never do anything like that."

I should like to emphasize here the extreme importance of differentiating fantasies from the actual carrying out of acts in keeping with such fantasies. It requires some fundamental alterations of the ego and its functions for such acts to take place (see Frosch, 1977b). Nonetheless, in some instances the fantasy of sharing a woman with another man as a means of making contact with the other's genitals may be lived out in actuality. McSweeny (1976), for example, reports five cases of men who had induced their wives to have affairs and had thereby achieved sexual gratification. On some occasions, the husband would select the man; on other occasions, the partner was randomly chosen. In several of these cases, the husband was actually present as a witness to the act and had intercourse immediately afterward, even using the same bed. McSweeny refers to this as triolism, where three persons participate in a series of erotic activities, with one partner watching as the other two perform. He points not only to the primal-scene material in this behavior, but also to the underlying homosexual gratification: "in effect he [the husband] and the other man meet sexually in the wife" (p. 176). Here he refers to the syndrome as the Tyndareus phenomenon.

According to the *Larousse World Mythology* (1965), Tyndareus was married to Leda.[1] Zeus came to Leda disguised as a swan. Soon after Zeus had lain with Leda, on the same night, Tyndareus entered her. Two sets of twins eventuated, one pair the offspring of Zeus and the other the offspring of Tyndareus. In suggesting that the Tyndareus myth relates to the pimp fantasy, I would underline the implied homosexual contact in the mutual entries, with the penises of both Tyndareus and Zeus occupying the same place. It is difficult to say who sought out this contact, since Zeus's proclivity to cohabitate with the wives of mortals was well known. For that matter, it seems to have been a habit of many of the gods. Wotan not infrequently roamed the earth in search of such opportunities, and was frequently successful—if he could escape the watchful eyes of Freya. Was it the unconscious homosexuality of the gods that led them to seek these experiences?

Another interesting example comes from *The Story of O* (Réage, 1954), a very controversial book which appeared in France some years ago. In this story a woman is held in bondage by her lover—a bondage she accepts as part of their love relationship. She submits to everything he demands of her. He induces her, for instance, to participate in all

---

[1] My thanks to Dr. Bernard Zuger for calling my attention to the Tyndareus myth.

kinds of sadomasochistic acts with other men. At times her lover also participates; at other times he looks on, as do some of the others. There are implications of unconscious homosexuality in the men sharing these experiences. In one instance, one man is performing painful oral sex on the woman, while another man is penetrating her rectally. At another point her lover persuades her to set up a relationship with his alleged stepbrother. She is to submit to any kind of sexual act that he demands. After several such acts (including repeated anal penetration), the woman perceptively points out that her body is only being used as a means of sexual contact between the two men. Admittedly, I am in no way able to evaluate the authenticity of the events described in this book; they may be the products of the author's very vivid imagination. But many of the incidents described contain features of unconscious homosexuality.[2]

A related point might be made about group sexual pleasure, which has been examined by Otto Sperling (1956). He reports, for instance, on two couples who had conjoint sexual intercourse, frequently exchanging partners. For Sperling's patient, one of the women, group sex became necessary for orgasm. Although she had originally been unwillingly led into these activities by her husband, she now only became sexual aroused by witnessing sexual intercourse of another couple. Eventually the husband induced her to be free with her favors for money. Sperling's interest lies in what he calls the parasitic superego, which permits patients to indulge in these perversions. He also calls attention to the scoptophilic and exhibitionistic features related to primal-scene material. Although he does not focus on unconscious homosexuality, I would suggest this was a contributing component.

I in fact had occasion to see two couples involved in switching. The curiosity and the search for something different was soon replaced by multiple comparisons of performance. Detailed reports were shared, which contributed to the sexual excitement. During intercourse with his wife, one of the husbands seemed as much interested in hearing about his male counterpart's activities as he was in his wife's current reactions. He was very much interested in what she felt, what she experienced, the detailed description of her orgasm. It was clear that part of the whole experience was an identification with the woman. (One of Schreber's fantasies concerned what it would be like to experience sex as a woman.)

I am indebted to Dr. Henry Greenbaum for his report of a middle-

[2] I am grateful to Dr. Arthur Zitrin for calling my attention to this material.

aged man, the father of three children, who came for psychoanalytic therapy because of marital difficulties. The chief cause of his difficulties was a compulsion to give his business associates his wife's telephone number for sexual purposes, and to encourage her to respond favorably to their telephone calls. When she resisted, he ridiculed her as being old-fashioned, and even displayed resentment and anger. When she finally surrendered to his demands for sexual promiscuity, he asked her to describe to him in minute detail her sexual experiences with the various men. He insisted on knowing what she felt during foreplay in the different erogenous zones, during penetration, and finally during orgasm. His identification with his wife in these experiences was quite evident. All this aroused him and led to sexual intercourse with her. During lovemaking his own feelings did not count. He was extremely attuned to his wife's emotions. He felt as if her pleasure, excitement, and orgasm were his. If she experienced displeasure or pain, he shared these feelings with her. He also masturbated with the fantasy of his wife having intercourse with other men. During the fantasy he concentrated his attention on her sexual activity and sexual excitement (see also p. 70).

Behind the wish for mutual genital contact, we occasionally encounter a more deep-seated fantasy — that the patient is in his mother's uterus while his father is having intercourse. The inserted penis is both a wish and a threat. One patient in analysis, for instance, would report in great detail his sexual activities with his mistress. When I began to pursue his motives in doing so, he recounted the following dream:

> I had a whole series of dreams last night, but one sticks in my mind. I was going down a tunnel, sort of against my will. It was like one of the sliding chutes. There is a bend in this tunnel, and as I reached this bend, a car is driving into the tunnel. It is a sports car, but at the same time, larger, like a Lincoln. The man driving it is dressed in sports clothes, but also more formally, sort of with a homberg. I continued to slide through the tunnel, against my will, and suddenly I came to the end, into the light and I awoke in a panic. My heart was pounding.

Although I will not report all the multiple associations, one related to a real incident the preceding day. The patient was driving his car out of a tunnel from the garage located underneath my office building. He saw me and fantasized, among other things, about the possibility of hitting me with the car, at the same time fearing that he too might be killed. Other associations led to fantasies relating to his mother, as well as to his resentment at the intrusion of a newborn brother and at his father's continuing contact with his mother.

This man's mother had frequently teased him about marrying her when he grew up. When I asked whether he had toyed with the idea of what it would be like to be in the vagina while his father had intercourse with his mother, he exclaimed, "Gee that's funny. When I woke from the dream, for some reason I thought of the vagina. It was kind of confusing. In one way it was like being born, but in a way, it was like being with my mother." I will not pursue the subsequent material, but it lent support to the implications in the dream of both him and his father sharing the same vagina and thus being in sexual contact. The dream also revealed the unconscious homosexual feelings toward me, which he hoped to fulfill by sharing his mistress with me.

I would like to make clear that in discussing the pimp fantasy I am not dealing with the psychology of the actual pimp. The factors in becoming a pimp are overdetermined, but I would not dismiss, as one component, the elements of the pimp fantasy I have described. I would thus like to refer to some reports on actual pimps. In some instances, it is quite clear that unconscious homosexuality was present.

James (1973) conducted a survey of the relationship between the prostitute and the pimp. For the prostitute, the pimp is a combination of husband, boyfriend, father, lover, agent, and protector. This is a role he readily accepts, especially the business part of the relationship. James views it merely as an exaggeration of the male-female relationship in the larger society. In this context, it might be appropriate to comment on the nature of the sexual relationship between the pimp and the prostitute. Some reports indicate that although they have intercourse, the prostitute does not have an orgasm. It is clear that in such instances it is not the sexual relationship that ties them together.

To illustrate the ambivalent relationship between the pimp and the prostitute, I would like to refer to the case of a 30-year-old woman who, from the age of 16 on, had a relationship with a pimp.[3] In the early years of this relationship, the two were involved in gambling, drug dealing, and prostitution. Currently the woman manages the man's various ventures, which include his pimping. She has had two children by him, although he lives in an upstairs apartment with another woman (with whom he has seven children). She admits to being very confused about the relationship and says she gets nothing out of it. She feels used and taken for granted. Yet she is unable to separate from him, although she

[3] I am indebted to Joan Feldman, Senior Psychiatric Social Worker at Brookdale, for this vignette.

has tried many times. She claims she cannot stand him and his treatment of her, and has at times wanted to kill him. Although tending to relate her difficulty in separating to the possibility of lack of economic support, it is clear that she is emotionally tied to him and seemingly held in thrall by him. This type of relationship is reportedly not uncommon between a prostitute and a pimp.

More directly related to my interest in the role of unconscious or overt homosexuality in the pimp and prostitute is a study on the life of a pimp by Hall and Adelman (1972). In this particular report, the pimp's reactions to homosexuality among his girls was quite vehement. As one of the prostitutes puts it:

> Silky [her pimp] hates girls with girls. I could be broadminded about relationships with girls if it wasn't for Silky. The problem for a pimp is his reputation. Fellows are put down who let their girls make it. Silky is threatened by a woman having love with another woman because he can't compete. He can compete with another pimp but how can be compete with a woman? All of Silky's girls have a bit of lesbianism. They need a man to prove they're not. If you're with a guy, that takes away all traces of doubt you might have about yourself. Jail sets you back because there aren't no men. I almost always get close to girls when I'm in jail [p. 141].

On one occasion, in a discussion between Silky and another pimp, the subject of homosexuality among their prostitutes comes up and leads to the analogy of homosexual relations between the two pimps. Silky reacts to both topics with marked vehemence and clearly rejects any possible relationship to the other pimp. It doesn't take too much psychoanalytic perception to discern the unconscious homosexuality in both pimps in this conversation.[4]

An even more explicit report is that by Choisy (1961). In reporting on her experience in treating actual pimps, she brings out the underlying homosexuality as an important factor. When she hinted at this to one pimp:

> He insisted again and again that he was not a "pansy." He went so far as to look for proofs. "In fact, I was once sexually excited — awfully excited — by Clairette (that's one of my girls). It happened on the night when I

[4] Prostitutes' hostility and even contempt for their customers has also been described. In some instances this relates to their homosexual preferences. Some women have the idea that sexual intercourse is humiliating for one or the other partner. Abraham (1920), in discussing penis envy, describes as one outcome the woman's vindictive wish to take revenge on the male by humiliating him. She wishes to humiliate him lest she be humiliated. Freud (1925b) points out that fantasies of being a prostitute may express both the idea of being humiliated and taking revenge for it.

stayed too late at her flat. One of her clients came in unawares. She had just time to hide me in her cupboard. I heard every little move of their love-making. It was terrific. When I was a kid I peered once through the keyhole of my parents' bedroom. But I didn't see half as many interesting things as this time. I actually heard how he moved up and down, with his penis in her, and the splashy sound it made. When he left I simply jumped on the bed and raped Clairette. That was the only time in my life I enjoyed sexual pleasure." I drew his attention to the fact that this orgasm was obtained through the instrumentality of another man. "Yes, but with a woman," he insisted sharply [p. 49].

Choisy describes another patient whose husband became very aroused when a man sitting next to her began feeling her legs and moving up to her genitals. She tried to move away, but her husband would not permit her to do so. While the man was touching her genitals, the husband put his own penis in her hand and ejaculated. He subsequently forced his wife to become a streetwalker. After these activities he was able to have orgastic intercourse with her. As he put it: "Well, you'll tell me afterward how it happened and how you satisfied your customers. You will show me all the money they gave you while I put my penis into you" (p. 37).

Choisy also takes the position that unconscious homosexuality underlies the customer's need for a prostitute: "A man, during the sexual act with a woman who has had many lovers, always partakes in some way of the forces and the fate of his predecessors. A boy who is in the habit of frequenting brothels and call girls gets mixed up with other men's forces (and we know through casework that such a boy has strong homosexual tendencies)" (pp. 116–117). She adds: "Perhaps a man does after all assimilate qualities whose origin may be in the other men who have been intimate with the same woman" (p. 130).

Freud (1910, 1912b), in discussing the choice of the degraded object, refers to the prostitute as a love object—"love for a harlot." Yet, he discusses this in the context of a split between the tender and the sensual components, which are gratified with different objects. He makes no reference to underlying homosexuality in the choice of the prostitute or the woman who is concurrently having other affairs, although he does describe one object choice in which one of the conditions for love is that the woman belong to someone else.

I would like to conclude by returning from the actual pimp to the pimp fantasy in individuals who are not pimps. This is the main focus of my presentation. I should point out that much of what I have described in the pimp fantasy is overdetermined, and many goals are achieved. The female is used to ward off attack by the male. At the same time, in this sharing of the woman, a wish for contact with the male's genitals is achieved, as well as a passive feminine identification with the woman. Although voyeuristic and primal-scene components are unquestionably present, I believe that the organizing principle — the "Dominante" (see p. 105) — in the pimp fantasy is unconscious homosexuality.

REFERENCES

Abraham, K. (1907), On the significance of sexual dreams in youth to the symptomatology of dementia praecox. In: *Clinical Papers and Essays on Psychoanalysis*. New York: Basic Books, 1955, pp. 13–20.
_____ (1908), The psychosexual difference between hysteria and dementia praecox. In: *Selected Papers on Psychoanalysis*. London: Hogarth Press, 1927, pp.
64–79.
_____ (1911), Notes on the psychoanalytic investigation and treatment of manic-
depressive insanity and allied conditions. In: *Selected Papers on Psychoanalysis*.
London: Hogarth Press, 1927, pp. 137–156.
_____ (1916), The first pregenital stage of the libido. In: *Selected Papers on Psychoanalysis*. London: Hogarth Press, 1927, pp. 248–279.
_____ (1920), Manifestations of the female castration complex. In: *Selected Papers
on Psychoanalysis*. London: Hogarth Press, 1927, pp. 338–369.
_____ (1922), The rescue and murder of the father in neurotic fantasy formations.
In: *Clinical Papers and Essays on Psychoanalysis*. New York: Basic Books, 1955,
pp. 68–75.
_____ (1924), Manic-depressive states and the pregenital levels of the libido. In:
Selected Papers on Psychoanalysis. London: Hogarth Press, 1927, pp. 418–419.
Alexander, F. & Menninger, W. C. (1936), The relation of persecutory delusions to
the function of the gastro-intestinal tract. *J. Nerv. Ment. Dis.*, 84:541–554.
American Psychiatric Association (1981), *Diagnostic and Statistical Manual, III*.
Washington, D.C.: American Psychiatric Association.
Andreyev, L. (1925), The seven that were hanged. In: *Best Russian Short Stories*.
New York: Modern Library, pp. 320–346.
Angel, K. (1965), Loss of identity and acting out. *J. Amer. Psychoanal. Assn.*,
13:79–84.
Arieti, S. (1974), *Interpretation of Schizophrenia*. New York: Basic Books.
_____ & Bemporad, J. (1974), Rare, unclassified and collective psychiatric condi-
tions: Psychose passionelle of Clérambault. In: *American Handbook of Psy-
chiatry*, 2nd Ed., ed. S. Arieti. New York: Basic Books, pp. 716–717.
Arlow, J. (1949), Anal sensation and feelings of persecution. *Psychoanal. Q.*, 18:
79–84.
_____ & Brenner, C. (1964), The psychopathology of the psychoses. In: *Psychoanalytic Concepts and the Structural Theory*. New York: International Universities Press, pp. 144–185.
_____ _____ (1969), The psychopathology of the psychoses: A proposed revision.
Int. J. Psycho-Anal., 50:5–14.
_____ _____ (1970), Discussion: The psychopathology of the psychoses: A proposed revision. *Int. J. Psycho-Anal.*, 51:159–166.
Aronson, G., Rep. (1974), Panel: The influence of the theoretical model of schizophrenia on treatment practice. *J. Amer. Psychoanal. Assn.*, 22:182–189.

Asch, S. (1971), Wrist scratching as a symptom of anhedonia: A predepressive state. *Psychoanal. Q.*, 40:603–617.

Bak, R. (1939), Regression of ego orientation and libido in schizophrenia. *Int. J. Psycho-Anal.*, 20:64–71.

———— (1943), Dissolution of ego, mannerism and delusion of grandeur. *J. Nerv. Ment. Dis.*, 98:457–468.

———— (1946), Masochism in paranoia. *Psychoanal. Q.*, 15:285–301.

———— (1954), The schizophrenic defense against aggression. *Int. J. Psycho-Anal.*, 35:129–134.

Balint, M. (1941), Reality testing during schizophrenic hallucinations. *Brit. J. Med. Psychol.*, 19:201–214.

Baumeyer, F. (1952), New insights into the life and psychosis of Schreber. *Int. J. Psycho-Anal.*, 33:262.

———— (1956), The Schreber case. *Int. J. Psycho-Anal.*, 37:61–74.

Beck, S. (1959), Schizophrenia without psychosis. *Arch. Neurol. Psychiat.*, 31:85.

———— (1965), *Psychological Processes in the Schizophrenic Adaptation*. New York: Grune & Stratton.

Bellak, L. (1958), *Schizophrenia: A Review of the Syndrome*. New York: Logos Press.

Bender, L. (1934), Anal component in persecutory delusions. *Psychoanal. Rev.*, 21: 75–85.

———— (1952), *Child Psychiatric Techniques*. Springfield, Ill.: Thomas.

———— (1954), *A Dynamic Psychopathology of Childhood*. Springfield, Ill.: Thomas.

Benedek, T. (1938), Adaptation to reality in early infancy. *Psychoanal. Q.*, 7: 200–214.

Benjamin, J. D. (1961), The innate and experiential in child development. In: *Lectures on Experiential Psychology*, ed. H. W. Brosin. Pittsburgh: University of Pittsburgh Press, pp. 19–42.

———— (1965), A developmental biology and psychoanalysis. In: *Psychoanalysis and Current Biological Thought*, ed. N. S. Greenfield & W. C. Lewis. Madison: University of Wisconsin Press, pp. 57–80.

———— (1972), In: The stimulus barrier in early infancy [by K. Tennes et al.]. *Psychoanalysis and Contemporary Science*, Vol. 1, ed. R. R. Holt & E. Peterfreund. New York: Macmillan, pp. 204–234.

Bennett, A. (1910), *Clayhanger*. Baltimore: Penguin Books, 1976.

Beres, D. (1956), Ego derivatives and the concept of schizophrenia. *Psychoanal. Study Child*, 11:164–235..

Bergman, P. & Escalona, S. (1949), Unusual sensitivities in very young children. *Psychoanal. Study Child*, 3/4:333–352.

Bibring, E. (1947), The so-called English school of psychoanalysis. *Psychoanal. Q.*, 16:69–93.

———— (1953), The mechanism of depression: In: *Affective Disorders*, ed. P. Greenacre. New York: International Universities Press.

Bion, W. R. (1957), Differentiation of the psychotic from the non-psychotic personalities. *Int. J. Psycho-Anal.*, 38:266–275.

———— (1959), *Experiences in Groups*. New York: Basic Books.

———— (1967), *Second Thoughts: Selected Papers on Psychoanalysis*. London: Heinemann.

Bleuler, E. (1906), *Affectivity, Suggestibility, Paranoia*. Utica, N.Y.: State Hospitals Press, 1912.

———— (1911), *Dementia Praecox or the Group of Schizophrenias*, trans. J. Zerbin,

New York: International Universities Press, 1950.

⸻ (1913), Criticism of Freud's theories. *Allgemeine Zeitschr. Psychiat.*, 70: 665–719.

⸻ (1916), *Textbook of Psychiatry*, trans. A. A. Brill. New York: Macmillan, 1924.

Blum, H. (1974), The borderline childhood of the Wolf Man. *J. Amer. Psychoanal. Assn.*, 22:721–742.

⸻ (1980), Paranoid and beating fantasies: An inquiry into the psychoanalytic theory of paranoia. *J. Amer. Psychoanal. Assn.*, 28:331–361.

Boyer, L. B. & Giovacchini, P. L., Eds. (1967), *Psychoanalytic Treatment of Characterological and Schizophrenic Disorders*. New York: Science House.

Brenner, C. (1980), The nature, classification and the sources of drives. Presented at meetings of American Psychoanalytic Association, December.

Brody, E. B. (1960), Borderline state, character disorder and psychotic manifestations: Some conceptual formulations. *Psychiat.*, 23:75–80.

⸻ (1961), Freud's theory of psychoses and the role of the psychotherapist. *J. Nerv. Ment. Dis.*, 133:36–45.

Brunswick, R. M. (1928), A supplement to Freud's "History of an infantile neurosis." In: *The Wolf Man by the Wolf Man*, ed. M. Gardiner, New York: Basic Books, 1971.

⸻ (1930), Reply to Harnik's critical remarks. *Int. Z. Psychoanal.*, 16:128–129.

Campell, M. (1926), *Delusion and Belief*. Cambridge: Harvard University Press.

Campion, J. (1981), Matricide·in schizophrenics. (Unpublished.)

Cancro, R. (1976), Comprehensive therapy of the schizophrenic syndrome. In: *Current Psychiatric Therapies*, 16:91–100.

⸻ (1979a), Genetic evidence for the existence of subgroups of the schizophrenic syndrome: *Schiz. Bull.*, 5(3):453–459.

⸻ (1979b), The genetic studies of the schizophrenic syndrome. A review of their clinical implications. In: *Disorders of the Schizophrenic Syndrome*, ed. L. Bellak. New York: Basic Books, pp. 136–151.

Cervantes, M. de (1605), The tale of foolish curiosity. In: *Great Spanish Stories*, ed. A. Flores, New York: Dell, 1962, pp. 40–80.

Choisy, M. (1961), *Psychoanalysis of the Prostitute*. New York: Philosophical Library.

Dansky, E. (1970), Reality testing. In: *Basic Psychoanalytic Concepts on Metapsychology*, Vol. 4, ed. H. Nagera. New York: Basic Books, pp. 156–167.

Deri, F. & Brunswick, D. (1964), Freud's letters to Ernst Simmel. *J. Amer. Psychoanal. Assn.*, 12:93–109.

Des Lauriers, A. M. (1962), *The Experience of Reality in Childhood Schizophrenia*. New York: International Universities Press.

De Souza, D. S. (1960), Annihilation and reconstruction of object relationship in a schizophrenic girl. *Int. J. Psycho-Anal.*, 41:554–558.

Diatkine, R. (1960), Reflections on the genesis of psychotic object relationships in the young child. *Int. J. Psycho-Anal.*, 41:544–547.

Dorpat, T. (1977), Depressive affect. *Psychoanal. Study Child*, 32:3–27.

Durkheim, E. (1897), *Suicide*. Glencoe, Ill.: Free Press, 1951.

Durrell, L. (1958), *Mountolive*. New York: Dutton, 1959.

Eidelberg, L. (1954), *An Outline of Comparative Pathology of the Neuroses*. New York: International Universities Press.

⸻ (1959a), The concept of narcissistic mortification. *Int. J. Psycho-Anal.*, 40:163–168.

⸻ (1959b), Humiliation in masochism. *J. Amer. Psychoanal. Assn.*, 7:

274–283.

———— (1959c), A second contribution to the study of the narcissistic mortification. *Psychiat. Q.*, 33:636–646.

———— (1961), *The Dark Urge*. New York: Pyramid Books.

Eissler, K. (1951), Remarks on the psychoanalysis of schizophrenia. *Int. J. Psycho-Anal.*, 32:139–156.

———— (1952), Remarks on the psychoanalysis of schizophrenia. In: *Psychotherapy with Schizophrenics*, ed. E. B. Brody & F. C. Redlich. New York: International Universities Press, pp. 130–167.

———— (1953), Notes upon the emotionality of a schizophrenic patient and its relation to problems of technique. *Psychoanal. Study Child*, 8:199–254.

———— (1954), Notes upon defects of ego structure in schizophrenia. *Int. J. Psycho-Anal.*, 35:141–146.

Elkisch, P. & Mahler, M. (1959), On infantile precursors of the "influencing machine." *Psychoanal. Study Child*, 14:219–235.

Engel, G. & Schmale, A. (1967), Psychoanalytic theory of somatic disorder: Conversion, specificity, and the disease onset situation. *J. Amer. Psychoanal. Assn.*, 15:344–365.

Fairbairn, W. R. (1941). A revised psychopathology of the psychoses and the psychoneuroses. *Int. J. Psycho-Anal.*, 22:250–279.

———— (1946), Object relations and dynamic structure. *Int. J. Psycho-Anal.*, 27:30–37.

———— (1954), *An Object-Relations Theory of the Personality*. New York: Basic Books.

———— (1956), Considerations arising out of the Schreber case. *Brit. J. Med. Psychol.*, 29:113–127.

———— (1963), Synopsis of an object-relations theory of the personality. *Int. J. Psycho-Anal.*, 44:224–225.

Federn, P. (1928), Narcissism in the structure of the ego. In: *Ego Psychology and the Psychoses*, ed. E. Weiss. New York: Basic Books, 1952, pp. 38–59.

———— (1932), Ego feeling in dreams. In: *Ego Psychology and the Psychoses*, ed. E. Weiss. New York: Basic Books, 1952, pp. 60–89.

———— (1943), Psychoanalysis of psychoses. In: *Ego Psychology and the Psychoses*, ed. E. Weiss. New York: Basic Books, 1952, pp. 117–165.

———— (1949), Depersonalization. In: *Ego Psychology and the Psychoses*, ed. E. Weiss. New York: Basic Books, 1952, pp. 241–260.

———— (1952), Psychoanalysis of psychoses. In: *Ego Psychology and the Psychoses*, ed. E. Weiss. New York: Basic Books, 1952, pp. 117–165.

Fenichel, O. (1931), Respiratory introjection. In: *Collected Papers*, 1:221–240. New York: Norton, 1933.

———— (1937), Early stages of ego development. In: *Collected Papers*, 2:25–48. New York: Norton, 1954.

———— (1945), *The Psychoanalytic Theory of Neurosis*. New York: Norton.

Ferenczi, S. (1911), Stimulation of the anal erotogenic zone as a precipitating factor in paranoia. In: *Final Contributions to the Methods and Problems of Psychoanalysis*. New York: Basic Books, 1955, pp. 295–298.

———— (1912a), On onanism. In: *Sex in Psychoanalysis*. Boston: Badger, 1916, pp. 185–192.

———— (1912b), On the part played by homosexuality in the pathogenesis of paranoia. In: *Sex in Psychoanalysis*. Boston: Badger, 1916, pp. 154–184.

———— (1913), Stages in the development of the sense of reality. In: *Sex in Psychoanalysis*. Boston: Badger, 1916, pp. 213–239.

_____ (1916–1917), *Disease or Pathoneurosis Theory and Technique of Psychoanalysis*. New York: Boni & Liveright, 1927.

_____ (1919), The phenomena of hysterical materialization. In: *Further Contributions to the Theory and Technique of Psychoanalysis*. New York: Boni & Liveright, 1927, pp. 89–104.

_____ (1921), Psychoanalytic observations on tic. In: *Further Contributions to the Theory and Technique of Psychoanalysis*. New York: Boni & Liveright, 1927, pp. 142–174.

_____ (1926), The problem of acceptance of unpleasant ideas: Advance in knowledge of the sense of reality. In: *Further Contributions to the Theory and Technique of Psychoanalysis*. New York: Boni & Liveright, 1927, pp. 366–379.

_____ (1930), Autoplastic and alloplastic. In: *Final Contributions to the Problems and Methods of Psychoanalysis*. New York: Basic Books, 1955, p. 221.

_____ (1933), The confusion of tongues between adults and the child. In: *Final Contributions to the Problems and Methods in Psychoanalysis*. New York: Basic Books, 1955, pp. 156–167.

_____ & Hollós, J. (1922), Psychoanalysis and the mental disorders of general paresis. In: *Final Contributions to the Problems and Methods of Psychoanalysis*. New York: Basic Books, 1955, pp. 351–370.

Fisher, C. (1953), Studies on the nature of suggestion. *J. Amer. Psychoanal. Assn.*, 1:222–255.

_____ (1966), Dreams and Sexuality. In: *Psychoanalysis: A General Psychology*, ed. R. M. Loewenstein et al. New York: International Universities Press, pp. 537–569.

_____ & Dement, W. (1961), Dreaming and psychosis: Observations on the dream sleep cycle during the course of an acute paranoid psychosis. *Bull. Phila. Assn. Psychoanal.*, 11:130.

_____ _____ (1963), Studies on the psychopathology of sleep and dreams. *Amer. J. Psychiat.*, 119:1160.

Freedman, A. (1962, 1964), Report: The nature of the psychotic process. Workshop held at meeting of the American Psychoanalytic Association, December 7, 1962. (Unpublished.)

Freeman, T. (1959), Aspects of defence in neurosis and psychosis. *Int. J. Psycho-Anal.*, 40:199–212.

_____ (1963), The concept of narcissism in schizophrenic states. *Int. J. Psycho-Anal.*, 44:293–303.

_____ (1969), *Psychopathology of the Psychoses*. New York: International Universities Press.

_____ (1970), The psychopathology of the psychoses: A reply to Arlow and Brenner. *Int. J. Psycho-Anal.*, 51:407–415.

_____ (1973), *A Psychoanalytic Study of the Psychoses*. New York: International Universities Press.

_____ (1977), On Freud's theory of schizophrenia. *Int. J. Psycho-Anal.*, 58:383–388.

_____ Cameron, J. L. & McGhie, A. (1966), *Studies on Psychoses*. New York: International Universities Press.

Freud, A. (1936), *The Ego and the Mechanisms of Defense*. New York: International Universities Press, 1946.

_____ (1952), A connection between the states of negativism and of emotional surrender [Abst.]. *Int. J. Psycho-Anal.*, 33:265–266.

_____ (1954), The widening scope of indications for psychoanalysis: Discussion. *J. Amer. Psychoanal. Assn.*, 2:607–620.

_____ (1963), The concept of developmental lines. *Psychoanal. Study Child*, 18: 246–265.

_____ (1965), *Normality and Pathology in Childhood*. New York: International Universities Press.

Freud, S. (1873–1939), *Letters of Sigmund Freud*, ed. E. Freud. New York: Basic Books, 1960.

_____ (1887–1902), *The Origins of Psychoanalysis: Letters to Wilhelm Fliess, Drafts and Notes*, ed. M. Bonaparte, A. Freud, & E. Kris. New York: Basic Books, 1954.

_____ (1891), *On Aphasia*. New York: International Universities Press, 1953.

_____ (1894), The neuro-psychoses of defence. *Standard Edition*, 3:45–61. London: Hogarth Press, 1962.

_____ (1895a), Draft H: Paranoia. *Standard Edition*, 1:206–212. London: Hogarth Press, 1966.

_____ (1895b), Project for a scientific psychology. *Standard Edition*, 1:295–343. London: Hogarth Press, 1966.

_____ (1896), Further remarks on the neuro-psychoses of defence. *Standard Edition*, 3:158–188. London: Hogarth Press, 1962.

_____ (1897), Draft N: Impulses. In: *The Origins of Psychoanalysis*. New York: Basic Books, 1954, p. 207.

_____ (1900), The interpretation of dreams. *Standard Edition*, 4 & 5. London: Hogarth Press, 1953.

_____ (1907), Delusions and dreams in Jensen's *Gradiva*. *Standard Edition*, 9:7–95. London: Hogarth Press, 1959.

_____ (1908), Letter to Sandor Ferenczi. In: *The Life and Work of Sigmund Freud*, Vol. 2, by E. Jones. New York: Basic Books, 1955, p. 418.

_____ (1910), A special type of choice of object made by men (Contributions to the psychology of love, I). *Standard Edition*, 11:163–176. London: Hogarth Press, 1957.

_____ (1911a), Formulations on the two principles of mental functioning. *Standard Edition*, 12:218–226. London: Hogarth Press, 1958.

_____ (1911b) Psycho-analytic notes on an autobiographical account of a case of paranoia (dementia paranoides). *Standard Edition*, 12:3–82. London: Hogarth Press, 1958.

_____ (1912a), Types of onset of neurosis. *Standard Edition*, 12:227–238. London: Hogarth Press, 1958.

_____ (1912b), On the universal tendency to debasement in the sphere of love (Contributions to the psychology of love, II). *Standard Edition*, 11:177–190. London: Hogarth Press, 1957.

_____ (1913a), The disposition to obsessional neurosis. *Standard Edition*, 12: 311–326. London: Hogarth Press, 1958.

_____ (1913b), Letter to Sandor Ferenczi. In: *The Life and Work of Sigmund Freud*, Vol. 2, by E. Jones. New York: Basic Books, 1955, p. 455.

_____ (1914a), On narcissism: An introduction. *Standard Edition*, 14:67–104. London: Hogarth Press, 1957.

_____ (1914b), Remembering, repeating and working-through (Further recommendations on the technique of psycho-analysis, II). *Standard Edition*, 12:145–156. London: Hogarth Press, 1958.

_____ (1915a), A case of paranoia running counter to the psycho-analytic theory of the disease. *Standard Edition*, 14:261–272. London: Hogarth Press, 1957.

_____ (1915b), Instincts and their vicissitudes. *Standard Edition*, 14:109–140.

London: Hogarth Press, 1957.

_____ (1915c), Repression. *Standard Edition*, 14:146–158. London: Hogarth Press, 1957.

_____ (1915d), The unconscious. *Standard Edition*, 14:159–216. London: Hogarth Press, 1957.

_____ (1916–1917), Introductory lectures on psycho-analysis. *Standard Edition*, 15 & 16. London: Hogarth Press, 1963.

_____ (1917a), A metapsychological supplement to the theory of dreams. *Standard Edition*, 14:222–235. London: Hogarth Press, 1957.

_____ (1917b), Mourning and Melancholia. *Standard Edition*, 14:237–258. London: Hogarth Press, 1957.

_____ (1919), A child is being beaten: A contribution to the study of the origins of sexual perversions. *Standard Edition*, 17:175–204. London: Hogarth Press, 1955.

_____ (1920), Beyond the pleasure principle. *Standard Edition*, 18: 3–64. London: Hogarth Press, 1955.

_____ (1921), Group psychology and the analysis of the ego. *Standard Edition*, 18:67–143. London: Hogarth Press, 1955.

_____ (1922), Some neurotic mechanisms in jealousy, paranoia and homosexuality. *Standard Edition*, 18:221–232. London: Hogarth Press, 1955.

_____ (1923), The ego and the id. *Standard Edition*, 19:3–66. London: Hogarth Press, 1961.

_____ (1924a), The loss of reality in neurosis and psychosis. *Standard Edition*, 19:183–187. London: Hogarth Press, 1961.

_____ (1924b), Neurosis and psychosis. *Standard Edition*, 19:149–158. London: Hogarth Press, 1961.

_____ (1925a), Negation. *Standard Edition*, 19:235–239. London: Hogarth Press, 1961.

_____ (1925b), Some psychical consequences of the anatomical distinction between the sexes. *Standard Edition*, 19:248–258. London: Hogarth Press, 1961.

_____ (1926), Inhibitions, symptoms and anxiety. *Standard Edition*, 20:77–124. London: Hogarth Press, 1959.

_____ (1927), Fetishism. *Standard Edition*, 21:149–157. London: Hogarth Press, 1961.

_____ (1930), Civilization and its discontents. *Standard Edition*, 21:59–151. London: Hogarth Press, 1961.

_____ (1933), New introductory lectures on psycho-analysis. *Standard Edition*, 22:3–182. London: Hogarth Press, 1964.

_____ (1936), A disturbance of memory on the Acropolis. *Standard Edition*, 22:239–248. London: Hogarth Press, 1964.

_____ (1937), Constructions in analysis. *Standard Edition*, 23:255–269. London: Hogarth Press, 1964.

_____ (1938), Splitting of the ego in the process of defence. *Standard Edition*, 23:271–278. London: Hogarth Press, 1964.

_____ (1940), An outline of psycho-analysis. *Standard Edition*, 23:141–208. London: Hogarth Press, 1964.

Friedman, P., Ed. (1967), *On Suicide*. New York: International Universities Press.

Fries, M. E. (1937), Factors in character development, neuroses, psychoses and delinquency. *Amer. J. Orthopsychiat.*, 7:142–181.

_____ (1977a), Longitudinal study — prenatal period to parenthood. *J. Amer. Psychoanal. Assn.*, 25:115–140.

_____ (1977b), Patients with archaic ego. Presented to psychiatric section of Westchester Medical Society, September.

_____ & Woolf, P. J. (1953), Some hypotheses on the role of the congenital activity type in personality development. *Psychoanal. Study Child*, 8:48–62.

Fromm-Reichmann, F. (1948), Notes on the development of treatment of schizophrenia by psychoanalytic psychotherapy. *J. Psychiat.*, 11:263–273.

_____ (1950a), *Principles of Intensive Psychotherapy*. Chicago: University of Chicago Press.

_____ (1950b), Provocation and manifestations of anxiety in schizophrenia: Panel discussion. *Bull. Amer. Psychoanal. Assn.*, 6:37–42.

_____ (1959), *Psychoanalysis and Psychotherapy: Selected Papers*. Chicago: University of Chicago Press.

Frosch, James P. & Gunderson, J. G. (1982), Studying therapists: Problems and proposals. (Unpublished.)

Frosch, John (1959), Transference derivatives of the family romance. *J. Amer. Psychoanal. Assn.*, 7:503–522.

_____ (1964), The psychotic character: Clinical psychiatric considerations. *Psychiat. Q.*, 38:81–96.

_____ (1966), A note on reality constancy. In: *Psychoanalysis — A General Psychology*, ed. R. M. Loewenstein et al. New York: International Universities Press, pp. 349–376.

_____ (1967a), Delusional fixity, sense of conviction, and the psychotic conflict. *Int. J. Psycho-Anal.*, 48:475–495.

_____ (1967b), Severe regressive states during analysis: Introduction and summary. *J. Amer. Psychoanal Assn.*, 15:491–507, 606–623.

_____ (1970), Psychoanalytic considerations of the psychotic character. J. Amer. Psychoanal. Assn., 18:24–50.

_____ (1973), Technique in regard to some specific ego defects in the treatment of borderline patients. *Psychiat. Q.*, 45:1–5.

_____ (1976), Psychoanalytic contributions to the relationship between dreams and psychosis: A critical survey. *Int. J. Psychoanal. Psychother.*, 5:39–63.

_____ (1977a), The mourning ruminative state — the flash phenomenon. *Int. J. Psycho-Anal.*, 58:301–309.

_____ (1977b), The relation between acting out and disorders of impulsive control. *Psychiat.*, 30:295–313.

_____ (1978), Emotional health and emotional illness. Presented to New York Psychiatric Society.

_____ (1981a), Neurosis and psychosis. In: *The Course of Life, Vol. III: Adulthood and the Aging Process*, ed. S. I. Greenspan & G. H. Pollock. Washington, D.C.: National Institute of Mental Health.

_____ (1981b), The role of unconscious homosexuality in the paranoid constellation. *Psychoanal. Q.*, 50:587–613.

Frosch, T. R. (1974), *The Awakening of Albion: The Renovation of the Body in the Poetry of William Blake*. Ithaca: Cornell University Press.

Fuchs, S. H. (1937), On introjection. *Int. J. Psycho-Anal.*, 18:269–293.

Furst, S. (1978), The stimulus barrier and the pathogenicity of trauma. *Int. J. Psycho-Anal.*, 59:345–375.

Gilbert, G. M. (1948), Hermann Goering: Amiable psychopath. *J. Abnorm. Soc. Psychol.*, 43:211–229.

Ginsberg, G. (1979), Psychoanalytic aspects of mania. In: *Manic Illnesses*, ed. B. Shopsin. New York: Raven Press, pp. 1–10.

Glover, E. (1925), The neurotic character. In: *On the Early Development of Mind*. New York: International Universities Press, 1956, pp. 47–66.

_____ (1932a), Medico-psychological aspects of normality. In: *On the Early Development of Mind*. New York: International Universities Press, 1956, pp. 235–251.

_____ (1932b), A psychoanalytic approach to the classification of mental disorders. In: *On the Early Development of Mind*. New York: International Universities Press, 1956, pp. 161–186.

_____ (1932c), The relation of perversion formation to the development of reality sense. In: *On the Early Development of Mind*. New York: International Universities Press, 1956, pp. 216–234.

_____ (1939), *Psychoanalysis*, 2nd Ed. New York: Staples Press, 1949.

_____ (1943), The psychopathology of prostitution. In: *The Roots of Crime*. International Universities Press, 1960, pp. 244–267.

_____ (1945), Examination of the Klein system of psychology. *Psychoanal. Study Child*, 1:25–118.

_____ (1958), Ego-distortion. *Int. J. Psycho-Anal.*, 39:260–264.

Goethe, J. W. von (1795), *Wilhelm Meister's Apprenticeship*. New York: Heritage Press, 1959.

Goldfarb, W. (1963). Self-awareness in schizophrenic children. *Arch. Gen. Psychiat.*, 8:47–60.

Gombrich, E. H. (1966), Freud's aesthetics. *Encounter*, 22(1):30–40.

Grauer, D. (1955), Homosexuality of the paranoid psychosis as related to the concept of narcissism. *Psychoanal. Q.*, 24:516–526.

Greenacre, P. (1941), The predisposition to anxiety. *Psychoanal. Q.*, 10:66–94, 610–638.

_____ (1952), *Trauma, Growth and Personality*. New York: International Universities Press.

_____ (1954), Problems of infantile neurosis: A discussion. *Psychoanal. Study Child*, 9:18–24.

Greenblatt, M. (1975), Foreword. In: *Borderline States in Psychiatry*, ed. J. Mack. New York: Crune & Stratton.

Greenspan, J. & Myers, J. (1961), A review of the theoretical concepts of paranoid delusions with special reference to women. *Penn. Psychiat. Q.*, 1:11–28.

Grinberg, L. et al. (1977), *Introduction to the Work of Bion*. New York: Aronson.

Grotstein, J. S. (1977), The psychoanalytic concept of schizophrenia: I. The dilemma; II. Reconciliation. *Int. J. Psycho-Anal.*, 58:403–452.

Guntrip, H. (1961), *Personality Structure and Human Interaction*. New York: International Universities Press.

_____ (1969), *Schizoid Phenomena, Object Relations and the Self*. New York: International Universities Press.

Hall, S. & Adelman, B. (1972), *Gentleman of Leisure: A Year in the Life of a Pimp*. New York: New American Library.

Hammet, V. B. O. (1961), Delusional transference. *Amer. J. Psychiat.*, 15:574–581.

Harnik, J. (1930), Kritisches über Mack Brunswicks Nachtrag zu Freuds "Geschichte einer infantilen Neurose." *Int. Z. Psychoanal.*, 16:112–117.

_____ (1931), Erwiderung auf Mack Brunswicks Entgegnung. *Int. Z. Psychoanal.*, 17:400–402.

Hartmann, E. (1967), *The Biology of Dreaming*. Springfield, Ill.: Thomas.

_____ (1979), Sleep dream research: The nightmare, ego boundaries and schizophrenia. Presented to discussion group at meeting of International Psycho-Analytical Association, July.

Hartmann, H. (1922), Ein Fall von Depersonalization. *Z. Gesam. Neurol.*, 74:593.

_____ (1939a), *Ego Psychology and the Problem of Adaptation*. New York: International Universities Press, 1958.

_____ (1939b), Psychoanalysis and the concept of health. *Int. J. Psycho-Anal.*, 20:308–321.

_____ (1947), Rational and irrational action. In:*Psychoanalysis and the Social Sciences*, ed. G. Róheim. New York: International Universities Press, pp. 359–392.

_____ (1950), Psychoanalysis and developmental psychology. In: *Essays on Ego Psychology*. New York: International Universities Press, 1964, pp. 99–112.

_____ (1951), Discussion of paper "On the development of Freud's concept of the attempt at restitution" by M. Katan [Abst.]. *Psychoanal. Q.*, 20:505–506.

_____ (1952), The mutual influences in the development of ego and id. *Psychoanal. Study Child*, 7:9–30.

_____ (1953), The metapsychology of schizophrenia. *Psychoanal. Study Child*, 8: 177–198.

_____ (1956), Notes on the reality principle. *Psychoanal. Study Child*, 11:31–53.

_____ & Betlheim, S. (1924), On parapraxes in the Korsakoff psychosis. In: *Essays on Ego Psychology*. New York: International Universities Press, 1964, pp. 354–388.

_____ & Kris, E. (1945), The genetic approach in psychoanalysis. *Psychoanal. Study Child*, 1:11–31.

_____ _____ & Loewenstein, R. M. (1946), Comments on the formation of psychic structure. *Psychoanal. Study Child*, 2:11–38.

_____ & Loewenstein, R. M. (1962), Notes on the superego. *Psychoanal. Study Child*, 17:42–81.

Hendin, H. (1969), *Black Suicide*. New York: Basic Books.

Herodotus (450 B.C.), *Histories*, Book I. New York: Heritage Press, 1958.

Hinsie, L. E. & Campbell, R. J. (1970), *Psychiatric Dictionary*. New York: Oxford University Press.

Hoedemaker, E. D. (1967), The psychotic identification in schizophrenia. In: *Psychoanalytic Treatment of Characterological and Schizophrenic Disorders*, ed. L. B. Boyer & P. L. Giovacchini. New York: Science House, pp. 189–207.

Hollós, J. (1928), *Behind the Yellow Wall*. Stuttgart: Hippokrates.

Holt, R. & Goldberger, L. (1959), Personological correlates of reactions to perceptual isolation. *USAF Wright Air Devel. Ctr. Tech. Rep.*, 59-737:1–46.

Holzman, P. & Ekstein, R. (1959), Repetition functions of transitory regressive thinking. *Psychoanal. Q.*, 28:228–235.

Hurvich, M. (1970), On the concept of reality testing. *Int. J. Psycho-Anal.*, 51:229–311.

Isaacs, S. (1946), *Social Development in Young Children*. London: Routledge & Sons.

Jacobson, E. (1953), Contribution to the metapsychology of cyclothymic depression. In: *Affective Disorders*, ed. P. Greenacre, New York: International Universities Press, pp. 49–83.

_____ (1954a), Contribution to the metapsychology of psychotic identifications. *J. Amer. Psychoanal. Assn.*, 2:239–262.

_____ (1954b), Transference problems in the psychoanalytic treatment of severely depressed patients. *J. Amer. Psychoanal. Assn.*, 2:595–606.

_____ (1957), Denial and repression. *J. Amer. Psychoanal. Assn.*, 5:61–92.

_____ (1959), Depersonalization, *J. Amer. Psychoanal. Assn.*, 7:581–610.

_____ (1964), *The Self and the Object World*. New York: International Universities Press.

_____ (1967), *Psychotic Conflict and Reality*. New York: International Universities Press.

_____ (1967), *Psychotic Conflict and Reality*. New York: International Universities Press.

_____ (1971), *Depression: Comparative Studies of Normal, Neurotic, and Psychotic Conditions*. New York: International Universities Press.

James, H. (1881), *Portrait of a Lady*. Boston: Houghton Mifflin, 1963.

James, J. (1973), Prostitute. *Med. Aspects Human Sex.*, 7:147–163.

Janet, P. (1906), *The Major Symptoms of Hysteria*. New York: Macmillan, 1929.

Jensen, V. W. & Petty, T. A. (1958), The fantasy of being rescued in suicide. *Psychoanal. Q.*, 27:327–339.

Jones, E. (1955), *The Life and Work of Sigmund Freud*. New York: Basic Books.

Jung, C. G. (1909), *The Psychology of Dementia Praecox*. Washington, D.C.: Nervous & Mental Disease Monographs.

Kafka, J. S. (1977), On reality: An examination of object constancy, ambiguity, paradox and time. In: *Psychiatry and the Humanities*, 2:133–158. New Haven: Yale University Press.

Kanzer, M. (1964). Freud's use of the terms autoerotism and narcissism. *J. Amer. Psychoanal. Assn.*, 12:529–539.

_____ (1979), Object relations theory: An introduction. *J. Amer. Psychoanal. Assn.*, 27:313–325.

Katan, M. (1949), Schreber's delusion of the end of the world. *Psychoanal. Q.*, 18:60–66.

_____ (1950), Structural aspects of a case of schizophrenia. *Psychoanal. Study Child*, 5:115–211.

_____ (1951), On the development of Freud's conception of the attempt at restitution. Presented to New York Psychoanalytic Society, February 27. (Abstracted by J. Lander, *Psychoanal. Q.*, 20:505–506.)

_____ (1954), The non-psychotic part of the personality in schizophrenia. *Int. J. Psycho-Anal.*, 35:119–128.

_____ (1960), Dreams and psychosis: Their relationship to hallucinatory processes. *Int. J. Psycho-Anal.*, 41:341–351.

Kernberg, O. (1967), Borderline personality organization. *J. Amer. Psychoanal. Assn.*, 15:641–685.

_____ (1969), A contribution to the ego psychological critique of the Kleinian school. *Int. J. Psycho-Anal.*, 50:310–333.

_____ (1975a), *Borderline conditions and pathological narcissism*. New York: Aronson.

_____ (1975b), Transference and countertransference in the treatment of borderline patients. *J. Natl. Assn. Priv. Psychiat. Hosp.*, 7:14–24.

_____ (1976a), *Object Relations Theory and Clinical Psychoanalysis*. New York: Aronson.

_____ (1976b), Technical considerations in the treatment of borderline personality organization. *J. Amer. Psychoanal. Assn.*, 24:795–830.

_____ (1980), The object relations theory of W. Ronald D. Fairbairn. *Bull. Assn. Psychoanal. Med.*, 19:131–135.

Kety, S. (1959), Behavioral theories of schizophrenia. *Science*, 29:3362–3363.

Khan, M. M. R. (1963), Ego ideal, excitement and the threat of annihilation. *J. Hillside Hosp.*, 12:195–217.

Klaf, F. (1961), Female homosexuality and paranoid schizophrenia. *Arch. Gen. Psychiat.*, 4:84–86.

Klein, G. (1959), Consciousness in psychoanalytic theory. *J. Amer. Psychoanal. Assn.*, 7:5–34.

Klein, H. & Horowitz, W. (1949), Psychosexual factors in the paranoid phenomenon. *Amer. J. Psychiat.*, 105:697–701.

Klein, M. (1928a), Early stages of the Oedipus conflict. In: *Contributions to Psychoanalysis*. London: Hogarth Press, 1948, pp. 202–214.

_____ (1928b), Early stages of the Oedipus conflict and of superego formation. In: *The Psychoanalysis of Children*. London: Hogarth Press, 1937, pp. 179–209.

_____ (1932), *The Psycho-Analysis of Children*. London: Hogarth Press, 1937.

_____ (1934), A contribution to the psychogenesis of manic depressive states. In: *Contributions to Psychoanalysis*. London: Hogarth Press, 1948, pp. 282–310.

_____ (1940), Mourning and its relation to manic depressive states. In: *Contributions to Psychoanalysis*. London: Hogarth Press, 1948, pp. 311–338.

_____ (1946), Notes on some schizoid mechanisms. *Int. J. Psycho-Anal.*, 27: 99–110.

_____ (1952), The mutual influences in the development of ego and id: Discussion. *Psychoanal. Study Child*, 7:51–53.

Klüver, H. & Bucy, P. C. (1937), Psychic blindness and other symptoms following bilateral temporal lobectomy in rhesus monkeys. *Amer. J. Physiol.*, 119:352.

Knight, R. (1940a), Introjection, projection, and identification. *Psychoanal. Q.*, 9:334–341.

_____ (1940b), The relationship of latent homosexuality to the mechanism of paranoid delusion. *Bull. Menninger Clinic*, 4:149–159.

_____ (1953), Management and psychotherapy of the borderline schizophrenic patient. In: *Psychoanalytic Psychiatry and Psychology*, ed. R. Knight & C. Friedman. New York: International Universities Press, pp. 110–122.

_____ (1954), Borderline states. In: *Psychoanalytic Psychiatry and Psychology*, ed. R. Knight & C. Friedman. New York: International Universities Press, pp. 97–109.

Kohut, H. (1971), *The Analysis of the Self*. New York: International Universities Press.

_____ (1977), *The Restoration of the Self*. New York: International Universities Press.

Kris, E. (1956), The personal myth: A problem in psychoanalytic technique. *J. Amer. Psychoanal. Assn.*, 4:653–681.

Kubie, L. S. (1953), The distortion of the symbolic process in neurosis and psychosis. *J. Amer. Psychoanal. Assn.*, 6:59–86.

Langs, R. (1966), Manifest dreams from three clinical groups. *Arch. Gen. Psychiat.*, 14:634–643.

Larousse World Mythology (1965), Leda and the Discursi. New York: Putnam's, p. 118.

Lebovici, S. (1960), A psychotic object relationship. *Int. J. Psycho-Anal.*, 41: 540–543.

Lehman, H. (1975), Schizophrenia: Clinical features. In: *Comprehensive Textbook of Psychiatry*, Vol. I, ed. A. Freedman, H. Kaplan, & B. Sadock. Philadelphia: Williams & Wilkins, p. 892.

Leveton, A. (1961), The night residue. *Int. J. Psycho-Anal.*, 42:506–516.

Lewin, B. (1950), *The Psychoanalysis of Elation*. New York: Norton.

_____ (1952), Phobic symptoms and dream interpretation. *Psychoanal. Q.*, 21: 295–322.

_____ (1954), Sleep, narcissistic neurosis and the analytic situation. *Psychoanal. Q.*, 23:487–510.

Lidz, T. et al. (1965), *Schizophrenia and the Family*. New York: International Universities Press.

Little, M. (1958), On delusional transference. *Int. J. Psycho-Anal.*, 39:134–139.

———— (1960), On basic unity. *Int. J. Psycho-Anal.*, 41:377–384.

———— (1981), *Transference Neurosis and Transference Psychosis*. New York: Aronson.

Loewald, H. (1951), Ego and Reality. *Int. J. Psycho-Anal.*, 32:10–18.

Loewenstein, R. M. (1965), Discussion of "A note on reality constancy" by J. Frosch. Presented to New York Psychoanalytic Society, December 12.

London, N. J. (1973), An essay on psychoanalytic theory: Two theories of schizophrenia. *Int. J. Psycho-Anal.*, 54:169–194.

Lustman, S. (1956), Rudiments of the ego. *Psychoanal. Study Child*, 11:89–98.

Macalpine, I. (1952), Psychosomatic symptom formation. *Lancet*, 1:278–282.

———— & Hunter, R. A. (1953), The Schreber case: A contribution to schizophrenia, hypochondria and psychosomatic symptom-formation. *Psychoanal. Q.*, 22: 328–371.

———— ———— (1955), *Daniel Paul Schreber: Memoirs of My Nervous Illness*. London: Dawson.

———— ———— (1956), *Schizophrenia 1677: A Psychiatric Study of an Illustrated Autobiographical Record of Demoniacal Possession*. London: Dawson.

Mack, J. (1965), Nightmares, conflict and ego development in childhood. *Int. J. Psycho-Anal.*, 46:403–428.

———— (1969a), Disordered ego functions in the dreaming of acute schizophrenic patients. (Unpublished.)

———— (1969b), Dreams and psychosis. *J. Amer. Psychoanal. Assn.*, 17:1–206.

———— (1969c), Nightmares and acute psychoses: A study of their relationship. (Unpublished.)

———— (1970), *Nightmare and Human Conflict*. Boston: Little, Brown.

Magnan, J. (1936), Delire chronique à evolution systematique. In: *A Textbook of Psychiatry*, by D. K. Henderson & R. D. Gillespie. New York: Oxford University Press, p. 236.

Mahler, M. S. (1960), Perceptual de-differentiation and psychotic 'object relationship.' *Int. J. Psycho-Anal.*, 41:348–553.

———— (1963), Thoughts about development and individuation. *Psychoanal. Study Child*, 18:307–324.

———— (1968), *On Human Symbiosis and the Vicissitudes of Individuation, Vol. I: Infantile Psychosis*. New York: International Universities Press.

———— (1971), A study of the separation-individuation process: And its possible application to borderline phenomena. *Psychoanal. Study Child*, 26:403–424.

Marcus, S. (1974), *Engels, Manchester and the Working Class*. New York: Random House.

McDevitt, J. (1965), Discussion of "A note on reality constancy," by J. Frosch. Presented to New York Psychoanalytic Society, December 12.

McGhie, A. (1966), Psychological studies of schizophrenia. In: *Studies of Psychosis*, ed. T. Freeman, J. Cameron, & A. McGhie. New York: International Universities Press, pp. 176–196.

McSweeny, A. J. (1976), The Tyndareus syndrome: Report of five cases. *Psychiat. Ann.*, 6:65–66.

Meissner, W. W. (1976), Schreber and the paranoid process. *The Annual of Psychoanalysis*, 4:3–40. New York: International Universities Press.

———— (1977), The Wolf Man and the paranoid process. *Annual of Psychoanalysis*, 5:23–74. New York: International Universities Press.

———— (1978a), *The Paranoid Process*. New York: Aronson.

———— (1978b), Theoretical assumptions of concepts of the borderline personality. *J. Amer. Psychoanal. Assn.*, 26:559–598.

_____ (1980), A note on projective identification. *J. Amer. Psychoanal. Assn.*, 28:43–67.

Melville, H. (1851), *Moby Dick*. New York: Heritage Pres, 1943.

Melzak, R. (1973), *The Puzzle of Pain*. New York: Basic Books.

Meng, H. (1934), Problem of the organ psychosis: Psychological treatment of patients with organic disease. *Int. Z. Psychoanal.*, 20:439.

_____ & Stern, E. (1955), Organ psychosis. *Psychoanal. Rev.*, 42:428–434.

Menninger, K. (1933), Psychoanalytic aspects of suicide. *Int. J. Psycho-Anal.*, 14: 376–390.

Meyer, A. (1913), *Modern Textbook of Nervous and Mental Diseases*. New York: White & Jelliffe.

Meyrinck, G. (1972), *The Golem*. Prague & San Francisco: Mudra.

Miller, I. (1962), Imitation and identification. Presented to meeting of American Psychoanalytic Association, New York, December.

Miller, M. H. (1965), On building bridges. In: *Psychoanalysis and Current Biological Thought*, ed. N. S. Greenfield & W. C. Lewis. Madison: University of Wisconsin Press, pp. 3–10.

Modell, A. (1968), *Object Love and Reality*. New York: International Universities Press.

Modlin, H. (1962), Varieties of intervention in psychotherapy. *Amer. J. Psychoanal.*, 22:58–63.

Moore, B. & Fine, B. (1968), *Glossary of Psychoanalytic Terms*. New York: American Psychoanalytic Association.

Nacht, S. (1958), Causes and mechanisms of ego distortion. *Int. J. Psycho-Anal.*, 39:271–273.

Niederland, W. (1960), Schreber's father. *J. Amer. Psychoanal. Assn.*, 8:492–499.

_____ (1968), Schrebcr and Flechsig. *J. Amer. Psychoanal. Assn.*, 16:740–748.

_____ (1974), *The Schreber Case*. New York: Quadrangle.

Nunberg, H. (1920), On the catatonic attack. In: *Practice and Theory of Psychoanalysis*, Vol. 1. New York: International Universities Press, 1961, pp. 3–23.

_____ (1921), The course of the libidinal conflict in a case of schizophrenia. In: *Practice and Theory of Psychoanalysis*, Vol. 1. New York: International Universities Press, 1961, pp. 24–59.

_____ (1922), States of depersonalization in the light of the libido theory. In: *Practice and Theory of Psychoanalysis*, Vol. 1. New York: International Universities Press, 1961, pp. 60–74.

_____ (1938), Homosexuality, magic and aggression. In: *Practice and Theory of Psychoanalysis*, Vol. 1. New York: International Universities Press, 1961, pp. 150–164.

_____ (1951), Transference and Reality. *Int. J. Psycho-Anal.*, 32:1–9.

_____ (1955), *Principles of Psychoanalysis*. New York: International Universities Press.

Oberndorf, C. P. (1934), Depersonalization in relation to erotization of thought. *Int. J. Psycho-Anal.*, 15:271–295.

_____ (1935), The genesis of the feeling of unreality. *Int. J. Psycho-Anal.*, 16: 296–306.

_____ (1939), On retaining the sense of reality in states of depersonalization. *Int. J. Psycho-Anal.*, 20:137–147.

Ogden, T. J. (1979), On projective identification. *Int. J. Psycho-Anal.*, 60:357–373.

Orgel, S. (1979), The influence of the theory and practice of psychotherapy on training for psychoanalysis: A summarizing statement. Presented to meeting of International Psychoanalytical Association, July.

Ovesey, L. (1954), The homosexual conflict: Adaptational analysis. *Amer. J. Psychiat.*, 18:243–250.

_____ (1955a), Pseudohomosexuality, the paranoid mechanism and paranoia. *Amer. J. Psychiat.*, 18:163–173.

_____ (1955b), The pseudohomosexual anxiety. *Amer. J. Psychiat.*, 18:16–26.

Pacheco, M. A. P. (1980), Neurotic and psychotic transference and projective identification. *Int. Rev. Psychoanal.*, 7:157–164.

Padel, J. H. (1977), Positions, stages, attitudes or modes of being. *Psychoanalysis in Europe (J. Eur. Psychoanal. Fed.*, Bull. 12).

Pao, P.-N. (1979), *Schizophrenic Disorders*. New York: International Universities Press.

Peto, A. (1967), Dedifferentiations and fragmentations during analysis. *J. Amer. Psychoanal. Assn.*, 15:534–550.

Prego-Silva, L. E., Rep. (1978), Dialogue: Depression and other painful affects. *Int. J. Psycho-Anal.*, 59:517–532.

Rado, S. (1928), The Problem of Melancholia. *Int. J. Psycho-Anal.*, 9:420–438.

_____ (1951), Psychodynamics of depression from the etiologic point of view. *Psychosom. Med.*, 13:51–55.

Random House Dictionary of the English Language (1966). New York: Random House.

Rangell, L. (1965), Some comments on psychoanalytic nosology. In: *Drives, Affects, Behavior*, Vol. 2, ed. M. Schur. New York: International Universities Press, pp. 128–157.

Rapaport, D. (1942), *Emotions and Memory*. New York: International Universities Press, 1950.

_____ (1951), *Organization and Pathology of Thought*. New York: Columbia University Press.

Rapoport, J. (1944), Fantasy objects in children. *Psychoanal. Rev.*, 31:1–6.

Réage, P. (1954), *The Story of O*. New York: Ballantine Books, 1981.

Reider, N. (1957), Transference psychosis. *J. Hillside Hosp.*, 6:131–149.

Reik, T. (1949), *From Thirty Years with Freud*. New York: International Universities Press.

Richardson, F. B. & Moore, R. A. (1963), On the manifest dream in schizophrenia. *J. Amer. Psychoanal. Assn.*, 11:281–302.

Rickman, J. (1926–1927), A survey: The development of the psycho-analytic theory of the psychoses, 1894–1926. *Brit. J. Med. Psychol.*, 6:27–94; 7:94–321, 321–374.

_____ (1928), *The Development of the Psychoanalytical Theory of the Psychoses*, 1893–1926. London: Baillere, Tindall & Cox.

Rosen, J. (1947), The treatment of schizophrenic psychosis by direct analytic therapy. *Psychiat. Q.*, 21:3–37.

_____ (1950), The survival function of schizophrenia. *Bull. Menninger Clinic*, 14:81–91.

_____ (1902), *Direct Psychoanalytic Psychiatry*. New York: Grune & Stratton.

Rosenfeld, H. (1949), Remarks on the relation of male homosexuality to paranoia, paranoid anxiety and narcissism. In: *Psychotic States: A Psychoanalytical Approach*. New York: International Universities Press, 1965, pp. 34–52.

_____ (1950), Note on the psychopathology of confusional states in chronic schizophrenia. *Int. J. Psycho-Anal.*, 31:132–137.

_____ (1952), Transference phenomena and transference-analysis in an acute catatonic schizophrenic patient. *Int. J. Psycho-Anal.*, 33:457–464.

_____ (1954), Considerations regarding the psycho-analytic approach to acute and chronic schizophrenia. *Int. J. Psycho-Anal.*, 35:'135–140.

_____ (1958), Discussion on ego distortion. *Int. J. Psycho-Anal.*, 39:274–275.

_____ (1964a), The psychopathology of hypochondriasis. In: *Psychotic States: A Psychoanalytical Approach.* New York: International Universities Press, 1965, pp. 180–199.

_____ (1964b), On the psychopathology of narcissism in psychotic states. In: *Psychotic States: A Psychoanalytical Approach.* New York: International Universities Press, 1965, pp. 169–179.

_____ (1965), *Psychotic States: A Psychoanalytical Approach.* New York: International Universities Press.

_____ (1970), On projective identification. *Sci. Bull. Brit. Psycho-Anal. Soc. & Inst. Psycho-Anal.* (London).

_____ (1978), Notes on the psychopathology and psychoanalytic treatment of some borderline patients. *Int. J. Psycho-Anal.*, 59:215–221.

Rosengarten, H. & Friedhoff, A. (1979), Enduring changes in dopamine receptor cells of pups from drug administration to pregnant and nursing rats. *Science*, 203:1133–1135.

Rosenhan, D. L. (1973), On being sane in insane places. *Science*, 179:250–258.

Sachs, D. M., Rep. (1977), Panel: Current concepts of normality. *J. Amer. Psychoanal. Assn.*, 25:679–692.

Sandler, J. (1960), On the concept of superego. *Psychoanal. Study Child*, 15: 128–162.

Schafer, R. (1968), *Aspects of Internalization.* New York: International Universities Press.

Schilder, P. (1933), Neuroses and psychoses. In: *On Neuroses: Paul Schilder*, ed. L. Bender. New York: International Universities Press, 1979, pp. 1–16.

_____ (1935), *The Image and Appearance of the Human Body.* New York: International Universities Press, 1950.

_____ (1942), Narcissism and social relations. In: *Goals and Desires of Man.* New York: Columbia University Press, pp. 184–197.

_____ (1951), *Introduction to a Psychoanalytic Psychiatry.* New York: International Universities Press.

_____ (1976), The psychoanalytic theory of psychoses. In: *On Psychoses: Paul Schilder*, ed. L. Bender. New York: International Universities Press, pp. 1–69.

Schreber, D. P. (1900), *Memoirs of My Nervous Illness*, trans. I. Macalpine & R. A. Hunter. London: Dawson, 1955.

Schultz-Heincke, H. (1931), Uber Homosexualitat [On homosexuality]. *Z. Gesaminte Neurol. und Psychiat.*, 140:(1–2).

Schur, M. (1955), Comments on the metapsychology of somatization. *Psychoanal. Study Child*, 10:119–164.

_____ (1965), Discussion of "A note on reality constancy," by J. Frosch. Presented to New York Psychoanalytic Society, October 12.

_____ (1966), *The Id and the Regulatory Principles of Mental Functioning.* New York: International Universities Press.

Schwartz, D. (1978), Aspects of schizophrenic regression: Defects, defense and disorganization in psychotherapies of schizophrenia. *Proc. 6th Int. Symp. Psychother. Schiz.*, ed. C. Muller (Int. Congress Series No. 464).

Schwing, G. (1940), *A Way to the Soul of the Mentally Ill.* New York: International Universities Press, 1954.

Scott, J. P. (1962), Critical periods in behavioral development. *Science*, 138: 949–958.

Searles, H. F. (1959), Integration and differentiation in schizophrenia. *Brit. J. Med.*

Psychol., 32:261.

_____ (1963), Transference psychosis in the psychotherapy of chronic schizophrenia. *Int. J. Psycho-Anal.*, 44:249–281.

Sechehaye, M. (1956a), *Autobiography of a Schizophrenic Girl.* New York: Grune & Stratton.

_____ (1956b), *Symbolic Realization.* New York: International Universities Press.

Shengold, L. (1967), The effects of overstimulation: Rat people. *Int. J. Psycho-Anal.*, 48:403–415.

Silver, A. (1981), Anxiety and defense in children with central nervous system dysfunction. (Unpublished.)

Silverman, S. (1978), The "innate given": A reconsideration in relation to some specific psychic phenomena, transference and treatment considerations. (Unpublished.)

Simmel, E. (1927), The opening of a psychoanalytic clinic in Berlin. *Z. Psychoanal.*, 13:245–246.

_____ (1929), Psychoanalytic treatment in a sanatorium [Abst.] . *Int. J. Psycho-Anal.*, 10:70–89.

_____ (1937), The psychoanalytic sanatorium and the psychoanalytic movement. *Brit. J. Med. Psychol.*, 1:133–143.

Sperling, M. (1955), Psychosis and psychosomatic illness. *Int. J. Psycho-Anal.*, 36:320–327.

_____ (1958), Pavor nocturnus. *J. Amer. Psychoanal. Assn.*, 6:79–94.

Sperling, O. (1956), Psychodynamics of group perversions. *Psychoanal. Q.*, 25:56–65.

Spitz, R. A. (1957), *No and Yes: On the Genesis of Human Communication.* New York: International Universities Press.

_____ (1964), The derailment of dialogue. *J. Amer. Psychoanal. Assn.*, 12:752–775.

_____ & Wolf, K. M. (1949), Autoerotism. *Psychoanal. Study Child*, 3/4:85–120.

Spring, W. J. (1939), Observations on world destruction fantasies. *Psychoanal. Q.*, 8:48–56.

Stärcke, A. (1920), The reversal of the libido sign in delusions of persecution. *Int. J. Psycho-Anal.*, 1:231–234.

Stein, M. (1966), Self observation, reality and superego. [Abst.]. *Psychoanal. Q.*, 36:148.

Sterba, R. (1946), Dreams and acting out. *Psychoanal. Q.*, 15:175–179.

Stokvis, B. (1952), "Organ psychosis" (Meng) in its importance to psychosomatic medicine. *Psyche* [Heid.], 6:228–240.

Stone, L. (1954), The widening scope of indications for psychoanalysis. *J. Amer. Psychoanal. Assn.*, 2:567–594.

Storch, A. (1924), The primitive archaic forms of inner experience and thought in schizophrenia. *Nerv. Ment. Dis. Monogr.*, 36.

Strachey, J. (1958), Editor's note. *Standard Edition*, 12:4, London: Hogarth Press.

Sullivan, H. S. (1953), *The Interpersonal Theory of Psychiatry.* New York: Norton.

_____ (1956), *Clinical Studies in Psychiatry.* New York: Norton.

_____ (1962), *Schizophrenia as a Human Process.* New York: Norton.

Sutherland, J. D. (1980), British object relations theorists: Balint, Winnicott, Fairbairn, Guntrip. *J. Amer. Psychoanal. Assn.*, 28:829–869.

Tausk, V. (1919), On the origin of the influencing machine in schizophrenia. In: *The Psychoanalytic Reader*, ed. R. Fliess. New York: International Universities Press, 1948, pp. 52–85.

Thomas, R. (1966), Comments on some aspects of self and object representation in a group of psychotic children: An application of Anna Freud's diagnostic profile. *Psychoanal. Study Child*, 21:527–532.

Trethowan, W. H. (1972), The couvade syndrome. In: *Modern Perspectives in Psycho-Obstetrics*, ed. J. Howells. New York: Brunner/Mazel, pp. 68–93.

Valenstein, A. (1981), A developmental approach to transference: Diagnostic and treatment considerations. Presented to Interdisciplinary Educational Conference, New York, November 21.

Van Ophuijsen, J. (1920), On the origin of the feeling of persecution. *Int. J. Psycho-Anal.*, 1:235–239.

Vogel, F. (1974). The Capgras syndrome and its psychopathology. *Amer. J. Psychiat.*, 131:922–924.

Waelder, R. (1951), The structure of paranoid ideas: A critical survey of various theories. *Int. J. Psycho-Anal.*, 23:167–177.

_____ (1960), *Basic Theory of Psychoanalysis*. New York: International Universities Press.

Walters, O. (1954), A methodological critique of Freud's Schreber analysis. *Psychoanal. Rev.*, 42:321–342.

Weinshel, E., Rep. (1966), Panel: Severe regressive states during analysis. *J. Amer. Psychoanal. Assn.*, 14:538–568.

Weisman, A. D. (1958), Reality sense and reality testing. *Behav. Sci.*, 3:228–261.

Weiss, E. (1947), Projection, extrajection and objectivation. *Psychoanal. Q.*, 16:357–377.

_____ (1950a), *Principles of Psychodynamics*. New York: Grune & Stratton.

_____ (1950b), Sense of reality and reality testing. *Samiksa*, 4:171–180.

_____ (1952), Introduction. In: *Ego Psychology and the Psychoses*, by P. Federn. New York: Basic Books, pp. 1–21.

Wexler, M. (1951a), The structural problem in schizophrenia: The role of the internal object. *Bull. Menninger Clinic*, 15:221–235.

_____ (1951b), The structural problem in schizophrenia: Therapeutic implications. *Int. J. Psycho-Anal.*, 35:157–166.

_____ (1971), Schizophrenia: Conflict and deficiency. *Psychoanal. Q.*, 40:82–99.

White, R. (1961), The mother-conflict in Schreber's psychoses. *Int. J. Psycho-Anal.*, 42:55–73.

_____ (1963), *Ego and Reality in Psychoanalytic Theory*. (*Psychol. Issues*, Monogr. 11.) New York: International Universities Press.

Will, O. A. (1961), Paranoid development in the concept of self: Psychotherapeutic intervention. *Psychiat.*, 24:74–86.

Winnicott, D. W. (1953), Transitional objects and transitional phenomena. *Int. J. Psycho-Anal.*, 34:89–97.

_____ (1970), Fear of breakdown. *Int. Rev. Psychoanal.*, 1:103–107, 1974.

Wolberg, A. R. (1973), *The Borderline Patient*. New York: Intercontinental Medical.

Zetzel, E. R. (1953), The depressive position. In: *Affective Disorders*, ed. P. Greenacre. New York: International Universities Press, pp. 84–116.

Index

Abraham, K., 3, 4, 16, 25, 52, 59, 77n, 78n, 86, 172, 180, 191, 361, 484n
  on hysteria and dementia praecox, 26n, 28, 59, 363
  on psychotic affective disorders, 179, 181
Acting out
  identity and, 270
  pimp fantasy and, 480, 481
Activation, 362, 364
Adaptation, 413–418
  autoplastic/alloplastic, 29, 414–416, 427; in character disorders, 415; in neurosis and psychosis, 415, 418; reality testing and, 415, 418
  average expectable environment and, 388, 398, 413, 414
  definition of, 413, 414
  psychosis and, 415, 417, 418, 427
  reality-syntonic/dystonic, 415–417, 418, 427
Adelman, B., 484
Adler, G., 4
Adolescent suicide, 192
Affects, 118, 177
  ambivalent, 179, 187
  dedifferentiation and, 198, 397
  definition of, 177, 178
  rudimentary, 164
  see also Psychotic affective disorders
Aggression, 83–88, 171–176
  death instinct and, 86
  death wishes against therapist and, 175–176
  neutralization defect and, 174
  in paranoid constellation, 83–86, 104, 172
Alexander, F., 77n
Alloplastic adaptation; see Adaptation
Ambivalence
  in depression, 179, 187–189

in paranoia, 85–86
reality development and, 290, 301
in paranoid constellation, 74–83
Anality in paranoid constellation, 74–83
  clinical examples of, 75–77, 79–82, 86
  with sadism and aggression, 83–88, 104, 172
Andreyev, L., 289
Angel, K., 270
Animism, 261, 288–290, 376
  in children, 288; psychotic, 373
  clinical examples of, 288–289
  isolation and, 289
  perceptual defects and, 293–294, 296, 377
  reality constancy and, 289–290
Anna O., 167
Anosmia, 352
Anthropomorphism, 261;
  see also Animism
Anticipation of gratification, 281–282
  depersonalization and, 330–331
  in paranoid, 282
  reality testing and, 340
Anti-libidinal ego, 362
Anxiety
  annihilation, 205
  basic, 1, 203–207, 212, 304, 382, 425, 426, 394
  cultural factors and, 381
  dedifferentiation and, 211–217, 310, 363, 366
  disintegration, 207–211, 310, 315, 310, 366
  neurotic, 205–206, 425
  organismic distress and, 206–207, 377, 394
  psychotic, 203–217, 310, 363, 366, 425, 426; see also Fusion fears
  schizophrenic, 173–174, 205, 376, 381
  self-dynamism and, 380

defenses against, 213, 216
dismemberment and, 209-210
in dreams, 40, 42
hypochondriasis and, 169
instinctual drive and, 175, 203, 207-208
matricide and, 210n
orgasm and, 76, 119n
survival-threatening experiences and, 394-395
Dismemberment, 209-211
Dominante, 105, 486
Dorpat, T., 186, 189
Dostoyevsky, F., 4
Dreams, 34-47
delusions and, 36, 45
of disintegration, 40, 42
ego boundaries and, 39
Freud on, 34-36, 41-44, 52-54
merging into psychosis, 43-46
nightmares, 38
presaging psychosis, 41-43
psychotic, 37-41
reality and, 39-44
residue of, 39
schlaftrunkenheit and, 44
secondary elaboration in, 44
similiarity to psychosis, 34-37
vividness of, 40
of Wolf Man, 45-46
Dual Instinct theory, 29-30, 171-196
on aggression, 86, 172-176
death instinct in, 86, 171, 173
on disintegration, 173, 175
on sadomasochism, 172
on schizophrenic anxiety, 173-174
Dual unity, 373
Durkheim, E., 192
Durrell, L., 280

Effectance, 238, 286, 339
Ego, 255-264
anti-libidinal, 362
archaic, 306
boundaries, 258, 315; diffusion of, 39, 212, 257, 259-261; solitude and, 261-262; *see also* Dedifferentiation
cathexis, 256, 262; loss of, 90, 114, 263, 274, 328, 405, 452
definition of, 256
delusional fixity and, 144-145

depression and, 187-188
feeling, 262, 318, 374n
nuclei, 21, 390
primitive, 134
reality and, 259, 269-355, 426-427
strength and weakness, 259-260, 362
undifferentiated potential of, 290, 411
Ego functions, 265-267
anticipation and, 281-282, 330-331
delay and, 338, 339
neutralization defect and, 267
psychotic versus neurotic, 266, 267, 313, 406
regression in, 266, 406
schizophrenic, 265
unequal development of, 265, 344
see also Defect-defense controversy, Reality testing
Eidelberg, L., 104, 188n, 479
Eissler, K. R., ix, 198, 309, 397, 436-438, 463-466
Ekstein, R., 445
Elkish, P., 134n
Empathy, 376, 463, 471
Engel, G., 193n
Engels, F., 402
English, O. S., ix
Environment
average expectable, 388, 398, 413, 414
holding, 398
maternal, 398
see also Cultural factors, Developmental factors
Erikson, E. H., 238
Erotomania, 99-100
Escalona, S., 145, 284, 294, 298, 397
Estrangement, 320, 376
in depersonalization, 320
in hypochondriasis, 162
Etiology, 387-404
biological factors in, 17, 163-164, 182, 184-185, 204, 297, 380, 388-394, 411, 474-475
constitutional factors in, 370, 387-394, 411, 423, 472
developmental factors in, 387, 388, 394-398
sociocultural factors in, 92-93, 259, 380, 381, 387, 388, 399-404
stimulus barrier and, 390, 396
twin studies in, 389, 393